THE TECHNICAL DELUSION

THE TECHNICAL DELUSION

Electronics, Power, Insanity

JEFFREY SCONCE

DUKE UNIVERSITY PRESS · DURHAM AND LONDON · 2019

© 2019 Duke University Press
All rights reserved

Designed by Matthew Tauch
Typeset in Adobe Jenson Pro by
Westchester Publishing Services

Library of Congress Cataloging-in-Publication Data
Names: Sconce, Jeffrey, [date] author.
Title: The technical delusion : electronics, power, insanity /
Jeffrey Sconce.
Description: Durham : Duke University Press, 2019. |
Includes bibliographical references and index.
Identifiers: LCCN 2018027896 (print)
LCCN 2018034463 (ebook)
ISBN 9781478002444 (ebook)
ISBN 9781478000761 (hardcover : alk. paper)
ISBN 9781478001065 (pbk. : alk. paper)
Subjects: LCSH: Mass media—Psychological aspects—
History. | Mass media—Technological innovations—
History. | Mass media and culture—History.
Classification: LCC P96.T42 (ebook) | LCC P96.T42 S38 2019
(print) | DDC 302.2301/9—dc23
LC record available at https://lccn.loc.gov/2018027896

Cover art: Richard Powers, *Portrait of Kafka*.
© The estate of Richard M. Powers.

FOR LYNN

CONTENTS

Acknowledgments ix

INTRODUCTION: On the Spectrums 1

1 · The Technical Delusion 21

2 · Chipnapped 82

3 · The Will to (Invisible) Power 117

4 · The System 175

5 · Targeted Individuals 237

EPILOGUE: The *Matrix* Defense 285

Notes 301

Bibliography 387

Index 419

ACKNOWLEDGMENTS

WRITING A BOOK in the twenty-first century is an increasingly delusional enterprise, and I have many people to thank for their help and advice as this symptom slowly cohered. First, my thanks to the many audiences who listened to presentations of this material over the past few years and offered feedback, as well as those who invited me to speak at their seminars, exhibitions, and events. In France, my thanks to Phillippe Baudouin, Jeff Guess, Pascal Rousseau, and Gwenola Wagon. In Germany, my thanks to Dagmar Brunow, Ole Frahm, Andreas Stuhlmann, and Babette Tischleder. Thanks also to Kass Banning, Brian Price, and Megan Sutherland at the University of Toronto; Jan Olsson at Stockholm University; and Nick Marx at Colorado State University. Earlier versions of this material appeared as "Ego and Ether: The Pulp Physics of Psychoanalysis," in *Broadcasting Modernism*, ed. Michael Coyle, Debra Rae Cohen, and Jane A. Lewty (2009), and as "On the Origins of the Origins of the Influencing Machine," in *Media Archeology*, ed. Erkki Huhtamo and Jussi Parikka (2011). A more ludic engagement of these issues appeared as "The Ghostularity," in *Communication +1*, ed. Bernard Geoghegan (2015). My thanks to all of these editors for the opportunity to rehearse this material. The cover art, by Richard Powers, is courtesy of John Davis, Kim Saxson, and the Powers Estate, and I thank them for the opportunity to share this extraordinary and as yet unpublished painting. I thank Dan Bashara, Eric Patrick, and Jocelyn Szczepaniak-Gillece for helping maintain some semblance of workplace sanity while finishing this project. Kate Choplin at the Indianapolis Public Library was kind enough to photograph a missing page of an important primary document. Finally, and most importantly, I thank Lynn Spigel for her advice, encouragement, and patience as the project proceeded, especially as there was good reason to suspect it would never be finished. It is to her that I dedicate this book.

On the Spectrums

INTRODUCTION

SHORTLY BEFORE HIS ADMISSION to a psychiatric ward in the mid-1950s, a man announced to his family that he was now a "television expert." This expertise had been acquired, apparently, through the man's ability to watch the family's new TV set for "hours at a time." Writing up the case in 1955 for the *Bulletin of the Menninger Clinic*, his psychiatrist described the nature of this expertise: "During a commercial the announcer said, 'Brush your teeth with _____ toothpaste,' while the picture showed a man brushing his teeth; the patient rushed to the bathroom and brushed his teeth."[1] Later, the patient is said to have scooped up water from a goldfish bowl in response to a hair tonic commercial. The psychiatrist supplied an appropriately sober diagnosis: command-automatism and echopraxia to television. No doubt this patient would be surprised at his diagnosis: *how can I be "crazy" when I am simply doing what television so clearly wants me to do?* Why did this brief and seemingly insignificant case merit attention within a venerated psychiatric publication such as the *Bulletin*? The editors were no doubt motivated in part by the novelty of the new medium, a technology becoming central to American life and thus of general interest to everybody—even psychiatrists. But this vaguely comical portrait of psychosis and television also confirmed a suspicion already ubiquitous at mid-century: *electronic media seek to control us, perhaps even to the point of commandeering the nervous system*. After all, how many billions of dollars do corporations and politicians spend each year hoping to cultivate just such unquestioning *command automatism* in their target audiences? For an advertising firm, what greater achievement is there than creating a slogan that evokes an *echopraxic* response in the viewer? Coke is thus the real thing, and there is nothing you can do to prevent it.

A practicing clinician contributed this case to the *Bulletin*, but one could easily imagine a similar assessment issuing from the pen of F. R. Leavis and appearing in the pages of *Scrutiny*—or, for that matter, sprung from the mind of William Gaines and published in the pages of *Mad Magazine*. This patient would also be at home in Harold Laswell's propaganda technique,

FIG I.1 In 1961, an ad parody from MAD *Magazine* speaks to television's privileged relationship with "insanity." SOURCE: MAD MAGAZINE, NO. 68. © E. C. PUBLICATIONS, INC.

Edward Bernays's "crystallized" public opinion, and Vance Packer's hiddenly persuaded.[2] Moving from the clinic to the culture at large, pronouncing media audiences to be "schizophrenic" or "psychotic" has been a staple of media criticism for many decades. "There is no question that television does what the schizophrenic fantasy says it does," wrote Jerry Mander in *Four Arguments for the Elimination of Television* (1977). "It places in our minds images of reality which are outside our experience. The pictures come in the form of rays from a box. They cause changes in feeling and . . . utter confusion as to what is real and what is not."[3] The belief that the media generate psychotic states of mind is greatly indebted to critical traditions that find anything pertaining to the "mass" a force of inauthenticity—in culture, thought, experience, and reality. No sooner had this thing conceptualized as the "public sphere" emerged in the eighteenth century, various commentators pronounced it a rather bovine entity, easily swayed by greed, stupidity, and passion. "Men, it has been well said, think in herds; it will be seen that they go mad in herds, while they only recover their senses slowly, one by one," observed Charles Mackay in his canonically misanthropic tome *Extraordinary Popular Delusions and the Madness of the Crowds* (1841).[4] Friedrich Nietzsche lamented the "herd instinct" and the "sum of zeros" he saw as empowering the weak-minded hoards over the extraordinary *Übermensch*. "Insanity in individuals is somewhat rare," he writes. "But in groups, parties, nations, and epochs, it is the rule."[5]

In the nascent field of sociology, Gustave Le Bon formalized this cranky disdain into "the law of the mental unity of crowds," arguing that once individuals form a mass, they take possession "of a sort of collective mind which makes them feel, think, and act in a manner quite different from that in which each individual of them would feel, think, and act were he in a state of isolation."[6] To become part of a crowd, in other words, is to enter another psychological reality, one of collective delusion and borderline hallucination. "The substitution of the unconscious action of crowds for the conscious activity of individuals is one of the principal characteristics of the present age," noted Le Bon, further predicting that this form of mass mental disassociation would only increase in prominence in the future.[7] In this respect, Max Horkheimer and Theodor Adorno's "mass deception," Daniel Boorstin's "pseudo-event," and Jacques Derrida's "artifactuality" all trace their origins to a belief, as old as modernity itself, that mass media, mass culture, and mass hallucination are inexorably bound together in a roiling stew of mass delusion.[8]

Deluded Technically Deluded

A "technical delusion" can be defined as a delusion about technology.[9] Such belief can focus on a device that does not exist (Venusian mind rays, presumably) or on a persistent and thus unreasonable conviction about an otherwise plausible practice (my neighbor spies on me through my computer's webcam). In either case, adjudicating what does and does not exist, or what is or is not reasonable, always remains open to some degree of debate.

Isolating a technical delusion involves a complex dialogue of historically situated beliefs, classifications, and assessments about technology, "madness," and their possible relationship. In this respect, technical delusions emerge at the intersection of the *deluded technically* and the *technically deluded*, two categories of assessment that are significantly informed by the historical production of knowledge about electronics and insanity. To be "deluded technically" is to express a profound conviction in a dubious technical affordance that, according to rather fuzzily calibrated scales of plausibility and conviction, attracts suspicion as to the individual's state-of-mind. *The radio can read my thoughts. Someone is using the Internet to put voices in my head. I must dutifully update my operating system every time the Apple Corporation tells me to do so.* If judged delusional by the psychiatric institution, said individual then becomes *technically deluded*—that is, the modern alliance of psychiatric evaluation and legal authority pronounces the individual authentically delusional and thus officially psychotic. Therapy must begin. Drugs must be administered. The patient must be renormalized. In this respect, the entire psychotic progression from the *deluded technically* to the *technically deluded* participates in a discursive negotiation of technical plausibility, probability, and possibility.

In psychiatric literature, few if any delusions are recorded about toasters, staplers, and riding lawnmowers. The majority of technical delusions center on electronics and electronic media. Such delusions began to emerge in the early nineteenth century as electricity (along with its more occult cousin, magnetism) became a privileged site for merging historical currents of theology, natural philosophy, physiology, parapsychology, engineering, and communications into the hard technologies that constitute "the media." Electronics in this sense can be thought of as *the politics of electricity*, a channeling of this raw energy into conceptual and technical forms that index a history of power, energetic and political. Those who find themselves deluded technically (or at least accused of being so) occupy the speculative fringes of this transformation from the electrical to the electronic, a struggle that, like psychosis itself, shadows the emergence of industrial modernity. The extraordinary social, economic, and cultural transformations of modernity are well known and well documented. Industrialism produced a new urban economy increasingly centered on wages, technology, and factory production. Urban expansion across the nineteenth century, in turn, produced new forms of social relations; changes in labor and the class system; new vectors of disease and crime; the beginnings of commercialized mass leisure; and new mechanisms for administering education, the law, health care, and other concerns of the newly aggregated social body. The population shifts, class relations, and emerging topographies produced by industrialism soon necessitated new mechanisms for maintaining social order within the body politic, thus leading to the emergence of what Michel Foucault influentially identified as the disciplinary state.[10] As the emerging hub of commerce and culture, meanwhile, the Victorian city produced a paradoxical new world of ever denser populations existing in increasingly atomized relations, a new social reality described rather unnervingly by Edgar Allan Poe in "The Man in the Crowd" (1840) and bloodily exploited by Jack the Ripper in 1888.[11] Social interventions that had once concerned only local or clerical authorities (addressing poverty, orphans, insanity, disasters) now fell to the administrative attention of larger governmental and bureaucratic power. This was not a mysterious process recognizable only to later historians. Those living through these transformations were acutely aware of their implications. As Georg Simmel observed at the end of the tumultuous nineteenth century, "Nietzsche may have seen the relentless struggle of the individual as the prerequisite for his full development, while Socialism found the same thing in the suppression of all competition—but in each of these the same fundamental motive was at work, namely the resistance of the individual to being leveled, swallowed up in the social-technological mechanism."[12]

The electronic politics of the nineteenth century often celebrated emerging sciences and technologies as tools for forging a future utopia.[13] Electricity, newly harnessed, was nothing less than miraculous, a force that promised to bring various forms of "enlightenment" to the entire planet.[14] In these earliest days of electrical science, a lone genius could serve simultaneously as inventor, experimenter, and theorist: Franklin, Volta, Faraday, Edison. In Jules Verne's *20,000 Leagues under the Sea* (1870), Captain Nemo assembles his fantastic submarine using only his singular intelligence, a workforce sworn to secrecy, and his mastery of electricity. "There is a powerful agent, obedient, rapid, easy, which conforms to every use, and reigns supreme on board my vessel," he tells a visitor to the *Nautilus*. "Everything is done by means of it. It lights, warms and is the soul of my mechanical apparatus. This agent is electricity."[15] Frank Baum's novel for children *The Master Key: An Electrical Fairy Tale* (1901) replaces the lone inventor with an actual genie to explore "the mysteries of electricity and the optimism of its devotees."[16]

With the new century, boyish enthusiasm for electrical experimentation gravitated toward wireless and other new electronic wonders. *The Wireless Boys*, *The Motion Picture Chums*, the *Tom Swift* series, and the many other "boy inventors" of this era debuted at a moment when a boy (and occasional girl) could still fantasize about making an extraordinary discovery in electrical science, looking to Edison, Bell, Marconi, Tesla, and the other putative fathers of modern electronics as a heroic model. Even then, however, the business of technical research and design was moving away from the motivated amateur toward corporate and governmental supervision.[17] By necessity, specialization in science and engineering disbursed the process of innovation across different departments. Advanced research also necessitated greater outlays of capital that were typically unavailable to lone researchers. As corporate electronics bottled the electrical genie, a variety of institutional players emerged with a proprietary interest in maintaining the secrecy of their goals, patents, and applications. Captain Nemo had exiled himself to the high-tech secrecy of the *Nautilus* as an escape from the stupidity and cruelty of the so-called civilized nations. A century later, submarines and other weaponry were firmly back under control of the nation-state. The ongoing alliances of the "military-industrial complex" became even more secretive in the postwar era as Cold Warriors pursued classified social and technological agendas. Accordingly, the second half of the twentieth century also witnessed rising suspicion about the motives and transparency of corporations and governments. Today, sane and insane alike fear the Defense Advanced Research Projects Agency (DARPA) as the most sinister of sinister high-tech cabals. Most citizens of technocracy believe as a matter of course that we now live within two realms of power: the power we see and the power we do not see—or, the power we can prove and the power we cannot prove.

With the Information Age, electricity has become the nervous fluid of the entire planet. Not only does electricity continue to power various gizmos and gadgets, it has also become the primary medium for circulating and archiving digital information. Most would concede that controlling the electrical array—both as raw power and as networked communications—is essential to maintaining social, economic, and political order. In the era of mass modernity, a *coup d'état* demanded seizing control of radio, television, and the military. Today, concern centers on a more cataclysmic sabotaging of the power grid and, with it, the data streams that control the "control society." Fearing a global decapitation of civilization's brainstem, survivalists prepare for a looming electromagnetic pulse (EMP) event they believe will shut down the power grid for months or even years, thus ushering in a prolonged period of anarchy as our technocratic order temporarily loses its autonomic and cerebral functions.[18] Cranks, perhaps, but they are not wrong. Once a divine, rarefied substance that made only fleeting appearances on humanity's stage, electricity, in its historical conversion into global electronics, describes a concurrent shift in the species from figurative to literal cyborgs.[19] This process may be gradual and radically uneven, but it appears equally inexorable. Some futurists look forward to a day when this migration will be complete, consciousness wiped from its flesh-and-blood platform to be uploaded as information into some iteration of electronic consciousness.

The politics of the electronic coincide with another historical trajectory within modernity: the conversion of insanity into *the politics of psychosis*. Determining who is and who is not mad, insane, psychotic, or schizophrenic continues to be a contentious debate, and, as Foucault argues, it is also one of the most political, especially as the medicalization of insanity afforded psychiatry and the disciplinary state increasing authority to intervene in the lives of those the "medico-juridical complex" deems mentally ill.[20] Psychiatric power, credentialed by training as a science and enforced by the courts as law, possesses a recursive authority to rewrite moral questions of social abnormality as settled matters of scientific pathology, produced and secured by a discourse of truth that historically has immunized itself from external critique. "In crude terms," writes Foucault, "psychiatric power says: The question of truth will never be posed between madness and me for the very simple reason that I, psychiatry, am already a science. And if, as science, I have the right to question what I say, if it is true that I may make mistakes, it is in any case up to me, and to me alone, as science, to decide if what I say is true or to correct the mistake. I am the possessor, if not of truth in its content, at least of all the criteria of truth."[21] Thomas Szasz offered a similar critique of "schizophrenia" as the twentieth century's preferred term for madness. Szasz argued that the literature on schizophrenia was flawed by a "single logical error: namely, all of the contributions to it treat 'schizophrenia' as if it were the shorthand *description* of a *disease*, when in fact it is the shorthand *prescription* of a *disposition*; in other words, they use the term schizophrenia as if it were a *proposition asserting* something about psychotics, when in fact it is a *justification legitimizing* something that psychiatrists do to them."[22]

Medical historians generally credit Emil Kraepelin with first isolating what would become known as schizophrenia. Kraepelin introduced the term "dementia praecox" (early dementia) in 1897 to distinguish a form of psychosis separate and apart from manic depression but not wholly identical to the senile dementia known to attack mental functions later in life. In 1911, the Swiss psychiatrist Eugen Bleuler introduced the actual term "schizophrenia" to further distinguish this illness from any lingering organic connection to the concept of dementia.[23] Bleuler reframed dementia praecox in the plural as the "schizophrenias," recognizing that there was still a great variety of presentation even within this newly isolated cluster of symptoms. Recently abandoned, these subcategories (hebephrenic, paranoid, and catatonic) were operative for a century.[24] The authority invested in medical science encourages us to believe that a thing like schizophrenia, once "discovered," is timeless, having existed for centuries misdiagnosed under other false names. But as Szasz has argued of Bleuler's intervention, "The claim that some people have a disease called schizophrenia ... was based not on any medical discovery but only on medical authority; that it was, in other words, the result not of empirical or scientific work, but of ethical and political decision making."[25] The schizophrenic, in other words, was a new category produced by the modern psychiatric eye, a bundling of symptoms unified not by the discovery of an etiological cause but through the process of naming. Schizophrenia is literally a *label*, a name invoked to index a presumed (but never proven) etiology underlying a group of distressing but not necessarily consistent symptoms. Or, as his fellow skeptic R. D. Laing wrote succinctly in 1967, "Schizophrenia is the name for a condition that most psychiatrists ascribe to patients they call schizophrenic."[26]

Foucault's *Folie et déraison: Histoire de la folie à l'âge classique* and Szasz's *The Myth of Mental Illness* both appeared in 1961, making them the two most visible figures in the so-called anti-psychiatry movement. David Cooper, Félix Guattari, and even the Church of Scientology offered their own critiques of modern psychiatry in this period.[27] Psychiatrists (and certain historians of psychiatry) often lump Foucault, Szasz, Laing, and other "anti-psychiatrists" together as ideologues immune to the clinical "facts" of psychosis, dismissing their critiques of the psychiatric institution as a *denial* of mental illness. But this would be a distortion of the many writers identified with such a project. In calling "schizophrenia" a psychiatric invention, Szasz expressed skepticism that psychodynamic theory was of any use in treating the condition that psychiatry itself had named schizophrenia. This did not prevent Szasz from endorsing the idea that the various symptoms commonly grouped together into a thing called schizophrenia might one day be isolated in terms of neurobiological causation. "If schizophrenia ... turns out to have a biochemical cause and cure," he writes, "schizophrenia would no longer be one of the diseases for which a person would be involuntarily committed. In fact, it would then be treated by neurologists, and psychiatrists then have no more to do with it than they do with Glioblastoma [malignant tumor], Parkinsonism, and other diseases of the brain."[28] His anti-psychiatry thus was entirely compatible with the dominant wing of contemporary psychiatric research that is indeed hoping to isolate the precise genetic markers and neurotransmitters implicated in schizophrenia. Foucault, meanwhile, for all his legendary suspicion of the entire psychiatric enterprise, did not question the very real suffering of those deemed "mad." His work centers more on the variable and contingent power relations involved in defining madness that pathologize a range of behavior as "abnormal." As Foucault notes, the initial purpose of modern psychiatry was not to "cure" the insane. It was instead to identify and segregate madness for the presumed protection of the larger social body. Much as Szasz's work is easily reconciled with contemporary neuropsychiatry, Foucault codified the doctrines of social epidemiology to argue that "madness," in all cases, invokes cultural frames of definition and diagnosis.

In the wake of Foucault, Szasz, Laing, and other critics of the psychiatric institution, the inherent ambiguity of schizophrenia has inspired a variety of disciplines to opine on its relation to the politics of modern culture and subjectivity. Philosophy, political science, sociology, art history, critical theory, science fiction, literary analysis—all have considered the schizophrenic as a symbolic challenger to the agents that frame consensus reality and enforce modern power. Accordingly, opining on the politics of schizophrenia has served as a prerequisite of sorts for inclusion in the pantheon of modern (and male) thought (occupying such renowned thinkers as Theodor Adorno, Antonin Artaud, Jean Baudrillard, Gilles Deleuze, Jacques Derrida, Félix Guattari, Fredric Jameson, Claude Lévi-Strauss, Friedrich Kittler, and Slavoj Žižek). Much of this work proposes a privileged, even determinative, link between modernity and schizophrenia. Louis S. Sass's canonical *Madness and Modernity* details clinical schizophrenia and aesthetic modernism as intertwined productions of a shared epistemological crisis marked by a growing hyperacuity of "selfhood" that takes shape in the late nineteenth and early twentieth century.[29] David Michael Kleinberg-Levin argues that modernity is the incubator, not only of schizophrenia, but also of the growth in narcissism and depression as contemporary psychosocial pathologies. As Kleinberg-Levin argues, "Suffering always has a historical dimension. . . . [I]t must be correlated very specifically with social structures, political institutions, and cultural ideology."[30] In *Mind, Modernity, Madness*, Liah Greenfeld argues that the Western ideology of personal freedom and the stressful imperative to achieve various forms of "self-fulfillment" are major factors in the West's higher incidence of schizophrenia and manic depression.[31] Angela Woods has suggested that the term "schizophrenia" has come to describe the fundamental inscrutability of its own existence. Woods has called schizophrenia "the sublime object of psychiatry," arguing that it serves as a "limit point for the discipline," a site of manifest unreason that seductively challenges the science that would seek to contain and understand it: "Eliding reason's colonization and existing beyond conclusive analytic explanation, schizophrenia serves both as an exemplary site of unreason upon which psychiatry can exercise an ongoing claim to scientificity, and as a challenge to the scientificity of those very claims."[32] These "cultural" critiques are elegantly summarized in Joel Kovel's contention that schizophrenia is a form of profound *alienation*, an estrangement from the social world that has implications that are both existential and political. Kovel argues that schizophrenia is not something one "has" (like the flu). It is, rather, something one "is" (profoundly alienated from both self and reality). While this distinction may seem to be incidental to the condition itself, the state of "being" schizophrenic rather than "having" schizophrenia better locates the syndrome within these larger social dynamics of capitalism and modernity. "Marx or Samuel Beckett can tell us more about schizophrenia than any medical text," Kovel writes, "even though neither Marx nor Beckett described schizophrenia as such."[33]

Following these critiques, medical historians have demonstrated the troubling elasticity of schizophrenia as a diagnostic category. Despite Bleuler's efforts to narrow conceptions of the illness, early adopters of the term used it rather broadly (supporting Szasz's polemical contention that psychiatry employs schizophrenia to classify and police behavior that a societal majority finds distressing or even just annoying). In 1931, the psychoanalyst A. A. Brill declared that Americans who spoke with a British "Oxford" accent were in fact "schizophreniacs," suffering from an "inferiority complex" and a "weakened intellectual state."[34] As Jonathan M. Metzl has demonstrated, psychiatry of the 1930s, '40s, and '50s regarded schizophrenia as primarily affecting introverted women incapable of coping with modern life and modern marriage (as epitomized in *The Snake Pit* [1948], the Oscar-nominated film adaptation of Mary Jane Ward's dramatized account of her own experiences in a psychiatric institution). Carol Warren has discussed how familial dynamics in America of the 1950s contributed to the institutionalization of depressed and anxious housewives as "schizophrenic."[35] By the 1960s and '70s, schizophrenia took on connotations of antisocial violence and quickly became the diagnosis of choice for African American men exhibiting "abnormal" belligerence and anger at perceived injustices in white society. As Metzl notes, this particular presentation of schizophrenia came to be known as the protest psychosis, so-called by the New York psychiatrists Walter Bromberg and Franck Simon, who, at the height of the nation's social unrest in 1968, advanced the claim that the rhetoric of the black liberation movement had the power to drive African Americans insane, producing "delusions, hallucinations, and violent projections in black men."[36] Adding weight to the politics of diagnostic bias, another study asked American and British clinicians to examine a set of identical case files and propose a diagnosis. Although they dealt with the exact same materials, the American clinicians pronounced twice as many patients to be schizophrenic as their British colleagues (the British possessing a much wider latitude for indulging the "eccentric").[37]

Current research in schizophrenia continues to emphasize genetic and neurochemical factors. There is, in this approach, a fundamentally organic dysfunction in the brain that causes the disruptive symptoms of the schizophrenic mind. Yet the fundamental ambiguity of schizophrenia remains. There is still no professional consensus within psychiatric medicine as to what actually causes or even constitutes schizophrenia. There is no blood test for schizophrenia. Heredity seems suggestive, but others argue this apparent link is simply a shield for the transmission of certain dysfunctional familial dynamics. Others believe that a stressor of some kind (relationship issues, financial trouble, drugs, trauma) is required to set the syndrome in motion (without necessarily addressing how said stressors are themselves a function of modernity). Age and gender also appear to be key factors, given that men in their late teens and twenties are now the most likely to be deemed schizophrenic. But even here it is unclear whether this correlation stems from physiology or structural social stressors specific to that population group. Those born in cities or during the winter appear to have a higher incidence for schizophrenia, although no one can yet explain why this might be so. In the search for a "smoking gun" of schizophrenia, even dirty cat litter gained temporary (paranoid) currency as a potential source of the condition.[38]

Epidemiologists often argue that schizophrenia affects one out of every hundred people around the world, regardless of race, class, or nationality. Yet a substantial body of research remains that complicates this 1 percent thesis. Several studies imply that schizophrenia—or, at least, its diagnosis—appears to afflict recent immigrants to a greater degree than the native-born, suggesting the condition has some basis in miscommunication, sociocultural alienation, and other dysfunctions of meaning that come from radical cultural displacement.[39] As early as the 1930s, meanwhile, researchers demonstrated that schizophrenia and other "mental disorders" tend to increase in proximity to urban centers, where they correlate strongly with levels of "poverty, unemployment, juvenile delinquency, adult crime, suicide, family desertion, infant mortality, communicable disease, and general mortality" (the closer one lives to the center of the city, argued the study, the more likely one is to become a paranoid schizophrenic—at least in Chicago).[40] Perhaps the most suggestive evidence of a modern or modernist pathology in schizophrenia can be found in a series of studies initiated by the World Health Organization. Beginning in 1967, these studies have "consistently found persons clinically diagnosed with schizophrenia and related disorders in the industrialized west (chiefly Europe and the United States) to have *less favorable outcomes* than their counterparts in 'developing' nations (countries in Africa, Asia, and Latin America)."[41] This differential has been widely debated. But many have argued that the greater incidence and particularly virulent progression of schizophrenia within the developed world implies that Western modernity is itself particularly conducive to triggering and sustaining psychotic episodes. Laing certainly suspected as much: "Our society may itself have become biologically dysfunctional and some forms of schizophrenic alienation from the alienation of society may have a sociological function that we have not recognized. This holds even if a genetic factor predisposes to some kinds of schizophrenic behavior."[42]

Current research on schizophrenia focuses on measuring levels of neurotransmitters such as serotonin and dopamine. Still, one could argue that adjusting neurotransmitters (whether in schizophrenia, depression, or other psychiatric conditions) is not in fact a "cure" for some abstract and objective illness but is instead a strategy for better aligning the patient with historically produced sociocultural "norms" that demand certain sensibilities, attitudes, and behavior. Shyness, for example, was once considered an admirable character trait, especially in women. In the self-branding world of neoliberal capitalism, however, shyness is now a "social anxiety disorder" that inhibits strategic self-promotion, a diagnosis greatly influenced, if not wholly invented, by a pharmaceutical industry that is ready, willing, and able to adjust neurotransmitters in response to changing standards of normative behavior.[43] One assumes, given the ascendance of a new sociomedical constellation, the shy might once again be allowed to stay home and read in peace.

Much of this controversy hinges on the unfortunate legacy of the nature-versus-nurture debate. Invoking nature versus nurture, in any sphere of human activity, assumes these categories are self-evident, mutually exclusive, and somehow "true" outside the cultural system that produced this binary in the first place. The fallacy of this division is especially evident in the popular understanding of genetics. With the mapping of the human genome, there seems to be an announcement almost weekly that a genetic predisposition or component has been isolated as the "cause" of any number of human conditions and behavior. Yet, as "predisposition" and "component" imply, possessing a gene for X does not necessarily mean that X will occur, only that one may be *predisposed* for X or that the genetic marker is a *component* in a larger complex of factors for X. As geneticists must continually remind the public, the expression of many genetic traits depends on a complex interaction of biological and environment factors.

The analyst Jacques Lacan was even more provocative in this recurring debate. Asserting that the human subject and its psychiatric disorders are a product of language, Lacan noted that a psychotic dysfunction cannot manifest without a subject already constituted within a world of meaning. Lacan invokes the example of "thought echo," a widely observed symptom indicative of schizophrenia in which a person hears his own thoughts repeated or echoed back. Those who would reduce all madness to genes, wiring, and chemicals have invoked thought echo as a purely neurological dysfunction, offered as evidence to refute psychodynamic accounts of psychosis. Such was the position of Lacan's mentor, Gaëtan Gatian de Clérambault, who had a significant influence on Lacan's earliest theories of paranoia.[44] "Let's agree with Clérambault that this is the effect of a delay produced by a chronaxic deterioration," Lacan proposes, "one of two intracerebral messages, one of the two telegrams, as it were, is impeded and arrives after the other, thus as its echo." But, Lacan continues, "For this delay to be registered, there must be some privileged reference point at which this can occur, from which the subject notes a possible discordance between one system and another." In other words, thought echo cannot be experienced as thought echo without a normalized "I" as the reference point for the perceived aberration of an echoing thought. So without a meaningful subject to hear and thus perceive the thought twice (as well as another meaningful subject to declare such experience to be pathogenetic), there can be no anomaly. (If, hypothetically, there were a society in which chronaxic deterioration was the norm, those who heard their thoughts only once would possibly be "psychotic.") "However the organogenetic or automatizing theory is constructed," Lacan continues, "there is no escaping the consequence that some such privileged point exists." Somewhat facetiously, no doubt, Lacan proposes that this privileged point is nothing other than "the Soul," a hyperbolically metaphysical statement that foregrounds the status of the ego as the soul's mortal (but equally fictional) cousin.[45] This observation, it should be noted, pertains regardless of whatever the latest biological "cause" of psychosis—chronaxic deterioration, dopamine levels, blocked receptors, parasites in cat litter, synaptic cascading, and so on. Regardless of what may be happening in the brain, psychosis—as a dysfunction of self—cannot exist without an ego spoken by the language of the symbolic.[46] Other animals can exhibit behavioral quirks, hallucinate, and react to traumatic memories. Only humans, it would appear, can become delusional—trapped in a constellation of meanings that in effect rewrite reality or portions thereof.

Like hysteria in the nineteenth century, schizophrenia has become such a moving target that some clinicians now question its utility as a diagnostic category. As Richard Bentall argues, "I think the concept is scientifically meaningless, clinically unhelpful and ultimately has been damaging to patients."[47] A decade later, Simon McCarthy-Jones echoed this sentiment: "The concept of schizophrenia is dying. Harried for decades by psychology, it now appears to have been fatally wounded by psychiatry, the very profession that once sustained it."[48] Bentall argues that schizophrenia "groups together a whole range of different problems under one label—the assumption is that all of these people with all of these different problems have the same brain disease."[49] Responding to these continuing uncertainties, the most recent edition of the *Diagnostic and Statistical Manual of Mental Disorders* (the DSM-V, which appeared in 2013) took limited steps in complicating this diagnosis by acknowledging the wide variability of schizophrenic presentations. As with autism, the DSM now recognizes schizophrenia as a "spectrum" disorder, thereby avoiding the binary yes-or-no logic of simple pathogenesis that early psychiatry imported from medical science. Moving to a spectrum does not necessarily solve or even improve the diagnostic process, but it at least foregrounds what have always been the more contentious questions in pronouncing an individual "schizophrenic." Yet even as a spectrum model allows for more flexibility in the diagnostic process, it also threatens to erase any pathogenetic "truth" thought to be at the center of schizophrenic etiology. If schizophrenia manifests along a spectrum, then everyone is, to some degree, schizophrenic. Over the past twenty years, the "neurodiversity movement" has advocated better accommodating those who function outside the standards and demands of so-called neurotypicals. Integrating the psychotic on his or her own terms would be difficult, probably impossible. But the idea of a schizophrenic spectrum suggests that the interplay of biology and culture thought to produce this thing called schizophrenia presents two pathways: (1) identify and label ever more precise diagnostic categories along the spectrum that in turn support ever more precise therapeutic (i.e., pharmacological) interventions; or (2) recognize that the politics of psychosis is necessarily bound to the structural toxicity of the modern social order.

Just how toxic is contemporary life? A study in 2015 by the *Journal of the American Medical Association* finds that the number of people in the United States taking antidepressants doubled between 2000 and 2012.[50] Several possibilities present themselves: improved screening procedures for depression, improved marketing strategies by the pharmaceutical industry, declining access to psychodynamic therapy. In terms of environment and genetic predisposition, however, a troubling and seemingly intractable political issue remains in this doubling. Perhaps life in the United States (and elsewhere) is becoming more stressful, unfulfilling, and thus depressing. A similar critique can be made of any and all psychiatric conditions thought to be increasing among a historical population. How many people, one wonders, would need to be diagnosed as clinically depressed, paranoid, and psychotic before attention turned away from individual pathology to social revolution? *Neoliberal subjects of the world, unite! You have nothing to lose but your Prozac!*

Modern Madness

As early as 1808, Joseph Haslam bemoaned not only the rising numbers of patients in his asylum, but also a proportionate increase in those attempting to treat the newly insane: "The alarming increase of Insanity, as might naturally be expected, has incited many persons to an investigation of this disease;—some for the advancement of science, and others with the hope of emolument."[51] Henry Maudsley found the situation in England no better sixty years later. "The popular opinion undoubtedly is, that insanity is increasing greatly in this country," he wrote in 1872. "The necessity, year after year, of enlarging the existing county asylums; the erecting of a second, or even of a third asylum in some counties, and of special borough asylums for large boroughs; and the still continuing cry for more accommodation, are facts sufficient to account for, and give much show of probability to, the opinion."[52] In the United States, meanwhile, state legislatures in the nineteenth century encountered the ongoing problem of building, funding, and then expanding facilities for their growing population of lunatics. By the late nineteenth century, physicians, philosophers, and the public widely endorsed the idea that the seemingly unending flood of insanity was an unfortunate consequence of civilization's progress. This alarm continued throughout the twentieth century as many worried, decade by decade, that schizophrenia was becoming pandemic in the United States. As one Cold War psychotic noted of her struggle, "At the rate at which schizophrenia is increasing, there is a reasonable chance that if the intercontinental missile doesn't get you, schizophrenia will."[53] More recently, Daniel Freeman and Jason Freeman nominated paranoia as "the 21st-century fear," arguing that it "permeates our society, more than we've ever suspected and possibly more than ever before."[54] Some individuals, it seems, simply cannot withstand the demands of a rapidly changing world that appears to grow more intrusive, frenetic, chaotic, unequal, unjust, atomizing, and alienating.[55] The *Boston Globe* observed in 1889, "As civilization advances new diseases are not only discovered, but are actually produced by the novel agencies which are brought to bear on man's body and mind. The increase in insanity through the world is unquestionably due to the 'storm and stress' of our crowded modern life, and almost every addition which science makes to the convenience of the majority seems to bring with it some new form of suffering to the few."[56]

As a corollary to the modernity-equals-madness thesis, commentators have long attributed this growing "storm and stress" to the media's acceleration, amplification, and accumulation of *information*. The advent of mass printing technologies in the 1830s, followed by their telegraphic weaponizing at mid-century, allowed a growing population to gather impressions from around the city, nation, continent, and world. This suffusion of information through ink, paper, and wire quickly led to the commonplace complaint that no one individual could possibly process so much data. In 1887, a dyspeptic Nietzsche described the modern European as succumbing to the exhaustion of an agitating cosmopolitanism, a sensibility "more irritable" and linked to "the abundance of disparate impressions." He complained, "The tempo of this influx *prestissimo*; the impressions erase each other.... [A] kind of adaptation to a flood of impressions takes place: men unlearn spontaneous action, they merely react to stimuli from outside."[57] Max Nordau echoed these sentiments by denouncing the nervous "degeneration" posed by the 6,800 newspapers operating in fin-de-siècle Germany: "The humble village inhabitant has to-day a wider geographical horizon, more numerous and complex interests, than the prime minister of a petty, or even second-rate state a century ago."[58] George Beard's dissection of "American nervousness" and Sigmund Freud's "principle of constancy" also spoke to a nervous system struggling to accommodate proliferating sources of stimulation. This theme continued throughout the twentieth century, as well. In 1970, Alvin Toffler described "future shock" as "the shattering stress and disorientation that we induce in individuals by subjecting them to too much change in too short a time,"[59] a shift measured in large part by new strategies for processing information. "One of the definitions of sanity is the ability to tell real from unreal," Toffler observed. "Soon we'll need a new definition."[60] Mark Andrejevic describes this new environment as "infoglut," arguing that the multiplication of media and information in the digital era produces a troubling paradox in everyday life. "At the very moment when we have the technology to inform ourselves as never before," he writes, "we are simultaneously and compellingly confronted with the impossibility of ever being *fully* informed. Even more disturbingly, we are confronted with this impossibility at the very moment when we are told that being informed is more important than ever before to our livelihood, our security, our social lives."[61] After taking office in 2017, President Donald J. Trump helpfully aided his supporters in negotiating this "infoglut" by labelling all information critical of his administration as "fake news."

Modernity's discourse of excessive information and escalating insanity, now some two hundred years old, can evoke accusations of presentism: *to be human is to believe, forever and always, that one's generational or centurial cohort is the most challenged, the most agitated, the most insane.* As a corollary thesis, every modern generation believes that the latest technical innovations will ultimately prove catastrophic to the individual and collective mind. (Invention x is making kids stupider, dismantling a sense of community, ruining my view of the Rhine.) But dismissing these critiques outright can lead to an equally specious form of universalism. To argue that human beings have always considered themselves stressed and yet, at the same time, eternally resilient in the face of technological upheaval is to posit a human subject standing outside of history. The narcissism of the ego is such that it projects itself across all of time, space, and history, imagining a continuity of human experience that, while generative of language, culture, and knowledge, somehow retains an essence that is impervious to such epiphenomena. The first caveman to build a slingshot and the astrophysicist working on gravitational mechanics are, in this perspective, essentially kindred spirits involved in the timelessly human project of promoting progress through technical innovation. Over the course of the past century, this humanist account of technology has been roundly critiqued by philosophers as diverse as Martin Heidegger, Jacques Ellul, and Bernard Stiegler. The ego, as the interface between internal instincts and external reality, does not remain pure, timeless, and untouched by its encounters with technology. Each technical innovation said to revolutionize human possibility—fire, language, the plow, computers—is not an inevitable step in the teleological destiny of humanity but, instead, a radically contingent deflection of the species as a historical cyborg. From this perspective, the ongoing association of modernity, media, and madness is not to be dismissed as a timeless human complaint about the nature of change and progress; rather, the actual and perceived increase in modern insanity should be seen as a historical symptom. The media, in this respect, may not necessarily be a determinative cause of modern psychosis, but they are certainly affecting how the ego (or self) conceptualizes itself in relation to a rapidly changing environment of energy, information, and power. "It is well known that the prognosis for patients with schizophrenia is better if they live in developing countries than in western industrialized societies," notes one psychiatrist. Addressing the plight of the Western schizophrenic, the study notes a recurring obstacle in treating these victims of modernity: *a constant inundation of delusional materials by television, radio, and the Internet*.[62]

The following pages consider the historical encounter between the politics of the electronic and the politics of psychosis, an amorphous conceptual space that hovers between the *deluded technically* and the *technically deluded*. Over the past two centuries, in the move from the raw electromagnetism of the nineteenth century to the global "Internet of things" (and beyond) that is our future, electronic media—broadly conceived as an alliance of energy, information, and technology—have come to stand as a primary location and signifier of *power*, energetic and political. Technical delusions frequently center on suspicions as to how these electronics might operate in the administration of power—semiotic, energetic, political. Such delusions frequently cast the electronic as a black box of power, a metonymy that reduces vast, abstract, and perhaps unknowable apparatuses of control into a single comprehensible device (even if this device is, to many, utterly insane). Such devices can be thought of as "power converters" working to transmute political force, physical energy, mediated information, and human consciousness. This conversion can be wholly physical, as when a victim believes she or he is the target of sinister electromagnetism, X-rays, microwaves, or some other energy deleterious to the body. Here the evil influencer has access to an energy weapon of some kind that allows power to be projected purely as *power*. But this conversion can also involve binding information to energy for the purposes of implanting voices, sending suggestions, or reading minds. Here influencing machines operate as *weaponized media*. In either application, the electronic stands as power under the control of power, the energetic face of semiotic and political control.

Delusions epitomize the unreal and irrational, yet their manifestation and evaluation remain grounded in material social processes. Accordingly, this project interrogates biophysical, electrotechnical, and sociopolitical models of "power," approaching technical delusions as speculative discourses that contemplate how these powers might intersect—conceptually and instrumentally. Such theories frequently proceed from a common question: *What is power capable of executing through electronics?* This question, in turn, implicates another series of questions that invoke the politics of psychosis. *At what point do technical speculations, beliefs, or convictions become so pathological that medical authorities must intervene? Who is to say, and by what authority, where plausible technical affordances end and psychotic delusions begin?* The goal here is not to provide a comprehensive history of madness, media, power, or psychiatry. It is instead to examine how technical delusions, over the past two centuries, have interrogated the historical relationship of electronics, power, and insanity. Such interrogation proceeds from a premise, once insane but now generally endorsed by all: *no transmission is innocent.*

The Technical Delusion

CHAPTER ONE

OCTOBER 4, 1986: Dan Rather, anchor of the CBS *Evening News*, walks home on Manhattan's Upper East Side. At Park Avenue he encounters an agitated stranger. "Kenneth, what is the frequency?" the man demands. Rather tells him he has "the wrong guy," but this only further agitates the stranger, who proceeds to punch Rather in the jaw. Rather runs into the lobby of a nearby building to elude his attacker, but the stranger follows and knocks Rather to the ground, repeating his question over and over:

> What's the frequency, Kenneth?
> What's the frequency, Kenneth?
> What's the frequency, Kenneth?

The building's superintendent comes to Rather's aid, and the attacker flees into the night. Police investigate the assault, but as there are no real leads to pursue in what appears to be the most random of random crimes, the case quickly goes cold.[1] Given the fame of the victim and the odd circumstances of the attack, however, Rather's assault immediately makes its way into the national news cycle—especially after a bruised and battered Rather addresses the incident himself on his evening newscast. Some speculate the entire affair is nothing more than a publicity stunt staged to boost Rather's ratings. "I got mugged," Rather muses of this odd incident. "Who understands these things? I didn't, and I don't now. I didn't make a lot of it at the time, and I don't now. I wish I knew who did it and why, but I have no idea."[2]

Gradually forgotten, "What's the Frequency, Kenneth?" returns in late 1994 as the title of the first single off a new album by R.E.M., the band's lyricist and lead singer, Michael Stipe, reveling in the dadaistic flavor of the incident. A week before R.E.M. officially releases the new single, William Tager, a motorcycle dealer in North Carolina, buys a 1986 Ford Taurus for a trip up the East Coast. Before leaving, Tager loads the car with an AK-47, a .22 caliber

Beretta, four banana clips, and 248 rounds of ammunition. After making a brief stop in Scranton, Pennsylvania, to visit the Steamtown USA train museum, Tager rents another car (believing the first one has been "bugged") and drives into Manhattan. Parking his rental on 49th Street, Tager dons a large smock, inserts a rifle in the sleeve, and walks toward the set of NBC's *The Today Show* at Rockefeller Center. There he is stopped at the door by technician Campbell Montgomery. Blocked in his mission to deliver "important information" to the network, a frustrated Tager retreats to his car and drives away. But he returns fifteen minutes later, and seeing Montgomery attempting to alert the police, he emerges from his car, assumes "a military stance," and shoots Montgomery in the back.[3] An ambulance takes Montgomery to Bellevue Hospital, but he dies in the operating room. Police, meanwhile, have little trouble apprehending Tager as he once again returns to his rented car. During a five-hour interrogation at the police station, Tager explains his motivations. "He says that the networks were watching him for 20 years," reports a detective. "He claims that they've been bugging him for 20 years. He claims that they tap his phone, they send rays on top of him, vibrations come out of the television. These are the terms he uses."[4] In November 1996, Tager receives a twelve-to-twenty-five-year sentence at Sing Sing prison.

A year later, TV critic Eric Mink of the *New York Daily News* speculates there may be a connection between Tager's murder of Montgomery and the still unsolved attack on Dan Rather. Mink shows a mug shot to Rather, and the newsman confirms Tager is most likely the same man. Still, there is no conclusive link between the two attacks. Finally, in 2004, some twenty years after Rather's initial assault, *What's the Frequency, Kenneth?* debuts as an Off-Broadway play. With the mysterious incident once again a topic of public speculation, the district attorney who prosecuted Tager for the murder of Campbell Montgomery writes a letter to the *New York Times*. "In the course of our prosecution, Mr. Tager made detailed statements admitting the earlier assault on Mr. Rather, who was one of a number of media figures Mr. Tager blamed for tormenting him. Mr. Tager's knowledge of nonpublic details of the attack on Mr. Rather, along with other facts and circumstances, left no doubt of his guilt." Although Rather's beating appeared "unsolved" for almost two decades, the prosecutor has never revealed this detail before; thinking like a DA, he has considered Tager's confession no longer important because the statute of limitations on Rather's assault has long since expired.[5] At Sing Sing, meanwhile, Tager enters a psychiatric program to address his decades-long struggle with paranoid schizophrenia.

He is paroled in October 2010, having served just under fourteen years for manslaughter in the first degree.

....

Delusions involving the media have been increasing steadily over the past century, to the point that many clinicians argue they now constitute the single most common symptom among those deemed psychotic, especially those classified as "schizophrenic" and "paranoid."[6] This is even more true if one regards "the media," as psychotics often do, not as an isolated technology but as a sinister alliance of energies, institutions, practices, and content. "People with schizophrenia can have delusions that seem bizarre," note the National Institutes of Health in educational materials from 2012, "such as believing that neighbors can control their behavior with magnetic waves. They may also believe that people on television are directing special messages to them, or that radio stations are broadcasting their thoughts aloud to others."[7] Wires, microphones, radios, televisions, computers, cable lines, antennas, satellites, microwave towers, cell phones, brain chips, and raw electromagnetism have all been implicated as sources of physical torment and mental control, as have the various agencies believed to possess the means and motives to employ these devices. The media are especially prominent in what psychiatry calls *delusions of influence* and *delusions of reference*. As the name implies, delusions of influence involve a person's sense that some external force is "influencing" his or her body. This influence can range from a vague sense that alien energies (rays, beams, frequencies, and so on) suffuse the body to a belief that one has lost all control over volition and movement. Beyond these effects on the body, delusions of influence can involve "thought insertion" and "thought broadcasting," two forms of transmission that exhibit a close affinity to the logic of electronic media. Those experiencing "thought broadcasting" believe their thoughts are leaking out in a type of involuntary telepathy with the surrounding world—perhaps even siphoned away by some external technology. Here the individual faces the daunting challenge of negotiating a social world in which he believes everyone knows what he is thinking. "Thought insertion," meanwhile, describes the sensation that thoughts inside the head are not one's own and thus must emanate from some other mind or place. Thought insertion often appears in conjunction with auditory hallucinations, although the two are not necessarily wholly equivalent phenomena. When hallucinatory voices are present, however, they typically issue commands, hurl abuse, repeat thoughts, and at times offer a continuous commentary on the individual's thoughts and actions.⁸

Delusions of *technical* influence over mind and body predate the advent of electronics proper, emerging within the rapid social transformations of the Industrial Revolution. As early as 1809, Joseph Haslam noted that his patients at London's Bethlem Royal Hospital frequently attributed their blasphemous inner voices to "hearkening wires."⁹ By the mid-nineteenth century, those charged with caring for the insane began to note that raw electricity and magnetism had become the primary villains in delusional persecution. In 1845, Jean-Étienne Dominique Esquirol reported several cases involving various forms of electrical assault or infusion, writing about one patient: "He pretends that they have taken possession of him by supernatural means, which spies,—selected from the most degraded of the French people,—employ by pouring upon his majesty, torrents of electricity, in order to annihilate him."¹⁰ As various technologies harnessed the powers of electromagnetism, so, too, did the psychotic, especially as devices such as the telegraph, telephone, and wireless married the physics of invasive electromagnetism with the politics of imperious communications. Observing that "celestial voices" had once been the predominant form of auditory hallucinations, a physician writing in 1887 noted that "the introduction of the speaking-tube was followed by a transferal of the voices to imaginary systems of tubing in the walls of the patient's apartment; the introduction of the telegraph was followed by the idea (heraldic of the telephone) that the voices were carried to the patients by systems of wires; this delusion latterly has been modified by the adoption of the name of the instrument."¹¹ By 1902, Charles Arthur Mercier's textbook on insanity had turned to the telephone in an effort to depict a typical "paranoiac" of the era. "Whatever he does, and whatever happens to him, that is in the least out of the ordinary course, is due to telephones," Mercier writes. "He plays billiard and loses; the telephone kept his balls out of the pockets and put his adversary's in. His nose begins to bleed; the telephones did it. He gets annoyed and throws his book across the room; the telephone prompted him, or possessed him and threw the book for him. He sees two strangers meet and chat on the opposite side of the street; the telephone is talking to them about him, or they are talking to him through the telephone, or the telephone is mixed up with them in some mysterious way."¹²

Already familiar to clinicians in the era of Edison, Marconi, and Freud, these delusions became even more widespread during the age of broadcasting. The advent of radio as both technology and institution provided a new model for comprehending how the influence of voice, sensation, and energy could invisibly colonize the ether. As a "net," the blanket distribution of radio content encouraged the fantasy of omnipresent (and perhaps omniscient) powers enveloping the world.[13] An anonymous letter sent to Harvard's Psychological Clinic in 1940 thus describes a man's ongoing struggle with "mind-reading pursuers" who had somehow learned to bind vocal soundwaves to radio's electromagnetic frequencies. "The vibration of their vocal cords, evidently generates wireless waves, and these vocal radio waves are caught by human ears without rectification," the letter explains.[14] Others found the very presence of this uncanny technology to be threatening, as in one schizophrenic's belief that the radio in his room would electrocute him.[15] In 1947, at the threshold of television's mass-diffusion across the United States, a concerned woman wrote to the Zenith Radio Corporation requesting the advice of a "television inspector": "I have been greatly disturbed by the television and the Magnaphone in my home, so much so that I get very little rest day or nite." She hoped the inspector might explain her "suffering," a "burning" of the feet and a sense of choking produced by a constant "talking, whistling, [and] ringing of bells from somewhere unknown" that, she implored, "has almost torn me into pieces."[16] This presentation has become so familiar, so emblematic, that popular culture recognizes the "tin-foil helmet" as the signature marker of the electronic paranoiac. Typically deployed for humor, tin-foil helmets are actually a rather desperate technology, an improvised attempt by the insane to seal the cranium from bombardment by the malevolent energies, signals, beams, rays, frequencies, and transmissions that seek to colonize brain and body. This "comic" figure actually has some foundation in clinical history. Emil Kraepelin, for example, recounts a patient who demanded pieces of tin to "insulate himself on all sides"—or, better yet, a "close-shut room with thick walls that no rays could penetrate."[17]

Historians of psychiatry generally credit Victor Tausk as the first to consider the significance of this technological turn within psychotic thought. One of Freud's most promising students (before his suicide in 1919), Tausk was also one of the rare members of the inner circle trained as a neurologist, a qualification that allowed him to gain clinical experience working with psychotic patients at the University of Vienna's psychiatric clinic. From this work, Tausk produced what remains the best-known account of technical control in psychotic delusions: "On the Origins of the Influencing Machine in Schizophrenia." Noting a recent increase in such ideation among his patients, Tausk summarized the effects of these delusional devices in five categories, complaints that have remained surprisingly consistent over the past century:

FIG 1.1 During the hard-fought presidential election of 2016, the Hillary Clinton campaign asked supporters to don a "tin-foil hat" that associated its opponent Donald Trump with fringe beliefs and possible insanity.
SOURCE: HILLARYCLINTON.COM.

1. It makes the patient see pictures.
2. It produces, as well as removes, thoughts and feelings by means of waves or rays or mysterious forces which the patient's knowledge of physics is inadequate to explain....
3. It produces phenomena in the body, erections and seminal emissions, that are intended to deprive the patient of his male potency and weaken him. This is accomplished either by means of suggestion or by air-currents, electricity, magnetism, or X-Rays.
4. It creates sensations that in part cannot be described, because they are strange to the patient himself, and that in part are sensed as electrical, magnetic, or due to air-currents.
5. It is also responsible for other occurrences in the patient's body, such as cutaneous eruptions, abscesses, and other pathological processes.[18]

Tausk focused primarily on the case of Natalija A., a former philosophy student who believed she was under the influence of an "electrical machine" in Berlin. She described the device as a coffin lid in the shape of her own body, lined in its interior with silk or velvet. The inner portion of the machine consisted of "electrical batteries" meant to "represent the internal organs of the body." Natalija A. not only saw the machine as a medium of control; she also invested it with the more primitive powers of animistic sympathy. For example, if someone were to strike the machine, she reported feeling the blow in the identical location on her own body in a type of electromagnetic voodoo. Natalija A. believed her apparatus to be in the service of a rejected suitor, a college professor who was motivated by jealousy (although there were also intimations that the police and other officials in Berlin might be involved). Although the machine at first influenced only Natalija A., she eventually came to believe that her mother, doctors, and friends were under the device's control, as well. Perhaps inevitably, she at last came to believe that Tausk was under its influence and that "they could no longer understand one another," thus bringing an end to their sessions.[19]

Long predominant in delusions of influence, the media have also become increasingly central in delusions of reference. Such delusions involve "a person's false belief that the behavior of others refers to himself or herself; that events, objects, or other people have a particular and unusual significance, usually of a negative nature; derived from an idea of reference, in which a person falsely feels that others are talking about him or her."[20] Mental health advocate Ken Steele recalls first hearing hallucinatory voices in 1962 at age fourteen. Immediately after a disc jockey finished playing Frankie Valli's anthem of adolescent humiliation-turned-falsetto bravado, *Walk Like a Man*, hostile voices began emanating from Steele's bedside radio: *Kill yourself . . . Set yourself afire. The world will be better off. You're no good, no good at all.* Terrified, Steele turned off his radio and ran into the hallway. But the voices followed him, apparently migrating from the receiver into the open air and into his head. Too frightened to wake his parents, Steele collapsed on the living room floor, where he eventually fell asleep for the night. But in the morning the voices continued, less insistent than before, yet still ever present in the background of his "normal" chain of thoughts. As he did every morning before school, Steele watched a few minutes of his favorite television program, NBC's *The Today Show*, but once again the voices took control. A newscaster announced dramatically, *Today Kenny Steele will kill himself.* A kindly Hugh Downs offered support: *Don't kill yourself, Kenny. Don't give up. Try not to do it.* Barbara Walters then appeared on-screen to conduct Kenny's posthumous interview: *Why did you kill yourself? Did you really mean to do it?* "They spoke in borrowed voices," writes Steele, "as if their own voices had been dubbed over by actors in a foreign film."[21] Keeping to the show's format, film critic Judith Crist followed with a segment discussing the merits of Kenny's death as a potential motion picture. The first of many hospitalizations soon followed. Steele's auditory hallucinations would continue for the next thirty years until one morning, miraculously, they simply ceased.

Steele's interrogation by *The Today Show* was more a hallucination than a delusion, given that it was a momentary alteration rather than a fixed system of belief. Delusions of reference typically involve more complex systems of meaning sustained with conviction over a long period of time. For the psychotic, the media's celebrated ability to simulate relations of intimacy with complete strangers has greatly enlarged the sphere of potential reference. Celebrity stalkers, for example, frequently hybridize delusions of reference with "erotomania," psychiatry's now rather quaint term for those who believe they are in a romantic relationship with someone they do not know or have never met. Pop music's trade in romantic fantasy has made it a formidable medium for mass-mediated erotomania, as in the case of two sisters institutionalized in 1937 who constructed a series of delusions around an assortment of radio crooners.[22] The younger sister, "H," believed she was engaged to the popular singer Rudy Vallee, a delusion fully supported by her older sister, "M," and their father. In fact, when H became convinced that Norman White, a singer on Detroit station WJR, was attempting to blackmail the family, the father wrote a letter to White demanding he cease and desist in harassing his daughter. As in so many other cases of media reference, the family believed the singers spoke to H each week through the coded messages of their song selections (White's rendition of "I'm Counting on You to See Me Through" was offered as evidence of his blackmail scheme). Fifty years after H and M crafted their crooner delusions, Charles Manson began telling his followers that the Beatles were sending enigmatic messages through the band's newly released *The Beatles* (commonly known as the White Album).[23] Facilitated or perhaps even wholly produced by the chemical-cultural psychosis of mixing lysergic acid diethylamide (LSD) and experimental pop music, Manson claimed the Beatles were asking him to contact them in London.[24] Whether psychotic or instrumental (or somewhere in-between), Manson's reading of the White Album illustrates how cults can also adopt reading strategies that transform otherwise anonymous media content into direct, meaningful communications. The Heaven's Gate cult, which committed mass suicide in 1997, is said to have shared an intense interest in *Star Trek: The Next Generation* and, in particular, the asexual android Data.[25] As John Caughey writes about the psychotic's inner world, "Although in entering another reality the individual may alter or even drop his actual social relations with others, he does not drop social relations in general. Far from it. On entering the psychotic world, the individual enters a social world, takes on a modified identity, meets others, and becomes entangled in complex systems of imaginary social interactions."[26] As is well known, John Hinckley's attempted assassination of President Ronald Reagan in 1983 stemmed from a desire to attract the attention of Jodie Foster, Hinckley acting out his own perverse version of Foster's film *Taxi Driver* (1976). Mark David Chapman's murder of John Lennon, meanwhile, was perhaps the inevitable outcome of the incredible psycho-electric vortex produced by the magnetic fame of the Beatles in the 1960s and '70s. (George Harrison would later be stabbed by a paranoid schizophrenic who believed the Beatles practiced "black magic.") Oddly echoing the plot of Martin Scorsese's fictional *The King of Comedy* (1982), David Letterman had repeated difficulties in the early 1990s with a stalker, Margaret Ray, who claimed to be his wife and once even stole his car.[27]

Although broadcasting is increasingly residual as an industrial practice, its power to influence and reference remains no less terrifying today. A survey of the sixty largest media markets in the United States found that almost half of the responding stations "indicated that they had received a letter, telephone call, fax, and/or e-mail from an individual asking them 'to stop sending voices to his/her head or to stop talking about him/her.'"[28] An employee of a TV station in Oregon responded that "dealing with people who hear voices" is "a daily part of my job," while a Texas station reported receiving around ten phone calls a week from the mentally disturbed. The complaints detailed in the study testify to the diversity of these delusions. A viewer in Ohio called a station to complain that its anchorwoman was sending messages "by the way she held her pencil." A viewer in Maryland reported the more common delusion that on-air personnel were watching her for the government. A radio listener in Oklahoma insisted that the theme music to a particular program "said bad things about her." A few employees reported disturbed individuals who made repeated attempts to enter the station's office building, one respondent noting that these visitors often arrived thinking they had made an appointment by speaking directly to someone through the TV set. Over the past twenty years, broadcast delusions have remained virulent, but they have also been augmented by delusional systems that incorporate the platforms and affordances of digital convergence. With the Internet taking up functions that range from virtual newspapers to private masturbation enclosures, psychotics now produce complex delusional systems of interactive paranoia. In 2005, for example, a man attempted suicide, believing that his friends "had placed a link between his Web page and his extremities and by hitting different keys, Web browsers could make his extremities jump." He also believed that pornographic images of himself were being published on the Internet and that the CIA "had placed Internet bugs in his ears that could read his mind and control his thoughts."[29] Another study cites a woman who achieved a type of symbiosis with the Internet. She complained that she was in fact "an Internet site as well as a 'live picture' living in the Internet. She believed that everyone with access to a computer was able to connect with her, monitor her and control her thoughts and actions."[30]

....

Despite the growing dominance of the media in delusional systems over the past century, psychiatry as an institution has demonstrated surprisingly little interest in addressing the *technicalities* of such delusions. In 1994, Alfred Kraus termed such presentations "technical delusion," but this is not an official psychiatric designation.[31] For most of its history, psychiatry has typically categorized delusions according to a limited number of thematic genres (persecution, control, erotomania, grandiosity, jealousy, and so on) or abstract experiences (influence and reference). The actual (il)logic of the belief—how the individual understands or explains his delusional experience—has remained surprisingly insignificant, at least diagnostically. In other words, psychiatry typically cares little whether a patient believes a demon, a TV weatherman, or an extraterrestrial is attempting to take control of his mind. Each is considered a variation of a more basic delusion of control or persecution. "Changes in the content of delusions in schizophrenic patients through time have frequently been reported, but have rarely been investigated," notes one study. At stake, argue its authors, is a long-standing divide within psychiatry between *pathogenesis* and *pathoplasticity*—that is, "which factors and influences are causal and intrinsically involved in the pathological processes of schizophrenia, and which are only coincidental colourings of its manifestations."[32] In less polysyllabic terms, delusions remain caught in the age-old divide between nature and nurture (with "nature" prevailing in most contemporary accounts). In relation to technical delusions, at least, much of psychiatry remains wedded to diagnostic criteria that have their roots in the late nineteenth century. Indeed, in a world where domestic terrorist bomber Timothy McVeigh could make the not implausible claim that the military had inserted a microchip in his buttocks for tracking and surveillance, psychiatry's language for assessing delusional technology has advanced little beyond Tausk's era of cranks, X-rays, and batteries.[33]

Psychiatry's lack of interest in the technicalities of technical delusions will strike many as counterintuitive. After all, attributing hallucinations to a covert CIA transmitter would seem a significantly different presentation from locating these voices in satanic demons. If nothing else, such differences in delusional logic align the individual with beliefs and communities—spiritual, cultural, scientific—that themselves participate in frequently antagonistic debates over defining the consensual boundaries of the real world. This lack of interest in delusional content can be explained, at least in part, by psychiatry's historical efforts to promote itself as an objective diagnostic science rather than a subjective interpretive art. Karl Jasper's *Allgemeine Psychopathologie* (*General Psychopathology*), first published in 1913, has been especially important in systematizing psychiatric approaches to delusions and their formation.[34] Working in a phenomenological tradition, Jaspers was less concerned with "what" a delusional individual believed than with "how" she or he experienced the world, a divide frequently described in terms of *form* ("how") and *content* ("what"). Accordingly, Jaspers introduced a distinction between what he called a "primary" and a "secondary" delusion. The primary delusion, for Jaspers, is the irreducible core of the psychosis, an original and thus foundational alteration in the phenomenological experience of the patient. Jaspers likened the primary delusion to "entering a new world."[35] Unexplained voices arrive. Thought seems to leak out of the head. The body is changing. An ego-alien force controls thought and action. This primary delusion is not a "cause" in an organic or psychodynamic sense; it is, instead, the initial and thus foundational alteration that signifies the onset of the psychotic episode. Secondary delusions, in turn, describe the "content" or delusional system that builds on the primary delusion's transformation of experience. Thus, an individual who hears voices or feels sensations of ego-alien control (a primary delusion) professes that the CIA is broadcasting signals into his brain and controlling his action by computer (secondary delusions). This distinction between primary form and secondary content has been debated throughout the century it came to dominate. Nevertheless, the idea that a primary delusional form underlies and is antecedent to secondary delusional content has remained a cornerstone of diagnostic practice, especially as biological approaches to psychosis have sought to displace psychodynamic traditions. Applications of the primary-secondary divide often align with a series of binaries that reinforce a fundamental divide between primary "forms" and secondary "content":

PRIMARY	SECONDARY
FORM	CONTENT
"HOW"	"WHAT"
PATHOGENESIS	PATHOPLASTICITY
BIOLOGY	CULTURE
NATURE	NURTURE

This particular reading of Jaspers is highly compatible with a neurobiological emphasis on organic dysfunction: the brain is "broken" (primary) and delusions emerge (secondary). The terms on the left are significant; those on the right are superfluous.

These binaries of form and content were further codified when Jaspers' student, Kurt Schneider, introduced his index of "first-rank symptoms" in schizophrenia, criteria often invoked through the mnemonic ABCD: auditory hallucinations, broadcasting of thought, controlled thought, delusional perception.[36] Schneider's A, B, C, and D provided a more neatly taxonomic version of Jaspers's primary forms, describing the most common experiential anomalies thought to generate the otherwise endless variations of secondary content.

Schneider's first-rank symptoms of schizophrenia continue to inform the criteria of the *Diagnostic and Statistical Manual of Mental Disorders* (DSM) and the International Classification of Diseases (ICD).[37] As in previous editions, the DSM-V (2013) diagnoses schizophrenia by confirming two of the following Criterion A (or "characteristic") symptoms as active for at least a month:

1. Delusions
2. Hallucinations
3. Disorganized Speech
4. Grossly Abnormal Psychomotor Behavior, such as Catatonia
5. Negative Symptoms (avolition, asociality, etc.)[38]

The DSM-V further adds that at least one of the two symptoms must be number 1, 2, or 3. This revision essentially formalizes the diagnostic weight hallucinations and delusions have always held in Criterion A for schizophrenia. Under earlier schema, a path theoretically remained to a schizophrenic diagnosis in the absence of hallucinations and delusions, but the DSM-V *requires* the presence of hallucinations, delusions, or disorganized speech to confirm the diagnosis.

To be schizophrenic is to manifest hallucinations and delusions. How, then, does one *confirm* the presence of hallucinations or delusions? Significantly, unlike physical symptoms such as fever or a rash, hallucinations and delusions can be known only through *discourse*. In the continuing absence of any definitive biological test for either predicting or confirming psychosis, diagnosing schizophrenia thus proceeds much as it did in the early twentieth century when Eugene Bleuler first introduced the term. A patient appears before a physician, clinician, or psychiatrist. The patient complains of or implies the presence of hallucinations. He expresses odd or unusual beliefs that indicate the possibility of delusional thinking. Hallucinations and delusions thus become bona fide symptoms only to the extent that the psychiatrist *validates their discursive presentation,* an interpretative judgment that is always haunted by a measure of uncertainty. After all, how can one person ever really know whether another person is hallucinating? By definition, hallucinations are only present and ultimately knowable to the individual said to be hallucinating. For everyone else, hallucinations can only be surmised through indexical evidence. Delusional systems are even more complex discursive exchanges. In a vernacular sense, a "delusion" is a manifestly incorrect belief that will not be surrendered by the delusional individual.

The current edition of the DSM-V formalizes this a bit by defining delusions as "fixed beliefs that are not amenable to change in light of conflicting evidence." But the editors also concede that "the distinction between a delusion and a strongly held idea is sometimes difficult to make and depends in part on the degree of conviction with which the belief is held despite clear or reasonable contradictory evidence regarding its veracity."[39] Of course, "reasonability," "contradictory," "evidence," "conviction," and "veracity" themselves are all qualitatively contentious terms. At the very least, a delusion requires a triangular social relationship to become a "delusion": two people in conflict is a disagreement, two people who interpret the world differently from a third open the door for delusional criteria. Obviously, these dynamics become even more complex in a heterogeneous social order stratified by power, environment, knowledge, language, and belief. As one study notes, "Delusions are associated with more than 75 distinct clinical conditions in the USA. Given the enormous variety and distinctiveness of ideas found in cultures across the world, the criteria by which distinctions are drawn are not easy to grasp."[40]

Delusions, as well as hallucinations, are considered "positive" symptoms in that they appear as an addition to the "negative" symptoms that early psychosis shares with other mental disorders (irritability, insomnia, depression, aphonia). As a positive symptom, hallucinations and delusions obey a more or less binary logic: they either exist or they do not. Yet as discursive phenomena, delusions are experienced, expressed, and encountered on the fundamentally ambiguous terrain of language and culture. This inherent uncertainty informs the ongoing legal concern that an individual might feign hallucinatory content in court to bolster an insanity defense or fake a delusion to earn a Section 8 discharge. Exploiting these vulnerabilities, journalists and assorted activists for many years have reveled in tricking psychiatric authorities into diagnosing them as "mad," thus allowing them access to institutions to expose abuse or fraud.[41] The prominence of language in assessing delusions as a pathology of belief installs a paradox at the center of the psychiatric project. Assembled from cultural building blocks of language and meaning, delusions are necessarily bound to the relativistic dynamics of society, history, and politics. So although psychiatry considers delusions a positive symptom of psychosis, their foundation in language precludes their providing any *positivist* proof of psychotic thinking. The ability of electronic media to provide ever more sophisticated simulations of voice and vision, often detached and disembodied from any discernible source, has only made the positivity of these symptoms more difficult to evaluate.

The Reflecting Machine

To the extent that psychiatry has demonstrated any interest in issues of content in delusional thought, technical or otherwise, the approach remains one of basic *reflectionism*. Delusions are said to "reflect" the world around them in the same way that literature, film, and other expressive forms are thought to "hold a mirror" up to society. In explaining the gravitation toward technical delusions in particular, psychiatry has long assumed that those whom we deem psychotic simply choose to blame or explain their difficulties through whatever new marvel happens to currently dominate public attention. As yet another exasperated psychiatrist observed at the turn of the twentieth century, "At the present day it is, as most people unfortunate enough to be thrown in contact with the insane know well, the telephone and the electric machine which have replaced in the visions of diseased minds the place once occupied by the Sabbat and the *grimoire*."[42] In the era of the telephone, lunatics had delusions about telephones. In the era of virtual reality, schizophrenics have delusions about virtual reality. This continuing emphasis on reflectionism has typically made psychiatry reluctant to recognize new delusional presentations. Not surprisingly, neurobiological accounts of psychosis appeal to a form of ahistorical humanism that universalizes all of human subjectivity. Brains break, and when they do, characteristic delusions emerge—whether in Neanderthals or astronauts. Rebuffing claims that culture and history have any meaningful impact on the delusional process, one study notes, "There are only a few themes of extraordinary anthropological importance for the organization of human relationships which can be found in every epoch and in different cultures (persecution, grandiosity, guilt, religion, hypochondria, jealousy, and love)." Responding specifically to the proposition that delusions involving technology might be an unprecedented presentation, the authors continue, "The 'new' themes, referring to the development of modern technology and the rapid changes of 'cultural patterns' turned out to be only the shaping of the basic delusional themes." The study's authors ultimately dismiss the impact of "technological and cultural innovations" in delusional content by appealing to a well-worn homily": proposing "new" delusions, they argue, is simply putting "old wine in new bottles."[43]

As a theory of technical content, reflectionism dates all the way back to Tausk's initial analysis of the schizophrenic influencing machine in 1919. As a student of Freud, Tausk was less concerned with engaging the historical or cultural significance of the influencing machine than with isolating an immutable process that would unify each and every presentation of these psychotic devices. In his analysis of Natalija A., the young woman who believed she was under the control of an anthropomorphic electrified coffin, Tausk sought to synthesize Freud's theories on paranoia with his own observations about schizophrenic projection. The influencing machine, Tausk argued, is a projection of the patient's *own* body, a way to externalize onto an ego-alien machine the disturbing internal sensations of physical and mental alteration that typify a psychotic episode. Again concurring with Freud, Tausk concedes that dreams of machines are almost always masturbatory in nature, the machine a "symbol" of the dreamer's genitalia: "In machine dreams the dreamer awakes, more often than not, with his hand on his genitalia, after having dreamed of manipulating the machine."[44] In psychosis, however, this displaced equation of body and machine can become *literal*,[45] apparently conforming to the widespread assumption that schizophrenics adopt "concrete thinking" over abstraction.[46] Tausk argues that the influencing machine is most often an anthropomorphic delusion: "The machines produced by the wit of man are fashioned after the likeness of the human body, an unconscious projection of his own bodily construction."[47] Unpacking the literalized metaphors of Natalija A.'s electric coffin, Tausk observes that the coffin's velvet lining demonstrated Natalija A.'s use of a common feminine metaphor for describing skin as feeling "silky" or like "velvet." The coffin's batteries he attributes to little more than the lesson taught to schoolchildren that the intestines constitute a "very complicated machine," although later he amends this somewhat to speculate that Natalija A.'s specific placement of batteries may represent a fetus in the womb.[48] When Natalija A. first discussed the machine, Tausk notes, the device was in the shape of a woman with fully articulated arms. But as time went on, she reported these arms to be only etchings on the lid of the coffin, leading Tausk to speculate that in the near future the machine would probably be without arms entirely. This progression he attributed to the defensive mechanisms of the ego as it attempted to distort the machine's true identity as a projection of Natalija A.'s body. It would, over time, become less like a recognizable body and more like a completely mechanical machine.

Such interpretative moves should not be surprising to anyone familiar with classical psychoanalysis. Yet an important question remains: *why should delusions of influence and persecution take the specific form of a machine?* Tausk is less forthcoming here, noting only that "patients endeavor to discover the construction of the apparatus by means of their technical knowledge, and it appears that with the progressive popularization of the sciences, all the forces known to technology are utilized to explain the functioning of the apparatus."[49] As is the case today, the technicalities of the technical delusion were of little interest to Tausk. In the end, the rise in technical ideation at the dawn of the twentieth century signaled, for Tausk, little more than "the need for causality that is inherent in man." Symptomatically and historically, then, the appearance of the influencing machine amounts to an accident or convenience; in fact, Tausk considered the influencing machine a *redundant* "terminal stage in the evolution of the symptom."[50] In this respect, an influencing machine is only an additional possible stage in the schizophrenic progression from an initial sense of alteration to more elaborate projections of external control. A patient experiencing influence may ultimately arrive at a mechanical explanation, but then again, perhaps not. This places Tausk in a somewhat paradoxical position. Granting that influencing machines were most certainly "symbols" that might be usefully subjected to the same techniques as dream analysis, Tausk nevertheless comes to the conclusion that this symptom is *a relatively arbitrary and redundant manifestation* of paranoid projection.

Reflectionism is perhaps the most influential school of historical interpretation because it is so obvious—tautologically so. Novels, paintings, or delusions involving electronics necessarily reflect a world in which electronics exist. In slightly more nuanced form, reflection theory borrows a page from vernacular psychoanalysis to imagine that novels, paintings, or delusions involving electronics reflect a world in which "anxieties" about electronics exist, allowing the text in question to become a puzzle of interpretative displacement. But as literary historian Raymond Williams has observed, the seemingly self-evident nature of reflectionism serves to repress the historical dynamics that actually shape cultural production (whether this production is judged "psychotic" or "sane"). Discussing these distortions in the realm of art, Williams writes, "The most damaging consequence of any theory of art as reflection is that, through its persuasive physical metaphor, it succeeds in suppressing the actual work on the material—in a final sense, the material social process—which is the making of any art work."[51] In other words, a novel, film, or painting does not simply appear out of nowhere to serve as a blank reflective surface that mechanically and thus passively records the surrounding world (or its attending "anxieties"); rather, such artifacts are the products of agents and forces actively producing, circulating, and consuming meaning from various positions within the social (and psychic) order. Van Gogh and Monet both painted flowers and landscapes in the late nineteenth century—if they did so "reflectively," they were clearly doing so on different planets. If images of plant life can be subject to such individualistic distortion, what does it mean to say a delusion "reflects" the surrounding historical environment?[52]

Reflectionism's statement of the obvious—that artists are a product of their times—camouflages the "material social process" by which artworks take shape. To counter reflection theory, Williams advocated the concept of "mediation." He conceded that in critical practice, mediation often functions as "little more than a sophistication of reflection."[53] Still, mediation at least attempts to frame cultural production as actively political rather than passively reflective. What is needed, Williams argued, is a concept of mediation that emphasizes the active process of material production without imagining self and social as two independent, autonomous realms that are bound by the cultural artifact; rather, the "work"—a painting on the canvas or words on the page—is a discourse, a meaningful transaction produced by the self and social in a situated dialogue of interdependent construction. The dynamics of delusional mediation can be demonstrated by moving from the art gallery to the art gallery in the asylum. Even as Tausk contemplated the psychoanalytic significance of Natalija A.'s animistic coffin, Robert Gie—institutionalized as "schizophrenic" only a few miles outside Vienna, in Rosegg—was producing a series of technical drawings that would eventually find a home in Jean DeBuffet's Collection de l'Art Brut. Gie appears to have produced the majority of his artwork around 1916, including his industrial portrait, *Distribution d'effluves avec machine centrale et tableau métrique* (*Distribution of Unpleasant Smells with Central Machine and Metric Table*). The drawing depicts a chain of men laboring in the service of a giant mechanized head, all in the apparent thrall of some inexplicable system of metrics. As with Gie's other drawings, an elaborate network of helmets and wiring connects the men to the central figure in what appears to be some type of electrified factory scenario (but who can say for sure?). At mid-century, the journal *L'Art Brut* would say of Gie, "Since he was unable to free himself of these currents that were tormenting him, he gives every appearance of having joined forces with them, taking passionate pride in portraying them in their total victory, in their triumph."[54]

Typically, the key to interpreting psychotic art is to know that the artist was at one time diagnosed as psychotic. Discussions of psychotic art approach the work much like psychiatry approaches a delusion: it stands as an index of an underlying psychosis. As David Maclagan argues, "Psychiatry's early interest in the paintings or drawings of psychotic patients stemmed from two overlapping needs: the desire to gain access to the mental world of the psychotic, and the wish to give as specific an account as possible of the

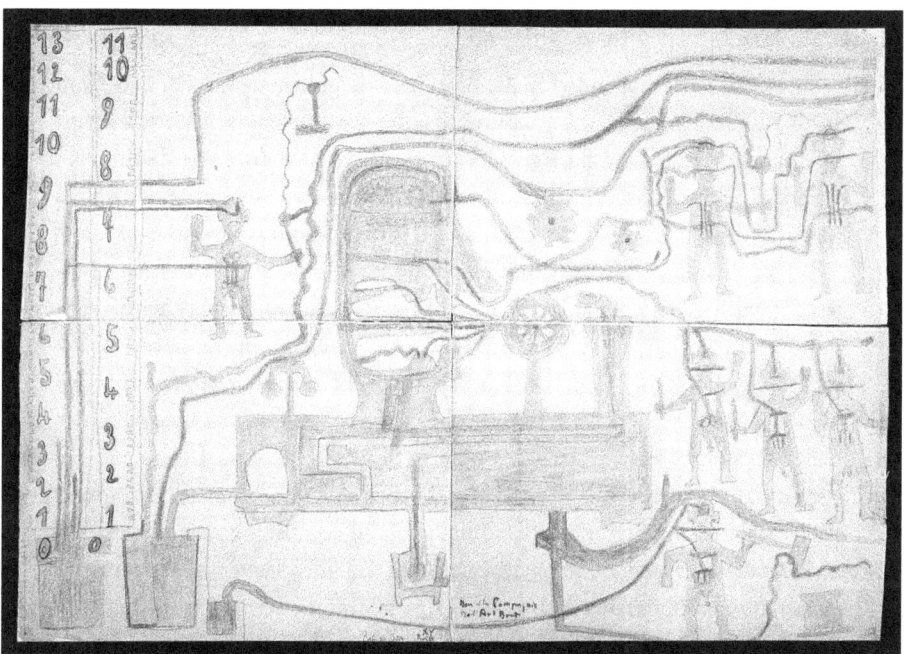

FIG 1.2 Robert Gie, *Distribution d'effluves avec machine central et tableau métrique* (circa 1916). Republished with permission from Collection de l'Art Brut.

various ways in which it departed from the normal."[55] These imperatives, still widely operative, encourage two common interpretations of the work. The art is thought to be either a record of things that "do not exist" (an illustration of hallucinatory or delusional material that the artist nevertheless takes to be "real") or it becomes an example of mimetic distortion (an attempt to capture the "real world" that has gone awry through psychotic alteration). In either case, there is a tendency to read psychotic art as something *other than art*—that is, a painting by a schizophrenic is often approached as if it is a direct, unrevised expression of the individual's subjective experience.[56] The "odd" style of art known to be "schizophrenic" thus becomes a two-way reflective mirror: on the one surface, a distorted reflection of the exterior world (Van Gogh's paintings thus "reflect" the agrarian world of late nineteenth-century Holland); and on the other surface, a reflection of the artist's distorted psyche (Van Gogh's paintings reflect his state of mind, his disturbed psyche).[57] The material work of creating the art *as art* (in dialogue with the era's larger conventions of signification) becomes little more than an autonomic reflex of insanity. As Francis Reitman observed of schizophrenic style in his study *Psychotic Art* (1951), "The difficulty arises in distinguishing aesthetic re-structuring of actuality from the re-structuring that occurs in the phantasies of normal individuals, both artistic and non-artistic, and from the qualitative alteration in the apprehension of reality that is taken as a defining characteristic of psychosis."[58] In other words, how does one distinguish the creative strategies of art ("aesthetic re-structuring") from the additional distortions of fantasy, schizophrenia, and schizophrenic fantasy?

By segregating art, fantasy, and psychosis as separate realms, Reitman suggests a pathogenetic essence might still be isolated somewhere within the pathoplastic style of a painting. But how, exactly, would one set about isolating this psychotic core from the shared practices of "aesthetic re-structuring"? Again, a painting becomes "insane" most often because knowledge of the artist's diagnosis ensures that his only option is to express a state of pure insanity. In the work of Robert Gie and other artists known to be variously *abnormal*, this impulse has contributed to the continuing romanticization of "outsider" art, psychotic or otherwise, as the final vestige of authenticity within the treacherously self-conscious sign play of modernity.[59] As Maclagan writes about psychotic and outsider art, "It acts like a magnified and exaggerated reflection of the post-Renaissance myth of the heroic artist. The triumph of the artistic power of invention over cultural restraints, the inherent power of the image to exceed rational explanation, and the anti-social inclination of individualistic expression, are all features that find an echo in the profile of psychotic art."[60] Henry Darger's penchant for drawing penises on little girls or Howard Finster's biblical graphomania thus amount to the same thing: they signify unadulterated, pure, unwavering, and thus authentic belief in a reality that is (for the sane tastemakers of the art world) beyond reason, in the "realms of the unreal" (personal perversion, in Darger's case; evangelical Christianity with Finster).[61]

Establishing a purity of psychotic style segregates the insane as an absolute Other, much as the isolation of a primary delusion is thought to index a psychosis that is wholly independent of any secondary cultural concerns. In doing so, this maneuver erases the continuities binding "sane" and "insane" culture as variously inflected mediations within a shared historical horizon. The 15,145 bloody pages of Darger's novel *The Story of the Vivian Girls, in What Is Known as the Realms of the Unreal, of the Glandeco-Angelinian War Storm Caused by the Child Slave Rebellion*, provides compelling evidence of an "abnormal" mind, yet the story also strives to emulate the Oz series of Frank Baum, the purported creative inspiration for Darger's epic. Similarly, one can examine Gie's complex of wired workers and assume he is attempting to capture, in most literal terms, what he imagines to be the scheme behind the altered phenomenology of his psychotic state. Thus does *L'Art Brut* present Gie as "having joined forces" with his electrical currents. Yet considered in terms of historical mediation, Gie's artwork seems equally in conversation with such fellow and highly eminent moderns as Georg Simmel, Max Weber, and Max Nordau. As an image of metrics, electronics, and industrialization, Gie's *Distribution of Unpleasant Smells with Central Machine* could easily serve as an illustration of Simmel's contention in "The Metropolis and Mental Life" that "punctuality, calculability, exactness are forced upon life by the complexity and extension of metropolitan existence and are not only most intimately connected with its money economy and intellectualist character. These traits must also color the contents of life and favor the exclusion of those irrational, instinctive, sovereign traits and impulses which aim at determining the mode of life from within, instead of receiving the general and precisely schematized form of life from without."[62] Gie's drawing of wired workers is just as much a cultural diagnosis as Simmel's lament over the "exclusion" of "life from within" (factory work under capitalism stinks): both are examples of a certain fin-de-siècle discourse on industrial modernity that emphasizes the "dehumanizing" toll of the new techno-economic order. Moreover, Gie and Simmel align themselves with a critique that stands in opposition to other prominent discourses of the era—namely, Taylorism, Fordism, and those other celebratory accounts of capitalist productivity that laud the increased efficiencies of mass industrialization. To say any of these discourses—Gie's paintings, Simmel's sociology, or Ford's boosterism—simply "reflect" the time period is to ignore how each statement mediates, from a very different position and agenda, the social, cultural, and economic transformations of the modern era.

One might argue that delusions are not really equivalent to paintings, novels, and other creative endeavors. Presumably, one does not *choose* to be delusional. But this does not mean that a delusion is any less a product of historical possibility than a poem. Despite exemplifying the unreal, the untrue, and the irrational, delusions nevertheless remain products of "material social processes," discursive activity bound to the dynamic negotiation of the self and the social in producing meaning. While reflectionism posits a very general link between delusional content and its historical moment, it is less persuasive in explaining the specificities of individual psychiatric presentations. One study, for example, details a woman under the delusion that her neighbor's satellite dish relayed romantic messages from Donald Duck.[63] To say such a delusion "reflects" a world in which satellite dishes and Donald

Duck both exist is essentially to say nothing. As we have seen, Tausk believed that the delusional arrival of an influencing machine was a redundant and essentially arbitrary component in the psychotic process. Why, then, do some primary delusions of influence cohere in the allegedly redundant content of an influencing machine (and cartoon duck) while others do not? Such questions speak to the mechanism of *delusional formation*. The process through which a person becomes delusional is no more settled an issue than what actually constitutes a delusion. One way to organize this question is around the issue of agency. Put simply, are individuals the active authors of their delusions, employing a deteriorating sense of reason and logic to explain the voices, sensations, and other phenomenological alterations of their psychosis? Or do delusions *find* the psychotic, cohering as an inescapable truth that is not so much chosen as imposed on the psychotic subject?

Reason or Revelation

In the first decades of the twentieth century, many respectable and seemingly reasonable people believed telepathy was an established scientific fact. The sciences of wireless and neurology were undoubtedly involved. All that remained was to identify that part of the brain involved in sending and receiving telepathic transmissions, as well as the waveform that carried the telepathic signal through the ether. Many offered speculation on the mechanics of this contact, from Sir Arthur Conan Doyle, the creator of Sherlock Holmes, to Sigmund Freud, the creator of the unconscious. "It seems more and more certain," wrote Maurice Maeterlinck in 1914, that "we are connected with everything that exists by an inextricable network of vibrations, waves, influences, of nameless, numberless and uninterrupted fluids."[64]

In 1910, Victor Thompson published his own monograph on the scientific foundations of telepathy: "Telepathic Vision and Sound." Like many of his contemporaries, Thompson believed that all psychic phenomena would eventually be traced to a single energy: "All psychic manifestations of the human intellect, normal or abnormal—insanity, hypnotism, somnambulism and telepathy—are related, and are to be referred to one general principle or law; these are facts resting upon a physiological basis, which, once understood, will remove it from the supernatural."[65] In meticulously researched and heavily annotated chapters, Thompson then surveyed the contemporary literature in hypnosis, insanity, hysteria, sleepwalking, epilepsy, and other "abnormal" psychological states with the goal of elucidating this universal synthesis of mental energy. After concluding his overview of contemporary psychology, Thompson moves on to the topic of wireless. Here Thompson provides detailed descriptions and even schematics of the various devices used across history to generate and transmit electricity. He summarizes the contributions of Alexander Graham Bell, Nikola Tesla, Thomas Edison, Valdemar Poulsen, Guglielmo Marconi, Reginald Fessenden, and other pioneers of electromagnetic science, pausing when appropriate to provide more detailed summaries of induction, coherence, and other electromagnetic principles.

With his theories of mind and electromagnetic contact in place, Thompson finally arrives at the topic of telepathy. Unlike the heavily researched and densely annotated chapters in the first half of the monograph, however, the chapter on telepathy merely reprints, verbatim, two letters written by Thompson in 1905. Both are addressed to Thomas Darlington, who was then serving as the commissioner of New York City's Board of Health. Hoping to provide assistance in combating a recent outbreak of meningitis in the city, Thompson advises Darlington, "It is hypnotization or telepathy at a distance, done by instruments undersigned and carried on for the last two years. The persons in telepathic communication can see and hear through a person."[66] Thompson then goes on to detail his own difficulties as the target of these instruments, troubles that eventually led to a brief hospitalization. Thompson gives a quick summary of his bodily ills during the period—fever, constipation, headaches—before moving on to the "psychological part" of his experience:

> My first impression was a man asking in my head: "Who are you?" "Is your name Thompson?" A strange fear came over me, and I thought that I was going crazy, knowing full well that the inner voices people hear are a common incident in delusional insanity. The next thing that happened, the extinct memory of images was suddenly restored, first the American and then Danish, down to my childhood; but here it happened that the voice asked me or my brain to explain the different images, and I was sure now that I was handled by other people, through instruments. I heard distinctly two voices, one explaining to the other; that is, one would say to the other, he means so or so, or it can be understood this or that way.[67]

At this point in the manuscript, then, the reader discovers rather abruptly that Thompson is completely mad. Like so many whom the century would soon deem "schizophrenic," Thompson recognized that his experiences might mark him as a lunatic, prompting him to offer a somewhat incoherent defense of his sanity: "Now I know that abnormal psychic activity is insanity, but in my case the sound or words that I hear is [*sic*] heard any place in the body, where the other parties please to place their telephones and microphones, etc.; in other words, through the sensation of hearing (the internal ear), the subjective mind working in direct opposition to it."[68] Following the reprinted letters to Darlington, Thompson's monograph then proceeds to explore various features of human anatomy, explaining how "telepathic instruments" can be used to "seize" control of the entire head and transform it into a type of wireless station: "It is possible to talk to a person many, many miles away, to go into his house, to see, and hear with him and to torture him. How the old torturers would have been glad to possess an apparatus which would have enabled them to torture their victim by an invisible force in his own home, enforcing with satanic ingenuity, a nightmare of unheard agony, and awful suffering and impossible escape."[69] Who would engage in such a nefarious project? "The persons handling the instruments are Danes," Thompson declares.

Thompson's monograph describes a familiar psychotic progression from growing unease to the formation of a truly singular delusion. Contrary to popular lore, psychosis typically does not arrive as a sudden "break" with reality and an instantaneous descent into madness. As clinicians must frequently remind the public, those whom we deem mad, insane, schizophrenic, or psychotic are not prone to running violently amok; nor do they necessarily evacuate the "real world" of their nonpsychotic peers. Most often, those on the threshold of psychosis experience a gradual but increasingly problematic change in their relationship with the world around them. As in Thompson's case, a growing hypochondria is common, as is a general sense that there has been some inexplicable change in one's relation to the world. Crucially, this "prodromal" phase of psychosis typically centers on an escalating *crisis of meaning*. As the analyst Darian Leader writes, "Delusions are almost always preceded by a period in which the person feels that there is some kind of meaning in the world, although it remains imprecise and elusive. A poster on the tube, an article in the paper or a TV advertisement seem to concern them, but they aren't sure in what way."[70] Whether the product of a neurobiological trigger or escalating psychodynamic alienation (or some combination), psychosis begins as a subtle "sensation of change" or "alteration." "The environment is somehow different," observed Jaspers in 1913, "not to a gross degree—perception is unaltered in itself but there is some change which envelops everything with a subtle, pervasive and strangely uncertain light."[71] In this "delusional atmosphere," prepsychotic individuals become increasingly sensitive to meaning itself. "Every detail and event takes on an excruciating distinctness, specialness, and peculiarity," writes Louis A. Sass. Crucially, however, "some definite meaning always lies just out of reach . . . where it eludes all attempts to grasp or specify it."[72] In January 2009, after US Airways Flight 1549 hit a flock of geese and made a miraculous emergency landing on the Hudson River, one young woman immediately recalled a recent online post related to the expression "A bird in the hand is worth two in the bush." Describing the anxious week that took her to the threshold of acute psychosis, she recalls, "I've never been one to say I predicted anything, but—for one thing, birds. Birds had taken down the plane. And then bush—President Bush. I thought, 'Oh my God, this is another 9/11, and I predicted the whole thing.'" Although she was a professed atheist, her thoughts over the next few days increasingly focused on memories from her Mormon childhood. Car horns in the street became the trumpets of revelation. Still precariously attached to reality, she realized she was ill and needed to check herself into a hospital. But she remembers she could not take the first taxi that she hailed: on the cab's roof was an advertisement for the Broadway production of *Wicked*. Concerned the taxi might actually take her to hell, she decided to wait for the next one.[73]

This period of looming significance often feels like a heightened state of nervous expectation. Klaus Conrad described this period as the "trema." A form of nervous anticipation akin to stage fright, the trema captures the escalating tension, perceptual hyperacuity, and elusive sense of significance typically encountered in early psychosis. Popular conceptions of psychosis frequently imagine the individual "losing touch with reality" as the boundaries of selfhood become confused and conflated.[74] But as Sass has argued, the "loss of self" experienced in schizophrenia "may develop *not* from a weakening of the observing ego or a lowering of consciousness but, to the contrary, from a hypertrophy of attentive, self-reflexive awareness."[75] In early psychosis, somatic and semiotic processing becomes more acute, leading to episodes of depersonalization and de-realization. Many have described these moments as an overwhelming encounter with the brute materiality of reality itself, a hyperawareness of the surrounding environment as raw matter momentarily detached from the invisible structures of meaning that secure the typically effortless integration of perception, thought, and action. A well-known account of this intense derealization can be found in Jean-Paul Sartre's canonical tale of existential angst, *La Nausée* (*Nausea*; 1938). Antoine Roquentin, a detached, bookish loner with little investment in the people and society that surround him (i.e., a classic schizoaffective personality), finds himself increasingly beset with moments of "nausea," an escalating crisis of disgust and alienation. Sitting in the park one day contemplating the knotted roots of a chestnut tree, Roquentin suddenly feels overwhelmed with a sense of dread and revulsion for the gross materiality of the nature that surrounds him: "The roots of the chestnut tree were sunk in the ground just under my bench. I couldn't remember it was a root any more. The words had vanished and with them the significance of things, their methods of use, and the feeble points of reference which men have traced on their surface. I was sitting, stooping forward, head bowed, alone in front of this black, knotty mass, entirely beastly, which frightened me."[76] Roquentin observes, "Usually existence hides itself. It is there, around us, in us, it is us, you can't say two words without mentioning it, but you can never touch it." But in his encounter with the tangled roots as abstract matter, a textured substance momentarily outside of language, Roquentin glimpses the ultimate angst of psychotic de-realization: "And then all of a sudden, there it was, clear as day: existence had suddenly unveiled itself. It had lost the harmless look of an abstract category: it was the very paste of things, this root was kneaded into existence. Or rather the root, the park gates, the bench, the sparse grass, all that had vanished: the diversity of things, their individuality, were only an appearance, a veneer. This veneer had melted, leaving soft, monstrous masses, all in disorder—naked, in a frightful, obscene nakedness."[77]

Shitij Kapur notes that the prepsychotic can continue for days, months, or even years "in this state of a subtly altered experience of the world, accumulating experiences of aberrant salience without a clear reason or explanation."[78] If and when this prodromal phase becomes acute, the "positive" symptoms of psychosis begin to appear. As in Thompson's case, an "ego-alien" voice may demand the subject narrate his memories or immediate experience, or multiple hallucinatory voices in conversation discuss the individual's thoughts and actions. As Leader writes, "It is in this period that the world starts to speak.... There is a mobilization of signifiers to treat the experience of enigma. Meaning can be established little by little or, more frequently, in leaps and bounds, moments when truth is suddenly discovered."[79] Conrad described this discovery of the truth as the "*Apophänie*."[80] Whether focused in a eureka moment or taking place in "leaps and bounds" over a longer period of time, apophany describes the final coherence of the delusion. Experiencing discomfort and alien voices for several days, Thompson enters the hospital where, one night in his bed, he suddenly understands what is happening: the Danes have developed "telepathic instruments" that "seize" control of the head and convert it into a type of wireless station. Sometime later, a meningitis outbreak confirms this fundamental insight, compelling Thompson, perhaps out of moral obligation, to share his knowledge of instrumental telepathy with New York City's Department of Health.

How, exactly, could a person come to believe so unfailingly that Denmark had deployed telepathic instrumentation capable of implanting voices and distributing meningitis? Two models of delusional formation are worth contrasting here, what might be distinguished as "reason" versus "revelation." The "reason" model has dominated modern psychiatry, dating as far back as 1690 in John Locke's "An Essay Concerning Human Understanding." Locke proposed that the "mad" have not "lost the faculty of reasoning, but having joined together some of the ideas very wrongly, they mistake them for truths.... For, by the violence of their imaginations, having taken their fancies for realities, they make right deductions from them."[81] As one might expect from one of the founding figures of the Enlightenment, the insane in this formulation are essentially Enlightenment thinkers led astray, allowing a moment of primary misapprehension to generate an entire secondary chain of logical yet errant ideas.

The "faulty reasoning" model has been described as an "explanationist" approach. Here an individual is thought to cultivate a delusion "in an attempt to explain or make sense of, an unusual experience."[82] *I hear voices arguing in my head. I surmise I am under the control of a telepathic instrument. I further surmise this instrument is employed by agents from Denmark.* Like reflectionism, explanationism is a persuasive theory, both in psychiatry and popular thought, precisely because it seems so obvious. From the perspective of the sane, the explanationist position is ultimately the most comforting. Who, after all, is more invested in championing the enduring power of reason than those who remain on the side of sanity, so much so that even a radical disruption of our consensual reality must be recuperated as the product of (misguided) reason? Explanationism and reflectionism, working in tandem, posit an individual who, suddenly beset with phenomenological or cognitive anomalies, sets out to understand what is causing his alteration, a search that in the modern era most often leads to some form of electronics or media as the culprit. This essentially linear account of the psychotic process, in turn, is highly compatible with the traditional division between primary form and secondary content. A pathological "form" occurs in the brain, leading to a faulty search for explanatory "content" within the culture. The chosen content is (as it must be) a "reflection" of its historical moment.

Despite appearing reasonable to those who are reasonable, however, this model of faulty reasoning fails to account persuasively for certain key features of delusional thought. If a delusion was indeed the product of somewhat logical reasoning based on a decidedly faulty premise (or even wholly organic dysfunction), why, then, is it so difficult to dissuade the psychotic of their delusional beliefs by continuing to appeal to this sense of reason and logic? With its model of sequential progression—a primary core that produces or seeks secondary content—the faulty reasoning position implies that the deluded individual might be open to further evidence and argumentation as a means of correcting the primary delusion. This rarely works.[83] In fact, one of the hallmarks of psychosis is the subject's inability or unwillingness to entertain the possibility that she or he is psychotic.[84] Thus returns what Jaspers called the "incorrigibility" of a delusion, its resistance to all counterarguments and counterevidence.

At first glance, technical delusions frequently appear to be the product of reason because psychotic discourse so often mimics the conventions of traditional scientific or sociological research. Thompson was certainly not alone in his extensive documentation of the technologies that assailed him. Paranoid psychotics, in particular, can be extremely dedicated in pleading their case, often generating voluminous narratives of the psychotic process. Examining these testimonies more closely, however, suggests that technical delusions are not necessarily the product of explanatory reason. Emil Kraepelin, for example, reported on a patient who was convinced that his sensations of persecutory electrification issued from a "treadle-machine" and eighteen-inch "horns" that his enemies concealed in their pockets. Knowing that shoemakers use treadle machines, the patient ordered several catalogues of electrical machinery in an attempt to isolate the precise model used by his enemies, a device he believed projected something he called a "sin-prognosis."[85] The patient sent away for electrical catalogues not to understand or explain how this operation *might* work, but to find confirmation of the exact machine that he *already knew* was responsible for his persecution. Tausk noted that patients invoke "all the forces known to technology . . . to explain the functioning of the apparatus."[86] Before this process of technical invocation begins, however, the certainty of a machine is already in place. When pressed, Nataljia A. supplied details about an electronic coffin that she already knew to be in existence. What appears to be a search for an explanation is actually more a form of "reverse engineering": machine first, blueprints second.

Thompson's claim that Denmark had developed a high-frequency device for transmitting meningitis would appear to epitomize a delusion born of faulty reasoning. But this distorts the chronology and apparent intent of

Thompson's manuscript. After revealing the Danish plot to Commissioner Darlington, Thompson goes on to describe the pivotal moment when he discovered the precise mechanism involved in this telepathic technology. While hospitalized for his hallucinations, Thompson recalls, he suffered pain from uneven pressure behind his eyeballs. But by giving one of them "a good whack," he was able to "unlock" his nasal cavity and momentarily suspend the sinus pain. The whack also temporarily silenced the voices in Thompson's head. In that exact moment, Thompson states, he suddenly understood, completely, that by using "a high-frequency apparatus ... in connection with a telephone system" certain individuals can transmit waves to the tissues and mucus of the nasal cavity, which then transport the signals to nerves in the eye, ear, and brain.[87] Inductive fields of high frequency thus enter the body, through the nose, to then take possession of the nervous system. Two years later, Thompson wrote to Darlington a second time, telling him he had hoped that sharing the plot in the previous letter would make the Danes stop, "but instead they started to torture me." Thompson then goes into further detail about the mechanics of this technology, noting that the city of New York could easily test his theory by "plugging up the nostrils of an animal and putting it under compressed air."[88] Thompson's apophany in whacking his eyeball suggests that his extensively researched and quite coherently written monograph was not a journey of explanation leading to a delusion; rather, it was a delusional reality in search of explanatory validation. Thompson explicates contemporary theories of electromagnetism, biology, and psychology to prove what he already knows to be true: that Danish nasal casting is threatening the city.[89]

While the (faulty) "reasoning" model assumes a psychotic subject actively explaining his or her experience, the revelation model inverts this process. Delusions are not reasoned so much as *revealed*, operating less as a convincing hypothesis than as an incontrovertible truth that suddenly unfolds around the individual. When Thompson whacked his eyeball, his enigmatic voices immediately had a source and purpose, a revelation so definitive that Thompson felt compelled to research and write a more thorough account of this extraordinary technology. Similarly, the woman who dared not take a "wicked" cab for fear of going to hell appears to have arrived at that crisis, not through considered logic, but instead through a chain of almost poetic associations (goose to bird to bush to Bush to 9/11 to *Wicked* to wicked to hell). When a taxi arrived bearing an ad for *Wicked*, this piece of the delusional puzzle was not evidence found and added to a hypothesis; rather, it was another link in a chain leading to a revelatory truth. Presumably, had she not sought help, this chain would eventually have delivered her, like Thompson, into some form of apophany, a fully realized delusion that would then make sense of the entire sequence.

The revelation position was most prominently argued by Jacques Lacan in his seminar on the psychoses, delivered in Paris at the Centre Hospitalier Sainte-Anne during 1955–56.[90] Lacanian theory is notoriously complex and resists tidy summarization.[91] Like all of his work, however, Lacan's approach to psychosis involves reframing Freudian concepts through the linguistic theories of Ferdinand de Saussure, the philosophies of Hegel and Heidegger, and even a touch of surrealism.[92] Lacan's project emphasizes the primacy of language, speech, and meaning in producing selfhood and its assorted dysfunctions. For Lacan, the seemingly self-evident "me-ness" of the ego is in fact a product of language, "spoken" by preexisting structures of meaning and social relations that Lacan designated as the "symbolic order." As Anthony Wilden writes, "It can be said very simply that the child begins outside the Symbolic. He is confronted by it, and the significant question—ultimately the 'Who (or what) am I'—is articulated on the problem of entry into it."[93] As a child enters into this constellation of signifiers, the ego assumes a functional position in terms of interior and exterior, me and you, fantasy and reality. All of humanity shares in this process, yet no two people enter into the symbolic in identical fashion. Unlike the perpetually miserable neurotic, psychosis exists as a *potentiality*—that is, an individual with a psychotic personality structure might adapt successfully for many years, even an entire lifetime, without manifesting the familiar symptoms of madness.[94] Lacan likens the psychotic personality structure to a rickety stool. "Not every stool has four legs," he writes. "There are some that stand upright on three. Here, though, there is no question of their lacking any, otherwise things go very badly indeed." The psychotic structure is like a stool with a missing leg (or two). By luck, miracle, and finesse, it might remain balanced for a period of time, but it will always be vulnerable to shifts that make it topple. "Well then, let me tell you that the significant points of purchase that uphold the little world of the solitary little men in the modern crowd are very few in number," he writes. "It's possible that at the outset the stool doesn't have enough legs, but that up to a certain point it will nevertheless stand up, when the subject, at a certain crossroads of his biographical history, is confronted by this lack that has always existed."[95]

Although psychiatry diagnoses many individuals with technical delusions as "paranoid schizophrenics," Lacan separated schizophrenia and paranoia as distinctive dysfunctions in calibrating self and other. As has been widely noted, those labeled schizophrenic often demonstrate problems in attributing the source of thoughts, voices, and sensations, phenomena that speak to a confusion of interior and exterior, self and other. Moreover, psychiatry has long identified schizophrenia with "flight of ideas," "word salad," "concrete thinking," and other forms of "disorganized" speech.[96] Rejecting characterizations of such speech as deficient or defective, Leader instead describes schizophrenic language as highly polysemic. The schizophrenic individual is "left at the mercy of too many meanings," he writes, becoming "overwhelmed and invaded by meaning. It is as if the rivets connecting signifier to signified have come apart, and the person hasn't been able to pin them back together again."[97] Paranoid psychotics, in contrast, suffer from the opposite problem. The boundary of self and other does not dissolve; instead, it becomes rigidly defined and tenaciously guarded by an individual who fixates on a threat (or threats) posed by the other. "Whatever the actual content of the delusion," notes Leader, "there is a solidity to the meaning ascribed to their situation.... The paranoia lies less in the idea itself than in the certainty and the rigidity with which it is held and broadcast, and the place it occupies in that person's life."[98] Schizophrenics overwhelmed and invaded by meaning can retreat into a type of defensive catatonia, limiting their contact with the outside world to minimize their distress. Paranoid psychotics, by contrast, often remain loquacious and engaged, sometimes manically so. This contributes to the convention, widespread in psychiatry and sensationalist fiction, of an individual who is seemingly coherent in affect, appearance, and speech who, in a single fleeting statement, reveals he is actually harboring a profoundly paranoid delusion.

Whether it takes the form of paranoia or schizophrenia, an acute psychotic episode depends on a *trigger*, an event or circumstance that topples the three-legged stool and thus disrupts the previous sense of stability of self and other in the social world. Lacanians place particular emphasis on those moments in life when an individual takes on a new identity or status. Leaving home, sexual encounters, marriage, parenthood, divorce, deaths of loved ones, promotions, demotions, terminations, relocations, sudden wealth, sudden bankruptcy—all are widely recognized as common triggers for psychotic episodes.[99] Leader notes that many of these trigger events are similar to the "rites of passage" in classical anthropology: "These were moments when the person had to 'face the world.' The fact that different cultures mark moments of transition with elaborate ceremonies and rituals suggested that symbolic framework was necessary to process them." If the symbolic order was not internalized during the Oedipal moment, Leader continues, "it would not be available to provide a network of meanings to process these moments of change. Rather than meaning, there would be an acute experience of a hole." The trigger, then, is an event that compels the psychotic structure to contend with a disruption in the typically normalized web of signifiers that hold "reality" together. "Since the symbolic was made up of signifiers that were all interconnected," continues Leader, "if one privileged term was felt to be missing, its effects would spread throughout the network."[100] "Aberrant salience," a "delusional atmosphere," the "trema"—all of these terms describing prodromal psychosis speak to a sudden sensitivity to meaning itself, a sense that something is "missing" and yet is also on the verge of revelation. "What is the subject ultimately saying, especially at a certain period of his delusion?" asks Lacan. "That there is meaning. What meaning he doesn't know, but it comes to the foreground, it asserts itself, and for him it's perfectly understandable."[101]

To be "delusional" is perhaps the single most familiar sign of madness, but Lacan—following Freud—argued that a delusion is not the illness itself but actually an attempt at recovery. In "Neurosis and Psychosis" (1924), Freud described a delusion as "a patch over the place where originally a rent had appeared in the ego's relation to the external world."[102] A delusion, in other words, is a scenario or premise that allows the psychotic ego to regain some functionality in its social interactions, even if this "patch" strikes observers as utterly bizarre and implausible. The arrival at a technical solution allows aberrant salience to resolve in delusional certainty. In explanationist accounts of this repair, a phenomenological anomaly compels a rational program of psychotic research and development, an effort to seek out and settle on the (delusional) hypothesis that seems most correct. A primary form presents itself, and secondary content is found to explain it. As in aesthetic theory, however, form and content are not necessarily so easy to disentangle. Form and content do not exist independently of each other, bound in the end by explanatory reason; rather, the psychotic process unfolds as a revelation, triggered by a disruption in the symbolic and eventually solved (delusionally) by arriving at a new constellation of meaning. "A delusion isn't deduced," Lacan writes. "It reproduces the same constitutive force."[103] So while the faulty reasoning model imagines a psychotic subject exercising reason (albeit faultily), the revelation model posits a subject *arriving* at a delusion, delivered by a chain of meanings that lead from the crisis of the trigger to a unique position of (delusional) understanding.[104]

Thompson's apophanic understanding of a Danish influencing machine is emblematic of this sudden arrival within meaning—*a whack of the eyeball, and everything suddenly makes sense.* But this process of revelation can also be seen in delusions of media reference. Peter Chadwick recalls how his own episode of acute psychosis began with a seemingly offhand but ultimately revelatory remark made on the radio. Chadwick recounts that his transvestism had already made him a figure of ridicule in his local community, contributing to an escalating sense of alienation and social detachment. One evening he happened to overhear a radio announcer on the BBC mocking "a cherub girl." Only days earlier, apparently, Chadwick had written a confidential letter to a friend using the exact same phrase in relation to himself and his lowly status within the neighborhood: "The idea of reference about 'a cherub girl' on the radio switched me from an internal locus of control, living my own life basically minding my own business (if giggled about locally) to feeling 'Hey! I'm being observed! It's on the media!' an external locus of control."[105] With this initial "reference" as an anchor, he continues, the idea of "being monitored externally induced an intense 'feeling of meaning' to everything I did and that was associated with me—even the headlines of newspapers lying on the pavement. Now 'signs' were everywhere."[106] This is a delusion based on a coincidence, obviously, but this coincidence assumes such profound importance only because it so uncannily calibrated a private transaction (Chadwick's letter) with the massive public apparatus (and agenda) of the BBC. Hearing someone else on the street use the phrase "cherub girl" might be somewhat unsettling, yet this could still be understood through an appeal to local gossip and shared social space. To hear the BBC use the phrase, however, veritably demanded a new reality, one in which the media—as a vast apparatus of power—were obviously and unquestioningly observing Chadwick's life. The profoundly uncanny, exhilarating, and perhaps terrifying recognition of this reference ensures that "signs" are "everywhere."

John Durham Peters has argued that the psychotic "ignore the contradiction between broadcasting's address (interpersonal) and distribution (mass)" and lack "a corrective cynicism or knowingness about the nature of the television apparatus."[107] "Each format or technology of communication implies its own disorders," he writes, arguing that schizophrenia's historical emergence and dominance parallels the entanglements of broadcasting and modernity. Most often, however, delusions of reference involving the media are the product of a complex reading protocol rather than sudden naïveté about the basics of the "television apparatus." Enigma leads to shifts in meaning that produce a new reality in which, incredibly, the mass media *do* engage in direct or coded address. Through a combination of prodromal alienation and extraordinary coincidence, Chadwick suddenly occupied a reality in which the BBC and other media outlets were discussing his life. No doubt he continued to understand how the BBC was *supposed* to work, that the media typically practice anonymous mass distribution—but this is what makes the revelation a *revelation*. When the media begin to speak to the psychotic, the addressee is not confused or duped but more often amazed and exhilarated by this extraordinary event, understanding that the phenomenon is truly *incredible*. Another recovered schizophrenic notes, "Sometimes the people on the television and radio would be speaking to me personally. This was a novelty at first and it got me quite excited. I couldn't believe it: the T.V. and radio giving me messages. These messages were pleasant at first but as the months passed they changed and left me feeling responsible for the disasters I heard about on the news programs. So I stopped watching television and listening to the radio and started going to the pub instead."[108] Unlike the delusion fabricated by faulty reasoning, the patch produced through revelation coheres as the *only possible solution* for repairing the "rent" between the ego and the external world. It is not an option, a theory, or a possibility. Delusions are *delusions* precisely because they function as a truth revealed, not as a reasonable hypothesis suspected. It is difficult to imagine how "reason" could lead to (and settle on) Danish nasal casting, Donald Duck, or an electronic coffin as a vector of paranoid persecution. Such a belief, held with fixed conviction, is the product of having this truth revealed *tout court*.

Meaning-Full Technologies

The distinction between Lockean reason and Lacanian revelation in delusional formation is as much philosophical as psychological. Working in the tradition of Nietzsche, Freud, and Heidegger, Lacan's account proposes a subject who, as an effect of language, finds himself at the mercy of the symbolic (or, at least, more so than the sane). "Do get it into your heads that language is a system of positional coherence," Lacan writes, "and secondly that this system reproduces itself within itself with an extraordinary, and frightful, fecundity."[109] To move through life is to move through meaning, the seemingly common signifiers of a culture that endlessly reassemble to produce unique subjective constellations. A fiction of language, the ego becomes psychotic through certain encounters within a social world of meaning. Delusions, in this formulation, are not freely chosen explanations for puzzling phenomena but are, instead, singular revelations of an incontrovertible truth. The individual does not employ meaning to explain; instead, meaning occupies the individual to reveal.[110] "With respect to what we might call the chain of the delusion," notes Lacan, "the subject seems to be both agent and patient. He undergoes rather than organizes the delusion."[111]

This "undergoing" of a delusion often presents, for the sane observer, a perplexing collision of manifest absurdity and inexplicable certainty. In his essay on the "uncanny," Freud notes this unsettling effect on sane observers, writing that "the ordinary person sees" in the mad "the workings of forces hitherto unsuspected in his fellow-man but which at the same time he is dimly aware of in a remote corner of his own being."[112] Madness can be seen as attracting uncomfortable attention to the already tenuous relationship between language and reality that organizes normative existence. No doubt this uncanniness also informs the Romantic equation of madness with genius: the mad are of our world and yet occupy it differently. This association has been widely critiqued, yet the defamiliarizing qualities of madness are difficult to dismiss entirely. Approached as a dislocation within language, madness rearticulates an entire constellation of meaning, opening associations and allusions typically unavailable to those operating wholly within the realm of historical sanity. Writing in the early 1960s, the Finnish analyst Martti Siirala saw in schizophrenia a process that "does not appear solely as something disturbing and destructive, something to be removed if possible; it also appears as a message about possibilities which have not yet entered a process of realization though reciprocity between the individual and his fellowmen."[113] Siirala proposed that schizophrenia is a "testimony of a special disposition," something akin to prophecy. "Traditionally regarded as 'deviating' from the normal in an inferior direction, this disposition would actually represent an unusual 'ability' to react fundamentally when confronted with something distorted, sick, or perhaps dead in our ways of living together, of being a society."[114] In 1975, following a decade in which schizophrenia seemed pandemic, Brian W. Grant aligned it with "social insight." Schizophrenia could be seen as a source of radical "newness," Grant argued, comparing and contrasting psychotic insight with scientific revolutions, poetic inspiration, and religious revelation. "A society has developed a mind-set, open to certain restricted possibilities," he wrote. "The schizophrenic, through the dramatic and painful restructuring of his own symbolic world, gains a new picture of reality. He communicates that picture, making available an inescapably forceful, intimate message about the possibilities the society is destroying."[115]

In the 1950s and '60s, a number of researchers hoped to replicate this displacement by comparing the thought processes of schizophrenia with the experience of ingesting LSD. Controlled studies administered "acid" to military personal, federal prisoners, autistic children, schizophrenics, and psychiatrists in the belief that the drug's distortions might therapeutically alter—or, at least, provide insight into—the neurochemical foundations of the ego.[116] The ability of schizophrenia and acid to distort relations of time, space, and self has made them, individually and in tandem, recurring topics of inquiry in relation to artistic inspiration and creativity.[117] As one might expect, the introduction of acid into the schizophrenic mind has generally proved a psychotic accelerant, and for one subject at least, it inspired a rather virulent technical delusion. While under the drug's effect, this individual professed a belief that he was controlled by "an indwelling television set." He complained that "the LSD had transformed him into a television set and that someone else was controlling him by sending out impulses which caused him to see pictures and induced sensations in his face and lips, which were misinterpreted as the fade out and ripples on a television screen." Moreover, he believed that same controlling individual "could even read his mind and everything that the individual was seeing." Eventually the subject came to the conclusion (not unwarranted) that this "controlling" presence was his physician, "who by using LSD may have gained this ascendency over his subject." The subject surmised, "Whoever could control the supply of LSD could control the rest of the world," an insight so profound that the patient demanded the immediate use of a phone to announce his discovery to the world.[118] This experiment chemically exacerbated a familiar psychotic response to television as an analog of consciousness. The patient suddenly made the cybernetic realization that the human brain—as a machine dealing in sound, image, and power—was not really all that different from a television set and thus could be flipped on and off by external agents who possessed the proper knowledge, tools, and access. In the mid-1960s, as Americans debated upgrading their black-and-white sets to color, a hippie button made these associations even more explicit: "Want Color TV? Try LSD."

When Norbert Wiener first proposed cybernetics as a founding science of the Information Age, he defined it as the study of "control and communication in the animal and machine."[119] Hoping to deflect humanist concerns over the scientific engineering of self and society, Wiener rather mercifully employed conjunctions to divide "control *and* communication" as well as "animal *and* machines." Once laden with acid, however, this test subject dissolved these meaningless distinctions. Animals are machines, and to communicate is to control. Another young man diagnosed as schizophrenic had a similar insight a decade later, even without the benefit of LSD: "Watching TV for hours on end and melting into it, I become the consumer of other people's fantasies." This "melting" into the set, he recognized, gave someone somewhere immense power. Much to the surprise of his therapist, the young man later announced he hoped to one day become a writer for television: "I got angry thinking about it and decided to write and make my own fantasies and force them down other people's throats." In the melty cybernetics of TV, it is better to communicate and control than to be controlled by communication. Or, as the patient said about this dynamic, "You either eat shit or make them eat yours."[120]

As these examples suggest, psychotic insight into the media is not merely a passive reflection. It is instead a singular mediation produced at the intersection of biographical and technical histories. A crisis in meaning emanating from schizophrenic dissolution or paranoid fortification resolves in the arrival of a *meaningful* technology as a *meaningful* solution. For example, a space station, a cell tower, or a microwave oven might figure as a psychotic theory for the sudden influx of alien influence over the body. Essentially interchangeable from a reflectionist perspective, these technologies actually propose very different configurations of "influence" in mediating power, information, and transmission. Mind beams from outer space, projected from a space station, imply a global—perhaps even an intergalactic—plot. Influence in this scenario involves agents who possess immense monetary resources, advanced technologies, and a vast bureaucracy committed to a secret plot of mass control. Influence via cell tower puts the individual in conflict with more proximate agents of power—perhaps municipal, state, or national officials seeking to control the citizenry (or to identify certain guilty individuals). Cell towers are the tent poles of a wireless mantle now enveloping the Earth, totems of power discreetly hidden away in the urban landscape so as not to draw attention to the virtual omnipresence of their invisible electronics. Microwave ovens, finally, constitute a down-and-dirty technology of electromagnetic warfare. There are, in fact, a surprising number of people who, sensing mysterious influence, come to believe nefarious neighbors have "weaponized" a microwave by removing the door and placing the device against a shared wall.

Technical delusions typically center on a device of some sort, but depending on the individual's psychic and historical horizons, associated (but never identical) chains of meanings also situate the delusional device as a specific mediation of power, control, agency, energy, consciousness, broadcasting, physiology, and those other meaningful domains associated with the transmission of energy and information by wire or wirelessly. The complexity of a delusion speaks to the amount of symbolic labor necessary to produce the patch that repairs the ego's disrupted relation to the external world. Some delusions operate within fairly common (though no less delusional) assumptions about technologies (as in believing that media corporations control reality, a premise widely endorsed by certain media theorists and many psychotics). Other delusions activate technologies according to more baroque and idiosyncratic chains of association (wireless plus voices plus nasal cavities plus Denmark equals Danish nasal casting). In either case, one might say—cribbing from Karl Marx—that psychotics make delusions "not under circumstances chosen by themselves, but under conditions directly encountered, given, and transmitted from the past."[121]

Media technologies are meaningful in and of themselves, obviously, but they are also significant as primary conduits for distributing larger networks *of* meaning. Part of the media's "meaning," in other words, is that they are significant purveyors *of* meaning. Over the past two centuries, electronics have become the privileged site for conceptualizing the control, concentration, circulation, and inculcation of meaning, especially in capturing the dynamics of the individual's contact with the larger social world. Of course, meaning is everywhere. But the media have come to stand as "meaning's" most material vessel, the place where meaning *happens* as these devices concretize the typically invisible (and thus normalized) processes of signification. When Marshall McLuhan reversed this formula by writing "the medium is the message," he located significance not in the flotsam of everyday content, but in the social and psychic transformations introduced by new technical affordances. Here, too, however, a primary message of the medium is its identity as a relentless generator of information. In the earliest years of radio and television, many described domestic media as an "electronic hearth." But whereas the hearths of old projected light and heat, radio, television, and their digital progeny now project an unending stream of audiovisual signifiers circulating in potentially infinite combinations. The "message" of these media is one of compulsory participation in various electronic and informational networks, from friends and family on a wireless calling plan to international streams of virtual capital to a global network of spectacle that circulates Hollywood blockbusters and beheading-by-terrorists videos. As a solution to psychotic disruptions in this world, delusions of influence typically draw on electronics as *meaningful technologies*, activating those associations that align the electronic with those powers thought to bind technology and the body through rays, beams, signals, impulses, and transmissions. Delusions of reference, in turn, frequently hinge on the media as *technologies of meaning*, devices that assault body and mind not only with the raw power of direct energetic influence, but also with the soft power of perpetual signification. The rise and eventual dominance of technical delusions over the past two centuries can be said, in banal terms, to "reflect" this historical era. Considered in terms of mediation, however, the ascendency of the technical delusion suggests that media electronics have assumed a determinative role in both disrupting and repairing the fundamental dyad of psychosis: self and other. In this defamiliarizing function, delusions about the media foreground the self's typically unexamined imbrication in various networks of influence, energetic and semiotic.

Prosthetic Irritation

In an oft-cited passage from "Civilization and Its Discontents," Freud observed, "Man has, as it were, become a type of Prosthetic God." This prosthesis, circa 1930, was the incredible precession of technologies that Freud had seen debut in his own lifetime: telephony, radio, cinema, X-rays, airplanes, automobiles, and so on. "When he puts on all his auxiliary organs he is truly magnificent," Freud continues, "but those organs have not grown on to him and they still give him much trouble at times."[122] Freud argued that mankind's technical prostheses had enabled humanity to come closer to the "fairy tale wishes" of "omnipresence and omniscience" that primitive man had imagined of the gods. An uncharacteristically optimistic Freud predicted that "future ages" would no doubt bring "unimaginably great advances" in civilization that would "increase man's likeness to God still more."[123] While Freud's prediction of this divine future might seem prescient of post-humanist theology, Freud remained Freud. He also noted in this passage that, as of 1930 at least, "we will not forget that present day man does not feel happy in his Godlike character."[124]

Freud's idea of the Prosthetic God has continued to inform much thinking about media and technology, perhaps most famously in McLuhan's observation that the media constitute an "extension of the human nervous system."[125] Fifty years after the halcyon days of McLuhanism, the prosthetic thesis returned in the work of the German media theorist Friedrich Kittler. For Kittler, the emergence of telephony, photography, radio, the cinema, and television constituted a new "discourse network" with profound implications for the status of the human subject.[126] Calling this era the "Second Industrial Revolution," Kittler observes that all of these media introduced an ability to encode the real world without any recourse to symbolization. All are media that "mediate," of course, but each also has a mechanical relation to reproducing material reality. Audio technologies "hear." Visual technologies "see." All mechanical recording technologies are archives that "remember." Like the earlier acquisition of language as a storage system, these media represent a prosthetic intervention in the production of the human subject. A hundred years after the Second Industrial Revolution, these crudely mechanical wax cylinders and hand-cranked cameras have been completely subsumed by the politics of the electronic, channeled into streaming flows of endlessly transmutable digital code. For many futurists, the digital doctrines of prosthetic extension constitute a horizon of limitless possibilities. Humans and information technology will soon achieve an irreversible symbiosis, one that will "free" humans of many mundane tasks, individual and collective, so that these fairy-tale wishes can be more readily attained. In the supreme fantasy of this future, the ego (*my ego!*) will live on forever as pure information, the brain and its resident "me-ness" encoded as digital data and stored for eons on the servers of virtual immortality. Then and only then will man achieve the omniscience and omnipotence of true Prosthetic Godhood.

But that which "extends" can also "converge." Electronic nerves stretching out into the world seem to perform the instrumental will of the individual ego, but these wires also converge countless tributaries of data into the body and conduct the electronic will of other individuals and institutions. In 1983, Baudrillard rather poetically described this energetic agitation as "the ecstasy of communication." "The promiscuity that reigns over the communication networks is one of superficial saturation, of an incessant solicitation, of an extermination of interstitial and protective spaces," he wrote. "Something that was free by virtue of space is no longer free. Speech is free perhaps, but I am less free than before: I no longer succeed in knowing what I want, the space is so saturated, the pressure so great from all who want to make themselves heard. I fall into the negative ecstasy of the radio."[127] Baudrillard diagnosed this "negative ecstasy" in the era of mass broadcasting, a period when this promiscuity manifested as unilateral emanations radiating from more localizable centers of power. The possibility remained in the scenario of maintaining some vestiges of interstitial and protective spaces. The ambitions of the media could still be deflected, perhaps completely avoided (with a well-crafted tin-foil helmet or by punching out Dan Rather). But turning off a device (or smashing it) is no longer a viable strategy for avoiding contact with those "who want to make themselves heard," locally or globally. "Video, interactive screens, multimedia, the Internet, virtual reality—we are threatened on all sides by interactivity," observed Baudrillard in 1997, once again anticipating a looming nightmare well before its full expression.[128] By 2020, one study predicts, 90 percent of the world's population older than six will have a smartphone, making us all proto-cyborgs of one kind or another. Humans who previously contended with the abstract possibility of electronic information adrift in the ether now find themselves chained to nearly ubiquitous networks of dispersed electronics and data.[129] There are progressive aspects to this decentering of the media, to be sure. Social media give voice to constituencies that previously had no public forum, be they organic kale farmers or middle-aged men upset because the remake of *Ghostbusters* (2016) had girls in it. Yet as the arrays, algorithms, and agendas of electronics increasingly elude the institutional choke points of the twentieth century, the networked potentials for prosthetic irritation continue to multiply. Anxieties over "imminent promiscuity" promise to intensify as the media move inexorably from figurative augmentation to literal penetration. Despite the comforting narcissism of the extension thesis, it should be abundantly clear to everyone by now that *the media have every intention of entering our bodies.* We will extend the media as much as, or more than, the media will extend us.

Our training for prosthetic integration began with telegraphy. Few had direct experience with the electromagnetic telegraph; nevertheless, the device introduced a basic concept of cybernetic being—the seeming ability to occupy multiple spaces in "real time." As Jane Feuer argues, an "ideology of liveness" has been an important corporate strategy for encouraging affective investment in the "nowness" of various media, even if this nowness was often illusory.[130] Following the telegraph, each new electronic marvel has promised an even more vivid experience of such liveness. Like so many media theorists, schizophrenics of the twentieth century recognized the ideology of liveness portends a new way of inhabiting the world. Recorded during a therapy session in 1955, a psychiatric patient pondered television's global extension of electronic presence: "I was thinking about five television sets in relation to Germany, Japan, and China; China, Japan, and Germany. I imagine a lot of these things are a small lapse of time, a small interval of time, probably retelecast themselves through many channels, and the importance, the high significant importance of these telecasts-to all those foreign nations." The patient went on to argue that "some television sets have a slight change of radio tubing, changes to be made, or slight change in vibration due to the location of the set itself, in some particular location or place, which affects the reception and the voluminous capacity of the television set itself.[131] Verging on incoherence, these ruminations nevertheless speak to a basic understanding of television as a machine that modulates space, time, vibrations, and volume in a continuous feed, a technology where "small intervals of time" and "slight changes" in position could have significant implications for these (and presumably all) of the world's nation states. A woman institutionalized in 1959 exhibited a more emotional response to television's call to mandatory ecstasy. She believed that television "controlled, persecuted, and tormented" her, and even hearing the word "television" provoked "an ecstatic terror on her face." Two years into her therapy, she at last revealed she had always heard the word "television" as "Tell a Vision," a break-through that allowed her doctors to understand that she saw TV as a "machine of infinite power which inexorably demands that ego alien material be told to it." While this revelation did not necessarily lead to a cure, at least her frequent assaults on the ward's television set could be "more readily comprehended."[132] To believe that the television is talking to you or about you is to be psychotic, and yet, *television is in fact frequently talking to us*—incessantly, urgently, and persuasively. This simulation of direct address can be extremely irritating. A British study from 1997 examined thirteen patients with delusions of reference related to television, manifesting as thought broadcasting, thought echo, or auditory hallucinations. Ten of the thirteen patients tried to avoid watching the news on television or watching the TV alone. Two of the patients expressed frustration that the television in the psychiatric ward could not be avoided.[133] Another study from 1997 found that schizophrenics were most troubled by game shows with studio audiences and comedies that featured "laugh tracks," given that those prone to paranoia often find this seemingly disembodied mirth to be "mocking, confusing, or derogatory."[134] Complaints made to the Federal Communications Commission (FCC) routinely involve accusations that certain television actors or characters are talking to or about the viewer.[135]

As Dan Rather unhappily discovered, newsreaders present a common focus of psychotic fixation.[136] Seated at a desk surrounded by a bank of monitors, the newsreader projects an imperious, perhaps omnipotent presence. He is the very emblem of power—electronic, corporate, political—who possesses the authority to summon subordinates from around the globe through His own superior prosthetic feeds. William Tager's belief that television sent rays and vibrations into his home was a classic delusion of raw energetic influence, but it also nominated Rather as the personification of the network(ed) power behind this attack. The ideology of liveness can also lead to delusions of intimacy that contribute to episodes of electronic erotomania. Thus did a "Mr. K" believe that "local and national newscasters spoke directly to him and controlled his thoughts. Mr. K wished to impregnate several local female newscasters. He believed that one specific local newscaster had killed his brother and was also conspiring to kill his father."[137] Psychotic paranoia can also convert individuals into savvy political economists, as in the case of a viewer who informed the FCC that "Rupert Murdoch, Mike Huckabee, and Roger Ails [sic]" of Fox News had waged "a continual campaign of terror against my family for over 10 years now." While many progressives might sympathize with this position, this viewer's complaints quickly veered into a (semi-)delusional logic that conflated various catastrophes with Fox's live coverage of the events. Of Murdoch, Huckabee, and Ailes, the complainant writes, "They are pretty much domestic terrorists, who have caused 1 billion [dollars] a month in storm and earthquake damage to the world for 10 years in a row, in doing false imprisonments, stalkings, burglaries, refrigerator poisonings, pretending people who are downright terrorists from India and Arkansas are people doctors, whom the people have never gone too [sic]."[138]

Compulsory participation in an expanding public sphere has irritated people since the beginnings of the daily newspaper. But as electronics both expanded and accelerated the collection of information from around the world, data and anxiety have entered into an amplified feedback loop. Baudrillard describes these cybernetic nervous breakdowns in terms of "superconductivity," events that overheat the global media array to trigger a cascade of electronic and physiological panic. The Ebola crisis, financial "flash crashes," terrorist attacks—all produce a superconductivity that overwhelms the communications grid to the point of irrational collapse, generating a panicked response in the intertwined nervous systems that now bind man and machine. "Information, crisis, and catastrophe," identified by Mary Ann Doane as television's primary modes of organizing time, have only further collapsed into one another as the Internet gradually subsumes television's role in organizing shared electronic time and space.[139] In this respect, the terrorist attacks of September 11, 2001, proved to be a benchmark not only in a realignment of geopolitical power, but also in further suturing electronic populations into networks of multi-mediated anxiety. Not only did 9/11 introduce unprecedented "wall-to-wall" coverage, but it also saw the proliferation of flowing "news crawls," graphic snipes, and "breaking news" alerts that saturated televisual space to the point of illegibility. Unsurprisingly, this traumatic eruption and overwhelming inscription of catastrophe had a profound impact on those already experiencing psychotic dysfunctions. One man believed his own family members had been killed at the Twin Towers, while in another case a man claimed signals delivered through the TV set were meant to activate him as a secret military operative against the terrorists.[140] "Live" television still evokes occasional episodes of mass presence (during catastrophes and sporting events, primarily), but the new "attention economy" typically disperses this monitoring function across a number of devices to create a more or less perpetual state of potential urgency. With perpetual interconnectivity, crises of various intensities—from failed presidencies to making dinner plans—remain in constant flux. Direct messaging, rapid refresh, "pushed" notifications—all signal that everything is happening all the time, and nothing is resolved—at least, not for very long. This technical vigilance is reminiscent of Freud's theory of anxiety as a psychic defense against the future eruption of trauma. No one wants to miss a "like" on Facebook (FB) or be the last to find out that the apocalypse is trending on Twitter. For many, very few moments of the day are spent "off the grid," an apt electrical metaphor that describes a cybernetic dynamic of general nervous tension spiked by occasional moments of fleeting relevance or superconductive terror. Even when off-line, however, there is no place to escape the global circulation of hypertrophic information. A few months after the 9/11 attacks, a family in Sacramento cited headaches, lupus, and "burned radar blankets" as evidence of an organized "9/11" electromagnetic conspiracy targeting their home. Convinced their house was under assault by radio waves, the family completely surrounded the home with corrugated sheet metal to repel further bombardment. Waves of traumatic information, apparently, had incubated a phobia of electronic contamination. Community complaints about the family's tin compound eventually attracted the attention of the Sacramento zoning commission and the local TV station KCRA. In a perverse irony, KCRA dispatched a news chopper to hover over the family's home and relay live images of their corrugated fortress for international consumption on CNN. Had the family turned on their TV set, their worst nightmare would have come true: an instrument of power hovering above their own house, gathering electronic sound and image to beam back into the inner sanctum of their metal fortress.

Anticipating future efforts to block such inundation, the media have also been working to reduce the transmission space (and attending complications) that separate sender and receiver. The Sony Walkman proved a relatively short-lived device emerging at the end of the analog era, but it was nevertheless an important harbinger for a new model of prosthetic integration in which the individuated skull would become the preferred theater for entertainment.[141] Headphones have subsequently devolved into the "ear bud," a plastic stopper in the auditory canal designed not for musical fidelity, but to signal a further sensory retreat from proximate social contact.[142] Similar efforts are under way in relation to the eye socket, with various technology firms looking to reduce the distance and distraction that separate eyeballs and information. This increasingly surgical targeting of the sensorium coincides with a shift toward a media economy based on egocasting. Broadcasting became narrowcasting became nichecasting becomes egocasting, described by Christine Rosen as "a world where we exercise an unparalleled degree of control over what we watch and what we hear. We can consciously avoid ideas, sounds, and images that we don't agree with or don't enjoy."[143] Eschewing the inefficient and obsolescent control mechanisms of mass address, media technologies now allow users to program elaborate delusions of reference, filtering information exposure to reinforce impregnable bunkers of lifestyle branding and political philosophy. Much as headphones and Oculus visors seek to eliminate the great cybernetic foil of "noise" between the points of transmission and reception, programmers of the future will employ data sets to better reduce and control erratic and unprofitable vicissitudes of taste. Today's toddlers, as second- and third-generation digital natives, are now in training to function as even better symbiotes to these technologies, suggesting that future iterations of egocasting may well be more prescriptive than descriptive, pediatric data management contributing to an actual *casting of the ego*.

In future histories of our cybernetic penetration, the iPhone may well be seen as the key transitional technology in this march toward compulsory prosthesis. Having quickly murdered such extracranial rivals as the camera, radio, Walkman, iPod, and television set, the so-called smartphone is, for all practical purposes, a brain chip that, for now at least, remains too large for actual implantation. Mandatory prosthesis portends an irritating future in which we will all be *answerable*—literally. The portability afforded by global Wi-Fi technology ensures that the processing of various data streams can proceed without interruption. This process of habituation is already so advanced that many now perceive the absence of cellular contact as akin to a terrifying form of cybernetic amputation. Some are so attached to their devices as to have "nomophobia," a profound anxiety provoked by the absence of a cell phone or a lack of cellular coverage.[144] A related study finds that the absence of a cell phone or network access is becoming a significant trigger in panic disorders.[145] Also growing is "ringxiety" (frequently imagining that one's phone is ringing when it is not). Some within the psychiatric community believe that "cell phone addiction" should be recognized as a distinct diagnostic category, a conclusion supported by research that demonstrates texting, social media updates, and web surfing can create a "dopamine loop" in smartphone users.[146] Once, the most chilling image of the addict was a mouse snorting itself to death with a limitless supply of cocaine; today, it is the texting teen wandering into traffic with a limitless data plan. (If nothing else, a brain chip could make walking and texting much safer.) The social media industry, meanwhile, aspires to the commodification of "automatic writing," a world of immediate and maximum sharing in which all vestiges of editorial revision or psychic repression are eliminated. Many already despair over digital technology's incessant demand to update software and replace obsolescent platforms, a free market choice (to update or not to update; that is the question) that increasingly is not really a choice, at least if one wants to remain seamlessly enfranchised in the electronic realm. How many citizens of the new century would already gladly accept a subcutaneous smartphone or universal remote—a key panel on the wrist, perhaps—if only to reduce the many hours lost to changing passwords, updating operating systems, and searching through couch cushions?[147] Imagine when these routines, driven by technical and political economies operating beyond any real human control, begin to make their demands from *within* the body. *Upgrading to Bobcat Omega X introduces new security features to Neural Netflix and stabilizes an earlier Tourette glitch in the Paris 3000 language chip. Click here to begin update.* Whoops, now you can't get the new U2 song out of your head—literally.[148]

Through the logic of technical analogy, psychotics of the previous century often believed that the radio could hear them or the television could see them. With the advent of webcams, Skype, FaceTime, and other audiovisual features, digital appliances *can* and *do* hear and see us, sometimes with permission, and sometimes without it. Going outside is no help, as the cities of the world are moving toward a dream of absolute visibility, a camera on every corner so that no transgression can escape unobserved. Having no other plausible choice, most confront this reality through a type of disavowal. Sure, in theory a remote agency might use my webcam to spy on me, but there *must* be mechanisms in place to prevent such abuse from happening on a massive scale. Even for the sane, however, unpleasant reminders of this vulnerability bubble to the surface from time to time. An unexpected ticket for running a red light arrives in the mail, reminding the offender that panoptic supervision (in traffic, at least) no longer depends on selective enforcement. Someone finds a micro-camera hidden in a public bathroom. A celebrity discovers footage of herself nude on the Internet, leading to the prosecution of the stalker-voyeur who installed a camera in the peephole of her hotel room.[149] A young man commits suicide after his college roommate "outs" him by secretly streaming a sexual encounter online.[150] In *Robbins v. Lower Merion School District*, school officials admitted to taking hundreds of covert photos of a fifteen-year-old sophomore that led them to accuse the student of trafficking in drugs. But the incriminating webcam photo did not show the student sorting amphetamine capsules, as the school district maintained; it was, in fact, an image of the accused eating Mike and Ike candy at his desk.[151] Worse yet, as more and more of "real life"—past and present—is translated into code, threats of unwelcome exposure transcend the immediate hazards of real-time surveillance. As *Star Wars* Boy, Anthony Weiner, and Mitt Romney all discovered, any embarrassing revelation captured by film, video, or cellphone in the seemingly distant past now has the power to return as the YouTube repressed, allowing millions of strangers not only to witness various secrets, fetishes, and revelations, but to also remix and repurpose them for their own cruel amusement.[152] Gone are the days when burning a letter or destroying a negative could bring peace of mind. Anything digitized and distributed will live forever, somewhere. As the panic over "sexting" suggests, digital natives are already adjusting to a new information order in which these older safeguards are irrelevant. Is it a good idea to employ digital networks to exchange nude pictures of oneself with a sexual partner? Raised in an erotic order that is still significantly informed by secrecy and shame, older generations say no, fearing this practice may lead to "revenge porn" or a Lifetime channel movie (especially now that digitized genitals are more indestructible than the earlier analog "mistake" of a tattoo). Young people who are better adapted to a culture of compulsory sharing and maximum visibility seem less concerned, especially as the mass aggregation of this photographic archive portends a future in which any one image will lose its singular power to embarrass or shame. In *The Circle* (2013), Dave Eggers's dystopic novel of the right now, a young woman beseeches her Google-esque employer to destroy footage of her facilitating an awkward hand job. The company refuses, citing her own mantra, "Secrets Are Lies; Sharing Is Caring; Privacy Is Theft."[153]

But this potential for a lifetime of ceaseless audiovisual surveillance is almost trivial compared with the much more terrifying translation of every human being on Earth into a data packet available for algorithmic management. Innumerable algorithms now analyze data streams looking for ways to make our behavior even more quantifiable and predictable. For now, a vestigial concern remains that one should make some attempt, no doubt perfunctory and perhaps even illusory, to control who has access to one's various streams of information, but security protocols are notoriously difficult to police, because the owners and architects of these platforms have a vested interest in their users' sharing as much information as possible with the widest possible audience. "Ubiquitous interactivity," argues Mark Andrejevic, "has the potential to facilitate unprecedented commodification of previously nonproprietary information and an aggressive clamp-down of centralized control over information sources." Herded into "digital enclosures," humans will be milked for data daily, generating petabytes of information that can be algorithmically mined for revelations that are otherwise invisible.[154] After all, we already live in a world in which a large retailer such as Target can surmise that certain data points have been impregnated and then address them accordingly.[155] Who can know what future algorithm will find a pattern in your data history, currently invisible, that will one day subject you to untold hardships? Computers suddenly figure out that a preference for Pepsi and biracial porn, when cross-indexed by Zip code and birth weight, makes certain people uninsurable, an enemy of the state, a potential "psychotic" necessitating psychiatric intervention.

For now, at the threshold of our mass prosthesis, the ego must continue to address its traditional negotiation of interior and exterior reality. But now it must also monitor the possible misadventures of its data *doppelgänger*, an electronic entity wandering the virtual realm and facing its own virtual disasters. While waiting to board an international flight, a woman tweets an unfortunate and apparently misunderstood joke. Unbeknownst to her, the tweet goes viral while she is in the air. When she lands several hours later, she reactivates her phone to discover she has been fired from her job.[156] Tormented tweens and teens once enjoyed the luxury of returning home after a day of taunting to strategize how to best handle a social conflict at school the next day. Today, perpetually interconnected through a variety of live platforms, adolescents must function as their own public relations department, available 24/7 to monitor their online selves and counteract the real-time nichecasting of teenage clique maintenance. In a number of high-profile cases, this constant stress has ended in suicide.[157] A woman who was hospitalized in 2005 recalled that her difficulties began when her credit card was refused in a store, "leading to a sense of unease and increasingly obtrusive thoughts." This is understandable, given that the refusal of credit—whatever its actual cause—signals a potentially catastrophic exile from the virtual terrain of capital. Tenuously suspended over vast chasms of debt (a virtual pit of non-money), those who are suddenly denied credit must consider the possibility of "identity theft" and, with it, the horror that it will take weeks, months, or even years to reabsorb this ectoplasmic tendril of escaped data back into its meaty owner. Later, this same woman went online to search for information about "phenylalanine" (an ingredient frequently used in breath fresheners), leading her to experimental studies featuring large amounts of numerical data. Entering sequences of personal relevance into the search engine eventually produced a website for Aramaic numerology, convincing the woman she had somehow stumbled upon "secret information about the Al-Qaeda terrorist network." In the manic episode that followed, she became convinced that certain agents had tapped her computer and telephone and bugged her home with microphones and cameras.[158]

For the structural administration of power, our collective acquiescence to the status of data opens exciting new possibilities for maximizing the collective efficiency of the labor pool. In the old manufacturing economy, a floor manager might catch an employee taking a seemingly exorbitant number of bathroom breaks. But in the information economy, a computer can monitor these breaks with the accuracy of an atomic clock, correlating productivity with "break time" to produce a useful metric for management's consideration. In the white-collar world, meanwhile, the rise of "cloud computing" now ensures that every work project is truly inescapable, the relevant documents and data following workers around the globe from computer to computer (like a dark cloud, always there to rain down unfinished labor). Once cybernetic integration approaches completion, any residual resistance, in theory or in practice, will be merely comical or annoying. This future can already be glimpsed in digital natives compelled to explain various technical practices to their elders. Max Horkheimer observed as early as 1957 that the changing demands of capitalism would gradually devalue the experience and wisdom of older employees in favor of the "accuracy and energy" provided by younger workers.[159] Thought, contemplation, consideration—these are generally impediments to the lightning-fast execution of corporate directives, policy initiatives, and other networked transactions. Older employees can perhaps take some comfort that this trend is ultimately a race to the bottom. Thus, much as human evolution positioned eighteen-year-old males to be maximally efficient as erection and ejaculation machines, cybernetic evolution will very likely produce systems to monitor when perceptual acuity and cognitive speed have peaked and begin their inexorable decline. Management tools that count keystrokes, for example, could easily measure reaction times and error ratios to evaluate degrees of project facilitation versus resistance, metrics that could be cross-indexed with cultural algorithms that measure entertainment choices and political beliefs. Together, this data profile will be able to chart, perhaps to the second, the exact moment an employee becomes irrelevant and counterproductive. With the erosion of permanent employees and long-term job security, moreover, "flexible labor" demands that workers remain in an even more acute state of perpetual access. After his arrest in March 2016 for allegedly shooting and killing six people in Kalamazoo, Michigan, Uber driver Jason Dalton told police that when he opened the Uber app, "a devil head popped up on his screen [and] that is when all the problems started." Melding Marxist alienation with cybernetic control, Dalton claimed he was "possessed" by the app, telling police, "You don't have to drive at all, the car just goes." When you "plug into" the Uber app, Dalton told officers, "you can actually feel the presence on you."[160] Some marveled that Dalton drove around Kalamazoo for several hours shooting random victims even as he continued to pick up fares for the ride-sharing service, as if the newly valued cybernetic capacity for "multitasking" should respect a line between rational productivity and homicidal psychosis.

Electronic leisure also aspires to increased efficiency. The advent of the consumer VCR in the mid-1980s allowed for time shifting, with consumer and product agreeing to rendezvous at some other part of the day. In the transition to the DVR, time shifting has taken on the additional function of stockpiling. With relative ease, digital devices now harvest and store decades' worth of entertainment products, an "on-demand" culture that ostensibly makes every individual a burdened curator. These blocks of entertainment can become so massive as to necessitate "binge watching," a Dionysian rite that gradually devolves into a Sisyphean nightmare. Confronting the daunting task of achieving a state of entertainment often provokes what John Ellis has described as "time famine" and "choice fatigue": "One aspect of the experience of time famine is the partial paralysis of choice: the hesitation between possibilities all of which seem equally attractive, in the knowledge that no time exists to savour them all."[161] Digital media's ability to facilitate quick previews and almost instantaneous switching of movies, television, and music often results in a fugue state of manic auditioning, ultimately leading to the catatonia of choice fatigue ("a combination of impatience, a great modern vice, and the sense of simply not wanting to be bothered," notes Ellis).[162] Netflix queues remain stagnant; playlists are made but never heard; books are downloaded but never read. This inhuman extension of the cultural archive brings with it a renewed despair over the still palpable limitations of human existence. Writes Ellis, "The existential difficulty of today's consumer is this lurking sense of mortality whilst being confronted by many attractive options, be they television programmes or leisure activities, commodities or ideas."¹⁶³ A smartphone can now easily store the entire work of Henry James for mobile reading, leading to the sobering realization that one will most likely not live long enough to read the entire work of Henry James, especially as said smartphone continues to remind you of other, more pressing obligations or diverting possibilities in your digital network. With any luck, in the fully prosthetic future, some form of neural "compression" will accelerate the DVR-to-brain transfer.

For the modern subject, romantic relations and sexual entanglements—real and imagined—already provided a fertile ground for triggering psychotic episodes. As flirtation and pair bonding continues to migrate to social media, dating apps, Big Data, and compulsory networking, new configurations of interpersonal and virtual libido promise entirely new forms of psychotic dysfunction. Despite early hopes that virtual sexuality might allow for polymorphous play, the main impact of these technologies so far veers more toward the self-objectification of sexual value in the form of virtual self-promotion, a phenomenon particularly prominent in the "swipe-right, swipe-left" culture of Tinder and other relationship apps. If one is not careful, one can also fall prey to "catfishing," defined by the online Urban Dictionary as an individual "having a fake Facebook profile, images and avatar in order to lure people to have romantic feelings." In Taiwan, a teenage girl becomes depressed after her "online boyfriend" in France commits suicide. Even after she spends several weeks in intensive therapy, her therapists remain unable to establish whether this French boyfriend actually existed. In the end, they decide it probably does not really matter.[164] For those in committed relationships, meanwhile, marriage counselors and divorce lawyers must contend with the vexing issue of adjudicating what is and is not appropriate in online relationships—most specifically, in the idea of "virtual infidelity."[165] While the issue of fidelity and disembodied sexuality is as old as "phone sex" (or even epistolary seduction), future media affordances portend unimaginable complications to human psychosexual dynamics. As one exasperated meat-wife said of her meat-husband's marriage to a virtual spouse in the online multiplayer game *Second Life*, "You try to talk to someone or bring them a drink, and they'll be having sex with a cartoon."[166]

Disentangling appropriate codes of embodied and virtual interaction will no doubt take generations of adjustment as digital natives gradually abandon obsolescent and yet, for now, still residual social and courtship practices. For prodromal psychotics—already prone to alienation, marginalization, and diminished social competence—negotiating the confusing, asymmetrical, and often volatile status of online contact can be especially difficult. A man in his mid-twenties, "Mr. X," entered therapy after exhibiting cyberstalking behavior in relation to a high school acquaintance. During his sessions, Mr. X revealed that social media dominated his day and that "the updates and activities posted by his FB 'friends' set the tone for his day. After working a night shift with minimal interpersonal contact, X returned home and pursued [SOCIAL MEDIA NETWORK] sites and online gaming. He did not have face-to-face interactions with peers; his only contact with 'friends' was via FB." Mr. X's cyber-stalking centered on a "Ms. A," a woman who had accepted his Facebook "friend" request several years earlier when they had shared a class together in high school. "The ease with which he learned details of her personal life may have fueled development of his underlying psychopathology," continue the authors. "He interpreted her general posted updates as evidence of her 'love' for him, requested a real-world relationship with her, and began to pursue her via phone and in person. These actions led to his arrest and hospitalization." Like so many social media users, Mr. X found it difficult to navigate the platform's oddly hybridized conventions of private and public space, a world where "friends" often do not even know each other and where some individuals will reveal intimate personal details to an audience of thousands. The authors of the study assert that adolescents and young adults with prodromal symptoms may be "particularly vulnerable" to this social media environment. "Motivated by loneliness, poor social skills and unpopularity," such individuals "seek out unrequited relationships with people with whom they have little or no prior relationship. Young people with emerging psychosis may have similar characteristics to 'socially awkward' stalkers. They may have age appropriate engagement in the online social world while simultaneously becoming increasingly isolated, lonely and confused by their intensifying psychotic symptoms."[167] In 1998, Tamaki Saitō proposed *Shakaiteki hikikomori* as a growing psychological disorder among Japanese youth. Saitō defines *hikikomori* as "a state that has become a problem by the late twenties, that involves cooping oneself up in one's own home and not participating in society for six months or longer, but that does not seem to have another psychological problem as its principal source."[168] First identified in Japan, cases of adolescents and young adults barricaded in their childhood bedrooms for months or even years, connecting to the outside world only through online gaming and the Internet, appear to be on the increase around the world.

While digital media wait to penetrate us in the transition from figurative to literal prosthetics, they also irritate through exponential increases in information. A study in 2013 found that 90 percent of the world's data had been generated in the previous two years.[169] Acolytes of Big Data celebrate the new information technologies as a weapon in instrumental reason's final victory over ignorance and superstition, but many have argued quite persuasively that technology's ability to provide massive amounts of information has not realized the Enlightenment fantasy of more knowledge and an improved society. "We live in a world of more and more information, and less and less meaning," observed Baudrillard in his canonical account of simulation.[170] The "truth" may have always been a fiction, but never has this artifice been so visible (or its nostalgia so untenable). Electrified and accelerated, information on the Internet functions like digital quicksand—unstable, shifting, bottomless, and often treacherous. Millions of individuals consult Wikipedia for basic information, an open site that allows users to revise entries and thus alter reality (if only for a few hours or days). Searching the Internet for information on even the most routine health symptom, such as a runny nose, can quickly escalate into the hypochondria of delusional reference, the ill surfer able to craft a compelling account of his or her impending death based on the Internet's bottomless pit of medical testimonials. Even as Big Data aspires to produce consensus truth through volume, the singularly anecdotal has never enjoyed more pataphysical opportunities for aggregation and amplification. A lone wolf now has the power to paralyze millions by engaging in even the most rudimentary performance of "terrorism." A few parents suspect that vaccination causes autism. Soon an entire movement is born that has a surprisingly strong cultural and epidemiological impact.[171] Turning to the various arms of the media in search of the "facts" concerning issues and controversies leads almost instantaneously into wholly concretized delusions that are often as implausible as they are incorrigible. "Information long ago broke through the truth barrier and moved into hyperspace where things are neither true nor false," writes Baudrillard. "You put out an item of information. So long as it is not denied, it is plausible. And, barring some happy accident, it will never be denied in real time and so will always remain credible. Even if denied, it will no longer ever be absolutely false, since it has once been credible. Unlike truth, credibility has no limits; it cannot be refuted, because it is virtual."[172]

As virtual credibility continues to expand, few historical events are now afforded the status of an actual historical event. After the terrorist attacks of 9/11, for example, pathologically and playfully paranoid "Truthers" took to the Internet in search of the *real* story behind the downing of the World Trade Center. The murder of twenty-six children and teachers at Sandy

Hook Elementary School immediately led to accusations of a "false-flag" operation. The entire event had been staged by actors, argued skeptics, or perhaps the government itself had engineered the massacre—all to create sympathy for more restrictive gun laws. In 2015, as the military prepared for a series of war games in the American Southwest, various right-wing groups proposed that the operation (Jade Helm 15) was in fact designed to secure an unconstitutional third term for Obama's already illegitimate presidency (by invading and "pacifying" Texas, likely to be the most resistant state in such a plan). Gun enthusiasts were certain the campaign would seek to disarm the populace to make them helpless in the face of Obama's unchecked powers. Abandoned Walmart stores were said to be internment camps in disguise, waiting to confine those captured in the fight against this tyranny. In older information orders, such a plot would easily have been dismissed as lunacy. But in the new "hyperspace" of virtual credibility, elected officials understood the need to appear in solidarity with those resisting this wholly delusional threat. Republican congressman Louis Gohmert of Texas flattered his constituency by stoking suspicion that Jade Helm 15 appeared to be targeting only the nation's "conservative" territories. In turn, Governor Greg Abbott mobilized the Texas National Guard, ostensibly to "monitor" the intentions and actions of the US military. Of course, witnessing the duly elected governor mobilizing the state military "just in case" only made the implausible seem that much more credible, spurring entirely new cycles of disinformation (further amplified by the theory's endorsement by martial arts star Chuck Norris, most famous for his CBS television series *Walker, Texas Ranger*).[173] A year after Jade Helm 15, Texas remained unpacified, and Donald J. Trump, himself a conspiracy enthusiast, was inaugurated as the forty-fifth president of the United States.

First-person accounts of psychotic episodes frequently distill the energetic and semiotic powers evoked and then defamiliarized by the psychotic process. Living alone in a remote area, Susan Weiner came to believe that signals from her TV set had revealed her "secret location" to malevolent authorities. Soon after, she "realized the people on the radio were talking to me, much the way one has an intuition about a geometry proof, a sudden dawning of clarity and understanding." A "live" TV signal reveals her position, and an electronic umbilicus places her in energetic rapport with "malevolent authorities." With this conceptual door opened, a living link established, a new formation of meaning begins to emerge intuitively, much like a "geometry proof": "I learned to communicate by deciphering bits of conversation, reading newspaper articles, and listening to songs on the radio."[174] From this contact, Weiner understood that an evil dictator was about to take control of the nation and that she was now working for a resistance movement to prevent some form of holocaust. Looking back, Weiner offers a Baudrillardian insight: "The movies, TV, and newspapers are alive with information for those who know how to read.... Schizophrenia is a disease of information."[175]

....

At the end of the twentieth century, cultural critics often invoked "schizophrenia" to diagnose all of mediated humanity. Continuing a theme prevalent since the early nineteenth century, this diagnosis linked modernity and madness in terms of dysfunctional communication. Baudrillard, for example, argued that the "ecstasy of communication" signaled "a new form of schizophrenia with the emergence of an imminent promiscuity and the perpetual interconnection of all information and communications networks. No more hysteria, or projective paranoia as such, but a state of pure terror which is characteristic of the schizophrenic, an over-proximity of all things, a foul promiscuity of all things which beleaguer and penetrate him."[176] In his influential work on postmodernism, Fredric Jameson arrives at a similar conclusion, deploying Lacan to describe an aesthetic tied to the "cultural logic of late capitalism." The culture of the late twentieth century, Jameson argued, was one of pastiche, blank irony, surface, and waning affect, indicative of an emerging subjectivity that is "schizophrenic" by virtue of its unmooring from historical agency. Overwhelmed by the immediate materiality of signifiers dislocated from the signifying chain that typically holds reality together, the postmodern subject is engulfed by "undescribable vividness" and vacillates between anxiety and euphoria.[177] While not engaging schizophrenia explicitly, Jean-François Lyotard's assessment of postmodernity as an era defined by the twilight of various "master narratives" posits a similar estrangement of self and meaning.[178]

Diagnosing the culture as schizophrenic typically involves the caveat that one is speaking figuratively and not literally (as if schizophrenia was itself an empirical thing). For much of the twentieth century, however, psychiatry speculated that schizophrenia—defined and aligned within modernity—was indeed the byproduct of environmental overstimulation, an illness inflamed or perhaps even caused by living in the modern world of relentless sensory assault. Ivan Pavlov proposed that schizophrenics were "weak genotypes" suffering neural damage from exposure to overtaxing environments. In 1936,

Pavlov speculated, "What would have happened if all these schizophrenics, of whom there are so many, just imagine this, if those schizophrenics would be, at the first sign of illness, put in a greenhouse to keep them away from the blows of life, of all the difficulties that life creates, well, would they then become real schizophrenics?"[179] This theory of "protective inhibition" still had resonance forty years later. A study in 1970 argued such theories shared the assumption that schizophrenia proceeds from "a low threshold for disorganization under increasing stimulus input. The arousal that results is broader than anxiety, in the usual use of the term, as it is contributed to by all sources of stimulation, including positive and negative affect, as well as external stimulation."[180] Such work essentially reasserted Pavlov's theory: "If the pre-schizophrenic is fortunate enough to be exposed to only limited anxiety-provoking situations, it is possible for him to lead his life as a schizoid individual and not experience schizophrenic breakdown. However, should a sufficiently anxiety-arousing situation arise, the spiral of reciprocal augmentation of anxiety and generalized fear is set into motion, and precipitates acute schizophrenic disorganization."[181] Many situations can be "anxiety-provoking," of course, from latent familial psychodynamics to escalating global tensions. But theories of protective inhibition focused especially on social situations and communicative transactions that threaten to become overwhelming. The normative ego, if placed in a position of escalating stress, disintegrates into schizophrenic confusion or calcifies into paranoid defense.

Before Freud opined on Prosthetic Godhood and the discontents of civilization, he endorsed speculation that the human sensorium evolved not to maximize access to information, but to protect the organism from encountering too much stimulation.[182] The eye limits the spectrum of light. The ear limits the spectrum of sound. Perhaps the ego, as a historical compromise with its environment, is itself a filter developed to accommodate a certain spectrum of meaning. One could argue that, so far, most citizens of modernity have learned to adapt, however miserably, to the demands placed on them by industrialization; scientific rationalism; technocratic administration; mandatory networking; spatiotemporal compression; and capitalisms early, mature, and late. But prosthetic irritation, whether it is mildly annoying or catastrophically psychotic, suggests that the ego is still adapting—phenomenologically, cognitively, existentially—to its new relationship with unbounded information and mutated meaning. Present-day man is "unhappy," in Freud's words, in that the ego has yet to adapt fully to the "god-like" attachments of the technical prosthesis. That the ego might be a malleable

FIG 1.3 *Hikikomori* describes the apparently growing global population of young men and women who remain sequestered for days, months, or even years in their bedrooms, most of their "contact" involving the Internet and online gaming. Image by Yuta Onoda, 2015. Republished with permission from Gerald and Cullen Rappart.

construct in structural transition counters the claim that psychoanalysis, like humanism and neuroscience, proposes an ahistorical model of selfhood (the psychoanalytic ego is male, white, Victorian, and Austrian/French). If the ego is itself a prosthetic implantation of the symbolic, as Lacan makes even more explicit, then its sense of identity and coherence is necessarily subject to historical and cultural forces. In her commentary on Lacan, Teresa Brennan addresses the historical specificity of the ego, emphasizing in particular the emergence of what she terms the "fundamental fantasy" of the *modern* ego. In this fantasy, the ego "conceives itself as the locus of active agency and the environment as passive."[183] She also writes, "To the extent that the fantasy dominates the subject's psyche, knowledge or experience of energetic connections between human beings and entities is foreclosed."[184] Brennan dates the "age of the ego" to the seventeenth century, the dawn of a "social psychosis" that, with technological assistance, remains operative in the present era.[185] Here Brennan links Lacan to Heidegger's critique of technology as a mind-set that transforms the world into "standing reserve," a material realm awaiting exploitation in the service of beings who perceive themselves as wholly autonomous from this external environment.[186] Mired in this fantasy, advocates of Prosthetic Godhood imagine that the modern ego will live forever in its current form—King Me eventually delivered into a blessed state of digital transcendence. Even if there is no body in the disembodied future of magical post-humanism, this ego will somehow persist as pure information. Proceeding from a resilient and generally normative model of the modern ego, futurists imagine the Singularized individual taking up prosthetics in active autonomy over the passive environment. But this prosthesis promises to be more a slow, painful, and stressful program of correction akin to mental orthodontics. As technologies enter the body, they cannot help but inscribe the material histories and power relations that brought them into being. Prosthetic Godhood may one day involve implantable knowledge chips, mechanized claws, and other affordances that add to a new and improved Human 2.0, but more likely, most will simply be happy to download a new ad-blocking app to defeat the marketers who ceaselessly target your retinal array.

Can the "age of ego" survive this transformation? In the journey from figurative to literal prosthetics, indexed by so many technical delusions, perhaps we are witnessing a threshold of neural or egoistic impedance, a breaking point at which the excesses and instabilities of meaning—digitized, multiplied, saturated—are overwhelming the modern ego's ability to reliably sustain its former fantasies of control. The electronic erasure of certainty, evident across so much of the contemporary media landscape, reveals that fantasy has always been as important as "reality testing" in suturing together the self and the social. To have so much of reality, perhaps even all of it, so quickly exposed as fantasy confronts the modern ego with a profound stressor.

Psychiatry has long understood the importance of stress in triggering psychotic episodes: an ego under duress begins to disintegrate, passing through various states of confusion, euphoria, insight, panic, paranoia, and catatonia. "Stress" is an especially appropriate term for describing the tensions that stem from a technical prosthesis. As Donna Haraway notes, the figure of the "stressed" human is indebted to the postwar cybernetic language of overtaxed systems and mechanical fatigue. "Associated with the notions of breakdown and obsolescence," she writes, "stress is also fundamentally part of the conceptual apparatus of cybernetic evolutionary biology. Stress limits and machine communication conceptually imply one another."[187] The origin of cybernetics in the language of engineering implies that stress is a purely physical force—too much electricity in the wires and too much nervous energy in the nerves. The source of this stress, in turn, is frequently attributed to energetic intensities in the ego's environment. Steam trains, urban density, the World Wide Web—all contribute to a stressful acceleration of everyday life (thus the antidotes of taking a walk in the country or periodically "unplugging" to reset the ego back to some imaginary baseline). Some forms of stress may very well be purely autonomic missives engineered by the limbic system. Getting chased by an angry bobcat, for example, is stress that both a human and a squirrel can understand. As residents of the symbolic, however, only humans can experience marriage, mortgages, and mortality as stressful. In other words, the stress that Lacan associated with psychotic triggering is not some purely physiological force of nature (that overheats and breaks the brain); it is, instead, inextricably bound to the social relations and technologies of meaning that have produced the ego in the first place. Only humans, after all, are condemned to walk the planet with their instincts entangled within semiotic structures of desire, morality, consequence, prohibition, guilt, and remorse. Accordingly, different historical and cultural structures for organizing social relations produce different potentialities for stress. In other words, although we often describe stress in terms of energetic anxiety, it is in fact *a product of meaning*, a consequence of how an individual understands, explains, and forecasts his or her relationship to the world.

Prosthetic extension (and convergence) brings with it new avenues of stress, especially as an older order of the ego is compelled to surrender foundational fantasies about the self and the social. In an essay on "bioelectronics," Ellen M. McGee provides a familiar portrait of future ego's engagement with the media prosthesis. New technical affordances "will enable humans to be constantly logged onto the internet, to cyberthink and to instantaneously retrieve encyclopedic stores of information. Building in these interfaces, surgically implanting them in the brain, will allow for greater energy, and efficiency, and will enable humans to operate without radios, or TVs, printed newspapers, cameras, GPS units, credit cards, computer workstations, ATM machines, wireless, corded or mobile phones, and other separate devices."[188] McGee concedes that this new bioelectronic world will present a challenge, especially to those who might remain attached to some residual illusion of a private self:

> The psychological impact on the self needs to be a subject of research since the boundaries between self and others and even groups will be eroded, if not eliminated. The boundaries between real and virtual world will blur, and a self constantly wired to the collective will be transformed. The emergence of a Borg type collectivity or hive mind, where personal

identity is lost and assimilation is the preeminent value is a real possibility. Selves will have relationships and interact in highly realistic virtual reality environments, transforming the sense of both the individual and reality. Whether this will be a benefit or burden is unclear.[189]

In this vision, widely shared by many futurists, bio-implants will eventually collapse such well-worn binaries as subject-object, private-public, interior-exterior, and real-virtual. Thought broadcasting and thought implantation, the signature curses of psychosis, will become deployable affordances as the classic psychotic dyad of self and Other dissolves into cybernetic collectivity. In effect, schizophrenia will be the new normal, and the Cartesian ego, the new insanity. If the ego, as Lacan argues, is a fiction held hostage to networks of meaning that both constitute and cohere its illusion of autonomy, then our forcible prosthetic integration into expanding fields of data, information, and meaning portends bold new horizons for becoming psychotic. An ego that once comfortably believed it was the agent of its own destiny will find itself buffeted from one provisional constellation of meaning to another, a "trema" exacerbated by the convergence of a technical prosthesis that demands faster and more immediate access to the body. More than ever, important meanings will hang in the air just out of reach, at least until cyber-thinking dissolves any lingering ambitions to maintain the modern ego. Philip K. Dick, himself no stranger to the borderlands of insanity, once observed, "There exists, for everyone, a sentence—a series of words—that has the power to destroy him."[190] Can the same be said of future encounters with the media? Are certain combinations of sound, image, and text, spinning like tumblers on a safe, lying in wait to deliver more and more transitional egos into toxic constellations of meaning?

Perhaps this is the price to be paid to achieve Prosthetic Godhood, the fairytale wish that technological extension endlessly promises and yet never seems to deliver. Freud likened the prosthetic impulse to the fantasy life of children, and for good reason: disempowered and dissatisfied, the child imagines a day when it, too, like parents and gods, will somehow enjoy greater, perhaps even absolute, power over space, time, and meaning. Various technologies continue to dangle this digital carrot, whether it is an Internet of Things that promises a seamless consumer utopia or a billionaire's bunkered mainframe that will one day archive his brain. Yet such prosthetics present a paradoxical horizon for the modern ego as we currently know and live it. In its classical form, the ego is a compromise, a zone for mediating internal and external conditions. If this ego were suddenly to become "omniscient" and "omnipresent," then it would no longer have anything to mediate. It would cease to exist, as would the wisdom, pleasure, and mastery the modern ego once imagined would accompany knowing all and seeing all. An ego that had continuous access to all possible information and endless positionalities of meaning (perhaps with digital "immortality" offered as a bonus affordance) might come to resemble a functional computer or a cut-rate god. But for an ego once dominant but now dissolved, the more likely response to Prosthetic Godhood would be sheer terror, followed by acute madness.

Chipnapped

CHAPTER TWO

THE SECRET OF THE BRAIN-CHIP, a graphic novel published in 2003, presents the story of a troubled college student named Paul.[1] As it opens, Paul is already having difficulties. A professor addresses him in class, but Paul feels disorientated and flees the room in confused anger. Another student tries to help, but she seems to be "far away," and Paul suddenly realizes he can no longer understand what she is saying. While walking home, Paul tries to understand why he has felt so "stressed" and "irritable" of late. The professor "seems to be up to something." His family is acting suspiciously. "All sorts of strange ideas have been running through my head," he says to himself, "as though something was about to happen." And then out of nowhere something *does* happen. Walking alone that night on a deserted street, Paul hears a voice: "*Hey idiot . . .* " At this juncture, with Paul experiencing his first auditory hallucination, the story pauses to provide psychiatric context, a voice of diagnostic authority speaking as black type on a plain white page: "A psychosis often starts slowly and quietly. Strange things happen to you. . . . You try to act normal. But gradually you become more and more anxious and confused, without even noticing it." A list of early "prodromal" symptoms follows: reclusiveness, forgetfulness, depression, insomnia, suspicion. "It is as though you have become unbearably sensitive to the rest of the world." Then comes a list of "early psychotic symptoms": alterations in sight, sound, and touch; thinking one has access to secret knowledge or information; a vague sense of influence from external sources. Paul's story resumes. The voices continue to plague him, despite his best efforts to go on with his daily routines. Then one night at his desk, Paul looks into the lens of a camera, and "the pieces of the puzzle [fall] into place."

"I was a guinea-pig in a horrible experiment," Paul realizes. "I was being observed all the time. Unscrupulous scientists were testing my reactions and influencing me by means of a chip they had implanted in my brain. Via satellites they could beam those voices at me. And everybody knew about it." After this moment of revelation, the story resumes, with Paul's father taking

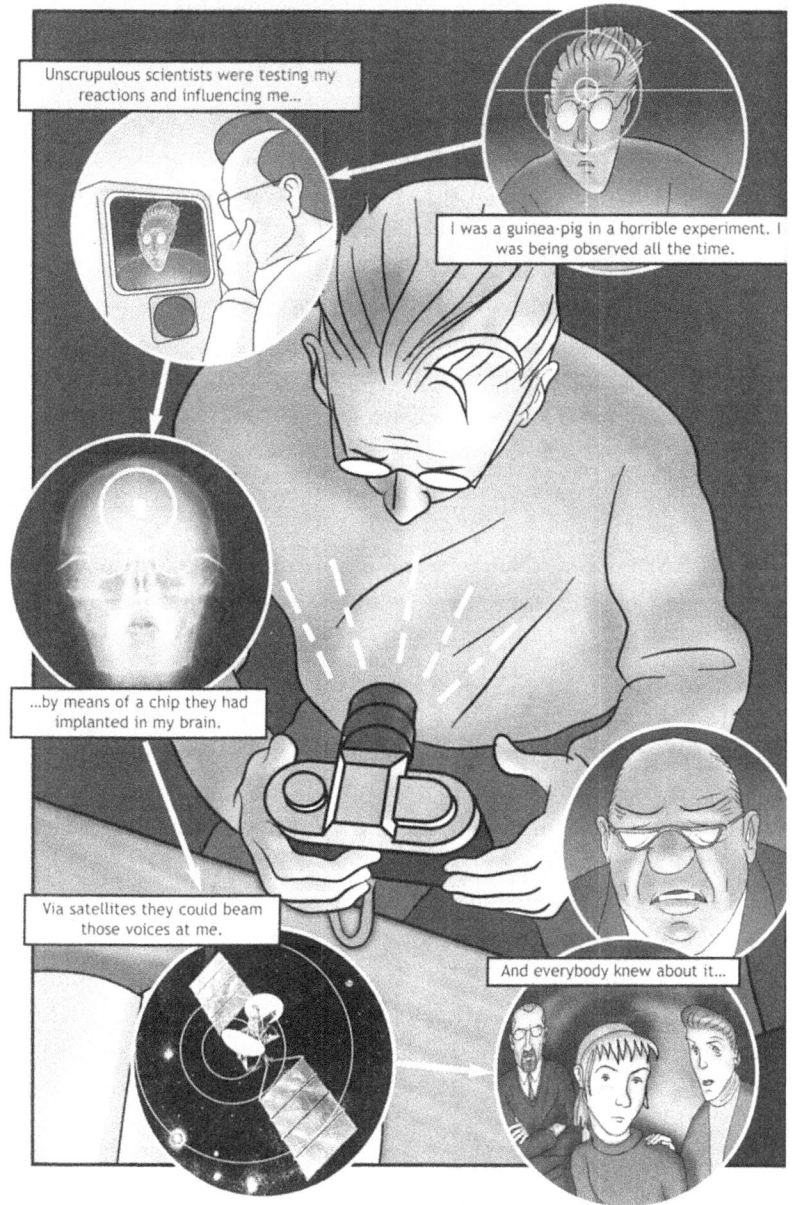

FIG 2.1 Paul's apophany in *The Secret of the Brain-Chip* (2003). Courtesy of EPO.

Paul to the doctor. But "there was no way I was going to cooperate," fumes Paul. "From now on everyone was suspect." Paul goes home to his parents, but hearing on the radio that pieces of a defective satellite are soon expected to fall back to Earth, he spends the next day at a local shopping mall so "the thick layers of reinforced concrete" will protect him from space debris. As he walks through the mall, tired and disheveled, almost every object he encounters becomes a significant clue warning of the looming disaster. Finally, Paul walks up to the display window of an electronics store, where a closed-circuit video camera feeds a bank of television sets. The spectacle of his face multiplied and staring back at him on a dozen TV screens confirms Paul's worst nightmare. He becomes acutely psychotic—so much so that security guards must subdue him. Later, he wakes ups in a psychiatric ward, still intensely paranoid. But through medication and psychotherapy, Paul slowly returns to the real world and begins to make sense of what has happened to him.

As a "Self-Help Guide for People Experiencing Psychosis," *The Secret of the Brain-Chip* is intended as a psychiatric prophylactic. Ideally, a counselor or physician gives a copy of the comic to an individual exhibiting the early symptoms of an impending psychotic episode. The book repeatedly stresses the need to seek help as soon as possible, emphasizing that psychosis becomes more protracted as an individual slips more deeply into his or her delusional system. "If you think you can solve this kind of problem yourself, you are making a mistake," the text warns somewhat ominously. As an intervention, *The Secret of the Brain-Chip* must thread a difficult needle. How does one signify psychosis to those becoming psychotic (in a world where consensus over psychosis itself is increasingly in doubt)? As an educational example for the potentially psychotic, Paul's brain chip must signify a delusion that is clearly *delusional*. Yet in attempting to capture a typical psychotic progression, the story employs a conceit that, for many, appears increasingly feasible. The comic book's prophylactic power is thus profoundly dependent on the *timing* of its reception. If encountered early in a psychotic progression, the reader perhaps will still have enough attachment to the social world to read the book as a cautionary tale and heed its advice. However, if a delusional system has already materialized, the distortive perspective of paranoid psychosis is likely to integrate the comic's message as yet another "sign," much like Paul's reaction to the random symbols at the shopping mall.

The timing of this comic book also has implications within the cultural history of technology. As of 2019, we the putatively sane can still generally agree that dentists working for the Illuminati are not injecting microchips into random molars. If reality is a "collective hunch," as Lily Tomlin and Jane Wagner once quipped, diagnosing a delusion involves exiling those hunches that are not so collective—and for the moment, at least, most believe our current social order does not include the possibility of covert brain chipping. But the self-evident insanity of the "chipnapped" (as these individuals occasionally refer to themselves) is certainly less self-evident now than it was in the 1950s and will most likely be even less self-evident in the coming decades. To even the casual observer, neuroscience and nanotechnology continue to make great strides, and many of us would certainly concede there are powers in the world that would *very much like* to have access to brain-chip technology. Are we certain *they* will not use it? Moreover, if this technology did exist, how would we know for certain *they* have not *already* used it? How well do you know your dentist, anyway? Our certainty that the chipnapped are insane depends on our generally unexamined commitment to a consensus narrative as to the probable parameters of technology and power, an account that the eccentric, psychotic, and otherwise "insane" choose for a variety of reasons not to endorse fully, if at all.

As we saw in the previous chapter, delusions constitute a particularly important, even paramount, criterion for diagnosing psychosis. But as we have also seen, a delusion cannot be identified and measured through any objective instrumentation. It must be interpreted through the imperfect medium of language. Vested with appropriate credentials, I, the psychiatrist, find what you have shared with me in our conversation to be delusional.[2] Published at a moment in which research in electronic prosthetics is accelerating, *The Secret of the Brain-Chip* foregrounds what has always been a challenge unique to isolating technical delusions: *Who is to say—and by what authority—which technologies do or do not actually exist? Who can say—and by what authority—how known technologies are actually being used? Who can know with any certainty what those in power will do with technologies of power to maintain their control?* These questions were already apparent during the Industrial Revolution as the first technical delusions took shape. As technocratic modernity further braided alliances of technical and political power, these questions became even more pressing. Today, as global flows of capital and information demand new structures of technical augmentation, these questions promise to become as insistent as they are unanswerable.

Strange but Plausible

Given the quantitative importance of delusions as necessarily qualitative symptoms, psychiatry has long sought to define them in the most precise and reliable terms possible. The DSM-IV (in authority from 1994 to 2013) defined a delusion as "a false belief based on incorrect inference about external reality that is firmly sustained despite what almost everybody else believes and despite what constitutes incontrovertible and obvious proof or evidence to the contrary. The belief is not one ordinarily accepted by other members of the person's culture or subculture."[3] To those trained in cultural history and critical theory, phrases such as "incorrect inference," "external reality," "false belief," "what everybody else believes," and "not ordinarily accepted" appear as red flags that mark potentially complex fault lines in terms of difference, power, and other socio-cultural vectors of political conflict. Reinforcing this rather fuzzy frame of consensus reality, previous editions of the DSM also distinguished between "bizarre" and "unbizarre" delusions. This was not an idle distinction. In the DSM-IV, a delusion deemed "bizarre" was sufficient *in and of itself* to arrive at a diagnosis of schizophrenia. If a patient exhibited a "non-bizarre" delusion, on the other hand, a second symptom was necessary to confirm the diagnosis. To coach clinicians in this close interpretative call, the "DSM-IV Guidebook" defined "unbizarre" delusions as "involving situations that occur in real life, such as being followed, poisoned, infected, loved at a distance, or deceived by a spouse or lover." "Bizarre" delusions, by extension, involved situations that the psychiatrist, as an ambassador of sane society, judged to be impossible (the "DSM-IV Guidebook" uses the example of an individual convinced his brain has been transplanted from another body). But the guidebook also acknowledged that clinicians might vary somewhat in their standards of "bizarreness": "Clinicians who primarily treat patients with Schizophrenia often think they have seen it all and tend to develop a relatively high threshold for labeling any delusion as bizarre. In contrast, clinicians with relatively little exposure to psychotic patients may consider virtually any delusion to be bizarre."[4] Distinguishing the "bizarre" from the "unbizarre" thus involved an interpretative judgment by the psychiatrist as to the *likelihood* of the patient's delusion, a decision that said as much about the life experience of the clinician as it did about the psychology of the patient. As the author of the guidebook concludes, "One person's bizarre is another person's *strange but plausible*."[5]

The DSM-IV's double-articulation of delusional thought, a system that first divides between the delusional and non-delusional and then, within the delusional, between the bizarre and the unbizarre, was an attempt to provide some semblance of objective calibration to what ultimately are subjective assessments of belief. But despite the hopes and dreams of those who believe psychosis to have a wholly organic cause and a strictly psychopharmacological cure, delusions remain inexorably bound up in the vicissitudes of meaning and the politics of culture. Technology only exacerbates the problem of finding a shared cultural frame for making a diagnosis, especially as the frontiers of technical development exceed the ability of any one person to speak from a position of absolute knowledge. Dr. Ronald Siegel recounts treating an aerospace engineer suffering from hallucinations that the patient attributed to a satellite called "POSSE." While this scenario is unlikely, Siegel nevertheless conceded that his patient's superior knowledge of physics, engineering, and contemporary orbital mechanics added a layer of doubt to the diagnostic process.[6] Technical delusions are particularly corrosive to the DSM-IV's distinction between "bizarre" and "unbizarre" delusions. Hoping to advise puzzled diagnosticians on the line dividing the bizarre and the unbizarre, the "DSM-IV Guidebook" advises, "One might make the judgment that a delusion is bizarre because it involves a mechanism that is *technologically impossible.*"[7] Believing that the government has tapped your phone is "unbizarre" inasmuch as everyone concedes such technology actually exists. Believing one's spleen has been teleported to the moon would be a "bizarre" delusion because almost everyone believes this is impossible. Many technical delusions, however, exist somewhere between these antipodes of possibility. Are there satellites orbiting the Earth, such as POSSE, that are capable of transmitting hallucinations directly into the brain? Most would say this is impossible. Yet like Siegel, most people making this judgment do not possess the technical expertise or security clearance necessary to make a definitive statement on the matter.

More troubling, there are already several known technologies capable of simulating psychotic symptoms. Thus, a teenager tells his doctor that he feels odd every time he goes to a local convenience store—irritated, upset, tense. Like Paul in *The Secret of the Brain-Chip*, he may be a prodromal psychotic experiencing the initial alterations that will eventually become acute madness. Then again, maybe he is simply a victim of the Mosquito. Invented by Howard Stapleton in 2005, the Mosquito is a small electronic device that emits an irritating high-frequency tone perceptible only to those younger than twenty-five (taking advantage of the fact that humans lose their upper-frequency hearing as they get older). Stapleton marketed the device as a security solution for dispersing teenagers who might otherwise loiter in front of stores or in public parks. Blasting a public space with a 17.4 kilohertz tone at 108 decibels makes the area generally intolerable to teenagers while leaving older adults blissfully oblivious of this sonic assault. What, then, are we to make of a teenager or young adult who reports feelings of unspecified irritation and fatigue, perhaps with the proto-delusion of hearing some type of control signal in the air? The Mosquito is particularly diabolical in that it targets the population believed to be most susceptible to a schizophrenic episode. For teenagers and young adults who are already experiencing some form of prodromal paranoia, how might they interpret the overall "bad vibe" perceived near locations using this technology?

Human rights activists have opposed the Mosquito as discriminatory to teenagers, but perhaps there should be an equal concern with the possibility that this readily available technology might prove to be only the first step in a whole series of electronic devices that provide anyone with the means to drive another person insane (or, at least, to highly annoy them). Various "spy shops" already market devices designed to inflict "electronic revenge" on one's clueless adversaries. There is the battery-powered Mind Molester, described with great enthusiasm by its marketer as emitting a "one-second electronic chirp every four minutes until the battery finally runs down. Due to the chirp's frequency, duration, and sound characteristics, it's a very, very difficult, time-consuming, frustrating and maddening task to locate the unit. And even if they find it, they'll still have absolutely no idea whatsoever as to what they've found. Is it a 'bug'? Is it a bomb? Only you know the truth!"[8] One might think of the Mind Molester as a simple mechanism for inducing the cascading snowball that becomes complex paranoia. For those who aspire to be even more annoying, there is also the Mind-Molester Ultra (so called because its chirps can be programmed into even more irritatingly unpredictable patterns) and the Off-the-Hook Mind-Molester (which randomly simulates the sound of a phone left off the hook, presumably to annoy the elderly).[9] Those seeking top-of-the-line electronic irritation, finally, can opt for a device called Sonic Nausea that "generates a unique combination of ultra-high frequency soundwaves which soon leads most in its vicinity to queasiness." It can also cause headaches, intense irritation, sweating, imbalance, nausea, or even vomiting: "Hiding this device in your inconsiderate neighbor's house might put an end to their late-night parties. Perfect for an abusive bureaucrat's office, the executive lunchroom, or for use on other office vermin."[10] At Thinkgeek.com, tormenters can purchase the Eviltron (or an entire Annoy-a-tron Prankster Pack). Once secreted within a target's home, the Eviltron randomly generates "unsettling creaking, uniden-

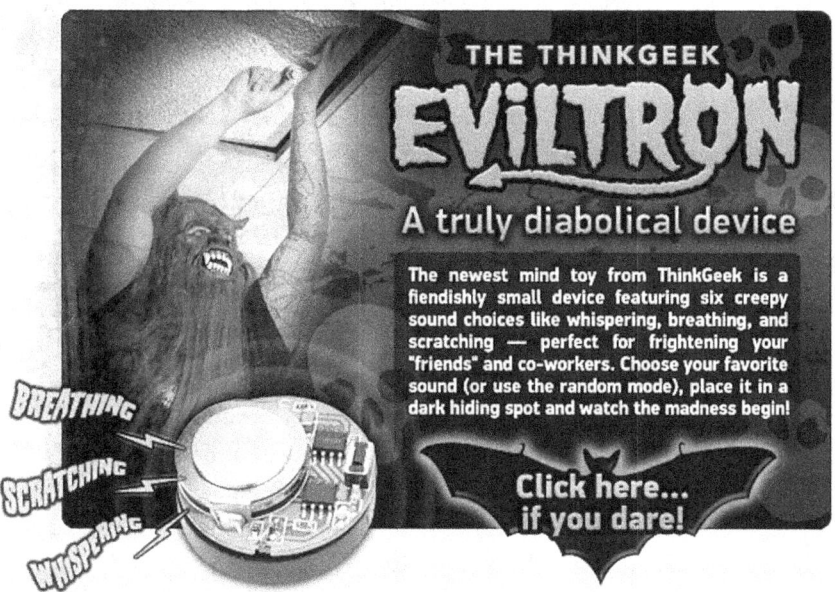

FIG 2.2 Once hidden by a prankster, the battery-powered Eviltron generates random odd squeaks, sinister laughter, and a whispering voice. Courtesy of ThinkGeek.

tifiable scratching sounds" and a "gasping last breath." A "sinister laughing child" and an eerie whisper ("Hey, can you hear me?") are also available options. Upping the hallucinatory ante, the Holosonics corporation markets "audio spotlight" devices that allow sound to be focused in a beam so that only one individual in a crowded room can hear it. Holosonics promotes the technology as reducing excessive noise in public spaces by micro-targeting individual listeners (at the grocery store, only the person standing next to the bananas hears messages about said bananas). Court TV, a cable network in the United States, quickly recognized the psychotic implications of this technology and deployed the devices in a guerrilla promotional campaign for its new series *Murder by the Book*. The campaign involved installing Holosonic devices in various coffee shops and bookstores in New York City. "As shoppers browsed the shelves," a reporter noted, "select shoppers would hear a faint whisper ask them: 'Hey. Do you ever think about *murder*? I do.'"[11]

Owners of boutiques, burger joints, and bookstores may have no long-term interest in driving their customers insane, but most will concede that the government would have few to no qualms about employing forms of sonic torture on its enemies. In fact, the US government already has an established track record in developing and deploying such technologies. Some of this torture has been explicit and crude, as when the US military blared Van Halen's song "Panama" over and over at high volumes in an attempt to flush the Panamanian dictator Manuel Noriega out of a church sanctuary in 1989. After the disastrous end to the government's siege of the Branch Davidian compound in Waco, Texas, in 1993, meanwhile, officials with the Federal Bureau of Investigation (FBI) admitted having conferred with Igor Smirnov, a Russian experimenter with electromagnetic frequencies whom *Newsweek* subtly described as "a subliminal Dr. Strangelove."[12] Smirnov specialized in embedding subliminal voices into electronic feeds, and the FBI apparently considered using his techniques to implant the voice of God—performed by Charlton Heston, no less—into cult leader David Koresh's phone line during their negotiations. More recently, the US military has deployed a device called MEDUSA (Mob Excess Deterrent Using Silent Audio). As described in the pages of *New Scientist*, MEDUSA uses short microwave pulses to "rapidly heat tissue, causing a shockwave inside the skull that can be detected by the ears. A series of pulses can be transmitted to produce recognizable sounds."[13] This shockwave is very unpleasant and causes the targeted skull to flee post haste. Ostensibly a device deployed for "nonlethal" crowd control, the possibilities for other forms of mischief are obviously endless.[14] Raytheon's Active Denial System (ADS), another "nonlethal" technology of crowd control, can transmit a microwave ray up to 1,600 feet, producing the effect of "intolerable heat" and causing "whoever it's pointed at to immediately start moving away." "They often scream," notes one report, despite the military's claims that "the chance of injury from the system is 0.1%."[15] This technology saw its first official deployment in Afghanistan during the summer of 2010. In 2015, plans were announced to mount the ADS system to the Air Force's new AC-130J Ghostrider gunship.

At the dawn of the twenty-first century, brain chips are slowly dissolving the distinction between "bizarre" and "unbizarre" delusions. After all, brain chips do now actually exist. Under the guidance of the Defense Advanced Research Projects Agency (DARPA), research in brain-computer interface (BCI) technology began at the University of California, Los Angeles, in the early 1970s.[16] In 2005, Matthew Nagle became the first recipient of Brain Gate, described by his doctors as a "mind-reading brain chip." After implantation, Nagle, who was paralyzed from the neck down in 2001, could manipulate a computer cursor *mentally*, allowing him to "think" his TV on and off and to move a prosthetic arm.[17] In 2004, another research team claimed success in developing a video game that could be controlled by brain waves.[18]

In 2009, two games arrived on the market using electroencephalography (EEG) Headset technology and biofeedback loops to simulate telekinesis. Force Trainer, a *Star Wars* tie-in, allows users to "levitate" a Ping-Pong ball in a plastic tower by producing brainwave patterns associated with intense concentration. In Mattel's MindFlex, players compete in guiding a small Styrofoam ball through an obstacle course using only the mind.[19] A new clinical trial in Brain Gate technology began in 2008, and in 2010 DARPA announced a $15 million initiative to continue refining BCI research. In September 2014, scientists announced the first successful transmission in "brain-to-brain" contact. The experiment involved a subject thinking a word, which a helmet of electrodes then translated into electromagnetic pulses. These pulses, transmitted over the Internet, were then received and decoded in the mind of Subject B. "It is a kind of technological realization of the dream of telepathy, but it is definitely not magical," announced theoretical physicist Giulio Ruffini. "We are using technology to interact electromagnetically with the brain."[20] In 2017, DARPA awarded a company $18 million to research a BCI capable of transferring information into the brain at speeds greater than one gigabit per second.[21] Today, announcements of new success in neural interfacing occur almost weekly, including the news that monkeys are now able to control wheelchairs with their minds.[22]

A growing number of individuals believe that brain chips, while not (yet) implanted in their own skulls perhaps, constitute a very real and looming danger for society at large. Some would say the dawn of the great implantation is already on the horizon. Privacy activists and other functional paranoids note with alarm that the Radio Frequency Identification (RFID) chip is opening the door to more invasive forms of data monitoring. Implanted in objects ranging from credit cards to cocker spaniels, RFID chips contain large amounts of embedded data that can be accessed by a scanner. One does not need to be a raving lunatic to foresee that RFID chips, in conjunction with cellular and GPS technology, may very well be introduced in the human population as a means of consolidating information about medical histories, consumer profiles, movement patterns, and citizenship status.[23] Activists argue that such chips, already used extensively to track lost pets, would initially be implanted under the guise of locating lost children.[24] These individuals would remain "in the system" through adulthood, and eventually, after a few generations, no one would remain "untagged."[25] It might seem as if the highly motivated could remove themselves from such surveillance with the aid of a pocketknife and a shot of whiskey, but *they* have already anticipated this. "Chips"—micro and nano—are growing smaller and craftier. Ongoing work in the Berkeley "smart dust project" seeks to further miniaturize tiny transmission chips, envisioning a future in which large swaths of territory (and the units that live in them) could be "dusted" (like crops) with chips capable of tracking movements and relaying waves of data gathered from the surface.[26] In 2012, both the United Kingdom and the United States approved the use of pills equipped with tiny RFID chips, ostensibly to monitor a patient's vital signs and supervise her medication schedule: "The sand-particle sized sensor consists of a minute silicon chip containing trace amounts of magnesium and copper. When swallowed, it generates a slight voltage in response to digestive juices, which conveys a signal to the surface of a person's skin where a patch then relays the information to a mobile phone belonging to a healthcare-provider."[27] Also in 2012, researchers at Stanford University announced success in creating a microchip capable of swimming through the bloodstream under wireless power and direction—perhaps into the brain.[28] Needless to say, such technologies and their possible affordances are of extreme interest to the "chipnapped." The chipnapped, in turn, would be quick to remind us that these technologies are all in the public record. Who knows what DARPA and other tech firms are doing in secret?

Delusional Evidence

Recognizing that cultural norms do not provide particularly stable ground for identifying delusions, technical or otherwise, the most recent revision of the DSM, published in 2013, shifts the definition of a delusion from the terrain of consensus and plausibility to that of *falsity and conviction*. Suppressing the contentious politics of normative thought, at least in terms of content, the DSM-V now recognizes delusions according to the individual's *depth of conviction, lack of insight*, and steadfast *resistance* to compelling counterevidence.[29] In a related revision, the DSM-V has also eliminated the distinction between the "bizarre" and "unbizarre." A delusion is now merely a delusion with no added weight assigned to the oddness or presumed impossibility of the belief.[30] On the one hand, the DSM-V's renunciation of "cultural standards" appears to be a concession, however oblique, to modernity's philosophical and sociological critiques of "normality." With the relativistic question of plausibility off the table, delusions can now be established by the patient's steadfast conviction in a belief that is untrue, even when presented with objective, empirical evidence of its falsity. As a reporter for *The Observer* describes the new criteria of the DSM-V, "The general idea is that delusions represent a problem with *how* you believe—that is, a problem with forming and changing beliefs—not a problem with *what* you believe. In other words, simply believing something strange or unusual should not be considered a problem but having 'stuck' beliefs that are completely impervious to reality suggests something is mentally awry."[31] Problem solved.

Or perhaps not. This shift is ultimately less a concession to issues of cultural/historical difference than an ingenious attempt to displace these politics onto the seemingly more defendable criteria of the demonstrably "untrue." In some respects, it resembles a return to the practices discussed at length by Michel Foucault in which physicians of the eighteenth century would attempt to cure a lunatic by enacting the absurdity of his conviction (as in striking a man who believes he is made entirely of glass with a hammer). In the DSM-V's new definition, the ambiguity of delusional thought has been acknowledged in terms of the variability of normative belief and yet has been put back under repression through an appeal to the empirical demonstration of falsehood. Eliminating the criterion of cultural consensus belies the fact that "depth of conviction" and "resistance to counterevidence" are themselves subject to implicit cultural standards, political norms, and historical tolerances. Put simply, a given society at a given historical moment remains amenable to indulging some (fantastical) beliefs more than others. The cultural politics of favoring certain forms of belief, in turn, has a direct impact on the standards for assessing conviction and counterevidence. The DSM's new definition of a delusion is thus highly synchronic—that is, it imagines a patient and clinician frozen in time and space, somehow cut off from the larger cultural and historical mechanisms that brought each actor (and their belief systems) into the diagnostic exchange. All that matters, in that moment, is the psychiatrist's assessment of what she or he believes constitutes reasonable counterevidence.

Under the new criteria, for example, what is to be done with Doreen Virtue, Ph.D.? On July 15, 1995, an "angel" warned Virtue that her car would be stolen that afternoon. Virtue, who in 1995 was a practicing psychotherapist and the founder of the Womankind Psychiatric Hospital in Nashville, Tennessee, ignored these warnings. Her website continues the narrative: "Despite this, the angel did not abandon Doreen in her most dire moment—as she was parking, two armed men, intent on a carjacking, brandished weapons and physically accosted the unsuspecting Doreen. The voice spoke to her again—it was loud, distinctly male, and it instructed her to scream with all her might. This time she listened, and her life was saved by passers-by who became alarmed and sent her attackers running."[32] From this epiphany,

Virtue went on to create a formidable business empire based on the concept of "angel therapy." She is the author of dozens of self-help books that hybridize angel-centric Victorian spiritualism with a range of mystical systems taken from across history, including numerology (*Angel Numbers 101* [2008]), Vedic philosophy (*Chakra Clearing* [2004]), and fantasy-inflected tarot (*Magical Unicorn Oracle Cards* [2005]).

Prior to a conversion to Christianity in 2017, Virtue conducted workshops around the world in spiritual healing and in 2013 organized an "Angel Messages Retreat" aboard an Alaskan cruise ship. Virtue also endorsed the reality of "Fairies," guardian angels for pets, and "indigo children." While angels do not appear in the text of Virtue's diet therapy book, *Losing Pounds of Pain* (2002), the cover nevertheless features a young woman sitting on a staircase crying as an invisible angel watches over her compassionately. Throughout Virtue's oeuvre, there is an emphasis on learning how to hear one's own angels speak, an irony that is not lost on Virtue herself: "I think it's ironic that I, a former psychotherapist who once worked in locked hospital psychiatric wards, now teach people how to hear voices!"[33] In fact, Virtue argues that many diagnosed as "schizophrenic" are in fact "star people," angels or extraterrestrials in human form.[34]

If she was sincere (and not simply a cynical huckster preying on the ignorant), Virtue would appear to fulfill the criteria for delusional thought under any and all iterations of the DSM. Yet for years she remained unimpeded by psychiatric and legal authorities for her purported belief that angels might assist a person picking lottery numbers. Of course, whether Virtue actually believed an angel prevented her from being carjacked is not the point. Her success in print and on the lecture circuit speaks to a general willingness to protect as sane those individuals who still maintain an archaic belief in instrumental angelic supervision. If an individual were to complain that the CIA monitored his activities twenty-four hours a day, and that he could see agents prowling in the bushes outside his house, said individual would no doubt be diagnosed as paranoid. Yet as a society, we continue to go to great lengths to accommodate as sane those individuals who appear to truly believe God observes everyone all the time, even if most would (at this point in history) consider surveillance by the CIA more plausible (if still highly improbable). This is not to say that all religious and supernatural beliefs are immune from suspicions of psychosis. Pronouncing oneself Jesus Christ, for example, will still earn a psychiatric admit. Typically, religious delusions have been defined as a matter of communicative direction. As Thomas Szasz observed in perhaps his most famous quotation, "If you talk to God, you are praying;

if God talks to you, you have schizophrenia."[35] But even this divide is not necessarily always true, given that many individuals continue to profess that God speaks to them directly. What an individual *really* means in claiming a dialogue with God remains, like a delusion, an ultimately unknowable gap between subjectivities attempting contact through the imperfect medium of language.

Slightly more modern but no less insulated from proofs of falsity are claims of extraterrestrial contact. In the spring of 1985, while sitting alone in a conference room at the Albuquerque Technical-Vocational Institute, Dr. Norma J. Milanovich heard a voice tell her to "pick up a pen."[36] She did. In the months that followed, Milanovich engaged in many sessions of voice-directed "automatic writing"—so many, in fact, that she soon had to switch to a computer to engage in automatic typing. Gradually transformed into a "multidimensional channel," Milanovich found herself under the tutelage of Beings known as "Monka and Kuthumi": "To my amazement, the transmission that came through stated that those communicating were Beings from Arcturus, who were riding on a Starship that was situated to the southeast of Albuquerque."[37] Later, by the telekinetic repositioning of a crystal on her desk, Milanovich began an extensive dialogue with the Arcturians, asking them about their home planet, nourishment, and clothing.[38] The Arcturians informed Milanovich that they were here for education and enlightenment. Their lessons, at one point, presented a classic construction of electromagnetic influence: "All thoughts are electrical impulses surrounded by an electromagnetic field of energy. This field of energy has the ability to move at speeds the human mind cannot even begin to comprehend." The ability to send telepathic thought, the Arcturians explained, involves a "force that propels and projects thoughts...based on a tensor equation. That tensor equation is made up of 2 parts electromagnetic energy and 1 part emotion."[39] Later, the Arcturians familiarized Milanovich and her friends with their invisible starship's thirty-five compartments, including "the old and new vaporizing chambers," "the Reunion Quarters for those who are in the reproduction mode," and "the duty free port" where the Arcturians exchange goods beyond those manifested "on the materialistic plane of the third dimensional reality of earth."[40]

Many "UFO religions" have revisited the Book of Genesis to produce an account of creation that might reconcile older conceptions of God with the revelations of twentieth-century physics. *The Urantia Book*, published in 1955 (but dictated during the 1930s and '40s by an anonymous "sleeping subject" in contact with "celestial beings"), combined Christian exegesis with modern cosmology to posit an "Isle of Paradise" at the center of the universe. This "Isle," in turn, is said to be surrounded by seven "superuniverses" that contain a billion perfect worlds. Scientology's mix of science fiction and self-help psychology also dates to the early 1950s. The pulp author-turned-seafaring guru L. Ron Hubbard founded the Church of Scientology in 1953. Those who become Scientologists begin by undergoing a process of "auditing." Employing the Hubbard Electropsychometer (E-meter), auditing involves purging new initiates of their "reactive mind" until they are "cleared."[41] Scientology also professes a belief in "implants," but as with so many other religions, it is difficult to know whether Hubbard meant for these implants to be interpreted literally or figuratively. The full cosmology of Scientology is too intricate to explicate in full here, but it essentially involves the contamination of our sector of the universe by "thetan" energies, soul-like entities blasted from their original bodies seventy-five million years ago by hydrogen bomb explosions ordered by Xenu, then the director of the Galactic Confederacy.[42] As the Thetans left their original bodies, they were captured in an "electronic ribbon" that Xenu had deployed around the earth (or "Teegeeack," as it was known then). These trapped spirits were then taken to a giant 3D movie complex where days of continuous screenings produced the implantation of the false reality that we inhabit today (the thetan souls having attached themselves to mankind once humanoids appeared on the planet).[43] While many Scientologists argue that this narrative of intergalactic 3D movie implantation should be read allegorically, much like the Old Testament, Hubbard nevertheless gave the various implants a very specific, technical nomenclature (such as the "R6" and "Helatrobus" implants, the latter installed by an ancient intergalactic government that spoke to living creatures by taking the form of clouds).[44]

Institutionalizing those who believe in angels, Arcturians, and Xenu would prove a very difficult medical and legal task. In the United States, the First Amendment to the Constitution allows a citizen to believe in any form of religious magic that he or she might choose, with wide latitude as to the intensity and irrationality of said magic. Meanwhile, appeals to teleportation, invisibility cloaks, mind beams, time travel, and other technological wonders allow aliens to elude any and all skeptical resistance to the reality of their existence.[45] In an odd twist for those who believe they are the victims of technical control, the utter implausibility of supernatural and super-scientific beliefs ("Angels will cry if I eat a Twinkie," "I am full of Thetans that once lived in a volcano prison on Hawaii") generally protects these systems from psychiatric assessment. The license afforded these magical systems is so great, in fact, that society allows them to offer and even enact rival theories of mental disorder. In evangelical circles, for example, there is a long tradition of explaining apparent psychiatric dysfunctions in terms of demons and possession. In *Schizophrenia, Obsession, Exorcism, Reincarnation, and Mediums* (1976), Francis Harber explains: "There are good invisible people and bad invisible people. The bad ones radiate harmful rays which cause the diseases and put evil thoughts into our mind."[46] Dr. Harber argues that schizophrenics are in fact "obsessed" by demons, providing a 119 point checklist of phenomena that suggest demonic intervention. An "obsessing spirit," we learn, can cause a variety of somatic complaints such as hay fever, constipation, migraines, hernias, colitis, and ulcers. Demons also have a hand in jaywalking, streaking, gambling, frigidity, homosexuality, and spontaneous demonstrations of a "Nazi salute."[47] Schizophrenics, Harder argues, are "potential mediums" who are "being harassed to put them on the spiritual path."

Lacking the ability to motivate their beliefs in the distant past or a faraway galaxy, the "fixity" and "conviction" of the chipnapped would appear to make them more vulnerable to being diagnosed as delusional. God and Xenu cannot be proved in any empirical sense; therefore, no "counterevidence" can be offered to disprove their existence. But a brain chip is a material object, made and implanted by fellow humans in the contemporary historical moment. Demonstrable proof of its nonexistence can be provided by showing the chipnapped an X-ray of his skull. Or can it? A technician you have never met emerges from another room and shows you an X-ray of your troubled brain. What does that prove? "An x-ray will prove nothing," opines an online commenter in a mind-control forum, "as these people are aware of what is going on, the same as most dentists, and are part of the deception and game."[48] Pivotal in developing brain-chip technology, the medical (and quite possibly psychiatric) community has a vested interest in denying the chip's existence. Submitting oneself to the professional protocols of anonymous institutional power is a futile act; in fact, one of the most effective strategies to convince the populace that brain chips are merely a paranoid delusion would be to deploy doctors and scientists as authorities denouncing such ideas as insane. Accordingly, many chipnapped individuals recognize that requesting an X-ray to locate a brain chip will likely earn them a psychiatric admission, forcing them to seek "friendly" physicians who might be more sympathetic and discreet.[49] None of this should be surprising. If there were an entity capable of injecting brain chips on a mass scale—whether it is the government, the Freemasons, or extraterrestrials—it stands to reason that this entity would also possess sophisticated techniques for concealing these powers.

Now that brain chips exist, the terrain for judging fixity and conviction has shifted from questions of technical feasibility to estimations of *political will*. Brain-chip delusions remain "psychotic" to the extent that the consensus reality of contemporary society must believe that no organization could actually succeed in such a scheme. Just as plausibility and bizarreness in technical delusions once depended on qualitative judgments as to likely technological affordances, the new standard of falsity and conviction depends on estimating the political powers possessed by those thought to be behind these technologies. Pressed about how a brain chip could make its way into the skull without an individual's knowledge, the chipnapped will argue that any surgical procedure, dental appointment, or even routine vaccination provides more than enough opportunity for an implantation.[50] Typical is the case of retired Marine Bill Burke, who claims to be under the control of a US military program called Dreamscape. In the late 1970s, Burke spent three days in a hospital in Barstow, California, for an operation on his ankle. He recalls waking up from surgery and finding "someone forcing something" into his nose. Three days later, while recovering at home, Burke saw "four uniformed military men standing by his bed: apparently a holographic or mental projection." Burke further claims that, beginning some three months after his surgery, computerized images have been transmitted to his electronic implant every day."[51]

Asked who is behind the random brain chipping of the population, victims nominate those suspects most associated with "black ops" capabilities: the FBI, the United Nations, the CIA, NASA, INTERPOL, MI6, the KGB. Particularly suspect are the classified projects of DARPA and the surprisingly candid marketing of IBM's VeriChip program. As the research division of the US Defense Department, DARPA brands itself with the thoroughly paranoid slogan, "Creating and Preventing Strategic Surprise." At IBM, meanwhile, VeriChip (an injectable RFID chip) received approval from the US Food and Drug Administration in 2006 for use in human beings. Calling the technology (with weirdly dark irony) "RFID for the People," IBM has opened the door on human implantation by touting the technology's value in storing medical information for patients who have difficulty communicating with physicians. Additional uses include "infant protection systems used to prevent mother-baby mismatching and infant abduction" and "wander prevention systems used for protection and location of residents in long-term care facilities."[52] In 2005, VeriChip filed with the Securities and Exchange Commission to become a publicly traded company but warned investors that certain risks were involved:

> Several of our systems incorporate the implantable VeriChip. The use of the implantable VeriChip, which is used in conjunction with a database containing a patient's vital statistics and other patient pre-approved information, may give rise to misperceptions about the use, and risk of misuse, of these systems, including misperceptions that the use of these microchips could intrude on privacy or allow "tracking." The use of the implantable VeriChip in humans is from time to time the subject of negative publicity. This publicity may negatively affect our ability to sell our systems, which may adversely impact our revenues.[53]

Hoping for just such an outcome, one activist invoked Pastor Martin Niemöller's famous poem about cowardice in the face of fascist aggression:

> When Verichip microchipped the Alzheimer patients I remained silent;
>
> > *I was not an Alzheimer patient.*
>
> When Verichip microchipped the Diabetic and AIDS patients I remained silent;
>
> > *I was not an AIDS patient nor a Diabetic.*
>
> When Verichip microchipped the Military I did not speak out;
>
> > *I was not in the Military.*
>
> When Verichip came for the activists I remained silent;
>
> > *I was not an Activist.*
>
> When they came to microchip me, *there was no one left to speak out.*[54]

Before going dark, the website also sold a DVD explaining "everything you need to know about the human microchipping agenda and how the media is using the science of gradualism to sell it to you!"[55]

Recognizing that the forces behind these technologies are unlikely to admit their involvement or reveal the extent of their actual powers, some have taken these issues to court, hoping (perhaps naïvely) that the judicial branch still retains enough autonomy to make Big Techno Power speak its truths. In 1974, George C. Jones, an inmate in the Georgia State Prison, sued the state for using "a machine or device by which [the] brain is probed and monitored by electric or parabolic sound waves designed to achieve behavioral control."[56] Jones sued under the First Amendment and Fourth Amendment, arguing that his freedom of thought had been restricted and that reading his mind violated his constitutional guarantee against "unreasonable search and seizure."[57] The judge, somewhat surprisingly, was not entirely unsympathetic to Jones's claims. At the very least, he considered it an interesting intellectual exercise, writing, "The Fourth Amendment contention raises the questions of whether thought interception by means of electronic brain-scanning is a search or seizure of one's person and whether or not thoughts by themselves constitute 'effects' within the meaning of such constitutional provision."[58] Injecting some skepticism into his ruling, the judge continued, "It would seem that a machine that represents a major breakthrough in metaphysics would have been patented in the United States Patent Office." Later, in the final order, however, he conceded that the court was "not unaware that prison authorities utilizing thought control machines are unlikely to reveal the existence or operation of so revolutionary a device."[59] Given that the victim of a brain chip, real or imagined, is often living in poverty or institutional confinement, many cases are dismissed under those portions of the US Legal Code pertaining to screening and evidence for proceedings *in forma pauperis*. Title 28 of the US Code allows the court to dismiss cases deemed "frivolous, malicious, or [that] fail to state a claim upon which relief may be granted."[60] Such was the case in the lawsuit of John Ginter, a prisoner at San Quentin who claimed that the associate warden, the "head" of the California Department of Corrections, and the "head" of the University of California, Berkeley, conspired in 1967 to "invade and rape" his mind with a device known as the "Magnetic Integrated Neron [sic] Duplicator" (MIND). The judge dismissed the case in 1994 as "beyond the realm of reality and possibility."[61] As this standard suggests, claims about brain chips are typically considered demonstrably false before they can even reach the court for adjudication, thus making it structurally impossible to prove their existence within the legal system. The chipnapped thus face twin threats of invisibility, denied "discovery" to gather more information on a device that is by definition "undiscoverable."

But the chipnapped have not been so easily dissuaded. In 1996, an associate professor at the University of Science and Technology in Hong Kong filed a $100 million suit against the US government for "implanting mind-control devices in his teeth.... Huang Si-ming charges that the devices were implanted during root canal work in 1991 while he was studying at the University of Iowa.... Another student at Iowa University who, like Huang, was born in China, had gone on a shooting spree, and the feds, Huang says, put the devices in his teeth to find out if he was involved." In his filing, Huang maintained that "one of the devices in his teeth [could] read his thoughts and talk to his mind when [he was] asleep. A second device ... transmit[ted] pictures of what he [saw] to a receiver for recording. The mind controller ... [could] drive him to 'bad' behavior."[62] At a hearing of the National Bioethics Advisory Board in 1998, Vicki Casagrande provided members with an explanatory booklet about electronic harassment and then offered public testimony about her own experiences of "telebiostimulation."[63] Jesus Mendoza has sued multiple parties, beginning in 1999, over his alleged harassment by electronic technologies.[64] The chipnapped and other victims of electronic harassment are especially enthusiastic about the case of James Walbert in Wichita, Kansas. Having invented an "antimicrobial sanitary seal for 12-ounce aluminum beverage cans," Walbert entered a business partnership to market his innovation. After the partnership dissolved, Walbert claimed that his former business partner immediately began to stalk him and his family members with "electronic and microwave devices," adding, in response to a court questionnaire, that the defendant's conduct had made him feel "stalked, the guy is straight creepy."[65] When the defendant did not appear in court to defend himself against these allegations, the judge granted Walbert his court order of protection, making Walbert the first known plaintiff to "win" a case of alleged electronic harassment.[66]

Walbert's court victory in Wichita was to some degree secured by a letter of support he obtained from former State Congressman Jim Guest of Missouri. "I have worked for 3 years with Microwave and Electronic Harassment victims throughout the US and overseas," Guest wrote. "It is hard for others to understand the technology that is being used to destroy people's lives. I know James because he contacted me for help."[67] The year before Walbert's case, Guest wrote to his fellow legislators to ask for their help "for the many constituents in our country who are being affected unjustly by electronic weapons torture and covert harassment groups. Serious privacy rights violations and physical injuries have been caused by the activities of these groups and their use of so-called non-lethal weapons on men, women, and even children."[68] During his time in the Missouri Legislature, Guest was the "go-to guy" for those experiencing electronic harassment.[69] In addition to filing lawsuits, the chipnapped and electronically harassed have a history of lobbying various legislatures to bring an end to these practices. In 2000, Congressman (and perpetual Democratic Party presidential candidate) Denis Kucinich of Ohio introduced legislation that would have outlawed direct energy weapons (DEWs), defined in the bill as any "means inflicting death or injury on, or damaging or destroying, a person (or the biological life, bodily health, mental health, or physical and economic well-being of a person) ... through the use of land-based, sea-based, or space-based systems using radiation, electromagnetic, sonic, laser, or other energies directed at individual persons or targeted populations for the purpose of information war, mood management, or mind control of such persons or populations."[70] The federal bill went nowhere. But in 2004, Michigan became the first state to criminalize harassment using electromagnetic radiation devices—a rare victory for the chipnapped.[71] In 2007, meanwhile, politicians and psychotics alike took notice at the confirmation hearings of the US Supreme Court nominee John Roberts when Joe Biden, the future US vice-president, asked: "Can a microscopic tag be implanted in a person's body to track his every movement? There's actual discussion about that. You will rule on that, mark my words, before your tenure is over."[72]

Legal protections against electronic implants and harassment became an even more pressing issue with the election of President Barack Hussein Obama in 2008. Convinced that America's first African American president was a stealth Muslim intent on destroying the United States and instituting a socialist welfare state, a sizeable portion of conservative Americans gradually descended into a form of collective insanity. As refracted through the paranoid-entertainment complex of right-wing radio and Fox News, the biracial, Ivy League–educated, upper-middle-class Obama provided a compelling demon for those alienated white men who perceived themselves as structurally disenfranchised in twenty-first-century America. Obama's reelection in 2012 is believed to have played a contributing role in defense contractor Albert Peterson's decision to murder his wife and children before committing suicide. "He felt that our God-given rights were being taken away," said a friend of the family. "He didn't like where the country was going."[73] All politics being local, as the saying goes, conservative lawmakers from districts gerrymandered for maximum paranoia have been very responsive to this voting bloc, including those who fear that "the government" might one day compel citizens to receive microchip and brain-chip implants.[74] Although he could cite no evidence that such implantations were actually taking place, or that any plans existed for such implantations to take place at any time in the foreseeable future, State Representative Ed Seltzer of Georgia argued he was simply being "proactive" in introducing a bill that would make it a misdemeanor to implant "microchips, sensors, transmitters or any other manner of tracking devices into individuals against their will."[75] Such paranoia also intersects with the agenda of Christian fringe groups who believe the biochip is the "mark of the Beast" predicted in the Book of Revelations (the mark of the Beast was previously thought to be the Universal Price Code).[76] This group, too, has found an advocate in the legislature. "I just think you should have the right to control your own body," State Representative Mark L. Cole of Virginia told the *Washington Post*. "My understanding—I'm not a theologian—but there's a prophecy in the Bible that says you'll have to receive a mark, or you can neither buy nor sell things in end times. Some people think these computer chips might be that mark."[77]

Understandably, this constituency was nearly apoplectic when, on April 2, 2013, President Obama announced his intention to sponsor a government-funded Brain Initiative. Described by the White House as "a bold new research effort to revolutionize our understanding of the human mind and uncover new ways to treat, prevent, and cure brain disorders such as Alzheimer's, schizophrenia, autism, epilepsy, and traumatic brain injury,"[78] the Obama Brain Initiative, as the project soon became known, promised to support the Human Connectome Project in its bid to produce the definitive map of the brain's neural networks (much as the Human Genome Project did with the genetic code).[79] For a community already convinced that even the seemingly innocuous suggestion that children should eat more vegetables provided evidence of social engineering, the purpose of the Brain Initiative could not be clearer: brain chips for everyone in preparation for the coming one world government. The participation of DARPA in the project ("Better understanding of the human brain supports national security," the agency argued in support of the Brain Initiative) only confirmed this plot, as did many of the materials included in the proposal. One researcher, for example, argued that it "will ultimately become feasible to deploy small wireless microcircuits, untethered in living brains, for direct monitoring of neuronal activity," not to mention "safely and transiently introducing engineered cells to make tight (transient) junctions with neurons for recording and possibly programmable stimulation, or a combination of these approaches."[80] In an interview with the *MIT Technology Review* in 2014, neuroscientist Joseph LeDoux addressed the prospect of employing brain chips to restore or even implant memories: "DARPA seems to be going full steam ahead on these kinds of technologies. What they plan to do is put chips in [the brain]. It would be like a prosthesis—instead of moving your arm, you're fixing memory."[81] Paranoids of the political left and right now find common ground in the understanding that technological innovation obeys the structural demands of global economics, shareholder bottom lines, and militarized paranoia—systems that proved long ago they are capable of eluding any attempts at human intervention. Now that algorithms and data mining exceed battalions and carpet bombing in their ability to shape the future, agents known and unknown have every incentive to continue miniaturizing and consolidating their technical powers.

Spectrum Disorders

In a world where the machinations of political and technological power aspire to invisibility, counterevidence is no more reliable than consensus as a ground for evaluating delusional ideation. What, then, is the psychiatrist of the near future to do when confronted with a person convinced he has a brain chip? Some clinicians advocate embracing the inherent ambiguity of all mental illness by abandoning the binary yes-no logic that early psychiatry imported from medical science. This would involve reframing several psychiatric categories in terms of a "spectrum," much like autism. In its revisions for 2013, the DSM-V took a step in this direction by inserting "spectrum" into its previous category of "Schizophrenia and Other Psychotic Disorders." A concession to cultural relativism, perhaps, the spectrum model has also been advocated by those who side with neurobiological causation (albeit for very different reasons). An individual can now be—in theory, at least—a little schizophrenic. The idea of a spectrum also has implications in terms of delusions. Approaching delusions as a spectrum would mean sidestepping the previous criteria of cultural consensus and counterevidence. As we have seen, the idea that a delusion is a "wrong" belief held with great conviction is difficult to defend. After all, almost everyone has certain beliefs that are in some sense "delusional," judged either by appeals to consensus reality or resistance to counterevidence.[82] A "spectrum" approach would instead emphasize the delusion's impact on the individual's daily life. Paranoia, for example, can manifest at many points along a spectrum of increasing dehabilitation, ranging from "prudent caution" (*I better not speed. I might get a ticket*) to "personality disorder" (*Everyone is out to get me*) to delusional psychosis (*I must find and remove the brain chip in my skull*). As a product of social relations, standards of acceptable paranoia can also exhibit great cultural and historical variability. In vernacular history, many believe that America was a more paranoid nation in the 1950s, citing the Red Scare and artifacts such as *Invasion of the Body the Snatchers* (1956) as the historical ground and reflective surface of this national delusion. Defining paranoia as "the unfounded belief that someone is out to hurt us," Daniel Freeman and Jason Freeman support the widespread impression that paranoia, as a general state of being, is once again on the rise. Nominating paranoia as the characteristic disorder of the twenty-first century, they argue that it permeates "our society, more than we've ever suspected and possibly more than ever before."[83] They cite a variety of possible causes for this increase, from alarmist media coverage to profound transformations in the global economy.[84] With no absolutes for isolating paranoia as a distinct pathology, Freeman and Freeman argue that an individual can be placed on a spectrum of paranoia by asking four questions: (1) How much does the person believe the paranoid thoughts? (2) How preoccupied is the person with the thoughts? (3) How distressing are the thoughts? and (4) How much do the thoughts interfere with everyday life?[85] Presumably, these questions could also be applied to other beliefs and possible delusions. In this scenario, an individual might be sincerely convinced he has a brain chip, but as long as he remains relatively calm about it and shows up for work, there is really no reason for anyone to intervene. Similarly, someone who is incredibly agitated many hours of each day believing that Mexicans, Muslims, or Martians are "out to get him" might benefit from psychiatric intervention.

History is also a "spectrum," of course, one that establishes the social and cultural baselines that become so important in evaluating the spectrum of delusional thinking. In 1965, Intel's co-founder Gordon E. Moore predicted that the number of transistors on an integrated circuit would double approximately every two years, thereby increasing exponentially the operating power of computer hardware. This "prophecy" (Moore's Law) has more or less held true: the power, speed, and capacity of media hardware continues to multiply at an unprecedented rate.[86] Given the prominence of electronic media in psychotic ideation, perhaps there should be a psychiatric equivalent of Moore's Law, a biennial doubling of reasonable technical paranoia to mirror the biennial doubling of technical affordances. For those on the borderline of delusional psychosis, brain chips signal a particularly decisive moment in this movement through the techno-historical spectrum. In mass modernity, technical delusions typically involved devices that were still exterior to the body, visible, and thus potentially vulnerable. If I believed the radio transmitted voices into my head, I could at least smash the radio. Even those who insist that the entire world is a virtual reality program can at least imagine the possibility of finding the source, short-circuiting the grid, and shutting down the spectacle.[87] The brain chip, however, aspires to be the optimum implantation of prosthetic power and thus the perfect delusion. When operating correctly, brain chips offer a real-time simulation of consciousness itself. As one implanted individual argues, "The modern day version of this system has the capability to read a person's mind in real time and give the victim the notion to do something, as if by command. Because this notion is perceived by the victim in the first person, the victim perceives this idea or way of thinking as a product of his own thought process. People that become the target of conditional mind control will be unable to discern and distinguish their own thoughts from those that are being projected to them."[88] Happily or unhappily for the acutely paranoid, brain chips have not yet achieved the ability to completely subjugate or counterfeit consciousness. If a brain chip were operating correctly, presumably, then one would never suspect he had one. To believe one has been chipnapped is to retain a residual core of the original bio-self that recognizes and resists the chip's alien agenda. As faulty technologies, brain chips remain the still unrealized Omega point of technocratic convergence.

At mid-century, this convergence still aspired toward forms of political totalitarianism. In the paranoid style of American politics, communists and fascists alike were thought to advocate for a state in which ideological obedience could be hardwired in the brain. Today the paranoid continue to expend great energy worrying about the CIA, the FBI, the National Security Agency (NSA), the Trilateral Commission, the New World Order and other shadowy forms of government control, but in truth, advertisers, marketers, and, eventually, consumers seem much more likely to realize the dream of biochip implantation. Brain chips would provide the perfect "digital handshake" to position humans within what Mark Weiser described in 1988 as "ubiquitous computing." For Weiser and other futurists, ubiquitous computing signals the era of "calm technology, when technology recedes into the background of our lives."[89] Today ubiquitous computing is better known by its slightly less Orwellian names, "the Internet of Everything" and "the Internet of You," hoping to suggest a unique individual enveloped by a benevolent marketplace of boundless provision. Embedding products, people, and processes with microchips capable of communicating directly within this all-seeing Internet, we are told, will provide humans with more time to go about the business of being human. No need to check on the quantity or quality of milk in the fridge—a chip will add it to the shopping list. A new filter for the furnace arrives at the door—the chip did it. Too drunk to drive the car? Your biochip will tell your ignition chip to block the starter. No longer will porn users be hostage to a crude "thumbs up-thumbs down" system of aggregated ratings for predicting quality of arousal. A brain chip can match browser histories with archived dopamine and beta-endorphin levels to focus attention on maximally stimulating erotica. A business report in the MIT *Technological*

Review in 2014 prognosticates, "As wearable devices get better-looking and more powerful, we'll trust them to monitor and control more of our lives." For now, though, "Many companies are still struggling to get anyone to put a wearable computer on."[90] No doubt, this resistance is vestigial. Once more and more people are comfortable with a "wearable computer," brain chips will be marketed as the ultimate advancement in "smart" and desirable interfacing with the global communications array. (Who will be the first celebrity to be enchipped?) It may well be that the chipnapping of the future will proceed with minimal resistance as these devices become positively associated through familiar marketing appeals to choice, convenience, and democracy. *If a brain chip puts me in touch with the things I want more quickly, so be it!*

If the "calm technology" of the Just Ubiquitous Internet of Computing Everything and You (JUICEY) succeeds, the media will effectively disappear, leaving the brain chip as the Holy Grail of both ubiquitous computing and paranoid psychosis. What technology could be more "calm" than an invisible prosthetic that seamlessly integrates the consumer mind with an array of data-monitoring systems? And once the media are invisible, so too are the power relations involved in securing this fantasy that the media are now calm to the point of invisibility.[91] Or, as a jaded commenter at an RFID website writes, "You don't really need to worry anyway, because when it all comes down to the true reality of it all, there is nothing you can do about it. You won't even be able to change the world, because my dear friend you are not in control. Just enjoy Babylon the best way you can, because in a decade you won't even remember ever writing your comment."[92] Significantly, the transition here is as much ideological as technological. Powered by capital, algorithms, and Big Data, the unchecked growth of JUICEY indexes a shift toward willing, even enthusiastic internalization of control. For most of the twentieth century, advertisers and consumers understood that their relationship was fundamentally adversarial. Corporations employed advertisers to sell people things they did not necessarily need or to promote more or different versions of the things they do require. Advertisers and merchants thus have always been interested in Psychological Operations (PsyOps) techniques to gain strategic advantages in the marketplace. Since at least the 1950s, retailers have been interested in the possibilities of "subliminal" messaging (despite a lack of evidence that such techniques work).[93] But these concerns speak to an older, perhaps even residual, model of paranoia in which the consumer transaction remained fundamentally suspect and hostile. The rise of digital platforms—and with them a generation of "digital natives"—has dramatically recalibrated these marketing relations. As social media and commerce continue to converge around the "networked hypersociality" and "participatory exhibitionism" of online culture, the prosumer culture predicted by futurist Alvin Toffler in 1980 has become a more or less continuous opportunity for market research. Particularly important is the imperative that young social media users share as much personal and consumer data as possible so marketers can better align targets in their digital crosshairs. As Michael Serazio observes, "Campaigns and platforms that draw upon user-generated content submissions are the industry's attempt at embedding commerce in that fabric of identity exploration that takes place on line."[94] The ultimate goal, of course, is not passive observation but active cultivation: "Soliciting ... self-expression can take a number of digital forms, which are fundamentally an effort at intertwining an emergent sense of self (and, for youth, this is still at an embryonic, unstable stage) with a *branded* identity."[95]

Cigarette and soft drink manufacturers have long understood the importance of establishing brand loyalty during the teenage years. A good ad campaign can thus ensnare a consumer for decades of routinized consumption. With the growing sophistication of Big Data and algorithmic prediction, the same loyalties might be cultivated for a whole complex of products. In 1956, Philip K. Dick's story "Minority Report" predicted a future in which mutant telepaths and computers could predict criminal behavior before it occurred, thus allowing the "pre-crime unit" to arrest these individuals before the crime itself actually transpired. Transposed into the world of marketing, imagine the value of algorithms that could predict, nurture, and eventually reinforce entire patterns of consumption, the Bourdieuian habitus of taste materialized as the architectural habitats of Big Data.[96] Amazon.com and other online retailers already attempt such groupings of products based on one's browsing history, but this strategy would prove even more lucrative if "taste" could be more scientifically inculcated and managed by early exposures to media. Not only could loyalty to beer and toilet paper be maintained; so could choices in the realm of entertainment and information. Introduced in the periodicals and penny dreadfuls of the nineteenth century, commercial seriality remains a crucial business strategy in the culture industries of today. Like the makers of Camel and Coke, entertainment manufacturers have a vested interested in capturing consumers during adolescence and then, through strategic marketing, holding them captive to a franchise for as many years as possible. The multigenerational and apparently lifelong commitments made to the Beatles, *Star Trek*, *Star Wars*, *Harry Potter*, and the universes of DC and Marvel comics demonstrate just how lucrative this strategy is and will continue to be for the culture industries. With the expansion of "on-demand" entertainment and the concurrent diffusion of mobile platforms (such as the brain chip), adolescents captured by a franchise could be effectively herded through a lifetime of consumption, thereby reducing risk and ameliorating cost for these industries in introducing new product lines. Here, too, consumers can gravitate toward the pleasures of familiarity and convenience. Why carry around a screen to watch a new movie when I can simply stream *Gremlins 2* directly from the cloud to my optic nerve?

When TiVo debuted in 1999 at the leading edge of new data-harvesting technologies, the company promoted its service to older, more affluent adopters by boasting about an almost uncanny ability to predict the personal tastes of its user. This flattering fantasy positioned TiVo as the discriminating viewer's cybernetic gatekeeper, providing a fig leaf of autonomy to that generational remnant still invested in the idea that a unique "self" might stand apart from the dross of mass culture. Nearly twenty years after this debut, however, the idea of having one's unique personal taste coolly aggregated and accurately predicted by various retailers no longer produces alarm, suspicion, or depression; nor does anyone particularly care that such closed loops of algorithmic surveillance corral consumers into more dependable circuits of consumption. In gothic lore, a vampire must be invited into the home before he can begin sucking the blood out of the resident. Today we routinely surrender our private data lives by "agreeing" to unread terms and conditions online, essentially baring the throat of our data self by allowing marketers access to our friends, contacts, photos, browser history, and other succulent information.[97]

Futurists might well dismiss such concerns as the residual complaints of cranky Marxists. And perhaps they are right. Given that Marxism itself displaced "man" as the engine of human history, who is to say the structural determinations offered by JUICEY might not orchestrate human existence more effectively than humans themselves? If our enchipment takes place under the current conditions of global capitalism, the "things" in the JUICEY will still depend on human survival to ensure the overall system's continuing operation (*You can't spell ubiquitous without "you"!*). For a human being to function effectively as the symbiote of an iPad or a riding lawnmower, she or he will need access to adequate nutrition, shelter, education, and health care to remain viable within these larger life cycles of manufacturing and consumption. Perhaps a community of networked machines, raised in the traditions of capitalism and dependent on the monetization of human desire for their own reproduction, will finally produce the just and humane world that humanity itself could never achieve. Rather than become our imperious overlord, the JUICEY might be a benevolent protector. The marketplace will decide, literally, in the form of hardwired instrumental reason. Subtle adjustments in key algorithms will allow humanity to maintain its cherished illusions of free will as the structural logic of market control gradually eases us into this system. In closed-circuit meetings, the competing interests of JUICEY will negotiate among themselves to arrive at rational accommodations with one another to maximize humanity's potential as a shared resource for consumer circulation. Interests that for decades fought one another according to the competitive logic of capitalism will achieve a type of data détente, producing a self-sustaining system that accommodates corporations each according to its abilities and each according to its needs. For example, precise algorithmic negotiations might generate a public health campaign that allows the real estate/beef complex currently known as McDonald's to finance the implantation of biochips in children so that health metrics can be continually monitored and stored for the family physician. No more needless deaths from sudden infant death syndrome: an App will notify mom that daughter's chicken pox will strike in three days. All that McDonald's asks in return is the right to monitor your child's blood-sugar levels and beam hamburger ads straight to the optical nerve whenever hunger cues begin emanating from the stomach. Incredibly precise actuary tables, meanwhile, will calculate the ideal number of visits a bio-replacement unit (a BRU, or child) can make to McDonald's to maximize his lifespan to burger consumption ratio (more nutritious and healthy consumer options will also have their say). As an additional convenience to parents, satellites could probe the BRU's toy chest to see exactly which Happy Meal toys are missing from his or her collection, activating an ancillary brain beam to junior that shows the missing figurine, entreating the BRU to visit McDonald's as soon as possible.

The toy manufacturer Mattel has already taken an interesting step in this direction by introducing a Barbie doll that records a child's private verbalizations, then uploads them for interactive analysis. Developed by the technology firm ToyTalk, Hello Barbie uses Wi-Fi technology to record and transmit the child's speech to the company's computer servers. Speech-recognition software analyzes the messages and then chooses—in less than a second—among thousands of verbal responses scripted by writers at ToyTalk and Mattel.[98] Over time, data analysis allows Hello Barbie to adjust to the child's characteristics and preferences, in effect customizing her responses for a maximum illusion of sentient interactivity. Inevitably, of course, researchers discovered that hackers could break into the system, either to eavesdrop on

FIG 2.3 Having ignored the terms and conditions of his online contract, Stan Marsh finds himself conscripted into a device that combines the iPad and *The Human Centipede*: the HUMANCENTiPad. SOURCE: SOUTH PARK STUDIOS.

FIG 2.4 Barbie: She wants inside your child's head. © 2015 Associated Press.

the child's private playtime or to steal information.[99] But these are minor and, again, vestigial concerns. Hello Barbie (and related toy lines) will allow parents to program more effective instructional protocols into the doll and, thus, the child. Barbie (or G.I. Joe or Optimus Prime) can make subtle suggestions: "Most children like having a clean room!" "Pretty girls don't wear boots, silly"; "One day your little brother might be bigger than you—remember that." Moreover, young children will no longer be burdened with performing the difficult psychosocial rehearsals of voicing both the self and a doll, a process that once helped integrate children into the intersubjective relations of identification and empathy that lubricated a more primitive form of humanism. As a machine that speaks for the aggregated hopes and quantified desires of a collective childhood experience, Hello Barbie presents a vanguard strategy for better integrating children into their destiny to socialize as interactive data packets. A brain chip would further liberate this relationship, exchanging Barbie's crude plastics for a fully interactive and perpetually available Barbie projection in the mind, a gateway to untold vistas of consumer dialogue.

....

The stakes of our seemingly inevitable rendezvous with the brain chip are vividly dramatized in the saga of Diane Napolis. In 2003, the State of California charged Napolis with one count of stalking and five counts of making criminal threats after she accused Steven Spielberg and his wife, Kate Capshaw, of implanting a chip in her brain. In her declaration to the Superior Court, offered in response to a court-ordered mental evaluation, Napolis described a familiar narrative of high-tech persecution. Napolis claimed her former position as a social worker in San Diego had led her to expose cases of "ritual abuse."[100] She believed this work had angered Satanists and other powerful figures who shared an interest in promoting the idea of false memory syndrome, a useful strategy for discrediting those who might access memories of childhood torture and molestation.[101] The account provided by Napolis links many individuals and organizations in this scheme, and while Spielberg and Capshaw are never mentioned by name, Napolis eventually invokes a "very wealthy Jewish Couple from Los Angeles" who, she feared, was about to come into possession of sophisticated technologies in "virtual reality, NSA tracking software, and more":

> This particular Jewish couple are known for their interest in Sci-Fi-like technology and their company specializes in unique special effects software.

This couple also has a reputation for being humanitarians, having funded a project that documented the testimony of Holocaust survivors many years ago. But unfortunately in their zeal to play God and destroy what they did not understand, they, along with a few of their friends, are guilty of a number of travesties. When confronted, they responded with an aggressive counter-play, consisting of misinformation and absurd claims to the court system and to the media which other media outlets repeated.[102]

In other words, Napolis was concerned that one of the culture industry's most powerful figures was about to access NSA-grade surveillance software, powerful brain chips, and the latest innovations in virtual reality. After Spielberg obtained a restraining order, Napolis somewhat inexplicably moved on to accusing actress Jennifer Love Hewitt of murder and mind control. Police finally arrested Napolis after she sent a threatening e-mail to a Hewitt fan site. Claiming Hewitt remotely manipulated her body through "cybertronic technology," Napolis vowed, "I plan on firing a gun at her heart and not missing." Pronounced delusional and a paranoid schizophrenic by court psychiatrists,[103] Napolis was committed to the Patton State Hospital and, upon release, given ten years' probation. In 2008, Napolis brought suit against Michael Aquino, a former member of Anton LaVey's Church of Satan and the founder, in 1975, of the Temple of Set. In her lawsuit, Napolis accused Aquino (along with six other people and San Diego State University) of conspiring to engineer the threat against Hewitt that resulted in Napolis's arrest and institutionalization.[104] Napolis has many defenders among "fringe" interest groups on the Internet, especially those concerned about the impact of satanic ritual abuse and covert government persecution.[105]

At the center of Napolis's theory and subsequent legal troubles was a device known as the Soul Catcher Chip, so called for its ability to record (and play back) the entirety of the human sensorium (and, thus, the "soul") of the implanted individual. Here Napolis appears to have suffered the misfortune of actually believing the predictions of a prominent figure in global telecommunications research. The Soul Catcher Chip was not a spontaneous hallucination on Napolis's part; it was, instead, the invention of Peter Cochrane, the head of British Telecom.[106] In 1999, Cochrane predicted the Soul Catcher Chip, a brain implant that would "act as an access point to the external world," was on the near-horizon and would allow individuals to "download the mind onto computer hardware" to create "a global nervous system via wireless Internet."[107] Cochrane further predicted that thoughts and emotions would be downloadable by 2050.[108] Another researcher at British Telecom argued it would soon be possible to "imbue a new-born baby with a lifetime's experience by giving him or her the Soul Catcher chip of a dead person."[109] "This is the end of death," observed Chris Winter, then head of British Telecom's Artificial Life Team and lead researcher on Soul Catcher 2025.[110] "By combining this information with a record of a person's genes, we could recreate a person physically, emotionally and spiritually."[111] British Telecom's resident "futurologist," Ian Pearson, expressed this affordance in terms of Moore's Law: "Over an 80-year life we process 10 terabytes of data, equivalent to the storage capacity of 7,142,857,142,860,000 floppy disks. If current trends in the miniaturization of computer memory continue at the rate of the past 20 years—a factor of 100 every decade—today's eight megabyte memory chips norm will be able to store 10 terabytes in 30 years."[112]

The residually sane recognize this discourse for what it is: a techno-futurist hubris prominent among Western scientists (in search of grants) and as old as H. G. Wells's *The Shape of Things to Come* (1933). For the borderline psychotic, however, it is difficult to imagine a more compelling explanation for the symptoms typical of prodromal schizophrenia. So even as a comic book such as *The Secret of the Brain-Chip* does its best to convince the prepsychotic that he or she *does not have a brain chip*, the head of British Telecom asserts with equal confidence, authority, and conviction that one's entire sensorium and "self" will soon occupy a chip implanted behind the eye. Ray Kurzweil, meanwhile, as head of engineering at Google, predicts that by 2040 "most of our thinking will be non-biological."[113] And who better than Spielberg to orchestrate the final crossing over from the Society of the Spectacle to the Society of the Brainstem?[114] He is a famous public figure, of course, but also widely regarded as the "Edison" of modern Hollywood, instrumental in creating the form of blockbuster spectacle that has come to dominate industrial output and audience imagination since the 1980s. In particular, his involvement in *Jurassic Park* (1993) foregrounded the magical possibilities of CGI technology, serving as a popular reference point in the public's understanding of the digital image. Who else would have such a driving ambition to create pure spectacle in the brain, movies in the mind that would at last achieve the "myth of total cinema" by circumventing vision for direct neural excitation?[115] The US military certainly understands the advantages of fusing the Spielberg aesthetic with computer imaging and tracking software. In 1999, the US Department of Defense partnered with the University of Southern California to create the Institute for Creative Technologies (ICT). As part of its mission, the ICT seeks to explore "techniques and technologies to improve the fluency of human-computer interactions and create visceral synthetic experiences."[116] Of course, the ability to program "visceral synthetic experiences" would be of immense interest to both the culture industry and the military-industrial complex, a synergistic opportunity actively promoted by the ICT. The institute notes that its location in Los Angeles "facilitates collaboration with major movie and game makers. ICT graphics innovations help create realistic computer-generated characters in Hollywood blockbusters and also enhance virtual characters for museum and military projects."[117] In a dream of vertical integration unimaginable to the old Hollywood studio system, the ICT promises to create immersive virtual reality scenarios that train soldiers for their physical deployment in theaters of war, experiences that—with just a little luck and talent—can then be adapted back into 3D IMAX extravaganzas and interactive gaming scenarios.

To make matters even more worrisome, Warner Brothers announced in March 2015 that Spielberg would direct the film adaptation of Ernest Cline's novel *Ready Player One* (2012). Riding a wave of dystopic young adult fiction, *Ready Player One* takes place in the mid-twenty-first century in a world where "real life" has become a desolate hellscape of poverty, crime, and collapsing infrastructure.[118] To escape, most spend their time in OASIS, a fully immersive virtual universe (literally—there are other virtual planets to visit by paying tolls that allow for shortcuts through this virtual time and space). A novel structured like a video game, *Ready Player One* chronicles Wade Watt's search for three "Easter eggs" hidden in OASIS by its creator James Halliday, who announces in his will that the first person to find all three Easter eggs (and solve the attending puzzles) will inherit his vast wealth, as well as administrative control of OASIS. Knowing that Halliday was a child of the 1980s and obsessed with that era's popular culture, Watts, his friends, and an evil corporation leverage their resources into mastering '80s pop ephemera in a search for clues. Entire runs of 1980s sitcoms such as *Family Ties* (NBC, 1982–89) must be reviewed like homework. Old video games such as *Centipede* and *Tank Battle* must be mastered. Nerd-film classics of the 1980s such as *War Games* (1983) and *Blade Runner* (1982) must be memorized line by line. The music of Duran Duran and Rush once again becomes current. Characterized as a dystopia for the novel's teen readership, the story as adapted by Spielberg promised to be a utopian windfall for the entertainment industry. Not only did the movie have the potential for substantial box office success in 2018; it also presented perhaps the most diabolical vector ever devised for the synergistic repurposing of the culture industry's vast archives. Younger viewers were introduced to the back catalogue of several franchises that have already proved quite lucrative for the entertainment industry. Older viewers, meanwhile, experienced the nostalgia of Spielberg applying the Spielberg aesthetic to properties that defined the era in which Spielberg helped introduce the Spielberg aesthetic that would come to colonize popular culture over the next forty years.[119] Popular history recounts that in 1945, just before the first test of the Atomic bomb, a group of scientists warned the US government that the weapon's fissile chain-reaction might not end, thus igniting the entirety of the atmosphere and destroying all life on the planet. In this respect, Spielberg's *Ready Player One* was ultimately a dud. But as a theoretical model, the film opened the door for future techno-cultural engineering that may eventually succeed in trapping future generations in hermetically sealed franchises capable of infinite cannibalization, a universe of *mise-en-abyme* sequels and transmedial franchising where the novelty of self-reflexive repetition becomes the last play of difference. If successful, implanting brain chips may very well become redundant.

To remain functional in our present reality, for the moment anyway, one simply *must* believe it impossible that Steven Spielberg and Jennifer Love Hewitt are installing brain chips to protect a ring of Satanists or to usher in a new era of neural entertainment franchises. For those who do believe in such a plot, however, appealing to consensus or counterevidence achieves little. Defining such ideas as "delusional" now depends on the spectrum-based criteria of "preoccupation," "distress," and "interference." In accusing Spielberg and threatening Hewitt, Napolis made the mistake of acting on her beliefs, thereby revealing the high levels of preoccupation and distress that earned her a psychiatric commitment. Yet if there was even the remotest chance that some alliance among Spielberg, Hewitt, DARPA, the ICT, the NSA, and Satan were about to plunge the world into the eternal "false consciousness" of the Soul Catcher Chip, what would be the *acceptable* levels of *preoccupation*, *distress*, and *interference* one could display without seeming insane? If one believes this future is even remotely possible, would it not be prudent to remain as distressed and preoccupied as possible?

The Will to (Invisible) Power

CHAPTER THREE

TOWARD THE END OF 1886, prominent New York attorney and already notorious "eccentric" Sterne Chittendale lapsed into an attack of electrical mania. Although Chittendale owned a bachelor apartment in Manhattan, he inexplicably took up residence at a hotel only a few blocks away; "his behavior in the dining room, where he accosted several ladies and told them he was full of electricity, was reported to the proprietor, who took steps to have his guest leave the hotel."[1] Undaunted, Chittendale moved to another hotel, where again he informed guests about "the storage of electricity in his body." A demented stroll down Broadway finally landed Chittendale in Bellevue's psychiatric ward. At his insanity hearing, Chittendale attributed his increasingly bizarre behavior to the electricity coursing through his system. Electrical currents also had a habit of gathering in his throat, he claimed, making it difficult for him to speak at times. A policeman testified that after his arrest, Chittenden would only consent to sitting on a nonconductive marble slab at the police station and refused to touch anything containing zinc.[2]

Electricity and madness have long been intertwined. A dream of Bethlem Royal Hospital, beheld in 1773, discovers in one of the cells "a philosopher, who has lost his reason in a fruitless attempt to discover the causes of electricity."[3] By 1858, another physician had described what had become, in his opinion, a "common" error of thinking in cases of acute mania: "Electric wires are sometimes imagined to pass through the head; and illusions producing blasphemous, obscene, and exaggerated expressions, are caused through this source of disturbance."[4] Brought to a Los Angeles police station in 1889, a "crank" imagined "he had a powerful battery in his right leg and that people were in danger of being killed by touching him."[5] One unfortunate woman projected her anxieties onto her doorbell, believing that each ring further "electrified" her room and body (leading her to the expensive habit of repeatedly breaking windows to vent this electrical flow).[6] In *Inferno* (1894), the autobiographical account of his own brush with madness, August Strindberg speculates that his escalating agitation might be the product of electricity. While visiting a small town in Sweden for rest under a doctor's care, Strindberg inspects his bedroom and finds, much to his horror, "an American bedstead of iron, whose four uprights were surmounted by brass knobs that resembled the conductors of an electric machine. In addition there was a flexible mattress, the springs of which mere made with copper wire, twisted into spirals like those of a Ruhmkorff induction coil."[7] A visit to the attic does little to assuage Strindberg's fears: "There, just to make matters worse, I found precisely one object, an enormous coat of chain mail, placed exactly over my bed. 'That is an accumulator,' thought I."[8] As Max Nordau observed of this era, "The physicists were still far from occupying themselves with magnetism and electricity, when the persons attacked by persecution-mania were already referring their own unpleasant sensations and hallucinations to the electric currents or sparks which their persecutors were supposed to cast on them through walls, ceilings and floors."[9]

Madness may be a disorder of the mind, but it is felt most palpably in the body, often provoking anxiety to the point of panic. Those who have experienced the full progression from early to acute psychosis report wildly fluctuating mood states and the corresponding physiological reactions.[10] In this vacillation between exaltation and panic, prodromal tensions can produce a heightened overall sensitivity to the usually unremarkable processing of the senses—sounds become more articulated and acute, the heartbeat more present and distracting, the skin more reactive to textures and temperatures. Then, too, there are the somatic symptoms of panic and anxiety: paresthesia, vertigo, hyperventilation, disorientation, partial amnesia, and *globus hystericus*. A body suffused with nervous tension or suddenly flooded with waves of panic experiences the physiology of nervous excitation (tingling, dizziness, and so on) most acutely—sensations that have long been described in the language of *electricity* and *electrification*. Psychotic delusions of "electrification" appear to emerge as a figurative understanding becomes literal conviction. "I 'feel' electrified" becomes "I *am* electrified." Electricity (and its ancillary energies) becomes the master code of the paranoid plot. "At once the old game recommences," laments Strindberg. "An electric stream seeks my heart; my lungs cease to work; I must rise or die."[11]

Psychotic electrification is most often persecutory, but not always. Victor Tausk briefly notes the case of Josef H., a frequently institutionalized patient in Belgrade who "felt electrical currents streaming through him, which entered the earth through his legs." Josef H. apparently enjoyed a natural symbiosis of alternating current with the Earth, a connection that suffused him with "power" even without the targeted beams of the typical influencing device. Tausk describes Josef H. as a "rare case" of electrical currents experienced "in the absence of the influencing apparatus."[12] Tausk adds that Josef H. claimed to generate the current "within himself," frequently "declaring with pride that that was his power!"[13] As the rare counterexample, Josef H. reaffirms the fundamental logic typically at work in delusional electrification: he believed he could *will* electrical power through his system—that is, he apparently saw himself as a walking personification of "willpower," that ineffable alliance between volition and energy that constitutes the active force of the ego. Drawn into intense self-contemplation of body, mind, and being, the psychotic understand perhaps better than anyone else that will and power are in fact supplementary forms. Any act of "will" requires some form of power to execute it. Any application of power, in turn, is under the direction of some form of will (ranging from a meddling neighbor to a sinister government or the implacable destiny of the cosmos). Psychotic willpower, as a dysfunctional binding of will and power, volition and energy, proceeds from a complex rewriting of the body and its nervous array during the eighteenth and nineteenth centuries. The electrified body dates to the rise of Enlightenment anatomy, shadowing the harnessing of electricity for instrumental applications by natural philosophy, science, engineering, and industrialization. The influencing machines of the nineteenth and twentieth centuries would exploit this parallel development of electrical empires, the self-regulating willpower of the ego resisting the networked willpower of technical others.

The Cartesian Corpse

The electronic body emerged from a series of mechanical analogies, many of which predated the electrical turn of modern anatomy. In 1632, for example, René Descartes famously described the body in terms of a hermetic clockwork, arguing that God "places inside [the body] all the parts needed to make it walk, eat, breathe, and imitate all those functions which can be imagined to proceed from matter and to depend solely on the disposition of our organs."[14] As Georges Canguilhem notes of Descartes, "The theory of the animal-machine is inseparable from 'I think therefore I am.' The radical distinction between the soul and body, between thought and extension, requires the affirmation that matter, whatever form it adopts, and thought, whatever function it fulfills, are each an undivided substance."[15] The concept of a unique human intellect or soul, in other words, depends on its remaining an essence that preexists and remains uncontaminated by its material housing in the body. Moreover, this essence of consciousness must remain a dynamic energy in *circulation*. To cease thinking is to *not* be. Variously critiqued over the past four hundred years, the essential riddle of the Cartesian subject remains for many an open question: Is there a "me" that exists independently of the body? What is the actual relationship between the immaterial self of the ego/mind and the tissue of the brain? Where is the "will," and where is the "power?" For centuries, anatomists had endorsed a theory of "animal spirits" circulating in the nerves as hollow tubules, a proposition introduced by Galen of Pergamum around AD 180. The Enlightenment's enthusiasm for medical dissection gradually mapped several distinct "systems" that circulate more material vitals through the organism. But while the arterial, lymphatic, and alimentary systems circulated tangible flows, the substance of nervous circulation remained more mysterious. "Altho' the minute structure of the nerves, the nature of their fluid, and those conditions on which depend their powers of fleeing and communicating motion to the body, lie much beyond our reach," observed Robert Whytt in 1765, "yet we know certainly, that the nerves are endued with feeling, and that as there is a general sympathy which prevails the whole system; so there is a particular and very remarkable consent between various parts of the body."[16] Over time, a theory of nervous vibration began to compete with the idea of a nervous fluid or spirit.[17] But even as accounts of the "animal machine" moved away from these more explicitly hydraulic models, modern anatomy remained significantly indebted to economic principles of equilibrium and balance. When sensation, circulation, nutrition, life and motion become "disconcerted" in the "animal machine," argued a physician of 1780, then "the vital functions of the Body depending upon them, must then be unduly performed. 'Where one Link's broken, the "whole chain's destroyed.'"[18]

Albrecht von Haller's experiments at mid-century had a significant impact on moving anatomy's conception of nervous communication away from vibrations and fluids toward a model of impulse and sensibility. While anatomists had long recognized that the nerves had a role in sensation and movement, von Haller demonstrated that the nervous system operated by conveying an impulse or energy as the result of stimulation. As Philipp Sarasin argues, Haller's thesis was that "the sensibility of the nerves and the contractibility of tissues are the fundamental principles of the body," a model that quickly replaced the Cartesian "clockworks" with a body that operates as a "stimulable, sensitive machine."[19] Crucially, the nervous system after von Haller moved away from conceptions of hydraulic circulation to a model based on *telecommunications* via *conductive stimulation*. The work of von Haller and other eighteenth-century anatomists also raised enigmas that were fraught with potentially troubling spiritual implications, especially as this branch of anatomy attracted the interests of materialist philosophy. In his notorious essay of 1748, *L'homme machine* (*Man a Machine*), Julien Offray de La Mettrie asked, "Who can be sure that the reason for man's existence is not simply the fact that he exists? Perhaps he was thrown by chance on some spot on the earth's surface, nobody knows how nor why, but simply that he must live and die, like the mushrooms which appear from day to day, or like those flowers which border the ditches and cover the walls."[20] Mettrie buttressed this attack on Christianity by invoking examples of uncanny physiology that appeared to contradict the Cartesian détente between the church and Enlightenment philosophers in stipulating that the brain was the "seat of the soul." "A frog's heart moves for an hour or more after it has been removed from the body, especially when exposed to the sun or better still when placed on a hot table or chair," Mettrie observed. The human heart was no less immune to this telltale persistence: "Bacon of Verulam in his treatise *Sylva Sylvarum* cites the case of a man convicted of treason, who was opened alive, and whose heart thrown into hot water leaped several times, each time less high, to the perpendicular height of two feet."[21] Equally strange, some creatures seemed capable of a lingering volition even with the brain severed from the body, the "will" seemingly cut off from all power and yet still residually active. In a case that would be familiar to most farmers, Mettrie cites a drunken soldier decapitating a rooster: "The animal remained standing, then walked, and ran: happening to run against a wall, it turned around, beats its wings still running, and finally fell down. As it lay on the ground, all the muscles of this rooster kept on moving. That is what I saw myself, and almost the same phenomena can easily be observed in kittens or puppies with their heads cut off."[22] These leaping hearts and headless kittens suggested an animating power wholly unrelated to any animating "soul" in the mind and body. Duly offended by this dethroning of the divine in both its worldly and godly forms, an anonymous author confronted Mettrie's "wicked and heretical treatise" the following year with the wittily titled retort, *Man, More than a Machine*, wherein "the immateriality of the soul is demonstrated by invincible arguments, which set this important truth in a clear, new, and different light."[23] In his *A Dissertation upon the Nerves* (1768), William Smith emphatically reaffirmed the soul's centrality in a nervous network of balanced equilibrium: "The soul is placed by the Almighty in the sensorium of the brain; as a center in a circle; the nerves are radii, proceeding from that center, whose axis must always be exactly parallel to that point. In this situation, they make their impulses fully, and in direct lines. But if the axis of the radii of any of the senses, is a little askew; then that sense, or senses, depending upon that radius, or radii, are imperfect, or entirely lost."[24] Mettrie died in 1751, supposedly after overindulging in a feast of truffles as a demonstration of his philosophical commitment to the materialist pursuit of sensual pleasures. But the materialist challenge would not be dismissed so easily, especially as natural philosophy transitioned toward the protocols of empirical science in the nineteenth century.[25]

By the late eighteenth century, these questions increasingly intersected with the era's growing fascination for electrical phenomena. The importance of electricity within Enlightenment thought is well documented, a pursuit most famously captured in the iconic portraits of Benjamin Franklin waiting with stoic resolve to be quite literally "enlightened" by a kite aloft in a thunderstorm.[26] As many social historians have noted, experiencing electrical phenomena became a form of edifying leisure in the late eighteenth century. Whether staged for polite contemplation in the salon or as sensational theatrics in the street, the electrical demonstration was a spectacle calculated to astonish by demonstrating the "electrician's" ability to conjure seemingly magical powers from the materials of the natural world.[27] Many of these "magical" spectacles involved exhibiting the innate electrical powers of living creatures. In London, for example, an advertisement from 1780 invited the curious to witness an Electrifying Eel available "to be seen, felt, heard, and understood, any hour of the day, at No. 9, Piccadilly." For half a crown, interested parties could witness how "this wonderful Gymnote rings bells, fires guns, and animates dead bodies. The very water in which it swims sets fire to combustibles, and gives an astonishing shock to any one who touches it."[28] In 1800, the naturalist Alexander von Humboldt reported witnessing horses attacked and killed by leaping electric eels in the Amazon.[29]

Electricity's demonstrable power to shock the body suggested that this wondrous fluid, if properly administered, might have therapeutic applications. By mid-century, physicians understood that an electrified muscle would flex independently of the patient's volition, suggesting muscle, nerve, and electricity might in some way cooperate in the production of movement. Accordingly, electricity's earliest therapeutic uses centered on revitalizing palsy and paralytics, adding energy to that which seemed to lack energy. In 1763, William Watson's apparently successful electrical treatment of an eighteen-year-old girl for "locked jaw" received wide notice,[30] while in 1767 Joseph Priestley recounted the case of a seven-year-old girl "who was first seized with a disorder occasioned by the worms, and by length by a universal rigidity of her muscles; so that her whole body felt more like that of a dead animal than a living one." After three months of electrical treatment, he reports, "every muscle of her body was perfectly flexible."[31] A short pamphlet of 1765 related the extraordinary case of the Reverent Mr. Winder, a "robust" man who, at fifty-four, was suddenly struck down by a paroxysm that left him without speech and weak in his legs. After taking the waters of Tunbridge in Kent, we are told, the patient showed some improvement but remained weak with palpitations, trembling, and bouts of vertigo. Happily for Mr. Winder, a year after the onset of his palsy, he had the good fortune to be struck by lightning as he lay in bed. He awoke completely cured of his ailments, leading the author to propose, "There is a antiparalitic Property, or Power hitherto unobserved, contain'd in, or conveyed with the Lightning (generally looked upon as an Enemy in Nature) similar in effect to something, that has been ascribed to the electrical Influence."[32] Despite such promise, results in electrical restoration remained inconclusive, leading Franklin to make a disappointed report on electricity's utility in palsy to the Royal Society in 1757.[33] By the 1770s, the application of "medical electricity" was so widespread that Thomas Percival could already note the public was disappointed that its "medical effects" were not more astonishing.[34] Francis Lowndes complained that many supposed electricity to act like "a charm" rather than as medicine and thus gave up on a course of electrical treatment too early.[35] Enthusiasts of the electrical fluid thus recommended extended courses of treatment, making these electrotherapeutic regimens a test of the patient's endurance. A physician in 1767 describes a prolonged series of shocks administered to a girl who, overcome with grief at the death of a close friend, found herself unable to stand or open her jaw. After several days receiving electrical shocks to her leg, temples, chin, throat, tongue, hip, and foot, "she spoke so as to be tolerably well understood, telling us that the shocks were frequently vastly severe for her to bear; but that, as she was fully sensible of the advantage she had already received thereby, she would gladly submit to my will, in hopes of further advantage."[36] Others were not so lucky or grateful. Percival relates the case of a man receiving daily shocks to treat a paralytic arm: "But by an unfortunate mistake in the position of the chain, the shock was one day conveyed through the epigastric region, and not along the paralytic arm, which rested upon it. A violent pain was instantly perceived in the stomach, which in a few minutes was succeeded by a profuse vomiting of blood."[37] Percival conceded this "misapplication" most likely contributed to the man's untimely death a few days later.[38]

Having both accidentally electrocuted themselves during their own experiments, Benjamin Franklin and the Dutch physician Jan Ingenhousz speculated that electricity applied to the head might be used to "restore the mental faculties when lost." In a letter to Franklin written in 1783, Ingenhousz recounted receiving a powerful shock that left him in a stupor for the rest of the day. The next morning, however, Ingenhousz made a surprising discovery: "My mental faculties were at that time not only returned, but I felt the most lively joye in finding, as I thought at the time, my judgment infinitely more acute. It did seem to me I saw much clearer the difficulties of every thing, and what did formerly seem to me difficult to comprehend, was now become of an easy Solution. I found moreover a liveliness in my whole frame, which I never had observed before."[39] Ingenhousz apparently had discovered, by painful example, the elementary principles of electroconvulsive therapy (ECT). Much as electricity appeared to have an intuitive relation to palsy and paralytics, so too did many believe it had an affinity for afflictions of the brain and mind. Elsewhere, surgeon John Birch reported mixed success in using electrical shocks to treat three melancholic patients. A singer close to suicide seems to have followed in the footsteps of Ingenhousz, his treatment followed "by a refreshing sleep, from which he awoke a new being.... He felt sensible of the powers of electricity every day after its application, being capable of mental exertions immediately."[40] Birch was less successful with a case of "moping melancholy" in a twenty-six-year-old who, after three increasingly massive shocks to the orbital bone, only had a slight headache to show for his troubles. Even this was not a complete failure, however, as it demonstrated to Birch just how much electrical force the brain could endure. "I was, myself, most surprised that I could practice so boldly, without any serious inconvenience to the brain," he observed, no doubt to the equal surprise of his patient. "Having carried the experiments as far as I wished," he continues, "I dismissed the patient, in the same unhappy state he had so long suffered."[41]

Although eighteenth-century electricians vacillated between success and failure, their collective efforts nevertheless established a seemingly fundamental link between electricity and the material force of life. In 1781, Tiberius Cavallo observed, "It seems that, independent of the already known parts of the human body, there is some other principle that accompanies the life of an animal, which is in a certain manner a conductor of electricity, and whose action ceases as soon as the animal becomes extinct."[42] For many, the body's conduction of electrical energy was part of a much larger cosmology. Toward that end, the German theosophist Friedrich Oetinger explained electricity's natural place in the divine order by subjecting the Book of Genesis to close textual explication, arguing that "the first light of the first day" could not be the sun, which Genesis designates as a product of the fourth day of Creation, but was instead "the electrical fire."[43] Variations on this model were still in circulation a century later: "Electricity is uncreated eternal matter, and the Deity himself could not have created the world but for its original and eternal presence."[44] Electricity, in other words, was as old as God himself, maybe even older and therefore more elemental. Even those without explicit religious motivation emphasized the omnipresence of electrical force in the natural, if not necessarily the divine, universe.

Luigi Galvani's publication of *Effects of Electricity on Muscular Motion* in 1791, while not necessarily answering or even addressing these enigmas directly, presented what appeared to be the definitive path forward toward further revelations.[45] In one of history's most famous episodes of scientific serendipity, Galvani discovered that the muscles in a frog's leg would twitch when touched with a metal knife. Further experimentation into this curious phenomenon led to Galvani proposing the existence of "animal electricity." The brain and nervous system, he argued, circulated this electricity through the body to power motion, volition, and thought. The implications of the theory made some contemporaries suspicious—most notably, Alessandro Volta, who argued that the nerves were not circulating a force intrinsic to the body but were merely conducting the electrical energy drawn from the metal implements of the experimenter. These debates would continue into the next century, making "Galvanism" a prominent actor in both Victorian physiology and philosophy. As the first exploratory bridge between anatomy and electrical science, galvanism imparted important lessons about the biological binding of volitional and electrical energy, will and power, in the body as a system of networked telecommunications. "Electricity is not only the connecting link between the Spiritual and Material Universe, but is the medium through which the Mind governs the Living Organism," wrote an awestruck electrician in 1862, adding, "The nervous system of man seems to be the great line of demarcation between his spirit and his body."[46] The neurologist Hugh Campbell made a similar endorsement in 1875: "Although this animal electricity is not life, it may be safely reckoned as its lieutenant. It is the power with which the operations of the vital forces are performed, and without which all the operations of the animal economy, from the nutrition of the meanest creature to the intellectual triumphs of the highest order of genius in man, would be arrested."[47]

In *The Human Machine*, Anson Rabinbach argues that Hermann von Hemholtz's *On the Conservation of Force*, published in 1847, had a significant impact across a number of Victorian disciplines with an interest in supervising various manifestations of energy. A landmark of modern physics, Hemholtz's article demonstrated that heat, light, electricity, and magnetism were all manifestations of a single energy (*Kraft*). "Interpreted through the dynamic language of Kraft, the body appeared as a field of forces, energies, and labor power," Rabinbach argues. "The metaphor of the machine underwent a change from that of a clockwork composed of diverse parts to that of the modern motor modeled on the steam engine or electric-powered technology."[48] Building on von Haller's divide of irritability and sensibility, Galvani's animal electricity facilitated a definitive shift in nervous anatomy from circulation to circuitry. What had previously manifested as sluggish or blocked flows of liquids, fluids, and liquors now became unbalanced or obstructed distributions of electrical energy. "The conducting power of the nerves ... would naturally lead us to regard the entire nervous system as an apparatus, through the medium of which, electricity, modified and restrained by certain laws, is made subservient to the purposes of existence," argued one physician.[49] In America, Dr. Benjamin Douglas Perkins quickly attracted both advocates and antagonists in proposing medical therapy by means of "metallic tractors." "Perkinsism," as this treatment came to be known in the early 1800s, involved applying two metallic poles (one copper, one zinc) to redistribute unbalanced electrical energy, thus bringing the galvanic body back into equilibrium. The tractors, Perkins argued, carried "the extra degree of energy to parts where it is diminished, or out of the system altogether, restoring the native law of electric equilibrium."[50] Perkins sold these tractors (at $25 a set) for home treatment, counting former President George Washington as one of his clients.[51] Perkinsism was eventually dismissed as quackery, having been found ineffective in an early example of "double-blind" testing and the "placebo effect."[52] But in the wake of Galvani's momentous discovery, "animal electricity" nevertheless continued to promise definitive answers to relationships that had remained wholly enigmatic for centuries.

Working along the "great line of demarcation between body and spirit," anatomists of the nineteenth-century continued to map the body's circuitry to better understand the exact nature of will and power. Extending Mettrie's fascination with the paradoxes offered by headless creatures, "Experiments on the Principle of Life," M. L. Gallois's widely translated study of 1814, detailed painstaking experiments in maintaining "life" in the torsos of decapitated animals. By introducing air into the lungs of a headless animal, Gallois found, "we may keep a decapitated animal perfectly alive, and that during a time which varies according to the species and age; and which, in very young rabbits, is at least a number of hours."[53] Gallois also noted that "portions" of the headless yet still "living" animal would die if one removed the "spinal marrow" controlling the nerves for that part of the body. Following this line of research, in 1817 the Austrian physician Karl August Weinhold claimed to have successfully removed the brain and spinal cord of a kitten and then refilled the empty cavities with a "metallic mixture" of zinc. Restarting the kitten's heart, Weinhold marveled, "Life appeared to be instantly restored— the animal lifted up its head, opened and shut its eyes, and, looking with a fixed stare, endeavored to walk; and whenever it dropped, tried to raise itself upon its legs. It continued in this state twenty minutes, when it fell down and remained motionless. During all of this time the animal was thus treated the circulation of the blood appeared to go on regularly the secretion of the gastric juice was more than usual, and the animal heat was re-established."[54] Other experimenters were interested in mapping these electrical mysteries from the extremities back to the supervising brain. Another unfortunate kitten found its spinal marrow divided, which "instantly stopped respiration. The animal was much agitated and gaped frequently. At the end of ten minutes, when sensibility had almost ceased, the larynx was divided from the os hyoids, and the lungs artificially inflated." Twenty-five minutes later, the physician divided the spine between the tenth and eleventh dorsal vertebrae, noting that the kitten retained "sensibility and motion" in both its front and hindquarters, "but all sympathy between them was destroyed, as an impression made upon the fore parts produced no effect on the hinder and vice versa." When it was "violently pinched" after fifty-two minutes, "no signs of life remained."[55]

 The most infamous and certainly most gruesome spectacles of galvanic animation were those performed in public on the bodies of recently executed criminals. Before England passed the Anatomy Act of 1832, only executed criminals could serve as medical specimens, a limited stock supplemented by the grave robbing of the Resurrectionists (as immortalized in Robert Louis Stevenson's tale "The Body Snatchers").[56] Cut down from the gallows, these bodies were prepared as quickly as possible to maintain the warmth and pliability of the corpse, which was then infused with electricity to demonstrate the function of various nervous pathways. In 1803, Galvani's nephew Giovanni Aldini arrived in London to perform a galvanic demonstration on the body of George Foster. For the immediate audience at Newgate Prison, as well as the larger reading public, this "performance" was a significant event. "On the first application of the process to the face, the jaws of the deceased criminal began to quiver," noted one account, "and the adjoining

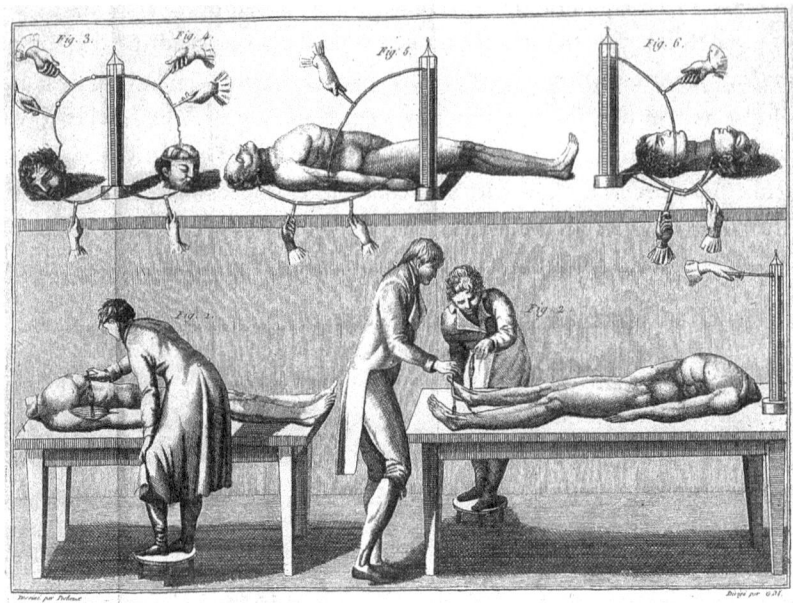

FIG 3.1 Illustration of experiments from Giovanni Aldini's *Essai théorique et expérimental sur le galvanisme* (1804). SOURCE: WELLCOME COLLECTION.

muscles were horribly contorted, and one eye was actually opened. In the subsequent part of the process the right hand was raised and clenched, and the legs and thighs were set in motion."[57] Elsewhere, Aldini described animating two decapitated heads at once, completing a circuit by connecting the condemned men through their ears.[58] In another showstopper, Aldini created an animating circuit by decapitating a dog, placing the head and body on a table covered with ammonia, and then throwing both head and body into violent convulsions by attaching wires to the ear and anus. Following in Aldini's footsteps, Dr. Andrew Ure of Glasgow provided a public demonstration of galvanism on the body of the murderer Matthew Clydsdale in late 1818. The spectacle received prominent coverage in both Europe and the United States, the *Weekly Recorder* describing the demonstration under the headline "Horrid Phenomena!" "The results were truly appalling," opined the report, before providing a horrific account of each experiment in vivid detail: dead legs made to kick, dead lungs made to inhale and exhale, a dead face compelled into grotesque contortions. Under such circumstances, who could resist speculating that even a dead body, if acted on quickly enough, might be brought back to life? This was in fact the reasoning of Ure himself, who, as the report concludes, "appears to be of the opinion that had not incisions been made in the blood vessels of the neck and the spinal marrow been lacerated, the criminal might have been restored to life!"[59]

Reanimation

When Aldini arrived in London in 1803 to perform his galvanic gymnastics, he had justified his bloody experiments on animals and corpses as necessary for demonstrating the value of his uncle's techniques in cases of "suspended animation," typically drowning victims who might be revived by electrical force.[60] By 1819, however, even Aldini claimed such experiments were no longer necessary: "I should think it a prostitution of galvanism, if it were only employed to cause sudden gestures, and to convulse the remains of human bodies; as a mechanic deceives the common people by moving an automaton by the aid of springs and other contrivances."[61] Aldini's invocation of the "automaton" here is telling. By equating galvanic reanimation with mechanical contrivances such as Wolfgang von Kempelen's chess-playing Turk and Jacques de Vaucanson's famous duck, Aldini acknowledged and was perhaps attempting to distance himself from the materialist implications of galvanism's "man-machine." While the galvanic turn in nervous anatomy did not necessarily foreclose Cartesian and Christian models of the self, it certainly complicated the idea that consciousness might exist as a motive force independent of the body's material frame. As James Delbourgo argues, the demonstrable impact of electricity on the functioning of both body and mind challenged "the sovereignty of mind or soul over matter (whether understood as Platonic, Christian, or Cartesian), by putting mind and matter into direct, convulsive communication."[62]

No single volume would prove more influential in dramatizing these issues than Mary Shelley's *Frankenstein*, which appeared in its first edition in 1818. As a story straddling the lines of philosophy, gothic horror, and even proto-science fiction, *Frankenstein* remains a touchstone of modernity. The most orthodox reading of *Frankenstein* frames the story as a cautionary tale of hubris that warns Enlightenment man, like Prometheus and Faust before him, not to "play God" in issues of life and death. Before embarking on *Frankenstein*, Shelley is thought to have read Humphry Davy's *A Discourse, Introductory to a Course of Lectures on Chemistry*, a manifesto of sorts on the utility of "chemical science" in understanding nothing less than all aspects of existence. Davy had also noted the power of natural philosophy to inspire the minds of "speculative philosophers" (and, one would assume, young novelists), especially in relation to recent revelations about the material operations of the body: "If the connection of chemistry with physiology has given rise to some visionary and seductive theories; yet even this circumstance has been useful to the public mind in exciting it by doubt, and in leading it to new investigations."[63] The genius of Shelley, only eighteen years old when she wrote her most famous work, was to intertwine the physiological and philosophical implications of these "new investigations," exciting the public mind in its "doubt" by presenting an elegantly balanced narrative equation: creature and creator as mirrored hostages to the unfolding disenchantments of Enlightenment thought.[64]

Conjured into existence, the creature's philosophical conundrum is well known: born of philosophical materialism, he wanders the world in dread and self-loathing. And like so many of his contemporaries, the creature must confront the sobering reality that he may be merely the product of a cruel mechanist trick. *Does the creature have a soul or not?* Whatever else the creature might signify historically, he is fundamentally *an animated corpse,* uncanny to the point of abjection. As Julia Kristeva writes in *The Powers of Horror,* "The corpse, seen without God and outside of science, is the utmost of abjection. It is death infecting life."[65] The creature is a hideous "thing" incommensurate with "man" as he imagines himself while wrapped in the mantle of his own language, culture, and imagination. Bereft of life, ego, and soul, Shelly suggests, the body is merely disgusting. "I collected bones from charnel-houses and disturbed, with profane fingers, the tremendous secrets of the human frame," recounts Victor Frankenstein, further describing his work as "filthy" and his laboratory a "workshop of filthy creation."[66] Once imbued with life, moreover, the creature is not a testament to the beauty and majesty of the human form, as Victor had hoped, but is instead a horrifying study in the body's raw materials made sickening and strange through the defamiliarization of Victor's craft. "His yellow skin scarcely covered the work of muscles and arteries beneath; his hair was of a lustrous black, and flowing; his teeth of pearly whiteness; but these luxuriances only formed a more horrid contrast with his watery eyes, that seemed almost of the same colour as the dun-white sockets in which they set, his shriveled complexion and straight black lips."[67] Shelley redoubles this horror in the violent destruction of the creature's bride, Victor tearing to pieces "the thing on which I was engaged."[68] Later he must summon the courage to confront his aborted handiwork: "The remains of the half-finished creature, whom I had destroyed, lay scattered on the floor, and I almost felt as if I had mangled the living flesh of a human being."[69] As Panagiota Petkou asks, "For what else is *Frankenstein* if not the coarse embodiment, in flesh and blood, of what has always been the utmost fear of the self? In calling the dead body back to our field of vision, Shelley works *against* . . . a sanitized view of the corpse and *for* the taint of brute materiality she plunges her reader into."[70]

Expanding the Faustian themes of the novel, innumerable readings of *Frankenstein* have centered on questions of body and spirit. Fabricated by a mortal man, does the creature have an immortal soul? Has Victor damned his own soul by daring to challenge God? But the truly evil genius of Shelley's story resides as much, if not more, in the existential challenge the creature poses to Victor and the reader. As the walking abject, the creature provokes disgust in his creator and audience not as an affront to God but, rather, as a repudiation of God's existence. Profaning God would at least mean that a God existed to profane, but *Frankenstein*'s abject rupture opens an even more terrifying void. Accordingly, Victor's first reaction to his triumph of galvanic reanimation is not blinding terror or moral remorse but a type of nausea, an immediate sickness. Witnessing the "dull yellow eye" and the creature's "convulsive motions," Victor flees to his bedchamber. This odd moment of nauseous dread is the subject of W. Chevalier's frontispiece for the 1831 edition. The etching pictures the newly "born" creature sitting on the floor, understandably stunned or baffled by his sudden emergence into raw existence, while the furtive Victor bolts from the room at what his knowledge has produced. Though he has just discovered the secret of life, Victor immediately falls into a troubled sleep in a second attempt to flee the burden his knowledge has just unveiled. But to no avail: the creature's abject being will not be denied. Victor is awakened by "the miserable monster whom I had created. He held up the curtain of the bed; and his eyes, if eyes they may be called, were fixed on me. His jaws opened, and he muttered some inarticulate sounds, while a grin wrinkled his cheeks."[71] This grinning insistence of the creature presents a much more uncanny moment than Shelley's elliptical treatment of the monster's actual creation. As Mettrie had suggested, perhaps the secret of life is that it simply is. Animating a corpse creates life, and that life is the animation of a corpse. Victor notes, "I had gazed upon him while unfinished; he was ugly then; but when those muscles and joints were rendered capable of motion, it became a thing such as even Dante could not have conceived."[72] The creature, too, learns this basic lesson: the abject body is a horrible thing. Having found the journal

FIG 3.2 Doctor Frankenstein flees after observing the first stirrings of his creature. Engraving by W. Chevalier after Theodor von Holst, 1831.
SOURCE: WELLCOME COLLECTION.

Victor kept in the months leading up to his monstrous "birth," the creature laments the horrors of his existence: "God, in pity, made man beautiful and alluring, after his own image; but my form is a filthy type of yours, more horrid even from the very resemblance."[73] If the corpse "without God and outside of science" is the epitome of abjection, as Kristeva suggests, then Shelley miraculously discovered a way to compound this horror by making the creature a composite of corpses. Though profoundly uncanny, a lone corpse at rest still allows the living to conjure the body's former ego, now evacuated but still coherent in some other plane of existence. Shelley's composite corpses further destabilize this already tenuous fantasy of unity. The fabrication of a creature and its bride, moreover, extends this abjection into the domain of sexual reproduction (if completed, would the bride eventually have borne the creature's child?).

Shelley's novel was a sensation, of course, inspiring the history of imitations, citations, and interpretations that would make the tale such a critical document of modernity. Many of these responses seem almost defensively therapeutic. The creature's grinning insistence that the reader, like Victor, join him in the void demanded that the creature be placed back under repression. An early and still favorite response was to simply ignore the godless implications of the story by maintaining an interpretation based on Cartesian fictions of body and mind. Robert Douglas's "A Story of Galvanism" amplified the Faustian aspects of Shelley's novel to the point of caricature. Douglas's story opens with a now elderly physician recalling a "science mad" colleague from his youth. This young colleague, we are forewarned, was both "a philosophical enthusiast" and an outspoken atheist: "His particular hallucination was electricity, with its collaterals, galvanism, and the sciences of heat and light."[74] The young man secures a loan from his father to perfect a device for better conducting galvanic experiments on the nervous system. The machine debuts in a famous surgical theater, the young inventor watching from the front row as a renowned anatomist receives a condemned corpse and, like Drs. Ure and Frankenstein before him, begins to manipulate its limbs with galvanic force. After a series of typical demonstrations, the corpse suddenly rises up from the slab and—much to everyone's shock and horror—extends a bony finger at the young inventor in the front row. Even worse, the young atheist recoils in terror as he realizes the performing corpse is none other than his father.[75] Unbeknownst to the son, his seemingly genteel father (the reader last encountered him trimming flowers on his country estate) has just been executed for a notorious series of robberies performed under an alias. These crimes provided the immense capital necessary for the son to create his galvanic apparatus. The son is so shaken by this "coincidence" that he collapses into unconsciousness, waking only long enough before dying to acknowledge that, despite his lifelong commitment to materialist science, in the end he must entertain the possibility of God's existence.

Humor provided another strategy for displacing the implications of an electrical body. In 1847, *Scientific American* published a purported press report from a distant European capital that detailed the visit of three guests to the home of a certain "Dr. Lube." When the men arrive, we are told, they find Dr. Lube seated at a pianoforte. An unknown fourth guest, a Mr. Eisenbrass, stands in the middle of the room. Greetings and introductions are exchanged. But after several more minutes of idle conversation among the group, one visitor notes that the doctor, who remains seated and vigorously playing the pianoforte, is not actually producing any music. Caught in his deceit, Dr. Lube makes a shocking revelation: "Mr. Eisenbrass" is in fact a talking and walking automaton operated by the keys of the pianoforte. The doctor explains the construction of his marvel: "The bones of a human subject were procured and clothed with a complete muscular system, composed of vulcanized caoutchouc. The consummate anatomical knowledge of Dr. Lube enabled him to do this with great success, at the same time adding a system of nerves made of fine platinum wire covered with silk."[76] Lube the anatomist has in effect combined recent marvels in rubber, electricity, and neurology to produce a cybernetic Frankenstein as party guest. As the article observes, "The accomplishment of all this was a matter of no small difficulty and ordinary minds would have shrunk from undertaking it. But Dr. Lube, with a zeal and perseverance worthy of all imitation, has mastered every obstacle, and produced a work the most extraordinary, ever constructed by mortal man."[77] There the article ends abruptly. While most readers of 1848 no doubt surmised the piece was a lark of some sort, no explicit frame is provided for evaluating the authenticity of "Mr. Eisenbrass." His absurdity is self-evident. Even if a genius like Lube were to succeed in such a difficult fabrication, the invention itself would remain essentially useless. (Eisenbrass is not even a good party guest, given that he goes slack and silent whenever Lube is not "playing him" at the keyboard.) Still, one can only imagine how a lunatic at mid-century might have responded to this report.

Galvanism presented theologians with a particularly difficult task. As the earthly custodians of the soul, religious leaders had a particular interest in offering a theory of "spirit" that could either repulse or integrate the implications of galvanism, especially after Shelley's novel so literally embodied the challenges of materialism in narrative form. Speaking to a congregation in Cleveland in 1851, Joel Tiffany invited his audience to contemplate the energies and networks of their own nervous system: "When I will to raise my arm, there is a power instantaneously communicated by which my arm obeys the mandate, and when I will to suspend that power, my arm falls to my side again. The origin of that power is in my will, which is a faculty of my mind or spirit. Independent of that will, my arm possesses no power to move itself." Addressing the uncanny aspects of galvanism, Tiffany then invited his audience to consider how elegantly the human mind could move a limb compared with the violent convulsions produced by the galvanic battery: "The difference between the two methods of moving the arm, consists in this; the electric or magnetic fluid is excited by the will in the one case, and by means of a common electric, magnetic, or galvanic battery in the other. There is also another difference growing out of the first; the excitation of the magnetic force, in the former case being under the direct spirit will, is more wisely and systematically directed in its action along the motory nerves and upon the muscles, than when under the mechanical action of a senseless battery."[78] Galvani may have stumbled upon one of God's secrets, but galvanism remained a crude, inferior imitation of the mechanics God imbued in man.

In his controversial study of 1845, *Anastasis*, theologian George Bush sought to reframe the Christian doctrine of bodily resurrection for those who might have been disenchanted by the continuing revelations of galvanic physiology. As traditionally promulgated by the church, Bush argued, resurrection was not supported by "reason or revelation."[79] The dead rot, Bush helpfully reminded his readers. But as galvanism (and *Frankenstein*) demonstrated so powerfully, there might be a covert energy within the body that lives on, perhaps dormant until revived at the point of death. "The precise boundaries between the *physical* and the *psychical* parts of our nature have never yet been determined," he argued. "In many points they seem to run into each other, and the progress of physiological science is continually multiplying the proofs of a most intimate relation between our sensations and the subtler physical agencies of nature."[80] Resurrection should thus be understood in terms of a "spirit body," argued Bush, a wholly immaterial and presumably energetic essence that evacuated the corpse at the moment of death. Bush thus presumed a type of galvanic reanimation, not in this world, but in the next—the electrical body rising from death to occupy a higher plane of electrical existence.

The most logical way to resolve these lingering Cartesian enigmas presented by galvanic neurology was also the most ghoulish. Why not interview a recently severed head? Perhaps a head suspended between life and death, if even for only a few seconds, might provide insight as to what transpires in the last moments of the nervous system's operation. In the wake of the French Revolution, opponents of the guillotine had maintained that death by the blade was not instantaneous, as was widely claimed by the device's proponents. Looking to build public sympathy, reformers circulated lurid stories of severed heads biting one another or trying to chew their way out of the receiving basket. The Belgian artist Antoine Wiertz was especially fascinated by the possibility of consciousness lingering after the fall of the blade, so much so that in 1848 he and a noted hypnotist attended an execution in the hopes of placing Wiertz *en rapport* with the decapitated criminal. Wiertz later offered two paintings on the subject: his large triptych "Last Thoughts of a Guillotined Head" in 1853, and the more intimate "Guillotined Head" in 1855. In *The Arcades Project*, Walter Benjamin translated Wiertz's meditations on the horror he imagined followed the severing of the head. First minute: "Astonishingly, the head lies here under the scaffold and yet still believes it is above, still believes itself to be part of the body. . . . Horrifying suffocation—Breathing impossible." Second minute: "Now the executed man first becomes conscious of his situation.—He measures with his eyes the space separating his head from the body and says to himself: So, my head is actually cut off." Third minute: "Not yet death. The head still thinks and suffers. And here a thought makes him stiff with terror: Is he already dead and must he suffer like this from now on? Perhaps for all eternity?"[81] On November 13, 1879, a trio of French physicians set out to disprove the continuing sensationalism of the guillotined subject, arranging an experiment with the condemned prisoner Théotime Prunier. Immediately after the execution, the physicians harvested Prunier's severed head and employed every stimulating force known to science to probe his mind for a last glimmer of consciousness: shouting in his face and ears, sticking pins into the skin, applying ammonia under his nose, and even burning his eyeball with a candle flame. As a willing participant in this experiment, Prunier might have been expected to manifest some sign of response through sheer power of will—to hold on to the vestiges of his consciousness in the interests of science and penal reform. But his head remained stolidly deaf and dumb; proving once again that the brain—once severed from the body—is instantaneously and unquestionably "dead," even if the body, in its spasms, convulsions, and contortions, might appear to possess lingering signs of life. As it is with the headless rooster, so it is with man. In the end the three physicians could report of Prunier only that his face "bore a look of astonishment"—a quite understandable countenance that froze in time the living ego's recognition of its imminent demise.[82]

Deanimation

Balancing the galvanic logic of the reanimated corpse was the uncanny terror of the de-animated body. In catalepsy, a type of waking paralysis, an individual's consciousness was thought to be trapped within the flesh of the body, the ego's willpower wholly severed from the galvanic pathways that enact volition. Most often, accounts of catalepsy presented an inert body that has lapsed into a state of suspended animation so deep as to be mistaken for death itself. Worse yet, cataleptics were thought to remain wholly conscious of their plight even as they could do nothing to signal they were still alive. In the most horrifying scenario of all, a cataleptic might end up in the graveyard, still conscious as his body was lowered into the grave or placed in the crematorium. As death shocked into something approximating life, Frankenstein's creature implied consciousness might be no more than an energetic illusion. As life drained into something approximating death, the cataleptic portended the claustrophobic horror of the ego suddenly exiled from its material platform.

Physicians of the nineteenth century considered true catalepsy to be an extremely rare condition, many professing never actually to have witnessed a case firsthand.[83] Vivid, highly sensationalized accounts of catalepsy, however, were more or less a staple of journalism and fiction throughout the nineteenth century, suggesting the condition was more a theoretical terror than an actual disorder. In a purportedly "real" case from 1801, for example, a young woman taken for dead was said to have escaped live burial only when the funeral party noticed she was perspiring: "She said, it seemed to her as if in a dream,—that she was really dead; yet she was perfectly conscious of all that happened around her. . . . She tried to cry out, but her soul was without power, and could not act on her body: she had the contradictory feeling as if she were in her own body and not in it, at the same time."[84] In Wisconsin, meanwhile, a girl of fourteen announced to her parents one night that "she was going to sleep, and that they must not bury her, as she should not be dead." Nineteen days later she remained in an unsealed coffin with no sign of life yet also no signs of decay.[85] Mrs. John Herbert, "Joliet's Cataleptic Lunatic," remained asleep for more than ten months, only briefly revived by a strong dose of cocaine that compelled her to recite menu items from the restaurant where she had formerly been employed as a waitress.[86] Journalistic accounts of catalepsy frequently played on the public's conflation of the condition with hypnotism, insanity, mind reading, mediumship, sleepwalking, Eastern mysticism, and other extraordinary mental states. These reports, many no doubt wholly fabricated, fully exploited the moral, comic, and horrific implications that might attend the mind's dispossession of bodily will: an aspiring hypnotist "tricks" a country girl into attending a ball while in a trance, with "tragedy" as the result; a Hindu "fire-worshipper" resides in Bellevue, neither "sane or insane, but in a state of seemingly unending auto-hypnosis"; three mysterious women place an entire town in Indiana under a trance; anticipating an oncoming cataleptic hibernation, a New Jersey man—"probably insane"—is found in the woods with his clothes stuffed with leaves and straw, planning to sleep there until the warm weather returned in the spring.[87] Most horrific of all were the many stories of pregnant women, believed dead, who were buried alive and then gave birth in the grave.[88] A case from Paris painted the tableau as vividly as possible, describing an exhumation for a criminal investigation: "At the feet of the corpse there was found the corpse of a new-born child; and all the circumstances connected with this proved that the woman had awakened, given birth to her child, and died in great torture. Her lips were bloody from the bites made by her teeth, and her hands pressed together as if in an excess of great pain."[89]

Concern over live burial is truly a primal fear, with folktales of premature internment dating back centuries.[90] Jan Bondeson traces this morbid obsession's "modern" form to the publication and subsequent translation of Jacques-Benigne Winslow's thesis *Morte incertae signa* (1740), a book that claimed "the signs of death used by the medical profession were unreliable and that people were at immediate risk of being buried alive."[91] For many years physicians had confirmed death by listening for a heartbeat and placing a mirror before the mouth to check for lingering respiration. Medical alarmists maintained that only visible putrefaction and decomposition could confirm that all vestiges of life had left the body. The French were thought to be particularly abysmal at judging death, leading to the frequent citation in the era that a full third to perhaps half of the "dead" were in fact buried alive (at least in France). Such alarmism understandably had a powerful impact on the popular ego's trepidation as to the already uncanny prospects of its demise. In response, Germany pioneered the *Leichenhaus*, a "waiting mortuary" where bodies could be monitored for several days before burial. Visible for public viewing, each corpse also featured a string tied around the finger so that the slightest twitch, even an inkling of residual will, might ring a bell in the monitor's office—a post that by law had to be staffed twenty-four hours a day.[92] Alert to this growth market of the uncertain dead, coffin makers debuted models that allowed the entombed to signal their living status even after burial. Not wanting to risk such a scenario, regardless of the alleged safeguards, others demanded in their last will and testament that quite specific tests for life be performed before the corpse entered the grave.

The popularization of galvanism provided a plausible, comprehensible, and thus troubling scenario for explaining the actual mechanics of catalepsy, especially after Shelley's *Frankenstein* gave such a compelling account of the

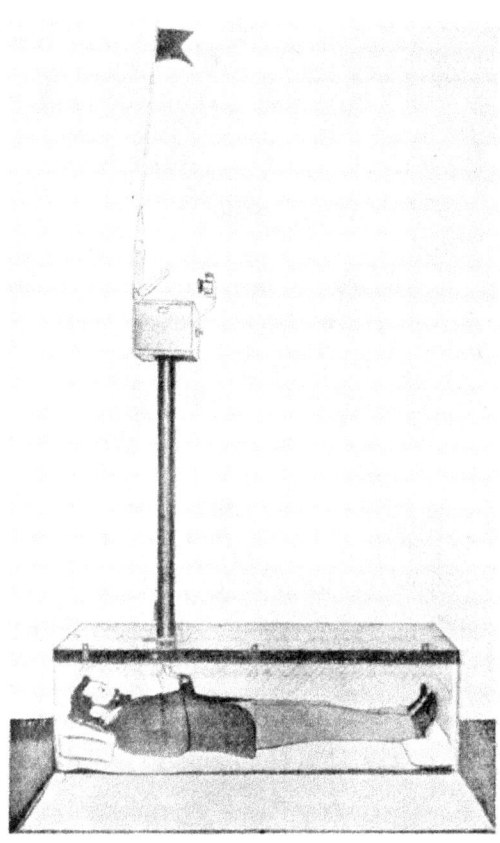

FIG 3.3 Karnicé-Karnicki's invention for allowing the prematurely buried to signal they are not yet dead, from William Tebb and Edward Perry Vollum's *Premature Burial and How It May Be Prevented: With Special Reference to Trance Catalepsy, and Other Forms of Suspended Animation* (1905). SOURCE: WELLCOME COLLECTION

electrified body. Like an electric toy deprived of its battery, the galvanic body might become drained of energy, its wires crossed or damaged. With the body's electrical wiring "burned out" or otherwise obstructed, the ego could no longer project its will through the nervous system (in fact, accounts of catalepsy at times referred to the condition as a "failure of volition").[93] Typical is Charles Lever's tale of 1836, "Post-Mortem Recollections of a Medical Lecturer." A teaching physician, having forgotten his lecture notes, engages in a hurriedly improvised address on the topic of insanity. Suddenly possessed of unprecedented clarity of vision, his lecture accelerates to a fevered pitch. Ideas and examples flood his mind, outpacing his ability to express them until they at last culminate in a most urgent thought that "rushed like a meteor flash across [his] brain." As he lectures his class on the topic of mania, he describes his accelerating flight of ideas as "like one who, borne on the rapid current of a fast flowing river, sees the foam of a cataract before him, yet waits passively for the moment of his destruction, without an effort to save."

To the amazement of his class, the narrator ends his lecture with a startling confession: "bursting forth into a loud laugh of hysteric passion, I cried—and I, and I—too, am a maniac." But the professor's horrors are only just beginning. Wholly overwhelmed by his manic thoughts about mania, he faints at the lectern. When next he resumes consciousness, he finds himself in bed paralyzed and unable to speak or move. Friends look on in pity and horror, and although his mind is completely conscious within his immobile body, he cannot so much as bat an eyelid to communicate the consciousness trapped within: "Was it that the nerves, from some depressing cause, had ceased to transmit influence of the brain?" He quickly surmises that he now suffers perhaps the most dreaded of all galvanic fates: catalepsy.[94]

Lever's story dramatized several common assumptions about nerves, insanity, and the galvanic economy circulating in the early nineteenth century. His catalepsy seems to be the product of his manic agitation, a "short-circuit" in the nervous system brought about by overexcitement. Obeying the electrical logics of polarity and charge, many considered catalepsy to be the radical reassertion of nervous equilibrium in the manic body. Physicians recognized that extraordinary discharges of nervous energy were sometimes necessary, but a healthy nervous system found a way to quickly restore itself to less volatile flows of this power. "Disease is nothing more than the efforts of nature to recover that lost equilibrium of health, which in the disturbed electrics or conductors, evince the labours of the electrical principle, to regain its natural state," argued Michael La Beaume in 1820.[95]

Significantly, Lever's paralyzed narrator is a professor and physician. Like Victor Frankenstein, he is thus particularly prone to the overexertion of mental flows that period neurology believed created disorder in the nervous system. He is what Jean-Étienne Dominique Esquirol would term, in 1845, a "monomaniac"—an individual driven to insanity by his fixation on a single topic.[96] As a psychiatric target, the monomaniac was a particularly diabolical specimen. Unlike the raving mad one might encounter at Bethlem, a monomaniac might go through most of life appearing entirely "normal." But should the object of his madness suddenly appear, the monomaniac could very well exhibit an instantaneous fit of insanity, perhaps never to return again to the world of the sane. Had Lever's physician narrator not forgotten his notes, perhaps he would have never attempted the improvised lecture on insanity that, ironically, unlocked his own monomaniacal encounter with madness. Lever's choice of specialty here was no accident. Throughout the nineteenth century, doctors of madness were widely considered the most likely candidates for becoming insane. This association was still strong forty years after Lever's tale first appeared, prompting a physician at Johns Hopkin in 1877 to write the editorial "Why Insanity Specialists Often Become Insane." It opens with an account of Dr. Emil Banta, an "insanity expert and resident alienist of the psychopathic branch of the Cook County Hospital in Chicago." Banta, we learn, went "insane" on the night of his honeymoon. After a terrified phone call from the new Mrs. Banta, police broke into the bridal suite to find the doctor raving, "I am the Son of God! I have received tonight a message from the Almighty! He has ordered me to perform a special commission and I intend to obey his commands! She is the object." Closing the ironic circle of insanity, the article concludes this episode by noting that Banta now resided among his former patients.[97] No doubt such lore was appealing to a public already anxious, yet also suspicious, about the allegedly rising levels of insanity in Victorian society. The fact that psychiatrists in particular were in danger of becoming insane suggested insanity itself might be an invention of the psychiatric mind, the insane "insanity expert" hoisted by his own diagnostic petard.

Happily for Lever's paralyzed narrator, the monomania that has plunged him into a cataleptic stupor also proves to be the means of his deliverance. Inevitably, the coffin arrives to take his body away to the cemetery. Still unable to signal that he is alive, the doctor adopts a new plan. If the nerves of volition no longer function, he reasons, his only hope is to somehow activate the other nervous networks at play in his body. Abandoning the circuitry of volition, the paralyzed physician instead attempts to commandeer his autonomic nervous system as a secondary channel for his willpower. In a supreme act of (galvanically displaced) concentration, he focuses all his internal nervous energy on agitating his heart, hoping its pounding might be perceived by a final mourner before closing the casket. As a galvanic self-diagnostic, he performs a detailed mental vivisection of his own nervous networks: "I set myself to think upon those nerves which preside over the action of the heart—their origin, their course, their distribution, their relation, their sympathies. I traced them as they arose in my brain, and tracked them till they were lost in millions of tender threads upon the muscle of the heart."[98] Luckily, his superior knowledge of the human nervous system allows him to translate mental images into nervous excitation to provide this alternate pathway of willpower. A mourner perceives his pounding heart, and the physician is saved.

The mysteries of galvanic conductivity also figure centrally in Samuel Warren's tale "The Thunderstruck," but in this treatment the author asks readers to imagine catalepsy's energetic chain from the opposite direction. Warren's tale begins with the citizens of London anxiously discussing a recent prophesy of the apocalypse, a prediction of particular interest to the young Emily, who spends much of her time pondering whether the end really might be near. A thunderstorm of unprecedented violence strikes the city, after which the tale's physician-narrator discovers Emily standing in a cataleptic trance. After the course of typical treatments fail, Emily seems to be drifting further way. In desperation, the doctor attempts to end the trance through violent confrontation, aggressively overstimulating every possible nervous pathway in the young woman's body: "I then took a penknife, and made a thrust with the open blade, as though I intended to plunge it into the eye; it seemed as if I might have buried the blade in the socket, for the shock or resistance brought forth by the attempt." Having failed at a simulated eyeball stabbing, the doctor moves on: "I pressed the back of the penknife upon the flesh at the root of the nail (as everyone knows, a very tender part), but she evinced not the slightest sensation of pain. I shouted suddenly and loudly in her ears, but with similar ill success." Discouraged, he waxes philosophical on the fate of all cataleptics: "the gloom of the grave and the light of life—both lying upon thee at once!"[99]

Written in 1836 during the early days of galvanic speculation, "The Thunderstruck" cultivates a certain hesitation regarding which electrical dysfunction best explains Emily's disconnection from the external world. Was she startled into her state by the proximity of the portentous lightning strike, literally frozen with fear? Or did her nerves suffer some type of electrical imbalance created by the instability and extreme volatility of the atmosphere on the day of the storm? Obsessed with the potential end of the world, perhaps Emily is the monomaniacal victim of religious fervor. Like Lever's narrator, she may have "burned out" her nervous system in her excitement for the prospects of the Second Coming—a monomania that reached its climatic crisis with the symbolic intervention of the lightning bolt. Emily is, after all, *thunderstruck*. Such explanations may seem more poetic than pathological, yet all three possibilities remained at the heart of medical speculation over cataleptic phenomena well into the nineteenth century. In his 1879 guide to diseases of the nervous system, the neurologist Moritz Rosenthal still attributed cases of catalepsy to, among other things, exposure to "a strong current of electricity," being "badly frightened," "over-excitement of the intellect," and "religious exaltation."[100]

By mid-century, these tales of morbid paralysis—underwritten by the principles of galvanic deanimation—were so prevalent as to earn the sarcastic attention of Edgar Allan Poe. In "How to Write a Blackwood's Article," an enthusiast of the notoriously sensationalistic Scottish journal recounts one of his favorite stories: "There was 'The Dead Alive,' a capital thing!—the record of a gentleman's sensations when entombed before the breath was out of his body—full of tastes, terror, sentiment, metaphysics, and erudition. You would have sworn that the writer had been born and brought up in a coffin."[101] Such ghoulishness inspired Poe's satirical sequel of 1838, "A Predicament," in which a woman experiences a slow-motion decapitation performed by an advancing clock hand, but not before suffering the indignity of having an eyeball pop out of its socket, the orb at once proffering a critique of the era's endless interrogation of human agency: "The loss of the eye was not so much as the insolent air of independence and contempt with which it regarded me after it was out. There it lay in the gutter just under my nose, and the airs it gave itself would have been ridiculous had they not been disgusting. Such a winking and blinking were never before seen."[102] The narrator's final decapitation is something of a relief: "I was not sorry to see the head which had occasioned me so much embarrassment at length make a final separation from my body. It first rolled down the side of the steeple, then lodged, for a few seconds, in the gutter, and then made its way, with a plunge, into the middle of the street."[103] Poe would return to a "Dead Alive" tale in "The Premature Burial," a story more comic than terrifying, despite its subsequent reputation in the annals of horror. Here Poe provides, in passing, yet another account of a seemingly dead man revived by galvanism on the dissecting table, before then moving on once again to the uncanny state of catalepsy. Poe's narrator is haunted by the fear that he will slip into a deathlike cataleptic state while among strangers and then be buried alive. His worst fears appear to come true when he wakes up in what he believes to be a coffin—panic ensues, until at last he remembers that he dozed off the night before in a rather narrow bunk in the hold of a ship. Happily, this horrific brush with a living death becomes a curative. "I took vigorous exercise," writes his narrator after confronting his phobia. "I thought upon other subjects than Death. I discarded my medical books."[104]

Despite cataleptics popping up in fiction more than mausoleums, several authorities earnestly took up the legal status of the cataleptic individual. As in the clinic, it is unclear how often these dilemmas arose in the legal system, if at all. Nevertheless, the legal status of the living dead certainly attracted the theoretical attention of the era's legal minds, either as an intellectual diversion or perhaps as a precaution should a case of catalepsy ever appear in court. How might lapsing into a cataleptic state affect contractual relations or criminal culpability? In a testament to just how difficult it was to either diagnosis or litigate such individuals, Francis Wharton's *A Treatise on Medical Jurisprudence* considered the legal implications of catalepsy alongside those of demonic possession, clairvoyant dreams, and "ghost ships" recently spotted on Lake Superior.[105] Meanwhile, a century of anatomical research and philosophical reflection had apparently done little to assuage the public's concerns over the possibilities of live burial. Another round of public panic erupted in 1896 with the publication of William Tebb and Edward Perry Vollum's *Premature Burial and How It Might Be Prevented* (answered quickly by *Premature Burial: Fact or Fiction?*). Tebb founded the London Association for the Prevention of Premature Burial that very same year, no doubt to the benefit of his book sales. In the US, New York State drafted the Premature Burial Act in 1898, and 1900 saw the chartering of the Society for the Prevention of People Being Buried Alive, an organization founded on the seemingly reasonable principle that "a supposed dead person should be treated as living until it is certain that he is dead."[106] Opined one supporter, "There is known to almost everyone in the range of his personal experience either a well-authenticated case of burial proceedings being interrupted by the revival of the person supposed to be dead, or the burial of some one concerning whom certain lingering appearances suggestive of life raised the awful answerless question, 'Was he buried alive?'"[107] "You Cannot Be Buried Alive," reassured a *New York Times* headline in an article recapping the latest medical safeguards in determining death, hoping—like Poe some forty years earlier—that the public might calm its fears over such an unlikely prospect.[108] Also hoping to ease the public's mind over such matters, a Dr. Tanner—renowned for his ability to fast through hypnosis—proposed to enter a deep cataleptic state and then remain buried in a coffin for a period of four weeks: "This I will do in the interest of science and to protect those prone to catalepsy from the fate of being buried alive." Tanner hoped to prove that humans were also prone to hibernation. But how, exactly, Tanner's being buried alive would protect others from a similar fate is never adequately explained.[109] And as Tanner's stunt only confirmed that a living man might in fact be taken as dead, accidentally buried, and survive as a cataleptic in a coffin for four weeks, his announcement was no doubt more terrifying than reassuring.

Flows to Fields

Frankenstein and the cataleptic presented two unnerving lessons in the galvanic anatomy of will and power, both elaborating on galvanic electricity as a fundamentally conductive energy of mental and physical animation. But the conductivity of "animal electricity" was not the only model of will and power circulating in the nineteenth century. Equally influential, though certainly more contested, were theories of "animal magnetism," a cosmology of power and the body introduced and promoted by the German physician Franz Mesmer. Like electricity, magnetism was central to the enigmas of natural philosophy throughout the eighteenth century. And while many (including Mesmer) suspected the two forces might be related, the exact nature of this bond would not be understood until the early nineteenth century. In promoting his discoveries, Mesmer summarized the basic principles of his practice thusly: "I set forth the nature and action of ANIMAL MAGNETISM and the analogy between its properties and those of the magnet and electricity. I added that 'all bodies were, like the magnet, capable of communicating this magnetic principle; that this fluid penetrated everything; that it could be stored up and concentrated, like the electric fluid; that it acted at a distance; that animate bodies were divided into two classes, one being susceptible to the magnetism and the other to an opposite quality that suppresses its action.'"[110] Or, as one of his acolytes described it, "Everything in nature has a communication by an universal fluid, in which all bodies are plunged."[111] Arriving in Paris in 1778, Mesmer created a sensation across Europe by claiming miraculous cures in body and mind through the manipulation of this magnetism, a process that we now recognize as the foundation of modern hypnotism. As word of his miraculous cures spread through Paris, Mesmer's doubters and opponents persuaded King Louis XIV to appoint a Royal Commission to investigate his claims. In 1784, the commission (which included the recently electrocuted Benjamin Franklin as a member) ultimately dismissed Mesmer's theories as having no empirical foundation.[112] Mesmer left Paris shortly after the inquiry (having allegedly been paid to do so). But his doctrines continued to attract advocates across Europe and North America.

Unlike many of his followers in the nineteenth century, Mesmer stopped short of endorsing animal magnetism as a means of instrumental telepathy or contact with the spirit world. He claimed only that this mechanism explained the more ineffable "covenant between two wills" known as "being in rapport."[113] Still, this "communication of will" provided an early theoretical model for telepathic broadcasting, even if the waves traded more in general affinities than specific messages. Although it was increasingly disreputable within early nineteenth-century science, mesmerism nevertheless remained a popular source of public spectacle, practiced by traveling mesmerists who claimed (either sincerely or performatively) to believe in Mesmer's larger cosmology. Charles Lafontaine, a touring Swiss mesmerist and the editor of *Le Magnétiseur*, arrived in London in 1840, where he staged several public performances and, in one dramatic display of mesmeristic power, "magnetized" a lion at the zoological gardens. In Manchester, his public demonstrations attracted the attention of James Braid, a Scottish surgeon whom Lafontaine invited on-stage to monitor the veracity of his performance. Braid would go on to become the founder of modern hypnosis (or "neuro-hypnosis," as he described it in 1841) by isolating the psychophysiological mechanism at work in mesmerism. Hypnosis, as practiced by Braid, had nothing to do with magnetism, fluids, clairvoyance, or any of Mesmer's other more sensational claims. And yet, despite bringing the practice into the domain of respectable science, hypnotism's inescapably uncanny disarticulation of will and power did little to dissuade opponents of the magnetic sleep. Particularly notorious was the very public battle between Braid and the Reverend Hugh M'Neile in 1842. M'Neile used Braid's visit to Liverpool in April of that year to deliver the long and impassioned sermon "Satanic Agency and Mesmerism." After the sermon received prominent coverage in the press, and after M'Neile refused to moderate any of his factual errors and baseless accusations, Braid published his own pamphlet defending the clinical use of hypnosis. M'Neile's attribution of "satanic agency" in the hypnotic state was not metaphorical. For many, the idea that one's own will could become so completely subordinated to the influence of another could only be explained by the intervention of demonic possession. As another Christian commentator warned, "under the influence of Mesmerism, the will of the responsible creature is completely prostrated before that of the mesmerizer. *If this is not evil*, we know not what *is*. This is sin—to suspend the will of the responsible creature, and yet give him power and action, and that action entirely under the sway of another, to do good or evil as he commands it."[114]

In galvanic fictions, the ego waxes and wanes according to its ability to negotiate the potential variability of animal electricity. Mesmeristic fictions, by contrast, invariably center on the ego's colonization by the will of another, an external force that somehow floods, possesses, overwhelms, or otherwise "influences" the subject's galvanic networks. The implications of this disarticulation of will from power received widespread literary treatment in the nineteenth century. Typical of such fiction is Timothy Shay Arthur's *Agnes; or, The Possessed* (1848). Written six years before his most famous title, *Ten Nights in a Bar-Room and What I Saw There,* Arthur's book begins with a brief preface foregrounding the basic evil that will be dramatized in the following pages. "The will of man is that in him which is inmost—it is that which really makes him a man. Can this be disturbed, laid quiescent, or be brought under the control of another, as is always the case in mesmerism, without some injury being sustained?" Shay answers his own question: "No truly reflecting man can for a moment question this. The thing is self-evident."[115] The story itself follows the eponymous Agnes who, after consulting a visiting mesmerist about her recurring headaches, is found to have extraordinary powers of clairvoyance. Before leaving town, the mesmerist implants a hypnotic suggestion in the young woman, telling her that in a month her headaches will return, and she should then visit him in Boston for further treatments. A month later, Agnes's headaches do in fact return, and she feels an overwhelming compulsion to leave for Boston, despite her fiancé's adamant objections. After arriving safely in Boston, Agnes suddenly goes missing. Florien, the suspect mesmerist, has kidnapped Agnes to conduct more tests with her extraordinary powers of clairvoyance. Working with a physician and his wife, Florian shuttles Agnes back and forth between Boston and New York while keeping her in a state of more or less constant mesmerization. Florien's motivations appear to be purely scientific, and Arthur avoids any direct discussion of sexual slavery. At one point, however, a momentarily lucid Agnes begs the physician's wife never to allow Florien to be in the room alone with her, a request that the now sympathetic wife accepts. Agnes eventually regains her freedom, of course, but learns the important lesson that the mesmerist—while undeniably powerful—trades in an art that is perverse and unholy.

The inappropriate power relations of mesmerism also informed many medical discussions of the practice, again focusing on the practice's unsavory potential to paralyze the (female) will and subordinate it to an external (male) power. A case appearing in the *Medical Examiner* in 1842 is typical. The editors reprint a history taken from France's *Gazette Medicale de Paris,* placed in the journal, we are told in a footnote, "for the edification of mesmerizers and miracle-mongers." The history itself recounts the case of a "Mademoiselle Melanie," a twenty-one-year old patient subject to alternating fits of hysteria and catalepsy. Finding the bedridden Melanie one day in a particularly deep and insensible cataleptic state, a Dr. Duvard places his hand on the epigastric region (i.e., her stomach) and notices she reacts with a look of slight discomfort. Although most might see this as a perfectly natural reaction to such an overture, medical or otherwise, Duvard decides this response instead necessitates a second "experiment." "I then placed my lips on the pit of her stomach, and asked her several questions; to my astonishment she answered correctly," reports Duvard. "During this first examination I made numerous experiments, which led me to conclude that there was a transposition of the five senses to the pit of the stomach."[116] After Melanie's midriff apparently responds to feathers, ringing bells, and noxious odors, the doctor speculates that a crossing of the nerves or nervous functions has thus led to taste, touch, hearing, sight, and smell manifesting on the "sensitive parts" of the lady's young and frequently comatose tummy. The doctor admits that while he had heard of such phenomena before, he had never believed it possible until confronted with this singular example. A host of other experiments (conducted in the presence of witnesses, we are informed, either out of a sense of propriety or in the spirit of empirical corroboration) "confirm" this remarkable thesis. Such accounts, dubiously sourced, may have been part of a larger effort in London to discredit Dr. John Elliotson's mesmeristic demonstrations with the sisters Elizabeth and Jane Okey in the late 1830s.[117] Two tracts from the early 1840s played on Elliotson's possibly "improper" relation with his female patients.[118] Many popular novels of the late Victorian era incorporated this lesson, as well, including George du Maurier's *Trilby* (1894), Bram Stoker's *Dracula* (1897), and Richard Marsh's *The Beetle* (1897). Given the mesmerist's powers of silent seduction, the ability to conquer prudish resistance by simply commandeering the will, it was perhaps inevitable that the device eventually appear in Victorian erotica. In *The Power of Mesmerism*, published in 1892, a libertine masters the art of mesmerism so that he can compel his sister, recently returned to the family estate, to join him in an unwitting program of wanton sexual experimentation.[119]

Historians of science often identify the discrediting of mesmerism as a key moment in natural philosophy's inexorable progress toward adopting the scientific method and ensuring the eventual triumph of science. But it would be more accurate to say that mesmerism, while perhaps "discredited" within a certain emerging sphere of scientific validation, nevertheless remained extremely influential as a conceptual space enabled by and resistant to the very paradigm that sought to discredit it. Robert Darnton argues that mesmerism's continuing appeal was in large part due to the reformers, skeptics, radicals, and political/scientific pariahs who rallied to the defense of mesmerism as a more populist school of healing. During the tensions leading up to the French Revolution, writes Darnton, a "radical strain" of

FIG 3.4 Playing on the salacious implications of mesmerism, the pamphlet promised to expose the "strange practices of Dr. Elliotson on the bodies of his female patients" (1842). SOURCE: WELLCOME COLLECTION.

"Mesmerist pamphlets constantly portrayed Mesmer as a dedicated man who arrived in Paris with a discovery that would put an end to human suffering and who naively turned to the leading academic and scientific bodies for support ... His system threatened a professional corps, which united with other vested interests to annihilate the threat, regardless of the cost in human suffering."[120] The science endorsed by church and state, in other words, did not serve the interests of the people, whereas mesmerism promised a populist revolution in knowledge, therapy, and healing.

As mesmerism moved into the nineteenth century, the assertion that the uncanny "magnetic sleep" was an index of a universal occult held great appeal for those opposed to scientific rationalism, religious dogma, and materialist disenchantment. Mesmerism, pollinated with the esoterica of various reformist visionaries in science and religion, found a most receptive audience within the modern spiritualist movement. By claiming empirical evidence of the afterlife, spiritualism became the fastest-growing religion of the nineteenth century. The central rite in this faith was mediumship—the ability of the dead to contact the living by "channeling" their energies through a sensitive medium.[121] The spiritualist séance, now regarded as a wholly occult practice, was in its early form promoted more as a scientific experiment in electromagnetic mysticism, communication conducted through the very real (though otherworldly) technology of the "spiritual telegraph." The affinity with mesmerism was clear: a spirit from the beyond, by harnessing an occult power permeating the universe, could take control of the medium's will, turning her into a passive "channel" for spirit communications. Indeed, to the observer little separated the "trance" of the mesmerized/hypnotized subject from the medium who yielded her body to the will of the dead.

The galvanism of Frankenstein and the cataleptic evoked a universe in which bodies rot and souls go dark in the nerves. The ability of mesmerism and hypnosis to cleave personal will and bodily power suggested a way out of this mortal dilemma, demonstrating that the ego—as an unquantifiable composite of will and power—might be able to migrate and survive through the inductive realm of unseen energies. Sheridan Le Fanu offered a particularly gruesome account of this energetic exchange in his short story "Green Tea," first published in 1869. The tale opens with a Reverend Jennings tormented by an evil monkey. At first Jennings sees the creature only fleetingly out of the corner of his eye, but gradually the monkey becomes more visible and aggressive. While visiting Jennings's home, a "metaphysical physician," Dr. Hessalius, finds that his patient for some time has been writing a book on ancient religious practices, a project that has led him deeply into mysticism and the occult.¹²² Discussing his symptoms, Jennings confesses that the "spectral illusion" of the otherworldly monkey first appeared as he began working long into the night on his book, often under the influence of powerful stimulants. Of late, he adds, the monkey has begun to speak. "Speak! How do you mean—speak as a man does, do you mean?" interjects the disbelieving Hessalius. "Yes; speaks in words and consecutive sentences, with perfect coherence and articulation," responds Jennings. "But there is a peculiarity. It is not like the tone of a human voice. It is not by my ears it reaches me—it comes like a singing through my head."¹²³ Although no one else in the congregation can see him, Jennings continues, the monkey often dances atop the open Bible during his sermons, taunting him and interrupting his thoughts with "dreadful blasphemies." Hessalius asks whether the creature is now in the room with them as they speak. No, Jennings responds, but he is certain the creature will return, as he always does, to torment him, "urging me to crimes, to injure others, or myself."¹²⁴ Intrigued, Hessalius agrees to take the case, and as he leaves he asks Jennings to inform him the moment the monkey returns. Later, when a note does arrive from Jennings, apparently once again at the mercy of the evil monkey, Hessalius rushes back to the house. But it is too late. Reverend Jennings has slit his own throat.

As an accomplished practitioner of the fantastic, Le Fanu allowed a variety of explanatory systems to compete as the ultimate source of Jennings's apparent "madness." Perhaps, as it appears to modern readers, he has indeed gone insane, overstressed by the demands of writing his tome on ancient religions and overcome by previously repressed denizens in his unholy imagination. Yet one cannot wholly dismiss those elements of "cosmic horror" that H. P. Lovecraft would mine so successfully in the next century. Perhaps this Christian minister, having dared to commune with the occult powers of a world beyond, has somehow incurred the wrath of an ancient primate demon.¹²⁵ The physician Hessalius advances his own theory. "It is the story of the process of a poison," he opines in the tale's closing pages, "a poison which excites the reciprocal action of spirit and nerve, and paralyses the tissue that separates those cognate functions of the senses, the external and the interior. Thus we find strange bed-fellows, and the mortal and immortal prematurely make acquaintance."¹²⁶ The doctor continues his postmortem assessment, describing the "normal" circulation of nervous and spiritual fluid. "Of this system, thus considered, the brain is the heart. The fluid, which is propagated hence through one class of nerves, returns in an altered state through another, and the nature of that fluid is spiritual, though not immaterial, any more than, as I before remarked, light or electricity are so." Normally, this spiritual fluid coursing through the nervous system is insulated and in balance. But, Hessalius continues, "By various abuses, among which the habitual use of such agents as green tea is one, this fluid may be affected as to its quality, but it is more frequently disturbed as to equilibrium. This fluid being that which we have in common with spirits, a congestion found upon the masses of brain or nerve, connected with the interior sense, forms a surface unduly exposed, on which disembodied spirits may operate: communication is thus more or less effectually established."[127] To review: excessive consumption of green tea leads to disequilibrium of spiritual "fluid" leads to irritation of nervous tissue leads to lesion leads to portal for otherworldly communication leads to phantom, homicidal monkey.[128] Within the context of its own narrative logic, the story's monkey demon is thus only apparently a hallucination, accredited in the end as a genuinely supernatural vision by a medical authority attuned to the possibilities of imbalanced energetic exchanges between our world and that which lies beyond. Had Jennings lived, Hessalius argues, his cure would have been found, not in the asylum, but in "dimming" and "sealing" the "inner eye" that the unfortunate man had "inadvertently opened." No doubt the first step in Jennings's recovery would have been strict avoidance of all caffeine.

Edward Page Mitchell's short story "The Professor's Experiment" (1880) provides a more humorous account of the Victorian obsession with the nervous debate between spiritualism and materialism. An American father travels to Germany with his daughter and the daughter's suitor. When the young man asks for the daughter's hand in marriage, the father cannot give his consent due to the suitor's unrelenting materialism. "No man who denies the objective verity of knowledge derived from intuition or otherwise by subjective methods—no man who pushes noumena aside in his impetuous pursuit of phenomena can make a safe husband for my child," he raves. Utterly convinced of his materialist principles, the young suitor is unable simply to renounce his convictions or, worse, feign insincere belief in the spiritual aspects of the universe. Knowing "belief" to be a function of the brain's hard wiring, however, the young man seeks medical consultation. Luckily, as they are in Germany (already well established in 1880 as the global center of neurophysiology), he quickly finds a trio of German physicians willing to advise him. Somewhat alarmingly, they tell him that the only way to definitively change his materialist convictions will be through trephination. Such an operation, they argue, will remove the pressure on the brain's gray matter that prevents the young man from crediting theological philosophy. Hearing of the suitor's impending sacrifice, the daughter and father rush to the surgical theater so they might be trepanned instead. "Although I cannot conscientiously accept him as a son-in-law while our views on the verity of subjective knowledge differ so widely," observes the father, "I can at least emulate his generous willingness to open his intellect to conviction. It is I who will trephined." Much to the disappointment of the eager Germans, however, in the end no one is trepanned. Waking from his surgical ether and believing the unperformed operation a success, the young man professes his newfound and steadfast belief in the power of the spiritual realm. "I have been floating in the infinite. I have been freed from conditions of time and space. I have lost my individuality in the immensity of the All," he excitedly exclaims. But this is just the ether talking—he remains in the end a materialist. Yet once the significance of their mutual sacrifice is made clear, the newly bonded father, daughter, and suitor exit, presumably to make plans for the wedding back in America. The bride-to-be has a final world for the scalpel-happy Germans: "'If you must trephine somebody for the sake of science, gentlemen,' she remarked with her sweetest smile, 'you might draw lots to see which of you shall trephine the other.'"[129]

Universal Nerve

Approaching the end of the nineteenth century, skeptics increasingly challenged the authority of spiritualism's theories of mediumship and the afterlife. Like so many other religions, spiritualism retreated into a more inscrutable mysticism that reframed its early narratives as enigmatic allegory. Meanwhile, "scientific" inquiry into spiritual phenomena fell to organizations such as the Society for Psychical Research (SPR), founded in London in 1882 by Fredric W. H. Myers, Edmund Gurney, and Henry Sidgwick.[130] Many prominent physicists of the late nineteenth century participated in the SPR in the hope that application of the scientific method might provide empirical evidence of psychic phenomena—or, failing that, at least expose the deceit of fraudulent mediums. In addition to "haunted houses," the early interests of the SPR focused on "thought transference" and telepathy (a term coined by Myers in 1882). As Roger Luckhurst notes in his history of telepathy, much of this work focused on radiant energy, electrical induction, and other "inter-phenomena" as a likely pathway for explaining mind-to-mind contact. Luckhurst places particular emphasis on an influential address by William Barrett, a physicist from Dublin, to the British Academy of Arts and Sciences in 1876. Barrett's paper, "On Some Phenomena Associated with Abnormal

Conditions of Mind," used the still mysterious physics of induction to argue, "When a person is thrown into a hypnotic or passive condition, the nervous action associated with thought can be excited by a corresponding action in an adjoining individual, and this across space without the intervention of recognized organs of sensation."[131] Frank Podmore's study of 1898, *Apparitions and Thought Transference*, was emblematic of the SPR's approach.[132] Seeking to demystify the premodern superstition of ghosts and hauntings, Podmore appealed to empirical evidence that supported the scientific validity of thought transference. Ghosts, Podmore concluded, were telepathically induced hallucinations, often "transmissions" projected by spikes in mental energy generated at the moment of death.[133]

Hoping to capture evidence of a bridge between the conductive networks of the body and the inductive fields of the atmosphere (and beyond), researchers employed many new devices and techniques to document otherwise invisible exchanges of energy. Advances in photography at the turn of the twentieth century held great promise for visualizing psychic activity. Spirit photography dated to the end of the American Civil War, photographers using basic "double-exposure" techniques to unite (for a fee) portrait sitters with departed loved ones and famous historical figures.[134] As Tom Gunning argues, by the end of the nineteenth century this mode of spiritual photography had transitioned from an emphasis on documenting "full-body materializations" to the "less spectacular but possibly uncannier" manifestation known as "ectoplasm." Gunning describes this mucous-like substance as "the prima materia . . . molded by spirit forces to create manifestations."[135] Thought to issue from the orifices of the medium, ectoplasm could take many forms. Most often, however, ectoplasm manifested as tendrils issuing from the medium's mouth. A bookend to the placenta and umbilicus of birth, this ectoplasmic cord presented its own odd compromise between the material and the spiritual, the visible and the invisible. Here was seemingly tangible matter, in the form of an undulating cord, that was somehow composed of spirit materials brought over from the invisible world.[136] In 1904, William Crawford offered a bioelectrical theory of the conversion at work in this process: "Operators are acting on the brain of the sitters and thence on their nervous systems. Small particles, it may even be molecules, are driven off the nervous system, out through the bodies of sitters at wrists, hands, fingers, or elsewhere." Crawford speculated that these particles, now "free" and suffused with a "considerable amount of latent energy," amplify their power by circulating around the séance circle. Eventually this circulating field of nervous particles enters the medium, who "is so constituted that

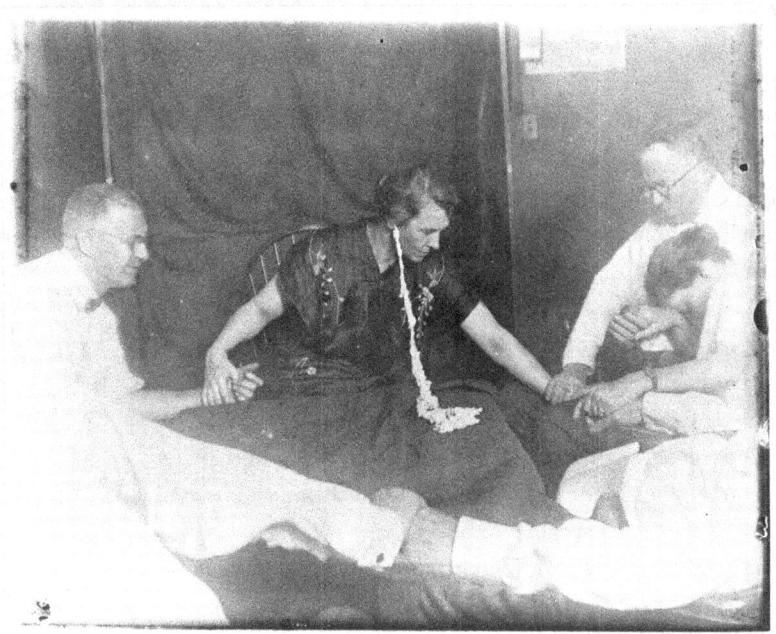

FIG 3.5 Ectoplasm emanates from the ear of a medium in a séance from the 1920s.
SOURCE: LIBRARY OF CONGRESS.

gross matter from her body can, by means of nervous tension applied to it, be actually temporarily detached from its usual position and projected into the séance room."[137] Crawford's theory involves multiple conversions between induction and conduction. Material nerves shed particles to produce a field or cloud of nervous energy, which in turn travels as an invisible circuit of amplification until, in the final moment, the medium transforms this invisible energy into a detachable object of "gross matter" that is, in the end, the willed form of spiritual beings.

In 1907, the physician Duncan MacDougall reported on an experiment designed to detect whether any perceptible loss of weight took place at the moment of death, evidence (he conjectured) of a spiritual substance exiting the body.[138] MacDougall's study involved six patients who, when death became imminent, had their beds transferred to a large but surprisingly precise scale. MacDougall was exacting in his attempt to account for non-soul-related substances. In his first subject, a man dying of tuberculosis, MacDougall calculated average hourly weight loss through perspiration. At the moment of death, MacDougall notes, "the bowels did not move, if they had moved the weight would still have remained upon the bed except for a slow loss by the evaporation of moisture depending of course, upon the fluidity of the feces. The bladder evacuated one or two drachmas of urine. This remained upon the bed and could only have influenced the weight by slow gradual evaporation and therefore in no way could account for the sudden loss." MacDougall also charged a colleague with the unpleasant task of lying down in the deathbed to see whether "forcible inspiration and expiration of air" might affect the scales. It did not. Less successful were the results obtained from a woman in a diabetic coma, with MacDougall citing "a good deal of interference by people opposed to our work." His last subject, finally, "was not a fair test," as the patient died "almost within five minutes after being placed on the bed . . . while I was adjusting the beam." From this limited pool of three successes and three failures, MacDougall proposed that the human body loses twenty-one grams of weight at the moment of death. "Is it the soul substance?" he asks. "It would seem to me to be so."

These efforts to photograph or weigh the soul shadowed Victorian attempts to demonstrate the materiality of thought. As early as 1867, the physician J. S. Lombard had captured variations in the temperature of the head in relation to intense mental effort.[139] In 1882, Angelo Mosso devised a "human circulation balance" to measure the redistribution of blood during mental activity, research cited by some psychic researchers (erroneously) as proving that thought itself had weight.[140] As the nineteenth century came to a close, Santiago Ramón y Cajal and Camillo Golgi advanced rival theories as to the interconnectivity of the brain's neural pathways, what one writer has evocatively distinguished as "the soup and the spark."[141] Golgi's "spark" model was essentially conductive, maintaining there was a physical connection between neurons that allowed information to continue flowing along the "wire." Cajal, meanwhile, eventually prevailed in demonstrating the more inductive "soup" model of the synapse, identifying a gap between neurons where the energetic pathway was—for a fleeting moment—suspended among potentialities, adrift in the psychochemical space of the neurotransmitter.[142] This "space" arguably remains one of the great occult mysteries of medical science: what transpires (chemically, psychologically, philosophically) in the infinitesimal gap between neurons? Efforts to provide scientific evidence of thought energy continued well into the twentieth century, even as the SPR's early confidence in the project began to wane. Still, as late as 1925 Sir Oliver Lodge continued to promote a comprehensive theory of the ether as a medium spanning the material and spiritual worlds, even as Albert Einstein's physics exiled this medium of invisible nothingness from the realm of science to that of poetry. "The Ether of Space is a theme of unknown and apparently infinite magnitude," wrote Lodge in the aptly titled *Ether and Reality*. "By a kind of instinct, one feels it to be the home of spiritual existence, the realm of the awe-inspiring and the supernal." And yet, as the physicist Lodge quickly reminded the giddy mystic, "the Ether is a physical thing."[143]

....

This instinct for the supernal was particularly strong in Judge Daniel Paul Schreber. In October 1893, Schreber left his appointment in Leipzig to become presiding judge of the Court of Appeals in Dresden, beginning a journey that would eventually make him the most analyzed psychotic of the twentieth century. Schreber recalls that he worked with "unquestionable efficiency" in his determination to earn the respect of his new (and slightly older) colleagues, a strain that gradually led to a state of mental "overtaxation." Unable to sleep, he began to hear odd, unexplained noises at night in his home. A physician advised him to take a week's leave, and Schreber, accompanied by his wife, returned to Leipzig in November 1893 to consult with Dr. Paul Flechsig, a renowned neurologist and the chair of psychiatry at Leipzig's University Hospital. Flechsig had supervised Schreber's successful recovery from a debilitating bout of hypochondria eight years earlier. After meeting with Flechsig in the morning to discuss a new plan of treatment, Schreber's condition deteriorated overnight—so much so that Flechsig returned the next morning to take Schreber back to the hospital. Schreber showed little sign of recovery, and his symptoms took a "supernatural" turn in February 1894. While his incredibly florid delusions resist tidy summary, in most basic terms he came to understand that his nerves had become entangled with those of God, a disruption in the "natural order of the universe" that not only threatened all of creation, but also had the odd side effect of gradually transforming Schreber into a woman.

After seven years of confinement, Schreber began to work on a manuscript that he hoped would aid in securing his release. Published in 1903, shortly after his discharge, *Memoirs of My Nervous Illness* interweaves a detailed account of Schreber's extraordinary experiences in the asylum with an equally extraordinary theory as to the true agents and mechanisms behind his various "miracles." Schreber opens with what is a foundational proposition of the *Memoirs*: "The human soul is contained in the nerves of the body" and "the total mental life of a human being rests on their excitability by external impressions."[144] In this, Schreber is wholly in line with the century of galvanic anatomy that opened the brain for the neural mapping of Victorian science. But

Schreber then adds a significant inflection to this familiar model of nervous conduction. There are, he argues, specialized "nerves of Intellect" within the overall nervous system charged with retaining mental impressions and serving as the "organs of will." Unlike the rest of the nervous system, these more specialized "nerves of intellect" (concentrated in the brain, naturally) possess a unique and most remarkable quality: "Circumstances seem to be such that *every single nerve of intellect represents the total mental individuality of a human being*, that the sum total of recollections is as it were inscribed on each single nerve of intellect."[145] The nervous system thus not only "conducts" energy (or "vibrations" in Schreber's model); it also serves as a massively redundant archive storing the entirety of one's stimulation, experience, memory, and "soul." But Schreber was not simply a massive hard drive of data. He was also a cosmic transmitter and receiver in dialogue with God. "God to start with is only nerve, not body, and akin therefore to the human soul," he observes. "But unlike the human body, where nerves are present only in limited numbers, the nerves of God are infinite and eternal." God as nerve (or nerve as God) is thus everywhere for all time. Much as electricity served as "eternal uncreated matter" in Oetinger's "theology of electricity," Schreber envisions "nerve" as the very substance of the universe. God's nerves, Schreber continues, "have in particular the faculty of transforming themselves into all things of the created world; in this capacity they are called rays; and herein lies the essence of divine creation."[146]

Like so many other psychics and psychotics of the era, Schreber was particularly interested in how these two forms of energy—the conductive nerve flows of the body and the inductive omnipresence of God (as Nerve)—might intersect. Schreber proposes that the privileged moment of this exchange occurs in death: "When man is alive he is body and soul together, the nerves (the soul of man) are nourished and kept in living motion by the body whose function is essentially similar to that of the higher animals." At death, however, the soul enters a type of hibernation, Schreber contends, existing as quiescent energy bound to the nerves and waiting to be retrieved by God. Schreber's notion of "soul" is reminiscent of the spirit body proposed by Bush and adopted by the spiritualists, a cohesive *doppelgänger* of spiritual materials hovering in the body and waiting, like a ghost, to emerge at the moment of death. But Schreber's variation on this model is decidedly more telegraphic. For him, ascendance into the afterlife does not involve a spirit body striding into heaven fully formed as a ghost or hologram; it is instead a transmission in which God extracts the dormant "soul" from the nerves of the corpse to draw it toward heaven. In making this transfer from the finite confines of the nervous system to the eternal blessedness of infinite nerve, souls travel as a form of energy in the process of purification, in effect traversing the emptiness of outer space until their final assimilation in heaven. On occasion, Schreber concedes, God makes temporary "nerve contact" with the living, typically to inspire poets or bless dreams: "But such 'nerve-contact' was not allowed to become the rule ... because for reasons which cannot be further elucidated, the nerves of living human beings, particularly when in a state of high-grade excitation, have such power of attraction for the nerves of God that He would not be able to free Himself from them again, and would thus endanger His own existence."[147] Significantly, "nerve" power precedes and exceeds the will of God Himself.

Schreber recalls that his "nervous illness" began shortly after he assumed his new position in Dresden, observing that the pressure of doing well in his new post had thrown his nerves into an acute state of "high excitation."[148] Schreber asserts that the magnetic attraction of his overexcited nerves was so strong, so singular, that it lured God into premature "nerve contact" with Schreber's still living body, thereby disrupting the "natural order of the universe." Schreber's many symptoms were thus "miracles" produced by the unceasing stream of God's "divine rays." Not only had Schreber tricked God, but his uniquely powerful nerves had also become a magnet for those countless souls traversing the universe, now caught in a limbo between heaven and Schreber's magnetic head. Complicating matters further, a renegade faction of Flechsig's soul (or perhaps the souls of his ancestors; Schreber is less than clear on this point) somehow appropriated a portion of God's divine rays and did not want to relinquish them. Nor did this faction wish to restore the natural order of the universe. These were the sources of the voices, thoughts, and compulsions that made Schreber appear insane, a plot that signaled nothing less than an attempt at "soul murder."[149] Thus did Schreber's cosmology equate the natural order of the universe with nervous equilibrium, a homeostasis disrupted by Schreber's extraordinarily charged nervous system and further agitated by Flechsig's nihilistic plot of appropriation. Mistaken in his attraction to Schreber's nerves and deceived by Flechsig's machinations, God has inadvertently transformed creation into an open circuit. How could God make such a mistake? Schreber's God is aloof and distant, we learn, and not generally interested in the daily affairs of creation. More important, however, Schreber asserts, "God did not really understand the living human being and had no need to understand him, because, according to the Order of the World, He dealt only with corpses."[150] Like so many other self-aware moderns, Schreber also acknowledged that his era was already one of "growing nervousness among mankind,"[151] a condition that presumably made God's task of differentiating live and dead circuitry on Earth that much more difficult. The God of the *Memoirs* is thus somewhat of a Luddite boob, caught unaware by the rapidly accelerating nervousness of his own creation and "tricked" by the powers of attraction in Schreber's still living nervous system.[152] Much like an overstressed worker in a phone exchange, God simply could not handle modernity's excessive nervous energies even as He was irresistibly attracted to it.

Electronics make only a few appearances in the *Memoirs*, but technical principles of induction, conduction, balance, insulation, resistance, and circuitry recur throughout Schreber's delusional system. Voices inform Schreber that the "mutual attraction of rays and nerves" obey the "principle of light telegraphy."[153] He speculates that at certain points during his confinement, noxious liquids introduced a "poison of intoxication" into his nervous tissue, while on other occasions, a kind of "paste" coated his nerves and rendered him temporarily insensible.[154] An attendant at the asylum would occasionally transfer a part of his soul directly into Schreber's body, producing a "jelly-like mass about the size of a cherry."[155] Other souls attempted to pull the nerves from Schreber's head, although they inevitably failed, given that "the staying power of my nerves proved the greater force and the half-pulled out nerves always returned to my head after a short time."[156] In one of the oddest physical manifestations in the *Memoirs*, Schreber reports attacks in the form of "little men," no more than a few millimeters tall. These little men would then "make mischief on all parts of my body, both inside and outside," running around on Schreber's head and often playing havoc with his eyelids. At times they stole tiny portions of food from his plate. At one point a brigade of these little men occupied Schreber's feet and tried to "pump out" his spinal cord, causing the nervous tissue to exit Schreber's mouth "in considerable quantity in the form of little clouds, particularly when I was walking in the garden."[157] In a postscript to the first edition of *Memoirs*, Schreber takes up the thorny question of cremation. If the soul does reside in the nervous tissue as data awaiting retrieval via divine ray, he speculates, perhaps it is best not to cremate the body before this transfer can take place (in addition to being a Luddite, God apparently is also lazy).[158]

This continual exposure to God's nerve rays had other consequences, as well. Schreber notes that the rays, on occasion, warped or temporarily thinned the bones of his skull. More significant, however, was the "unmanning" effect of this contact. There is, he asserts, "a tendency, innate in the

Order of the World, to *unman* a human being who has entered into permanent contact with the rays. This is connected on the one hand with the nature of God's nerves, through which Blessedness is felt, if not exclusively as, at least accompanied by, a greatly increased feeling of voluptuousness."[159] Related to this voluptuousness, Schreber recalls an episode shortly before the onset of his crisis in 1893: "One morning while still in bed (whether still half asleep or already awake I cannot remember), I had a feeling which, thinking about it later when fully awake, struck me as highly peculiar. It was the idea that it really must be pleasant to be a woman succumbing to intercourse."[160] This is in fact where Schreber's delusion eventually leads. His "unmanning" by divine ray is a process of physical transformation. "For myself I am subjectively certain that my body—as I have repeatedly stated in consequence of divine miracles—shows such organs to an extent as only occurs in the female body."[161] During the early years of his confinement, Schreber struggled with this "unmanning" by fighting these sensations of female "voluptuousness," believing that these changes to his body and mind constituted a strategy to humiliate and defeat him. But in November 1895, he came to accept that he must assume the form of a woman to maintain the order of the universe. "Everything feminine attracts God's nerves," he observes toward the end of *Memoirs*, necessitating that Schreber reconcile himself to his cosmic voluptuousness. "I could see beyond doubt that the Order of the World imperiously demanded my unmanning, whether I personally like it or not, and that therefore it was common sense that nothing was left to me but reconcile myself to the thought of being transformed into a woman."[162] With the original order of the universe disrupted—permanently, it would appear—by God's attraction to Schreber's highly excited nerves, a new Order of the Universe depends on restoring a certain gendered economy to the energies of the universe. In perhaps his supreme moment of grandeur, Schreber in effect must become God's bride and enact an energetic doctrine of Victorian complementarianism. The only logical conclusion, he observes, is that his unmanning is preparation for his "fertilization by divine rays for the purpose of creating new human beings."[163]

Shortly after his transfer to the asylum at Sonnenstein, when Schreber still believed he might resist these forces, he devised a plan to liberate the countless souls caught in the "position of so-called middle instances between myself and God's omnipotence."[164] By drawing down these souls into his own nervous system, Schreber conjectured, God could then draw them all up en masse and restore the order of the universe. In a demonstration of cosmic willpower, Schreber writes, "I succeeded with immense mental effort in temporarily drawing down to myself all impure ('tested') souls; it would only have required a thorough 'covering with rays' for my recovery through one nerve-restoring sleep and with it the disappearance of the impure souls."[165] But this effort at restoration presents a threat to Flechsig and his allies in the "so-what party."[166] Schreber writes, "In consequence Flechsig's soul took special measures to exclude the recurrence of such a danger to its existence and to that of other impure souls. It resorted to *mechanical fastening* as an expedient"—or what Schreber calls "tying-to-rays"—which appear to be (who can really know for sure?) a literal binding of soul energy to mechanical anchors. When this first method fails and souls continue to fall into Schreber's body (where they then dissolve), Flechsig's renegade soul devises a second strategy, which Schreber describes as the "tying-to-celestial bodies." Once physically bound to distant stars, these souls of the universe could not be drawn into Schreber's body and dissolved by his powers of attraction. "I realize that such a conception, according to which one must think of my body on our earth as connected to other stars by stretched out nerves, is almost incomprehensible to other people considering the immense distances involved; for me however as a result of my daily experiences over the last six years there can be no doubt as to the objective reality of this relation."[167] Schreber's "tethering" to distant celestial bodies had a variety of alarming effects, most unpleasant of which was his frequent sensation that his nerves were being torn from his body through the top of his head: "One can form some picture of the disagreeable sensations these happenings cause if one considers that these are the rays of a whole world—somehow mechanically fasted at their point of issue—which travel around one single head and attempt to tear it asunder and put it apart in fashion comparable to quartering."[168]

Schreber's insistence on a physical, conductive tethering in this scheme of celestial tying presents a delusional inflection on the state of the energetic ego at the close of the nineteenth century. The "untested souls" of the universe are not simply caught between heaven and Earth (or, more accurately, between heaven and Schreber's head). They are also in flux between two energetic states. For Schreber's delusion to function properly, souls could not be lost in an undifferentiated cloud of cosmic energy, an inductive field that would align them more closely to God as infinite nerve than to Schreber's (poorly) insulated nerves. So while in transit, departed souls remained discrete packets of information, egos that are physically tethered and in conductive rapport with Schreber's brain. Unaware of this struggle,

God as infinite nerve continues to draw these souls, like an antenna, to the forecourts of an inductive heaven, even as Schreber works to plug each and every conductive cable into his head.[169]

Quantum Cathexis

Part legal document, part autobiography, part cosmological treatise, *Memoirs* first appeared in a limited press run by a publisher who specialized in religious and occult esoterica.[170] An early reader was Carl Jung, the member of Freud's inner circle who was most sympathetic to mysticism (and psychotics). Jung passed the book along to Freud, who in 1911 published his own "textual" analysis of the book-patient, "Psychoanalytic Notes upon an Autobiographical Account of a Case of Paranoia" (Freud, as many critics have noted, never met with Schreber for traditional analysis; his assessment proceeds wholly from the text of the *Memoirs*).[171] Introduced into critical circulation via Freud, the Schreber case went on to become one of the most discussed, debated, and dissected presentations of the twentieth century, of relevance not only to Freudians, but also to a larger intellectual community interested in the psychosocial dynamics of modernity.[172] Once a curiosity found only in rare book shops, Schreber's *Memoirs* have been reprinted and reread to the point that they now function as both a primary document of psychiatric history and a multilayered enigma of modernist *écriture*. While James Joyce's *Finnegan's Wake* stands at the *ne plus ultra* of modernist fiction, Schreber's *Memoirs* have attained a similar status in the literature on pathological modernity.

For many years, Freud's essay was best known for nominating homosexual repression as the central mechanism in paranoia, a linkage that remained psychoanalytic doctrine well into the 1960s.[173] At some ineluctable juncture, however, practitioners and historians of psychoanalysis began to hoist Freud by his own analytic petard, subjecting his work, life, and relationships to its own symptomatic analysis.[174] In this quest, many diagnosticians have been drawn to Freud's concluding remarks in the Schreber essay. Here Freud confesses an unnerving similarity between Schreber's delusional universe and Freud's own theory of libido. "Schreber's 'rays of God,'" Freud concedes, "are in reality nothing else than a concrete representation and external projection of libidinal cathexes; and they lend his delusions a striking similarity with our theory." Freud was so concerned about these similarities, apparently, as to offer, in print, a witness as to the primacy of his intervention: "I can nevertheless call a friend and fellow-specialist to witness that I had developed my theory of paranoia before I became acquainted with the contents of Schreber's book."[175] Freud ends with a rhetorical device that his supporters and his opponents would deploy repeatedly over the next century: "It remains for the future to decide whether there is more delusion in my theory than I should like to admit, or whether there is more truth in Schreber's delusion than other people are as yet prepared to believe."[176]

Rhetorically, at least, Freud's concluding remarks open the door for considering the delusional aspects of psychoanalysis, an invitation that many have been eager to accept. In his influential reading of the case, Friedrich Kittler locates this delusional affinity as the legacy of Victorian psychophysics, a connection that triangulates Schreber, Flechsig, and Freud in a shared effort to diagram—cosmically, neurologically, psychoanalytically—a mechanics of the psyche. As Kittler writes, "It did not take private religious illuminations to reduce, in the first sentence of the book, the soul to nervous tissue and to the language of nervous tissue."[177] Three years after the publication of *Memoirs*, for example, Sir Oliver Lodge offered a cosmic model of nerve that was every bit as fanciful as that of Schreber: "It has been surmised . . . that just as the corpuscles and atoms of matter, in their intricate movements and relations, combine to form the brain cell of a human being; so the cosmic bodies, the planets and suns and other groupings of the ether, may perhaps combine to form something corresponding as it were to the brain cell of some transcendent Mind."[178] Kittler's reading of the *Memoirs* emphasizes Schreber's role as a multifunctional media instrument. A bundle of nerves circulating and storing information, Schreber is a camera. He is a gramophone. He is a telephone. "The paranoid machine operates like an integrated system of all the data-storage devices that revolutionized recording circa 1900."[179] This twofold capacity to *conduct* and *store* information makes Schreber an emblematic figure in what Kittler designates the "discourse network" of 1900, a new complex of technology and information that operates "without *Geist*" and constitutes, for Kittler, a "second industrial revolution."

There is an undeniably conductive, mechanical, and, thus, *Geist*-less logic at the heart of psychoanalysis from its very origins. Introduced in Freud's collaboration with Joseph Breuer on hysteria, the economics of cathexis—the neuronal circulation and binding of psychic energy—would remain operative throughout Freud's career. So would the "principle of constancy," a legacy of Victorian equilibrium and regulation that, in Freud's version, posited that organisms seek to maintain psychic homeostasis. Immediately after the publication of *Studies on Hysteria* in 1895, Freud began to work on "Project

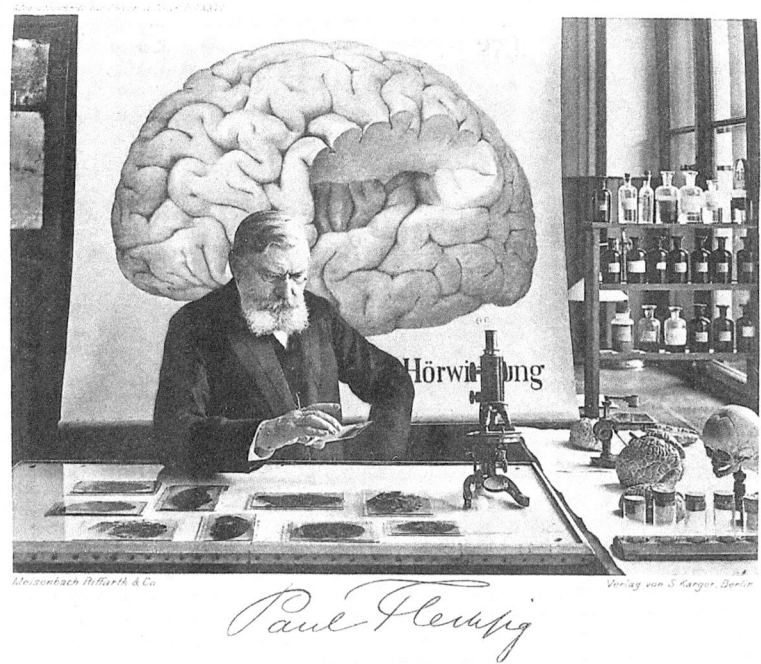

FIG 3.6 Following the work of Zvi Lothane and Friedrich Kittler on the Schreber case, this photograph of Paul Flechsig, Schreber's physician and psychic tormenter, has assumed greater significance. Taken in 1909 at Flechsig's clinic in Leipzig, it captures figuratively and perhaps literally why Schreber might have installed Flechsig at the domineering center of his theory of "nerve energy."

for a Scientific Psychology," his attempt to outline a "psychology which shall be a natural science."[180] Eventually abandoned (and unpublished in Freud's lifetime), "Project for a Scientific Psychology" nevertheless introduced an "economics of nerve forces" that would recur throughout Freud's writing."[181] But Freudian theory and Schreberian delusion also shared an interest in the transmission and conversion of more occult energies. As detailed earlier, Schreber's delusional universe combined divine cosmology with Victorian psychophysics to produce what Kittler dubbed a "neurotheology."[182] Freud, by contrast, confined these interests primarily to the seemingly psychoanalytic-adjacent areas of telepathy and "thought transference." In this respect, Freud's delusional theory and Schreber's theoretical delusions have a common foundation in "magical thinking," described by Freud as that period in childhood development when the relationship between internal thought and external events remains ambiguous.[183] Magical thinking not

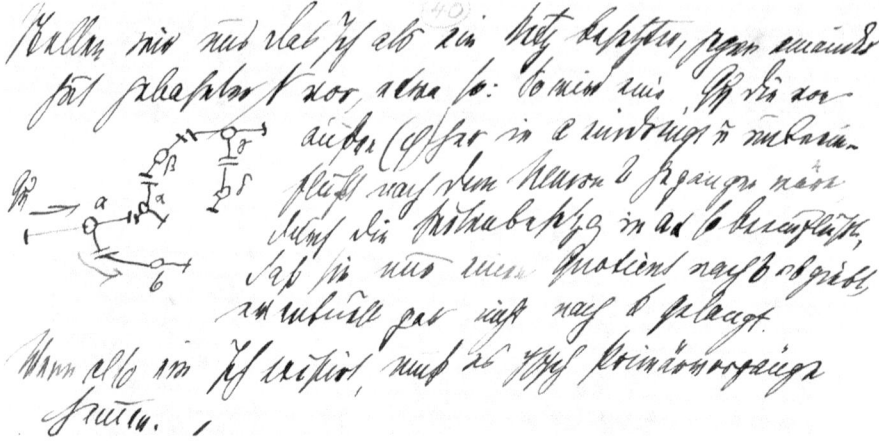

FIG 3.7 Detail from Freud's handwritten manuscript for *Entwurf einer Psychologie* (*Project for a Scientific Psychology*), 1895. On the left side of the page, Freud diagrams the possible neuronal mechanism of cathexis. SOURCE: LIBRARY OF CONGRESS, MANUSCRIPT DIVISION, SIGMUND FREUD PAPERS.

only defined the earliest history of the ego, Freud argued, but could also be seen in "primitive" societies, regressed neurotics, and, significantly, psychotics. As Pamela Thurschwell argues, "magical thinking" was a cultural dominant in the late nineteenth and early twentieth centuries, pervading a variety of scientific and artistic discourses. Psychoanalysis and psychic research both emerge in this era, argues Thurschwell, as sciences interested in "occult forms of intimacy and transmission."[184] While psychic research imagined the possibility of providing empirical verification of occult transmission, psychoanalysis vacillated between "inviting and disavowing" magical thinking. This ambivalence can be seen not only in Freud's ludic invocation of the psychotic Schreber as an analytic peer, but also in Freudianism's complicated engagement with occultism.

Once considered a relatively minor motif of the *Standard Edition*, the "occult" aspects of Freudianism are now well known. Recognizing an affinity between the Freudian unconscious and his own idea of "subliminal consciousness," Frederic Myers invited Freud in 1911 to align with the SPR. Myers was also the key figure in bringing Freud's work on hysteria to England. Many members of Freud's inner circle were proponents of applying psychoanalytic technique to occult phenomena—most notably, Carl Jung and Sándor Ferenczi.[185] A strong dissenter was Freud's future biographer Ernest Jones, who consistently dissuaded Freud from publicly associating psychoanalysis with the only slightly less reputable field of psychic inquiry. "You ask me of the Society of Psychical Research," he wrote to Freud in regard to Myers's invitation. "I am sorry to say that in spite of the good names in it, the society is not of good repute in scientific circles. You will remember that they did some valuable work in the eighties on hypnotism, automatic writing, etc., but for the past fifteen years they have confined their attention to 'spook-hunting,' mediumship, and telepathy, the chief aim being to communicate with departed souls."[186] Histories of the psychoanalytic movement revel in anecdotes of a paranoid Freud fretting over the attribution of ideas and even the possibility that his work might be stolen through "thought transference." Ironically, these suspicions were apparently particularly acute in relation to Victor Tausk, the first theorist of the paranoid influencing machine.[187]

Freud's writing on telepathy was very conflicted—perhaps he was hedging his bets until all the science was in—even as it gradually moved from suspicious rivalry to a more deliberate inscrutability. Thus, in the unpublished paper "Psychoanalysis and Telepathy" (1921), the not yet convinced Freud regarded recent popular interest in the occult as a noxious irritant, grouping it with the insubordination of the newly antagonistic Jung and Alfred Adler. "We do not seem destined to work in peace on the development of our science," he complained.[188] A year later, Freud was more coy on the topic: "You will learn nothing from this paper of mine about the enigma of telepathy; indeed, you will not even gather whether I believe in the existence of 'telepathy' or not."[189] The essay "The Occult Significance of Dreams" (1925) saw Freud moving a step closer in indulging the phenomenon: "One arrives at a provisional opinion that it may well be that telepathy really exists and that it provides the kernel of truth in many other hypotheses that would otherwise be incredible."[190] Finally, in 1926, the year of his seventieth birthday, Freud apparently had become convinced—personally, if not publicly—of telepathy's reality. "If anyone should bring up with you my Fall from grace," he wrote to a no doubt horrified Jones, "just answer calmly that my acceptance of telepathy is my own affair, like my Judaism and my passion for smoking, etc., and that the subject of telepathy is not related to psychoanalysis."[191] Having in his career documented "omnipotence of thought" as a neurotic mode of infantile regression; having textually diagnosed Schreber's telepathic horrors as psychotic paranoia; and having as recently as 1919 praised Tausk's work on the paranoid delusion of "influencing machines," Freud in the mid-1920s was nevertheless prepared to consider telepathy science rather than symptom.[192]

Freud argued that psychoanalysis had little to say about the demonstrable reality of telepathic thought but could be of value in subjecting allegedly telepathic material, such as dreams, to rigorous analytic dissection. But this disavowal denied a physiological theory of telepathy already implicit in the energetic foundations of the Freudian project. Psychoanalysis *could* in fact validate telepathic energy in the dynamics of cathexis. Freud was thus true to neurology, psychic research, and psychoanalysis when he accepted as a matter of course that the passivity of sleep, a time of lower (and thus less "positive") electrical activity in the brain (as well as the ego's most undefended moment), would naturally create "favorable conditions for telepathy."[193] By 1925, Freud believed he had located the exact transmission point of telepathic phenomena, one that again must be seen in terms of cathexis and energy transfer: "On the basis of much experience I am inclined to draw the conclusion that thought transference . . . comes about particularly easily at the moment at which an idea emerges from the unconscious, or, in theoretical terms, as it passes over from the 'primary process' to the 'secondary process.'"[194] Given the prominence of repressive energies in the analytic session (for both the analyst and the analysand), Freud and his followers came to be concerned with telepathy as manifest chiefly at the moment of analytic countertransference. This was the explicit topic of Helene Deutsch's "Occult Processes Occurring during Psychoanalysis" (1926),[195] and it speaks to what John Forrester describes in *The Seductions of Psychoanalysis* as the discipline's fascination with "leaked communication." Forrester writes, "Once the psychoanalytic situation has been conceptualized as a semi-permeable discursive membrane, telepathy becomes a threat to that situation. The aim of the rules of analytic discourse is to regulate the flow across the membrane; telepathy represents a direct threat to this attempt at discursive regulation."[196]

Particularly sensitive to such "leakage," the Hungarian analyst Istvan Hollos took a most active interest in studying telepathic countertransference, proposing, after Freud, that these telepathic exchanges almost always involved a message "connected with a wish which is not yet in a state of repression, but is in the process of being repressed."[197] Working in dialogue with Ferenczi and an unnamed physicist, Hollos proposed a neurological theory that blended the Freudian thesis on primary and secondary processes, William Barrett's foundational speculation on telepathic induction, and Cajal's demonstration of synaptic transfer. The result was a kind of *quantum cathexis*, a process in which psychic material, much like electrons, gave off energy when "jumping levels"—in this case, between the orbitals of the primary and secondary process. At the heart of the theory was the inductive biophysics of "crossed nerve bundles," nodal points in the nervous system capable of transferring impulses through inductive association rather than conductive networking. "There is a genuine logical nexus between the explanation of the crossing of nerve bundles by means of 'neuromotor induction' and the induction process of the unconscious," argues Hollos. "In other words, this theory implies that if an intraindividual nerve induction exists, then an interindividual one may also exist."[198] Thought transference, in other words, occurred when the inductive mysteries of the unconscious, that absent yet influential realm of the psyche, surged forth and escaped from the inductive gap of the synapse. Receiving a "transferred" thought apparently reversed this process: the thought, as energy in a not yet understood form, accessed a similarly unguarded synaptic juncture of an individual whose thoughts also lingered on the cusp of the unconscious.

Freud identified "magical thinking" as the province of psychotics (as well as of children, neurotics, and primitive societies). In "On Narcissism" (1914), Freud introduces the idea that psychotic delusions represent an attempt at "restoration," a redirection of libidinal energy to external objects that assumes either a hysterical or paranoid form.[199] In this formulation, the magical thinking seen in so many technical delusions represents an intersection between restoration and the scientific marvelous, the psychotic individual adopting technical assistance in the struggle to remap the internal and external worlds. This association of psychosis and magical thinking found fuller exploration in Géza Róheim's *Magic and Schizophrenia* (1930). Róheim proposed that schizophrenic delusions have their foundation in "imagination magic," a logic not unlike the totemistic beliefs of preliterate cultures.[200] By way of illustration, Róheim discusses a schizophrenic patient who seems emblematic of Freud's restorative thesis. This patient believed he could "cure" people with a radium tube: "I put a lens into the tube. It is like a phosphorous ball, with rays. Then I look at a person and make him a new head. I can make your head nice and round and normal."[201] Róheim does not identify who this patient sought to cure; nor does he share whether the patient had actually fabricated the device or if it was itself a figment of the imagination. From the description, however, it appears this tube had the power to focus the patient's vision into a curative ray gun, making material the familiar iconographic strategy in comic books for visualizing vision as a straight line (whether it is Wimpy spying a fortuitous cheeseburger or Superman's scalding ocular heat rays). Thus does a diffuse field of vision become a focused sight line as the ego wills a conductive stream of energy out into the inductive expanse of the world."[202] Róheim's patient also offered to "cure"

Róheim, advising, "I was to put my soul (in the shape of a miniature human being) before me on the table; by thinking of my soul I could make it feel good; and after putting the soul back, my entire body would feel good."[203] Here we have an even more uncanny validation of Freud's account of libidinal withdrawal and restoration. The soul (ego), as an internal state, was to be temporarily extracted from its housing in the brain so it could take an external, articulated form as a miniature human being—standing on a table, no less. Directing good thoughts outward toward this anthropomorphic soul would infuse it with good feelings. Returned to the body, like a gingerbread man to the oven that baked him, the newly recharged soul would radiate inductive goodness back through the nerves and tissues of its host.

Reversing the polarity of this energetic fog, William Rouse's story "The Dead Man's Thoughts" (1921) opens with a poor but happy newlywed couple receiving a surprise visit from the bride's former suitor, a brilliant scientist who vanished shortly before the couple's wedding and has been missing for three months. After giving his blessing to the young couple, the scientist describes his current research project. "I shall be able to demonstrate in the laboratory exactly what 'stuff dreams are made of,' and the minds that dream them, and the bodies that carry the minds," he boasts, adding "no thought, no feeling, is ever manifested save as the result of physical force."[204] Months later, a telegram arrives announcing the scientist's untimely death. Knowing the couple would be too proud to accept money from his estate, the dead scientist instead offers them the free use of his home so the husband can complete his studies without financial strain. He asks only that Phyllis, his former love, place fresh roses in the study every afternoon in his memory. Over the following weeks, Phyllis becomes increasingly depressed, no doubt partly because the roses she leaves each day in the study die each morning before dawn. Theories of ghosts and hauntings are considered, but eventually the husband discovers a letter explaining an elaborate revenge plot afoot in the house. "The thought of death has its own ethereal vibration," explains the scientist in this letter from beyond the grave. "Hate also travels by vibration. . . . More than Marconi did for telegraphy I have done for the conscious transmission and direction at will of thoughts and emotions."[205] The husband reads on to discover that an apparatus has been concealed in the study where Phyllis goes each day to replace the roses, a device that broadcasts "thoughts of suicidal despair" (powerful enough, apparently, to drive even non-sentient flowers to their death). With only seconds to spare, he runs to Phyllis and saves her from an impending suicide attempt. Returning to the study to find and destroy the apparatus, he discovers instead the scientist, who has rather improbably been disguised as the household servant during their time in the house. Confident that his scheme for revenge has worked, that his rival will also know the torture of losing Phyllis, the scientist sits in a chair dying from the effects of choral hydrate. His final comfort is in knowing that his rival is now locked in the room with him and that he will eventually die from the effects of the suicide machine's transmissions. Instead, the husband breaks through the wall and uncovers the device, "a mass of delicate and intricate apparatus from which countless antennae arose." He empties a revolver into the machine and, suddenly feeling "happier than he ever had before," returns to attend to the still shaken Phyllis.

As the story of a living dead man who seeks to eliminate all traces of desire, to destroy himself and the young lovers who look forward to a life of home, hearth, and family, "The Dead Man's Thoughts" is uncannily evocative of Freud's own foray into pulp fiction, the perplexing "Beyond the Pleasure Principle" (1920).[206] Ostensibly inspired by the clinical experience of traumatized veterans compulsively reliving moments of battlefield stress, the real protagonist of "Beyond the Pleasure Principle" is a primordially embattled vesicle, "a living organism in its most simplified form . . . susceptible to stimulation."[207] Freud locates the origins of human consciousness in the nervous fate of our single-cell ancestors. Bombarded by external stimuli, Freud postulates, the vesicle would develop a "crust which at last will have been so thoroughly 'baked through' by stimulation that it would present the most favorable possible conditions for the reception of stimuli."[208] Herein lie the evolutionary origins of the sense organs—eyes, ears, and suggestively, the antennae that "are all the time making tentative advances toward the external world and then drawing back from it." Perhaps symptomatic of Freud's alleged paranoia, he casts this evolutionary process as more defensive than exploratory: "*Protection against* stimuli is an almost more important function for the living organism than *reception of* stimuli."[209] Freud goes on to describe the fate of this vesicle in a language that would no doubt resonate with many anxious subjects of modernity: "This little fragment of living substance is suspended in the middle of an external world charged with the most powerful energies; and it would be killed by the stimulation emanating from these if it were not provided with a protective shield against stimuli."[210] Endorsing, like Schreber, the familiar thesis that nervousness was on the increase within modernity, Freud suggests that the modern world's compression of space and time presents a fundamental challenge to the "baked crust" of defensive consciousness. If Freud did not fully see the implications of the media on these economies of stimulation, Marshall McLuhan most certainly did.

In *Understanding Media*, McLuhan revisits "Beyond the Pleasure Principle" with minimal distortion. "With the arrival of electric technology, man extended, or set outside himself, a live model of the central nervous system itself," he writes. "To the degree that this is so, it is a development that suggests a desperate and suicidal autoamputation, as if the central nervous system could no longer depend on the physical organs to be protective buffers against the slings and arrows of outrageous mechanism. It could well be that the successive mechanizations of the various physical organs since the invention of printing have made too violent and overstimulated a social experience for the central nervous system to endure."[211] McLuhan in essence formalizes Freud's earlier theories of prosthesis and cathexis, proposing an electronic psyche that continues to seek internal constancy even as expanding electromagnetic connections threaten to overamp the psychic array.

....

In a postscript to *Memoirs*, Schreber imagined himself as a cosmic telephone operator. Of the countless souls tethered to his head, he observes, "It is presumably a phenomenon like telephoning. The filaments of rays spun toward my head act like telephone wires; the weak sound of the cries for help coming from an apparently vast distance is received only by me in the same way as telephonic communication can only be heard by a person who is on the telephone."[212] In 1912, the year following his essay on Schreber, Freud also invoked the telephone to explicate his own science of the mind. In "Recommendations to Physicians Practising Psycho-analysis," Freud sought to explain psychoanalytic technique to potential practitioners.[213] The analyst, he writes, "must turn his own unconscious like a receptive organ towards the transmitting unconscious of the patient. He must adjust himself to the patient as a telephone receiver is adjusted to the transmitting microphone." Analyst and analysand thus take their positions at opposite ends of a shared line of conduction: "Just as the receiver converts back into soundwaves the electric oscillations in the telephone line which were set up by sound waves, so the doctor's unconscious is able, from the derivatives of the unconscious which are communicated to him, to reconstruct that unconscious, which has determined the patient's free associations."[214] For Schreber, the souls of the dead cohered in a telephonic line that conducted their cries across the void of space. For Freud, the neurotic's unconscious cohered in the vehicle of speech, a conductive syntagm that the analyst, properly attuned, could use to reconstruct and possibly understand the occult field of energies that animated these messages. But transmission was not without its hazards. Extending a wire to connect the unconscious voids of analyst and analysand might lead to unwitting moments of telepathic transference. Renegade energies in the psyche, not yet repressed, might leap from the neural networks of conductive circulation to radiate as an inductive field. For Schreber, meanwhile, millions of souls tethered to the stars as nervous cables threatened, daily, to rip off his head.

The iteration of psychophysics shared by Freud and Schreber may now be obsolescent, but galvanic will and mesmeristic power continue to forge a poetic alliance. Galvani's electrical conduction remains an instrument of coherence and rational administration. A visible line connects point A to point B in a direct application of power. Lightning connects heaven and earth, a wire connects outlet and appliance, a nerve connects finger and brain. Affixing a lightning bolt to a football helmet, guitar amp, sports drink, condom, or mud flap warns that the object and its owner are in some way awesomely "supercharged" with excesses of explosive power, electricity that cannot be contained within the conduits of its standard circulation. Comedic electrocutions, meanwhile, strobe the victim's skeleton to reveal the body's boney platform, a flesh-and-blood capacitor momentarily almost overwhelmed by an excessive flow of power. Magnetic induction, in turn, is in every aspect the uncanny supplement of conductive electricity. As any child who has played with a magnet knows, magnetism can be witnessed only indexically—iron filings made to move across a table; metals irresistibly summoned through the open air; two magnets that palpably resist making contact, despite the apparent "nothingness" that divides them. When associated with the body, magnetism ("animal" and otherwise) is a radiant energy that suffuses and surrounds. Auras, vibes, ghosts, telepathy, telekinesis, astral projection—all depend on an undulating field of occult influence. Cartoon images of the mesmerized, hypnotized, bewitched, and brainwashed often depict this alteration through the convention of eyeballs transformed into spinning spiral discs, a signifier that the individual has been enthralled by some external, invisible power. Willpower draws on both energies, capable of assuming both forms. In conductive terms, mind supervises rational will as applied power, the ego directing instrumental energy through the body's nervous networks toward a specific goal or target. Inductively, the mind uses occult power to project its will as an uncanny emanation that floats within or beyond the physical body.

This alliance of rational conduction and occult induction would become especially central to modern psychosis. As Michael Eigen argues, the "mental ego" in psychosis finds itself vulnerable to the "permeability and penetrability of the subject by an alien mind." Of psychotic experience, Eigen writes, "Space and physical boundaries become meaningless. Thoughts can instantaneously be everywhere and anywhere." This is essentially the environment facing all citizens of modernity and beyond, especially as electronics have accelerated conversions between conduction and induction. It is in such an environment that "influencing machines" begin to emerge as a solution. Writes Eigen, "The patient's greatest fears seem to focus not merely on a reduced and mechanized body (the latter is almost comforting), but also on the electrifyingly impalpable threat of invisible mental power as such."[215] To become a machine or to fall under a machine's influence is "comforting" to the extent that the mental ego repairs its immediate relationship to the surrounding world. Less certain, however, are the agents who produce the "impalpable threat of invisible mental power as such." By definition, an influencing machine implies the presence of an *influencer*, a motive operating behind the mechanism.

The System

CHAPTER FOUR

IN *AUTOBIOGRAPHY OF A SCHIZOPHRENIC GIRL* (1951), Renee Sechehaye provides a vivid account of the tension encountered in her childhood and teenage years: "Suddenly a wave of anxiety would creep over me, the anxiety of unreality. My perception of the world seemed to sharpen the sense of the strangeness of things. In the silence and immensity, each object was cut off by a knife, detached in the emptiness, in the boundlessness, spaced off from other things. Without any relationship to the environment, just by being itself, it began to come to life."[1] Sechehaye also describes a sense of "deadness" while walking the streets, a common prodromal sense of depersonalization that renders the external world into a type of static movie set: "I was rejected by the world, on the outside of life, a spectator of a chaotic film unrolling ceaselessly before my eyes, in which I would never have a part. In these awful moments, without protection, inexplicably ill, I could only submit."[2] During therapy sessions with her analyst and eventual adoptive mother, Marguerite Sechehaye, Renee recalls a similarly anxious nightmare from her childhood:

> A barn, brilliantly illuminated by electricity. The walls painted white, smooth—smooth and shining. In the immensity, a needle—fine, pointed, hard, glittering in the light. The needle in the emptiness filled me with excruciating terror. Then a haystack fills up the emptiness and engulfs the needle. The haystack, small at first, swells and swells and in the center, the needle, endowed with tremendous electrical force, communicates its charge to the hay. The electrical current, the invasion by the hay, and blinding light combine to augment the fear of a paroxysm of terror and I wake up screaming, "The needle, the needle!"[3]

Renee's nightmare involves no "finding" of the needle in the haystack. Instead, it presents the irresistible radiation of that which typically should remain hidden, buried, submerged. But the needle remains, charging the hay, no matter how large the surrounding haystack. The meaning of this radiating needle appears fairly straightforward, at least from a psychoanalytic perspective:

a girl at the threshold of puberty confronts the horrors of a needle "swelling" with "tremendous electrical force." Elsewhere in the autobiography, Renee recalls how she developed an acute fear of bright electrical light very early in her childhood. The "brilliantly illuminated" barn is thus another anxious figure in the dream. "Enlightenment" (*éclairer*) is a key term throughout Renee's account of her illness. *Éclairer* can mean "enlighten," as in the realization of knowledge—an epiphany, an awareness, an understanding. But in the original French, *éclairer* also connotes *illumination* and *electrification*. Renee's nightmare of the electric needle in the bright light of the barn is thus an epiphany of illuminations displaced, the realization of a terrifying psychosexual secret that cannot be hidden within the radiating electrical forces of enlightenment. No little girl can escape the phallic needle of electrified anxiety. Significantly, Renee refers to her waking episodes of derealization as entering the "land of light," a somewhat perverse use of this Enlightenment metaphor to signal her entrance into an utterly incomprehensible world of brutal alienation. "It was as if an electric current of extraordinary power ran through every object," she writes, "building until the whole blew up in a frightful explosion."[4]

Renee gradually cultivates a fantasy to explain the sinister *agency* behind this program of terrifying electrical illumination. She described her tormentors simply as "the System": "I thought of it as some vast world-like entity encompassing all men. The System organized the world in a hierarchy of interdependent guilt and punishment, binding all men under 'the scourge of culpability.'"[5] Renee's curse—her illness—is to recognize the existence of the System, a social reality that is invisible to most. Drifting into more acute psychosis, Renee devises an ingenious defense against the System: "In dreams and in waking fantasies I constructed an electric machine to blow up the earth and everyone with it. But what was even worse, with the machine I would rob all men of their brains, thus creating robots obedient to my will alone. This was my greatest, most terrible revenge." Overwhelmed by the System's blinding illuminations of unreality, Renee in effect constructs a type of "anti-influencing machine" at the often perilous border between childhood fantasy and teenage delusion, an elegantly direct form of defensive projection-turned-*defensive protection*. But in the end, this "electrical machine" would have its revenge against Renee. Although she created it as a protective fantasy, she eventually realized that the "machine" was in fact her external persecutor: she did not control the electrical machine; the electrical machine controlled her. "The ring closed," she remembers. "The land of enlightenment was the same as the System."[6]

As with influencing technologies, the influential agents who control the System have shifted over time. In the premodern era, lunatics enduring imaginary persecution located the source of this tormenting power in either local or cosmic terms. The influencer might be a family member or a neighbor, or it could be God or Satan (or some combination of these agents). Industrialism's harnessing of steam, electricity, and other modes of power produced not only a rapid sequence of technological innovations, but also a public discourse preoccupied with predicting the impact these devices might have on society. Key to such discourse was the question of instrumental power. Which agents and agencies would be the forces innovating, guiding, and supervising these new technical powers? Accordingly, the psychotic "influencer" begins to assume new identities. While local and cosmic threats were still abundant, increasingly common were persecutors drawn from the more anonymous ranks of bureaucracy, science, industrialism, and the government, the functionaries associated with the emergence of the "disciplinary" state. As Michel Foucault argues in his canonical account of this shift in political power, the eighteenth and nineteenth centuries witnessed the emergence of a complex network of knowledges, practices, and technologies designed to administer to the health, safety, and security of the newly recognized "social body." Foucault argues that this transition depended in large part on the implementation of an institutional "power over life," knowledge that proceeded from two overlapping moments in the redefinition of the "body politic." The first moment "centered on the body as a machine: its disciplining, the optimization of its capabilities, the extortion of forces, the parallel increase of its usefulness and its docility, its integration into systems of efficient and economic controls, all this was ensured by the procedures of power that characterized the *disciplines: an anatomo-politics of the human body."*[7] Foucault then describes a second but crucially interdependent moment involving the "social" or "species" body: "the body imbued with the mechanics of life and serving as the basis of the biological processes: propagation, births, mortality, the level of health, life expectancy and longevity, with all the conditions that can cause these to vary. Their supervision was effected through an entire series of interventions and regulatory controls: *a bio-politics of the population."*[8] The first power reframed conceptions of the biological body not just in anatomy and medicine, but also in a wide range of disciplines that had an interest in exploiting its functions. Here is where the energetic body, the self as a type of machine, would take hold as a popular concept (and, at times, a psychotic delusion). The second power involves a more governmental and scientific administration of the social body. Here the individual becomes the vector of larger forces (disease, crime, poverty, insanity, deviance, and so on) that must be monitored by the state for the overall protection of society. Man the machine becomes subject to the machinery of the social order: bureaucracy, administration, the System.

The dynamics of *will* and *power* were of interest to both of these politics, the body and the social body bound through mysterious dynamics of motivation, energy, and control. As we have seen, popular logics of conduction and induction produced an energetic framework for understanding flows of energy and fields of consciousness, making the nervous system a pivotal network in imagining the "anatomo-politics" of the body. In the nineteenth century, these logics gradually became aligned with a cybernetic integration of body and machine as mirrored systems of regulation and control. In terms of sane metaphor and psychotic delusion, then, media technologies became the conduit intermediating the nervous system and the System as "an entire series of interventions and regulatory controls" for the biopolitical management of the social body. Those who had previously negotiated relations of power that were primarily local and interpersonal now increasingly contended with the "powers that be," more anonymous agents of supervision and control that, in the logic of the biopolitical, were assuming more and more authority within and over the social body. This is the Kafkaesque core of the System—a sinister bureaucracy in which no one individual occupies a determinative position of power. The System is everywhere and nowhere at the same time, impossible to isolate or meaningfully engage at any particular nodal point and yet virtually omnipotent in its ability to control an individual's social spaces and actions. The rise of the modern influencing machine and other technical delusions could not happen without the rise of modern technology, certainly, but equally crucial to this paranoid invention was the advent and dominance of the biopolitical systems believed to have access and authority in shaping electricity through the politics of the electronic. Paranoid psychotics, it would seem, have been remarkably sensitive to the occult integration of anatomo-political and biopolitical systems. For example, Renee recalls writing a letter as she slipped more deeply into her psychosis to "the unknown author of my suffering." Renee hopes that a reasonable, heartfelt letter addressed to the agents in the System behind her terrifying symptoms will bring an end to her electrifying torments. But as Renee finally realizes, "Because I did not know where to send my letter, I tore it up."[9]

Institutionalized

While many lunatics of the early nineteenth century continued to attribute their persecution to friends, family, and assorted supernatural presences, a growing number focused their anxiety on the figure newly empowered to judge madness as a pathology: the physician. There is a long history of popular suspicion over the expertise and competence of the healer, apothecary, and physician. But this antagonism took a new form in the early nineteenth century as doctors of body and mind, variously defined and educated, began working toward more consecrated professional identities and, with this recognition, increased authority over the "medico-juridical" fate of an individual patient. Crucial to the implementation of disciplinary bio-power was the widespread implementation of new standards in the education, regulation, and evaluation of medical professionals. Thomas Percival's *Medical Ethics, or a Code of Institutes and Precepts, Adapted to the Professional Conduct of Physicians and Surgeons*, first published in 1803, is widely regarded as a key text in formalizing the standards of medical education.[10] In the United States, the *New England Journal of Medicine and Surgery and Collateral Branches of Science* (now known as the venerable *New England Journal of Medicine*) began publication in 1812 as an official organ of medical science. *The Lancet* performed a similar function in England beginning in 1823. The accreditation of the physician produced a system for diagnosing and, if necessary, confining a patient as insane, often against the patient's will. For those suspected of lunacy, the physician thus became the embodied representative of the larger institutions of power that assumed authority over the individual in the eighteenth and nineteenth centuries. The supervising physician also wielded an assortment of potentially terrifying technical powers over the institutionalized patient. These interventions varied from "bleeding" (still practiced as late as the eighteenth century) to "rotational therapy" (spinning in a chair) and the "bath of surprise" (dunking the insane, without warning, into ice-cold water as a means of "shocking" their system back to reason).

Patients learned quickly that resisting these interventions would only make their plight that much worse; indeed, this lesson was central to the therapeutic strategies of early psychiatry. In his lectures on psychiatric power, delivered the year before the landmark publication of *Discipline and Punish*, Foucault invokes a historical tableau that vividly captures this newfound authority at the close of the eighteenth century. In 1788, a manic and seemingly mad King George III was removed to a private asylum for treatment by the famed expert on insanity Thomas Willis. The physician and his

FIG 4.1 Rotational therapy machine for the treatment of the insane, from Alexander Morison's *Cases of Mental Disease* (1828).

attendants stripped "all trappings of royalty" and consigned the king to an "isolated place." "The person directing the treatment tells him that he is no longer sovereign," Foucault writes, "but that he must henceforth be obedient and submissive." Worse yet, "Two of his old pages, of Herculean stature, are charged with looking after his needs … but also with convincing him that he is entirely subordinate to them and must now obey them."[11] The manic king hurls his feces at his former servants. But these commoners now have absolute power over their (temporarily) displaced king: "One of the pages immediately enters the room without saying a word, grasps by his belt the delirious madman … [and] forcibly throws him down on a pile of mattresses, strips him, washes him with a sponge, changes his clothes, and, looking at him haughtily, immediately leaves to take up his post again."[12] Important to the success of this therapy is the psychiatrist's ability to project his authority and instill his will into the patient. In other words, a most basic tactic was to create, as quickly as possible, an imbalance of power between the physician and his charge, what Foucault describes as "the substitution of a 'foreign will' for the patient's will." The patient must feel himself immediately confronted by something in which all the reality he will face in the asylum is summed up and concentrated in the doctor's foreign and omnipotent will."[13] As a physician commented in 1842, the "raving lunatic" must be confronted with a powerful gaze. "Under the rebuke of a deportment of command, and masterly eye, he quails and retreats."[14]

It is perhaps not surprising that so many lunatics, confronted by this "foreign will," would imagine the physician as the mostly likely architect of their symptoms and the most powerful agent over their fate. In the political turmoil of the French Revolution, Jean-Étienne Dominique Esquirol noted that a fear of imprisonment or civil punishment often made the insane "express as much dread of the tribunals of justice, as they formerly entertained of the influence of demons and of evil spirits."[15] While visiting the Bethlem asylum in 1821, meanwhile, an American reported of its inmates: "Many took us aside with coherent well-told tales of the treacherous devices by which they had been trepanned into a place of confinement:—some of which really sounded so probable, that if this were not known to be the commonest of delusions that prevail in these cases, it would have been difficult to withhold belief from such very circumstantial details."[16] Adjudicated as insane, these lunatics nevertheless recognized quite correctly that their incarceration somehow issued from the collaborative authority of the physician and the state—however inchoate remained the exact function and power of the two agents. The association of medicine with technologies of electrification also made the physician a consistent suspect for implementing nervous influence over the patient. A physician writing in 1835 recalled a patient suffering "neuralgic pains" who "fancied that the physician to whose care he was confided had the power of torturing him by electricity, and that invisible wires were spread through every part of the house as conductors of the fluid, which was used at night as the instrument of cruel and tyrannical persecution."[17] The basic paranoid relationship of patient and physician has remained a familiar theme in psychotic ideation ever since. "Electricity Was Her Nemesis" blares a headline from 1897. "The electricity is in the house of my physician," testified Elizabeth Turner during her own commitment hearing. "He is a good man, but he keeps electricity in his house and people come and go to his house and get the electricity and come to me to put it in my blood and bones." In the end, Turner was deemed a "proper subject for the lunatic asylum."[18]

The late eighteenth and early nineteenth centuries also saw the rise of "protest literature": letters and essays written to appeal unjust confinement. Institutionalized in a madhouse between 1778 and 1795, William Belcher recognized that his "real lunacy" was actually a product of the asylum and its practices, insisting that the "trade" in madness was "a horrible disgrace to government and to society." In his missive, titled *Address to Humanity, Containing a Letter to Dr. Munro, a Receipt to Make a Lunatic, and Seize His Estates, and a Sketch of a True Smiling Hyena* (1796), Belcher pledged to devote his remaining years to reforming this corrupt public institution: "In a nation in which such outrages as I have experienced are practiced with impunity, and their prosecution discountenanced, no man is safe from living or dying in a strait waistcoat."[19] Diabolically, the most damning proof of one's insanity was the fact that he or she had already been confined as insane. Even worse, the success of a patient, once in the asylum, in proving his sanity could only present an embarrassing failure to the psychiatric enterprise as a whole. In a practice so dependent on the performance of authority, any admission of a mistake necessarily lessened the power and credibility of the physician, giving him little incentive—financially or professionally—for reversing a diagnosis. Belcher gets to the Foucauldian heart of psychiatric power: "Another dreadful aggravation is that every degree of resentment against the authors of their ruin, is considered as a presumption of remaining insanity in the sufferer, who has hardly any chance of restoration without their consent."[20] An American critique of the madhouse industry from 1834 makes a similar argument: "His very denial is considered as evidence against him, and his moderation is regarded as the proverbial cunning with which the lunatic endeavors to effect his escape."[21] Or, as still another institutionalized patient of the era noted, "How do those commissioners arrive at the knowledge that the patients are actually insane? . . . This is the grand secret."[22]

A brief notice in the *London Observer* from 1849 documents just how vague this "grand secret" remained at mid-century, especially when it encountered the equally vague secrets of electricity.[23] Edwards Vicars, a distiller from Liverpool, escaped from an asylum after two years of confinement. "His delusion was an enormous faith in the powers of electricity," noted the *Observer*. This, however, did not necessarily mean that Vicars was insane: "Considering how little is known of that science, even by the learned themselves, [this] will not appear irrational to the uninterested reader." The editorial continues, "He believed, for instance, that electricity made men mad." But this, too, was not necessarily an "unreasonable belief," the paper continued, "if the identity of that fluid and animal magnetism be once admitted." Vicars was also said to harbor the delusion that "magistrates, doctors, and lawyers were leagued together to drive people insane." Even this was an entirely reasonable supposition, argued the *Observer*, noting that Vicars was only professing "a faith in which he has many sincere fellow believers." Vicars in fact presented a rather coherent and, for many, quite plausible account of the era's new configuration of biopolitical power: lawyers, judges, and doctors, in league with one another, constituted a type of insanity industry. Each had a vested interest in producing the insane to motivate profitable litigation, confinement, and treatment. For Vicars, electricity was the medium of influence that allowed this conspiracy to continue, a not unreasonable assumption (judged the *Observer*), given how many still associated this energy with the larger occult mysteries of magnetism and metaphysics. Not only did this cabal conspire to drive people insane, Vicars reasoned; they had also wired his asylum with "telegraphic wires" to keep the inmates in a constant state of madness. In the end, a jury agreed with the editors and found that, while Vicars "might be a free liver ... , he was no lunatic." The *Observer* invoked Vicars's case as further evidence of the potential for abuse in England's thriving system of private asylums. For the *Observer*, the Vicars case was yet another example of the appalling lack of standards and supervision in diagnosing and confining the so-called insane. All asylums should be public, the paper argued, but even then, there "can be no wise law of lunacy until the limits between eccentricity and madness are clearly laid down; until the theory of 'delusions' is philosophically enunciated, and finally, in a word, insanity is defined."[24] As now happens every decade or so in revising *The Diagnostic and Statistical Manual of Mental Disorders*, the *Observer* called for a greater consensus on diagnostic criteria: "Until then the lunacy law is a tragi-comedy, and the lunacy commissioners are but the chief actors—their theatres being the private asylums of the country."[25]

Issues of psychiatric authority also figured heavily in what is generally regarded as the first documented case of a psychotic influencing machine. On December 30, 1796, James Tilley Matthews disrupted a debate in the British House of Commons by shouting accusations of treason from the gallery. His target was Robert Banks Jenkinson, soon to become Lord Liverpool and then, in 1812, prime minister of England. After his outburst, Matthews was escorted from the gallery and taken into custody for questioning. He explained that Jenkinson had betrayed the nation by continuing a needless war with France for purely political reasons. Matthews claimed to have firsthand knowledge of this deceit because he had personally conducted a diplomatic mission to Paris in an attempt to prevent the war. While this may sound like ravings of delusional grandeur, Matthews's claim was essentially true.[26] Rightly or wrongly, Matthews had indeed made a trip to Paris and appeared to believe he had the unofficial backing of Lord Liverpool. A month after publicly accusing Jenkinson of treason, Matthews entered the confines of Bethlem Royal Hospital. He would remain institutionalized as a lunatic until his death in 1815.

After a year of confinement, Matthews was judged incurable. His family petitioned for a second opinion, leading to a brief hearing. Back at Bethlem, the diagnosis reaffirmed, Matthews asserted the trip had been nothing more than a "pretext to implant a magnet into his brain."[27] The family made another attempt to free Matthews in 1809 by submitting affidavits testifying to his sanity and demanding the right of habeas corpus. Arguing against Matthews's release was Joseph Haslam, the apothecary of Bethlem who also served as its de facto supervisor. Haslam had been in charge of Matthews's case for a decade, during which time he had encouraged Matthews to write his own account of his story. Matthews's writings (and drawings), as edited and presented by Haslam, became the central documents in demonstrating to the court that Matthews continued to be insane.[28] As refracted through Haslam, Matthews disclosed the details of an elaborate device he believed was responsible for his misfortunes: a machine he called the "air loom." Matthews was so certain of this device's existence, in fact, that he was able to draft a detailed schematic illustrating its design and operation. The air loom produced "magnetized gases" that could be guided through the atmosphere to target unwitting enemies. Matthews believed that the air loom was controlled by a "gang of villains profoundly skilled in Pneumatic Chemistry" operating from an apartment near London Wall.[29] The gang, working for the Jacobin French, consisted of seven members, a motley band distinguished by a proto-Dickensian attention to character type and detail: "Bill the King," "Jack the Schoolmaster," "Sir Archy," "Middle Man," Augusia, Charlotte, and "Glove Woman." Matthews believed that the air loom was capable of a number of extraordinary interventions, many of which appear to anticipate contemporary schizophrenic delusions of paranoia somatica. These miraculous affordances included "thigh talking" (compelling the victim to believe that his hearing has been transposed to the "external part of the thigh"), "lobster-cracking" (tightening the magnetic energy around a victim to strangle circulation and vital energy), and "apoplexy-working with the nutmeg-grater" (forcing fluids into the head to produce "small pimples on the temples").[30] Beyond these rather noisome physical symptoms (the machine could produce bladder stones, as well, we are told), the air loom implemented phenomena akin to thought insertion and thought broadcasting. In "kiting," "magnetic impregnations" place an extraneous idea in the brain that the victim is unable to banish from his thoughts.[31] "Voice sayings" are communications made between the gang and the victim directly through the auditory nerve, "without producing the ordinary vibrations of the air."[32] Especially complicated was the process of "thought-making," a seemingly self-explanatory procedure that in fact in-

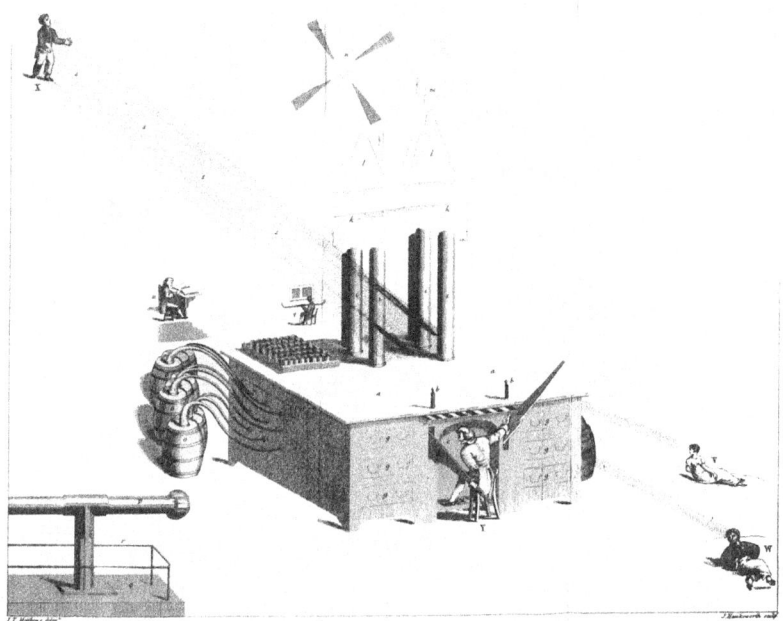

FIG 4.2 James Tilley Matthews's rendering of the air loom, published as evidence of Matthews's insanity in Joseph Haslam's *Illustrations of Madness* (1810). Republished with permission from Bethlem Museum of the Mind.

volved one member of the gang "sucking at the brain of the person assailed, to extract his existing sentiments" while another forced into his mind "a train of ideas very different from the real subject of his thoughts."[33] Matthews described the air loom as a keyboard-controlled device capable of quantifying, manipulating, and then targeting the occult powers of mesmerism. By sitting at an organ with keys and stops, a member of the gang in effect "played" the device by mixing various gases (made from such substances as "horse gas" and "seminal fluid") and then transmitting them up to one thousand feet.

After prevailing before the court, Haslam published much of his evidence in 1810 as *Illustrations of Madness*. Many regard Haslam's monograph as the first extensive case study in psychiatric history, but as Mike Jay argues, this misunderstands the purpose of the document. *Illustrations of Madness* was not a "case study" in the modern sense as an overview of symptoms presented for diagnosis. It was instead a missive aimed directly at the physicians who had dared to pronounce Matthews sane, thus leading to the court proceedings of 1809 and the demand that Haslam defend his judgment. As Jay notes, the full title of Haslam's monograph reiterates Matthews's fundamental insanity

FIG 4.3 "Nellie Practices Insanity at Home," from Nellie Bly's *Ten Days in a Mad-House* (1887).

while also taking a swipe at the authorities who had challenged Haslam's professional opinion: *Illustrations of Madness: Exhibiting a Singular Case of Insanity, and No Less Remarkable Difference in Medical Opinion: Developing the Nature of Assailment and the Manner of Working Events; with a Description of the Tortures Experienced by Bomb-Bursting, Lobster-Cracking, and Lengthening the Brain.* In his preface, Haslam announces that his aim in publishing the book is perhaps to "turn the attention of medical men to the subject of professional etiquette, and to a consideration of those nice feelings and reciprocal charities, which confer on practitioners of medicine the amiable distinction of a fraternity."[34] Mad or not, Matthews found himself at the center of a medico-juridical battle in which issues of professional standards, political favor, and legal authority were in dramatic contestation.

Suspicion about the motives of evil physicians, psychiatrists, and asylum directors remains a prominent mode of paranoid ideation. Over the past two centuries, anxiety over "psychiatric power" has even produced an entire subgenre of popular suspense fiction. The protest literature of the eighteenth and nineteenth centuries, often a fusion of lived experience and gothic convention, did much to fashion the horrors of the sane suffering through involuntary confinement. There is thus the panicked asylum patient, unjustly committed, desperately hoping to make the most of his limited contact with the supervising physician to prove his sanity. There is also the inmate who, held prisoner by the System of the asylum, must find a way to plead her case to someone outside the medico-juridical circuit of power that enforces her confinement. Nellie Bly's *Ten Days in a Mad-House* (1887) popularized the idea of an undercover investigator feigning madness to gain admittance to the asylum (in some variations, proximity to madness actually drives the undercover investigator insane).[35] There is also the bureaucratic horror of the sane investigator unable to prove his real identity, trapping him in the System for days, months, or years. In the "mad doctor" plot, the chief psychiatrist or director of the asylum himself has gone insane, using his patients for hideous experiments, perhaps under the guise of curing mental illness, or perhaps not. Edgar Allan Poe explored similar territory in "The System of Doctor Tarr and Professor Fether" (1845), in which a man visiting an asylum discovers in the end that the lunatics have imprisoned their keepers and have been masquerading as the staff.[36] Such "reversal" narratives speak to a popular recognition of insanity's relativity and public suspicion about the new institutions that were in the process of assuming such absolute power over diagnosis and confinement.[37] Even today, mistaken-insanity plots hinge less on the diagnosis than on the incredible challenge of extricating oneself from the psychiatric system. Those wrongly accused of a crime can be cleared by additional evidence or another's confession, but those wrongly institutionalized as insane face a narrative dilemma that can be solved only by "outsmarting" the powers behind the institutionalization or beyond the asylum walls.

Disordered Bodies

The earliest technical delusions emerged from this relatively simple alliance between psychiatric and electronic power. Typically direct and localized, these plots imagined an electrification of the physician's "foreign will." As the disciplinary state matured, with its technologies of power more firmly entrenched, the dynamics of will and power began to trigger new delusional presentations. Supporting these new delusional forms was an implicit equation between biological and social disorder, a biopolitical schematic that promoted the mirroring of the body and body politic in terms of a homeostatic ideal. Introducing his 1733 treatise on "nervous diseases of all kinds," George Cheyne invited the reader to envision the human apparatus in which such "disorder" could take hold. He described the body as "a Machin of an infinite Number and Variety of different Channels and Pipes, filled with various and different Liquors and Fluids,—perpetually running, [gliding], or creeping forward, or returning backward, in a constant' Circle, and sending out little Branches and Outlets, to moisten, nourish, and repair the Expenses Of Living."[38] Cheyne's treatise addressed "the English Malady," which he defined as "a Reproach universally thrown on this Island by Foreigners," alleging that the British were particularly prone to "nervous distempers, Spleen, Vapours, and Lowness of Spirits."[39] Cheyne wished there were not "good grounds for this reflection," but quickly conceded that a third of the English population did indeed suffer from various "nervous disorders." There were many culprits: the moisture in the air, the variability of weather, the richness of the food. But Cheyne also turned the tables on England's derisive neighbors. The English Malady was a malady, certainly, but such disordering was to be expected, given England's superior "wealth and abundance," an advantage secured by "the inactivity and sedentary occupations of the better sort (among whom this evil mostly rages)." The center of this prosperous disordering was London, of course, which Cheyne then vividly rendered as a city so dynamic in its activities as to have created a stagnant atmosphere of sulfurous fires, fetid oil, stinking breath and perspiration, diseased animals (intelligent and unintelligent), crowded churches, putrefying bodies, sinks, butcher houses, stables, and dunghills. This stench, he observed, "must alter, weaken, and destroy the healthiest Constitutions of Animals of all Kinds," an infectious air that "transubstantiated into the Habits" of those living in a great city.[40] *The English Malady* in effect pits two bodies of circulation against each other: human pipes, channels, and vibrations in a state of hypothetical balance confronted by the city as a putrid symphony of disorder (channeling many of the same noxious substances only just recently in the human body). Without proper precautions (or occasional respites to the country for those so able), the sheer excrescence of the city would inevitably unbalance the "constant circle" of balanced flows and vibrations in the body, a disequilibrium portrayed by Cheyne, in the pre-Galvani era, as a disruption of the body's stabilizing binaries (dry and wet, hot and cold, flexible and brittle, and so on). The body, like the city, would become blocked, sluggish, foul, and out of balance.[41]

In a now distant language and logic, *The English Malady* presented the basics of a "cultural epidemiology," a nascent sociology seeking to make connections between illness and environment. In 1808, physician Thomas Trotter continued these explorations in his study *A View of the Nervous Temperament: Being a Practical Inquiry into the Increasing Prevalence, Prevention, and Treat-*

ment of Those Diseases Commonly Called Nervous, Bilious, Stomach and Liver Complaints, Indigestion, Low Spirits, Gout, &c. Endorsing many of Cheyne's observations, Trotter was even more detailed in his social survey of nervous disorder.[42] He began by comparing the daily stresses of life in a "savage state" with those of "modern times" to establish a psychosocial theme that would dominate the next two centuries—namely, that advances in civilization introduce the potential for an excessive stimulation of the nerves. Also like Cheyne, Trotter placed particular emphasis on the city as the capital of nervous disorder. But Trotter's "pollution" presented a fundamentally different hazard from Cheyne's foul air and alleyways, a menace that Trotter captured by illustrating the "life cycle" of a city. "A narrow port is by degrees widened into a capacious harbor," Trotter began. As commercial trade increased, so, too, did the "coffeehouse, the inn, and the tavern." Things go downhill quickly:

> Then the rout commences, to teach the young the arts of gaming; and the midnight masquerade initiates them into the wiles of intrigue. The riot disturbs sleep; the drunkard is seen staggering home, in danger of robbery and death; and the woman of the town, deserted by her destroyer, is seeking reprisals, and looking for prey in the streets. Now the hospital and bedlam appear in the suburbs; the first to receive the poor, sick, and lame; and the other to confine the more wretched in mind.... Morals and health are alike committed in this vortex of wealth and dissipation.[43]

This is the London of George W. M. Reynolds, the Paris of Eugene Sue, and the Philadelphia of George Lippard, cities that "may be truly called a hot-bed for the passions; all the vices that more particularly enervate the constitution and injure health, can be there practiced long without suspicion or restraint, and indulged to the utmost: thus the young and inexperienced are quickly initiated into every fashionable folly, and a vortex of dissipation."[44] In the late eighteenth century, nervous disorders became a function of sensitivity, an overstimulation of nervous tension that transformed the system's natural "irritability" into the disorders of "irritation." As Foucault notes, this made the "nervous" more culpable in their illness "as everything to which they were attached in the world, the life that they led, the affections that they had had, the passions and fantasies that they had nourished with excessive indulgence, all melted into the an irritation of the nerves, where they found their natural effect and their moral punishment."[45] Bad climate, air, and food still had a place in disordering the nerves, but to this list were added the excessive stimulation of "reading novels, theatrical spectacles, an immoderate zeal for the sciences, an excessive passion for sex," and various other vices enabled by the city and the so-called advance of civilization.[46] Or, as Trotter succinctly writes, "The more complicated and various the pleasures and business, which man is to pursue in life, he will be the more liable to defeat and disappointment; and the more ardent his passions, they will the sooner terminate in exhaustion and disgust."[47] Trotter's solution, predictably, was that Great Britain could protect its "commercial greatness" only by returning to a "simplicity of living and manners." If it did not, Britain would become—like Rome—easy prey of its invaders, who would then "ultimately convert us to a nation of slaves and idiots."[48]

With the advent of the electromagnetic telegraph in the mid-nineteenth century, the exciting and excitable body politic received its own galvanic nervous system. Analogies of circulation, now energized by the example of galvanic conduction, attached themselves to the telegraph to conceptualize the electronic binding of information and power within the social body. Like the nervous system, the telegraph was a conduit for energetic power and a network for electronic messaging. As Iwan Rhys Morus argues, the nervous system and the telegraph were "systems that seemed to transmit intelligence instantaneously," and within this affordance, "both systems were to do with regulation."[49] The striking parallel between the "nervous system" and the "telegraphic network" was immediately apparent to all manner of Victorian thinkers. "The thousands of miles of electric wire which already span our globe, cannot fail to strike every one as the equivalents of those nerves, which unite in sympathy all the members of the body," wrote George Wilson in 1860. And just as the nervous system represented the "last and highest development of every organism," the spread of telegraphy heralded the arrival of mankind's coming apotheosis: "The analogy is no far-fetched one, but presses itself upon every thoughtful man's notice."[50] All analogies are reversible, of course, allowing anatomists to explain the body's nervous system as a network of telegraphic communications. A public lecture on anatomy thus describes the cerebellum as "a sort of switchboard for the telegraph wires running from the motor area of the brain to different parts of the body."[51] Through decades of repetition, the telegraph analogy of nervous wiring would become so ubiquitous as to eventually appear self-evident: nerves are the communications network of the body, and wires are the nerves of the machine.

Telegraphy's rapid expansion around the world also produced a new type of *public* and, with it, a new terrain for imagining the administration of energetic and political power. As a functioning technology, the telegraph physically connected more and more localities into a public circuit of instantaneous telecommunications, laying the groundwork for all subsequent communications networks to follow. At the same time, telegraphy as a concept encouraged individuals to reimagine their interface with the larger body politic, rethinking the relationship between the individual and the social.[52] Benedict Anderson has described this transformation in terms of the "imagined community," a psychic empire that is generally equivalent to the idea of the nation-state.[53] As Anderson argues, modernity witnessed a move from premodern investments in the power of "religious community" and "the dynastic realm" to a growing self-recognition of social membership through emerging bonds of an imagined nation-state. For Anderson, the imagined community depends on citizens' recognizing their mutual investment in relations of abstract simultaneity: "that each person is but one subject nevertheless linked to the simultaneous invisible activities of their social others."[54] Anderson argues that this community is "imaginary" in that most members will never meet one another. It is "limited" in that no matter how large the community, it has "finite, if elastic, boundaries." And it is a "community" in that, "regardless of the actual inequality and exploitation" in the nation-state, it remains a "deep, horizontal comradeship."[55]

This new sense of community had already begun to take shape with the rapid growth of print media in the late eighteenth and early nineteenth centuries. The focus of nineteenth-century realist fiction, for example, in Europe and the United States increasingly centered on protagonists entering into and exploring the larger networks of contemporary society. Newspapers contributed even more immediately to this visualization of the public. The explosive growth of the city during the Industrial Revolution produced economies of scale that allowed daily newspapers to reach what was arguably the first mass audience. As Anderson argues, the very date on the masthead provided "the essential connection—the steady onward clocking of homogenous, empty time" for a nation briefly gathered around the ritualistic consumption of the day's "news."[56] At mid-century, with telegraphy poised for mass diffusion across the nation and world, commentators began to anticipate how this device would radically transform this evolving sense of a public sphere. "The wires of the Telegraph will be the nerves of the press, vibrating with every impression received at the remotest extremities of the country," noted one enthusiast in 1846.[57] With telegraphy, the already familiar analogy of nerve and wire increasingly focused on the idea of territorial equivalency:

It is almost certain that within a few months the Magnetic Telegraph, which is literally material Thought and flies as swift, absolutely annihilating space and running in advance of time, will be extended to all the great Cities in the Union—so that a net-work of nerves of iron wire, strung with lightning, will ramify from the brain, New-York, to the distant limbs and members,—to the Atlantic sea-board towns, to Pittsburgh, Cincinnati, Louisville, Nashville, St. Louis and New-Orleans,—and that every commercial, political, or social event transpiring at either of these points, will be known at the very instant it happens, in all!"[58]

In this expansion and acceleration, the telegraph thus produced a new public in a most material sense: a world that had not existed (at least in terms of instantaneous participation) suddenly became manifest, a social body powered by the cabled nerves of this new communications complex. As Michael Garvey observed of telegraphy in 1852, "This marvelous agent seems destined to consolidate and harmonize the social union of mankind, by furnishing a sensitive apparatus analogous to the nervous system of the living frame, which will make men conscious of their mutual dependency, and diffuse throughout every division and portion of our race that primary instinct which combines all the organs and faculties of the living being for the preservation of that union which is their life."[59] Circulation and equilibrium, so central to the human organism, would now prevail in the social body through the regulated flow of telegraphic power.

Just as the mechanics of the human brain somehow hosted the mysterious presence of the human mind, analogic thinking assumed that telegraphic nerves hosted the equally occult dynamics of the public mind. In 1860, *Scientific American* observed, "These wires interlace our hamlets, towns and cities, and, in the same manner as the impulses of the human mind are conveyed along the nerves of the body, so are the volitions of the public mind communicated by telegraphic instruments along the 'electric nerves' which ramify the national telegraphic system."[60] Writers knew this was an analogy and therefore should not be seen as a literal equivalency, yet the analogy itself was so persuasive, so vivid, that the line between literal and figurative consciousness in the body politic was consistently blurred. In the introduction to *The Body Politic*, written in the immediate aftermath of the American Civil War, William Horatio Barnes argued that the "public mind" was not unlike the "'vital spark of heavenly flame' which glows within the human breast. Did we know the deep foundations of the individual soul, and its mode of existence, we might comprehend the public mind."[61] A system of nervous communication, he wrote, "is essential to the health and safety of the body politic, for without it our country would be little better than contiguous masses of plains and mountains."[62] Without telecommunications to give the social body cohesion, in other words, it would be little more than the unanimated body parts of Victor Frankenstein's creature. Barnes, a Unionist seeking to promote a new homeostasis in the body politic, described the Confederacy's brief secession as a "galvanic shock": "In medical practice the galvanic battery is sometimes used with good effect upon nervous and paralytic patients. The batteries of rebellion brought to bear upon the body politic, with intent to produce dismemberment, had the contrary effect. The Republic, aroused from lethargy and divested of foolish fears, met the emergency with a strength and calmness which astonished all beholders. The vigorous effort gave strength and tone to disordered nerves, and restored health and soundness to the public mind."[63]

Even more exhaustive in exploring this analogy was the British philosopher Herbert Spencer. Today Spencer is remembered as a primary architect of social Darwinism. His essay "The Social Organism" (1860) certainly contributes to this tradition, describing society's development from a primitive embryonic state to the fully functioning complexities of (British) civilization. Spencer offered four principles that linked the biological and social bodies, not limb for limb or organ for organ in an anthropomorphic mirroring, but as abstract "organisms" that nevertheless exhibit similar trajectories of gestation and development.[64] These common features can be summarized as (1) massification; (2) structuration; (3) interdependence; and (4) reproduction. Spencer argued that a division between the "governing" and "governed" classes could be found in all societies through human history, an evolutionary divide that Spencer paralleled to the organs of "sensitivity" in the living organism. "Though the units of a community are all sensitive, they are so in unequal degrees," he wrote. "The classes engaged in laborious occupations are less susceptible, intellectually and emotionally, than the rest; and especially less so than the classes of highest mental culture."[65] Happily, this more lumpen class was useful in mining, manufacturing, and the distribution of commodities, which Spencer likened to the "circulatory" and "alimentary" systems of the body (money and consumables circulate like blood, while the transport, manufacture, and distribution of commodities through the industrial process is like the nation's digestive tract). The highest and most refined system, predictably, involves the "nerves," which Spencer aligned with the history of governmental power as the body's regulatory and executive functions. In the most primitive societies, he argued, a chief or chief's council decided and then acted on their edicts, the "directive" and "executive" functions of the social order confined to one person, or perhaps a few people. For Spencer, the history of society is the history of power's increasing specialization within the social organism, a process that began with the cleaving of the directive and executive functions: "In those larger and more complex communities possessing, perhaps, a separate military class, a priesthood, and dispersed masses of population requiring local control, there grow up subordinate governing agents; who, as their duties accumulate, severally become more directive and less executive in their characters."[66] All civilized roads culminate in England, of course, which Spencer celebrated as having advanced to the highest of all mammalian cerebral functions: a complex and fully articulated nervous system. "To kings and their ministries have been added, in England, other great directive centres," he wrote, "exercising a control which, at first small, has been gradually becoming predominant: as with the great governing ganglia which especially distinguish the highest classes of living beings." Here Spencer describes, in biosocial terms, the decentralization of absolute authority into the various ministries, agencies, bureaus, schools, prisons, hospitals, and other "directive centers" of power now charged with administering the day-to-day order of the state. "Strange as the assertion will be thought," he continued, "our Houses of Parliament discharge, in the social economy, functions which are in sundry respects comparable to those discharged by the cerebral masses in a vertebrate animal."[67]

At the highest levels, the social organism evolves an "internuncial apparatus"—that is, the neurons of this social tissue begin to form more intricate connections, allowing for more abstract thought. For Spencer, this internuncial apparatus is the telegraph: "After a long period during which the directive centres communicate with various parts of the society through other means, there at last comes into existence an 'internuncial apparatus,' analogous to that found in individual bodies. The comparison of telegraph-wires to nerves is familiar to all. It applies, however, to an extent not commonly supposed. Thus, throughout the vertebrate sub-kingdom, the great nerve-bundles diverge from the vertebrate axis side by side with the great arteries; and similarly, our groups of telegraph-wires are carried along the sides of our railways."[68] Spencer's division of the directive and executive functions becomes, in electronic form, a telegraph system endowed with "central" and "autonomic" nervous functions. Cerebral messages of commerce, state, or personal correspondence course through the executive cables of the system, while a separate line attends to the autonomic monitoring of the nation's "arteries," regulating the traffic of goods and citizens circulating through the railway system. Recognizing just how rich the telegraph wire and nerve analogy might be, Spencer concluded, "Probably, when our now rudimentary telegraph-system is fully developed, other analogies will be traceable."[69]

Back inside the human body, meanwhile, physicians posited a similar class divide between hydraulic labor and electrical thought. The laboring classes might risk injury and sore muscles, but a professional class of "brain-workers" faced an even more catastrophic hazard. "The suns of our best men go down at noon," observed *Scientific American* in 1864. "The men of intense thought—men of letters, men of business who think and speculate, men of state who are ambitious to rule, these men are sacrifices." Such men were vulnerable because their brains had to supervise not only their own bodies but also "a hundred other brains, and the muscles thereto appended." The editors explained the physics involved: "An electric battery works a single wire from the city to Brighton, and does its work well, and goes on for some months before it is dead or worn out. Can it do the work of a hundred wires? Oh yes, it can, but it must have more acid, must wear faster, and will ultimately die sooner."[70] In his widely read study *American Nervousness* (1881), physician George Beard codified this already familiar analogy. He gave popular identity and scientific credence to these weary brainworkers in the figure of the *neurasthenic*—that despondent soul who responded to modernity's cataclysmic changes with fatigue, despair, and insomnia (among other symptoms). Primarily male, neurasthenics were subject to dampened affect and a paralysis of will, overtaxed by a world that demanded more of their nervous economy than that of any previous generation. Energizing the environmental and moral dissipation of Cheyne and Trotter, Beard is concise in his thesis: "Nervousness is strictly deficiency or lack of nerve-force. This condition, together with all the symptoms of diseases that are evolved from it, has developed mainly within the nineteenth century, and is especially frequent and severe in the Northern and Eastern portions of the United States.... The chief and primary cause of this development and very rapid increase of nervousness is *modern civilization*."[71] Americans were more prone to nervousness due to the volatile weather and low humidity of the North American continent. Beard reasoned, "Moisture conducts electricity, and an atmosphere well charged with moisture, other conditions being the same, will tend to keep the electricity in a state of equilibrium, since it allows free and ready conduction at all times and in all directions."[72] The moister British therefore had a lower environmental propensity for nervousness, whereas Americans—especially in the dryer Rocky Mountain regions—served as veritable lightning rods for electrical imbalance. Significantly for Beard and the many who followed him, the neurasthenic did not suffer from a single overwhelming discharge of nervous energy. Instead, a steady expenditure of nerve force (due to the demands of modern life) typically left him without a sufficient "reserve" if a real crisis arrived. "Men, like batteries, need a reserve force," he wrote, "and men, like batteries, need to be measured by the amount of this reserve, and not by what they are compelled to expend in ordinary daily life."[73] In a section titled "Analogy of the Electric Light," Beard echoed the logic of *Scientific American* from a decade earlier, writing, "When new functions are interposed in the circuit, as modern civilization is constantly requiring us to do, there comes a period, sooner or later, varying in different individuals, and at different times of life, when the amount of force is insufficient to keep all the lamps actively burning; those that are weakest go out entirely, or, as more frequently happens, burn faint and feebly—they do not expire, but give an insufficient and unstable light—this is the philosophy of modern nervousness."[74]

A similar electrical economy animated the hysteric as the other great nervous patient of the nineteenth century. While the overstimulation of brainwork had the effect of slowly draining the reserves of the typically male neurasthenic, the female hysteric responded through a variety of dysfunctions that suggested a more "sensitive," explosive, and thus erratic nervous economy. In the mid-nineteenth century, this constitutional "sensitivity" had allowed women to assume the power of mediumship, making them the most likely terminals for channeling the invisible energy of the "spiritual telegraph." Women were thought to be no less sensitive by the end of the century. But outside occultist spheres, the excitable nerves of women remained more a constitutional weakness. In *Functional Disorders of the Nervous System in Women* (1896), for example, Timothy McGillicuddy argued that the primary nervous problem facing women was that they were women: "Every woman suffers more or less, and many almost constantly, from functional derangement of some of the organic structures of the body. We are frequently consulted by those who, although suffering from no gross pathological condition, nevertheless require our aid for the great discomforts, both physical and mental, which these various functional disturbances entail, and we should make every effort to afford them consolation and relief."[75] Male physicians, in other words, should always be patient in dealing with their female clients, who as a rule always have something wrong with them, real or imagined.

Beard proposed five aspects of modern civilization that he believed to be the most enervating: "steam-power, the periodical press, the telegraph, the sciences, and the mental activity of women."⁷⁶ Beard's list may strike modern readers as humorous, no doubt because of its odd selectivity, explicit instrumentality, and unexamined sexism (steam, newspapers, telegraphy, science, and educated women are driving the world insane). Considered more abstractly, however, Beard's list proposes a thesis that many commentators would still find reasonable today: changes in daily life produced by a new technological environment make for a more stressful, nervous, and thus "insane" world, especially in the United States. To illustrate the "nervousness" provoked by the telegraph, Beard turned to the era's acceleration in the flows of capital. "The telegraph is a cause of nervousness the potency of which is little understood," he wrote. "Before the days of Morse and his rivals, merchants were far less worried than now, and less business was transacted in a given time; prices fluctuated far less rapidly, and the fluctuations which now are transmitted instantaneously over the world were only known then by the slow communication of sailing vessels or steamships.... Now, prices at each port are known at once all over the globe."⁷⁷ While Beard's account of a strained nervous economy did not have universal support among his fellow physicians, it was nevertheless widely adopted in psychological and popular theory during the 1880s and 1890s. "Electro-therapeutics," a belief that willpower could be recharged as actual energy, became medical dogma, drawing on what T. Jackson Lears has called a principle of "psychic scarcity," a mental economy that likens a "person's supply of nervous energy to a bank account."⁷⁸ Electrophysiologists offered a number of professional devices for electrification, including what one therapist described in 1890 as a class of influence machines (also known as the Holtz machine).⁷⁹

Especially popular were the seemingly endless variations on the "galvanic belt." Patents for new and improved versions of the electro-galvanic belt increased greatly in the 1880s (around the publication of Beard's work, not coincidentally) and continued into the 1920s. As Carolyn Thomas De La Peña argues, the electric belt would become especially central to promises of restoring masculine vitality sapped by urbanism, industrialism, and the demands of modern life: "Electricity infused the body with a palpable force. As a result, many saw electric health aids as capable of driving power directly into the nerves and muscles, leaving the body with more reserve force."⁸⁰ Such devices promoted cures to a variety of illnesses, although the proximity of belt to groin (some with a scrotal pouch) suggests these devices were particularly convincing for men looking for relief from impotence, prostatitis, and incontinence.⁸¹

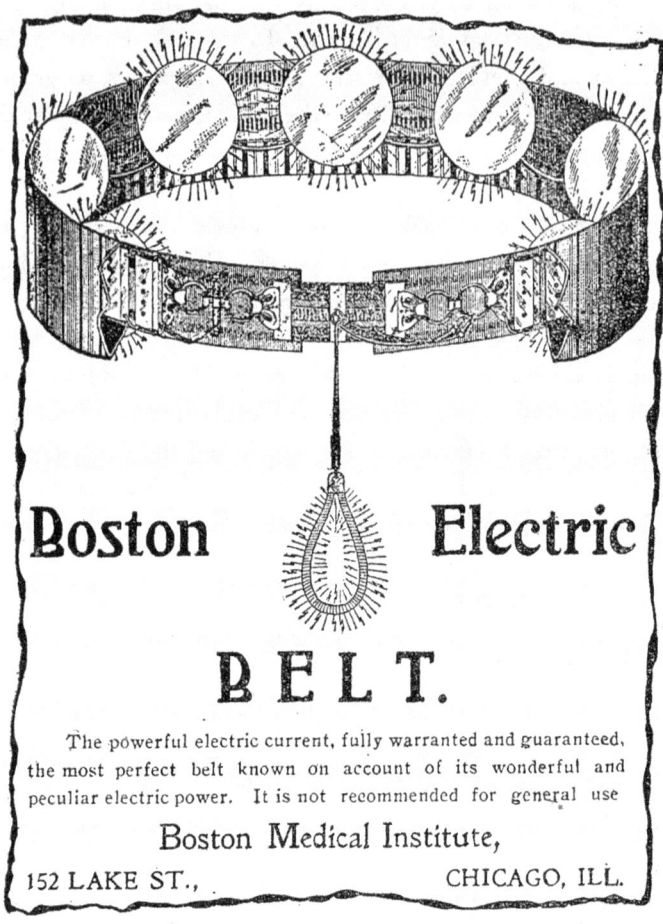

FIG 4.4 The Boston Electric Belt (1911), one of countless revitalizing devices of the late nineteenth and early twentieth centuries promoting galvanic principles. SOURCE: WELLCOME COLLECTION.

Telephonic Insanity

The actual infrastructure of telegraphy was such that very few people had direct experience with the technology. For many, the revolutionary impact of the device took the form of two iconic illustrations: (1) the lone operator, invariably tense, hunched over the key to create a literal interface of copper wire and nervous finger; (2) a bustling room of multiple operators struggling to keep up with this new network's incessant demands. At the end of the century, however, the telephone presented an agent of nervous disorder that allowed growing numbers of people to actually experience rather than merely contemplate the newly accelerated world of electronic telecommunications. How many people, if any, were actually driven to insanity by the telephone is difficult to say. But anecdotal accounts of telephonic insanity were certainly widespread at the close of the nineteenth century, suggesting that a range of specialists in medicine, sociology, labor, and other disciplines believed that the telephone *should* drive individuals insane. For men, telephonic insanity typically stalked the world of commerce. Bad connections and overloaded switchboards were thought to be a source of constant exasperation for middle- and upper-class professionals, this technology of acceleration frequently failing to keep up with the world it had itself created. A German "commissioner in lunacy" thus testified at an insanity hearing that "even phlegmatic men might have their mental balance upset by exasperation at getting no reply from 'Central,'" noting the case of a prominent doctor who became "completely insane through telephone exasperation."[82] For the common laborer, meanwhile, telephonic insanity centered more on successful rather than thwarted communications. In one account, a reporter in Cincinnati had the good fortune of entering a drugstore just as a young man wandered into the establishment to make a series of loud and seemingly deranged phone calls. The druggist explained that the young man was formerly a shipping clerk in New York City but had become a monomaniac in relation to the telephone: "He had become so worried, being of an excessively nervous temperament, by the constant ringing of the telephone all day in his ears that, though sane on all other subjects, he is crazy on this, and runs into drug stores and uses telephones in a nervous, unstrung manner, calling the name of his former sweetheart, long since dead." A high-stress job lost in the big city, a dead sweetheart, forced migration westward to find work—"His case is a curious psychological study," concluded the reporter.[83]

Telephonic insanity also targeted women, of course, often as an implicit punishment for violating Victorian codes of decorum. Thus, in London a woman "employed in the chorus of one of the theatres" (i.e., a chorus girl) was found wandering the streets with "her hands to her mouth and ears in telephonic fashion," conversing with Saint Peter. After being taken to the police station, she claimed to hear "celestial music" and "Saint Cecilia playing the piano" through her imaginary phone.[84] In 1896, meanwhile, newspapers in Chicago saw fit to report on the case of a young shop girl recently abandoned by her morally suspect suitor, Harry, an itinerant "drummer who sold cigars." The girl had become nervous and brooding. "I am not ill," she claimed, "but everyone annoys me so. They have put a telephone through my head so I can talk to Harry, but now they won't let me use it."[85] A similar fate befell a woman in Philadelphia, who claimed betrothal to a local physician. One morning she arrived at the insane department of the almshouse telling "a strange story of how she often, day and night, heard a voice speak to her through a mysterious telephone, and direct her how to remind Dr. Williams of his promise."[86] In a world where men and women could converse by telephone with greater frequency, freedom, and intimacy—often "inappropriately"—it is not surprising that fallen and falling women should incorporate the device of their moral doom in their delusional ravings.

The telephone's powers of enervation were so great, in fact, that just thinking about the new technology too much could apparently trigger a bout of insanity. A notice from 1892 describes a man who imagined himself "filled with electric wires," a delusion said to have evolved from his exceedingly keen interest in telephony: "Before the telephone was in actual public service, he became very much interested in the accounts of the scientific experiments in connection with the then imperfect instrument." When he finally heard a voice through the new technology, "his wits completely deserted him. At the present time he imagines that a telephone is secreted within him and he holds conversation with an imaginary individual at the other end of the wire." In the end, this "news story" reveals itself to be an advertisement for Paine's Celery Compound, a medicine said to purify the blood and strengthen the nerves (which all agreed were obviously more sensitive in the new telephonic age).[87]

Newspapers reveled in accounts of telephony that emphasized its foundation in the elemental powers of electricity, making electrocution particularly symbolic in relation to the hazardous (often fatal) binding of the human nervous system to electronic communications network.[88] As frontline workers in spreading telephony's nervous networks, telephone linemen appeared to have an elevated risk for developing telephonic insanity through electrocution. In 1892, for example, a worker for the Chicago Telephone Company went insane after being struck by lightning through a phone line. Oddly, this accident happened not while the man was on a pole fixing the line, but while he was calling headquarters (making the story more terrifying for the everyday user of the telephone). Following a galvanic logic of electrification, the strike transformed the man into a type of mad Frankenstein's monster. After regaining consciousness, the paper reports, the lineman "was a raving maniac. His strength was superhuman, and none of the attendants in the house could control him. He bit and snapped and kept crying, 'Hello! Hello! Ring off!' until help arrived."[89] These dangers were so well known, in fact, that some advocates of electric-

FIG 4.5 The electrocution of the Western Union lineman John Feeks, October 11, 1889. Drawing by D. Dumon for Émile Desbeaux's *Physique populaire* (1891).

ity complained about a certain kind of hypochondria taking hold among the public. Philip Coombs Knapp's foundational study *Accidents from the Electric Current* (1890) reminded readers that electricity, coursing through lines strung with "customary American carelessness," had indeed become much more powerful over the previous decade.⁹⁰ But Knapp also grumbled that the newspaper industry's fascination with stories of electrocution, both fatal and miraculous, had contributed to a type of electronic hypochondria. "It would be strange if, when the newspaper reports of electrical accidents have produced a feeling of panic in many minds," he wrote, "the actual victims of such accidents should not develop many nervous symptoms which often have a distinctly psychical origin."⁹¹ As a testament to the conceptual power of electricity to trigger insanity, Knapp cited the case of "a man of fifty [who] saw a fatal electrical accident. Two weeks later he was struck by a dead wire carrying no current. He fell unconscious and a few hours later was found to have typically traumatic hysteria."⁹²

Of all the moderns made nervous by the telephone, however, none were more at risk than the growing army of switchboard operators, primarily women, who facilitated the overall *prestissimo* of modern life. Experts of all types agreed that operating a switchboard was demanding, even punishing work. "Telephone work is carried out under conditions that are most 'trying' to people's nerves," observed one psychologist. "A telephone operator is subjected to a constant strain of attention, and it is to be feared that the stress of the harassing work carried out is not always lessened by the sympathy of the public."[93] One report claimed that in 1890 alone, no fewer than nine "telephone girls" had been driven mad by the many hours spent on the exchange as operators.[94] "Telephonic insanity is gaining firm hold among the young women who operate the talking machines," reported another paper that same year, this time focusing on a nineteen-year-old operator who, after two years on the exchange, "found herself shouting 'Hello' and 'All right' and 'Busy,' and such things, in elevated trains and other public places."[95] Andreas Killen discusses a notorious "telephone accident" in Berlin in 1902 at the world's newest and largest switchboard system. Unfamiliar with the new equipment, the operators quickly became overwhelmed until "one of the[m] tore her phone set from her head and fell into hysterics, an example which was infectious. A few minutes later, the room was a mass of screaming and howling women."[96] This spectacle of harried operators quickly plugging and unplugging connections at the switchboard proved an ideal figure for illustrating a deterministic relationship between the telephone and the accelerations of modernity. The switchboard montage would remain a staple of Hollywood dramaturgy for many decades, the image of hurried (but efficient) operators enabling complex narrative connections in a complex city in a complex age. At the turn of the twentieth century, however, the spectacle of "Central" as the telephonic nerve center of the new mechanical age remained notable as a tableau in which the female operator and her nerves became a sympathetic synecdoche for the nervous economies of both the telephone and the social world it was thought to transform.[97] "For those already obsessed with speed and complexity," Killen argues, "exchanges seemed to suggest a future in which technology and the human body would become ever more closely fused in a single organism."[98]

Intermedial Delusions

With the nervous electrification of the body politic through telegraphy and telephony, new villains awaited the paranoid and psychotic. The perfidious physician or evil mesmerist had been primarily a localized and highly personalized antagonist. Though capable of incredible mischief, this influencer's grievances, tactics, and ambitions generally remained contained within the immediate psychodynamic realm of the patient. But the overlay of biological, technical, and social systems at the close of the Victorian era produced the delusional vectors of biopolitical power that would establish the modern influencing machine. As Victor Tausk himself noted of this persecution through remote technologies, "It is noteworthy that the persecutors are all persons who live at some distance from the patient, whereas the persecuted belong to the closest circle of acquaintanceship and ... represent a kind of constantly present family."[99]

In 1888, in a case study published by the New York Academy of Medicine, Frederick Peterson analyzed the diary of a "paranoiac" as he recounted his electromagnetic entanglement in these new economies of power. The subject's voices, helpfully, took a keen interest in electromagnetic physics. "I heard a great deal about 'inducting,' 'conducting,' 'sphere of influence,' sometimes even 'poles,' positive and negative, and my brain was constantly compared to a magnet," his diary reads. "I could find no better explanation myself for a long time than the theory of a fluid, similar to or the same as electricity, uniting brains."[100] The diary goes on to detail a delusional system that might best be described as *intermedial*, drawing on two overlapping logics of technological and social power. Behind the plot to turn his brain into a magnet, we learn, is yet another physician. But this physician assumes a much different role than the more immediate tormentors of the early nineteenth century. For one, this particular physician is English. It is unclear from the diary whether the English physician still resides in England or is conducting his experiments from somewhere in the United States. But in either case, it is clear that his exact identity remains unknown to the patient—the physician is, crucially, *a stranger*, a man of medicine and science operating from a remote space of medicine and science. He is thus emblematic of a new delusional menace that was emerging in the late nineteenth century: an ambassador of a "science" that has an agenda, perhaps for the public good, perhaps not, who operates from a position of power that is unanswerable to the patient.

The patient's voices inform him that this physician had somehow become aware of "magnetic properties" in his brain that have made him an excellent subject for telepathic experimentation: "He was stated to have been the first to form a perfect communication with the inducted brain, and he had drawn off my entire memory back to childhood." The English physician is thus a mind reader (or, to reverse this equation, the paranoiac is a thought broadcaster). The public nature of this paranoia becomes even more acute in the second phase of the "experiment." Having drawn off the patient's memories, the English physician then "delivered it verbally in the presence of reporters from the city who had taken it down."[101] The paranoiac's delusion of thoughts extracted and then rendered in newsprint compel him to enter, unwillingly, a paranoid public sphere. In this respect, his delusion reimagines a process that Anderson argues is central to constructing the new imagined communities of the nineteenth century. Commenting on the act of reading a newspaper, Anderson notes, "It is performed in silent privacy, in the lair of the skull. Yet each communicant is well aware that the ceremony he performs is being replicated simultaneously by thousands (or millions) of others whose existence he is confident, yet of whose identity he has not the slightest notion."[102] In imagining that his memories and thoughts have been transmitted telegraphically and then transcribed into newsprint, the magnetic-brain paranoiac in effect actualizes this typically sympathetic understanding of the public sphere.

His delusional system does not end there, however: "[The English physician] continued in communication with my thoughts, and that wherever he went, every one to whom he told the story of the new marvel was also set in connection with the magnetic currents flowing from my head, and began to participate in my thoughts.[103] This presents a significant shift in technical logic that foregrounds the transitional aspects of this delusion even more acutely. While the English physician functioned as a telegraphic terminus in the initial presentation of this system, receiving the telepathic memories of the patient so that he could distribute them to the press for public consumption, in this second iteration, the English physician becomes more a "tuner," in effect linking the public—one by one—to the extraordinary broadcast apparatus in the patient's head. What had been, with the English physician alone, an apparently shielded conductive mode of contact now becomes a more inductive field of radiation (albeit one that the physician still must "connect" one link at a time). One could even argue that the patient's diary anticipates "wireless" as a technical principle and "radio" as a social institution. Equating telepathy with wireless is perhaps less than remarkable; indeed, the arrival of Guglielmo Marconi's breakthrough in 1895 was, for many, simply a confirmation of the telepathic potential many already believed implicit in radiant energy. Anticipating the use of wireless telepathy to link a "vast network" of strangers, however, presents a "broadcast" use of the technology that corporate interests would not fully realize, conceptually or technologically, until the early 1920s.[104]

This turn toward villains working within or above the public becomes a recurring feature of technical delusions in their modern form. In 1883, for example, authorities asked another individual why his "secret tormentors" could not be seen or heard by others. "The dogs have established a special connection with me by means of some secret invention in electricity," responded the patient. Besieged by a "rascally crew of thieves and murderers" who worked incessantly to "violate" his body and mind, the patient believed this "combination of electricity and ventriloquism" could be stopped by only one man: Thomas Edison. Who better, after all, to solve an enigma of technological torment than the leading technical genius of the era? Other delusions were more suspicious of Edison. In 1901, for example, the deputy clerk of Cook County, Illinois, received word that his brother, missing for several years, had just been arrested for attempting to gain entrance to Edison's home in New Jersey. The man, who had been a printer, claimed that Edison had "appropriated" his invention and was using it to have "a potent influence over his life and happiness." The device "is filling my brain with magnetism and I cannot regain my full mental faculties until I see that machine and touch it," he told police. "I must have an interview with Mr. Edison and make him leave me alone or restore my patent to me."[105]

Edison frequently found himself at the center of delusional ideation in the late nineteenth century, not simply because he was famous, but also because so many of his inventions bordered on the uncanny. Edison's wizardry featured prominently in popular fiction of the era. Garrett P. Serviss's *Edison's Conquest of Mars* (1898), an unauthorized sequel to H. G. Wells's *War of the Worlds*, imagined the famous inventor creating an antigravity device and a disintegration ray to avenge the Martian attack on Earth.[106] A fictionalized Thomas Edison Jr. pursued his own adventures in a dime novel series published in 1891–92. Slightly more displaced were the many serials trading in "Edisonades," defined by John Clute and Peter Nicholls as tales involving "a young US male inventor hero who ingeniously extricates himself from tight spots and who, by so doing, saves himself from defeat and corruption, and his friends and nation from foreign oppressors."[107] Some Edisonades bordered on the hallucinatory, such as "Electric Bob's Big Black Ostrich," in which "Electric Bob" constructs a "Big Black Ostrich"— outfitted with a machine gun, no less—to cross into Mexico and find a lost gold mine.[108] Developing alongside the fictionalized legend of Edison was a very material empire. In concrete terms, new electrical power plants springing up across the nation, often emblazoned with his name on the side of the building, demonstrated to all that Edison had power *over power*.

Edison also figured centrally in the delusional system of a fifty-three-year-old man admitted to the State Hospital for the Insane in St. Peter,

FIG 4.6 On a quest for Mexican gold, a mechanized electrical ostrich fights its way across the desert in Robert Toomb's tale "Electric Bob's Big Black Ostrich," published by the *New York Five Cent Library* in 1893.

Minnesota. For a number of years prior to his admission in 1891, the patient had been troubled by his knowledge that the powers of "animal magnetism" could be greatly amplified when men pool this energy by gathering in large groups. In the months preceding his institutionalization, he had come to believe that "the Odd Fellows and Free Masons were societies which existed for the purpose of centralizing and concentrating this mysterious force, which he denominated as magnetism or phenomenal power." Believing he was unjustly incarcerated in the asylum, he wrote a series of letters pleading his case. To the governor of Minnesota he provided a classic account of "thought broadcasting": "My difficulty is an outgo of my silent thought.... I have but to think a thought and it reaches other minds in sound without an effort on my part, and is sounded for a distance, I suppose, of two or three miles."[109] His tormenters are notable for their identity as occulted groups secreted away among the public at large. Already somewhat suspect in American political life, the Odd Fellows and Freemasons presented a threat to this patient (and the nation) because of their secretive agenda. Such individuals were dangerous enough on their own, reasoned the patient, but if they continued to systematically "centralize and concentrate" their occult energies and practices, who could know what evil they might be capable of perpetrating? As skilled practitioners of the magnetic arts, they would be able to pool, and thus amplify, their power, significantly expanding their sphere of telepathic influence. In terms of political power, meanwhile, Odd Fellows and Freemasons represent another stratum of anonymous tormentors that were emerging in the modern nation-state, a secretive body within the public at large believed by many to possess inordinate influence in the government and economy. As the patient's letter-writing campaign continued, his delusional system turned to Edison and the electric light. In this Gilded Age of speculation and cornered markets, the Wizard of Menlo Park was able to invent the electric light bulb only after first harnessing all of the "personal magnetism" in the world. After 1893, the hospital's director observed, the patient did nothing but discuss these ever more bizarre theories—with others, when possible, and with himself when not. The prognosis was not good. "Dementia is his destiny," his physician concluded.[110]

For those concerned about the malevolent implications of magnetism, the arrival of wireless telegraphy was both a miraculous revelation and a terrifying confirmation. The suspected physics of telepathy were already well established when Marconi succeeded in 1901 in sending a wireless signal across the Atlantic Ocean. For many, wireless did not suggest telepathy might be possible; rather, it verified that telepathy was a scientific principle. "I will not attempt to take up your time in endeavoring to convince you of the existence of Telepathy," wrote William Walker Atkinson in 1900. "Psychic science has made such wonderful strides of late, that not only are its students fully aware of the truth of telepathy, but the general public as well are fully posted on the subject, and generally accept it as an established fact, as readily as they do the X-Rays or Wireless Telegraphy."[111] Atkinson was a leading figure in the burgeoning New Thought movement, centered in Chicago, that promoted "mental science" as the key to success in business, romance, and life generally.[112] At the center of this science was the universal existence of "a dynamic mental principle, a mind-power—pervading all spaces—immanent in all things—manifesting in an infinite variety of forms, degrees, and phases."[113] Such belief in a universal force occupying all space and matter is consonant, of course, with any number of other religious traditions—be it Jesus or the Jedi—a point that was not lost on Atkinson. "The universe is alive, and has mind and Mind-Power in every part and particle of itself. This is not an original idea of my own, of course, the leading scientific thinkers admit it today, and the Hindu philosophers have known it for fifty centuries."[114] "Mental science" sought to master the dynamics of this mind power by isolating and operationalizing the "laws of attraction in the thought world." The goal was to harness will to power in a positive projection of thought, all the while remaining on guard against the "negative thoughts" and "injurious thought attraction" projected by others. More secular than spiritualism and more practical than psychoanalysis, New Thought was a philosophy of mentation ideally suited for the Gilded Age, especially as this period of economic transition moved into a more nervous twentieth century. Advocates promised more overall happiness, of course, but their primary concern was to train men to succeed in the world of commerce. New Thought writers thus careened effortlessly from theories of Universal Mind to principles of effective salesmanship, from advice for neurasthenics to strategies for promotion. Mind power, variously conceived, would lead in many different directions over the course of the century, from Dale Carnegie's best-selling *How to Win Friends and Influence People* (1937) to theories of national psychic unity; from Norman Vincent Peale's *The Power of Positive Thinking* to Cold War experiments in the possibilities and principles of "psychic warfare"; from occult interest in the concept of "aura" to the post-hippie New Age of good and bad vibes.[115]

Bolstered by the recent discoveries of physics and neurology, the New Thought movement shared with other mental sciences of the early twentieth century a belief in thought as a physical force. But Atkinson went beyond the familiar equation of telepathic and inductive energy, arguing that the science of mind power brought with it certain inevitable social realities. Wireless was key to Atkinson's thinking on this point. "It seems that when a message is sent from the Marconi transmitter, the vibrations travel in all directions, and not alone in the direction of the person to whom the message is sent," he wrote. "It would seem to the reader, at first, that any instrument, in any direction from the sender, could and would be affected by the vibrations and would take up and record them."[116] Such indiscriminate reception is not the case, argues Atkinson, due to the human ability to "tune in" only those who possess a similar "mental keynote": "People whose minds are attuned to a certain pitch will receive the vibrations from the minds of others whose mental keynote is the same."[117] Much like the paranoid patient concerned that urban Masons and Odd Fellows were amplifying their collective mental power, Atkinson argued that thought waves tend to be denser and in constant collision around the Earth's population centers in a type of sociophonic aggregation. "The resonance of like-minded thought-waves" explained the "mental atmosphere of places, towns, houses, etc." When opposing vibrations came into contact, meanwhile, the two waves were in conflict and "each [would] lose in proportion to its weakness, and the result [would] be either a neutralization of both or else a combination having vibrations of an average rate."[118] Atkinson thus proposed an atomic foundation to social atomization, describing the attraction and repulsion of atoms and particles as arising from states of "like and dislike, love and hate, pleasure and pain."[119] Like so many humans of the modern era, Atkinson's emotional atoms lived a rather lonely existence, hovering through "a space that separates them—which never can be traversed or overcome." There is "always a 'keep your distance' or 'thus far and no further' principle in nature which holds every particle of matter individual and alone," he writes. "The ions composing an atom are akin to a minute solar system, each ion being attracted to the other and yet "kept at its distance, the combined pull and push of desire and the 'keep off,' respectively, tending to cause them to circle round and round each other."[120]

In yet another odd iteration of Freud's libido theory, Atkinson posited willpower as a force generated by two opposing poles: desire and will. The desire pole of desire-will is connected with emotion and feeling and is always in a "coiled up" state of tension.[121] Not all desires are acted on, noted Atkinson, leaving us to ponder the limbo zone where desire does or does not cross over the threshold to become will. "Just where desire passes into will is impossible to decide," he wrote. "The chances are that they blend into one another."[122] To better illustrate this dynamic, Atkinson invoked a story he called "The Fable of the Mentative Couple," a gendered parable that captures the paranoid necessity of mastering Atkinson's mental science. Volos, the husband, we are told, is "stern, inflexible, strong, positive, apt to stick to a thing once begun; full of the will to live and vitality," while his wife, Emotione, is "impressionable, imaginative, emotional, fanciful, full of desire, curious, sympathetic, and easily persuaded." One day, Volos leaves the castle unguarded, and even though he has instructed Emotione to keep the gate closed tight while he is away working on "some arduous enterprise," his wife yields to the temptation of "an attractive stranger with a fascinating smile on his lips." When Volos returns home that evening, he finds that Emotione has "subscribed to a set of books on Modern Art, a beautiful work published in 824 weekly parts, at the nominal price of $5 a part—739 parts of which were already out, and would be delivered shortly.... Volos cried aloud to the gods of his land—but it was too late, the contracts had been signed."[123] Later absences from the home on Volos's part result in furniture, rugs, and "a baby-grand, self-playing, automatic, liquid-air-valved, radium carburetter, piano-playing, Organette." When Volos resolves to remain on guard day and night at the gates of the castle, a motley assortment of characters distract him through spectacle and flattery, allowing the handsome salesman access once again to the gullible Emotione. In Atkinson's version of Victorian complementarianism, the economy depended on men without desire and women without will locked in a battle of the sexes, to be resolved only if and when masculine will and feminine desire found reconciliation. (In fact, according to Atkinson's fable, the actual necessity of "feminine desire" is never really explained. Masculine will is clearly the more important force.)

For ambitious practitioners of mental science, however, the most coveted role in this fable was to be the fascinating salesman, the man of will who burdens the woman (and cuckolds her husband) with encyclopedias, organettes, and other generally useless commodities. In the historical struggle between exploiter and exploited, adherents of mental science would have a clear advantage in becoming successful influencers rather than ciphers in the passive mass of the influenced. "The teachers of Business Psychology very ably instruct their pupils in the art of suggestion in the process of making sales," Atkinson noted approvingly. "People are positively told to do certain things in these advertisements. They are told to 'Take home a cake of Hinky-dink's Soap tonight; your wife needs it!' And they do it."[124] Atkinson and his peers in effect rewired Friedrich Nietzsche's "will to power" into a schematic of electrical domination of the marketplace. All that was required was to acknowledge and seize this power. Such responsibility, however, made life itself a twenty-four-hour-a-day job. In depicting the mind as a lazy employee or an inefficient technology, advocates of mind power imagined a world in which the daily social struggles of labor, worth, and economic anxiety dominated the subject's interior life, as well. No longer could one come home and rest on the couch after a long day's work; instead, every man interested in wealth, marriage, and status had to worry about whether he was getting maximum productivity from his brain, sending out the positive mental induction that would secure his will over the weaker minds around him. In theory, universal thought power was available to everyone. In practice, of course, those with superior "power of will" would take charge to implement their agendas, while the deficient were doomed to buy unwanted encyclopedias.

Accumulating this power could take the truly ambitious well beyond success in the marketplace of soap. Atkinson contended that great leaders of "statesmanship, politics, business, finance, or military life" provided tangible evidence of thought power radiating across the social landscape. Powerful leaders, he observed, "send out the Thought-Waves consciously and deliberately, erecting the mental image, and holding strongly to it, so that in time their sweeps of mental currents reach further and further away and bring a greater number of people under the influence and into the field of attraction." Such men of power could, in essence, transform their will into ideology—radiating their beliefs and desires to the public at large. "They 'treat' the public 'en masse' by holding the strong mental picture of that which they desire, and then sending out strong thought-currents of desire in all directions, willing that those coming within their radius shall be attracted toward the ideas expressed in the Mental image projected in all directions."[125] Even for the most industrious believers, however, potential obstacles to success remained. For one, this mental Darwinism implied that another devotee of mental science might have greater or more positive powers, allowing him to dampen or even cancel out the projections of the less accomplished. More distressing, there was the sinister menace of *negative thought*. This could manifest as doubt or recrimination in one's own mind, of course, but it could also take the form of negative thought projection emanating from one's rivals and adversaries. In addition to training believers in positive thought, Atkinson offered advice on "repelling" the negative thoughts emanating from what he called the "human wet-blanket."[126]

More active in this regard were occultists with an explicit lineage in magic and witchcraft. *Psychic Self-Defense*, published in 1930 by the celebrated British occultist Dion Fortune, is an early and still widely circulated work among those concerned with the possibilities of psychic attack.[127] The spreading influence of New Thought was a primary motivation for Fortune. Surveying the literature, she cited New Thought's craven appeals to success in business and romance, accusing mental science of ignoring the spiritual aspects of these techniques. "Their exponents advertised that they would teach the art of salesmanship," she complained, "of making oneself popular and dominant in society, of attracting the opposite sex, of drawing to oneself money and success."[128] Not only is this a trivialization of occult powers, she reasoned; it also introduces neophytes to a potentially dangerous realm they ultimately will not be able to control.[129]

How does one know she or he is under "psychic attack"? Fortune identifies three recurring "subjective symptoms": (1) characteristic dreams (and, in particular, dreams of "weight" on the chest); (2) a sense of fear and oppression; and (3) nervous exhaustion and mental breakdown. (This last symptom, Fortune notes, is particularly common among "white people.") To this Fortune adds a number of less common physical symptoms, including bruises (while sleeping), "evil odors," inexplicable outbreaks of fire, mysterious footprints (generally leading nowhere), and the "precipitation of slime." Psychic attacks can be the work of skilled occults, such as witches, or they can be the accidental side effect of occupying a space recently suffused with negative psychic energy. Citing the case of a veteran performer suddenly seized with stage fright, Fortune noted that earlier in the day, on the same stage, auditions had been held for a number of novice (and very nervous) performers. "It may well be that the 'microphone panic,' so well known to broadcasters, is caused by the thought-atmosphere generated by a succession of nervous people who have stood upon the same spot," she wrote.[130] The modus operandi for all psychic attack, Fortune argued, is a telegraphic projection of emotional states: "Experimental psychologists are already suspecting that emotion is closely akin to electricity; they have proved conclusively that emotional states alter the electrical conductivity of the body. The occultist believes that emotion is a force of an electrical type, and that in the case of the ordinary man it radiates out from him in all directions, forming a magnetic field; but in the case of the trained occultist it can be concentrated into a beam and directed."[131] Particularly noxious is the dynamic of "psychic vampirism," a phenomenon Fortune observed in many couples. "Knowing what we do of telepathy and the magnetic aura," she wrote, "it appears to me not unreasonable to suppose that in some way which we do not as yet fully understand, the negative partner of such a rapport is 'shorting' on to the positive partner. There is a leakage of vitality going on, and the dominant partner is more or less consciously lapping it up, if not actually sucking it out."

Fortune first became aware of psychic vampirism while training in London to become, perhaps unsurprisingly, a psychoanalyst. Looking back at her experience with the talking cure, Fortune recalled that she and her fellow analysts in training found certain cases "exceedingly exhausting to deal with. It was not that they were troublesome, but simply that they 'took it out' of us, and left us feeling like limp rags at the end of a treatment." Later, Fortune discussed this hazard of analytic fatigue with a nurse working in the hospital's "electrical department," who noted that these very same patients "equally 'took it out of' the electrical machines and that they could absorb the most surprising voltages without turning a hair."[132] This anecdotal and rather implausible detail typifies the era's intuitive depiction of the Freudian unconscious as an energetic abyss, an absent presence that behaves like a gravitational field in the mind.[133] As we have seen, Freud described the ideal analytic exchange as the unconscious of analyst and analysand tethered by a phone wire, two phantom voids that, through the practice of free association, might temporarily and even telepathically align with each other. Wireless provided a much more compelling model for this process and spread quickly among those attempting to capture any mysterious function of mind that appeared outside the realm of consciousness. The non-Freudian Morton Prince describes a patient aware of "two strata" at work in her mind, leading Prince to liken the "subconscious" to invisible particles emitted by a radioactive plate that "can only be inferred from the effects they produce."[134] Wilhelm Stekel, one of Freud's earliest converts and a staunch advocate of telepathy, described the sleeping mind as having to fight off countless "wireless telegrams from all over the world" seeking entrance to the psyche.[135] Playing on these mysterious associations even as he hoped to demystify them, James Oppenheim titled his layman's guide to psychoanalysis *Your Hidden Powers* (1923). "Why does radio interest you?" he asked his readers. The answer, for Oppenheim, was that radio promised to make people happier, their lives more wonderful, even though the technology itself was something, Oppenheim felt compelled to explain, that existed "outside yourself." But, he continued, "suppose someone came to you and said: 'Science has discovered something greater than radio. It has made a discovery in human nature. It is discovering you.'"[136] The key to one's hidden powers, of course, was psychoanalysis: "Perhaps you have dismissed it as some new cult, some form of religion, something to do with spiritualism, or what is called the 'occult.' It is none of these."[137] So deep, apparently, were the popular associations of psychoanalysis and the supernatural that Oppenheim felt obligated to assert a final time that Freud's work, though it dealt with the "hidden," was not a product of occult mysticism. "I merely want to point out that true scientists have made these discoveries in exactly the same way scientific discoveries have always been made," he wrote, as if both radio and *Die Traumdeutung* had issued from the labs at RCA.[138]

Proponents of telepathy, New Thought, psychic vampirism, and psychoanalysis found validation in a series of experiments conducted in 1926 by the neurologist Ferdinando Cazzamali at the University of Milan. Cazzamali, noted the *New York Times*, "treated the human brain as a broadcast station ... to see what radio signals sent out by the brain could be picked up by delicate radio receivers." His experiments depended on "highly excitable persons as subjects" who, once under hypnosis, emitted signals "at the extremely low wave length of from four to ten meters," sounds that were "similar to wireless signals, but were often accentuated until they resembled whistling or the tones of a muted violin."[139] Playing on the decade's popular fascination with the new phenomenon of broadcasting, the reporter noted that Cazzamali's chief obstacle in this experiment was "electrical interference," an annoyance familiar to most wireless enthusiasts: "The difficulty is not in detecting the supposedly feeble wave impulses sent out by the brain. It is in avoiding the simultaneous detection of hundreds of other electromagnetic impulses which are being sent out by other parts of the human body, by any other living creatures in the neighborhood, even by a variety of inanimate objects close at hand."[140] So astounding was this apparent verification of the brain as radio transmitter that Edmund Shaftesbury, the noted health enthusiast (and founder of Ralston-Purina), reprinted an earlier volume on thought power with a new preface detailing the work of Cazzamali. But even as Shaftesbury extolled the wondrous potentials of mental control and influence, he also recognized the horrifying implications of a world in which frequencies integrated the brain into a larger network of public surveillance and indoctrination: "Imagine what the world would be if the workings of the mind could be detected with scientific accuracy.... There would be no privacy of thought. Your brain would makes noises for all the world to hear.... There would always be someone 'listening in.'"[141]

The eerie credibility of these claims was no doubt greatly enhanced by the newfound ability to sit near a radio set in the living room and hear voices emanating from across the nation and even around the globe—or, just as often, to listen to the otherworldly swirls of static and interference that seemed to hold these voices hostage in the ether. While wireless had long existed in the public consciousness as an abstract concept, the 1920s saw the actual diffusion of radio as a broadcast technology in the home. Broadcasting itself, pioneered in large part by the pre-war networking activities of amateur wireless enthusiasts, rather quickly became a corporate and governmental concern as the United States and Europe negotiated how this new practice, wholly unforeseen a mere decade earlier, would be regulated.[142] The founding of the BBC in the United Kingdom in 1922 and of NBC and CBS in the United States in 1926 and 1927, respectively, signaled a new soundscape for the young medium that would solidify centralized, unilateral transmission for the rest of the century. The 1920s also saw the emergence of technicians dedicated to the science of controlling public opinion. Echoing Fortune's distaste for Atkinson's mental mercantilism, some early media critics warned of the dark forces soon to be unleashed by mass electronic media. In *The Science of Power* (1919), Benjamin Kidd observed, "It is clearly in evidence that the science of creating and transmitting public opinion under the influence of collective emotion is about to become the principle science of civilization, to the mastery of which all governments and all power interests will in future address themselves with every resource at their command."[143] In *Man, the Puppet* (1925), Adam Lipsky warned that the "large concentrations of capital" involved in radio and film production ensured continued control by "relatively few men."[144] Much of this early work on public opinion endorsed a fundamental irrationality in the public mind, an inheritance of Charles Mackay and Gustave Le Bon's earlier work on "the crowd" and its penchant for madness. Lipsky, for example, fused Mackay with Gramscian hegemony to observe, "The truth that government is fundamentally a contrivance for the preservation of conditions favorable to those who have been successful in getting what they want, is ... revealed in lightning flashes." Such moments, Lipsky observed, compel those in power to "convince the majority of people that the chances are against an improvement of their lot by reshuffling the cards" and that "ill-luck, force, and fraud would not be wiped out by a new deal, a new distribution of places, property and privileges."[145] The emergence of networked media would only make these moments of crisis more profound. "Crowds are subject to mass contagion and stampede," Lipsky observed. "It should not be forgotten that crowds are crowds just as truly though they be invisible and dispersed—especially under the conditions of modern rapid communication."[146] In this respect, public opinion constituted the unconscious of the public mind. An occult field, the individual unconscious was a hidden power encountered obliquely through dreams, parapraxis, and neurotic symptoms. The mind of the public was an equally occult presence that could be measured obliquely but never fully understood, even as it manifested its own "neurotic" symptoms in the form of unforeseen political shifts, inexplicable fads, and mysterious trends in taste.[147] "The conscious and intelligent manipulation of the organized habits and opinions of the masses is an important element in democratic society," wrote Edward Bernays in his study *Propaganda* (1927). Bernays's reasonable and even self-evident thesis quickly veers into occult devices and powers: "Those who manipulate this unseen mechanism of society constitute an invisible government which is the true ruling power of our country. We are governed, our minds molded, our tastes formed, our ideas suggested, largely by men we have never heard of." If "the ego is not master in its own house," as Freud observed, the same is true of the body politic's mass ego, a collective psyche controlled (imperfectly) by what Bernays described as "our invisible governors."[148]

These new configurations of mass power seeking to control both the body and the body politic inevitably found their way into the delusional systems of mid-century psychotics. While older, residual logics and actors remained in circulation, delusions increasingly integrated not just media technologies, but also the technicians and the "invisible governors" believed to have expertise and control over issues of will, power, and transmission. Diagnosed as a schizophrenic in 1935, "Maria S.," an immigrant from Germany, began a program of therapy that involved writing for two hours a day, five days a week, in a private room at New York's Pilgrim State Hospital.[149] Maria S.'s difficulties began in 1929 after she wrote a letter to the editors of a newspaper in Berlin. Although the letter was never published, Maria S. became convinced that the editors were mocking her in the reader's forum by implicitly answering her letter and parodying her writing style. She also became anxious because she included her full address in the letter, a vulnerability that made her increasingly suspicious of other German immigrants in New York City. When another German couple moved in upstairs, Maria S. suspected they were using a Dictaphone to record her phone conversations and demanded that her husband find a new apartment. After another minor crisis in the new home, Maria S. believed that "wires" had been put in the walls to transmit her every word to the neighbors, revealing to everyone what a bad mother she was.

Somewhat inexplicably, Maria S. continued to write letters to German-language newspapers in New York and Berlin. Eventually a paper did publish one of her letters—in this case, an editorial protesting the rise of the National Socialist Party in her homeland. Her paranoid wish fulfillment came true when, a few days later, she received a letter with "Heil Hitler!" written on the envelope. The letter inside threatened to denounce her to the police, the anonymous author claiming to "know all about" Maria S. and her activities. The German papers made her even more nervous when Joseph Goebbels, the Nazi minister of propaganda, made a passing remark about "an hysterical city woman." This apparently produced an apophany of psychotic reference, transitioning Maria S. from a general state of paranoid anxiety into acute psychosis. Convinced now that the Nazis were indeed targeting her, Maria S. quickly concluded that she was due to inherit $93 million from a German aristocrat who shared her maiden name. The Nazis had wired her apartment with shortwave radio to monitor her, hoping eventually to steal the money for themselves.

Like so many paranoiacs, Maria S. sought to uncover and understand the mechanisms behind her persecution. Convinced her mind was "on the air," she began reading deeply in psychology and, like so many other mental scientists of the era, gradually crafted her own personal theory of mental telepathy. This became a theory of metaphysics, as well, leading Maria S. to argue that the diaphragm was "the seat of the soul" and that the spirits of Chopin, Voltaire, and Milton, among others, conversed with her by resting in her chest. After an exhaustive but unsuccessful quest to rip out the wires she believed were hidden in her walls, Maria S. resolved to stop thinking about microphones and radios. But then, four months before her institutionalization at Bellevue, she had a vivid dream:

> I dreamt a man slept with me and I had intercourse with him. I got out of bed, turned the electric-lamp on near the writing table and lighted a cigarette.
>
> "How was this dream possible?" True enough my husband and I slept in two separate rooms, but I had no desire for another man, at the present, I believed, I had no sexual desire at all.
>
> Who influenced me in such a way? I looked at the smoke of the cigarette—and sudden [sic] there was an answer! Freud, Dr. Freud from Vienna was sitting by a radio—and had influenced my dream while I was asleep.... I became all excited over the insult done to me. In the morning when I cleaned up my rooms I talked to the walls. I called Dr. Freud terrible names like "gorilla" and "pig" and told him to go back to Vienna, where he can make his experiments with sweet Viennese girls.[150]

Thus did Maria S. produce a paranoid condensation of Freudian theory, telepathic influence, and radiophonic technology. A dream turns to defense ("I had no sexual desire at all") turns to Freud, who stands as an overdetermined figure of occult mentation in its many modern forms.

Maria S. eventually came to her senses, however, realizing that Freud could not possibly spend all of his time monitoring a lone woman in New York City on his radio set. The only reasonable possibility, she concluded, was that Freud received help from Alfred Adler and Carl Jung, presumably in the form of rotating shifts. She became increasingly convinced, she wrote, that Adler had been hired by the Nazis to "influence me by means of thoughts and through the wire to send me out in the night on the street, so that I could be arrested on the ground of prostitution." Having had "no sexual desire at all," Maria S., via psychoanalytic paranoia, was now under pressure to become a prostitute.

Unlocked by Freud and threatened by Hitler, Maria S. and her mental radio station began to attract other prominent technicians of power. The American industrialist J. P. Morgan seemed particularly concerned about whether Maria S. was a communist. "'No—I said—I am not," she wrote. "What I would like to do is search and find a *new* Marx—and inspire him to write out a new economical system for the 20 Century (sic).' Mr. Morgan thought I have splendid ideas."[151] During the summer of 1935, Maria S. grew even more deranged. In the manuscript, she recalled several conversations with the "spirits" of Freud, Jung, Bertrand Russell, Jules Romains, and other prominent psychologists. Her manuscript ends with an account of the final confrontation that brought her to Bellevue for psychiatric evaluation. Maria S. related this part of her story in the form of a play, complete with stage directions for herself, her husband, a policeman, and the many luminaries listening on the wire. When Maria S.'s husband expressed concern over her odd behavior, Jung warned Maria "on the strong wire" that her husband was planning to phone a Nazi physician and that she should refuse any further examination. Albert Einstein then interrupted the proceedings to announce "the discovery and manufacturing of the new wire, on which thoughts were sounding, and spirits could talk." Einstein proclaimed this "the greatest discovery ever made! For we have discovered *die fünfte Dimension!*"

MARIA: Victory! We have discovered the fifth dimension!

(MR S AND THE POLICEMAN)

MARIA: What do you want—?

(POLICEMAN SMILES)

MARIA: Do you come about the wire—? . . .

DOCTOR: Alright! You tell your troubles to the doctor in the Bellevue Hospital.

MARIA: Bellevue Hospital . . . ? No, No! Leave me alone!
(I SLAPED [sic] THE DOCTOR IN HIS FACE).

After that I felt as I was put into iron chains and was carried out of the apartment.[152]

Whether Maria believed she was writing for the stage or for radio is unclear. In either case, narrating her final crisis as a public performance provides an apt resolution to the newly electrified public forums of thought broadcasting. While most targets of broadcasting remained anonymous to the point of invisibility, Maria S.'s mental radio station enjoyed a grandiose connection with Freud, Morgan, Einstein, and other titans of modern power, forging a nexus of theoretical psychology, capital, and science.

The predominance of radio in Maria S.'s delusional system incorporates not only the technical affordances of wireless (a technology that itself makes space and physical boundaries "meaningless"), but also the power relations shaping this technology as a confluence of occult thought, advanced capital, and global tension. Tentative excursions into the public sphere via newsprint open a delusional door that transform Maria S.'s head into a wireless salon, hosting many luminaries in dialogue before assuming, at last, the form of a public presentation in scripted format. Initially concerned that her anonymity within the imagined community of the German diaspora might be compromised, Maria S. eventually embraces—at the height of her crisis—a form of thought broadcasting that assumes the actual form of radio broadcasting. If one cannot escape the emerging global system of occult politics, a domain of power colonized by Freud, Einstein, and the Nazis, why not embrace the logic of "invisible mental power" by serving as its tuner?

Other delusional systems at mid-century were equally invested in the invisible machinations of power. Barbara O'Brien awoke one morning to find three "soft, fuzzy ghosts" standing next to her bed: Burt, Hinton, and a small boy named Nicky. The trio were emissaries of a sort, visiting O'Brien to inform her that she was now the subject of a controversial experiment. Human beings, Burt tells her, exist in two forms: Operators and Things. Most Things live their lives blissfully unaware of the Operators, even as the Operators continuously observe and manipulate Things for sport. Barbara, unfortunately, is a Thing. The trio tell her that her Operator, a man named Hadley, has selected her to see what will happen once a Thing learns "the facts of the Operators' world." Not everyone approves of Hadley's idea, however, leading other Operators to intervene in an attempt to shut down the experiment. As the first Thing in direct contact with the Operators, Barbara becomes an object of struggle as various networks of Operators compete over her fate. For the next year of her life, O'Brien crisscrosses the country as a telepathic fugitive until, at last, a therapist diagnoses her as schizophrenic and begins the process of restoring her to sanity.

Published in 1958 by Ace, best known for its science-fiction pulps, O'Brien's *Operators and Things* presents a fantastic account of an utterly banal delusional community.[153] Despite their incredible telepathic powers, the Operators are not extraterrestrials or spirit beings. Instead, they circulate as ordinary people among Barbara's co-workers, neighbors, and fellow citizens. But Operators possess a single and determinative advantage. "Operators are born with special brain cells known as the battlement," says Burt. "With these cells, an Operator can extend and probe into the mind of a Thing. He can tap the Thing's mind and discover what is going on there, and even feed thoughts to the Thing's mind in order to motivate."[154] Mere humans (albeit with extra brain cells), the Operators demonstrate the same variability in morals, beliefs, and intelligence as Things. But the "battlement" imbues them with such a sense of innate superiority that they cannot help but regard Things much as Things regard cats and dogs: as mere playthings that exist at and for the pleasure of the Operators. Some Operators are benevolent and protect their Things. Others revel in teasing, tormenting, and even torturing their Things. Particularly sinister is the practice of "hook operating." Operators, we learn, compete for points (and to keep their wits sharp) through elaborate games of manipulation designed to put another Operator's Thing in jeopardy. The Thing's "owner," in turn, must institute countermoves, leading to further interference by the hook operator. When Things experience the ups and downs of romantic and professional life, they often as not are merely executing the directives of the hook operators, pawns in an invisible game of Thing chess. The game continues until one of the Operators concedes the contest (and the points).

This fundamental division of power between Operators and Things, a telepathic aristocracy and their puppet-like pawns, is further codified by a complex system of Operator contracts and litigation. Although Operators are vastly superior to Things in terms of telepathic power, their own community is an unexpectedly mundane mirror of the world of Things. Operators trade Things like commodities, buying and selling their "contracts" in open and black markets. This can lead to disputes, obviously, so governmental and juridical entities exist that are empowered to adjudicate Operator relations. Hadley's decision to "open" Barbara's mind, for example, is not supported by the local city council—"the highest legal authority for Operators in any city."[155] Much to Barbara's chagrin, the city council wishes to shut down the experiment, not out of concern for her welfare, but in fear that she will tell other Things about the true nature of their Thing-like existence. Strategizing on how to relocate Barbara to California without the interference of various local councils, O'Brien's escorts file for a "bill of resuscitation," a legal maneuver executed when a Thing, "pretty far gone," needs to be "revived" for further play.[156] City councils are important to Operator relations because the effective range of Operators' telepathy is about "two city blocks," making Operator-Thing relations subject to localized control, instrumentally and politically. Eventually, more benevolent Operators succeed in holding off those who believe Barbara must be eliminated. They even escort her daily to the door of her analyst in San Francisco. Concerned that Barbara's voices have not left, despite six months of intensive therapy, her psychiatrist recommends trying electroshock therapy. O'Brien reluctantly agrees. That night, various Operators debate whether her cure would be better secured by decapitation or setting her head in concrete. The next morning, Barbara wakes up to find the Operators have left for good.

In the second half of her narrative, O'Brien contemplates what led her to this schizophrenic encounter with the Operators. She considers classically psychoanalytical explanations, but when a French Freudian accuses her of being sexually repressed (suggesting that a woman her age should have had at least 125 sexual relationships), she discounts his assessment.[157] But O'Brien nevertheless endorses the unconscious as the driving force behind her psychosis, transposing it from the domain of sexual repression to that of gendered suppression. O'Brien begins her narrative by describing her life "before the Operators," narrating the events that led to her psychotic episode. She sees a direct correlation between the hook operators revealed in her delusion and the practices of the corporate workplace. "Considering the amount of hook operating that goes on in business organizations, it is surprising how little understanding of it exists among young people before they enter business," she notes.[158] After several talented and hardworking co-workers are passed over for promotion, Barbara begins to understand the strategies that allow the unqualified but ruthless to advance up the corporate ladder. Women want more money, O'Brien observes, but men are always in search of more power, making them the most likely to engage in hook operating. "A Hook Operator has a nose for power," she observes, "and as soon as he enters an organization, he follows his nose until he comes upon the individual who is giving off the strongest odor."[159] This would be the "Powerman." The hook operator will advance in the workplace by locating the powerman's "soft spot" and sinking his hook accordingly.

O'Brien's mental health had been fine, apparently, until a schism developed over the future direction of the company at which she was employed. In a battle of office politics, she had sided with her talented mentor, but he was ultimately driven out by the dull-witted son of the company's founder. This unexpected shift in status understandably left O'Brien feeling exposed and uncertain, triggering an escalation of anxious symptoms. Only a few days later, the ghostly trio of Operators appeared at the foot of her bed to educate her about the actual mechanisms of power guiding corporate America, municipal politics, and the lowly life of the toiling Thing. A century earlier, delusion systems had frequently centered on extraordinary individuals employing extraordinary devices. In O'Brien's paranoid vision of 1950s America, power was no longer a singular intervention. It had become a routinized system in which Things fought for money and Operators competed for points, all subject to complex contract law and invisible government administration. While deep in her psychosis, O'Brien laments her fate as a Thing. "Are you shocked because Things are exploited?" responds an incredulous Operator. "Doesn't your kind exploit every form of life it can exploit? There's nothing more ruthless than a Thing. Your kind is in no position to criticize."[160]

The Ego Machine in a World of Shit

By the mid-twentieth century, even children had some understanding of technology's role in mediating the anatomo-political and the biopolitical. Tormented by recurring nightmares about an electrified needle in the haystack, Renee Sechehaye fantasized about creating "an electric machine to blow up the earth and everyone with it." In this, Renee aspired to the status of an Operator: "with the machine I would rob all men of their brains, thus creating robots obedient to my will alone." But in the end, Renee proved to be only another Thing, powerless and submissive to the demands of the System. Hoping to unlock productive analytic material, Renee's analyst asked her to draw a picture of a person. Her drawing depicts a figure impaled by a "hay straw," a curious detail that her therapist describes as "a narrow wire passing through the body, or rather through the mind, representing the tension of unreality and at the same time recalling the nightmare of the needle in the haystack."[161] An exemplar of Freudian displacements, straw, needle, wire, and nerve are all bound by "tremendous electrical current" in a circuit of substitutions around Renee's core psychosexual anxiety, a tableau that plugged her wired body into the larger circuitry of the System.

Asking children to draw pictures of the human body (or of their families) is a standard diagnostic test in child psychiatry. Distortions in these drawings are thought to provide insight into the child's ego development. In 1952, psychologist Paula Elkisch conducted a study of this diagnostic tool and discovered, much to her surprise, that spontaneous drawings of the human body were "very rare," at least among boys age nine to eleven. Left to their own devices, boys of the 1950s were much more likely to draw machines "or anything pertaining to a machine."[162] This is not surprising, given that Western modernity provides boys in particular with innumerable opportunities to identify with machinery, from the dominating power promised by various gadgets to the pleasure of performing one's role in the "well-oiled machine" of a team sport (like war). Elkisch's study focused on two young boys in particular, Adison and Joe, chosen as polar opposites in terms of socialization and temperament.[163] Adison was the most popular boy in his school, whereas Joe suffered the "rather unusual occurrence" of scoring a zero on the popularity scale. Adison, we are told, "not only depicted all sorts of machines and mechanisms; he also expressed the spirit of the machine, its potency, its dynamic explosive power, its uncanniness." Joe's machines, meanwhile, had "no relationship between the parts, no dynamic interchange. These machines stand still and it is questionable whether, if put to the test, they would function. If the inanimate organism stands for the animate, this organism is dead."[164] Elkisch argued that drawings of machines might be more useful than the standard test of the human figure, at least in young boys: "This means that we will have to understand a boy's machines in terms of his interest in his own body, and its relationship to other bodies—and, furthermore, as an attempt on the part of the child to solve his relationship to reality, to the outside world. We will have to 'reverse' his machines, these enigmatic beings, into the image of his own body, thus perhaps reading the level of his ego state."[165]

The most famous "boy-machine" in psychoanalytic literature is undoubtedly Joey, the Mechanical Boy, discussed at length by Bruno Bettelheim in *The Empty Fortress* (1967).[166] Bettelheim's book presented three case studies of infantile autism drawn from his time as director of the Sonia Shankman Orthogenic School in Chicago.[167] Although the full essay on Joey appeared in 1967, Bettelheim contributed a condensed case history to *Scientific American* in 1959, which in turn earned a brief notice in the *Los Angeles Times*.[168] Admitted to the Orthogenic School at nine, Joey brought with him an elaborate array of electromechanical routines designed to mediate his autistic interactions with the social world. Eating required bringing "big motors, tubes, and electric wires into the dining room," as did Joey's trips to the toilet. Bettelheim describes Joey's first weeks in the school's dining hall: "Laying down an imaginary wire he connected himself with his source of electrical energy. Then he strung the wire from an imaginary outlet to the dining room table to insulate himself, and then plugged himself in. . . . These imaginary electrical connections he had to establish before he could eat, because only the current ran his ingestive apparatus."[169] Joey's bed, meanwhile, had all manner of mechanical devices (made out of cardboard and tape) designed to "sleep" him at night, including a battery, a motor, and a "carburetor" that permitted him to breathe. Bettelheim's assessment of this behavior casts Joey as quite conversant in the lessons of galvanic conduction, his selfhood suspended somewhere between anatomical circulation and mechanical circuitry:

> Just as the infant has to make contact with his mother to be able to nurse, so Joey had to connect with electricity, had to plug himself in, before he could function. Electricity that seems to flow through the wire, he made run through his body. It connected him to a power source larger than his own, much as the child in his mother's arms becomes part of a larger circle, becomes connected to a larger source of energy.[170]

Joey's mastery of galvanic anatomy was remarkably sophisticated. Bettelheim relates an episode in which a frustrated teacher hoped to dissuade Joey from his persistent belief that objects are alive. Joey, angry and frustrated, threw a toy block across the room. The teacher retrieved the block and placed it back on the table, telling Joey, "This block cannot move. If you put it down on the table it cannot get up and walk away." Joey responded, "It CAN move. The nerve impulses cause the muscle to move."[171] Bettelheim invoked the widely held theory of the era that autism was the product of distant parents (popularly known as the "refrigerator mom" thesis) and imagined Joey employing electrical logic to compensate for a childhood of emotional poverty.[172] Denied the nurturing circle of human bonding, Joey engineered his own emotional circuitry: "Since human beings had failed him, machines were now his protectors and controllers. Since human beings did not 'feed' his emotions, electricity would have to do it. Since he felt excluded from the circle of humanity, he plugged himself into another circle that nourished—the electrical current."[173] But Joey's electrical economy involved more than simple pantomime. During his first year at the school, Joey carried radio tubes or light bulbs wherever he went. For most of the day, Bettelheim writes, Joey would remain so motionless and withdrawn as to seem almost "nonexistent." But several times a day, this long span of nonexistence was interrupted by the machine "starting up, getting into ever higher gear, until its climax was reached in a shattering 'explosion.'"[174] These explosions involved Joey throwing his tube or light bulb to shatter against the wall while screaming "Crash! Crash!" or "Explosion!" When electrical emotions became too much, an "explosion" tripped the fuse and reset the homeostasis of Joey's mechanical being.

Bettelheim's account of Joey's explosion routine placed the boy between two competing paradigms of emotional regulation. Joey, it seems, enacted a textbook illustration of Freud's "principle of constancy," perhaps better known as the "pleasure principle." Although the principle is often distorted to suggest a constant search for pleasure, a more fatalistic and thus Freudian interpretation is that organisms seek to avoid *displeasure*. As discussed earlier, Freud remained consistent in his allegiance to a mechanist economy of cathexis, a system of charge and discharge regulating the psyche's libidinal energies. From this perspective, Joey's daily cycles from "nonexistence" to shattering explosions present an almost parodic performance of cathexis, with Joey quite literally charging and discharging when confronted with emotional discomfort. But Bettelheim's portrait of Joey also evokes the more dystopic implications of cybernetics. Unveiled by Norbert Wiener in *Cybernetics: Of Control and Communication in the Animal and the Machine* (1948), this new field promised a revolutionary approach to understanding communication and information theory. For Wiener, animal and machine were self-regulating systems involved in various circuits of information processing, obeying a more or less shared schematic of "communication and control": sender to message to receiver to feedback. Extrapolating from the mechanics of the telephone line to the architecture of the cosmos, Wiener argued that animals and machines were both systems of temporary order resisting (futilely) the inevitable entropy of the universe.[175] "Life is an island here and now in a dying world," Wiener observed. "The process by which we living beings resist the general stream of corruption and decay is known as homeostasis."[176] Like Joey, Wiener proposed that the only possible solution to the terrifying entropic chaos of the non-me world was to focus on the temporary refuge offered by mastering loops of more or less predictable inputs, outputs, signals, and feedback. Joey's strategy for negotiating the treacherous demands of socialization endorsed one of the central tenants of cybernetic theory. "When I give an order to a machine, the situation is not essentially different from that which arises when I give an order to a person," Wiener writes. "In other words, as far as my consciousness goes I am aware of the order that has gone out and of the signal of compliance that has come back. To me, personally, the fact that the signal in its intermediate stages has gone through a machine rather than through a person is irrelevant and does not in any case greatly change my relation to the signal."[177] Attempting to seduce a (human) sexual partner and programming a dishwasher are thus essentially the same activity: a system of messages and feedback that can be described in terms of the inputs, outputs, signals, and noise that define the entirety of social life.

Throughout the 1950s and '60s, many disciplines looked to cybernetics as a possible unified field theory for understanding any and all phenomena, from quantum physics to Shakespearean sonnets. For many, cybernetics held the promise of providing a schematic to the universe, establishing what Bernard Geoghegan has called the "cybernetic apparatus." As cybernetics expanded its influence, argues Geoghegan, its "mathematical procedures, diagrammatic strategies, and technologies" became "immaterial ideals" that "enabled the strategic alliance of researchers and institutions across disciplinary, political, and national borders." As Geoghegan's history demonstrates, the "quasitranscendental powers of cybernetic instruments" made this science of equal interest to the Rockefeller Foundation and French structuralism.[178] Wiener opined that cybernetics might even be of use in rethinking approaches to psychopathology, including psychoanalysis. While lobotomy and shock treatment were valuable in correcting dysfunctions in "circulating memories" (i.e., the conscious mind), argued Wiener, psychoanalysis was better suited for accessing "permanent memories" stored in neuron pools that are not immediately available to patient or psychiatrist (i.e., the unconscious).[179] Despite this magnanimous overture to absorb Freud, tension remained between cybernetics and psychoanalysis throughout the 1950s. N. Katherine Hayles highlights the increasingly acrimonious exchanges between the analyst Lawrence Kubie and the neurologist Warren McCulloch at the annual Macy conferences, an ongoing forum for the interdisciplinary consideration of cybernetic possibilities. In "The Past of a Delusion," his address to the conference in 1953, McCulloch castigated Freud as motivated by greed and dismissed psychoanalysis as unscientific charlatanism. So acrimonious was the attack that Kubie apparently "interpreted the speech as a sign of McCulloch's own psychological distress," even going as far as "to arrange for psychoanalysts in the Boston area to meet with McCulloch 'on a social pretext if necessary,' with a view to getting him the 'help' that Kubie thought he needed."[180]

There is no explicit mention of Wiener or cybernetics in Bettelheim's account of Joey, but there is also little attempt to disguise the author's suspicion of mental models that would emulate the rationalist agenda of postwar engineering. Bettelheim explored these suspicions more thoroughly in *The Informed Heart: Autonomy in a Mass Age*, published in 1960 as Bettelheim was in the middle of his clinical work with Joey. Bettelheim opens with a poetic conceit that speaks almost directly to Joey's plight: "We are in great haste to send and receive messages from outer space. But so hectic and often so tedious are our days, that many of us have nothing of importance to communicate to those close to us."[181] For most of the book, Bettelheim reflects on his experiences as a prisoner at Dachau and Buchenwald, hoping to theorize the adaptive dynamics of individual personality traits when confronted by radical changes in social environment. Bracketing this narrative, however, is a more general thesis about modernity. "Modern man suffers from an inability to make a choice," he writes, "between renouncing freedom and individualism, or giving up the material comforts of modern technology and the security of a collective mass society."[182] Bettelheim resists the label of Luddite, however, arguing that humanity should not renounce the television set, dishwasher, or even the advantages of a computerized "punch-card" society but should, instead, recognize the effects of these technologies on human relations to better integrate and mitigate their potentially dehumanizing impact. Humans are conforming to the demands of the machine, he warns, by accepting their fate as mere cogs in the greatest machine of all: society. Similarly to *The Empty Fortress*, Bettelheim does not invoke Wiener or cybernetics directly, referring instead to a qualitative change wrought by modernity's seemingly inexorable embrace of efficiency and control: "Many manipulations of men that would ordinarily arouse great resistance in the manipulator, if not open refusal, are carried out without qualms, because all the manipulator has to do is feed anonymous cards into a pre-sorting machine."[183] Wiener anticipated such resistance when he published *The Human Use of Human Beings* (a title that oddly confirms even as it attempts to refute the implications of cybernetic dehumanization). To those who advocate (or fear) a totalitarian society based on the scientific engineering of "communication and control," Wiener observes that the "aspiration of the fascist for a human state based on the model of the ant results from a profound misapprehension both of the nature of the ant and of the man."[184] Humans can learn, ants cannot, he argues, adding, "If the human being is condemned and restricted to perform the same functions over and over again, he will not even be a good ant, not to mention a good human being."[185] In an oblique reference to Wiener, Bettelheim concludes his book on concentration camps, dishwashers, and the tedium of everyday life with a chapter titled "Men Are Not Ants."[186]

Morally, ethically, and politically, Bettelheim and Wiener shared similar tenets of postwar Western liberalism. But in the arena of human relations and emotional life, Bettelheim remained resistant to the scientific ambitions of cybernetic ego management. After all, Joey is a practicing cyberneticist, and he is miserable. Bettelheim explicitly offers Joey not only as a case study in a psychoanalytic theory of autism, but also as a parable of postwar anxiety over the growing influence of science and technology in daily life. Echoing his thesis in *The Informed Heart*, Bettelheim writes, "Just as the angels and saints of a deeply religious age help us to fathom what were man's greatest hopes at the time, and the devils what he trembled at most, so man's delusions in a machine would seem to be tokens of both our hopes and our fears of what machines may do for us, or to us."[187] Bettelheim sides more with fear than hope in describing Joey's case. Freudian cathexis, as a "natural" process of the human mind tied to qualitative emotional investments, might be guided by therapy to the interpretative breakthroughs of psychoanalysis. But Joey's slavish rehearsal of a machine caught in a cybernetic loop spoke to the obvious poverty of the life that technology had in store for humanity.[188] Here Bettelheim placed Joey on the horns of a robotic dilemma well known to readers of pulp science fiction. As everyone knows, the best way to disrupt a robot's dehumanized performance of "communication and control" is to pose an impossible paradox. When confronted with human imponderables, the panicked robot (or mainframe) cries, "Does not compute! Does not compute!" Suffering an oddly human existential crisis, the befuddled device smokes, shakes, and eventually explodes. Bettelheim assigned a similar function to Joey's daily shattering of bulb and tube, arguing that the boy was only truly "alive" when he offered these brief but dramatic moments of resistance to the mechanical complex that "ran him":

> As the master sorcerer's apprentice he had long ago invented these machines to run his body which he felt could not run by itself. But long ago too, the machines had taken over and were now running him. Overpowered by the machines that controlled his body and mind, and exasperated by how they ran him by their own laws and not his own wishes, Joey reasserted himself in a fury. When "exploding" the light bulbs or tubes that power the Joey-machine he became for an instant a real person. . . . It was the one supreme instant of his being alive. But as soon as he had shattered the machine all life ebbed away and anxiety set in. The circuit was broken.[189]

Joey never actually exploded, happily, but in Bettelheim's account, the boy's cries of "Crash! Crash!" signaled a violent disruption of his hard-fought homeostasis as a machine and presented a fleeting opportunity to engage Joey as "real person."

The general psychodynamics that produced Joey's autism were not difficult for Bettelheim to understand—bad parenting. More mysterious were the origins of Joey's mechanical symptom. When and why did this young boy turn to the logic of electronics to regulate his emotional neglect? How did a child of nine master cybernetic theory? After Joey had undergone several weeks of therapy, one of his counselors used a scar on the boy's arm to dislodge a formative moment of trauma. While visiting at a neighbor's house, Joey had become very angry with his older sister and shattered a television screen with a hammer. "There was a tremendous television tube and one of the small persons had a sledge hammer," recalled Joey (speaking of himself in the third person). "It was a big tube, and it was so round. It was the biggest thing I ever saw." In displacing his anger through vandalism, Bettelheim speculated, Joey "had tried to punish an electrical device for having flooded him with overwhelming feelings." When he was harshly disciplined for smashing the TV, Joey learned that his parents "counted machines more important than his feelings. He was expected to keep his feelings in check for the sake of an electrical device, and once again this flooded him with feeling." Later that day, forbidden from taking out his aggression on the TV, Joey put his arm through a pane of glass and required seventeen stiches to sew up the wound (thus the scar). Bettelheim speculates that this episode contributed to Joey's realization that machines, with their ability to switch on and off, did not have feelings and were thus worthy of emulation. As one might expect of a good analysand, accessing this memory of the broken screen allowed Joey to bond more closely with his caregivers at the school. A few days later, a session involving play with a stuffed kangaroo inspired a fantasy in which Joey saw himself protected in the pouch (with the counselor as his surrogate kangaroo mother).[190] As their relationship grew, one of his counselors offered, "You're afraid everything will explode because we won't take care of you, and you'll get hurt." Joey agreed, adding, "I think everything will explode. . . . Vagina. Somebody's vagina will explode. Explode us all." Working to create interpretative suspense, Bettelheim at this point withholds comment on this odd chain of associations from exploded TV to exploding vagina—mediated by a marsupial pouch, no less—and merely observes, "Surely nothing good can have come from an exploding vagina, and his life was certainly no good."[191]

For many months, Bettelheim and his team struggled to find a way to disrupt Joey's cybernetic loop of explosion and homeostasis, hoping to find some channel that might allow Joey, in his fleeting moments as a "real person," to remain engaged and outwardly directed to his surrounding environment. Eventually, an opportunity to escape the circuitry arrived in the form of shit. Joey's use of the toilet initially involved an elaborate series of "preventions" to ward off potential threats to the integrity of his bodily system. While on the toilet, Joey held in one hand the imaginary tubes and wiring that "ran him," using his other hand to either pinch his urethra (while defecating) or plug his anus (while urinating). To not do so, Bettelheim reasoned of Joey's reasoning, was to risk having his "stuffing" fall out: "All his preventions safeguarding intake were connected to, and dependent on, his anxiety about output—and both were based on the conviction that his metabolic processes were run by mechanics."[192] In an effort to make Joey less dependent on these mechanical precautions, Bettelheim's team decided to restrict the amount of "technology" Joey could take with him to the dining table and toilet. This intervention met with great resistance, but a year later, Joey had sublimated these routines into his artwork. Joey's oeuvre consisted of fecal-filled dinosaurs, oil wells that spewed shit, and diagrams of technologically assisted defecation. Less dependent on the cybernetic monitoring and self-regulation of his internal systems, Joey slowly turned his attention to the surrounding environment. "The result was the Joey now saw feces coming out everywhere," Bettelheim writes. "Though there was little change in his actual toilet behavior, he now saw the world as containing essentially nothing but feces."[193] Joey's fascination with shit eventually allowed him to bond with an older boy at the school, Ken (whom Joey nicknamed "Kenrad" in honor of his favorite brand of radio tube).

As his attachments to the surrounding social world increased, Bettelheim writes, Joey entered into a period of gradual transition from boy-machine to boy-in-control-of-machinery. To document this transition, Bettelheim offered a series of drawings by Joey depicting his changing relationship to the machines that "ran him." Early drawings show Joey occupying what he called "an electrical papoose," a figure that condensed his fascination with electronics, pouches, and vaginas. In an early version of the papoose, a "terribly small and lonely" Joey is wholly barricaded within a small compartment that appears precariously perched high in the air. A device resembling an antenna gathers either energy or communications, depicted in the familiar telecasting convention of lines spiraling through the air. A subsequent drawing shows Joey still isolated but more securely connected by physical wiring to the machine that "lived" him. Eventually Joey began drawing a contraption he called the "Connecticut Papoose," significant to Bettelheim in that these images show "for the first time the papoose is not merely an entity run by a machine" but one that "also runs the machine." In this iteration, a still wired Joey remains encased in what resembles a train car, wheels added to the "papoose" that imply greater mobility. Joey now runs the machine rather than the machine running Joey. Thus, observes Bettelheim, Joey "was no longer a collection of wires in a glass tube but a person, though still encased and protected by glass, connected and cut off at the same time (Connect-I-cut)."[194] Joey's faith in cybernetics was apparently waning, allowing him to entertain a figurative rather than literal equation of boy and machine. There then followed a transitional fascination with birds and eggs, inspiring Joey to draw a "chicken-hen" with an "exploding womb" as well as a vehicle he called "the hen electric." The latter was a bird-shaped car that Bettelheim saw as "pregnant with an electrical fetus."[195] The trajectory here, whether psychoanalytic or novelistic (or both), should be clear. Joey, the boy who once lived as a machine, prepared for his symbolic rebirth as an organic human being. Sure enough, Joey finally tells his counselor, "The tubes were burning too long. I don't need them anymore." Rescued by a fateful encounter with shit, Joey was now a real flesh-and-blood boy.

....

Cybernetics aspired to a universe of systems within systems. A doctrine of information in circulation, cybernetics also signaled a historical benchmark in the ongoing suturing of the anatomo-politics of the human body and the biopolitics of the population. Humans have always produced and lived within systems, cyberneticists would say, but with the advent of Wiener's distinctly American philosophy, every person on Earth does or eventually will consider themselves to be ego machines negotiating systems of modulated inputs and outputs. The body is a machine; thought is energy; and both are variously connected to the machinery of power. This terror, once actively resisted by a modern ego under siege, is now openly embraced. A few vestigial pockets of humanism may no longer promote cybernetics as the key to all known truth, but it remains the de facto religion of science, communications, information studies, and all other positivist endeavors that believe the qualitative dynamics of subjectivity and meaning can be mastered through the quantitative administration of objective data. Today this faith is most pronounced among the various futurists associated with "post-humanism," a movement best known through Raymond Kurzweil's

FIGS 4.7, 4.8, AND 4.9 Drawings curated by Bettelheim demonstrating Joey's gradual emergence from his cybernetic loop: (*above*) the "electrical papoose"; (*opposite top*) the "Connect-I-cut papoose"; (*opposite bottom*) the "hen electric."

HEN ELECTRIC

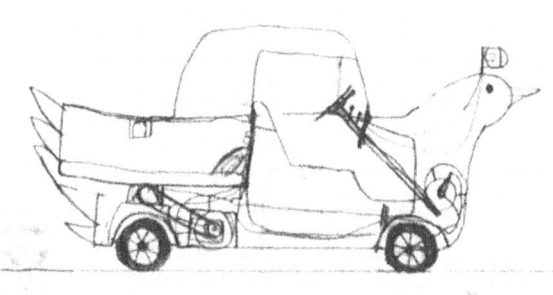

influential proposition that humanity is approaching the "singularity," a historical tipping point when the integration of information technologies will at last produce a type of cyborg subject and forever alter what it means to be "human."[196] A journey that began with primate ancestors throwing rocks at one another will soon culminate in artificial intelligence that can (and *will*) think for and beyond the limited perspective and capabilities of the human brain. For now, the singularity is taking its first baby steps into capitalist integration, as in smart toilet paper rolls that automatically reorder themselves via the "Internet of Things." But cybernetic post-humanism envisions many more miracles in the future of the species. Humans, these prognosticators believe, will one day exit the human body entirely, weaning egos bred of carbon and oxygen into complexes of silicon and electricity. Wiener himself endorsed such a prospect: "Theoretically, if we could build a machine whose mechanical structures duplicated human physiology, then we could have a machine whose intellectual capacities would duplicate those of human beings."[197]

The idea that the ego, as the brain's information packet, might be loaded into a computer is a familiar theme of science fiction that predates Wiener in the many "brain-in-a-jar" stories of the 1920s and '30s. Sadly, wiring a brain with electrodes and floating it in an aquarium proved a dead end, thus ending dreams of transplantation and instead opening the door to the possibilities of *translation*. For those so inclined, the advent of digital media has made this fantasy of an indestructible ego seem plausible once again.[198] Significant money and attention is now going into whole brain emulation (WBE), a project that might be described as the cybernetic Rapture. Jeff Lichtman and J. L. Morgan of Harvard write, "We think the computer analogy gives us a lead. The computer can be turned off and on without losing much data because the instructions that make it work are embedded in its 'static' physicality. A deep understanding of how information is stably stored in the structure of hard discs, the input and output wires of each chip, the physical structures that explain the working of those chips and so on would be enormously helpful in making sense of a computer. Might the same be said of nervous systems?"[199] Brain emulators say yes. The "human mind and its conscious experiences" are "purely computational phenomenon," observes one study. "We are broadly similar to an intelligent robot. Our body is analogous to the robot's mechanical body. Our brain is analogous to the robot's computer hardware including the physical hard drives which contain its control software." The cybernetic quest for "mind uploading," we are told, would involve copying one robot's software and transferring it to another, producing "a similar behaving robot with a similar tokening of internal data structures." Much like humanists who no longer feel compelled to cite Freud when discussing the unconsciousness, scientists and engineers invoke Wiener's cybernetic consciousness as a self-evident thing. The study concedes that this cybernetic brain-computer model is based on an analogy that is perhaps "deeply flawed"; nevertheless, it is "an analogy that rests at the core of all of our research in cognitive science, neuroscience, and even biology itself."[200] Flawed or not, in other words, *we all believe it.*

The impulse guiding these cybernetic dreams of escaping our foul, disgusting, and deteriorating bodies is not difficult to understand. Nature wants us dead, as Freud helpfully reminded readers in "The Future of an Illusion," and the ego will do anything to fantasize defenses against the limitations of its own knowledge and existence.[201] In this respect, cybernetic fantasies of WBE constitute a return of the *Frankenstein* repressed. Enlightenment science challenged the comforting fiction of the Cartesian soul, demonstrating that selfhood might be little more than a trick of tissue and nerve. Embracing this material finitude, cybernetic post-futurism hopes to preserve this Cartesian illusion in the form of code. As Hayles argues, cybernetics proved instrumental in producing a new essentialist divide, not between body and mind, but between materiality and information. Inherited from the cybernetic debates of mid-century is the doxa that "information and materiality are conceptually distinct and ... information is in some sense more essential, more important and more fundamental than materiality."[202] Underlying the cybernetic dream of uploading consciousness is a magical positivism born of panicked materialism, a belief that any and all questions can be resolved through the accumulation of sufficient data. In this post-human universe of secular data management, the immateriality of information replaces the ontological infinitude of God as the occult field of magical omniscience, promising its acolytes, through the transubstantiating miracle of magical positivism, the possibility of deliverance from the mortal humiliations of material existence.[203] Egos, gathered by modernity into cities and besieged by the electronics of nervous irritation, will use the very same electronics to escape into the bodiless peace that comes with virtual immortality.

In this respect, there is a certain poetry on Bettelheim's part in casting shit as the medium that delivers Joey from his cybernetic prison. Foul, protean, and for the most part useless, shit is the amorphous paste that routinely foils human attempts to maintain systems of rational order. There is little that is systematic about shit. As modern-day Schopenhauerians frequently observe, "Shit happens," a reference to the unpredictable and ineluctable muck that catastrophically intervenes to befoul the best laid plans of mice, men, and machines. Shit is the supreme emblem of organic entropy, an unpleasant reminder that the mental ego, whatever its exalted self-image, remains hostage to the embarrassments of the body. Shit is also decidedly analog or, put another way, nondigital. The radical contingency of each shit, from bolus to turd, evokes an organic secretion so complex in composition that it implicitly mocks any possibility that the ego, as another bodily secretion, might be reduced to a manageable information profile. Can human memory really be archived on chips and *being-in-the-world* transcribed into electronic flows of discrete integers? How much data is necessary to avoid compression loss when moving, copying, and running this ego? Even if these questions of existential engineering are answered, most likely shit will continue to complicate this antiseptic fantasy of clean data and disembodied being. In the short term, there is the material shit of the political, industrial, and governmental economies necessary to make such a fantasy a reality (securing research funding, adjudicating new legal issues, subordinating a meat-based workforce to maintain the mainframes, and so on). And in the long term, there is the more ontological question: Can *Dasein* really be digitized? Or is it inextricably linked to the inductive shit lurking between the 1s and 0s of a digital data stream?

Targeted Individuals

CHAPTER FIVE

AT SOME INDETERMINATE MOMENT in the early 1960s, attorney Francis E. Dec appears to have crossed over into something resembling insanity. Convicted and disbarred by the State of New York in 1958 for mishandling $400 in a Nassau County divorce case, Dec began the new decade involved in a lengthy and increasingly deranged series of legal appeals, eventually filing a petition for a writ of certiorari with the Supreme Court. A parole violation in 1961 landed Dec in New York's Pilgrim State Hospital for a sixty-day psychiatric evaluation, and his mental state appears to have continued to deteriorate over the next several years. Apparently suffering an acute psychiatric crisis, Dec made a failed attempt in 1965 to flee the United States and return to his family's homeland in Poland. But after a brief detention at the Canadian border (during which time he would later claim to have been beaten and tortured), Dec was unceremoniously returned to his house in Hempstead, New York. He would live there, more or less alone, for the next twenty-five years, growing ever more reclusive, paranoid, and delusional, increasingly obsessed with a sinister plot he believed to be operating all around him. When not scraping "CIA paint" off the walls of his house with a razor blade, Dec spent his free time typing screeds and manifestos describing his ongoing persecution.

Dec's troubles may have begun within the limited jurisdiction of the Nassau County court system, but over time he found himself locked in deadly battle with what he called the worldwide Communist Gangster Computer God (CGCG). Through a strange array of electronic devices, Dec argued, the CGCG controlled almost all activity on Earth, from the major events of global history to seemingly random cars tactically backfiring on the street near Dec's home. Truly a *lunatic*, Dec believed that the CGCG implemented this control from a complex of "brain banks," computers, and other sinister media operating on the dark side of the moon:

> Four billion worldwide population—all living—have a Computer God Containment Policy Brain Bank Brain, a real brain, in the Brain Bank

Cities on the far side of the moon we never see. Primarily based on your lifelong Frankenstein Radio Controls, especially your Eyesight TV sight-and-sound recorded by your brain, your moon-brain of the Computer God activates your Frankenstein threshold Brainwash Radio—lifelong inculcating conformist propaganda. Even frightening you and mixing you up and the usual "Don't worry about it" for your setbacks, mistakes—even when you receive deadly injuries! THIS is the Worldwide Computer God Secret Containment Policy![1]

The CGCG's goal was to implement a "Frankenstein Slave State," and Dec saw evidence of this conspiracy everywhere—in the media, of course, but also in the courts, the government, the food supply, the medical profession, and even the traffic patterns in his neighborhood. The plot dated back centuries, born of a scheme to displace the "Astrocist religion" and contaminate the bloodline of the "Slovene People."[2]

Dec distributed photocopies of his screeds by nailing them to telephone poles, placing them under windshield wipers, and mailing them to TV and radio stations across the country. Having mailed hundreds of these fliers in the 1970s and 1980s, Dec and his paranoid defiance of the CGCG eventually began to attract an audience, albeit a following united more in amazed disbelief than sympathetic solidarity. The cartoonist Robert Crumb devoted an entire issue of *Weirdo Comix* to Dec in 1983. Three years later, Milwaukee disc jockey Doc Britton gave voice to Dec's prose in a series of dramatic readings, creating a bootleg tape that would be sampled and mixed into a variety of outré recordings for the next twenty years. A Soho stage play about Dec premiered in 1999, and Dec received prominent treatment in Diane Kossy's book *Kooks: A Guide to the Outer Limits of Human Belief* (1994).[3] Today, a website works to collect, archive, and share the entirety of Dec's oeuvre, not just his ephemeral photocopied fliers, but also the official documents attending his increasingly incoherent legal appeals during the 1960s.[4] Whether or not Dec was aware of this notoriety late in life is unclear. In 1995, a "fan" paid a visit to Dec in his nursing facility to ask him about his various theories, but by that point Dec had become wholly catatonic. According to one's perspective, Dec either passed away quietly or was "exterminated undetectably" in 1996 at a Veterans Administration hospital in Queens.

Diagnosing Dec based only on his fliers and a brief stint in a psychiatric ward would be difficult. His writing certainly conveys a lifetime of relentless persecution at the hands of yet another nebulous System, but as the composite powers of the CGCG suggest, this paranoia was somewhat unfocused.

In a dense, single-spaced flyer from the mid-1980s, Dec greets the reader with a crude drawing of a cranium, the skull opened, we are told, for the insertion of "Frankenstein formfitting controls":

> LOOK AT THE PICTURES!!! See the skull, the part of bone removed, the "master-race" Frankenstein radio controls, the Brain-thoughts Broadcasting Radio, the Eyesight Television, the Frankenstein Earphone Radio, the Threshold Brainwash Radio, the latest new skull reforming to contain ALL Frankenstein Controls, even in THIN skulls of WHITE PEDIGREE MALES! Visible Frankenstein controls! The synthetic nerve-radio directional antennae loop! Make copies for yourself! There is NO ESCAPE from this worst gangster police state, using ALL of the deadly gangster Frankenstein controls![5]

While this array of odd technologies may seem somewhat redundant (the Frankenstein Slave State employs not just one but three types of radio), Dec's precise nomenclature suggests that each device performed a unique function, at least in (or to) Dec's mind. In addition to rendering strange such familiar technologies as radio and television, Dec made frequent reference to a series of devices—never fully explained—that apparently made sense only to him. Describing the challenges of his daily life on Long Island, Dec cites "DEADLY ASSAULTS, even in my yard with knives, even bricks and stones, even DEADLY TOUCH TABIN or ELECTRIC SHOCK FLASHLIGHTS; even remote electronically controlled around-corners-projection of DEADLY TOUCH TARANTULA SPIDERS!"[6]

Whatever Dec's mental status, his writing speaks to a feature of technical delusions that became increasingly prominent in the second half of the twentieth century. With the exponential explosion of media electronics and media content after World War II, isolating a definitive plot involving a specific persecutor who operates an isolated technology is ever more difficult, perhaps impossible. Psychotic delusions have always been malleable, capable of adjusting to new information and circumstances. But as technology and information themselves become more promiscuous, bound together in the service of techno-semiotic systems that aspire to remain invisible, deniable, and thus unanswerable, locating any discernible enemy to function as the paranoid ego's traditional foil poses a significant challenge. Dec's screeds are emblematic in their careening, amplified panic over imperious yet chimerical powers that seemingly are everywhere all the time and yet can never be fully confronted or understood. Accordingly, Dec's grand composite Other, the Communist Gangster Computer God, draws on every significant axis of

FIG 5.1 A typewritten flyer by Dec warning of "'master-race' Frankenstein radio controls." Image courtesy of Peter "zero" Branting, Official Francis E. Dec Fanclub, http://www.bentoandstarchky.com/dec/rants.htm.

modern power imaginable—a "thing" (or is it a principle? a metaphor?) that draws on politics, law, technology, and religion. This excess of power, in turn, manifests across an excess of platforms. Dec does not simply hear voices on a hallucinatory radio like the lunatics of old; instead, an assortment of radios, in league with television, print, and computers on the dark side of the moon, orchestrate a never-ending campaign of inescapable persecution. Dec came to believe that even the installation of new curbs in his neighborhood indexed a sinister plot: "First in the entire world all corner sidewalk curbs are being replaced with smooth corner driveways for non-existent baby carriages and wheelchair pedestrians in this ghost town, ideal for vehicles to drive up on the sidewalk from any direction for the computerized Computer God undetectable extermination."[7]

To the modern ear, Dec's manic rantings are undeniably comic. But this humor, like so much comedy, stems in large part from our own sublimated anxiety. Dec's insane screeds about the CGCG are funny because they allow the smugly sane to disavow a basic truth at the heart of Dec's universe. Most recognize, in some form and by some name, the existence of something akin to the "Worldwide Computer God Secret Containment Policy," an abstract field of power, perhaps unrecognizable even to itself, that is nevertheless determinative in shaping our experiences and the horizons of possibility. After living with disciplinary power for some two centuries, today's technocratized citizens understand that authority once vested in a single person, a certain machine, or even a residual nation-state is now disbursed not only across the everywhere and thus nowhere of administrative control, but through endlessly proliferating vectors of dissimulation, camouflage, and evasion. Once a thing to be possessed and implemented, power is now for many simply an abstract force of nature to be endured. Dec's writing is funny in large part because he is naïve enough to believe that this modern form of power might actually be named, its plots actually exposed. This hubris is even more hilarious given Dec's incongruous collisions between the minor frustrations of life on Long Island and a massive bank of computers orchestrating reality from the dark side of the moon. (The CGCG, never asleep and always lurking, possesses the malicious precision to program even traffic jams and curb cuts in downtown Hempstead.) Laughing at Dec's delusional portrait of the Frankenstein Slave State relieves us from confronting our own implicit theory of the ego's subordination to techno-semiotic power. Sure, the idea of a Communist Gangster Computer God working as master puppeteer is amusing, but is it any more or less ridiculous than any other attempt to comprehend the machinations of contemporary society?

CGCGVALISHAARP

Framed as an exemplar of "psychotic" discourse, Dec's typewritten fliers do appear truly insane. Dec's hyperbolic paranoia in recounting his forced repatriation to Long Island in 1965, for example, would appear the quintessence of psychotic écriture:

> While "my" return-trip 707 Boeing jet airliner was being serviced for "my" return trip, I quickly walked into the airplane and saw a CIA GANGSTER with a small electric hairdryer-type blower pumping DEADLY POISON NERVE-GAS SMOKE into SECRET COMPARTMENTS under the ashtrays in the arms of the chairs where later I was ordered to sit in the airplane full of CIA UNDERLINGS, "passengers", my assassins, who GIGGLED as they watched me dragged in chains by the airplane by the Gangster CIA Police Gangsters! These deadly Gangster CIA passengers, they PRESSED THE FRONTAL PANEL OF THE ASH TRAYS IN THE SEAT ARMS to release the DEADLY POISON NERVE GAS SMOKE! Indubitably, all of the other deadly CIA underling GANGSTERS upon this staged-return flight, they ALL had taken the TOP-SECRET POISON NERVE GAS ANTIDOTE PILL™, immuning them from the deadly poison nerve gas smoke! Deadly poison nerve gas smoke was sprayed at me from CIGARS, CIGARETTES and even from BALL-POINT PENS also from the WIG of a woman sitting next to me, even the Swiss cheese-type ice cubes were evaporating into poison nerve gas smoke in all of the "free" drinks![8]

Manifestly demented, Dec's writings also exhibit a pronounced dialogism. In sharing his concern that wigs, pens, and ice cubes might spray him with nerve gas, for example, Dec invokes the obligatory scene in every James Bond novel wherein MI6 reveals the latest (secret) high-tech toys available for 007's new mission. As in all dialogic exchanges, Dec's tortured text also reframes the significance of Ian Fleming's oeuvre, highlighting the paranoia already lurking in the genre's source materials. Fleming did not invent the spy novel, of course, but his introduction of James Bond as the paragon of British masculinity, suavely defending the Anglophonic empire, epitomizes a postwar fascination with the secret operation of technocratic power. Bond's "toys," moreover, speak to a core premise in many psychotic delusions about technology: those who occupy positions of power, variously defined, do indeed have access to secret technologies employed in covert operations, whether it is a super-villain's high-tech plan to blow up the moon or MI6's ingenious concealment of machine guns behind the headlights of Bond's

Aston Martin. Equally intriguing here is Dec's seemingly gratuitous inclusion of a trademark symbol (™) to brand the TOP-SECRET POISON NERVE GAS ANTIDOTE PILL, a comic gesture aligning Dec with any number of postwar cynics (from the yippies to MAD *Magazine*) disgruntled by America's quest to commodify, brand, and trademark all of human existence. Quotation marks, used liberally by Dec throughout his writing to signal the general deceitfulness of the objects around him, here call into question just how "free" the "free" drinks on this airplane actually were: free of cost, perhaps, but chilled with deadly nerve-gas ice.

Dec's prose also draws heavily on the era's bestsellers in crypto-archeology and Christian eschatology. Erich von Däniken's *Chariots of the Gods?* (1968) proposed that the wonders of the ancient world were in fact the product of extraterrestrial intervention, a thesis that inspired a wave of popular imitators to publish their own claims that "God was an astronaut."[9] Though widely dismissed as bad histories based on junk science, books like *Chariot of the Gods?* succeeded as entertainment by cultivating an eerie sense of cosmic paranoia, combining H. P. Lovecraft and *National Geographic* to implicitly suggest that the Ancient Ones would one day return. Von Däniken's reading of the Nazca Lines in Peru, for example, argued that these large hieroglyphs, dating to around 500 BC, are legible only from the sky. Therefore, they *must constitute a landing field for ancient astronauts*. Dec confronted Von Däniken on his own turf, proposing a Polish-inflected theory regarding the construction of the Mayan pyramids of Chichen Itza. "Like ALL of the pyramids, the pyramids in the Torrid zone in Central America were built by Slovenic Astrocism, with C. God Frankenstein Skull Cap Controls, under the direct rays of the sun lite, to eliminate slanted diffusion etc. with no snow to curtail operations year round, with endless growing season to sustain life, with no intelligent nearby population to interfere or spread the secret, not even an interfering nite glow, smoke, dust, etc. from any population."[10] While Von Däniken mined an archeological vein of paranoia, Hal Lindsay's *The Late, Great Planet Earth* (1970) examined the turbulent global events of the 1960s and '70s through the Book of Revelations, warning readers that the End Times were near. Even more alarmist were the comic tracts of Jack Chick, morality tales that cast the unsaved as one acid trip, TV show, or rock concert away from eternal damnation. Lindsay and Chick were especially popular among those evangelical sects eager for the Rapture,[11] a constituency that in many cases still fights the battles of the Reformation by casting Catholicism as a false religion working in service of the Antichrist. One of Chick's more technically deluded tracts, for example, asserts that a "big computer in the Vatican" records the name of every Protestant church member.¹² Dec also had an interest in the grand arc of Christianity and the chicanery of "Mafia Communist Catholicism." Exploiting suspicions of papist subterfuge spanning from *Melmoth the Wanderer* (1820) to *The Da Vinci Code* (2003), Dec lambasted Catholicism as "THE FIRST TOTALITARIAN SUPERSTITION COMMUNISM RELIGION," a conspiracy that had labored throughout its history "FOR CONTROL AND MANIPULATION OF THE HUMAN RACE INTO THE OVER ALL PLAN *to explore and control the entire Universe*."¹³ Dec was no less suspicious of Judaism. Through some inexplicable logic, Dec apparently came to believe that human aging was not a natural process but was instead a Jewish plot. "Worldwide, systematic instant plastic surgery BUTCHERY MURDER, fake ageing so ALL people are dead or useless by age 70!" he wrote. "Done at night to YOU as a Frankenstein slave!" For Dec, Jewish control of new technologies and global interbreeding foretold a bleak future: "Eventual brain lobotomization of the entire world population for the Worldwide Deadly Gangster Communist Computer God overall plan, an ideal worldwide population of light-skinned, low hopeless and helpless Jew-mulattos, the communist black wave of the future."¹⁴

The CGCG conducted this lobotomy campaign by taking unwitting humans to hospitals or "camouflaged miniature-hospital van trucks." Dec blamed "Jew doctors" for this plot, but the surgery itself appears to have been highly automated. "The Computer God Operating Cabinet has many robot arms," Dec wrote, "with electrical and laser beam knife robot arms. With fly-eye TV cameras watching your whole body, every part of you is monitored—even through your Frankenstein Controls! Synthetic blood; synthetic instant-sealing flesh and skin, even synthetic electrical heartbeat to keep you alive are some of the unbelievable Computer God Instant Plastic Surgery Secrets.™"¹⁵ Brain control through psychosurgery was a familiar Cold War concern in the 1950s and '60s. American propagandists routinely accused the Soviets of using psychosurgery to either quiet dissidents or research strategies of mass control. On the home front, meanwhile, Walter Freeman performed thousands of transorbital lobotomies in the 1950s and '60s, earning him the rather ghoulish nickname "Dr. Icepick."¹⁶ The sinister possibilities of psychosurgery were certainly familiar to many psychotics of the era. In his memoirs, CIA agent David R. McLean recalls the various "cranks, nuts, and screwballs" who routinely contacted the agency: "One disturbed gentleman from Buffalo claimed the Communists had kidnapped him, cut open his head, removed his brains, and inserted a radio."¹⁷

Dec's account of "Frankenstein threshold brain radio" also evokes the plot of Sam Katzman's *Creature with the Atom Brain* (1956). In this staple of the late-night creature feature, an exiled mobster employs a Nazi scientist to create an army of radio-controlled zombies, powered by atomic energy, to restore him to power.[18] That schizophrenia and science fiction should share an interest in brain control is no coincidence. When Eugen Bleuler introduced "schizophrenia" to psychiatric literature in 1911, he formalized a type of madness that gradually had been moving toward diagnostic recognition during the last decade of the nineteenth century. This period roughly coincides with the emergence of science fiction as a distinct literary genre. Jules Verne and H. G. Wells are typically credited as the so-called fathers of the genre, but in truth, science fiction (or, better, science as fiction) drew on a number of writers operating along many speculative frontiers.[19] Although they were more concerned with social structure than technology, the various utopian novels of the eighteenth and nineteenth century contributed much to the genre.[20] Verne imagined the Baltimore Gun Club "shooting" the first man to the moon in 1865, but by 1883, a Madam Ehrenborg had published an account of her own very real expedition to Mars, a spiritualist journey that took advantage of the less ballistic and more plausible theory of "magnetic currents that connect the planets in our solar system."[21] In 1900, psychologist Theodore Flournoy published a study that would go on to become a classic of psychology, spiritualism, and science fiction: *From India to the Planet Mars: A Case of Multiple Personality with Imaginary Languages*.[22] Flournoy's object of study was the famous trance medium Miss Helene Smith, a woman who—in addition to being the reincarnation of a Hindu princess and Marie Antoinette—claimed to speak both Sanskrit and "Martian," the second language acquired during her visits to the Red Planet. Operating within a historical moment when the precise boundaries of spiritualism, science fiction, and psychosis had yet to cohere, Smith, Ehrenborg, and other mental travelers foregrounded the challenges facing the consecration of each of these three discourses.

Bound by a common interest in speculative theory and industrial progress, Victorian authors, assorted madmen, and those charged with distinguishing the two frequently operated at the frontiers of technological possibility. All were attracted to what Tzvetan Todorov has termed the "scientific marvelous"—a technical/narrational strategy that emerged in nineteenth-century literature as a means of providing rational explanations to otherwise fantastic enigmas. In his canonical study of "fantastic" fiction, Todorov describes the genre in terms of "hesitation," stories calculated to suspend the reader for as long as possible between two systems of explanation: the natural and the supernatural.[23] The "fantastic" is the effect produced through such hesitation. In the nineteenth century, the scientific marvelous emerged as a strategy for resolving this fantastic hesitation through the invocation of a natural, techno-scientific solution. So while a gothic novelist in the Radcliffe tradition might ultimately reveal a ghost to be no more than a mad nun running around in a sheet, practitioners of the scientific marvelous could resolve a similar enigma by attributing the apparition to a magic lantern or a distorting mirror.[24] What we now call science fiction is this scientific marvelous pushed beyond merely providing plausible explanations to Victorian conundrums, having become an entire genre based on interrogating the marvelous nature of science itself. Developing alongside early twentieth-century interest in wireless, telepathy, physics, neurology, and psychology, pulps such as *Amazing Stories* and *Weird Tales* frequently traded in tales of synthetic "madness"—the seemingly psychotic discovered to be under the influence of a scientifically marvelous machine. These stories ranged from the cosmic horror of H. P. Lovecraft to more mundane exercises in technologies of telekinesis and psychosis. Hugh B. Cave's "The Murder Machine" (1930) imagines a device capable of transmitting "hypnotic thought-waves" that provoke targets to commit homicide.[25] In "The Radio Mind-Ray" (1934), a scientist discovers that, after injecting morphine and adrenaline into the nervous system, the "electrical rays given by the brain might be increased many times in power and intensity." His first experiment involves compelling his wife "to undertake or not undertake certain things against her normal inclinations."[26] In the awkwardly technical conspiracy tale "The Ray of Madness" (1930), the president of the United States is almost driven to insanity after a foreign spy targets his pillow with weaponized moonbeams.[27]

By the 1950s, a large arsenal of science-fiction devices were available not only for the adult psychotic, but also for emotionally troubled adolescents on the precipice between childhood fantasy and teenage delusion. In his work with the psychotic, analyst Rudolf Ekstein frequently encountered the scientific marvelous in the fantasy worlds of "borderline" children. An adolescent girl convinced that her mother sought to kill her spoke in "terrified outbursts about the invasion of the earth by horrible moon creatures intent on attacking and kidnapping her."[28] Another "severely disturbed girl" broached the topic of alienation by engaging her therapist in a discussion of *Invaders from Mars* (1953) and *The Devil Girl from Mars* (1954), both recently shown on television. "I saw one about a girl that came from another

FIG 5.2 The "devil girl" from *The Devil Girl from Mars* (1954) provides a point of identification for a troubled teenager. SOURCE: DANZIGER PRODUCTIONS.

planet.... She was a devil girl, I mean, she was horrible," offered the girl, marveling at the alien's cruelty to the people of Earth. Recognizing in the patient a point of identification with the "devil girl," the therapist suggested, "I wonder if one could help such a girl, you know, this girl from the other planet, to take on our characteristics and be like us."[29]

Ekstein was not the only critic to note an affinity between psychosis and science fiction. In 1954, psychoanalyst Robert Plank addressed this connection directly in "The Reproduction of Psychosis in Science-Fiction." An interview with Plank later appeared in *Time* magazine with the title, "Is Science-Fiction Off Its Rocket?"[30] Plank agreed, to a point, arguing that science-fiction writers routinely trade in themes also found in schizophrenic delusions, especially "delusions of grandeur, of persecution, and of superhuman influence."[31] Plank argued that these themes were symptomatic of a schizophrenic personality structure shared by the author and his readers. But Plank was no Frederic Wertham, the famed crusader against violence in comic books.[32] Plank did not argue that reading science fiction would trigger a schizophrenic episode—quite the opposite, in fact. Trained as a psychoanalyst, Plank believed the genre helped writers and readers sublimate their latent schizophrenic impulses, making the stories a safety valve of displacement. By "objectifying his fantasies in a work which has existence outside his mind, the writer is able to rid himself of fantasy material, but if not so handled, might indeed get a quite more personal hold on him and emerge as a symptom."[33] Readers, too, enjoyed the benefit of seeing their (schizo)fantasy structures externalized and shared. "Psychologist Plank would not go so far as to say that science-fiction writers are 'crazy' because they reflect schizophrenic trends," continued *Time*. "Rather, he argues, these signs are becoming more conspicuous in a mechanized civilization. Science fiction may be bad science and worse fiction, but to a good wig-picker it 'is a sensitive barometer of our changing mental climate.'"[34] Plank's research was at the center of a paper presented by Franklin D. Jones at Walter Reed Hospital in 1965. Jones was also interested in the possible connection between schizophrenia and science fiction, leading him to conduct a "content analysis" of the first six anthologies of *Galaxy* magazine (published from 1952 to 1962). This task involved reading 123 short stories, constituting 2,042 pages of text. From this survey, Jones proposed sixteen recurring categories of content, many of which intersect with the familiar symptoms of schizophrenia.[35]

By the 1960s, science-fiction writers were hailing the schizophrenic as a potential ally in critiquing "mechanized civilization." A type of "schizophrenia" entered the genre as both a stylistic device and a manifest theme. In his study of the author Michael Moorcock and the British science-fiction magazine *New Worlds*, Colin Greenland notes the gradual turn in the early 1960s away from the unexamined aesthetic of "realism" that had dominated the genre since its inception. As Greenland writes, the authors at *New Worlds* "recognized that the trend in physics as in psychology had been away from absolutes towards the relative and contingent.... For the artist realism was out of the question because reality was losing ground, to possibility. Conspiracy theory became popular; schizophrenia, it seemed, was now useful."[36] This trend can also be seen in the revolutionary impact of artist Richard Powers. As the de facto art director for Ballantine Books, Powers introduced modernist elements of surrealism, cubism, and primitivism to paperback design, displacing the more representational style that had previously dominated the pulps.[37] Given mid-century science-fiction's interest in alternative realities, philosophical inquiry, and subjective defamiliarization, the schizophrenic's "bizarre" relationship to time, space, language, self, and reality made him a useful ally in crafting speculative universes, reinvigorating the "fantastic" origins of the genre and defamiliarizing the institutions of mid-century technocracy.[38] As the more or less techno-rational path out of fantastic literature, science fiction turned to the schizophrenic as a means of reintroducing an element of fantastic hesitation. Is this world "real" or is it not?

This hybridization of science fiction and schizophrenia was particularly prominent and self-conscious in the work of Philip K. Dick. Best known as the author of *Blade Runner* (1982; adapted from Dick's 1968 novella *Do Androids Dream of Electric Sheep?*), Dick repeatedly returned in his work to the ambiguities dividing "hallucination as reality" and "reality as hallucination,"[39] using all manner of scientifically marvelous devices (androids, cryonic suspension, virtual reality, time travel, psychotropic drugs) to problematize the self's typically self-evident experience of selfhood and reality. A modern autodidact with a lifelong interest in issues of philosophy and theology, Dick frequently collided spiritual, scientific, and schizophrenic hesitation most explicitly, using the figures of the mystic and the psychotic to stage commentaries on the illusory nature of the material world. In *Martian Time-Slip* (1964), the schizophrenic protagonist emigrates to Mars, where he encounters a psychotherapist who believes his psychosis may indicate an altered relationship to time.[40] In *Clans of the Alphane Moon* (1964), an orphaned psychiatric colony creates its own civilization based on the different "clans" of mental illness. In *The Three Stigmata of Palmer Aldrich* (1965), bored off-world colonists use an illegal drug (Can-D) to facilitate communal hallucinations involving a Barbie-like doll (Perky Pat) and dollhouse. *We Can Build You* (1982; written in 1962) includes not one but three schizophrenic characters (including a robot of Abraham Lincoln), with the last third of the novel involving hallucinatory therapy at a mental hospital. Dick describes the "fixed idea" of his work as "the pleasant illusory skin stretched over a dreadful reality ... plus the theme: I am not (or he is not) what I think (I am) he is—in particular my (his) true identity is obscured by fake memories."[41] This relentlessly paranoid vision of a suspect, destabilized reality made Dick, alongside William S. Burroughs and J. G. Ballard, central to debates over postmodernity and science fiction in the 1980s and '90s. (Like so many visionaries, Dick has had many more readers in death than he did while he was alive.)

These thematic interests became especially personal for Dick on February 20, 1974.[42] While recovering from a wisdom tooth extraction, Dick opened the front door of his home to receive a delivery of pain medication. At the door was a young woman wearing a Christian Ichthys pendant (better known as the fish symbol). Dick would later claim that sunlight reflecting from the pendant mesmerized him with a "pink beam," ushering the author into a prolonged period of profoundly meaningful hallucinations. Dick came to believe he was living two lives at the same time: that of the science-fiction writer Philip K. Dick in the twentieth century and that of a persecuted Christian named "Thomas" in first-century ancient Rome. He also came to believe in the existence of a "transcendentally rational mind" guiding human experience, an entity or agency that Dick referred to as "Zebra." After recovering from the intense psychological disruptions of 2-3-74 (Dick's shorthand for the momentous events of February-March 1974), Dick continued to theorize these experiences until his death in 1982. *The Exegesis of Philip K. Dick*, a dense compendium of letters, notes, diagrams, and rough drafts chronicling Dick's search for what often seems like a "unified field theory" of all reality, appeared in 2011. Dick's evidence ranged from absurd anecdote (early in *The Exegesis*, he notices that at night his cat will only look to the sky, not at the ground, suggesting that he is receiving a sidereal transmission) to new interpretations of religious, philosophical, occult, and psychedelic texts.[43]

What exactly "happened" to Dick in the final decade of his life remains unclear. Dick himself certainly considered schizophrenia a possibility: "Schizophrenia is the breaking through of the collective archetypal forms and world.... Viewed in this way, a mere ego-constructed world is the private world we mistakenly (evidently) label as a sane—i.e., normal (rational)—world. But maybe our entire civilization is wrong.... We moderns are half-brained men: we are deformed, and the only place we can turn to for wholeness is the balancing right hemisphere of our own brains—which is where the unconscious is where dreams *and* schizophrenia originate."[44] Dick writes at one point that he has adopted a regimen of soluble vitamins recommended to help schizophrenics bring their left and right brains into better alignment. Pamela Jackson and Jonathan Lethem, the editors of Dick's *Exegesis*, suggest that those interested in a "medical, psychiatric, neurological, or pharmacological context" for *The Exegesis* "will be spoiled for choice."[45] Whatever explanation one favors, however, Dick's *Exegesis* reads in many places as a transmission from the most distant borderlands of science and schizophrenia (all in the service of finding God or His equivalent). Throughout *The Exegesis*, Dick invokes ideas of interstellar transmission and cosmic communications. At one point, he contemplates the significance of a dream in which "your Zenith TV set a circuit detects when Christ in his invisible form returns ... [and] it causes three lights to come on." Dick continues:

> You then remove the spindle and base and take from it a dark green cellophane strip and replace it in the TV set, where presumably the 3 lights

come on even more or anyhow some further development occurs, in line with the event. I ask myself, Why 3 lights? And it occurs to me that 3 lights equal three eyes, the coming on the 3rd eye, which means the restoration of the original faculty, taken away at the Fall, of sight. Unless the 3 lights simply refers to the trinity and nothing more, that is most likely what is signifies; also, the removal of the strip of very dark green cellophane suggests the removal, at the right time, of an occluding membrane which filters out most of the light, allowing only a token amount to filter through.... The veil must be torn aside for the light, which has returned, to shine. In the dream I was extremely surprised to find I had such a circuit in my TV set; I called the multitude that I might show them, but none was interested.[46]

Dick's dream is an odd collision of First Corinthians ("through a glass darkly") and *Winky Dink*, a popular show of the 1950s that allowed children to draw on the TV screen by placing a layer of protective cellophane over the glass. The Zenith dream is in line with a gradually developed thematic in *The Exegesis* that casts Dick (and perhaps all of humanity) as a type of receiver, terminal, or cosmic antenna for the emanations of Zebra. Dick goes on to describe his experience of 2-3-74 in cybernetic terms, writing, "One of my circuits which is usually dormant will light up! No one else has it! Power flowing through an electrical (wiring) circuit for the first time to light up lights is a good mechanical analog for first neural firing along a circuit of the brain."[47] Elsewhere, Dick contends with the cybernetic foil of "noise," imagined here in cosmic terms: "Considering the distance over which these packets of information travel, and their velocity, much contamination, signal-loss and other familiar invasion of the material must take place— cross-talk from other fields, so that when the tachyons at last impinge on us even if our transduction is superb (as in the case of mystics and saints) there would be something quite less than a perfect meaningful construct."[48]

At some point, Dick became convinced that his novel *Ubik* (1969) was in some way a direct transmission from the entity Zebra, a cosmic revelation that Dick "tuned in" much like a broadcast signal. "I don't feel I was 'picked' by a Future Force, as its instrument," he wrote, "any more than when you are watching a TV program the transmitter has picked you. It is broadcast; it just radiates out in all directions and some people tune in, some do not."[49] Over the course of writing *The Exegesis*, *Ubik* becomes the central parable of the "transcendentally rational mind's" attempts to contact Dick (and thus the Earth) to communicate the true order of the universe and deliver humanity from its fallen state as captives in the Black Iron Prison, or BIP. This leads to a sometimes confusing equation of *Ubik* the novel with the force known as Ubik, which is akin to Zebra. Adding another mirror to this delusional hallway, Dick eventually recounted this period in his life in two autobiographical novels, *Radio Free Albemuth* (1976) and VALIS (1981). An acronym for Vast Active Living Intelligence System, VALIS was the narrative instantiation of Dick's Zebra, which also appeared to Dick in the form of Ubik. As Dick writes, "The entity VALIS is the entity Ubik, which in all the time of writing VALIS I never realized! And VALIS exists; therefore Ubik exists; therefore *Ubik* as a novel is, like VALIS, basically veridical, even though when I wrote it I didn't (yet) know it."[50] Dick eventually described VALIS as a satellite system originating in the constellation of Canis Major, transmitting "pink laser beams" to Earth. He occasionally invokes the physics of energetic transmission, suggesting that VALIS is an actual technology. Early speculation centered on "tachyons," which Dick (following Arthur Koestler) describes as "particles of cosmic origin which fly faster than light and consequently in a reversed time direction."[51] Tachyon bombardment explains, for Dick, how VALIS could "talk to us from the future" not as a cosmic metaphor, but as a working transmission link operating according to known physics: "The vitalistic principle of the force Ubik is also sentient. It impinges on transmissions such as TV, phones. Has to do with ions."[52] Like so many psychotics, scientists, and science-fiction writers before him, Dick marveled at an atmosphere saturated with energy and information. Echoing Baudrillard's account of the "negative ecstasy of radio," Dick wrote, "Entity in ionosphere due to growth of radio signal patterns? An AI bounce-back to us? Obtains information from our electrical impulses, and this is the noösphere? The entire pattern of our radio signals and their information, have formed a living, or anyhow sentient entity which is why the noösphere came into being."[53]

Read dialogically, *Ubik*, VALIS, and *The Exegesis* produce a hall of mirrors so thoroughly mad and confusing that it becomes impossible to isolate any definitive relationship between Dick and his material. Whatever the exact flow chart of (un)reality that informed Dick's universe, however, his work supports Plank's observation that science fiction is really less interested in science than in the issue of *communication*.[54] For Plank, this interest mirrored the genre's growing disenchantment with modernity. Following World War I, Plank argues, disillusionment with the mounting failures of scientific rationalism produced a new form of science fiction that was interested in the possibilities of communication that might exist beyond language. As a result, communication in science fiction increasingly shunned instrumental utility in favor of "magical thinking," imagining technologies and practices "perpetrated by methods which are outside of normal human experience, if not outside of experience all together."[55] This is a key feature of Dick's work, certainly; he frequently focused his fiction on impasses and odd breakthroughs in making various forms of contact. Plank was especially interested in the prevalence of telepathy in science fiction, a device he located in the "omniscience of thought" frequently attributed to magical thinking in children and schizophrenics. As scientific interest in telepathy faded in the 1920s and '30s, science fiction adopted the telepath as a symbol of future deliverance. Plank notes that both utopian and dystopian science fiction of the twentieth century asserted the inevitability of omniscient communications but proposed different timelines for these technical and telepathic innovations. In visions of the near-future, such as George Orwell's *1984* (1949), technology provided instruments of oppressive surveillance and control. The state (or some equivalent) employs technical magic to confirm the suspicions of many a paranoid schizophrenic: *Big Brother (or Big Something) is watching you*. This pessimism has remained central to the genre ever since, as in the various "tech noir" scenarios that bedeviled Arnold Schwarzenegger throughout his Hollywood career. There is the "bread and circuses" state of *The Running Man* (1987), in which the government contains political unrest by uniting the nation through televised spectacles of violence. *Total Recall* (1990), based on Dick's "We Can Remember It for You Wholesale," provides yet another scrambling of political power through a collapse of real and simulated worlds. In *The Terminator* (1984), human ingenuity produces Skynet, a technology that (like so many other AI devices) determines that its own preservation depends on exterminating all of humankind.

Telepathy, however, most often appears in science fiction of the far distant future, signaling the emergence of a new social order that no longer has need of secrets, repression, or technology. Arthur C. Clarke's *Childhood's End* (1953) and John Wyndham's *The Chrysalids* (1955) are exemplary in this regard, each portraying the emergence of telepathy among the young as a sign of evolutionary advancement. Combining the two future timelines, some novels envision telepathy arriving as a genetic mutation in the wake of a nuclear apocalypse, implying that mankind must literally blow itself up before advancing to a higher level of consciousness. Considered as a metatext of the past century, the paranoid and telepathic arms of science fiction envisioned a common future passing through two stages of magical fantasy: the immediate paranoid crisis of external powers monitoring a vulnerable

FIG 5.3 In a bubblegum card from 1962, Martians send a very direct message via ray gun: burning flesh! Topps® Mars Attacks Series card, used with permission from The Topps Company, Inc.

subject (childhood) and the more utopian fantasy of a world united through the adult mastery of telepathic communion (childhood's end).

Despite these various misdirects in *The Exegesis*, at the heart of the Zebra/Ubik system is the pulp mainstay of the "ray gun," a scientifically marvelous technology for transmitting energy or information. H. G. Wells introduced the idea of a "heat ray" in *War of the Worlds* (1898), but as William J. Fanning Jr. notes, interest in ray weapons really began to flourish only in the years following World War I. Fanning attributes this fascination not only to public interest in electricity, X-rays, and radium but also to widespread speculation in the popular press about the possible weaponry and tactics of "the next war."[56] Nikola Tesla's work on the wireless transmission of electrical power has led to his association with secret plots that range from miraculous energy weapons to UFO propulsion systems.[57]

Ray guns allow for particularly crude and direct forms of "influence." Character A need only to point the gun at character B, and with the squeeze of a trigger, character B quickly receives the powerful message that he is now disintegrated, heated, frozen, shrunk, enlarged, dissolved, suspended, mutated, transported, levitated, sterilized, de-boned, mind read, time traveled, sex changed, brain switched, made invisible, made insane, or otherwise transformed. Ray action is also scalable, of course, allowing various mad men across the genre's history to threaten entire cities, continents, planets, and galaxies with the influencing potential of an energy beam. In every iteration, however, the fundamental equation remains: influencer plus power (political/energetic) equals influence. *Star Trek*'s phaser and *Star Wars*'s light saber are essentially ray guns, as is *Star Trek*'s transporter system, a technology that "shoots" people through space as a beam of energetic information. A "ray gun" is central even to the esoteric art cinema of Stanley Kubrick's *2001: A Space Odyssey* (1968). Debating the symbolism of the black monolith in *2001* is a familiar rite of passage for young cinephiles. Whatever else the monolith may represent, its most manifest function is one of influence. Installed by some superior power—whether God or aliens—the monolith triggers evolutionary intelligence, "influencing" its primate audience to take up the building of tools (and the bashing of skulls). Perhaps the monolith does so simply through the purity of its example, its metric perfection and machined surfaces awakening the ape brain to the concept of techne. Then again, the monolith's apparent function as a beacon—activated by the alignment of the planets—casts it once again as machine for focusing energy and information (on the ape brain). Kubrick reinforces this energetic quality by scoring the scene with Gregory Ligeti's "Requiem," a swelling choral wall that functions as a siren song of radiating presence.

Injected into the world of politics, the ray gun made a derisive return in the 1980s as a mocking pronunciation for Ronald Reagan, the fortieth president of the United States. "The Gipper," as he was also known, earned the additional nickname "Ronnie Ray-Gun" after appearing on national television in March 1983 to announce his Strategic Defense Initiative (better known as SDI).[58] Quickly envisioned in the press and popular imagination as a satellite system that could detect and then destroy Soviet missiles by shooting lasers through space, SDI became known to its critics as "Star Wars" (and thus Reagan as Ray-Gun). Whether Reagan and his military advisers thought such a missile shield was really possible is unknown. Some have speculated that SDI was created not to build killer satellites, but to bankrupt the Soviet Union as it attempted to keep pace with America's military spending. Still others believed (and continue to believe) that the SDI program concealed a more disturbing avenue of research: electromagnetic mind control. Alex Constantine takes up the issue in his essay "Blue Smoke and Lasers," arguing, "Masers, not lasers, are the hidden thrust of 'Star Wars.' The weapon is an extremely sophisticated mind and body machine capable of thought transfer, manipulation of emotions and muscle control. Images, even dreams, can be beamed to a subject. A human or cybernetic controller can carry on a conversation telepathically, and at the same time instill physical sensations, subliminal commands, emotions and visual and aural hallucinations." If this seems far-fetched, Constantine adds, "Computerized EM [electromagnetic] devices that talk and transmit images to the brain were current when Reagan delivered his first SDI pitch in 1983."[59] From this perspective, Reagan's great hope for SDI was to produce a schizophrenia ray gun, perhaps to drive the enemy insane, or perhaps to better control the unruly (liberal) citizens of American democracy. As evidence, the conspiratorially minded maintain that several SDI "whistleblowers" have been systematically targeted by the very weapon they were asked to perfect. Most notable here were the "'colorful' suicides of 23 SDI engineers in Great Britain" between 1982 and 1986.[60] A website devoted to the mysteries of SDI recounts the fate of Alistair Beckham, a software engineer with Plessey Defense Systems: "It was a lazy, sunny Sunday afternoon in August 1988. After driving his wife to work, Beckham walked through his garden to a musty backyard toolshed and sat down on a box next to the door. He wrapped bare wires around his chest, attached the end to an electrical outlet and put a handkerchief in his mouth. Then he pulled the switch."[61]

Like schizophrenia and science fiction, "conspiracy theory" frequently invokes the scientific marvelous to resolve perplexing enigmas of agency, power, and control. Conspiracy theory is most famously associated with the mysteries surrounding Lee Harvey Oswald's (alleged) assassination of President John F. Kennedy in 1963. Gary Allen and Larry Abraham's *None Dare Call It Conspiracy* (1971) proved pivotal in moving conspiracy theory toward global plots of financial and technological subterfuge, as did the circulation in the mid-1970s of a document known as the Gemstone File.[62] Conspiracy theory in its modern form often describes a borderland between psychosis and science fiction. For example, Cathy O'Brien's *The Trance Formation of America* (1995) purports to be an authentic account of O'Brien's life as a government operative turned "CIA mind control slave." At one point in her narrative, O'Brien describes how George H. W. Bush, soon to be the forty-first president of the United States (and father to the forty-third), used the popular children's television show *Mister Rogers' Neighborhood* to "scramble/confuse young victims' memory of contact with him and his sexual abuse." As evidence, O'Brien cites the abuse of her own daughter, Kelly, "who ran 104–6 degree temperatures, vomited, and endured immobilizing headaches for an average of three days." Her account continues:

Kelly's bleeding rectum was but one of many physical indicators of George Bosh's [sic] pedophile perversions, I have overheard him speak blatantly of his sexual abuse of her on many occasions. He used this and threats to her life to "pull my strings" and control me. The psychological ramifications of being raped by a pedophile President arc [sic] mind-shattering enough, but reportedly Bush further reinforced his traumas to Kelly's mind with sophisticated NASA electronic and drug mind-control devices. Bush also instilled the "Who ya gonna call?" and "I'll be watching you" binds on Kelly, further reinforcing her sense of helplessness.[63]

Where was Ronnie Ray-Gun in all this? Reagan informs O'Brien that George H. Bush "is like a director. He makes sure the stage is set to implement the New World Order as I envision it.... All the world's a stage. I'm the Wizard. But he is directing the show so you better pay attention and learn your part well from him."[64]

Mark Fenster argues that a central appeal of conspiracy theory lies in its ability to reduce the complexities of structural power and political struggle into a more manageable populist narrative of "antagonism between the people and the powerful elites." In so doing, "conspiracy theory substitutes instrumental power, one part of the historical process, for the whole."[65] The incomprehensible contingencies of history, in other words, become an occult (but potentially knowable) precession of mysterious murders, secret machines, and unseen alliances. Much as the influencing machine makes manifest the transmission of technosemiotic power, conspiracy theories thus allow believers to conceptualize the otherwise unfathomable administration of political power. Over the past few decades, the paranoid continuum separating conspiracy theory and psychotic delusion has been gradually compressed. Dec's concern over the "communist black wave of the future," the "evil metric system conspiracy," and traffic signals controlled by the CGCG already presented a hyperbolic version of what Richard Hofstadter, in 1964, famously dubbed the "paranoid style in American politics." In the great centrist tradition of American public discourse, Hofstadter emphasized that either the left or the right could lapse into a paranoid fear of the Other.[66] Over the past half-century, however, the American right appears to have been particularly receptive to conspiracy theory's accounts of malevolent elites and secret power. The election of William Jefferson Clinton, the first Democrat in the White House after twelve years of Republican rule, inspired "paranoid" responses that ranged from a rapid growth in the militia movement to rumors that First Lady Hillary Clinton was somehow responsible for the murder of the White House aide Vince Foster. Entering the twenty-first century, the end of consensus broadcasting mirrored a similar collapse in the consensus model of American politics. In this new environment of partisan nichecasting, Rupert Murdoch's Fox News (founded in 1996) became among the most successful of all cable networks by targeting older, whiter viewers with a conspiratorial battle that pitted conservative common sense against leftist elites who actively worked to undermine the nation. The American right had long suspected that liberals, immigrants, feminists, homosexuals, teachers, unions, Hollywood, professors, and various other Others were destroying the homeland, either by diabolical design or as "useful idiots" manipulated by America's enemies. The election of the nation's first biracial (and thus "black") president in 2008 further validated these suspicions, especially as a concurrent shift to Web 2.0 allowed growing numbers of conspiracy theorists to produce their own media content.[67] Fox News adjusted to this new information order by reporting on, and thus amplifying, various "controversies" and conspiracies initiated by right-wing bloggers. Particularly virulent was the so-called birther movement and its claim that President Barack Obama was not actually born in the United States. Calls for the president to produce his birth certificate began at the fringes of American political life and eventually became a talking point for elected conservatives. (Predictably, once the document was released, it was dismissed as a forgery.) In the 2016 election cycle, the paranoid style went mainstream with the candidacy of Donald J. Trump, the real estate developer-turned-reality TV star who opportunistically joined the birther cause to launch his own political ambitions. Trump's willingness to trade in conspiratorial discourse, about both Obama and his opponent Hillary Clinton, proved a central component of his campaign.[68] Trump prevailed and became the forty-fifth president of the United States. A few weeks later, an agitated man discharged an AR-15 rifle at the Comet Ping Pong pizzeria in suburban Washington, DC. He had gone there, he told police, to investigate claims that Hillary Clinton, having miraculously avoided indictment for Foster's murder in the 1990s, was now using this otherwise nondescript pizza joint to run a child pornography ring.[69]

TI, V2K, and DEW

In an older, more stable techno-semiotic order, science fiction was fictional. Conspiracy theory was theoretical. Delusions were delusional. The implosion of these three discourses, especially in relation to paranoid electronics, testifies to modern power's success in cloaking, not only its agents and operations, but also the very terrain of reality itself. Over the past twenty years, the merging of psychotic, science-fiction, and conspiratorial discourse has become particularly prominent within a group known as "targeted individuals," or TIs, as they call themselves. Although they vary in the intensity of their paranoia, TIs are united in the claim that they are targets of energetic persecution by agents known or unknown. Some TIs, plagued by fatigue, endorse conspiratorial accounts of long-standing concerns over electromagnetic field (EMF) pollution and microwave poisoning.[70] Other TIs present symptoms that are often indistinguishable from paranoid psychosis. A central figure in the community is Harlan Girard, who began hearing voices in 1983 while living in Los Angeles. In a profile published in 2007 in the *Washington Post Magazine*, Girard recalls how he suddenly became a target of unusual harassment. Strangers gathered under his window at night. He could hear someone in his crawlspace. He found himself in random confrontations with angry motorists. Shortly thereafter, Girard began to hear voices, which he attributed to a recording studio with "four slobs sitting around a card table drinking beer." The voices were "crass but also strangely courteous," recalls Girard. The voices gradually became more frequent and more hostile, taunting Girard for being "abnormal" and asking him repeatedly "why he wasn't dead yet." Despite this seemingly classic presentation of psychosis, Girard completed a graduate degree at the University of Pennsylvania and remained functional in day-to-day life.[71] After receiving a large inheritance that freed him from having to work, Girard dedicated his life to researching and exposing the motives and technologies behind this form of harassment.

As a pioneer of the TI movement, Girard has enabled hundreds, if not thousands, of people to come forward with similar experiences. One of the more visible is Gloria Naylor, the author of the best-selling novel *The Women of Brewster Place*. Following the success of that novel (which included a film adaptation produced by Oprah Winfrey), Naylor rented a home in South Carolina to begin her next writing project. As related in her autobiographical novel *1996*, Naylor believes that a dispute with a new neighbor over a wayward tomcat led her eventually to become a target of government surveillance.

In an interview on National Public Radio, Naylor described her relationship to the protagonist of *1996*:

> Since many of these things did happen to the real Gloria Naylor, by using myself as a protagonist, I was able to have the book act partly as a catharsis. Basically, what *1996* is about, it's about our loss of privacy in this country, that the government has moved well beyond just the simple following of people, and the tapping of their phones. But they now have technology that is able to decode the brain patterns, and to detect what people are actually thinking. And they have another technology called microwave hearing, where they can actually input words into your head, bypassing your ears.[72]

In 2010, actor Randy Quaid and his wife, Evi Quaid, claimed to be targets of the "Hollywood Star Whackers," a nebulous group of agents, lawyers, and producers who, the Quaids believe, murdered Heath Ledger and David Carradine.[73] Beyond these high-profile paranoids there are a number of self-identified TIs who have published e-books detailing their accounts of harassment through unknown electronics.[74]

Those who identify as TIs frequently report that their harassment began as a conflict with a neighbor, doctor, relative, or even complete stranger. Following an incident, major or minor, the TI begins to note numerous odd occurrences in daily life that suggest a pattern, leading to a suspicion of gang stalking. A hybrid of workplace mobbing and cause stalking,[75] "gang stalking" is the TI term for a coordinated program of abuse perpetrated by a rotating team of harassers. One TI writing under the pseudonym Elizabeth Sullivan describes a common revelation among the gang stalked: "I thought for a long time that they were really pathetic spies because they were so obvious. A car would pull out behind me and follow me for miles, even if I made a wrong turn.... Apparently, the instructions for the group are not to get caught or identified and to make sure the targets know that they ARE being watched and followed. That is part of their protocol."[76] Early forms of harassment also include odd break-ins and bizarre disruptions in the home and at work. John Hall, formerly an anesthesiologist in San Antonio, maintains that gang stalkers began breaking into his house and his girlfriend's apartment to disassemble appliances, shorten interior doors (to extend the sight line of cameras in the baseboards), and leave needle punctures in his beverage containers.[77] Other frequently reported gang-stalking activities include random threats by strangers, mysterious cars parked by the house, increased traffic in the neighborhood, stolen mail, frequent "hang-up" phone calls, dead pets, coordinated noise campaigns (constant sirens, truck noise, car alarms), and suspicious neighbors. Targeted individuals also refer to a subset of gang stalking called street theater: stalkers staging elaborate public performances designed to annoy and frighten the target. Sullivan witnessed street theater in a failed attempt to pick up a Disneyland-themed cake for her daughter. When she arrived at the bakery, Sullivan was told the electricity was out and that the store's electronic doors would not open. While waiting in the car for the electricity to be restored, Sullivan was informed by another waiting stranger that a market down the road also featured nice birthday cakes. Sullivan left and made do with the alternative cake—much to the disappointment of her eight-year-old daughter. Looking back, Sullivan concludes that this entire episode was staged to introduce yet more strife and anxiety into her already tense home. If that seems "crazy," TIs would be the first to agree. As a sympathetic psychologist writes about gang stalking, "The techniques used against these targeted individuals are purposely designed to make the victim appear to have a mental disorder in order to invalidate any claims of wrongdoing by the perpetrators. It is a highly organized and multi-faceted attack that is used by many political and religious extremists, by corporations and businesses, and even by organized crime."[78]

Many TIs believe that this harassment eventually escalates to electronic intervention, the persecutors mobilizing all manner of directed energy weapons—DEWs, in TI parlance—to amplify the target's daily mental and physical distress. Depending on the scope of the plot and the power of the persecutor, these DEWs can range from a weaponized microwave oven in the next apartment (the door removed and the unit place against a common wall) to mind-control satellites orbiting the Earth. A widely circulated document within the TI community describes the impact these DEWs are thought to have on the body. Effects include thought reading and broadcasting; waking visions; vivid controlled dreams; drained battery watches; heart palpitations; forced "muscle-quaking"; violent no-rash itching; forced orgasms; sudden overheating; microwave burns; severe facial distortions; and narcolepsy. As evidence that they are in fact "targets," some TIs claim these symptoms will temporarily vanish if they make a sudden change in their daily routine, such as staying overnight in a hotel (after a day or so, however, the agents behind the targeting locate the victim and the symptoms begin again).[79] In the most advanced form of this harassment, finally, the TI begins to hear voices that appear to emanate from within or just behind the head. As in schizophrenia, these voices are typically hostile, offering abusive commentary on the TI's daily routine and even encouraging the subject to commit suicide (as with Girard's tormenting by the "four slobs" at the card table). This particular subset of technologies is known within the TI community as Voice to Skull, or V2K.

A crucial document in the TI universe is Allan Frey's "Human Auditory System Response to Modulated Electromagnetic Energy," published in the *Journal of Applied Physiology* in 1962.[80] Widely cited in the community, Frey's article is foundational for its description of the microwave auditory effect (MAE). Building on the observation that radar operators in World War II frequently heard clicks and buzzing in the head while near their equipment, Frey demonstrated an ability to use "extremely low average power densities of electromagnetic energy" to induce the "perception of sounds in normal and deaf humans."[81] In other words, Frey demonstrated it was possible to transmit the "perception of sound" directly to the inner structure of the ear through microwave targeting. "The RF [radio frequency] sound has been described as being a buzz, clicking, hiss, or knocking, depending on several transmitter parameters, i.e., pulse width and pulse-repetition rate. . . . The apparent source of these sounds is localized by the subjects as being within, or immediately behind, the head. The sound always seems to come from within or immediately behind the head, no matter how the subject twists or rotates in the RF field."[82] A TI translates this into her own phenomenology: "It was an irregularly pulsed 'humming' sound, impossible to tell which direction it came from, seeming louder when one was lying down and filling the air with a menace inimical to life, a sense of crushing weight and oppression, and shock waves like a beating. It reverberated most in the area just behind the ear, the mastoid bone area which is filled with air pockets, and caused my eyes to ache and forehead to feel fuzzy and interfered with."[83]

Frey's work transmitted electronic pulses only, not "voices," but for the TI community the implications are clear: any number of nefarious individuals and organizations would have an interest in projecting voices directly into the skull. While some TIs trace their persecutors back to centuries-old societies such as the Illuminati and the Freemasons, many more see their torture as related to postwar technologies secretly researched and implemented by the US and USSR in their competition for global influence in the 1950s–70s. At the core of this concern is the nebulous science of "psychotronics," the theory and practice of using electronics to affect mood and behavior or even transmit information through a form of "synthetic telepathy." Targeted individuals have gradually coalesced around the same counterhistory of the twentieth century that has so long animated the conspiracy community. Both groups frequently contend that the government's interest in psychotronic technology began as World War II was coming to an end. In Operation Paperclip, the US sought to recruit German scientists both to aid in American research and, equally important, to keep their knowledge out of Soviet hands.[84] For the conspiratorially minded, this meant eliding distinctions between apolitical German researchers and dedicated Nazis, the latter bringing with them not only the specter of fascism, but also Hitler's purported interest in theosophy and the occult.[85] Given the American image of communism as a state of drone-like conformity, many posited that the ultimate goal of the Soviets was to create a form of electronics that could serve as a medium of direct mind control (as opposed to the indirect "mind control" of radio and television). In 1958, Leonard Carmichael of the Smithsonian Institution warned an audience that he possessed four volumes, each the size of the "Manhattan phone directory," titled "Selected Articles on the Central Nervous System and Behavior, 1957." It had been translated from Russian.[86] Many believed Soviet neurology sought methods to better operationalize the "brainwashing" techniques practiced by China during the Korean War. Pavlov's famous salivating dogs, trained to have an involuntary reaction to arbitrary stimulus, presented one face of godless communist indoctrination, but so, too, did the Soviets' purported research in nervous energy, telepathy, remote viewing, and telekinesis.[87] In the introduction to the English translation of L. L. Vasiliev's *Mysterious Phenomena of the Human Psyche* (1965), Felix Morrow notes that Vasiliev, by then in his seventies, had survived Stalin's ban on parapsychological research to head his own research lab in Leningrad. Long interested in the possibilities of "brain broadcasting," Vasiliev claimed that Soviet scientists had constructed a mechanical hand that could be operated by mental impulses.[88] *Psychic Discoveries behind the Iron Curtain* (1971) further contributed to the idea of an "ESP gap" in American defenses.[89] In 1975, officials claimed that the US Embassy in Moscow had been under Soviet microwave bombardment for fifteen years, ostensibly to "recharge" listening devices implanted in the embassy's walls and to jam US attempts to monitor Soviet communications.[90] As members of the TI community are quick to point out, personnel who served at the embassy during those years complained about "strange ailments during their tenure in Moscow, ranging from eye tics and headaches to heavy menstrual flows."[91]

Those familiar with the Soviet interest in remote viewing and remote influence surmised that this microwave bombardment may have had an even more sinister goal: covert manipulation of American brains within the embassy's walls. Such anxieties continued well into the 1980s, especially after the Soviet Union constructed a mammoth electromagnetic array near Kiev, in the Ukraine. The exact purpose of the installation, nicknamed the Russian Woodpecker (for its continual "pecking" disruptions of global shortwave radio transmissions), was unclear.[92] Most believed that the array was an early missile defense warning system, but the psychotronic community speculated the Woodpecker was a prototype for broadcasting a control signal across the continent.[93] In 1978, the US Army initiated the Stargate Project to test the efficacy of psychic powers for espionage and military applications, especially remote viewing (RV) and remote influence (with the hope that these techniques might be used to visualize or influence activities behind enemy lines). In 1980, *Military Review* published an article titled "The New Mental Battlefield" that argued, "There are weapons systems that operate on the power of the mind and whose lethal capacity has already been demonstrated. The psychotronic weapon would be silent, difficult to detect, and would require only a human operator as a power source."[94] Stargate officially ended in 1995, but many TIs assume that this research continues under the auspices of the Defense Advanced Research Projects Agency (DARPA).

Not all TIs believe that the government is out to get them, but many, if not most, endorse the theory that the CIA was the lead actor in developing the basic technologies of electronic torment. Like conspiracy theorists, many TIs are conversant in a standard history of the CIA's covert operations. Starting in 1951, Project ARTICHOKE investigated how hypnosis, electronics, and drugs might be used to facilitate enemy interrogations. Many believe ARTICHOKE was also an attempt to "program" agents for covert espionage, leading to the widespread theory that John F. Kennedy's assassin, former marine Lee Harvey Oswald, was in fact a product of the project. Project ARTICHOKE quickly merged with what remains the most notorious of these classified programs: MK-ULTRA, a CIA project that explored seemingly every electronic, psychic, and chemical strategy possible in an effort to develop (and defend against) various "mind-control" techniques. The program was in official operation from 1953 to 1973. With the CIA program under congressional investigation by the US Senate Select Committee to Study Governmental Operations with Respect to Intelligence Activities (known as the Church Committee) in 1975, the agency's director, Richard Helms, admitted to ordering the destruction of all MK-ULTRA documents in 1973. But seven surviving boxes of records surfaced in 1977, leading to a joint hearing on August 3, 1977, before the Senate Subcommittee on Intelligence. As the CIA's efforts at mind control became more widely known, many stepped forward to claim involvement in the program—perhaps most famously, the model and 1940s pin-up girl Candy Jones, who, under hypnosis, claimed to have trained with the CIA under an alternative personality, "Arlene," for a number of missions in East Asia.[95]

Targeted individuals assign particular significance to a series of experiments in the 1950s and early 1960s supervised by the psychiatrist Donald Ewen Cameron at McGill University. Funded under the auspices of MK-ULTRA Subproject 68, Cameron's research developed techniques of "psychic driving" and "depatterning."[96] Promoted as a possible cure for schizophrenia, psychic driving involved placing patients in a drug-induced coma for hours, days, or even weeks while also compelling them to listen to loops of taped noise and repetitive statements, all in an effort to "erase" the schizophrenic components of the personality. Later, Cameron introduced the even more disruptive practice of depatterning, a treatment that combined induced sleep with an intensive program of electroshock therapy, the goal being an absolute erasure of the subject's sense of self (and, with it, his schizophrenic symptomology). Cameron described three stages to the process. In the first stage, typically achieved after about five days, there are "marked memory deficits but it is possible for the individual to maintain a space-time image."[97] (In other words, he still knows who and where he is.) The second stage arrives after about ten to twenty days of this treatment. Here "the patient has lost his space-time image, but clearly feels that there should be one. He feels anxious and concerned because he cannot tell where he is and how he got there."[98] Stage three, finally, arrives at some indeterminate point afterward: "In the third stage, there is not only a loss of the space-time image but loss of all feeling that should be present.... In more advanced forms, he may be unable to walk without support, to feed himself, and he may show double incontinence. At this stage all schizophrenic symptomatology is absent. His communications are brief and rarely spontaneous, his replies to questions are in no way conditioned by recollections of the past or by anticipations of the future."[99] After maintaining stage three for about a week, a gradual diminution of the induced sleep and electroshock was to bring the patient back to stage two, stage one, and then, finally, his new and, it was hoped, improved state. There is scant evidence that psychic driving proved therapeutic for individuals diagnosed with schizophrenia, leading Naomi Klein to cast Cameron as a pivotal architect (unwittingly, perhaps) of KUBARK, the CIA's counterintelligence interrogation manual of 1963.[100]

Targeted individuals are also extremely concerned with MK-ULTRA's possible sponsorship of psychosurgery and electronic brain implants. Pivotal here is the work of José Manuel Rodriguez Delgado. Although Delgado has never been explicitly linked to MK-ULTRA, TIs believe his research contributed greatly to the government's ongoing quest for mind-control technology. In "Intracerebral Radio Stimulation and Recording in Completely Free Patients" (1968), Delgado and his coauthors demonstrated how electrodes implanted in the skull—what Delgado dubbed a "stimoceiver"—could be used to record brainwave activity and stimulate neural pathways. "Free patients" in this context meant that the entire process could be done by remote transmission, without tethering the subject to the usual wiring employed in brainwave scans.[101] The study also used the stimoceiver to charge various parts of the brain to elicit certain behavior: "One of the main objectives in telemetric recording of intracerebral activity is the search for correlations between electrical patterns and behavioral manifestations."[102] In fact, Delgado had once demonstrated his device by stopping a charging bull—in a bull ring, no less—by activating its implant. The study monitored and stimulated four psychiatric patients confined because of fits of explosive violence, including a man who "became enraged if other cars cut in front of him and ... would go miles out of his way to force them off the road."[103] During electrical stimulation, one patient reported feelings of "fainting, fright, and floating around," while another, after seven seconds of stimoceiver transmission, "interrupted spontaneous activities such as guitar playing, and in a fit of rage threw herself against the wall, paced around the room for several minutes, and then gradually resumed her normal behavior."[104]

In 1969, Delgado published the ominously titled *Physical Control of the Mind*, a book that argued not only the benefits of electronic brain stimulation for the mentally disturbed, but also the possibility of an advanced "psychocivilization" in which stimoceivers would produce "a happier, less destructive, and better society."[105] While most of Delgado's book examines the nuts and bolts of electronic brain stimulation, he closes with an unapologetic defense of the wider possibilities of physical intervention in the brain. Delgado notes that there are essentially two options for intervening in human behavior: (1) chemical and physical agents to induce changes in neurophysiological behavior; and (2) the "use of positive and negative social reinforcements, based on the sensory relations between the subject and his environment."[106] Delgado saw no ethical reason to favor the latter technologies (ideology, brainwashing, psychoanalysis) over the former (drugs and electronic brain stimulation). In a characteristic rhetorical move of scientists, Delgado also argued that the techniques of radio-controlled cerebral stimulation were neither "good" nor "bad" in and of themselves but depended on the motivations and politics of the operator. The technology raised many ethical, legal, and political questions, Delgado conceded. But he reminded readers that "human happiness

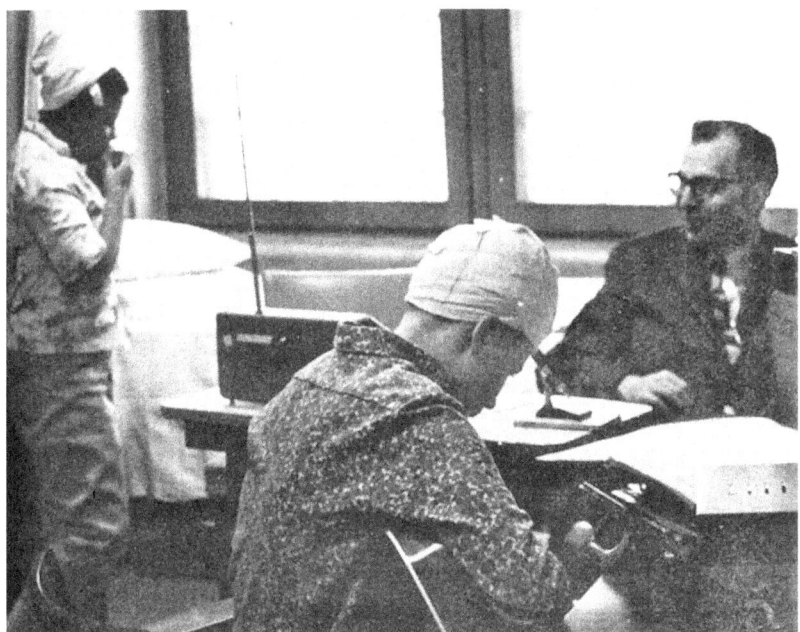

FIG 5.4 Jose Delgado (on right) working with patients implanted with stimoceivers, from *Journal of Nervous and Mental Disease* (October 1968). Republished with permission from Wolters Kluwer Health, Inc.

is a relative value and depends as much on mental interpretation as on environmental reality."[107] And while Delgado had proved that his technology could regulate aggressive behavior in monkey colonies, he did not foresee that his techniques would necessarily translate into a workable solution for "juvenile delinquency" or "international tensions."[108]

Proponents of brain implants and psychosurgery often framed the practice as a last resort in combating cases of unpredictable violence. The same year that Delgado published his manifesto for a psychocivilized society, Vernon Mark, a professor of surgery at Harvard Medical School, and Frank Ervin, a professor of psychiatry at the University of California, Los Angeles, published *Violence and the Brain*.[109] Focusing on "dyscontrol syndrome," Mark and Ervin argued that destroying parts of the limbic system that demonstrated abnormal electrical activity was the most promising treatment for those who displayed a penchant for recurring acts of violence. As Jonathan Metzl argues, this emphasis on "bad" brains coincided with a racialized shift in the definition and diagnostic frame for schizophrenia. By the 1960s and '70s, schizophrenia had taken on connotations of antisocial violence and quickly became the diagnosis of choice for African American men who exhibited "abnormal" belligerence and anger at perceived injustices in white society. In the wake of widespread racial uprisings in the summer of 1967, Mark, Ervin, and their colleague William H. Sweet published an open letter in the *Journal of the American Medical Association* titled "The Role of Brain Disease in Riots and Urban Violence." The letter speculated that many of those participating in civil unrest in Watts, Detroit, Cleveland, Chicago, New York City, Atlanta, and other American cities were in fact mentally ill. The New York psychiatrists Walter Bromberg and Franck Simon dubbed this "the Protest Psychosis," claiming that the rhetoric of the black liberation movement had the power to drive African Americans insane by producing "delusions, hallucinations, and violent projections in black men."[110] Anticipating potential accusations of racism, Bromberg and Simon noted that the great majority of African Americans facing similar social and economic injustice did not resort to violence. Thus began (or even continued) a research program in how those "predisposed" to urban delinquency and violence might be identified and treated before they acted on these impulses.[111] In 1972, Sweet received a $500,000 grant to study how psychosurgery, implants, and drug therapy might help better "manage" those judged prone to aggressive or criminal behavior. Recognizing that much of this work was directed at controlling inner-city violence associated with young black men, *Ebony* magazine labeled this line of research a "new threat to blacks," observing that such tactics once again shifted responsibility for urban crime away from structural disenfranchisement to a "disease" of individual responsibility.[112]

Lately, many TI's have turned their attention to the menace of "chemtrails" as a vector for mass social engineering. A chemtrail is a jet contrail that is (allegedly) impregnated with chemicals, metals, and other particulate matter to modify the atmosphere. Theories about the motives behind this campaign vary. One recurring explanation holds that chemtrails accelerate the process of global warming, thereby generating the environmental crisis that will eventually justify the installation of a One World government.[113] Others contend that chemtrails function as atmospheric reflectors for the High Frequency Active Auroral Research Program (HAARP) in Alaska. Like the notorious Area 51 in Nevada and other remote government installations, HAARP generated much speculation about its primary purpose during the facility's operation between 1993 and 2015.[114] Some people speculated that HAARP provided an improved method for generating extra-long frequency (ELF) signals that could communicate with US submarines deployed on the other side of the Earth. Openly discussed by the government was the facility's Ionospheric Research Instrument, a high-frequency radio transmitter that could temporarily heat and thus "excite" sections of the ionosphere. One of the more fantastic theories involved the reelection of President Obama in 2012. As Election Day approached, writers for Alex Jones's influential Infowars.com website speculated that HAARP, deployed by the incumbent administration, was responsible for the timely arrival of Hurricane Sandy. Two weeks before the election, as the hurricane made its still unpredictable way up the Atlantic coast, "Infowarrior" Kurt Nimmo offered, "If Sandy strikes Virginia, Maryland, Pennsylvania, New York and New Jersey, it will undoubtedly produce widespread chaos and present an ideal opportunity for Obama to come off as a strong and decisive leader marshaling [the Federal Emergency Management Agency] and the federal government's 'emergency management' apparatus into action."[115] Calling Sandy "the perfect storm," Nimmo further predicted, "The establishment media will naturally provide all the propaganda Obama needs to sweep the election on Tuesday, November 6, a week after the hurricane is projected to hit." Of course, many would argue that this is precisely what happened. Hurricane updates stalled whatever momentum Obama's challenger Mitt Romney might have had going into the election, and Obama did indeed earn positive news coverage in the wake of the disaster (especially in his "bipartisan" tour of the storm damage with New Jersey's Republican Governor Chris Christie).

Elana Freeland likens HAARP to a modern Manhattan Project—one that will eventually provide the government (US or United Nations) with an ability to exert "full spectrum dominance of Planet Earth."[116] Freeland notes that installations similar to HAARP now circle the Earth, east and west, north and south. Each installation appears to make use of US patent 4,686,605, registered in 1987 as "Method and Apparatus for Altering a Region in the Earth's Atmosphere, Ionosphere, and/or Magnetosphere." The stated "method and apparatus" in the patent seeks to increase the "charged particle density" of a "selected region above the earth's surface." To what end? In fairness to the conspiracy community, the patent does cite "weather modification" as a potential use, accomplished by "altering upper atmosphere wind patterns or altering solar absorption patterns by constructing one or more plumes of atmospheric particles which will act as a lens or focusing device."[117] The patent is also quite candid about its goal to deliver the missile defense system first promised by Ronald Reagan in 1983. Rather than using space lasers, HAARP promises atmospheric manipulation to "disrupt not only land based communications, both civilian and military, but also airborne communications and sea communications. This would have significant

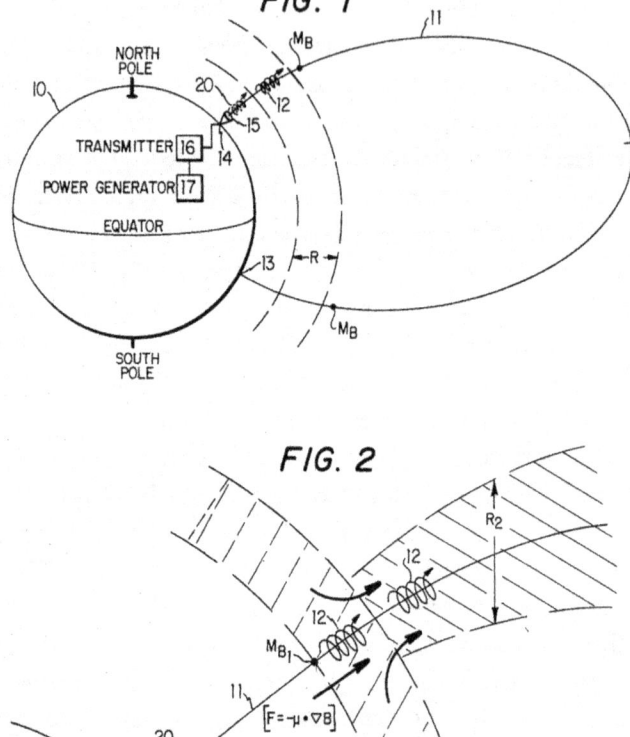

FIG 5.5 Diagram illustrating US patent no. 4,686,605, registered in 1987 as "Method and Apparatus for Altering a Region in the Earth's Atmosphere, Ionosphere, and/or Magnetosphere." SOURCE: US PATENT OFFICE.

military implications, particularly as a barrier to or confusing factor for hostile missiles or airplanes."[118] But HAARP's powers do not end with jamming communication and subjecting incoming missiles to unpredictable forms of aerodynamic drag: "By knowing the frequencies of the various electromagnetic beams employed in the practice of this invention, it is possible not only to interfere with third party communications but to take advantage of one or more such beams to carry out a communications network even though the rest of the world's communications are disrupted."[119] In other words, not only can HAARP scramble the world's communications array; it can also serve as the one remaining open channel for its operator to coordinate global action. By varying frequency and magnitude, moreover, HAARP can allow for "positive communication and eavesdropping purposes at the same time."[120] For TIs, chemtrails promise a more precise targeting and amplified application of HAARP's powers, whatever they may be. Ionizing and heating variable sections of the ionosphere, inflected by the chemicals and metals seeded through chemtrails, will open incredible new horizons for military and industrial exploitation of the atmosphere. Writes Freeland, "Our post-industrial, post-Atomic age atmosphere is now being plasma-ized. Unstable, energetic, high-velocity particles are being cycled into our atmosphere from the stratosphere and ionosphere, then activated by microwaves for military-industrial agendas, all in the guise of ameliorating 'climate change.'"[121]

Freeman confines her indictment of the technology to the hypothetical dangers accompanying climate warfare, including mass poisoning by excessive electromagnetic fields and the growing scourge of "Morgellons disease."[122] But the science-fiction promises of HAARP—whether they are realizable or a propaganda tool of deterrence—have inspired others to even more inventive speculation. For targeted individuals, HAARP is of interest for its presumed ability to transmit symptoms of somatic distress, V2K phenomena, and, eventually, a global mind-control signal. The mechanics here are less than clear. Jerry Smith's *HAARP: The Ultimate Weapon of the Conspiracy* is willing to entertain a variety of possibilities, arguing that HAARP is the "ultimate" technology to issue from the historical chain linking Nazism, the CIA, MK-ULTRA, LSD, Frey, Cameron, Delgado, and conspiracy theory's other usual suspects. Smith argues that nebulous "elites," informed by German materialism, Pavlovian conditioning, and behaviorist sociology, feel an obligation to administer the masses for their own good.[123] Possible methods include the broadcasting of hypnotic suggestions, a more generalized manipulation of mass brain waves and mental states, targeting of the hypthothalmic "pleasure center," and stimoceiver implants wired to global control signals. All of these plots basically cast HAARP in the same role, making it the most massive "power converter" in human history, a device that essentially translates the globalist agenda of the US, United Nations, or some other imperious actor into a literalized ideological atmosphere enveloping the entire globe.

Asked why they have been targeted by HAARP or related DEW and V2K technologies, TIs will argue that the random selection of otherwise ordinary citizens speaks to the New World Order's ambitions to perfect techniques of surgical manipulation. Controlling the masses through vast walls of EMF energy may be the ultimate goal, but in the meantime the architects of this system must experiment on technologies for perfecting control at the level of the individual. The only factor uniting TIs, it seems, is their collective powerlessness—technologically, culturally, economically. Typically invisible in American politics, the issue of class is a manifest concern in TI discourse, albeit in a binary opposition that reduces the world to mysterious "elites" and everyone else. Population control is a recurring theme: "Targeted individuals are being used as lab rats or are being inconspicuously murdered in order to cut back on the Earth's population and retain a controllable number of people, whom the criminal leaders of this program, perceive as being more elite."[124] As we have seen, the racial identity, cosmopolitan history, and global engagement of President Barack Obama have made him a figure of significant concern to paranoid nationalists. But while much of the political right casts Obama as a stealth Muslim and socialist, many in the TI community see him as an extension rather than a disruption of the One World agenda. Addressing the Obama administration's alleged culpability in ignoring electronic torture, one TI commentator observes, "This has a lot to do with the military industrial complex funding of everything from wars for profit to military research to political campaigns. Due to the citizens united supreme court ruling, corporations are now thought of as people and can contribute unlimited amounts of money to political campaigns." Utterly corrupt yet legally protected, he continues, American corporations "have all the traits of the psychopathic personalities, featuring a stunning lack of empathy. We are in effect objects on a chess board and life has become cheap."[125] These sentiments are not all that different from those expressed by supporters of Donald Trump and Bernie Sanders in the 2016 presidential election. In this populist wave, disenfranchised elements of the political right and left sought to answer power by isolating elite nodal points (bankers, congress, Hollywood) or, in more extreme visions, secret puppet masters (the Bildenburgs, the Trilateral Commission, global capitalism). In this respect, the alliance between the conspiracy community and TIs produces an account of global power that is not different from the influential intervention of Michael Hardt and Antonio Negri in *Empire* (2001).[126] These communities also understand that political agency and determination can no longer be isolated according to the traditional villains offered by Marxist and colonialist theory. The "elites" in control of this new configuration of power have many possible motives—social engineering of the "sheeple," satanic magic, protecting markets and wealth—but their actions cannot be charted in terms of simple causality. Traveling back a bit further in Marxist history, these communities postulate that the "soft" power implicit in Louis Althusser's model of the Ideological State Apparatus is now assuming, through technology, the more hardwired controls afforded by a Repressive State Apparatus that seeks global stateless control.[127] Much as the state, as a classical theater of Marxist struggle, must occasionally supplant ideology with weaponry, the New World Order is in the process of introducing psychotronic technologies that weaponize ideology itself.

Why Me?

On July 20, 2012, James Egan Holmes entered a theater in Aurora, Colorado, during the midnight premiere of *The Dark Knight Rises*, the third installment in a particularly paranoid rebooting of the *Batman* franchise. Twenty minutes into the film, say witnesses, Holmes left through a front exit door, then returned a few minutes later equipped with tactical gear, tear gas canisters, and multiple firearms. After lobbing tear gas into the audience, Holmes allegedly opened fire, killing twelve people and injuring seventy more. At the police station, Holmes warned that his apartment was booby-trapped, leading to an evacuation of the complex as the bomb squad worked for two days to disarm thirty hand grenades and ten gallons of gasoline connected to a trip wire and central control box. Accused of the largest mass shooting in Colorado since Columbine, Holmes powered the cable news universe for several days.[128] His mug shot quickly went viral online as an icon of insanity: with his hair dyed bright orange, Holmes looks into the camera with a blank, dazed stare. Four months after the shooting, Barack Obama defeated Mitt Romney in the 2012 presidential election. A month after that, Adam Lanza shot and killed twenty elementary school students and six staff members at Sandy Hook Elementary School in Newtown, Connecticut.

The court of public opinion judged Holmes and Lanza insane. For those occupying the more excitable fringes of the American right, however, common responses to the Aurora and Newtown shootings involved suspicion or even vigorous denial. A surprisingly sizeable faction of this community believed the shootings were a "false-flag" operation staged by the government to build opposition against advocates of the Second Amendment.[129] Either the mass shootings did not happen at all and were only elaborate examples of left-wing stagecraft, or the shootings were actually engineered by the Obama administration (with Aurora helping Obama to win reelection and Newtown inaugurating a second-term push for radical gun seizures). This theory suggested that Holmes, in particular, was a patsy, a Manchurian candidate of the twenty-first century to take the baton from the older regime's Lee Harvey Oswald. Skeptical websites noted a seeming disparity between the placid photo on Holmes's student ID and his insane-looking mug shot. A close comparison of the eyes in the two images (presented side by side for analysis) "proved" the two photos were of different people. While some claimed that the vast difference in appearance was evidence of an imposter, others explained the contrast as evidence of government mind control: Holmes's "crazed" look was clearly the result of profound alteration by drugs, hypnosis, or technical control.[130] Armchair detectives sifted through press and police accounts in search of other potential clues. How could an unemployed college student afford almost $10,000 worth of sophisticated military armaments? Could a lone graduate student really have the knowledge and resources to install a series of booby traps so sophisticated that it took the FBI two days to disarm them? An inmate who spent four hours with Holmes immediately after his arrest seemed to corroborate that Holmes was under some form of "control": "He felt like he was in a video game," the inmate claimed, and said he had been "programmed" to kill by an evil therapist.[131]

But the conspiracy did not stop there. In the days that followed the shooting, it was revealed that the alleged shooter's father, Robert Holmes, was the "lead scientist" at the credit score company FICO, a corporation with immense power over the economic destinies of everyday citizens. Before that, the senior Holmes had worked at HNC Software in San Diego, a company that many believed was partnering with DARPA to develop "cortronic neural networks," described on the website BeforeItsNews.com as a project to produce "machines that someday might be able to reason like humans."[132] Even more alarming, for many, was the academic background of the alleged shooter. By most accounts an excellent student, James Holmes had majored in neuroscience at the University of California, Riverside. Admitted to the doctoral program in neuroscience at the University of Colorado Medical Campus, Holmes secured $21,000 in funding from the National Institutes of Health. Reporters eventually unearthed a videotape of an eighteen-year-old Holmes making a presentation at Miramar College in San Diego. The talk centered on "temporal illusions," which Holmes defined as "an illusion that allows you to change the past."[133] This revelation led more inventive minds to speculate that Holmes had been experimenting in neural time travel, perhaps backed by funding from DARPA. As one poster on a prominent conspiracy site suggested, "He carried out the shootings so he could undo it later by changing the past within his mind. This is why the government sealed the file on James Holmes. This is also why Holmes looked totally spaced out at the court appearance. He's in the process of mentally rewriting the past and entering a different timeline. The government's scared shitless that he succeeded in time travel."[134]

Pursuing the logic of delusional reference, conspiracy theorists (and, in some cases, the mainstream media) did their best to find meaningful connections between Holmes and the diegetic universe of Batman, the Joker, and other denizens of *The Dark Knight Rises*. The film's release on DVD and Blu-Ray in autumn 2012 allowed for meticulous frame-by-frame analysis, leading some to argue the film actually *predicted* both the Holmes and Lanza shootings. Eagle-eyed viewers discovered a building in the Gotham City skyline with AURORA emblazoned in red letters at the top. Later in the film, a map of Gotham City shows a neighborhood labeled "Sandy Hook." At Infowars.com, the web extension of Alex Jones's popular radio show, a posting on the "mysterious coincidences plaguing the movie" invoked the concept of "predictive programming": "Classic predictive programming is usually set in motion to desensitize a target audience to a concept, a possibility, or an event—so when an idea is finally introduced into society, or when an event actually occurs, they have been carefully foreshadowed, pre-programmed you might say, in the minds of people."[135] The "pre-programming" in this case related to satanic magic, practiced among certain economic and cultural elites, that demands ritualistic sacrifices such as mass shootings and mass terrorists attacks such as 9/11: "There can be no question that occult magic is in practice in the upper-most tiers of secret societies and that it is continuously being researched and experimented with using us, the unwitting public, as disposable guinea pigs."[136]

Mainstream media sources were no less aggressive in pursuing a link between *Batman* and Holmes's rampage. Holmes's bright orange hair was clearly an homage to Heath Ledger's Joker, the charismatic nemesis of the previous installment in the *Batman* series (this despite the fact that Ledger's Joker had green hair). Holmes's battle gear, meanwhile, evoked "Bane," Batman's new opponent in *The Dark Knight Rises*. Violent video games were also a suspect, of course, especially after Lanza's shooting spree in Newtown a few weeks later. In the following weeks, gun advocates and Hollywood fought a pitched battle over the impact of guns versus the representation of guns, a public relations war that was essentially a Baudrillardian struggle over the representation of the representation of guns. The media gradually framed Holmes's costuming and armaments as evidence of his delusional relationship to video games and *Batman*. Alarmingly, several people in the audience that evening apparently thought Holmes—dressed in tactical gear and armed to the teeth—was either an overzealous fan playing dress-up or an actor hired as a promotional stunt. But Holmes's selection of the *Batman* screening was based more on tactical practicality. A notebook recovered from his apartment contained diagrams of all sixteen theaters in the Century complex. Holmes chose theater nine not for what was on the screen, but for the advantages it offered in maximizing the attack. As to motivation, the notebook indexes Holmes's descent into a psychotic Hamlet: "The question: what is the meaning of life? What is the meaning of death?" Stick figures marked in the binary code of 1 and 0, life and death, suggest an unsuccessful effort to solve this equation.[137]

Theories of the Aurora and Newtown shootings demonstrate the impossibility of disentangling the precise mechanisms that now bind governmentality, global finance, neurology, and other modes of power known and unknown. These shootings also show how quickly the Internet can both disburse and consolidate information, regardless of its source or status. For those predisposed by politics or psychosis (or both) to imagine that these mass shootings were anything but mass shootings, the Internet became an aggregator of evidence and an accelerator of collective deduction. Beneath the various theories offered, however, operated the deep schematic of the classic influencing machine: secret power—secret technology—influenced victim. But Holmes's ability to motivate links, however specious, among Hollywood, DARPA, neurology, time travel, and Wall Street made him a perfect figure for bridging the speculative interest of conspiracy theory and the lived distress of targeted individuals. Even more alarming, since the Aurora tragedy mass shooters themselves now increasingly claim status as targeted individuals to explain their killing sprees. On September 16, 2013, Aaron Alexis shot and killed twelve people at the Washington Navy Yard in Annapolis. Two weeks before the shooting, Alexis had contacted a prominent TI support group for help regarding his ongoing persecution by ELF energy. The FBI reported that Alexis's shotgun had several phrases etched

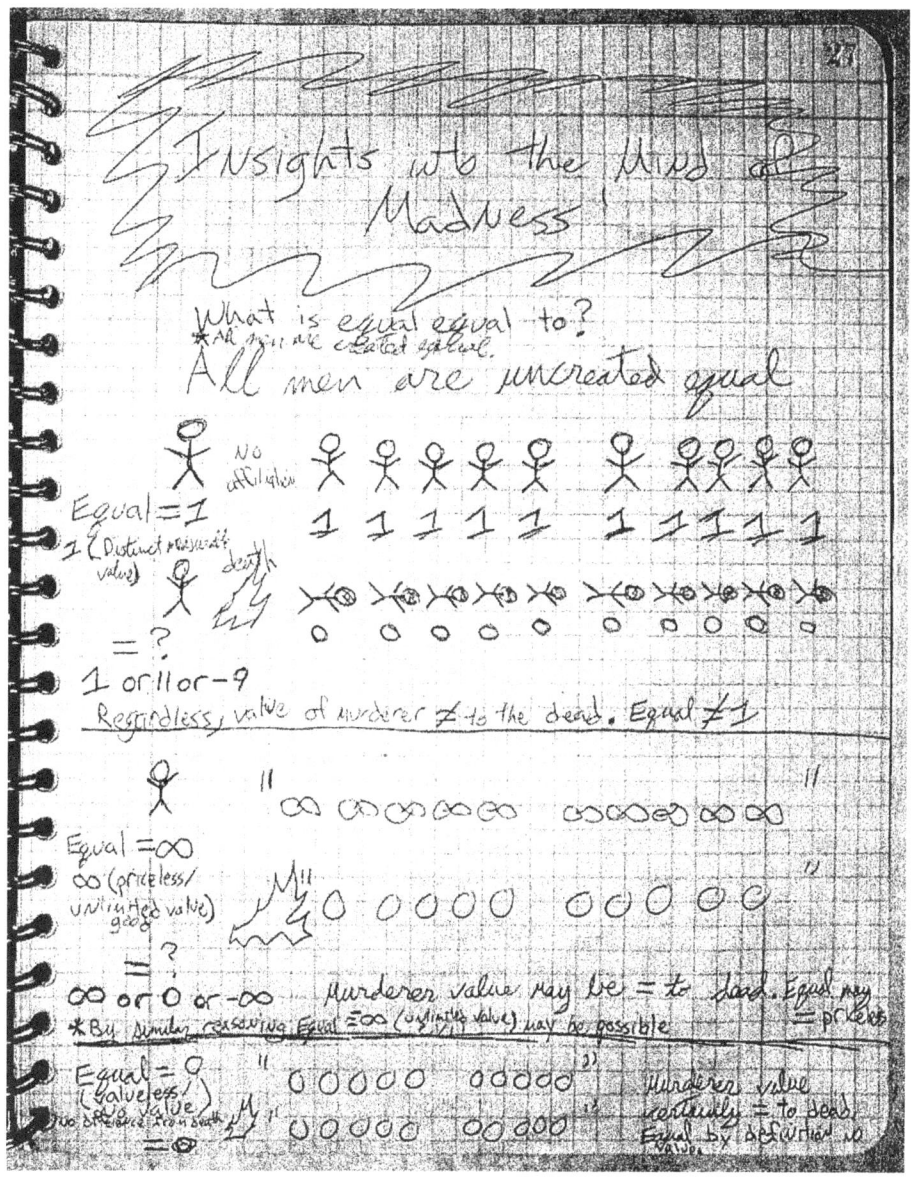

FIG 5.6 A page from the journal of James Holmes titled "Insights into the Mind of Madness." The drawing assigns living stick figures a value of one and dead stick figures a value of zero, under the statement "All men are uncreated equal." SOURCE: COLORADO JUDICIAL DEPARTMENT.

into the barrel and receiver, including "End to the torment!" "Not what y'all say!" "Better off this way!" and "My ELF weapon!"[138] On October 6, 2014, attorney Myron May abruptly quit his job at the district attorney's office in Dona Ana, New Mexico, and made his way back to his childhood home in Florida. Throughout November he posted on Targeted Individuals International's Facebook page, asking on one occasion, "Has anyone here ever been encouraged by your handler to kill with a promise of freedom?" May also made repeated attempts to contact Renee Pittman, a prominent figure in the TI community.[139] On November 19, May entered the Strozier Library, on the Tallahassee campus of Florida State University (FSU), and began shooting. He wounded three students before being shot and killed by FSU police. After the shooting, Pittman and nine others received packages in the mail containing a USB flash drive loaded with May's personal testimony as a TI and a sample letter that sympathetic activists could send to Congress. His motivation was to draw attention to the plight of fellow TIS: "I am making a sacrifice so that others in my same position might have a chance at a normal harassment-free life. I realize that my methods are not the best selection—and probably will not be perceived as the selection of a Christ-follower—but I have prayed incessantly for months to no avail. There are targeted individuals that have endured this torture for decades without any relief, and what targeted individuals need more than anything is media attention."[140] Finally, on July 17, 2016, former marine Gavin Eugene Long shot and killed three police officers in Baton Rouge, Louisiana. Long's attack followed in the wake of the department's questionable shooting of Alton Sterling, a thirty-seven-year-old African American man well known in the neighborhood for selling compact discs near a local convenience store. Only a few days before Long's shooting, Micah Xavier Johnson ambushed and killed six police officers in Dallas during a protest march in support of the Black Lives Matter movement. The timing of Long's attack led many to assume he was motivated by racial injustice. Subsequent investigations revealed that Long believed he suffered from post-traumatic stress disorder (although his official diagnosis by the Veterans Administration was unclear). Long also associated with a variety of anti-government groups, including the black sovereign citizen movement known as Washitaw Nation. In three self-published books, Long offered a program of self-help for "melanated people."[141] In 2015, Long joined a group advocating for so-called targeted individuals and appeared on an online discussion program discussing the plight of those targeted and tracked by the US government.

By forming support groups and online forums, TIs constitute what one study describes as an "extreme community," defined as a group that attempts to "reframe what would otherwise be classified as 'mental disorder' in an entirely different light." Alluding to psychiatry's historical difficulties in defining the boundaries of delusional thought, the study advises that "therapists should be aware of the amount of information available on the internet that aims to justify almost any sort of conspiracy theory, fringe belief, or anomalous experience. The definition of a delusion as a belief not adequately justified by supporting evidence may have to take into account that anyone who spends 30 minutes online can find plenty of 'justifying evidence,' regardless of its validity or source."[142] The growing number of TI-related shootings speaks to the potential dangers of self-diagnosis and self-therapy conducted in an echo chamber, online or otherwise. But as in all cases of delusional formation, the role of "cultural content" is ambiguous here. Would these individuals engage in acts of mass violence regardless of the cultural and historical context? Or, by providing forums for negotiating collective consensus, does the Internet function as both an enabler and an accelerant of psychotic projection? This question is bound up in the larger politics of the Internet as the platform for a democratic public sphere. Like so many other self-identified communities on the Web, targeted individuals appear less interested in open dialogue than in occupying hardened silos of information and belief that validate the reality of their social world. A study from 2006 confirmed that "mind control communities" do in fact traffic a limited number of websites and endorse a repertoire of information as core "facts." The study also noted the authority of thought leaders in this community for their significant impact on assessing evidence and arbitrating action. The Internet remains the primary venue for maintaining TI mythology, but the continuing growth of the community has led to an increase in face-to-face meetings and conferences.[143] In 2011, at a Presidential Committee Hearing on Bioethical Issues held in New York City, all but one of the seventeen participants who spoke during the public session claimed to be under attack by secret electronics.[144]

Like those deemed officially psychotic, targeted individuals typically do not resort to violence, opting instead to research, document, and share their experiences of torture by energy weapons and V2K technologies. While the Internet may play some role in concretizing delusional content among those who do eventually engage in violence, the network of TI websites (and their conspiratorial cousins) also provide an archive, forum, and therapist's couch for those who believe they are under some form of electronic attack. Ironically, TIs have embraced the Internet as a space for interrogating the governmental and technological agents that invented the Internet in the first place. Sharing stories of electronic persecution further validates the shared TI narrative, perhaps to the point of motivating acts of violent retribution. And yet these forums also provide TIs with some degree of attachment, however precarious and pathological, to a shared social world. If a delusion, as Freud argues, repairs the psychotic ego's relation to external reality, then these forums function as collective delusions that provide a spectrum of individuals with a common frame of reference. Websites and forums for TIs thus facilitate an international "group therapy" session, but with one important difference: there is no therapist at the center to challenge the legitimacy of the TI scenario. Trolls, cranks, and even well-meaning clinicians may join the debate to question the psychiatric status of the TI experience, but they are generally ignored or rebuffed by the sheer unanimity of TI experience. As the community has expanded, moreover, many veterans use these websites to assist the newly targeted. One WikiHow page advises TIs about how to accept the "social isolation" that so often comes with the TI experience, providing an eleven-step program of self-therapy:

1. Acknowledge your current situation, but know that it is not the end of the world. . . .
2. Recognize that you are not alone. . . .
3. Research and learn all you can about being a targeted individual. . . .
4. Acknowledge the pain you feel associated with being targeted, rejected and lonely. . . .
5. Express gratitude for the people and the things you still have in your life. . . .
6. Find online T.I. support. Network and form friendships with other T.I.'s. There are online support groups and daily conference calls for T.I.'s.
7. Do not allow yourself to become depressed. . . .
8. Human beings need human interaction. Continue to try to interact with other people even if it's not a long-term interaction. . . .
9. You may want to communicate via social media (Twitter, Facebook, etc.). Join on-line social groups and forums (there are TI groups and forums on-line). . . .
10. Look for volunteer opportunities. . . .
11. Be the real you. Don't let anyone or anything sink your good side.[145]

Significantly, no "step" is included here to recommend a basic medical or psychiatric evaluation: visitors to the site are greeted and immediately validated as fellow members of the TI community.[146] These websites are obviously not a substitute for actual psychiatric care, but it could be argued that this "community" provides a way to forestall further psychic disintegration. Unlike the acute psychotics of the past century, targeted individuals appear to have a great capacity for remaining functional and integrated within the demands of everyday life. Many have jobs, spouses, children. It should be noted that this eleven-step guide to dealing with TI isolation is not dissimilar to the advice a therapist might offer someone in the prodromal phase of a potential psychotic episode. The targeted are basically advised to acknowledge their situations and feelings; seek out more information on their condition; and remain socially integrated through friends, volunteerism, work, and—crucially—fellow TIs on the Internet. One could argue that the sharing of TI history and experience provides a framework that allows many of these individuals to remain variously functional. Of course, the paranoid threat of the Other is never far away, so even as many TIs recommend social media as a way to cope with their situation, others eventually become suspicious of the medium. "There appears to be TI forums set up to entrap us, destroy evidence and inflict more harm as well as sites that intentionally misinform us," one TI has posted. "Listen closely to your own HEART and instincts above all else. And make lists of all the perpetrators (puppets) you encounter—their day of judgment WILL come."[147] Taking a more Foucauldian approach, another website warns the new TI to maintain, as much as possible, an outward appearance of normality. "*For some reason, you—the new TI, have been chosen to be 'It.'* You may not know the reason, but it's important to understand what's going on. The 'game' is this: They pretend you are crazy and a threat to other people. Their role is to get you to be a danger to yourself or someone else, or to get you to do something that is illegal. Why? So they can trick you into giving up your rights. They want you in jail or in a mental hospital."[148] Of course, this has arguably been the challenge that many at the margins of modern society have faced since the early 1800s—avoiding the attention of "power" in either its electronic or its political mode.

....

Perhaps the greatest single validator of TI experience is also the most powerful: the marketplace. Over the past decade, businesses that had previously catered to environmentalists concerned about EMF pollution have graciously directed their marketing toward those who believe they are targets of DEW or V2K harassment. A TI's first priority is to shield mind and body from attack by various radio frequencies, creating a growth market for RF-repellant boxer shorts, socks, T-shirts, and even a "hoodie" advertised as "tested to 90% or better RF attenuation over the frequency range from 1 GHz to 8 GHz."[149] The more fashion-conscious target can select a pink sleeveless blouse that achieves "a respectable 35 dB shielding" or jeans equipped with copper-lined pockets designed to reflect cell-phone radiation. The QuWave company offers a line of Personal Defenders, said to "produce a Scalar Field specially tuned to protect your body and brain against 'Psychotronic Attacks' and Electronic Harassment." It provides defense against "ELF, HAARP, Implants, Microwaves, psychic attacks, Remote Viewing/Manipulation, V2K, Mind Control," and, crucially, "etcetera." One might think that would be enough, but there is more: not only does the QuWave protect against these energies, it also converts "electronic and psychic attacks to positive energy" to "strengthen the human Bio-Field" and "beam" these powers directly to the "sub-conscious." But can QuWave be trusted? For only ten additional dollars, the company will add a "Security Seal" to your order that will show whether the "unit was tampered with during shipping."[150] Of course, wearing or carrying anti-EMF gear every hour of the day can be an inconvenience. Luckily, another manufacturer now offers the Quiet Zone Retreat, an eight-by-eight-by-seven-foot enclosure that allows the TI to remain shielded while not wearing protective clothing. Interested parties are assured that the enclosure is "big enough for a king mattress, small dining table, or several upholstered chairs." For those who deem these options too expensive, offered without any sense of irony whatsoever is a "handsome baseball style hat ... designed to shield the head from frequencies from below AM through microwave, including cellular phone frequencies." This cap will "provide your brain a quiet place without interference to your mental processes from RF radiation."[151]

While some might find it a bit exploitative to market tin-foil baseball caps to the seemingly insane, it could be argued that these products provide a palliative or even therapeutic function during a time of delusional transition. Support groups for targeted individuals and the monetization of RF-repellant clothing suggest a shift on the fulcrum balancing the deluded technically and technically deluded. In an earlier era, fashioning a hat from aluminum foil signified exile from the boundaries of sanity and civilization. Buying a lead-lined baseball cap, by contrast, serves as a sarto-

FIG 5.7 In this promotional video posted at QuWave.com, a young man finds himself besieged by electronic harassment, psychotronics, and psychic attacks. Courtesy of QuWave Technology.

rial index of an emerging and increasingly accepted techno-semiotic reality. Science fiction, conspiracy theory, and technical delusions originated within modernity as speculative discourses of the scientific marvelous, staking out positions that described a spectrum of credulity from fiction to speculation to conviction. This marvelous became more banal, however, as energetic, informatic, and political power became more entrenched and insidious. Will and power, forces that for many years were at war in clearly articulated networks of nerve and wire, are now fully integrated within the invisible cybernetics of administrative power. While many technical delusions remain fixated on bizarre and mysterious technologies, this would appear to be a residual formation, tied to modernity's initial fascination with seemingly magical properties of technology. Targeted individuals suggest an emerging formation that centers more on bizarre and mysterious plots. Speculation (and psychotic conviction) has turned toward the covert plots of control animating the overt complex of electronics that increasingly enforce the agenda of global capital and the neoliberal state. No doubt, some TIs are profoundly disturbed and require immediate medical intervention. But how many others are negotiating a prolonged prodrome of anxious displacement, on the verge of an acute psychotic episode, yet somehow able to remain more or less functional by investing in the TI mythos as a preemptive fantasy? Being forced to fashion a tin-foil hat from kitchen scraps is humiliating. But the ability to purchase a stylish lead-lined hat or metal camisole fully integrates TIS into the only fantasy of collective solidarity allowed under neoliberal administration: the illusion that one can take power and take care by being a wise consumer.

The *Matrix* Defense

EPILOGUE

BY THE CLOSE OF 2003, no fewer than four homicides in the United States claimed an interface with *The Matrix*, the new millennium's ambitious science-fiction trilogy featuring Keanu Reeves as a lowly hacker-turned-avenger of reality. Framing the global simulacrum as an opportunistic CGI infection, the three films embedded their cyber-stoner premise in the visual kinetics of a prolonged arcade fight: Neo, the seeker of material truth, battling an unending digital stream of sober-suited authoritarians—Agents Smith, Jones, Brown, and so on. In May 2000, less than a year after the first and most explicitly paranoid installment of the trilogy, Vadim Mieseges murdered, skinned, and dismembered his landlord before leaving her body in a dumpster in San Francisco's Golden Gate Park. The lawyers defending Mieseges, a former mental patient and obviously still troubled computer science student, convinced the court that the murder was the product of a psychotic break triggered by a volatile combination of crystal meth and Mieseges's delusion that he had been "sucked into the Matrix." Tonda Ansley appears to have been suffering similar delusions when she murdered Sherry Lee Corbett, a professor at Miami University in Ohio. "They commit a lot of crimes in 'The Matrix,'" Ansley told police moments after shooting Corbett in broad daylight on the streets of Hamilton, Ohio. "That's where you go to sleep at night and they drug you and take you somewhere else and then they bring you back and put you in bed and, when you wake up, you think that it's a bad dream."[1] The local press noted the connection to *The Matrix* during an early court appearance, writing, "The science-fiction film, acclaimed for its impressive special effects, suggests reality may not be as it appears,"[2] a description that no doubt captured Ansley's hallucinatory state of mind, as well. The court eventually found Ansley not guilty by reason of insanity and institutionalized her in a maximum-security psychiatric facility. Just a few months before the final verdict in Ansley's trial, a nineteen-year-old named Josh Cooke attracted international attention when he murdered his adoptive parents with a twelve-gauge shotgun, selected, it was argued, for its resemblance to Neo's weapon of choice for dispatching the datacrats of *The Matrix*. "Defendant Cooke harbored a bona fide belief that he was living in the virtual reality of 'The Matrix' at the time of the alleged offenses," argued his attorney in a pre-trial motion, adding that her client "could not distinguish right from wrong or understand the nature, character and consequences of his alleged acts."[3] Cooke's defense team later abandoned this approach, but even after his conviction, his lawyers promised to introduce evidence of the young man's obsession with the film during the sentencing phase of the trial. Cooke kept a life-size poster of Neo in his bedroom, they argued, and frequently wore a version of the hero's signature trench coat. Most damning, Cooke had the desire and capacity to watch *The Matrix* and play the video game *Grand Theft Auto* for six hours at a time.

The "*Matrix* defense" circulated as a minor moral panic in the US media in the early years of the new century. On the surface, psychotic gravitation toward *The Matrix* would appear to vindicate Jean Baudrillard's theories of a world rewritten in terms simulation and hyperreality. These associations were certainly encouraged by the directors of *The Matrix*, Laurence and Andrew Wachowski. In the first instalment of the trilogy, Neo hides an illegal computer disc in a hollowed-out copy of Baudrillard's *Simulation and Simulacrum*. The filmmakers even invited Baudrillard himself to appear in one of the sequels, but he declined their offer. Having served as the king of simulation for some three decades, Baudrillard no doubt was reticent to contribute further to a common misreading of his work. "The most embarrassing part of the film," he observed in a later interview, "is that it confuses the new problem raised by simulation with its arch-classical, Platonic treatment. This is a serious flaw. The idea that the world is nothing more than a radical illusion has challenged every great culture, and it has been resolved through art and symbolization. What we invented in turn, in order to tolerate this kind of suffering, is a simulated real capable of supplanting the real and bringing about a final solution: a virtual universe from which everything dangerous and negative has been expelled." *The Matrix*, for Baudrillard, remained invested in the belief that a "real world" untouched by signification could be located outside the walls of electronic simulation, when, of course, it cannot. "*The Matrix* is the kind of film about the Matrix that the Matrix itself could have produced," he quipped.[4]

The one person associated with the *Matrix* defense who apparently understood Baudrillard was Lee Boyd Malvo. In October 2002, police arrested the seventeen-year-old Malvo and his mentor, John Lee Muhammad, forty-two, for a series of sniper attacks in Washington, DC, that killed ten people and injured three others. The "Beltway Sniper," as the duo came to be known, provoked three weeks of nonstop panic in the nation's capital and cable system before Malvo and Muhammad were captured while asleep in Muhammad's 1990 Chevy Caprice. (The vehicle's trunk had been converted into a sniper's perch.) Malvo told his court-appointed psychiatrists they could better understand him and his beliefs by viewing *The Matrix*, which, like many of his comrades in the cyber-docket, he claimed to have seen more than one hundred times. Searching for a plausible defense, Malvo's lawyers embraced the strategy of "radical illusion." Clearly Malvo believed he was "in the Matrix" and was thus psychotic. At one of the shootings, police found a tarot card with the inscription, "For You Mr. Policeman. Call Me God. Do not tell the media about this." Lawyers suggested that this demonstrated that Malvo, as a shooter, thought he was in a giant video game playing in the "God Mode," a code cheat that allows the player's avatar immunity from all attack—that is, virtual immortality. As it turns out, however, Malvo and Muhammad's agenda had more to do with Hollywood than holography. They hoped the tarot card would better "brand" their crime spree, all in an effort to generate greater mystique and publicity for their cause. While waiting to go on trial, Malvo produced dozens of jailhouse sketches that gave further clues to the nature of their mission. Seeking racial, social, and economic revolution, Malvo and Muhammad combined the high-tech paranoia of *The Matrix* with the low-tech interventions of revolutionary Islam in an eerie reversal of Charles Manson's plans for "Helter Skelter."[5] They hoped the sniper terror, amplified by the media, would provoke martial law, which in turn would "incite a racial revolution over the 'continued oppression of black people.'"[6] Manson imagined that a looming race war would end with his "family" of white hippies emerging from a secret cave to rule over the black victors. Malvo and Muhammad sought the establishment of "a utopian black colony in Canada based on racial and social justice."[7] Malvo's drawings were later introduced in court as evidence of his "indoctrination" at the hands of the older Muhammad, the Morpheus to Malvo's Neo. The drawings depicted a diversity of subjects, from global jihad and Tupac Shakur to Neo in combat, surrounded by a haze of random numbers. Malvo and Muhammad apparently took to heart Baudrillard's observation that terrorism's primary goal is not violence against people but violence against meaning. Malvo did not see himself as trapped "in the Matrix," held hostage by invisible persecutors. Instead, he aspired to be the Matrix, an information trap that would generate superconductive terror, leading to an escalating political crisis. Malvo and Muhammad ultimately failed in their effort to overthrow the government through mass-mediated panic. Fifteen years later, the propagandist Steve Bannon and his protégé Donald J. Trump would be much more successful in "smashing the administrative state" through disinformation. Like Malvo, Bannon understood that dramaturgy about Washington, DC, was infinitely more important than anything actually happening in Washington, DC, leading him to declare the media, not the Democrats, as "the opposition party" and predicting that the "war" between Trump and the press would only grow worse.[8] Trump did his part by tweet-doodling his own schoolboy taunts, dismissing the "lamestream" media as "fake news"; ridiculing the *New York Times* as a "failing" enterprise; and subjecting various journalists at his Orwellian rallies to an official "two minutes hate."[9] So successful was this strategy that seven months into the new administration, with Trump's approval rating at a historic low, an ardent supporter took to the airwaves to argue that "the media," backed by the Illuminati and Freemasons, had deployed a unique frequency (440 hertz) known to "rot organs" and "change DNA." It was also this expert's considered opinion that this control signal was responsible for turning people against President Trump.[10]

The spectrum uniting Malvo, Bannon, and Trump signals the realization that, in terms of power, it is better to project meaning than to receive it. This equation of power with personal broadcasting finds its apotheosis in Trump's purported thrill when posting disruptive tweets and then immediately turning on the cable news networks to watch their coverage of his missives. As in so much psychopathology, Trump's "tweetstorms" are the extreme that define a "new normal"—to live without some degree of libidinal investment in electronic projection, real or imagined, is to be dead. In 2008, psychiatrist Joel Gold inspired a wave of press coverage by proposing an emerging and genuinely unprecedented form of psychotic projection, which he termed the "*Truman Show* delusion" (TSD). In this broadcast cousin of the *Matrix* delusion, a patient comes to believe that his entire world is cast with actors and staged by producers for a national television audience. "I realized that I was and am the centre, the focus of attention by millions and millions of people," said one patient in the study. "My family and everyone I knew were and are actors in a script, a charade whose entire purpose is to make me the focus of the world's attention."[11] This patient also apparently believed that the only way to end the charade was to climb to the top of the Statue of Liberty to meet his true love. If she did not appear, he planned to jump to his death.[12] In another case, a college student believed he was competing on a reality TV show. The voices in his head, critiquing his performance and issuing "challenges," were producers looking to maximize his entertainment

FIG E.1 Malvo's Neo. SOURCE: FAIRFAX COUNTY CIRCUIT COURT.

appeal for the audience. If he successfully completed these tasks, he stood to win $100 million.[13] Teaming up with his brother Ian Gold, a professor of philosophy and psychiatry, Joel Gold proposed a new theory of delusional formation in *Suspicious Minds: How Culture Shapes Madness* (2014).[14] The *Truman Show* delusion was unprecedented, they argued, not so much in its mechanism as in its expression. Adhering to Karl Jaspers's division between primary form and secondary content, the Golds argue that the TSD is basically a familiar paranoid delusion of control expressed within a new technical terrain of paranoia: "The *Truman Show* delusion expresses the fear that one is being controlled, not by force, but by what people know. The *Truman Show* delusion is a delusion of control in the age of surveillance."[15] Gold and

Gold then invoke Michel Foucault's work on panopticism as a prelude to the familiar argument that contemporary media constitute an even more pervasive form of electronic panopticism: "The *Truman Show* delusion represents a confluence of two seismic cultural changes: the loss of privacy and the new porousness of social life. Many human beings are now exposed to a far greater number of unknown others than ever before—strangers who can know a lot about us with a few clicks of the mouse—and the *Truman Show* delusion is a pathological fear about what those strangers might do with the new knowledge they have."[16] The TSD, in other words, is a reflection of the technological anxieties facing us all. "One doesn't have to be remotely disposed to persecutory delusions to be scared as hell about the brave new electronic world that is forming around us," they write. "The social environment is larger today than it has ever been before in human history, and we are exposed to a greater variety of malicious intentions and new methods for acting on them than ever before."[17]

No doubt, there is a paranoid strain in the *Truman Show* delusion, as there is in delusions of being sucked into the Matrix. But there is also a new iteration of grandiosity in this presentation, one that significantly inflects the power relations of surveillance. The TSD proposes a target worthy of perpetual monitoring by an anonymous audience; the *Matrix* delusion, not so much, if at all. (Once you are trapped in the Matrix, whoever trapped you may or may not care to observe you.) Even more elemental in joining these delusions is their shared crisis of agency within a world of electronic artifice. These delusional presentations may still have a foundation in radical illusion and the belief that a true reality is lost behind a mirage, but the more immediate concern involves negotiating the information puzzle of everyday life as a virtual environment, a realm that increasingly equates action with meaning. Psychotics once located power in the instrumental affordances of the influencing machine, a marvelous device capable of extraordinary interventions into the ego (whether through broadcasting or implantation). This was the classic technical delusion described by Victor Tausk: I, a formerly private ego, am under assault by an external agent. As electronics became more ubiquitous, such delusions began to emphasize the power behind the power—the murky agents and agencies, from Thomas Edison to MK-ULTRA, that enacted their agenda through these ordinary (yet still extraordinary) devices. Psychotic concern over influencing machines and influencers is still widespread, obviously, leading many disturbed individuals on intellectual or even violent quests to locate the source of their remote torment. But with the new millennium and a new information order, individuals both sane and insane are learning to think of themselves as avatars operating within the field of information, understanding that power's most salient location is now information itself. "How should I behave?" becomes "How should I signify?" In this respect, a popular iteration of Norbert Wiener's cybernetics appears to be taking hold. As we have seen, the psychotic delusion of being a machine, or being under a machine's control, dates back many decades. This ideation stems, in part, from the frequent association of nervous and electrical energy, nervous system and electrical grid, as analogous economies that in some sense are interchangeable—or, at least, capable of transfer and transmutation. Virtual delusions center less on the man-machine analogy than on the realization that man and machine are both involved in the production, circulation, and reception of information.

One might say that, with the rise of virtuality, more and more individuals aspire to *be* the influencing machine. Put in more vernacular terms, crazy people used to think the media was talking to them; now, more and more people believe they *are* the media or, at least, the media's puppet master. This was Malvo's plan, apparently: *I will be the external agent that uses the media to influence others.* Maturing in a world of perpetual mediation, algorithmic management, and strategic egocasting, digital natives are already quite comfortable with externalizing and translating themselves into data for both public consumption and neoliberal self-diagnostics. The taking and posting of "selfies" suggests a fundamentally different relationship between the self and the environment, an affordance that allows posters to fantasize that they are "out there" being noticed by some iteration of a public sphere. Accordingly, self-help manuals advise readers to self-actualize in terms of Twitter followers and favorable impressions (measured in the concise metrics of "impressions," "likes," and "retweets"). Bloggers work tirelessly on web pages that attract little to no traffic, understanding that it is still better to be an active producer of information than merely a passive receiver. Personality quizzes are as old as ego psychology and modern publishing. But in the digital economy, one can submit one's personality traits and lifestyle choices to instant analysis (knowing full well the data are being harvested by marketers) and then quickly share the results online. (Which Beatle are you? I'm a Ringo!) Facebook encourages users to list "likes" and "dislikes," not as interior details to be revealed slowly in a seductive staging of friendship or intimacy, but as a "bill-of-sale" produced up front to calculate the value of future virtual interactions. Social media allow people to perform their "best self": *I'll post this picture of me in Italy so people will know and envy the fact that I'm in Italy.* In the crazed male mind, "dick pics" cut to the chase in sexual marketing:

this is what I have to offer you. Entire networks now exist to indulge the once shameful task of networking. Like so many other modern binaries, Erving Goffman's influential divide of "front-stage" and "back-stage" has imploded to produce a virtual stage on which the info-ego is encouraged to pursue a twenty-four-hour cycle of working and preening. As Joshua Gamson writes, "The unwatched life is not worth living."[18]

Older critics frequently dismiss such developments as a symptom of millennial narcissism. But this is to judge by the obsolescent standards of an increasingly obsolescent modern(ist) ego. The compulsion toward maximum visibility and, with it, a fantasy of acting the influencer rather than the influenced is a structural imperative of a system that recognizes power's migration into the information complex: *information seeks to control me, so I will control information.* For some, this influencing fantasy can take more extreme forms. In 2008, the Republican campaign volunteer Ashley Todd reported a robbery and assault to the Pittsburg Police Department. Todd told police she had been robbed at an ATM by a tall African American man who, when he saw a bumper sticker for Republican candidate John McCain on her car, carved the letter "B" in her cheek and told her, "You are going to be a Barack supporter." With less than two weeks to Election Day and eager to believe this potentially game-changing story, a number of right-wing news sites promoted Todd's claim. Some predicted it might even stall Barack Obama's momentum in the polls. Todd's estimation of the information economy was sound. In the end, her hoax was foiled only by her own human error. Police became suspicious when (1) a surveillance camera at the ATM contained no footage of the robbery; and (2) the "B" on Todd's face was backward, suggesting she had carved it herself with the aid of a mirror. This proved correct.[19]

In 2002, Lucas Helder, a college student in Wisconsin, devised a plan to educate the world about capitalism, marijuana, and immortality. His chosen platform was a unique combination of pipe bombs and pixels. Like the Unabomber before him, Helder wrote a manifesto explaining his views and motivation, sending the document to his college newspaper.[20] All the miseries of the world, Helder argued, stemmed from man's fear of death, a premise that Helder elaborated into a fairly coherent Marxist-Freudian critique of the contemporary social order. "In fearing death, you are forced to work (in turn providing for the government), and conform to society," he wrote. "You work to buy food, provide shelter, entertainment, etc. You conform to society because you will receive negative emotion/pain/death (jail/death penalty) if you don't. You fear, therefor [sic] you conform."[21] Money animated this system; therefore, Helder wrote, "fear of death results in the ability of the government to make money, on the people/on precious consciousness/on you!" Interested in ghosts, dreams, and astral projection, Helder wished to announce that death was an illusion, a revelation he believed would lead to the elimination of all greed and exploitation. Recognizing the superconductive potential of explosions in post-9/11 America, Helder's plan involved setting off a series of pipe bombs across the American Midwest. At each rural bombsite, Helder left a flyer titled "Explosions! A Bit of Evidence for You!" in which he expounded his views, signing off as "someone who cares." Handwritten at the bottom: "Knowledge is Power." Leaving a paper trail of typewritten notes may seem an oddly low-tech strategy for global enlightenment, but Helder's plan involved a more sophisticated intervention in the information ecosystem. His pipe bombs were deployed not in some random campaign of menace, but to create coordinates (or "dots") that, once connected, would draw a giant "smiley face" on the map of the United States. Helder, in other words, borrowed a convention from cinematic variations on the Zodiac killer (a spatial method in the madness) to imagine how his string of explosions, once transferred onto a map on the evening news, would gradually reveal this whimsical and darkly ironic figure. The plan was never completed, however, as police triangulated Helder's cell phone signal and apprehended him in Nevada on his way to the next coordinate.

Offered as a symbolic solution to a psychotic crisis, technical delusions have always offered insight into technologies of power. Virtual delusions recognize that the translation of the world into the binary code of 0 and 1 presents the most elegant and diabolical binding of power and information yet imagined. In other words, virtual delusions—as an emergent psychotic formation—suggest a thesis on which Jacques Lacan, Baudrillard, and innumerable science-fiction writers might agree: *To control electronics is to control the power of meaning, and to control meaning is to control the power of electronics.* Mediating this exchange is the ego, once modern and in control but now increasingly aware that it is, potentially, merely an effect of a cybernetic system—electronic, semiotic, or perhaps both. The first step to mastering or (in a more residual modernist mode) defeating such a system is to recognize, embrace, and mobilize one's identity as a data packet.

....

Despite its frequent association with electronic counterfeiting, Baudrillardian simulation was always concerned more with meaning than with technologies of radical illusion. Virtual reality and other forms of spectacular fascination doubtless will figure in humanity's mediated future. But the main agenda of contemporary information technology is not to create an immersive virtual reality program that "tricks" us with radical illusion. It is, instead, to enact a positivist drive toward explaining, actualizing, and controlling the world as data. Here Baudrillard proposes a psychotic possibility that is infinitely more terrifying than mere suspension in a virtual realm of digital code. In a series of short essays bundled under the title *The Perfect Crime* (1996), he describes this process of realization as the "murder" of reality. Aphoristic and elliptical, Baudrillard's procedural mystery can be interpreted in many ways. But a recurring suspect is the virtual's impulse toward the positivist actualization of (a) reality in terms of massive data sets. The world has always existed in radical illusion, Baudrillard argues, a play of appearances that is "never identical to itself, never real."[22] Subject, object, language, distance, desire, seduction—all are products of inhabiting a world that remains shrouded in the mysteries of illusory surfaces and unfathomable consciousness. But quantitative ambition threatens to extinguish these qualitative mysteries and, with them, all phenomena associated with our fundamental "alter-ation" within radical illusion.[23] This "alter-ation," writes Baudrillard, "tends to diminish with increasing information and ... will, in the end, be eliminated by absolute information; the worlds' equivalence to the world—the final illusion, that of a world which is perfect, fully realized, fully effectuated, a world which is consummated and has attained the height of its possibilities."[24] While it may seem desirable to "fully effectuate" the world, Baudrillard's warning here—like so much science fiction—is that human subjects, as shades wandering through a life of radical illusion, should be careful what they wish for. What Baudrillard describes is a false utopia where radical illusion evaporates and is replaced by an isomorphic equivalence of the world with information about the world: "The perfect crime is that of an unconditional realization of the world by the actualization of all data, the transformation of all our acts and all events into pure information; in short, the final solution, the resolution of the world ahead of time by the cloning of reality and the extermination of the real by its double."[25] Crucially, this realization of the world is not equivalent to the Enlightenment fantasy of achieving some form of absolute knowledge. Instead, it describes an encoding logic in which the information double of a (but not the) reality locks humanity within a static, closed system of positivist actualization. In an effort to dispel doubt, danger, death, inefficiency, and the other entropic contingencies of our incomprehensible existence, humanity deploys virtuality, not as an electronic mirage, but as an arrested circuit of information, the world and the equivalency of a world frozen as data. Sealing the gap between reality and its information double slays not only radical illusion but also any possible occult dynamics of subject and object. In the end, the objects win by transcribing us according to their needs and protocols. We are left with a transition from "objective reality—reality related to meaning and representation" to what Baudrillard termed "integral reality, a reality without limits in which everything is realized and technically materialized without reference to any principle or final purpose whatever."[26] Our digital terrarium will present not radical illusion or even a simulation of radical illusion but, instead, a homeostatic cybernetics perfected through positivist equations and administrative procedures.

Integral reality proposes radically new possibilities for the symbolic order, perhaps even its ultimate annihilation. As we have seen, Lacan posited a "lack" at the center of human existence (and a "hole" at the center of psychosis). The technology of language produces a symbolic order that inscribes a fundamental alienation in the subject as it enters into a system of meaning and representation, a world where signifier and signified obey a logic of endlessly displaced difference. Many of us share a language, but no two people share the same iteration of the symbolic (just as one can ever return to the hypothetical unity believed to exist before language). Constituted by and within a world of articulated meaning, the ego lives a series of fantasies as it pursues its unique life trajectory through the symbolic. For the psychotic, drawn into the hole of meaningful disruption, the ego's function as the normalizing interface between inside and outside falters. Positivism, of course, abhors the idea that human existence could be so capriciously attached to mere vicissitudes of meaning. With enough reason, rationalism, and data, offers the positivist, language's unpredictable structures of deferral and difference might be calibrated to craft a denotative mirror that at last stabilizes an objective reality. Inside the data terrarium, the ego of old will be rescued from its fundamental lack and alienation by constructing an environment wherein the play of signifiers and signifieds is at last arrested in the best practices of data and the data of best practices: no more relativism, no more contingency, no more translation errors—only a universal protocol for validating data and its processing. Of course, such a system would need to function as a perfect economy, hermetically sealed off from any and all new data, given that the introduction of any new or unstable term would threaten to disrupt the overall system. But even if disaster erupts, opening once again a rent of difference and doubt, positivist protocols will be in place to repair these occasional cracks in the glass. This environment would not involve a radical illusion in that nothing would necessarily be concealed (which, indeed, is the entire point of positivism). The elimination of lack and a scientific standardization of the symbolic would also, at long last, eradicate that human swamp of irrationality known as the unconscious (if, indeed, one could find a positivist who believes the unconscious exists and is thus in need of eradication). In a world visualized and calibrated through data, nothing will be left to repress or foreclose. The neurotic and psychotic will vanish, along with the tenuously meaningful subject that once incubated them.

Such a project would involve siphoning as much interiority as possible from the modern ego, a process that is arguably already well under way. New technical economies encourage syntagmatic connectivity over the poetic or psychotic agonies of paradigmatic contemplation. As Fredric Jameson argued in relation to postmodernism, late capitalism no longer needs coherent subjects to enact its agenda.[27] This incoherence has only accelerated with the move toward virtualization, prosthesis, and global data management. Already, even the most residual forms of thought, reflection, and doubt are proving to be impediments of an increasingly transactional socioeconomic order. Quickly fading, it would seem, is any need to curate deep archives of individual knowledge through the protocols of language (i.e., reading, writing, speaking, thinking). More useful in the dynamics of contemporary power is a subject rendered into a nodal point for the timely relay of information. To think is to fail—or, at least, retard—and so information technologies are working to open up as much processing space as possible in the brain by compressing the resistances of subjective depth into a more superficial nexus that is better suited to entertaining incessant connectivity. The "perpetual present" once bemoaned by Jameson as a hazard of postmodernity now stands as a valued affordance for the entire data-political network.

This fate may seem far-fetched. But as religion, capitalism, and other structural disasters suggest, humans have proved quite ingenious at producing massive economies of control from which it becomes extremely difficult to escape. Being trapped in a world of rationalist data management is no less absurd than an existence ruled by sky gods or the occult mechanisms of exchange value. Admittedly, the modern ego has led to much unhappiness and destruction, from the perpetual fog of neurotic despair to the Anthropocene's acceleration toward global annihilation. Considering this less than stellar history, some futurists argue there should be no nostalgia for the ego of old and that the post-human subject will leave behind sexism, racism, homophobia, and other regressive formations in history's repressive politics of difference.[28] Digitizers imagine the brain rendered into a 3D avatar capable of storing human consciousness—data encoded within data—where hygienic simulations of difference, a virtual gap of virtual self and other, somehow supplants the messy biological exchanges of sociopolitical intercourse.[29] Faced with a binary choice of gyno-feminist spirituality and electronic augmentation, Donna Haraway proposed it would be better to be a "cyborg" than a "goddess," choosing an unknown future over a depressingly familiar history that has already proved exploitative.[30] In a work Foucault blurbed as a blueprint for "anti-fascism," the two-part study of "capitalism and schizophrenia" (*The Anti-Oedipus* [1972] and *One Thousand Plateaus* [1980]), Gilles Deleuze and Félix Guattari proposed a radical rerouting of psychical energy that would actively rewire the human subject as a psychotic.[31] Written when the circuitous energies of the technical delusion were already more than a century old, *The Anti-Oedipus* embraced the schizophrenic fascination with mechanics and technology to propose the idea of the "desiring-machine." Rejecting the pessimism of Freud's universal neuroticism and Lacan's location of desire in lack, Deleuze and Guattari instead expressed a preference for the free-flowing "desiring-production" of the schizophrenic. Freed from the tyranny of lack, tomorrow's "schizo" would engage desire not as an unattainable phantom bound up in signification but, instead, by pursing affective intensities wherever they might lead, obeying the logic of a machine capable of generating endlessly productive interfaces with other devices. "Desiring machines are binary machines," they observe, "obeying a binary law or set of rules governing associations: one machine is always coupled with another. The productive synthesis, the production of production, is inherently connective in nature."[32] A glass of milk is thus rendered in reverse: "The anus-machine and the intestine-machine, the intestine-machine and the stomach-machine, the stomach-machine and the mouth-machine, the mouth-machine and the flow of milk of a herd of dairy cattle ('and then ... and then ... and then ...')."[33] "Intensities," a production of ceaseless connections and ruptures, would overflow the regulated conductive streams of the Freudian economy to produce an ocean of bliss, a "body without organs" that speaks a "language without articulation."[34] In this early iteration of their panic materialism, Deleuze and Guattari sought to disrupt the previous centuries' investment in fixity and homeostasis with an active program of molecular becoming and interstitial possibility.[35]

The dream of *The Anti-Oedipus* was to stop making sense, a fantasy not unfamiliar to many modernists and Romantics over the past few centuries. Recognizing that language, history, culture, society, and meaning constitute a straitjacket of sorts, humans have long struggled to imagine modes of existence and (non)self that could invoke the sublime, the irrational, the unknown, the uncontrollable, the unnamable. Such anarchic calls to psychotic liberation no doubt seemed more plausible in the late twentieth century—and, indeed, Deleuze's later writings on the contemporary sociopsychic-economic order were less optimistic.[36] The schizo culture of the untethered desiring machine remains unrealized, retarded for the moment (and perhaps forever) by the "society of control." Supplanting Foucault's disciplinary society, the society of control is the administrative complex that will be charged with installing integral reality. As Deleuze argues, the binary of individual and mass, so central to disciplinary power, is no longer needed. Replacing this foundational dialectic of modernity is a more granular dispersion of power into patterns of data management that are global in scope yet extremely localized in actualization. "Individuals" are no longer central to this system, replaced instead by "'dividuals" who figure within "masses, samples, data, markets, or 'banks.'"[37] Deleuze notes that the disciplinary societies of the nineteenth and twentieth centuries depended on institutional spaces in which "one was always starting again (from school to the barracks, from the barracks to the factory)," stages on the modern ego's way as it pursued its biopolitical path to become a productive individual within a civic and economic mass. While the mass remained as the hypothetical aggregate of these individuals, disciplinary institutions nevertheless addressed and produced its charges as individuals with unique (though structural) trajectories within the biopolitical. In the society of control, meanwhile, "one is never finished with anything," producing a dynamic of "limitless postponement" in which "the man of control is undulatory, in orbit, in a continuous network." Interstitial becoming, once at the heart of Deleuze's liberating agenda, now functions as the engine of capitalist renewal on the global stage. For now, at least, "connectivity" does not describe a schizo sensually coupled to a Rube Goldberg network of flowing ecstasies; rather, "connectivity" captures the plight of pre–post-humans bound to virtual flows of information where *becoming data* portends an interstitial oblivion of nonexistence. In the society of control, the human transformation into desiring machines appears blunted by the machining of desire, not in the sense of Lacanian lack, but in integral reality's drive toward recasting all exchanges through the positivist plentitude of data. The radical delusion of the Matrix at least counterfeited some possibility of enjoyment. (In fact, given the choice, many would gladly take the metaphorically loaded "blue pill" of fantasy over the harsh "red pill" of actuality.) Integral reality's enactment of a positivist utopia does not even offer this delusional escape. Instead, there are only cycles of delirium and depression as residual subjects assimilate to a perfect language of 0 and 1, a system that slowly erases all of the messy fractionalizations of qualitative doubt.

Post-human schematics typically imagine a subject (or society) that chooses, of its own relatively free will, to produce new and improved post-subjects. Little thought is given, however, to the reigning relations of power that aspire to deliver us to this era of post-ness. Despite its name, the singularity is not an inevitable or singular rendezvous of brains and bytes. Instead, it will arrive as a necessarily contingent move from the biopolitical to a possible iteration of the data-political. Once accomplished, however, this path toward integral reality cannot be reversed, especially as data administration slowly erases the "human" formation that imagined it wanted to be posthuman in the first place. Imagining a digi-king empowered to conjure goods, services, and information out of thin air, advocates of the Internet of Everything neglect to consider how this radical realignment of space, time, and desire might affect what is "needed" and how it is "wanted."[38] Looking further down the road of data deliverance, brain uploaders imagine millions of minds entering a mainframe that somehow maintains the pleasures of the embodied ego while defeating the treachery of the body.[39] Whereas the ego of old, confronted with its mortality, experienced the existential angst of imagining nonexistence, the data-ego will eventually confront the equally horrifying prospect of having to manufacture new and diverting libidinal attachments for thousands and thousands of years. Virtual immortality, like heaven, is a place where nothing ever happens—or, at least, nothing can *continue* to happen once the virtual ego, exhausted from centuries of maintaining the charade of its embodied origins, has an even more crippling digistential crisis.

Unlike futurists who imagine humanity's ongoing prosthesis as a benign and freely chosen augmentation, the psychotic appear much more sensitive to the function of power, figurative and literal, in mediating these speculative-turned-operational encounters between self and technology. Over the past two centuries, the psychotic frequently have served as conscripts in exploring how electronics might come to mediate society and subjectivity in ways that are, quite suddenly and catastrophically, something other than what they were. Implicit in these insane delusions about the media is a recognition that any form of prosthesis will necessarily concretize and expand the agenda of power charged with implementing such augmentation. So far, the history of the technical delusion has been generally terrifying, the residual subject compelled to negotiate a meaning system refracted through an increasingly byzantine hall of electronic mirrors. The singularity, brought to life within the society of control, promises to recalibrate these terrors, absolving the residual subject of any aspiration to contemplation, comprehension, purpose, or any other potential operating error in the emerging cybernetic assemblage. Psychosis as we know it may well decrease during this process of crossing over as the modern ego, once so intent on achieving Prosthetic Godhood, finds itself less transcendent than evaporated. In this respect, those who today see themselves in the Matrix, on reality television, or involved in other delusions of influencing may signal a final stand against the encroaching homeostasis of integral reality. The fantasy of generating media, while perhaps no less a dead end than the terror of serving as a target, at least gives residual subjects a strategy for confronting the slow historical drift into cybernetic catatonia.[40]

Introduction

1 Celestine Hay, "Command-Automatism and Echopraxia to Television," *American Journal of Psychiatry* 112, no. 1 (1955): 65.
2 Harold D. Lasswell, "The Theory of Political Propaganda," *American Political Science Review* 21, no. 3 (1927): 627–31; Edward L. Bernays, *Crystallizing Public Opinion* (New York: Boni and Liveright, 1927); Vance Packard, *The Hidden Persuaders* (New York: David McKay, 1957), 157–66.
3 Jerry Mander, *Four Arguments for Eliminating Television* (New York: William Morrow, 1978), 86. For his part, the philosopher Stanley Cavell was not convinced by Mander's jeremiad:

> Perhaps the most astonishing stretch of what I have been able to read of this book is its section in praise of Victor Tausk's description of the "Influencing Machine." Mander is convinced that television is the realization of the ultimate influencing machine. But the point of Tausk's extraordinary paper is that to think there are in reality such machines is symptomatic of schizophrenia. I cannot tell whether Mander knows this, and whether, if he does, he is declaring that he is schizophrenic, and if he is, whether he is claiming that television has driven him so, even as it is so driving the rest of us, and perhaps claiming that it is a state in which the truth of our condition has become particularly lucid to him. Without telling these things, I am still prepared to regard this book, the very fact that numbers of reasonable people apparently

take it seriously, as symptomatic of the depth of anxiety television can inspire. (Stanley Cavell, "The Fact of Television," *Daedalus* III, no. 4 [Fall 1982]: 94).

4 Charles Mackay, *Extraordinary Popular Delusions and the Madness of Crowds* (London: Richard Bentley, 1841), xviii.
5 Friedrich Nietzsche, *The Will to Power*, trans. Walter Kaufmann and R. J. Hollingdale (New York: Vintage, 1968), 33.
6 Gustave Le Bon, *The Crowd: A Study of the Popular Mind* (London: T. Fisher Unwin, 1893), 29.
7 Le Bon, *The Crowd*, 5.
8 See Max Horkheimer and Theodor Adorno's "The Culture Industry: Enlightenment as Mass Deception," in *Dialectic of Enlightenment*, 94–136 (Palo Alto, CA: Stanford University Press, [1944] 2007); Daniel Boorstin, *The Image: A Guide to Pseudo-Events in America* (New York: Atheneum, 1962); Jacques Derrida and Bernard Stiegler, "Artifactualities," in Jacques Derrida and Bernard Stiegler, *Echographies of Television* (Cambridge: Polity, 2002), 41–55.
9 The first formal use of this term that I have been able to find appears in Alfred Kraus, "Phenomenology of the Technical Delusion in Schizophrenics," *Journal of Phenomenological Psychology* 25, no. 1 (1994): 51–69.
10 Michel Foucault, *Discipline and Punish*, trans. Alan Sheridan (New York: Vintage, 1979).
11 Edgar Allan Poe, "The Man of the Crowd," *Burton's Gentleman's Magazine*, December 1840, 267–70. Jack the Ripper is believed to have murdered five women in London's East End between August 31 and November 9, 1888. Despite a century of speculation, the cases remain unsolved.
12 Georg Simmel, "The Metropolis and Mental Life" (1903), in *The Sociology of Georg Simmel*, trans. Kurt Wolff (New York: Free Press, 1950), 409–24.
13 See Leo Marx, *The Machine in the Garden: Technology and the Pastoral Ideal in America* (Oxford: Oxford University Press, 1964); James W. Carey and John J. Quirk, "The Mythos of the Electronic Revolution," *American Scholar* 39, no. 3 (1970): 395–424.
14 David E. Nye, *Electrifying America: Social Meanings of a New Technology, 1880–1940* (Cambridge, MA: MIT Press, 1992).
15 Jules Verne, *20,000 Leagues under the Sea*, trans. Anthony Bonner (New York: Bantam, [1870] 1962).
16 Frank L. Baum, *The Master Key: An Electrical Fairy Tale Founded upon the Mysteries of Electricity and the Optimism of Its Devotees. It was Written for Boys, but Others May Read It* (New York: Bowen-Merrill, 1901).
17 The definitive history of this transition in wireless radio remains Susan Douglas, *Inventing American Broadcasting, 1899–1922* (Baltimore: Johns Hopkins University Press, 1989).
18 Peter Vincent Fry has written several books on the possibilities of an EMP disaster: see Peter Vincent Fry, *Apocalypse Unknown: The Struggle to Protect America from an Electromagnetic Pulse Catastrophe* (CreateSpace Independent Pub-

lishing Platform, 2013); Peter Vincent Fry, *Blackout Wars: State Initiatives to Achieve Preparedness against an Electromagnetic Pulse (EMP) Catastrophe* (CreateSpace Independent Publishing Platform, 2015); Peter Vincent Fry, *Electric Armageddon: Civil-Military Preparedness For An Electromagnetic Pulse Catastrophe* (CreateSpace Independent Publishing Platform, 2013).

19 Electromagnetic Pulse (EMP) Commission, "Report of the Commission to Assess the Threat to the United States from Electromagnetic Pulse (EMP) Attack: Critical National Infrastructures," monograph, April 2008, http://www.dtic.mil/dtic/tr/fulltext/u2/a484672.pdf.

20 Foucault's canonical early study, *Folie et déraison: Histoire de la folie à l'âge classique*, interrogated how, in the late eighteenth and early nineteenth centuries, "madness" became an "illness" produced by and subject to the authority of psychiatry as a medical discourse, a body of knowledge empowered by the state to produce binding truths in relation to the body of the patient. Foucault returned to the question of "psychiatric power" in a series of lectures at the Collège de France in 1973 and 1974. Here Foucault reiterated that psychiatric disorders are not so much discovered in the body as *produced* through discourse—existing in a symbiotic, supplementary relationship with the "science" that defines and diagnoses them. The lectures provide an interesting bridge between *Folie at déraison* and *Discipline and Punish*, Foucault's equally canonical work on the carceral power of the state to survey, individuate, and thus regulate populations through disciplinary tactics of normalization: see Michel Foucault, *Psychiatric Power: Lectures at the Collège de France, 1973–1974*, vol. 1 (New York: Macmillan, 2008).

21 See Foucault, *Psychiatric Power*, 134.

22 Thomas S. Szasz, *Schizophrenia: The Sacred Symbol of Psychiatry* (Syracuse, NY: Syracuse University Press, 1988), 88. In keeping with the revolutionary spirit of the era, Szasz approached the psychiatrist-patient relationship as one of oppressor and oppressed, citing involuntary psychiatric institutionalization as an issue of basic civil rights: see Thomas S. Szasz, "Involuntary Hospital Commitment," in *Ideology and Insanity: Essays on the Psychiatric Dehumanization of Man* (Syracuse, NY: Syracuse University Press, 1991), 113.

23 Eugen Bleuler, *Dementia Praecox or the Group of Schizophrenias* (New York: New York International Universities Press, [1919] 1952).

24 The DSM-V abandoned these subcategories. Clinicians have demonstrated that an individual patient often manifests all three of these phases over the course of a psychotic episode.

25 Szasz, *Schizophrenia*, 3.

26 R. D. Laing, *The Politics of the Family, and Other Essays* (London: Routledge, 1971) 44.

27 David Cooper introduced the term "anti-psychiatry" in 1967. In addition to his collaborations with Gilles Deleuze, Félix Guattari championed innovative therapies for schizophrenic patients at the La Borde clinic in France. In 1969, Szasz and the Church of Scientology established the Citizen's Commission

of Human Rights to investigate claims of psychiatric injustice. Szasz later attempted to distance himself from the church's agenda. For an account of Szasz's relation to Scientology, see Geoff Watts, "Thomas Stephen Szasz," *The Lancet* 380, no. 9851 (2012): 1380.

28 Thomas S. Szasz, *The Therapeutic State: Psychiatry in the Mirror of Current Events* (New York: Prometheus, 1984).

29 Louis A. Sass, *Madness and Modernism: Insanity in the Light of Modern Art, Literature, and Thought* (New York: Basic, 1992).

30 David Michael Kleinberg-Levin, *Pathologies of the Modern Self: Postmodern Studies on Narcissism, Schizophrenia, and Depression* (New York: New York University Press, 1987).

31 Liah Greenfeld, *Mind, Modernity, Madness* (Cambridge, MA: Harvard University Press, 2013).

32 Angela Woods, *The Sublime Object of Psychiatry: Schizophrenia in Clinical and Cultural Theory* (Oxford: Oxford University Press, 2011), 27.

33 Joel Kovel, "Schizophrenic Being and Technocratic Society," in *Pathologies of the Modern Self: Postmodern Studies on Narcissism, Schizophrenia, and Depression*, ed. David Michael Kleinberg-Levin (New York: New York University Press, 1987), 335.

34 "Oxford Accent Poseurs Called Schizophraniacs," *New York Herald Tribune*, November 5, 1931, 19.

35 Carol Warren, *Madwives: Schizophrenic Women in the 1950s* (New Brunswick, NJ: Rutgers University Press, 1987).

36 Jonathan Metzl, *The Protest Psychosis* (Boston: Beacon, 2009), 100. See also Walter Bromberg and Franck Simon, "The 'Protest' Psychosis: A Special Type of Reactive Psychosis," *Archives of General Psychiatry* 19, no. 2 (1968): 155. For more on the relationship between race and psychiatric diagnosis, see Dinesh Bhugra and Oyedeji Ayonrinde, "Racism, Racial Life Events, and Mental Ill Health," in *Clinical Topics in Cultural Psychiatry*, ed. Rahul Bhattacharya, Sean Cross, and Dinesh Bhugra (London: RCPsych, 2010), 39–51.

37 The Cross-National Project was established by the United Kingdom and United States in 1965: see Barry J. Gurland, Joseph L. Fleiss, John E. Cooper, Robert E. Kendell, and Robert Simon, "Cross-National Study of Diagnosis of the Mental Disorders: Some Comparisons of Diagnostic Criteria from the First Investigation," *American Journal of Psychiatry* 125, no. 10S (1969): 30–39; Morton Kramer, "Cross-National Study of Diagnosis of the Mental Disorders: Origin of the Problem," *American Journal of Psychiatry* 125, no. 10S (1969): 1–11; John E. Cooper, "Psychiatric Diagnosis in New York and London: A Comparative Study of Mental Hospital Admissions," Maudslay Monograph no. 20 (London: Oxford University Press, 1972).

38 E. Fuller Torrey and Robert H. Yolken, "Could Schizophrenia Be a Viral Zoonosis Transmitted from House Cats?" *Schizophrenia Bulletin* 21, no. 2 (1995): 167.

39 B. E. Gavin, B. D. Kelly, A. Lane, and E. O'Callaghan, "The Mental Health of Migrants," *Irish Medical Journal* 109, no. 1 (2016); F. Bourque, E. Van der Ven,

and A. Malla, "A Meta-analysis of the Risk for Psychotic Disorders among First- and Second-Generation Immigrants," *Psychological Medicine* 41, no. 5 (2011): 897. There is even literature to suggest that the "culture shock" of international travel can be strong enough, in certain circumstances, to trigger psychotic behavior: see Stanley Shapiro, "A Study of Psychiatric Syndromes Manifested at an International Airport," *Comprehensive Psychiatry* 17, no. 3 (1976): 453–56; Marcel A. H. Monden, "Development of Psychopathology in International Tourists," in *Psychological Aspects of Geographical Moves: Homesickness and Acculturation Stress*, ed. Miranda A. L. van Tilburg and Ad J. J. M. Vingerhoets (Tilburg, Netherlands: Tilburg University Press, 1997), 229. M. Uemoto, N. Moriyama, H. Hamada, M. Onishi, K. Fujiya, A. Koizumi, and S. Watanabe, "Maladies mentales chez les Japonais à Paris," *Annales Médico-Psychologiques* 140, no. 7 (1982): 717–27.

40 Robert E. Lee Faris and Henry Warren Dunham, *Mental Disorders in Urban Areas: An Ecological Study of Schizophrenia and Other Psychoses* (New York: Hafner, 1939).

41 Kim Hopper and Joseph Wanderling, "Revisiting the Developed versus Developing Country Distinction in Course and Outcome in Schizophrenia: Results from ISoS, the WHO Collaborative Follow-Up Project," *Schizophrenia Bulletin* 26, no. 4 (2000): 835–46.

42 R. D. Laing, *The Politics of Experience* (New York: Ballantine, 1968), 120.

43 Christopher Lane, *Shyness: How Normal Behavior Became a Sickness* (New Haven, CT: Yale University Press, 2008).

44 Jacques Lacan, *The Seminar of Jacques Lacan, Book III: The Psychoses, 1955–1956*, ed. Jacques-Alain Miller, trans. Russell Grigg (New York: W. W. Norton, 1993), 34.

45 Lacan, *The Seminar of Jacques Lacan, Book III*, 34–35.

46 Even studies that rather studiously avoid Lacanian theory often come to something approximating this Lacanian conclusion. Joseph LeDoux writes, "It is, in my opinion, the structuring of cognition around language that confers on the human brain its unique qualities." LeDoux describes language as a "revolution" rather than an "evolution of function," one that allows humans to embellish and store "working memory," which in turn allows for human "consciousness.... When I use the term consciousness, I usually am referring to the special qualities of human consciousness, especially those made possible by language": Joseph LeDoux, *Synaptic Self* (New York: Penguin, 2002), 197–98.

47 Richard P. Bentall, *Madness Explained: Psychosis and Human Nature* (London: Penguin, 2004).

48 Simon McCarthy-Jones, "The Concept of Schizophrenia is Coming to End— Here's Why," *The Conversation*, August 24, 2017, https://theconversation.com /the-concept-of-schizophrenia-is-coming-to-an-end-heres-why-82775.

49 Bentall, *Madness Explained*.

50 Elizabeth D. Kantor, C. D. Rehm, J. S. Haas, A. T. Chan, and E. L. Giovannucci, "Trends in Prescription Drug Use among Adults in the United States

from 1999–2012," *Journal of the American Medical Association* 314, no. 17 (2015): 1818–30.
51 John Haslam, *Observations on Madness and Melancholy: Including Practical Remarks on Those Diseases; Together with Cases: and an Account of the Morbid Appearances on Dissection* (London: J. Callow, 1809), v–vi.
52 Henry Maudsley, "Is Insanity on the Increase?" *British Medical Journal* 1, no. 576 (1872): 36.
53 Barbara O'Brien, *Operators and Things* (New York: Ace, 1958), 15.
54 Daniel Freeman and Jason Freeman, *Paranoia: The 21st-Century Fear* (London: Oxford University Press, 2008), 8.
55 "Nervous Strain: JAMA 100 Years Ago," *Journal of the American Medical Association* 45 (1905): 404.
56 "Telephone Diseases," *Boston Daily Globe*, November 24, 1889.
57 Nietzsche, *The Will to Power*, 71.
58 Max Nordau, *Degeneration* (Lincoln: University of Nebraska Press, [1892] 1993).
59 Alvin Toffler, *Future Shock* (New York: Random House, 1970), 2.
60 Toffler, *Future Shock*, 236.
61 Mark Andrejevic, *Infoglut: How Too Much Information Is Changing the Way We Think and Know* (New York: Routledge, 2013), 2.
62 L. Scher, "Sociopolitical Events and Technical Innovations May Affect the Content of Delusions and the Course of Psychotic Disorders," *Medical Hypotheses* 55, no. 6 (December 2000): 507–9; Jens Bohlken and Stefab Priebe, "Political Change and Course of Affective Psychoses: Berlin 1989–1990," *Psychiatry Research* 37, no. 1 (1991): 1–4; M. A. Marcolin, "The Prognosis of Schizophrenia across Cultures," *Ethnicity and Disease* 1, no. 1 (1991): 99–104; P. Kulhara, "Outcome of Schizophrenia: Some Transcultural Observations with Particular Reference to Developing Countries," *European Archives of Psychiatry and Clinical Neuroscience* 244, no. 5 (1994): 227–35.

Chapter 1. The Technical Delusion

1 Robert D. McFadden, "Park Ave. Assault on Rather Leaves Mystery as to Motive," *New York Times*, October 6, 1986, B3.
2 Denis Brian, *Sing Sing: The Inside Story of a Notorious Prison* (Amherst, NY: Prometheus, 2005), 235.
3 State of New York, Executive Department, Division of Parole, Sing Sing Correctional Facility, "Inmate Status Report for Parole Board Appearance," William Tager, NYSID7771999N, DIN 96A7476, December 2006, https://archive.org/stream/239143-william-tager-parole-documents/239143-william-tager-parole-documents_djvu.txt.
4 Robert McFadden, "Police Say Murder Suspect Thinks TV Networks Spied on Him," *New York Times*, September 2, 1994, A1. See also "Headliners," *New York*

Times, October 12, 1986, E9; Adam Nossiter, "Man Pleads Guilty in Shooting of Stagehand on Midtown Street," *New York Times*, July 26 1996, B3; The novelist Paul Limbert Allman explores an alternative explanation for Rather's attack, implicating, of all people, the literary icon Donald Barthelme: see Paul Limbert Allman, "The Frequency," *Harper's Magazine*, December 1, 2001, 69–72. Allman eventually elaborated his thesis as a play at the Edinburgh Fringe Festival in 2004. The production imagines Rather and Barthelme crossing paths in Houston during Hurricane Carla in 1961, forever linked by some odd quantum fluke opened by the storm: Marilyn Stasio, "Review—What's the Frequency, Kenneth?," *Variety*, October 26, 2004, 4.

5 "No Doubt in Rather Case," *New York Times*, November 5, 2004, A30.

6 Psychiatry's general lack of interest in the content of delusional thought has resulted in relatively few attempts to document the history of delusional ideation. A study from 2011 looking at delusional content in a single psychiatric hospital over the course of the twentieth century produced results that are "consistent with reports in the literature" that "persecutory content" is "the most common delusional category," adding that "technology" has emerged in recent years as a dominant in persecutory delusions: see Brooke Cannon and Lorraine Masinos Kramer, "Delusion Content across the 20th Century in an American Psychiatric Hospital," *International Journal of Social Psychiatry* 58, no. 3 (2012): 323–27. A similar study from Slovenia examined delusional content in schizophrenics between 1881 and 2000, noting that delusions of "outside influence" and "control" increased after the introduction of radio in the 1920s and increased even more after the introduction of television in the 1950s: see B. Skodlar, M. Z. Dernovsek and M. Kocmur, "Psychopathology of Schizophrenia in Ljubljana (Slovenia) from 1881 to 2000: Changes in the Content of Delusions in Schizophrenia Patients Related to Various Sociopolitical, Technical and Scientific Changes," *International Journal of Social Psychiatry* 54 (2008), 101–11. Alfred Kraus notes several studies documenting an "important increase in themes" involving technologies in delusional thought: see Alfred Kraus, "Phenomenology of the Technical Delusion in Schizophrenics," *Journal of Phenomenological Psychology* 25, no. 1 (1994): 51–69. Kraus cites studies from Austria (Hermann Lenz, *Vergleichende Psychiatrie* [Vienna: Wilhelm Maudrich, 1964], 37–720); from Czechoslovakia (M. Bouchal, "Changes in the Thematic Content of the Symptoms of Schizophrenia and Paraphrenia under the Influence of Social and Historic Development," *Ceskoslovenská psychiatrie* 54, no. 3 [1958]: 149–53; from Finland (Karl Aimo Achté, *Der Verlauf der Schizophrenien und der Schizophreniformen Psychosen: Eine vergleichende Untersuchung der Veränderungen in den Krankseitsbildern, der Prognosen und des Verhältnisses zwischen dem Kranken und dem Arzt in den Jahren 1933–1935 und 1953–1955* [Copenhagen: Ejnar Munksgaard, 1961]); from Germany (Heinrich Kranz, "Das Thema des Wahns im Wandel der Zeit," *Fortschritte der Neurologie und Psychiatrie und Grenzbeibiete* 23, nos. 1–2 [1955]: 58–72): from Italy (Enzo Agresti, "Studio delle varianti cliniche dei temi e dei

contenuti deliranti in epoche diverse. Confronto dei vari tipi di delirio a distanza di circa un secolo," *Rivista di Patolologia Nervosa e Mentale* 80 [1959]: 845–65).

7 See "What Is Schizophrenia?" National Institutes of Health, http://www.nimh.nih.gov/health/publications/schizophrenia/what-are-the-symptoms-of-schizophrenia.shtml.

8 Not all individuals who report "thought insertion" also hear voices. While often co-present as symptoms, they are not necessarily equivalent: see Christoph Hoerl, "On Thought Insertion," *Philosophy, Psychiatry, and Psychology* 8, nos. 2–3 (June–September 2001): 189–200.

9 John Haslam, *Observations on Madness and Melancholy: Including Practical Remarks on Those Diseases, Together with Cases, and an Account of the Morbid Appearances on Dissection* (London: J. Callow, 1809), 68.

10 Jean-Étienne Dominique Esquirol, *Mental Maladies: A Treatise on Insanity* (Philadelphia: Lea and Blanchard, 1845), 307. Esquirol also notes having encountered several cases in which patients believed "electricity and magnetism" were being employed to produce pain in the intestines: Esquirol, *Mental Maladies*, 197.

11 Edward Charles Spitzka, *Insanity: Its Classification, Diagnosis and Treatment* (New York: E. B. Treat, 1887), 53.

12 Charles Arthur Mercier, *A Text-Book of Insanity* (New York: Macmillan, 1902), 142–43. Mercier's tone echoes the comic exasperation frequently found in nineteenth-century psychiatric discourse, a sense of disbelief that the patient could remain so deeply committed to ideas that are so patently ridiculous.

13 Radio's "etheric ocean" was of great interest to physicists, psychic researchers, and the psychotic in the early twentieth century as the most likely abode for spirits, telepathy, and other unexplained phenomena. For a more detailed discussion, see Jeffrey Sconce, "The Voice from the Void," in Jeffrey Sconce, *Haunted Media: Electronic Presence for Telegraphy to Television* (Durham, NC: Duke University Press, 2000), 59–92.

14 L. Percy King, "Criminal Complaints: A True Account by L. Percy King," in *The Inner World of Mental Illness*, ed. Bert Kaplan (New York: Harper and Row, 1964), 135.

15 Joel Milam Hill, "Hallucinations in Psychoses," *Journal of Nervous and Mental Disease* 83, no. 4 (1936): 405–21.

16 "Letter to the Zenith Radio Corporation," July 8, 1947, Zenith Electronics, LLC, Lincolnshire, IL. Perhaps, she offered, Zenith might have a "pay as you watch" system that would help relieve her from the pain associated with a television set that she believed remained in continual operation in the home.

17 Emil Kraepelin, *Lectures on Clinical Psychiatry* (New York: Wood, 1917), 167. Always on the lookout for cutting edge research opportunities in new technology, graduate students at the Massachusetts Institute of Technology studied the effectiveness of such helmets in blocking electromagnetic waves. The re-

search found instead that such helmets actually attract and focus energy from electromagnetic fields, a finding that should be obvious to anyone who still remembers using "rabbit ears" on a television set: see Ali Rahimi, Ben Recht, Jason Taylor, and Noah Vawter, "On the Effectiveness of Aluminum Foil Helmets: An Empirical Study," Massachusetts Institute of Technology, Cambridge, MA, February 17, 2005.

18 Victor Tausk, "On the Origin of the 'Influencing Machine' in Schizophrenia," (1919), in *The Psycho-Analytic Reader*, ed. Robert Fliess (New York: International Press, 1948) 33–34.

19 Tausk, "On the Origin of the 'Influencing Machine' in Schizophrenia," 42.

20 Benjamin J. Sadock and Virginia A. Sadock, *Kaplan and Sadock's Synopsis of Psychiatry: Behavioral Sciences/Clinical Psychiatry* (Philadelphia: Lippincott, Williams, and Wilkins, 2011), 283.

21 See Ken Steele and Claire Berman, *The Day the Voices Stopped: A Memoir of Madness and Hope* (New York: Basic, 2001), 1–4.

22 A. T. Kibzey, "Folie à deux: A Case of Familial Psychosis," *Psychiatric Quarterly* 22, nos. 1–4 (1948): 718–28.

23 The influence of the White Album has become core mythology in the Manson narrative, although it is unclear whether Manson really believed the Beatles were sending him secret messages or, instead, his claim to secret communications with the band was only another strategy to exert psychological control over his "family." For a more detailed account of Manson's interpretation of the White Album, see Ed Sanders, *The Family: The Story of Charles Manson's Dune Buggy Attack Battalion* (New York: E. P. Dutton, 1971), 136–40. Interestingly, this delusional relation to media figures can have a cascading effect. In his book *Imaginary Social Worlds*, John Caughey relates the case of a man who became fascinated by how Manson, as such an "insignificant" figure, could nevertheless "garner such devotion from the women in his clan." The man, a teacher of folklore and mythology, set out to use his knowledge of "the occult," "therapeutic processes," and "eye psychology" to control the young women in his classes: see John Caughey, *Imaginary Social Worlds: A Cultural Approach* (Lincoln: University of Nebraska Press, 1984), 62–63.

24 In 1969, rumors circulated that Paul McCartney had died in a car accident (and had been replaced in the band by the winner of a McCartney "look-a-like" contest). At the height of the "Paul Is Dead" rumor, some fans argued that holding a mirror up to the cover of the band's *Magical Mystery Tour* album revealed a secret phone number. Calling this number, it was said, gave fans the opportunity to converse with Paul's spirit, procure free LSD, or receive two tickets to the mythical kingdom of "Pepperland."

25 A basic overview of the history of Heaven's Gate can be found in Rodney Perkins and Forrest Jackson, *Cosmic Suicide: The Tragedy and Transcendence of Heaven's Gate* (Dallas, TX: Pentaradial Press, 1997).

26 Caughey, *Imaginary Social Worlds*, 201.

27 Frank Bruni, "Behind the Jokes, a Life of Pain and Delusion," *New York Times*, November 22, 1998, 45.

28 E. Fuller Torrey, Peter Lurie, Sidney M. Wolfe, and Mary Zdanowicz, "Threats to Radio and Television Personnel in the United States by Individuals with Severe Mental Illnesses," HRG Publication no. 1501, Public Citizen's Health Research Group, Washington, DC, and Treatment Advocacy Center, Arlington, VA, December 15, 1999.

29 See Vaughn Bell, Ethan Grech, Cara Maiden, Peter W. Halligan, and Hadyn D. Ellis, "Internet Delusions: A Case Series and Theoretical Integration," *Psychopathology* 38, no. 3 (2005): 144–50.

30 Dusan Hirjak and Thomas Fuchs, "Delusions of Technical Alien Control: A Phenomenological Description of Three Cases," *Psychopathology* 43, no. 2 (2010): 96–103.

31 Kraus, "Phenomenology of the Technical Delusion in Schizophrenics"; see also Hirjak and Fuchs, "Delusions of Technical Alien Control."

32 Skodlar et al., "Psychopathology of Schizophrenia in Ljubljana (Slovenia) from 1881 to 2000," 109.

33 Michael Barkun, "Religion, Militias and Oklahoma City: The Mind of Conspiratorialists," *Terrorism and Political Violence* 8, no. 1(1996): 50–64.

34 Karl Jaspers, *General Psychopathology*, trans. J. Hoenig and Marian W. Hamilton (Chicago: University of Chicago Press, [1913] 1963).

35 Jaspers, *General Psychopathology*, 99.

36 Kurt Schneider, *Clinical Psychopathology* (New York: Grune and Stratton, 1959).

37 As the title suggests, *The Diagnostic and Statistical Manual of Mental Disorders* confines itself to psychiatric diagnosis. The International Classification of Diseases provides criteria for all varieties of disease, mental and physical. In psychiatric evaluation, the DSM and ICD frequently overlap in terms of criteria (although key differences remain). The DSM (created by the American Psychiatric Association) is dominant in North America; the ICD (created by the World Health Organization), in Europe. The DSM is currently in its fifth edition (DSM-V); the ICD is now in its tenth edition (ICD-10).

38 American Psychiatric Association, ed., *The Diagnostic and Statistical Manual of Mental Disorders*, 5th ed. (DSM-V) (Washington, DC: American Psychiatric Association, 2013), 99.

39 American Psychiatric Association, ed., *Schizophrenia Spectrum and Other Psychotic Disorders: DSM-V Selections* (Washington, DC: American Psychiatric Association, 2016).

40 Dinesh Bhugra and Kamaldeep Bhui, "Cross-Cultural Psychiatric Assessment," in *Clinical Topics in Cultural Psychiatry*, ed. Rahul Bhattachary, Sean Cross, and Dinesh Bhugra (London: RCPsych, 2010), 256.

41 Nellie Bly's *Ten Days in a Mad-House* (New York: Ian L. Munro, 1887) is an early exemplar of this genre. Particularly infamous in psychiatric circles was the "Rosenhan Experiment" of 1973. In his article "On Being Sane in Insane

Places," Rosenhan described an experiment designed to evaluate the criteria for psychiatric diagnosis as practiced by large urban hospitals. Rosenhan recruited volunteers, all "sane," to present themselves at various hospitals and claim they had been "hearing voices" during the previous week. Based on this claim alone, all were admitted as suffering from a "psychiatric disorder." Once in the psych ward, each volunteer behaved normally, telling the attending staff each day that they felt fine and that they no longer heard any voices. On average, volunteers remained hospitalized for nineteen days before physicians cleared them for release. Disputing the results, one hospital dared Rosenhan to send more imposters, vowing this time they would be intercepted. After a period of several months the hospital proudly announced that it had identified forty-one potential imposters. Rosenhan then announced that he had in fact sent no volunteers during this period, only adding to the hospital's embarrassment: see David L. Rosenhan, "On Being Sane in Insane Places," *Science* 179, no. 4070 (1973): 250–58.

42 F. Legge, "The Nature of Hallucinations," in *The Living Age*, vol. 235 (Boston: Living Age, 1902), 249.

43 Thomas Stompe, Gerhard Ortwein-Swoboda, Kristina Ritter, and Hans Schanda. "Old Wine in New Bottles? Stability and Plasticity of the Contents of Schizophrenic Delusions," *Psychopathology* 36, no. 1 (2003): 6–12.

44 See Tausk, "On the Origin of the 'Influencing Machine' in Schizophrenia," 40.

45 This literalization of body and machine can take several forms. In what many argue to be a variation of Capgras delusion (believing one is a corpse), some individuals come to believe they are robots. In other cases, the individual remains human but finds himself surrounded by robots: see Karel W. De Pauw and T. Krystyna Szulecka, "Dangerous Delusions: Violence and the Misidentification Syndromes," *British Journal of Psychiatry* 152, no. 1 (1988): 91–96.

46 "Concrete thinking" describes a tendency observed in schizophrenia to render language in most literal terms. As part of the diagnostic process, individuals are asked to interpret a series of proverbs (such as "a rolling stone gathers no moss") to check for "concretism": see Alfred Barth and Bernd Küfferle, "Development of a Proverb Test for Assessment of Concrete Thinking Problems in Schizophrenic Patients," *Der Nervenarzt* 72, no. 11 (2001): 853–58.

47 Tausk, "On the Origin of the 'Influencing Machine' in Schizophrenia," 45.

48 Tausk, "On the Origin of the 'Influencing Machine' in Schizophrenia," 43.

49 Tausk, "On the Origin of the 'Influencing Machine' in Schizophrenia," 33.

50 Tausk, "On the Origin of the 'Influencing Machine' in Schizophrenia," 35–36.

51 Raymond Williams, *Marxism and Literature* (London: Oxford University Press, 1977), 97.

52 "If art reflects life," Brecht once quipped, "it does so with special mirrors": Bertolt Brecht, "A Short Organum for the Theatre" (1949), *Brecht on Theatre: The Development of an Aesthetic* (New York: Bloomsbury, 2013) 204.

53 Williams, *Marxism and Literature*, 99.

54 Jean Dubuffet, ed., *L'Art Brut*, vol. 3. (Lausanne: Collection de l'Art Brut, 1965), 63.

55 David Maclagan, "Has 'Psychotic Art' Become Extinct?" in *Arts, Psychotherapy and Psychosis*, ed. Katherine Killick and Joy Schaverien (New York: Routledge, 2003), 134.

56 Maclagan cites the work of Louis Wain, invoked in psychiatric literature for a series of cat paintings that became increasingly abstract and complex over time, a progression interpreted as a "direct 'window'" on his psychotic deterioration": Maclagan, "Has 'Psychotic Art' Become Extinct?" 135.

57 Also notable in the context is the work of the British painter Mary Barnes (1923–2001). Working with R. D. Laing and D. G. Cooper at Kingsley Hall, Barnes discovered herself as a painter while undergoing regression therapy for her schizophrenia. She would later co-author a book of her experiences with her therapist Joseph Berke: see Joseph Berke and Mary Barnes, *Mary Barnes: Two Accounts of a Journey through Madness* (London: MacGibbon and Kee, 1971).

58 Francis Reitman, *Psychotic Art* (New York: International Universities Press, 1951) 8.

59 This impulse dates back to Jean Debuffet's introduction of the term *l'art brut* in 1949. Debuffet writes, "Here we are witnessing an artistic operation that is completely pure, raw, reinvented in all its phases by its author, based solely on his own impulses. Art, therefore, in which is manifested the sole function of invention, and not those, constantly seen in cultural art, of the chameleon and the monkey: Jean Dubuffet, "L'art brut préféré aux arts culturels" (Paris: Galerie René Drouin, 1949).

60 See Maclagan, "Has 'Psychotic Art' Become Extinct?" 139.

61 For an introduction to his work, see John M. MacGregor, *Henry Darger: In the Realms of the Unreal* (New York: Delano Greenidge, 2002). Howard Finster, inspired by God, created more than 46,000 works of art for his "Paradise Gardens" near Summerville, Georgia. For an overview of his work, see Howard Finster and Tom Patterson, *Howard Finster, Stranger from Another World: Man of Visions Now on this Earth* (New York: Abbeville Press, 1989).

62 Georg Simmel, "The Metropolis and Mental Life" (1903), in *The Sociology of Georg Simmel*, trans. Kurt Wolff (New York: Free Press, 1950), 409–24.

63 Garrett B. Ryder, "Delusional Dish Syndromes," *Irish Journal of Psychological Medicine* 9, no. 2 (November 1992): 134.

64 Maurice Maeterlinck, *The Unknown Guest and Other Essays* (London: Methuen, 1914), 92. Maeterlinck, awarded the Nobel Prize for Literature in 1911, may have been drawn to these beliefs by his experiences with Muhammad, a German horse said to be capable of addition, multiplication, and calculating square roots: Maurice Maeterlinck, "The Eberfeld Horses," in Maeterlinck, *The Unknown Guest and Other Essays*, 181–300.

65 Victor Thompson, *Telepathic Vision and Sound*, pamphlet, 1910, 4. Thompson's monograph appears to have been self-published. Two copies survive: one at the New York Public Library, and the other at the Indianapolis Public Library.

Thompson's belief that a unifying energy would eventually explain all physical and psychic phenomena was widespread at the turn of the twentieth century. As Alex Owen writes, "What united many of these different trends and factions was a loosely Neoplatonic belief in an occluded spirit realm and a broadly conceived sense of an animistic universe in which all of creation is interrelated and part and expression of a universal soul or cosmic mind": Alex Owen, *The Place of Enchantment: British Occultism and the Culture of the Modern* (Chicago: University of Chicago Press, 2007), 21.

66 Thompson, *Telepathic Vision and Sound*, 53.
67 Thompson, *Telepathic Vision and Sound*, 53.
68 Thompson, *Telepathic Vision and Sound*, 54.
69 Thompson, *Telepathic Vision and Sound*, 93.
70 Darian Leader, *What Is Madness?* (London: Penguin, 2011), 71.
71 Karl Jaspers, *General Psychopathology* (Chicago: University of Chicago Press, 1963), 98.
72 Louis A. Sass, "The Land of Unreality: On the Phenomenology of the Schizophrenic Break," *New Ideas in Psychology* 6, no. 2 (1988): 223–42.
73 Rachel Aviv, "Which Way Madness Lies: Can Psychosis Be Prevented?" *Harper's Magazine*, December 2010, 41.
74 See George E. Atwood, Donna M. Orange, and Robert. D. Stolorow, "Shattered Worlds/Psychotic States: A Post-Cartesian View of the Experience of Personal Annihilation," *Psychoanalytic Psychology* 19, no. 2 (2002): 281–306.
75 Louis A. Sass, "Introspection, Schizophrenia, and the Fragmentation of Self," *Representations* 19 (1987): 10.
76 Jean-Paul Sartre, *Nausea* (New York: New Directions, 1964), 127.
77 Sartre, *Nausea*, 127.
78 Shitij Kapur, "Psychosis as a State of Aberrant Salience: A Framework Linking Biology, Phenomenology, and Pharmacology in Schizophrenia," *American Journal of Psychiatry* 160, no. 1 (2003): 15.
79 Leader, *What Is Madness?*, 173.
80 Whereas an "epiphany" describes a sudden realization of the truth, an "apophany" captures the sudden but delusional insight of the psychotic: see Klaus Conrad, *Die beginnende Schizophrenie. Versuch einer Gestaltanalyse des Wahns* (Stuttgart: Georg Thieme, 1958).
81 John Locke, *An Essay Concerning Human Understanding* (1690) (London: T. Tegg and Son, 1836), 94.
82 Elisabeth Pacherie, Melissa Green, and Tim Bayne, "Phenomenology and Delusions: Who Put the 'Alien' in Alien Control?" *Consciousness and Cognition* 15, no. 3 (2006): 566–77.
83 This "incorrigibility" of delusional thought is at the center of Milton Rokeach's study *The Three Christs of Ypsilanti*. As an experiment in personality theory and social psychology, Rokeach arranged for three men who each professed to be the divine singularity that is Jesus Christ to live in the same ward at the Ypsilanti

State Hospital. Rokeach's book documents how, over the course of a year, the "Three Christs" adjusted to accommodate one another's delusions, all the while maintaining their own status as the one true Christ: see Milton Rokeach, *The Three Christs of Ypsilanti* (New York: NYRB Classics, 2011).

84 This phenomenon is often called "lack of insight" (anosognosia). Recent studies suggest that anosognosia has, in some cases, a basis in neurological dysfunction. As with so many psychiatric terms, however, "lack of insight" appears to exist on a spectrum with no definitive etiological mechanism. For a recent overview of this debate, see Rose Mary Xavier and Allison Vorderstrasse, "Neurobiological Basis of Insight in Schizophrenia: A Systematic Review," *Nursing Research* 65, no. 3 (2016): 224–37.

85 Kraepelin, *Lectures on Clinical Psychiatry*, 164.

86 Tausk, "On the Origin of the 'Influencing Machine' in Schizophrenia," 33.

87 Thompson, *Telepathic Vision and Sound*, 55. Later, in a section titled "The Mystic Veil Is Lifted," Thompson summarizes his findings:

> Substitute a human being into a wireless apparatus with a Poulsen singing arc (undamped waves), this person is called the "medium," place on him an inhibition current, in the form of a telephone circuit, and connect this with the "operator" (there can be more than one operator), placing the telephones in the same spots as on the "medium," and we have the inside apparatus. The outside person, the "detector," is prepared—that is, the nasal membranes are hardened, or the discharges from the arterial system stopped; this is done by a drug, unknown to him. As soon as the ear of the outside person responds, the muscle reading commences, this consists in repeating all that is said on the outside, through the telephone system; by degrees composite impressions are formed, the operator is going "with" the outside person, taking off the images and words, if he does not know an image; all he has to do is to name it, viz., mother, brother, etc., if he goes against, it is torture. You may say, "how can he get the images?" I refer then to the eye, as said before the pressures are formed in the choroid or the blood; in other words, the telephones inhibits on the arteries of the eyelids, temporal, etc., they must go through a human being to be produced. (Thompson, *Telepathic Vision and Sound*, 92)

88 Thompson, *Telepathic Vision and Sound*, 55.

89 In a handwritten letter dated June 21, 1913, Thompson made a gift of his monograph to the editor of the *New York Evening Journal*. "This is not a literary work," he wrote, "but it explains a subject that perhaps may interest you. If not, throw it into your bookcase, because someday, it may come up." Thompson also asked the editor not to publish any of the monograph's contents without his consent, "because my brother in law is Prime Minister of Denmark (Klaus Berntsen)": Victor Thompson to Editor, *New York Evening Journal*, letter, June 21, 1913, Indianapolis Room Collection, Indianapolis Public Library.

90 Jacques Lacan, *The Psychoses: The Seminar of Jacques Lacan, Book III, 1955–1956*, ed. Jacques-Alain Miller, trans. Russell Grigg (New York: W. W. Norton, 1993).

91 As Anthony Wilden writes, "Lacan is not prone to define or employ his terms unambiguously": Jacques Lacan, *Speech and Language in Psychoanalysis*, trans. Anthony Wilden (Baltimore: Johns Hopkins University Press, 1981), 159. Perhaps the most concise appraisal of Lacan's impenetrability comes from Lacan himself. Addressing an audience of frequently baffled analysts in training, Lacan observed,

> I'm not surprised that my discourse may have created a certain margin of misunderstanding. This is because in addition, if one is to be consistent in practice with one's ideas, if all valid discourse has to be judged precisely according to its own principles, I would say that it is with a deliberate, if not entirely deliberated, intention that I pursue this discourse in such a way as to offer you the opportunity to not quite understand. This margin enables you yourselves to say that you think you follow me, that is, that you remain in a problematic position, which always leaves the door open to a progressive rectification. (Lacan, *The Psychoses*, 164)

92 Lacan associated with many modernist luminaries of the 1930s, including such surrealist and surrealist-adjacent figures as André Breton, Georges Bataille, Salvador Dali, and Pablo Picasso. Dali made reference to Lacan's recently completed dissertation in the first issue of the surrealist journal *Minotaure*, in which Lacan himself would publish early in his career.

93 Lacan, *Speech and Language in Psychoanalysis*, 177.

94 As Leader notes, psychiatry has gradually come to ignore its once active interest in "quiet madness," the idea that an individual can "be mad" for his or her entire life without ever necessarily "becoming mad": see Leader, *What Is Madness?*, 9–34.

95 Lacan, *The Psychoses*, 203.

96 The phrase "flight of ideas" describes the onset of rapidly changing, disjointed thinking. In extreme forms, this can lead to the seemingly meaningless statements known as word salad. Psychiatry has also associated schizophrenia with concrete thinking, described as a diminished capacity for understanding metaphor, simile, and other forms of figurative language.

97 Leader, *What Is Madness?*, 100.

98 Leader, *What Is Madness?*, 77.

99 Eric Santner's discussion of the noted psychotic Daniel Paul Schreber provides an exemplary account of shifts in status as a psychotic trigger: Eric Santner, *My Own Private Germany: Daniel Paul Schreber's Secret History of Modernity* (Princeton, NJ: Princeton University Press, 1998).

100 Leader, *What Is Madness?*, 175.

101 Lacan, *The Psychoses*, 21. Jacques-Alain Miller observes, "In some way we can say that, in the moment of perplexity, the meaning doesn't appear to be satisfactory.

It is a moment of waiting for meaning, that is enigmatic, and that does not satisfy": Jacques-Alain Miller, "The Invention of Delusion," *International Lacanian Review* 5 (2008): 19, http://lacancircle.net/JAMinventionofdelusion.pdf.

102 Sigmund Freud, "Neurosis and Psychosis" (1924), in *The Standard Edition of the Complete Psychological Works of Sigmund Freud*, 24 vols., ed. James Strachey (London: Hogarth, 1961) 19:149–53.

103 Lacan, *The Psychoses*, 21. Jaspers himself wrote of the primary delusion as an "immediate intrusive knowledge of meanings," suggesting that delusional meaning is not so much actively discovered as revealed: Jaspers, *General Psychopathology*, 99.

104 Miller provides a detailed examination of Lacan's relation to Clérambault, Jaspers, and the concept of the "elementary phenomenon": Miller, "The Invention of Delusion."

105 Peter K. Chadwick, "Peer-Professional First-Person Account: Schizophrenia from the Inside—Phenomenology and the Integration of Causes and Meanings," *Schizophrenia Bulletin* 33, no. 1 (2007): 169.

106 Chadwick, "Peer-Professional First-Person Account," 169.

107 John Durham Peters, "Broadcasting and Schizophrenia," *Media, Culture, and Society* 32, no. 1 (2010): 124.

108 Alistair McIntyre, *A Journey into Madness* (London: Chipmunka, 2007).

109 Lacan, *The Psychoses*, 226–27.

110 Countering "explanationism," Pacherie, Green, and Bayne identify a radically different tradition they call the endorsement position. The endorsement position proposes a less linear account of the psychotic process, removing the intervening moment of deductive reasoning between primary and secondary to argue that "the person believes—that is, doxastically endorses—the content of their perceptual state, or at least something very much like the content of their perceptual state": Pacherie et al., "Phenomenology and Delusions."

111 Lacan, *The Psychoses*.

112 Sigmund Freud, "The 'Uncanny'" (1919), in Strachey, *The Standard Edition of the Complete Psychological Works of Sigmund Freud*, 17:218–56.

113 Martii Siirala, Silvano Arieti, and Harold Kelman, "Schizophrenia: A Human Situation," *American Journal of Psychoanalysis* 23, no. 1 (1963): 44.

114 Siirala et al., "Schizophrenia," 46.

115 Brian W. Grant, *Schizophrenia, a Source of Social Insight* (Westminster, UK: John Knox, 1975), 171

116 In 1956, Charles Savage and Louis Cholden noted the growing professional interest in lysergic acid diethylamide (LSD) among psychiatrists, writing that it fulfilled Kraepelin's dream of "a psychosis in miniature": Charles Savage and Louis Cholden, "Schizophrenia and the Model Psychoses," *Journal of Clinical and Experimental Psychopathology* 17, no. 4 (1956): 405. For an example of LSD research involving US military personnel, see H. A. Abramson, M. E. Jarvik, and M. W. Hirsch, "Lysergic Acid Diethylamide (LSD-25): X. Effect on Re-

action Time to Auditory and Visual Stimuli," *Journal of Psychology* 40, no. 1 (1955): 39–52. The late 1950s and early 1960s also saw experiments in psychotherapy using LSD. Perhaps the best-known case is recounted in Constance Newland, *My Self and I* (New York: Coward-McCann, 1962).

117 For additional work on the similarities of schizophrenia and LSD, see Stefano Belli, "A Psychobiographical Analysis of Brian Douglas Wilson: Creativity, Drugs, and Models of Schizophrenic and Affective Disorders," *Personality and Individual Differences* 46, no. 8 (2009): 809–19; Malcolm B. Bowers Jr. and Daniel X. Freedman, "'Psychedelic' Experiences in Acute Psychoses," *Archives of General Psychiatry* 15, no. 3 (1966): 240; George S. Glass, "Psychedelic Drugs, Stress, and the Ego: The Differential Diagnosis of Psychosis Associated with Psychotomimetic Drug Use," *Journal of Nervous and Mental Disease* 156, no. 4 (1973): 232–41; Murray Korngold, "LSD and the Creative Experience," *Psychoanalytic Review* 50, no. 4 (1963): 152; Michael M. Vardy and Stanley R. Kay, "LSD Psychosis or LSD-Induced Schizophrenia? A Multimethod Inquiry," *Archives of General Psychiatry* 40, no. 8 (1983): 877.

118 Charles Savage, "Variations in Ego Feeling Induced by D-Lysergic Acid Diethylamide (LSD-25)," *Psychoanalytic Review* 42, no. 1 (January 1955): 10–11.

119 Norbert Wiener, *Cybernetics: Control and Communication in the Animal and the Machine* (New York: John Wiley and Sons, 1948).

120 Sheldon Bach, "Narcissism, Continuity, and the Uncanny," in *Narcissistic States and the Therapeutic Process* (New York: Rowman and Littlefield, 1985), 126.

121 Karl Marx, *The Eighteenth Brumaire of Louis Bonaparte* (1852) (New York: International Publishers, 1963), 15.

122 Sigmund Freud, "Civilization and Its Discontents" (1930), in Strachey, *The Standard Edition of the Complete Psychological Works of Sigmund Freud*, 21:92.

123 Freud, "Civilization and Its Discontents," 92.

124 Freud, "Civilization and Its Discontents," 92.

125 Marshall McLuhan, *Understanding Media: The Extensions of Man* (New York: McGraw-Hill, 1964).

126 Friedrich A. Kittler, *Discourse Networks 1800/1900*, trans. Michael Metteer (Stanford, CA: Stanford University Press, 1992).

127 Jean Baudrillard, *The Ecstasy of Communication* (New York: Semiotext(e), 1983), 24.

128 Jean Baudrillard, *Screened Out*, trans. Chris Turner (London: Verso, 2002), 176.

129 If future science discovers that EMF pollution is an actual hazard, as many psychotics suspect, the physical and affective consequences are likely to be catastrophic. (We already willingly drive cars knowing they may well kill us. What will the acceptable risk be for the brain tumors and synthetic ADHD cultivated by mobile telephony?)

130 See Jane Feuer, "The Concept of Live Television: Ontology as Ideology," in *Regarding Television: Critical Approaches*, ed. E. Ann Kaplan (Los Angeles: American Film Institute, 1983), 12–23.

131 Donald L. Burnham, "Some Problems in Communication with Schizophrenic Patients," *Journal of the American Psychoanalytic Association* 3, no. 1 (1955): 67–81. The patient continues, "And the metamorphosic change of the television set doesn't give what the human understanding of that would be, either by an individual or a group of individuals. And just wouldn't have the necessary response, I suppose, in some way, either to that person's satisfaction or to the television set's perfection."

132 Joseph Robert Cowen, "A Note on the Meaning of Television to a Psychotic Woman," *Bulletin of the Menninger Clinic* 23 (1959): 202–3.

133 Ivan Leudar, Philip Thomas, D. McNally, and A. Glinski, "What Voices Can Do with Words: Pragmatics of Verbal Hallucinations," *Psychological Medicine* 27, no. 4 (1997): 885–98. Two other patients reported they experienced hallucinations only in relation to specific channels (BBC 1 and BBC 2 for one patient, and Channel 4 for the other.)

134 See M. G. Smyth, "A Glossary of Television-Related Symptoms in Psychosis," *Psychiatric Bulletin* 21 (1997): 545–46.

135 In a complaint filed on April 21, 2013, a viewer accused the comedian Craig Ferguson, *The Simpsons*, and Tyler Perry of making direct references to his life. The viewer hoped the matter could be resolved "in a manner that keeps Me from going to jail": indecency complaint to the FCC, Consumer Information Management System control no. 00003643361, June 5, 2013. Ostensibly complaining about the situation comedy *The Big Bang Theory*, a woman claimed that a commercial run during the series mentioned, and thus threatened, both of her elderly aunts by name. The FCC dutifully responded, leading the woman to write, "Thank you! But I've already contacted the police and the FBI who are currently assisting me": indecency complaint to the FCC, Consumer Information Management System control no. 00003204235, August 22, 2011.

136 See Stephen G. Noffsinger and Fabian M. Saleh, "Ideas of Reference about Newscasters," *Psychiatric Services* 51, no. 5 (2000): 679.

137 Noffsinger and Saleh, "Ideas of Reference about Newscasters," 679. "Mr. K wished to kill this newscaster in retribution for the perceived killing of his brother and to prevent the newscaster from killing his father. Previously, Mr. K approached the office of a local television station to verbalize his grievances to the newscaster. He was unarmed and peacefully left the premises when confronted by security staff members."

138 Indecency complaint to the FCC, Consumer Information Management System control no. 383269, July 5, 2015.

139 Mary Ann Doane, "Information, Crisis, Catastrophe," *Logics of Television: Essays in Cultural Criticism* (Bloomington: Indiana University Press, 1990), 222–39.

140 Anand Pandya and Peter J. Weiden, "Trauma and Disaster in Psychiatrically Vulnerable Populations," *Journal of Psychiatric Practice* 7, no. 6 (2001): 426–31; Victoria A. Franz, Carol R. Glass, Diane B. Arnkoff, and Mary Ann Dutton, "The Impact of the September 11th Terrorist Attacks on Psychiatric Patients: A

Review," *Clinical Psychology Review* 29, no. 4 (2009): 339–47; Ronnie G. Stout and Rokeya S. Farooque, "Negative Symptoms, Anger, and Social Support: Response of an Inpatient Sample to News Coverage of the September 11 Terrorist Attacks," *Psychiatric Quarterly* 74, no. 3 (2003): 237–50; Mark Taylor and Kym Jenkins, "The Psychological Impact of September 11 Terrorism on Australian Inpatients," *Australasian Psychiatry* 12, no. 3 (2004): 253–55.

141 Debates about the social impact of the Walkman begin in the immediate wake of its widespread adoption in the early 1980s. In the opening paragraph of his essay "The Walkman Effect," Shuhei Hosokawa cites an interview with Phillip Sollers in which Sollers recalls a journalist asking teenagers wearing the devices "whether they are losing contact with reality" and "whether they are psychotic or schizophrenic." The teenagers, we are told, informed the journalist these were the wrong questions. "All of these problems of communication and incommunicability . . . belong to the sixties and seventies," a teen replied. "The eighties are not the same at all. They are the years of autonomy. Soon . . . you will have every kind of film on video at home, every kind of classical music on only one tape. This is what gives me pleasure": Shuhei Hosokawa, "The Walkman Effect," *Popular Music* 4 (1984): 165–180.

142 The Walkman and subsequent personal audio systems such as the iPod/iPhone have actually become useful tools for those experiencing auditory hallucinations, providing a sonic distraction that blocks, or at least mutes, the intrusive "voices." As a manual on cognitive therapy observes, "The most effective counter-stimulation strategy for auditory hallucinations is the use of a Walkman to listen to music. Although some types of music may be more effective in blocking hallucinations than others, in practice people typically listen to what they most enjoy. However, if hallucinations are triggered by the patient's choice of music, the therapist should intervene and suggest that other music should be tried instead (e.g. nonvocal)": Nikolaos Kazantzis, Frank P. Deane, Devin R. Ronan, and Luciano L'Abate, eds., *Using Homework Assignments in Cognitive Behavior Therapy* (New York: Routledge, 2005), 240.

143 Christine Rosen, "The Age of Egocasting," *New Atlantis* 7 (Fall 2004–Winter 2005): 52.

144 Manjeet Singh Bhatia, "Cell Phone Dependency—A New Diagnostic Entity," *Delhi Psychiatry Journal* 11, no. 2 (2008): 123–24.

145 Anna Lucia Spear King, Alexandre Martins Valença, Adriana Cardoso Silva, Federica Sancassiani, Sergio Machado, and Antonio Egidio Nardi, "'Nomophobia': Impact of Cell Phone Use Interfering with Symptoms and Emotions of Individuals with Panic Disorder Compared with a Control Group," *Clinical Practice and Epidemiology in Mental Health* 10 (2014): 28.

146 Susan Weinschenk, "Why We're All Addicted to Texts, Twitter, and Google," *Psychology Today* (blog), posted September 11, 2012, https://www.psychologytoday.com/blog/brain-wise/201209/why-were-all-addicted-texts-twitter-and-google.

147   In 2014, Ben Slater, an advertising executive in Brisbane, Australia, had a microchip implanted between his thumb and forefinger so he could "control electronic devices with just a wave of his hand." It was also his hope that the next generation of iPhones would have the capability to read the embedded microchip: "Australian Man Who's Had a Microchip Inserted into His Hand so that He Can Do More with the iPhone 6 . . . Maybe," *Daily Mail*, September 7, 2014. Microchip implantation has also become a growing interest among artists. In 1997, the Brazilian artist Eduardo Kac implanted a microchip, registered with a US data bank via the Internet, in his ankle. He chose this location because "it is an area of the body that has traditionally been chained or branded": Arlindo Machado, "A Microchip Inside the Body," *Performance Research* 4, no. 2 (1999): 8–12. In August 2017, forty-one employees at Three Square Market in Wisconsin allowed themselves to be microchipped to "open doors, log into computers and buy snacks from the break room with a wave of their hand": Chris Morris, "Wisconsin Company Holds Party to Implant Workers with Microchips," *Fortune*, August 2, 2017, http://fortune.com/2017/08/02/wisconsin-company-holds-party-to-implant-workers-with-microchips/.

148   The iPhone 6, introduced in September 2014, included a free (and mandatory) copy of the Irish rock band U2's new album *Songs of Innocence*, installed in the phone's iTunes library. Many were not happy with this "gift." Apple eventually introduced a "one-click" option for users looking to delete the album: Ellie Zolfagharifard, "'Oops, I'm Sorry': Bono Apologizes for U2 Album Being Automatatically Added to Apple iTunes Libraries After iPhone 6 Launch," *Daily Mail*, October 15, 2014. Equally disturbing for the prospects of prosthetic implantation, in 2009 the marketing behemoth Amazon.com digitally erased illegal copies of George Orwell's *1984* and *Animal Farm* from users' devices (citing copyright violations). The irony of the situation was apparent to all, leading Amazon to admit that the deletion was a bad idea. "We are changing our systems so that in the future we will not remove books from customers' devices in these circumstances," said a spokesman: Brad Stone, "Amazon Erases Orwell Books from Kindle," *New York Times*, July 17, 2009.

149   Such was the fate of the sportscaster Erin Andrews. In 2016, a jury awarded Andrews $55 million in damages in her lawsuit against the hotel that had apparently revealed her room number and allowed her stalker to book the adjacent suite (to install his camera in the peephole): Maane Khatchatourian, "Erin Andrews Awarded $55 Million in Peephole Video Lawsuit," *Variety*, March 7, 2016.

150   Lisa W. Foderaro, "Private Moment Made Public, then a Fatal Jump," *New York Times*, September 29, 2010. See also Patrick McGeehan, "Conviction Thrown out for Ex-Rutgers Student in Tyler Clementi Case," *New York Times*, September 9, 2016.

151   Robert Mackey, "School Accused of Using Webcam to Photograph Student at Home," *New York Times*, February 19, 2010.

152 *"Star Wars* Boy" refers to a video made by Ghyslain Raza in 2002, documenting Raza imitating a light-saber battle from *Star Wars: The Phantom Menace*. Discovered by a classmate and posted to the Internet without Raza's consent or knowledge, the video become a viral exercise in comic derision. Congressman Anthony Wiener, meanwhile, was forced to resign his seat in the House of Representatives when it became apparent that he was sending pictures of his penis to a variety of women under the pseudonym "Carlos Danger." Many believe that Mitt Romney's presidential ambitions were thwarted in the election cycle of 2012 when a bartender covertly recorded his speech at a Republican fundraiser. During the talk, Romney lamented that his opponent, President Barack Obama, already enjoyed the support of the "47 percent." Romney said, "All right, there are 47 percent who are with him, who are dependent upon government, who believe that they are victims, who believe the government has a responsibility to care for them, who believe that they are entitled to health care, to food, to housing, to you-name-it." Video leaked by *Mother Jones*, September 12, 2012.
153 Dave Eggers, *The Circle* (New York: Vintage, 2013), 328.
154 Mark Andrejevic, "Surveillance in the Digital Enclosure," *Communication Review*, 10 (2007): 295–317.
155 In a story that should make even the borderline paranoid shudder, "predictive analysts" for the big box retailer Target (target!) were able to determine that a high-school student was pregnant before she told her parents by using a "pregnancy prediction" score based on the teen's purchasing of twenty-five products associated with women in their second trimester. This triggered a personalized mailing of prenatal coupons congratulating the teen on her new baby, and a flyer was intercepted by the girl's surprised father: Charles Duhigg, "How Companies Learn Your Secrets," *New York Times*, February 16, 2012.
156 Jon Ronson, "How One Stupid Tweet Blew up Justine Sacco's Life," *New York Times*, February 12, 2015.
157 See Sameer Hinduja and Justin W. Patchin, "Bullying, Cyberbullying, and Suicide," *Archives of Suicide Research* 14, no. 3 (2010): 206–21.
158 Bell et al, "Internet Delusions."
159 See Max Horkheimer, "The Concept of Man" (1957), in *Critique of Instrumental Reason*, trans. By Matthew J. O'Connell (London: Verso, 2012), 18.
160 "Man Charged in Kalamazoo Shootings Says Uber App Took Him Over," *Chicago Tribune*, March 14, 2016.
161 John Ellis, *Seeing Things: Television in the Age of Uncertainty* (London: I. B. Tauris, 2000), 170.
162 Ellis, *Seeing Things*, 171
163 Ellis, *Seeing Things*, 170.
164 See Joseph Kuo and Hai-Gwo Hwu, "Internet-Related Delusional Disorder," *Taiwanese Journal of Psychiatry* 21, no. 1 (2007): 68.

165 Andreas Vossler, "Internet Infidelity 10 Years On: A Critical Review of the Literature," *Family Journal* 24, no. 4 (2016), 359–66.

166 "Is This Man Cheating on His Wife?" *Wall Street Journal*, online ed., August 10, 2007.

167 Nithin Krishna, Bernard A. Fischer, Moshe Miller, Kelly Register-Brown, Kathleen Patchan, and Ann Hackman, "The Role of Social Media Networks in Psychotic Disorders: A Case Report," *General Hospital Psychiatry* 35, no. 5 (2013): 576.

168 Tamaki Saitō, *Social Withdrawal: Adolescence without End*, trans. Jeffrey Angles (Minneapolis: University of Minnesota Press, 2012).

169 "Big Data, for Better or Worse: 90 Percent of World's Data Generated over Last Two Years," *Science Daily*, May 22, 2013, www.sciencedaily.com/releases/2013/05/130522085217.htm.

170 Jean Baudrillard, *Simulations* (New York: Semiotext(e), [1981] 1994), 79.

171 After Disneyland proved to be the vector of a measles epidemic in 2014–15, health officials assigned much of the blame to the "anti-vaccine" movement, estimating that the vaccination rate now hovers between 50 percent and 86 percent (with 96–99 percent necessary to maintain "herd immunity"): Karen Kaplan, "Vaccine Refusal Helped Fuel Disneyland Measles Outbreak, Study Says," *Los Angeles Times*, March 16, 2015.

172 Jean Baudrillard, "Information at the Meteorological Stage," in Baudrillard, *Screened Out*, 85.

173 Lisa Suhay, "What Is Jade Helm 15 (and Should Chuck Norris Be Worried)?" *Christian Science Monitor*, May 5, 2015.

174 Susan K. Weiner, "First Person Account: Living with the Delusions and Effects of Schizophrenia," *Schizophrenia Bulletin* 29, no. 4 (2003): 878.

175 Weiner, "First Person Account," 877.

176 Jean Baudrillard, *The Ecstasy of Communication*, 26–27.

177 Fredric Jameson, *Postmodernism, or, the Cultural Logic of Late Capitalism* (Durham, NC: Duke University Press, 1991), 26–27.

178 Jean-François Lyotard, *The Postmodern Condition: A Report on Knowledge* (Minneapolis: University of Minnesota Press, 1984).

179 Pavlov, quoted in George Windholz, "Pavlov's Concept of Schizophrenia as Related to the Theory of Higher Nervous Activity," *History of Psychiatry* 4, no. 1 6 (1993): 511–26.

180 Seymour Epstein and Margaret Coleman, "Drive Theories of Schizophrenia," *Psychosomatic Medicine* 32, no. 2 (1970): 113–40.

181 Epstein and Coleman, "Drive Theories of Schizophrenia." A more recent study should give all parents pause, especially those who have come to depend on electronics as a reliable tactic for distracting unruly toddlers: see D. A. Christakis, J. S. B. Ramirez, and J. M. Ramirez, "Overstimulation of Newborn Mice Leads to Behavioral Differences and Deficits in Cognitive Performance," *Scientific Reports* 2 (2012): 546.

182 Sigmund Freud, "Beyond the Pleasure Principle" (1920), in Strachey, *The Standard Edition of the Complete Psychological Works of Sigmund Freud*, 18: 1–64.
183 Teresa Brennan, *History after Lacan* (London: Routledge, 2002) 11.
184 Brennan, *History after Lacan*, 12.
185 Brennan, *History after Lacan*, 39.
186 See Martin Heidegger, *The Question of Technology and Other Essays*, trans. William Lovitt (New York: Harper and Row, 1977).
187 Donna J. Haraway, *Primate Visions: Gender, Race, and Nature in the World of Modern Science* (New York: Routledge, 1989), 102.
188 Ellen M. McGee, "Bioelectronics and Implanted Devices," in *Medical Enhancement and Posthumanity*, vol. 2, ed. Bert Gordijn and Ruth Chadwick (New York: Springer Science and Business Media, 2008), 207.
189 McGee, "Bioelectronics and Implanted Devices," 207. M. T. Anderson's young adult novel *Feed* (2002) unequivocally casts this new "hive" mentality as a burden. Anderson's dystopic take on the Internet and social media envisions a world in which children are outfitted with neural interfaces at a young age (the titular "feed"). The interface allows Internet content to enter the brain directly, turning one's field of vision into a type of desktop.
190 Philip K. Dick, *Valis* (1981) (New York: Mariner Books, 2011), 68.

Chapter 2. Chipnapped

1 Marc De Hert, G. Magiels, and E. Thys, *The Secret of the Brain-Chip: A Self-Help Guide for People Experiencing Psychosis* (Brussels: EPO, 2003).
2 Freud believed psychotic patients were incapable of transference, making them poor candidates for psychoanalytic therapy. For Jacques Lacan, transference requires the patient to accede to the analyst's presumed ability to know the significance of his discourse, making the analyst the "subject supposed to know" (*sujet supposé savoir*). An individual manifesting a technical delusion would have particular difficulties in entering into this relationship. The analyst might (1) occupy a position revealing that she or he has no access to the truth of the technical plot, thus undermining the presumed position of power inherent in becoming *le sujet supposé savoir sur technologie*; or (2) she or he may be under the instrumental control of the technical plot, or even a robot, thus providing evidence that only further consolidates the delusional system. For Lacan's discussion of *le sujet supposé savoir*, see Jacques Lacan, *The Four Fundamental Concepts of Psychoanalysis: The Seminar of Jacques Lacan, Book XI*, trans. Alan Sheridan (London: Hogarth and Institute of Psycho-Analysis, 1977), 223–24.
3 American Psychiatric Association, *The Diagnostic and Statistical Manual of Mental Disorders*, 4th ed. (DSM-IV) (Washington, DC: American Psychiatric Association, 1994), 765.

4 Carl C. Bell, "DSM-IV Guidebook," *Journal of the American Medical Association* 274, no. 22 (1995): 184.
5 Bell, "DSM-IV Guidebook," 184, emphasis added.
6 See Ronald K. Siegel, "Dr. Tolman's Flying Influence Machine," *Whispers: The Voices of Paranoia* (New York: Simon and Schuster, 1996), 53–89. In the end, Siegel traced the patient's delusion back to a college screening of the psychedelic cult film *El Topo* (1970). Siegel's experience with this patient evokes what Brendan Maher has called the "Martha Mitchell effect." The wife of John Mitchell, the attorney-general for President Richard Nixon, Martha Mitchell was deemed mentally ill for her conviction that the White House was engaged in some form of illegal activity. The subsequent revelations of Watergate proved her correct. The Martha Mitchell effect is a cautionary reminder to psychiatrists that some delusions, no matter how unlikely, may actually be true: see Brendan A. Maher, *Anomalous Experience and Delusional Thinking: The Logic of Explanations* (Somerset, NJ; John Wiley and Sons, 1988).
7 Bell, "DSM-IV Guidebook," 184, emphasis added.
8 This device, available at SpyMall.com, is described under the product category "Electronic Revenge": see http://www.spymall.com/catalog/revenge.html.
9 "Electronic Revenge," http://www.spymall.com/catalog/revenge.html. More recent iterations of this technology are marked as "Annoy-a-tron: Periodic beeps and sounds make your friends crazy hunting for that ANNOYING NOISE"; "Ringtone Annoy-a-tron: RINGING AND BUZZING will drive friends bonkers looking for the missing phone!"; and "Eviltron: Unsettling spooky sound effects SCARE THE CRAP out of your friends."
10 "Electronic Revenge," http://www.spymall.com/catalog/revenge.html.
11 F. Joseph Pompei, "Spotlight of Sound: Bringing Audio in Retail Environments into Focus," *Sound and Communications*, vol. 55, no. 7, July 20, 2009, 54–57, 68.
12 Dorinda Elliott and John Barry, "A Subliminal Dr. Strangelove," *Newsweek*, August 22, 1994, 57.
13 David Hambling, "Microwave Ray Gun Controls Crowds with Noise," *New Scientist*, July 3, 2008, https://www.newscientist.com.
14 MEDUSA evokes the lore of the "brown note." Among fans of heavy metal, rumors have long circulated that extreme amplification of a certain frequency, somewhere between 5 hertz and 9 hertz, will trigger an involuntary constriction of the human bowels. These possibilities, it is said, were of particular interest to Lemmy Kilmister, the bass player for Hawkwind and Motörhead. Research has yet to confirm the existence of the so-called brown note: see Geoff Leventhall, Peter Pelmear, and Stephen Benton, *A Review of Published Research on Low Frequency Noise and Its Effects* (London: Nobel House, 2003).
15 Dan Cairns, "US Army Heat Ray Gun in Afghanistan," BBC *Newsbeat*, July 15, 2010, http://www.bbc.co.uk/newsbeat/article/10646540/us-army-heat-ray-gun-in-afghanistan.

16 As one of the government's most secret and "sci-fi"–like agencies, DARPA figures prominently in contemporary conspiracy theories and psychotic delusions. For a classically conspiratorial accounting of DARPA's agenda, see Jim Marrs, *The Trillion-Dollar Conspiracy: How the New World Order, Man-Made Diseases, and Zombie Banks Are Destroying America* (New York: William Morrow Paperbacks, 2011).

17 David Ewing Duncan, "Implanting Hope," *Technology Review* 108, no. 3 (2005): 48–54.

18 Notorious "early adopters" of technology, the gaming community appears to be very excited at the prospect of controlling a video game with brainwaves: see Minjin Ko, Kyoungwoo Bae, Gyuhwan Oh, and Taiyoung Ryu, "A Study on New Gameplay Based on Brain-Computer Interface," DIGRA '09: Proceedings of the 2009 DIGRA International Conference: Breaking New Ground: Innovation in Games, Play, Practice and Theory (Brunel University, 2009), http://www.digra.org/digital-library/publications/a-study-on-new-gameplay-based-on-brain-computer-interface/; Danny Plass-Oude, Boris Reuderink, Bram van de Laar, Hayrettin Gürkök, Christian Mühl, Mannes Pohl, Anton Nijholt, and Dirk Heylen, "Brain-Computer Interfacing and Games," *Brain-Computer Interfaces* (London: Springer, 2010): 149–78.

19 As yet, there has been no conclusive study to determine whether *Force Trainer* and *MindFlex* have at last confirmed the reality of telekinesis or whether the entertainment value of the games depends more on the basic psychological mechanism of magical thinking: see A. F. Rovers, L. M. G. Fejis, G. J. M. van Boxtel, and P. J. M. Cluitmans, "Flanker Shooting Game: Model-Based Design of Biofeedback Games," *Proceedings of the International Conference on Designing Pleasurable Products and Interfaces* (2009): 483–94.

20 Carles Grau, Romauld Ginhoux, Alejandro Riera, Thanh Lam Nguyen, Hubert Chauvat, Michel Berg, Julià L. Amengual, Alvaro Pascual-Leone, and Giulio Ruffini, "Conscious Brain-to-Brain Communication in Humans Using Non-Invasive Technologies," *PLoS One* 9, no. 8 (2014): e105225.

21 Greg Walters, "High-Speed 'Brain Modem' Could Restore Vision, Speech, and Movement, Seeker.com, August 28, 2017, https://www.seeker.com/tech/high-speed-brain-modem-could-restore-vision-speech-and-movement.

22 Nathaniel Scharping, "Watch a Monkey Control a Wheelchair with Its Brain," *Discover Magazine*, March 3, 2016, http://blogs.discovermagazine.com/d-brief/2016/03/03/monkey-control-wheelchair-mind/#.WviNj9MvxBw.

23 Nadeem Raza, Viv Bradshaw, and Matthew Hague, *Applications of RFID Technology* (London: Institute of Electrical Engineers, 1999).

24 See Paul Liao, Alexis Smith, and Connie Wang, "Convenience and Safety vs. Privacy: The Ethics of Radio Frequency Identification (RFID)," in *Confronting Information Ethics in the New Millennium*, ed. Laurie Burkhart, Jake Friedberg, Trevor Martin, Kavitha Sharma, and Morgan Ship (Boulder, CO: Leeds School of Business, 2007), 115–23.

25 Dan Newling, "Britons Could Be Microchipped like Dogs in a Decade," *Daily Mail*, October 30, 2006. Speculative pieces such as this one contributed to the rumor, circulating in early 2014 among the radical right of the United States, that the European Union would require the implantation of biochips into all newborns beginning in May of that year.

26 This project is under the direction of Kris Pister. See Brett Warneke, Matt Last, Brian Liebowitz, and Kristofer S. J. Pister, "Smart Dust: Communicating with a Cubic-Millimeter Computer," *Computer* 34, no. 1 (2001): 44–51.

27 Amy Maxmen, "Digital Pills Make Their Way to Market," July 30, 2012, http://blogs.nature.com/news/2012/07/digital-pills-make-their-way-to-market.html.

28 Matt Bettonville, "Chip Moves Wirelessly in Bloodstream," *Stanford Daily*, February 23, 2012, https://www.stanforddaily.com/2012/02/23/chip-moves-wirelessly-in-bloodstream. Eugene Thacker discusses the history and ethics of nanomedicine and nanotechnology as a new form of industrialism that approaches the body as "programmable matter" based on a theory of "atomistic reductionism": see Eugene Thacker, *Biomedia* (Minneapolis: University of Minnesota Press, 2004), 115–40.

29 "Delusions are fixed beliefs that are not amenable to change in light of conflicting evidence": American Psychiatric Association, *Diagnostic and Statistical Manual of Mental Disorders*, 5th ed. (DSM-V) (Washington, DC: American Psychiatric Association, 2013), 87. "Depth of conviction" refers to how deeply the individual believes in his or her delusion. In other words, does the individual still have some doubt (or can doubt be introduced by others), or is she or he steadfast in maintaining the truth of the delusion? "Lack of insight" refers to the deluded individual's inability to recognize that she or he is deluded, psychotic, and in need of treatment.

30 American Psychiatric Association, DSM-V, 87. See also M. Cermolacce, L. Sass, and J. Parnas, "What Is Bizarre in Bizarre Delusions? A Critical Review," *Schizophrenia Bulletin* 36, no. 4 (2010): 667–79.

31 Vaughan Bell, "You Needn't Be Wrong to Be Called Delusional," *The Observer*, August 3, 2013, https://www.theguardian.com/science/2013/aug/04/truly-madly-deeply-delusional.

32 "About Doreen Virtue," http://www.angeltherapy.com/about.php. As of March 2016, Virtue's bio shortened this more florid account to read, "Doreen worked as a psychotherapist specializing in healing eating disorders, until her life was saved by divine intervention on July 15, 1995 during an armed carjacking."

33 Doreen Virtue, *How to Hear Your Angels* (Carlsbad, CA: Hay House, 2007).

34 Virtue, *How to Hear Your Angels*.

35 Thomas Stephen Szasz, *The Second Sin* (London: Routledge and Kegan Paul, 1974), 101. Long before Szasz's famous pronouncement, the directionality of spiritual communications inspired a legal brief that arrived at a similar conclusion: see Matthew D. Field, "Is Belief in Spiritualism Ever Evidence of Insanity Per

Se?" *Medico-Legal Journal* 6 (1888): 194. In a finding repeated many times since, Field argued that an individual who believes it is possible to talk to God is sane, whereas an individual who believes he actually talks with God is likely insane.

36 Norma J. Milanovich, Betty Rice, and Cynthia Ploski, *We, the Arcturians* (Albuquerque, NM: Athena, 1990), 20.

37 The idea of "the Arcturians" as the most developed civilization in the universe comes from the work of the psychic Edgar Cayce, apparently derived from a series of psychic readings Cayce performed in the 1920s and '30s. Beings of the so-called fifth dimension, the Arcturians are said to occupy the star group that Jesus traveled to after leaving Earth, making them interstellar ambassadors of Christian enlightenment. As to their physical appearance, Noel Huntley writes, "They are three to four feet tall; very wispy and slender. They all look very much alike. This was chosen since they are past comparisons and judgement, and being different no longer appeals to them. Skin is greenish in colour, but strictly they state they have a colour which does not register on our planet. They have two very large almond-shaped eyes. They have three fingers on each hand which they call projectiles. They may be used to touch and guide object which they normally move psychokinetically": Noel Huntley, *ETs and Aliens: Who Are They? and Why Are They Here?* (Bloomington, IN: Xlibris, 2002), 113–14. Many adherents to the Arcturians describe them as guardians of a stargate. David K. Miller writes about the Arcturian stargate, "This powerful passage point requires Earthlings who wish to pass through it to complete all lessons and Earth incarnations associated with the third-dimensional experience. It serves as the gateway to the fifth dimension. New soul assignments are given there, and souls can then be sent to many different higher realms throughout the galaxy and universe": David K. Miller, *Spiritual Technology for the Fifth-Dimensional Earth* (Flagstaff, AZ: Light Technology, 2008), 226.

38 Milanovich's friends also queried the alien visitors, leading to this odd exchange about Arcturian clothing: "We think that you might be 'dipped' in the fabric or the garments might be applied electrically. Cynthia also hypothesizes that you can penetrate the garments by dematerializing and then materializing within them." The Arcturians respond, "No, but we appreciate your attempting to answer this puzzle. Actually, the way that we move in and out of these garments is through passing our form from the fifth dimension to the fourth dimension and then to the third dimension of time and space": Milanovich et al., *We, the Arcturians*, 49.

39 Milanovich et al, *We, the Arcturians*, 105. Not all extraterrestrials are benevolent sky beings, of course, as many ufologists believe aliens have come to Earth to mutilate cattle and probe human orifices. Interestingly, those who believe they are in actual communicative contact with aliens typically find this to be a pleasant and instructive experience. Such was the case of Ida Kannenberg, an antique dealer in Oregon who believed she was in more or less constant telepathic rapport with a being known as Hweig. Although Kannenberg's account

of Hweig strongly suggests an auditory hallucination, Kannenberg stated that Hweig was here for the explicit purpose of *preventing* mind control: see George C. Andrews, *Extra-Terrestrials among Us* (Woodbury, MN: Llewellyn, 1986). Among the first to claim abduction by a UFO, Kannenberg passed away in 2010 at ninety-five. Her books include *The Alien Book of Truth: Who Am I? What Am I Doing? Why Am I Here?* (1992), *UFOs and the Psychic Factor* (1992), and *My Brother Is a Hairy Man: An Extraterrestrial View on Bigfoot and Human Genesis* (co-written with Lee Trippett; 2013).

40 Milanovich et al., *We, the Arcturians*, 162. The idea of a duty-free room for exchanging goods that exist beyond the material plane of our third-dimensional reality suggests that taxation remains even at higher planes of existence. Intergalactic taxation also figures centrally in L. Ron Hubbard's account of Scientology.

41 Although Scientologists are notoriously antagonistic to psychiatry and psychoanalysis, the notions of the reactive mind and clearing are nevertheless extremely similar to the Freudian concepts of the unconscious and resistance. In Scientology, the E-meter renders "resistance" into a literal energy.

42 Lawrence Wright's *Going Clear: Scientology, Hollywood, and the Prison of Belief* (New York: Vintage, 2013) provides an excellent history of Scientology's formation and its beliefs. Hubbard argued that Xenu used tax inspection as a ruse to gather, capture, and exile these citizens of the Galactic Confederacy. Hubbard himself was for many years an ongoing target of investigation by the Internal Revenue Service.

43 The Church of Scientology has been very aggressive in litigating the revelation of certain church doctrines. For many years, the narrative of Xenu and the hydrogen bombing of the volcano banks on Earth ("Incident III," as it is known in Scientology) was known only through court records generated by the church's attempts to protect Hubbard's copyrighted material. A six-part series in the *Los Angeles Times* by the reporters Joel Sappell and Robert W. Welkos in 1990 also brought more of this material to light: see Joel Sappell and Robert W. Welkos, "The Scientology Story," *Los Angeles Times*, June 24–29, 1990. In the past decade or so, many more documents have been made available by former members of Scientology. A large library of these materials can be accessed through WikiLeaks, including the very important series titled "The Technical Bulletins of Dianetics and Scientology." For an index of these writings, see https://wikileaks.org/wiki/Category:Scientology.

44 In a lecture in 1963, Hubbard hinted at the origins of these implants:

> Now, the technological win is tremendous and there are only about five percent of the cases you're going to run into that are going to give you a bit of a thetan ache because they don't have what I choose to call now, because it was the nation or small government that did these things—Helatrobus—not to be confused with Helatrobe. Helatrobe is the Galactic Confederation. It's Helatrobus. Call these things the Helatrobus Implants for lack of a better designation because 43 trillion isn't accurate for all cases, don't you see, and

that sort of thing. You can't give it by a time date and there is no reason to keep calling it by a time date. Let's call it by something that was less well known, but that we can identify. Call them the Helatrobus Implants and it tells you these are the implants which begin with the electronic clouds over planets and—and the dichotomy, plus and minus, and so forth, and sweep on through in a certain series. (L. Ron Hubbard, "The Helatrobus Implants: A Lecture given by L. Ron Hubbard on 21 May 1963," https://wikileaks.org/wiki/Scientology_censored_Helatrobus_lectures_%281963%29.)

45 The concept of "lost time," as old as Betty and Barney Hill's notorious claim of alien abduction in 1961, provides a particularly ingenious defense against rationalist counterclaims—that is, "My groggy inability to remember what happened is proof that something did indeed happen."

46 Francis Harber, *Schizophrenia, Obsession, Exorcism, Reincarnation, and Mediums* (New York: Vantage, 1976), preface.

47 Other obsessing spirits are particularly petty, as in those that cause "a person who is wearing glasses to see blurred and give him the idea his lenses are smudged," thus causing the tormented to "constantly take off his glasses to clean them." If you "feel that . . . trousers are too tight sometimes; other times . . . pants feel just right," you might be obsessed by a demon. "An obsessing spirit causes a person who has a full-time job to do a lot of free work after working hours or work at a second job in order to exhaust him physically, and mentally and kill him off." At the same time, however, an obsessing spirit can cause a man "to go fishing in all his spare time": see Harber, *Schizophrenia, Obsession, Exorcism, Reincarnation, and Mediums*, 35–40.

48 "How to Detect and/or Disable an Implanted RFID Chip," http://www.godlikeproductions.com/forum1/message1190061/pg2.

49 Michael Bell, a self-professed victim of chip implantation, describes the obstacles involved in contacting the medical community. After traveling from the United States to Spain to consult with a radiologist willing to search for implantable devices, Bell found his own doctors unwilling to remove the devices seen in the magnetic resonance imaging (MRI) scans. Those who have "strong ultrasound or MRI images suggesting a foreign body may also have to hire an attorney to assist them in getting the foreign body removed," he writes. "If the Target gets lucky and finds a surgeon willing to remove the foreign object, they must remember to photograph it and have the doctor acknowledge what this foreign body is. Without the doctor acknowledging an implant as a non-therapeutic device that was placed in the victim without their knowledge or consent, then the entire process will be a wash and nothing will come from it and it cannot be used as evidence in a court of law." Bell later discovered that the radiologist in Spain would no longer see covertly implanted patients. "The radiologist was scared for his own safety, and did not want to risk the safety of his own life or that of his family": Michael F. Bell, *The Invisible Crime: Illegal Microchip Implants and Their Use against Humanity* (Chandler, AZ: Brighton, 2011), 55–56.

50 Bell describes the process of implantation this way:

> The chosen victim is drugged through food, drink, or directly exposed to ether gas within their very own homes. Illegal, covert surgery is either performed in the Target's house or apartment or they are alternately moved to an undisclosed location. Surgery can also be performed in a van parked close to the victim's residence. [They are] caught completely off guard; and they are fully anesthetized while surgery or multiple operations are performed—all with neither the victim's knowledge or consent. A small cosmetic surgery cut or incision is made behind one or both of the victim's ears. These small cuts are designed to heal quickly, without stitches by using a cosmetic surgery aid known as Dermabond. The incisions in the future, when healed, will resemble a natural fold in the skin. Then, a tiny plated electrode is slid beneath the skin, on top of the skull. Using EEG technology, this tiny repeater or transmitter can, at the speed of light and in real time, record and send out the signal coming from the human being's brain within the pre-speech center. The victim who has these implants installed can now, with the aid of a converter capacity computer system, actually have their every thought read in real time and as they occur. A tiny speaker is inserted within each ear canal which enables the controller or perpetrator to hear all sounds which the victim hears, also in real time. (Bell, *The Invisible Crime*, loc. 548 of 2426, Kindle)

51 See Jim Keith, *Mass Control: Engineering Human Consciousness* (Lilburn, GA: IllumiNet, 1999), 233.

52 VeriChip Corporation, Form S-1, filed with U.S. Securities and Exchange Commission, December 29, 2005, https://www.sec.gov/Archives/edgar/data/1347022/000119312505250388/ds1.htm.

53 VeriChip Corporation, Form S-1. The warnings continue: "In addition, we cannot assure you that our business and operations will not be harmed by any misperceptions or negative publicity that prompts legislative or administrative efforts by politicians or groups opposed to the development and use of human-implantable RFID microchips. We cannot assure you that legislative or administrative restrictions directly or indirectly delaying, limiting or preventing the use of human-implantable RFID microchips or the sale, manufacture or use of such systems will not be enacted in the future."

54 http://www.wethepeoplewillnotbechipped.com. This website has been shuttered since I conducted this research in 2014, with the webmaster observing, "I basically fear for my safety after being under intense pressure from the adversary. I have come to realise this is not my war, it is Gods [sic]."

55 Advertisement at http://www.wethepeoplewillnotbechipped.com.

56 *George C. Jones v. Dr. Allen L. Ault*, 67 F.R.D. 124 (S.D. Ga. 1974). See the discussion of this case in Sean Munger, "Bill Clinton Bugged My Brain: Delusional Claims in Federal Courts." *Tulane Law Review* 72 (1997): 1809–50. Jones was quite specific in his account of the device's impact on the body: "The

waves particularly attack the pituitary gland which, petitioner says, is the most important portion of the 'emotional brain.' However, they are directed at various other parts of his body, causing such symptoms as itch between the legs and his private parts and in the rectal area; hunger after eating; sleeplessness; sexual self-excitation; loss of memory; sluggishness; depression; paranoia; fire in the stomach and chest; migraine."

57 *George C. Jones, Petitioner v. Dr. Allen L. Ault et al., Director of the Georgia Board of Correction and Offender Rehabilitation and Members thereof, and Joe S. Hopper, Warden, Georgia State Prison, Reidsville, Georgia, Respondents* (two cases), nos. CV474–279 and CV474–293, U.S. District Court for the Southern District of Georgia, Savannah Division (67 F.R.D. 124; 1974 U.S. Dist. LEXIS 5710; 20 Fed. R. Serv. 2d [Callaghan] 972). The previous case invoked by the judge was *Boyce v. U.S. Parole Board* (S.D. Ga., C.A. 3224, 1975).

58 *George C. Jones, Petitioner v. Dr. Allen L. Ault et al.*

59 *George C. Jones, Petitioner v. Dr. Allen L. Ault et al.*

60 28 U.S. Code 1915A: Screening.

61 *John M. Ginter v. California Dept. of Corrections, et al.*, No. Misc. 94-097-WBS, U.S. District Court, Eastern District of California (April 13, 1994). Ginter continued to assert the reality of his assault by magnetic integrated neuron duplicator until his death from lung cancer in 2007.

62 "Hong Kong Professor Sues U.S. for Mind Control," *Chemical and Engineering News*, February 5, 1996. In March 2014, Brandon Jacobs sued the Institute of Electrical and Electronics Engineers (IEEE) for implanting a brain chip, as well as for the institute's "alleged failure to live up to an alleged agreement to give him a link to his alleged profile on its website. The lawsuit says all other program participants have 'a master web site for their Big Brother chip'": Daniel June, "IEEE Sued in Los Angeles Superior Court for Implanting Big Brother Microchip into Victim's Head," *JD Journal*, March 20, 2014, https://www.jdjournal.com/2014/03/20/ieee-sued-in-los-angeles-superior-court-for-implanting-big-brother-microchip-into-victims-head. In his statement, Jacobs claimed, "I have the x-rays that clearly show the Palacos cement in my forehead at Edison imaging located in New Jersey. The radiologist did not specify anything abnormal in the radiology report though. The cement is clearly visible though. The company needs to testify and be punished by perjury if they speak untruth." Given that Jacobs's claim suggested possible negligence on the part of Edison Imaging, this case also attracted the interest of the radiology community: see Steve Millburg, "Lawsuit: Radiologist Missed Sinister Brain Chip," *Highlights in Radiology*, March 24, 2014, http://www.radiologydaily.com/daily/neuroradiology/lawsuit-radiologist-missed-sinister-brain-chip.

63 Casagrande testified:

> I am here as a representative of victims of telebiostimulation and control. If you'll turn your page, I have a definition just for those of you who aren't familiar with the technology, and what it's all about. Telebiostimulation and

control is the manipulation of biological processes by the use of telemetry. This technology tapped into the networks of research or targeted living organisms and input signals into the organisms neuronetworks. Telebiostimulation and control were used in neural networks where the brain goes beyond simply recording thoughts as they are processed within the mind. Instead, technology is capable of placing thoughts, feelings, sounds directly into the mind and relaying signals to muscles, making them contract and/or release. A little bit about myself. I am an engineer. I have a master's degree. I have worked for one of the Big Three in Detroit. This technology is being used on myself, and subsequently I have lost a lot of my life. (Vicki Casagrande, public testimony at the 21st Meeting of the National Bioethics Advisory Committee, Case Western Reserve University, Cleveland, Ohio, May 19, 1998)

64 Mendoza's persecution appears to have started during his second year at the Thomas M. Cooley Law School in Lansing, Michigan. At his website, Mendoza alleges he

> presented to the Dean of the law school, Don Leduc, a former attorney for the US Dept. of Justice concrete and specific evidence showing how the President of the law school and former Chief Justice of the Michigan Supreme Court Thomas E. Brennan and Michigan Court of Appeals Roman S. Briggs were using the school to defraud students of their federal loans while giving away law degrees to those affiliated with government agencies. Neither Judge Brennan, nor Judge Briggs denied or engaged the evidence of fraud. Instead, Mendoza was the subject of pervasive harassment, illegal searches, attempts of entrapment, and attempts to run over. On October of 1997, Mendoza was found with unexplained swollen heart at the emergency room. On July 13, of 1998 two individuals were trying to brake [sic] into Mendoza's apartment around 3:00 am. The same day, Mendoza left the state and returned home, Mission, Texas. Mendoza left the law school in full compliance with the Honor Code and in good academic standing. (http://jesusmendoza1.blogspot.com/2010/05/jesus-mendoza-update.html)

What follows is a list of lawsuits Mendoza has filed since leaving Michigan: *Jesus Mendoza v. the University of Texas Pan-American*, U.S. District Court, Southern District of Texas, case no. M-05-408, U.S. Court of Appeals for the Fifth Circuit, case no. 06-41453; *Jesus Mendoza Maldonado v. Social Security Administration*, U.S. District Court, Southern District of Texas, Mcallen Division, case no. M-05-133; *Jesus Mendoza v. Justice of the Peace Ismael "Melo" Ochoa*, 398th District Court, Hidalgo County, Texas, cause no. C-013-08-1, Court of Appeals, 13th District of Texas, cause no. 13-08-00588-CV; *Jesus Mendoza v. Pedro S. Montano, MD, and JP Ismael Ochoa*, 13th Court of Appeals, 13th District of Texas, case no. 13-07-00146-CV; *Jesus Mendoza v. the Texas Department of Assistive and Rehabilitative Services*, 345th District Court, Travis County, Texas, cause no. D-1-GN-09-002538; *Jesus Mendoza v. Dr. David Moron, et al.*,

U.S. District Court, Southern District of Texas, McAllen Division, case no. 7 05-CV-184, U.S. Court of Appeals, Fifth Circuit, case no. 06-40671; *Maldonado v. Ashcroft*, U.S. Court of Appeals, Fifth Circuit, case no. 04-40095; *Jesus Mendoza Maldonado v. Alberto R. Gonzales*, U.S. Supreme Court, case no. 04-9908; *Jesus Mendoza Maldonado v. the Thomas M. Cooley Law School, et al.*, U.S. Court of Appeals, Sixth Circuit, case no. 02-2095; *Jesus Mendoza v. William Rea et al.*, 389th District Court, Hidalgo County, Texas, cause no. C-1615-02-H.

65 "Final Order—Protection from Stalking," December 30, 2008, in *Walbert v. Redford*, District Court, Sedgwick County, Kansas, case no. 2008-DM-008649.

66 The extent to which the judge actually endorsed Walbert's claims is unknown. It is equally probable that the judge was penalizing the defendant for not taking the proceedings seriously enough to appear in the courtroom. (The defendant was also ordered to pay Walbert's legal fees.) It should be noted that Walbert's invention of an "antimicrobial sanitary seal" for cans of beer and soda pop suggests concerns over contamination, a frequent complaint of the paranoid. Also, since "winning" his case, Walbert has gone on to sue the Wichita police force, claiming they have engaged in an organized plot against him since winning his court order in 2008. The case was dismissed in the U.S. District Court: *Walbert v. Wichita Police Department*, civil action no. 10-1234-MLB, U.S. District Court, District of Kansas, U.S. Dist. Lexis 66030, June 21, 2011.

67 "Final Order—Protection from Stalking."

68 Jim Guest to Missouri Legislature, letter, October 29, 2007, http://www.stopthecrime.net/jimguestletteroctober102010.pdf.

69 David Hambling, "Court to Defendant: Stop Blasting that Man's Mind!" *Wired*, July 1, 2009, https://www.wired.com/2009/07/court-to-defendant-stop-blasting-that-mans-mind.

70 *Space Preservation Act of 2001* (HR 2977)

71 See Michigan Public Acts (2003), Acts 256–257. The definition of such devices is provided in section 256(k): "'Harmful electronic or electromagnetic device' means a device designed to emit or radiate or that, as a result of its design, emits or radiates an electronic or electromagnetic pulse, current, beam, signal, or microwave that is intended to cause harm to others or cause damage to, destroy, or disrupt any electronic or telecommunications system or device, including, but not limited to, a computer, computer network, or computer system."

72 U.S. Congress and Senate Judiciary Committee, "Confirmation Hearing on the Nomination of John G. Roberts, Jr., to Be Chief Justice of the United States," 109th Cong., 1st sess. (September 15, 2005). Given the Roberts court's ruling that corporations enjoy the same rights as citizens, one can only imagine the court's position on the constitutionality of any law that would seek to take away a corporation's freedom to implant its speech in the frontal cortex of employees or customers.

73 Emily Annie Epstein, "'Beautiful' Family Slain Hours after Church by 'Mentally Ill Father Who Was Tormented by the Prospect of Obama Winning the

Election," *Daily Mail*, September 27, 2012. Two days after the election, a man in Florida made good on his threat to "not be around" if Obama won a second term. Police found him in his home, dead and surrounded by empty prescription pill bottles. A message on the wall read, "Do not revive. Fuck Obama": Meena Hart Duerson, "Florida Man who Warned He Wouldn't 'Be Around' if Barack Obama Was Reelected Kills Himself after the Election," *New York Daily News*, November 14, 2012.

74 Ever fearful of the socialist practices of Europeans, this community began in 2014 to trade in the rumor that all babies born in the European Union as of May 2014 would undergo compulsory RFID implantation. The claim appears to have originated at the dubious "news" site Topinfo Post, in an article by Vlad Dimitrievich titled "All European Newborn Babies Will be Microchipped from May 2014." The article contains no sources.

75 Alan Greenblatt, "Lawmakers Are Working on Anti-Brain-Chip Bill," April 15, 2010, https://www.npr.org/sections/alltechconsidered/2010/04/15/126023516/breathe-easy—ga—lawmakers-are-working-on-anti-brain-chip-bill. Classifying the insertion of involuntary microchips in another's body as a "misdemeanor" provides a clue to Seltzer's sincerity in passing this law.

76 For more detail on this perspective, see Jeffrey R. Grant, *Surveillance Society: The Rise of the Antichrist* (Colorado Springs, CO: WaterBrook Press, 2003). As Grant explains, the Book of Revelations calls for the "mark" of the Antichrist to appear on either the forehead or the right hand. Grant sides with the forehead thesis, reasoning that "some individuals may not have a right hand, due to an accident. In addition, if electronic scanners are used to detect the Mark at a distance, a right hand might be out of sight. The forehead will almost always be in plain view": Grant, *Surveillance Society*, 238. In 2001, however, minister Arno Froese dismissed the likelihood of this connection, noting, "The under-the-skin chip theory presumes that this technology is the epitome of sophistication.... By the time you read these lines, the capability of computer science will have multiplied many times": Arno Froese, *The Coming Digital God* (West Columbia, SC: Midnight Call Ministries, 2001), 199.

77 Fredrick Kunkle and Rosalind Helderman, "An Issue of Privacy or Sign of the Apocalypse?" *Washington Post*, Feb 10, 2010, B1.

78 "The BRAIN Initiative: Brain Research through Advancing Innovative Neurotechnologies," April 2, 2013, https://obamawhitehouse.archives.gov/node/300741?.

79 On April 2, 2014, exactly one year after President Obama's announcement of the BRAIN Initiative, a research team announced the first successful map of the "mouse connectome": Seung Wook Oh, Julie A. Harris, Lydia Ng, and Brent Winslow et al., "A Mesoscale Connectome of the Mouse Brain," *Nature* 508 (April 10, 2014): 207–14.

80 A. Paul Alivisatos, Miyoung Chun, George M. Church, Ralph J. Greenspan, Michael L. Roukes, and Rafael Yuste, "The Brain Activity Map Project and the Challenge of Functional Connectomics," *Neuron* 74, no. 6 (2012): 970–74.

81 Brian Bergstein, "Q&A: Joseph LeDoux," MIT *Technology Review*, June 17, 2014, 30–33. Supporting LeDoux's contention (and perhaps paranoia) is a study demonstrating that a brain implant could turn memories "on and off" in mice: see Benedict Carey, "Memory Implant Gives Rats Sharper Recollection," *New York Times*, June 17, 2011. Similar results were reported with monkeys the following year: see Benedict Carey, "Brain Implant Improves Thinking in Monkeys, First Such Demonstration in Primates," *New York Times*, September 14, 2012.

82 For example, as political ideologies continue to align more closely with issues of identity and lifestyle, partisan beliefs have become notoriously impervious to reality and counterevidence. A study in 2013 demonstrated that partisan allegiances had a significant impact on an individual's ability to solve a math problem correctly: Dan M. Kahan, Ellen Peters, Erica Dawson, and Paul Slovic, "Motivated Numeracy and Enlightened Self-Government," *Behavioural Public Policy* 1, no. 1 (May 2017): 54–86.

83 See Daniel Freeman and Jason Freeman, *Paranoia: The 21st-Century Fear* (London: Oxford University Press, 2008). See also Joseph Triebwasser, Eran Chemerinski, Panos Roussos, and Larry J. Siever, "Paranoid Personality Disorder," *Journal of Personality Disorders* 27, no. 6 (2013): 795–805.

84 In the summer of 2016, the victories of "Brexit" advocates in the United Kingdom and Donald Trump as the Republican candidate for the US presidency added anecdotal support to this thesis. Both victories stemmed in large part from media-assisted paranoia over allegedly open national borders and unchecked immigration, anxieties that in turn spoke to the global displacement of the manufacturing sector in both the United Kingdom and the United States.

85 Freeman and Freeman, *Paranoia*, 42.

86 Entering the twenty-first century, the long-term prospects of Moore's Law are in doubt. The ability to continue miniaturizing circuits has apparently hit a wall in terms of both capacity and fabrication. It should be noted, moreover, that Moore's Law was never a mystical truism of the universe but is itself linked to a very specific material economy: see Christopher Mims, "The High Cost of Upholding Moore's Law," MIT *Technology Review*, April 20, 2010, 71–72.

87 This is a recurring theme in the Matrix trilogy (1999–2003) and serves as the basis for the climax of *The Hunger Games: Catching Fire* (2013).

88 Bell, *The Invisible Crime*, loc. 1564 of 2426, Kindle. It is worth noting that, in granting brain chips the power to produce a perfect simulation of real-time consciousness, such accounts provide a cybernetic version of the philosophical homily "Turtles All the Way Down." In other words, if a brain chip generates a self-sustaining illusion of consciousness, then an infinite number of these mediated levels potentially exist, with no way to discern which (if any) constitutes the ultimate "true" horizon.

89 See Mark Weiser, Rich Gold, and John Seely Brown, "The Origins of Ubiquitous Computing Research at PARC in the Late 1980s," IBM *Systems Journal* 38, no. 4 (1999): 693–96; David Rose, *Enchanted Objects: Design, Human Desire, and the*

Internet of Things (New York: Simon and Schuster, 2014). In one of his early "sociological" studies, Jean Baudrillard proposed an inversion of subject-object relations under consumer capitalism, predicting an environment in which commodities reproduce human social relations to ensure the commodity's own replication and survival: see Jean Baudrillard, *The System of Objects* (London: Verso, 1996).

90 Rachel Metz, "The Internet of You," MIT *Technology Review*, May 14, 2014, 77–78.

91 Anyone who has ever been forcibly routed to a new home page or search engine after performing a computer system update can only imagine what such shenanigans would be like in the age of ubiquitous computing.

92 "How to Detect and/or Disable an Implanted RFID Chip."

93 For a history of advertising's interest in subliminal techniques, see Charles R. Acland, *Swift Viewing: The Popular Life of Subliminal Influence* (Durham, NC: Duke University Press, 2012). A patent from 1983 promised the ability to curtail shoplifting through subliminal audio messages embedded in the retailer's ambient music: Rene R. Lundy and David L. Tyler, "Auditory Subliminal Message System and Method," U.S. Patent no. 4,395,600, July 26, 1983. The impact, if any, of ambient music on consumer shopping behavior remains a central debate among marketers. For a recent discussion, see Daniel Gaygen, "Effects of Ambient Music Exposure on Simulated Buy Decisions," *International Journal of Business and Social Science* 4, no. 4 (2013): 184–94.

94 Michael Serazio, "Selling (Digital) Millennials: The Social Construction and Technological Bias of a Consumer Generation," *Television and New Media* 16, no. 7 (2015): 608.

95 Serazio, "Selling (Digital) Millennials," 608.

96 Pierre Bourdieu, *Distinction: A Social Critique of the Judgement of Taste* (Cambridge, MA: Harvard University Press, 1984).

97 In the episode "The HUMANCENTiPad" (2011), *South Park* satirized the widespread online practice of agreeing to "terms and conditions" without actually reading the many paragraphs of information to which one is acceding. The episode's avowed satirical target is our cavalier and often lazy engagement with online transactions. But one could also argue that the refusal to thoroughly review online terms and conditions is a type of surrender, born from the implicit understanding that the user does not, and will never, have the power to contest these terms (even if one took the time to interpret their byzantine legalities). Less a sign of laziness, our perfunctory "checking of the box" signals an acquiescence to corporate power.

98 James Vlahos, "Barbie Wants to Get to Know Your Child," *New York Times*, September 16, 2015.

99 See Donell Holloway and Lelia Green, "The Internet of Toys," *Communication Research and Practice* 2, no. 4 (2016): 1–14.

100 The belief that witches, in the service of Satan, cannibalize and otherwise ritually abuse children dates as far back as Heinrich Kramer and James Sprenger's

Malleus Maleficarum, the foundational witch-hunting manual written in 1486. Popular accounts of occultism in the nineteenth century and early twentieth century (most famously, Joris-Karl Huysmans's *La Bas* of 1891) further codified the iconography and dramaturgy of such abuse. The publication of Lawrence Pazder's *Michelle Remembers* in 1980 greatly contributed to the modern moral panic over satanic ritual abuse (SRA). Based on his therapy sessions with Michelle Smith (whom he eventually married), *Michelle Remembers* united pop occultism with the basic tenants of Freudian repression. Pazder and Smith made two appearances on *The Oprah Winfrey Show*, imbuing SRA with even more popular legitimacy by speculating that hundreds, if not thousands, of individuals had repressed their memories of childhood abuse at the hands of Satanists. The central claims of *Michelle Remembers* were all eventually debunked, but not before Pazder served as a consultant on hundreds of ritual abuse cases, most famously the McMartin Preschool trial in which several workers at a Southern California daycare facility were accused of Satanic child abuse. At its conclusion in 1990 (with no convictions and all charges dismissed), the McMartin trial was the most expensive court case in US history. By the time Napolis got involved, SRA was both well known and highly dubious: see Lawrence Pazder, *Michelle Remembers* (New York: Pocket Books, 1980); Colin A. Ross, *Satanic Ritual Abuse: Principles of Treatment* (Toronto: University of Toronto Press, 1995). See also George A. Fraser, ed., *The Dilemma of Ritual Abuse: Cautions and Guides for Therapists* (Washington, DC: American Psychiatric Press, 1997); Matt Johnson, "Fear and Power: From Naivete to a Believer in Cult Abuse," *Journal of Psychohistory* 21, no. 4 (1994): 435–41.

101 For a summary of Napolis's activities in this area, see Paul Bocij, *Cyberstalking: Harassment in the Internet Age and How to Protect Your Family* (Westport, CT: Greenwood, 2004).

102 See "Declaration of Diana Napolis, in Response to the Recommendations of the Board of Behavioral Science," Superior Court of California, case no. 171331 (February 19, 2003).

103 *The People, Plaintiff and Respondent, v. Diana Napolis, Defendant and Appellant*, D041854, Court of Appeal of California, Fourth Appellate District, Division One 2003 Cal. App. Unpub. Lexis 9972 (October 23, 2003).

104 In her amended complaint, Napolis claims:

> In October 2002, due to threats made by Plaintiff's perpetrators that they would kill her by nonlethal technology, it caused Plaintiff to write a pseudo-threat to a Hollywood figure to ensure that she would be placed in the custody of law enforcement, in efforts to save her life. Due to Plaintiff's eventual plea to "stalking," and subsequent notoriety, it resulted in further ruination of Plaintiff's reputation and career and revocation of her MFT [marriage and family therapy] license. These malicious actions by Defendant Aquino and others caused Plaintiff to be misdiagnosed as "mentally ill" after which she was forced by the criminal justice system to take psychotropic

medication. While being monitored by San Diego Probation Department, Defendant Loftus and other Does conspired to make a false police report about Plaintiff accusing her of activity which had never occurred which caused significant emotional distress for Plaintiff due to the extensive efforts it took to correct these misrepresentations. After May of 2007, Plaintiff experienced enough psychological recovery to allow her to file a complaint against Defendants. (U.S District Court, Southern District of California, case no. 08CV557 WQH-NLS)

105 There is still a sizable community on the Internet invested in the reality of SRA as a genuinely widespread phenomenon, many of whom cite Napolis as a victim of both satanic and governmental persecution. Napolis went on to start a blog and has since seemingly shifted her concerns from Spielberg, Hewitt, and Satanists to theories of alien overlords and global simulation. Under the heading "Report about Finds to Date in San Diego County," her entry for September 20, 2010 reads,

> We are in an artificial biosphere. The "Sun" and "Moon" are artifacts—apparently made by the aliens—These are not planets or stars. We cannot see any stars in San Diego County. They have placed a tight net around the County. Inside this net is a quantum computer program; I am told there are multiple nets around the planet—I would assume as a working hypothesis that these too house a similar program. The enemy are flanging the sky, mountains, buildings—and people from an angle—top and bottom in multiple places as this diagram shows. They are making planes disappear and they seem to have control over the airports. They can create simulated realities, send people into strange spaces, and they are attacking the public en masses—unknown to them. They can teleport and "time travel." They go into the top of peoples [sic] heads or into their rectums as these "aliens" inhabit toilets. I've seen a child pulled off a mountain into the field and then disappear. They routinely remove astral bodies. They pull animals into this field and also make them disappear. I've seen their helicopters fly into mountain tops. This is Armageddon—they also tell me this—and they are intent on spiritually and physically killing life on this planet, after which they will sometimes inhabit the victim's body. As previously written they are adept at identity theft and will take over communications by fraud. Because of the Good vs. Evil war that is occurring, they have managed to access grand spiritual beings via this program and believe they derive power from torturing them nightly—for the past 10 months. You would cry at knowing their identities. We need help desperately—they can't hold on for much longer, but please, wage a very smart war." (Diana Napolis blog, https://diananapolis.wordpress.com)

106 Peter Cochrane, *Tips for Time Travelers* (New York: McGraw-Hill, 1999).

107 Katina Michael and M. G. Michael. "Homo Electricus and the Continued Speciation of Humans," in *The Encyclopedia of Information Ethics and Security*, ed. Marian Quigley (Hershey, PA: Information Science Reference, 2007), 312–18. In *Wired* magazine's 1999 list of "The Wired 25," Cochrane shared that the inspiration for the Soul Catcher Chip came from his father's death at sixty-one. He "longed to keep his dad's spirit accessible in any form. His mother was revolted by the idea, and his wife had a similar reaction when he asked her how many parts of himself he could replace with synthetic components before she rejected him as a machine": "The Wired 25," *Wired*, November 1, 1998, 109–33.

108 Michael and Michael, "Homo Electricus and the Continued Speciation of Humans."

109 *Daily Telegraph*, July 18, 1996. When Winter argues it will soon be possible to "imbue a new-born baby with a lifetime's experience by giving him or her the Soul Catcher chip of a dead person," what would that involve? Does the baby subject, once chipped with the dead subject's experience, instantly enter the Symbolic order, fully conversant in the dead subject's knowledge of wine, computer coding, and mortgage escrow (thus producing the "uncanny" effect of the adult baby)? Or does the baby subject eventually learn, at appropriate moments, to get advice by accessing the dead person's experiences through a firewall or partition of some sort? Do baby subject and dead subject merge into some kind of dead-baby subject? Or does the dead subject simply commandeer the baby meat to live for another generation (and then again and again after that)? This last option—immortality through continuous subjectivity across a sequence of bodies—is, of course, a familiar plot in movies about Satanists, the very group Napolis believed was sponsoring Spielberg (and Hewitt) in a campaign of Soul Catcher implantation.

110 Clive Crickmer, "Liven Up . . . Death Has Had Its Chips," *Daily Mail*, July 18, 1996, 20.

111 "Connected," *Daily Telegraph*, July 18, 1996.

112 Pearson continues, "An implanted chip would be like an aircraft's black box and would enhance communications beyond current concepts. For example, police would be able to relive an attack, rape or murder from the victim's viewpoint to help catch the criminal": Pearson, quoted in "Connected."

113 Andrew Griffin, "Humans Will Become Hybrids by 2030, Says Leading Google Engineer, with Tiny Robots Scurrying around Our Brain to Help Us Think," *The Independent*, June 4, 2015, https://www.independent.co.uk/life-style/gadgets-and-tech/news/humans-will-become-hybrids-by-2030-says-leading-google-engineer-with-tiny-robots-scurrying-around-10296200.html.

114 Admittedly, Jennifer Love Hewitt's contribution to this project is more difficult to discern.

115 André Bazin, "The Myth of Total Cinema," in *What Is Cinema?*, vol. 1, trans. Hugh Gray (Berkeley: University of California Press, 1967), 17–22.

116　Institute of Creative Technologies website, http://ict.usc.edu.
117　Institute of Creative Technologies website.
118　Ernest Cline, *Ready Player One* (New York: Random House, 2011).
119　It could be argued Netflix achieved the first success on this front with *Stranger Things* (2016–), a series set in the early 1980s and heavily influenced by the Spielberg universe.

Chapter 3. The Will to (Invisible) Power

1　"Overwork Causes Insanity: Lawyer Sterne Chittenden's Eccentricity Changes to Mania," *New York Times*, January 10, 1887, 5.
2　"Declared to be Insane: More about Sterne Chittenden's Singular Delusions," *New York Times*, January 18, 1887, 8.
3　"A Visit to Bedlam: A Vision," *Weekly Miscellany; or, Instructive Entertainer*, December 12, 1774, 257.
4　Joshua Burgess, *The Medical and Legal Relations of Madness; Showing a Cellular Theory of Mind, and of Nerve Force, and also of Vegetative Vital Force* (London: John Churchill, 1858), 37.
5　"A Crazy Woman: Thought She Was Wealthy and Acted Accordingly," *Los Angeles Times*, July 20, 1889, 2
6　John S. Marshall, "Communications," *Medical and Surgical Reporter* 54, no. 1327 (March 1886): 388.
7　August Strindberg, *Inferno and From an Occult Diary* (New York: Penguin, 1979), 189.
8　Strindberg, *Inferno and From an Occult Diary*, 189.
9　Max S. Nordau, *Degeneration* (New York: D. Appleton, 1895), 218.
10　Anthony P. Morrison, "A Cognitive Analysis of the Maintenance of Auditory Hallucinations: Are Voices to Schizophrenia What Bodily Sensations Are to Panic?" *Behavioural and Cognitive Psychotherapy* 26, no. 4 (1998): 289–302.
11　Strindberg, *Inferno and From an Occult Diary*, 200. As Strindberg's anxieties intensified, he attributed his symptoms to an "electric girdle" and the possibility of an "electrical machine" concealed beneath his bed: "Hunted from hotel to hotel, pursued everywhere by electric currents which lift me from my chair, or out of bed, I deliberately set about planning my suicide. A knife falls from a table. So it is electricity!"
12　Victor Tausk, "On the Origin of the 'Influencing Machine' in Schizophrenia" (1919), in *The Psycho-Analytic Reader*, ed. Robert Fliess (New York: International Press, 1948) 31–64.
13　Tausk, "On the Origin of the 'Influencing Machine' in Schizophrenia."
14　René Descartes, *Treatise on Man* (1632) (New York: Prometheus Books, 2003), 22.
15　Georges Canguilhem, "Machine and Organism," in *Incorporations* (New York: Zone, 1992), 52. Hanns Sachs takes up the relationship between the machine

and unconscious projections of man's bodily structure in "The Delay of the Machine Age," *Psychoanalytic Quarterly* 2, nos. 3–4 (1933): 404–24.
16 Robert Whytt, *Observations on the Nature, Causes, and Cure of Those Disorders Which Have Been Commonly Called Nervous, Hypochondriac, or Hysteric: To Which Are Prefixed Some Remarks on the Sympathy of the Nerves* (Edinburgh: Becket, Du Hondt, Balfour, 1765), v.
17 Matthew Cobb, "Exorcizing the Animal Spirits: Jan Swammerdam on Nerve Function," *Nature Reviews Neuroscience* 3, no. 5 (2002): 395–400.
18 *A Dissertation upon the Nervous System and Its Influence upon the Soul* (London: Privately Printed, 1780): 2.
19 Philipp Sarasin, "The Body as Medium: Nineteenth-Century European Hygiene Discourse," *Grey Room* 29 (2007): 55.
20 Julien Offray de La Mettrie, *Man a Machine* (Cambridge: Cambridge University Press, [1748] 1996), 23.
21 Mettrie, *Man a Machine*, 27.
22 Mettrie, *Man a Machine*, 27. In 1945, a farmer in Colorado beheaded a chicken, only to discover that the animal would live long past the ordinary point of collapse. "Mike the Headless Chicken" lived for eighteen months without a head and became a minor sensation, even making it to the pages of *Life* magazine (October 22, 1945). Scientists determined that the decapitation had left Mike's brain stem intact, thus allowing the chicken to continue its basic physiological processes. In the end, Mike passed away not from any lingering effects of his headlessness, but from choking on a kernel of corn.
23 Anonymous [Elie Luzac], *Man, More than a Machine* (London: W. Owen, 1752), frontispiece.
24 William Smith, *A Dissertation upon the Nerves* (London: W. Owen, 1768), 60–61.
25 Joseph Priestley, *A Free Discussion of the Doctrines of Materialism, and Philosophical Necessity, in a Correspondence between Dr. Price, and Dr. Priestley. To Which Are Added, by Dr. Priestley, an Introduction, Explaining the Nature of the Controversy, and Letters to Several Writers, etc.* (London: J. Johnson and T. Cadell, 1778).
26 See, e.g., Benjamin West's painting *Benjamin Franklin Drawing Electricity from the Sky*, oil on slate, 1816, no. 158-132-1, Philadelphia Museum of Art. Like so many iconic moments in the American imagination, Franklin's kite experiment may not have actually ever taken place: see Tom Tucker, *Bolt of Fate: Benjamin Franklin and His Fabulous Kite* (New York: Public Affairs, 2003).
27 James Delbourgo, *A Most Amazing Scene of Wonders: Electricity and Enlightenment in Early America* (Cambridge, MA: Harvard University Press, 2006), 90.
28 "Electrifying Eel," *Morning Chronicle and London Advertiser*, no. 3212, September 4, 1779, n.p.
29 Recent research demonstrates that von Humboldt's claims, long thought to be apocryphal, may well have been true: see Kenneth C. Catania, "Leaping Eels Electrify

Threats, Supporting Humboldt's Account of a Battle with Horses," *Proceedings of the National Academy of Sciences* 113.25 (2016): 6979–84.

30 William Watson, "Observations upon the Effects of Electricity Applied to a Tetanus, or Muscular Rigidity, of Four Months Continuance," *Philosophical Transactions* 53 (1763): 10–26.

31 Joseph Priestley, *The History and Present State of Electricity* (London: J. Dodsley, J. Johnson, B. Davenport, and T. Cadell, 1767), 411.

32 John Wilkinson, *The Case of Mister Winder, Who Was Cured of a Paralysis by Flash of Lightning* (Göttingen, Germany: Podwig and Barmeier, 1765), 22. See also Cheney Hart, "An Account of a Cure of a Paralytic Arm, by Electricity: In a Letter from Cheney Hart, MD, to Mr. William Watson, FRS," *Philosophical Transactions* 49 (1755): 558–63.

33 Stanley Finger, "Benjamin Franklin, Electricity, and the Palsies: Historical Neurology," *Neurology* 66, no. 11 (May 23, 2006): 1559–63.

34 Thomas Percival, *Essays Medical and Experimental*, vol. 2. (London: J. Johnson, 1773), 150.

35 Francis Lowndes, *Observations on Medical Electricity: Containing a Synopsis of All the Diseases in which Electricity Has Been Recommended or Applied with Success* (London: D. Stuart, 1787), 49.

36 Edward Spry, "Account of a Locked Jaw, and Paralysis, Cured by Electricity: By Dr. Edward Spry, of Totness, in a Letter to Charles Morton, MD Sec. RS," *Philosophical Transactions* (1767): 88–91.

37 Percival, *Essays Medical and Experimental*, 183.

38 Sherry Ann Beaudreau and Stanley Finger, "Medical Electricity and Madness in the 18th Century: The Legacies of Benjamin Franklin and Jan Ingenhousz," *Perspectives in Biology and Medicine* 49, no. 3 (Summer 2006): 330–45.

39 Jan Ingenhousz to Benjamin Franklin, letter, 1783, quoted in Beaudreau and Finger, "Medical Electricity and Madness in the 18th Century," 337. Franklin's "electrocutions" were produced not by the famous kite, but in attempts to "electrify" a turkey and, later, apply charges to a paralyzed patient.

40 "A Letter from Mr. John Birch, Surgeon, on the Subject of Medical Electricity," in George Adams, *An Essay on Electricity, Explaining the Principles of that Useful Science; and Describing the Instruments, Contrived either to Illustrate the Theory or Render the Practice Entertaining* (London: J. Dillon, 1799), 550.

41 "A Letter from Mr. John Birch," 552.

42 Tiberius Cavallo, *An Essay on the Theory and Practice of Medical Electricity* (London: Elmsly, Dilly, Bowen, 1781), 116.

43 Ernst Benz, *The Theology of Electricity: On the Encounter and Explanation of Theology and Science in the Seventeenth and Eighteenth Centuries* (Eugene, OR: Pickwick, 1999), 45–46.

44 B. Brown Williams, *Mental Alchemy: A Treatise on the Mind, Nervous System, Psychology, Magnetism, Mesmerism, and Diseases* (New York: Fowlers and Wells, 1852), 141.

45 Luigi Galvani, *Effects of Electricity on Muscular Motion* (Norwalk, CT: Burndy Library, [1791] 1953).
46 O. K. Chamberlin, *Electricity, Wonderful and Mysterious Agent* (New York: John F. Trow, 1862), 4.
47 Hugh Campbell, *A Treatise on Nervous Exhaustion and the Diseases Induced by It* (London: Henry Renshaw, 1875), 28.
48 Anson Rabinbach, *The Human Motor: Energy, Fatigue, and the Origins of Modernity* (Berkeley: University of California Press, 1992), 66.
49 Squier Littell, "On the Influence of Electrical Fluctuations as a Cause of Disease," *Littell's Living Age* (October 10, 1857): 699.
50 Benjamin Douglas Perkins, *The Influence of Metallic Tractors on the Human Body* (London: J. Johnson, 1798), 94.
51 William Snow Miller, "Elisha Perkins and His Metallic Tractors," *Yale Journal of Biology and Medicine* 8, no. 1 (1935): 41.
52 John Greenway, "Galvanism as Therapeutic Agent: Perkins's 'Metallic Tractors' and the Placebo Effect," ANQ 14, no. 4 (2001): 24–37.
53 M. L. Gallois, "Experiments on the Principle of Life: Especially on That of the Motions of the Heart, and on the Seat of this Principle," *New England Journal of Medicine, Surgery and Collateral Branches of Science* 3, no. 1 (1814): 11–20.
54 "Power of Galvanism," *The Lancet* 2 (1842–43): 815. For a more detailed discussion of Weinhold's experiments, as well as their influence on the writing of *Frankenstein*, see Stanley Finger and Mark B. Law, "Karl August Weinhold and His 'Science' in the Era of Mary Shelley's *Frankenstein*: Experiments on Electricity and the Restoration of Life," *Journal of the History of Medicine and Allied Sciences* 53 (1998): 161–80; Karl August Weinhold, *Versuche über das Leben und seine Grundkräfte auf dem Wege der Experimental-Physiologies* (Madgeburg, Germany: Creutz, 1817).
55 William E. Horner, "Observations and Experiments on Certain Parts of the Nervous System," *Philadelphia Journal of the Medical and Physical Sciences* 1, no. 2 (July 1, 1820): 285. Public distaste for vivisection gained momentum throughout the nineteenth century, leading eventually in England to the Cruelty to Animals Act of 1876 and in the United States to the publication of Frances Cobbe's *Vivisection in America* (1890). So widespread was the medical community's interest in nervous vivisection at the beginning of the nineteenth century that an early editor of the *New England Journal Medicine and Surgery*, while applauding much of the work performed on "inferior animals," nevertheless opined, "But when we observe the whole rising race of candidates for fame rushing impetuously, with knives, needles, saws and poisons, on the living animals around them,—in order to find out some new phenomenon during their torturous experiments, we must pause, and ask, is this the way to clothe the profession in the character of wisdom and humanity as well as science?": "Physiological Experiments," *The Medico-Chirurgical Review* 1, no.2 (London: G. Hayden, 1824), 440.

56 Alexander White, "Corporeal Contraband: A History of the Resurrectionist Movement in Britain and Canada," *University of Toronto Medical Journal* 86, no. 3 (2009): 113–16. See also James Blake Bailey, *The Diary of a Resurrectionist, 1811–1812: To Which Are Added an Account of the Resurrection Men in London and a Short History of the Passing of the Anatomy Act* (London: Swan Sonnenschein, 1896). Bailey observes, "The newspapers of the day contain many proposed solutions of the difficulty. One correspondent gravely suggested that as prostitutes had, by their bodies during life, been engaged in corrupting mankind, it was only right that after death those bodies should be handed over to be dissected for the public good. Another correspondent proposed that all bodies of suicides should be used for dissection, and that all those persons who came to their death by duelling, prize-fighting, or drunkenness, should be handed over to the surgeons for a similar purpose": Bailey, *The Diary of a Resurrectionist*, 31.

57 Giovanni Aldini, *An Account of the Galvanic Experiments Performed by John Aldini on the Body of a Malefactor Executed at Newgate* (London: Cuthell and Martin, 1803).

58 Giovanni Aldini, *General Views on the Application of Galvanism to Medical Purposes; Principally in Cases of Suspended Animation* (London: J. Callow, 1819), 19–20.

59 "Horrid Phenomena!" *Weekly Recorder*, no. 5, April 9, 1819, 35. For an even more thorough account of galvanic manipulation followed by autopsy, see "Experiments upon the Body of Morris, Executed Jan. 15, 1841," *Medical Examiner* 4, no. 4 (January 23, 1841): 58.

60 In *Essay on the Recovery of the Apparently Dead*, Charles Kite noted that bodies "suspended" by drowning still responded to electrification for up to four hours. While they could not yet be fully revived, Kite nevertheless believed such experiments proved "electricity is the most powerful stimulus we can apply": Charles Kite, *Essay on the Recovery of the Apparently Dead* (London: C. Dilly, 1751), 166. For a more detailed accounts of these efforts, see Don Shelton, *The Real Mr. Frankenstein: Sir Anthony Carlisle, Medical Murders, and the Social Genesis of Frankenstein* (Auckland, New Zealand: Portmin, 2012).

61 Aldini, *General Views on the Application of Galvanism to Medical Purposes*, 26.

62 Delbourgo, *A Most Amazing Scene of Wonders*, 26.

63 Sir Humphry Davy, *A Discourse, Introductory to a Course of Lectures on Chemistry* (London: Johnson, Cadell, Davies, 1802).

64 While the Romantic fascination with electricity certainly figures throughout the novel, Shelley remained elliptical in describing the actual process by which the creature is born. (Shelley's technical specifications as to Victor's secret are limited to a brief reference to the "instruments of life.") She does write about "the kites, wires, and strings" used "to draw down that fluid from the clouds." Within the 1818 edition's inventory of electrical wonders, however, there is no explicit mention of Galvani and his science of "animal electricity"; in fact, the first edition assigns more weight to the chemist than to the electrician in solv-

ing the riddles of existence. Asked to recount the origins of her notorious creature for the standard edition of 1831, however, Shelley emphasized galvanism's influence on her imagination, particularly its suggestion that "the component parts of a creature might be manufactured, brought together, and endued with vital warmth": Mary Shelley, *Frankenstein: Or the Modern Prometheus* (London: Colburn and Bentley, 1831).

65 Julia Kristeva, *Powers of Horror*, ed. Leon S. Roudiez (New York: Columbia University Press, 1982), 4.
66 Mary Shelley, *Frankenstein; or, The Modern Prometheus* (London: Lackington, Hughes, Harding, Mayor and Jones, 1818), 91.
67 Shelley, *Frankenstein* (1818), 1:98.
68 Shelley, *Frankenstein* (1818), 3:43–44.
69 Shelley, *Frankenstein* (1818), 3:53.
70 Panagiota Petkou, "Getting Dirty with the Body: Abjection in Mary Shelley's *Frankenstein*," *Gramma* 11 (2003): 31–38.
71 Shelley, *Frankenstein* (1818), 1:100.
72 Shelley, *Frankenstein* (1818), 1:101.
73 Shelley, *Frankenstein* (1818), 2:106.
74 Robert Douglas, *Adventures of a Medical Student* (New York: Burgess, Stringer, 1848), 47.
75 In *Diary of a Resurrectionist*, Bailey comments on this convention, saying, "Writers of fiction have made use of body-snatching, and have given a gruesome turn to their stories by making the body, when uncovered, turn out to be that of a relation or friend of some one of the party engaged in the exhumation": Bailey, *The Diary of a Resurrectionist*, 16.
76 "Automaton Extraordinary," *Scientific American* 48, no. 3 (March 25, 1848): 272.
77 "Automaton Extraordinary," 272.
78 Joel Tiffany, *Lectures on Spiritualism: Being a Series of Lectures on the Phenomena and Philosophy of Development, Individualism, Spirit, Immortality, Mesmerism, Clairvoyance, Spiritual Manifestations, Christianity, and Progress, Delivered at Prospect Street Church, in the City of Cleveland, during the Winter and Spring of 1851* (Cleveland, OH: J. Tiffany, 1851), 171.
79 George Bush, *Anastasis: or, The Doctrine of the Resurrection of the Body, Rationally and Scripturally Considered* (New York: Wiley and Putnam, 1845), 73.
80 Bush, *Anastasis*, 73–74.
81 Antoine Wiertz, "Thoughts and Visions of a Severed Head" (1870), in Walter Benjamin, *The Work of Art in the Age of Its Technological Reproducibility, and Other Writings on Media* (Cambridge, MA: Harvard University Press, 2008), 249–51.
82 Charles Desmaze, *Histoire de la médecine légale en France: D'après les lois, registres et arrêts criminels* (Paris: Charpentier, 1880), 206.
83 Isaac Baker Brown, *On the Curability of Certain Forms of Insanity, Epilepsy, Catalepsy, and Hysteria in Females* (London: Robert Hardwicke, 1866), 48.

84 "Remarkable Instance of the Failure of Volition," *Connecticut Magazine; or, Gentleman's and Lady's Monthly Museum of Knowledge*, March 1801, 153.

85 "Singular Case of Catalepsy," *Chicago Tribune*, January 27, 1869, 1.

86 "Joliet's Cataleptic Lunatic," *Chicago Daily Tribune*, September 10, 1887, 3. Mrs. Herbert's case is further elaborated in "Asleep Seven Months," *New York Times*, August 17, 1887, 5.

87 "Goes to a Ball while Hypnotized," *Chicago Daily Tribune*, August 17, 1895, 9; "Ichangier Cola's Disease," *New York Times*, July 20, 1898, 7; "A Remarkable Case of Catalepsy in an Indiana Town," *New York Times*, April 5, 1875, 2; "To Sleep the Winter Out," *New York Times*, December 11, 1896, 1.

88 "A Child Born in a Grave," *New York Times*, January 3, 1878, 2.

89 Franz Hartmann, *Buried Alive: An Examination into the Occult Causes of Apparent Death, Trance, and Catalepsy* (Boston: Occult, 1895), 63.

90 Both vampires and zombies have been attributed to superstitions surrounding catalepsy. Noting "there are no vampires save in countries where the dead are buried," Henry Steel Olcott advanced the theory that vampires were "half-dead" cataleptics who preyed on the living either bodily or through astral projection: Henry Steel Olcott, *The Vampire* (Wheaton, IL: Theosophical, 1920).

91 Jan Bondeson, *Buried Alive: The Terrifying History of Our Most Primal Fear* (New York: W. W. Norton, 2001), 53; Jacques-Bénigne Winslow and Jacques-Jean Bruhier, *The Uncertainty of the Signs of Death, and the Danger of Precipitate Interments and Dissections, Demonstrated* (Dublin: George Faulkner, 1746).

92 In his travel guide for Europe, William Pembroke Fetridge included one such facility as a worthy tourist site: see William Pembroke Fetridge, "Germany," in *Harper's Hand-book for Travellers in Europe and the East* (New York: Harper and Brothers, 1871), 342.

93 Lever's tale was undoubtedly inspired by purportedly real examples of premature burials narrowly avoided, as in an notice from 1801 given the rather understated title "A Remarkable Instance of the Failure of Volition," *Lady's Monthly Museum; or Polite Repository of Amusement and Instruction*, vol. 5, 1801, 149; "The Buried Alive," *Ladies' Literary Cabinet*, January 12, 1822, 76; "Early Burials," *New York Mirror*, January 15, 1825, 2, 25.

94 Charles Lever, "Post-Mortem Recollections of a Medical Lecturer," *Dublin University Magazine*, June 1836, 625.

95 Michael La Beaume, *Remarks on the History and Philosophy but Particularly the Medical Efficacy of Electricity* (London: F. Warr, 1820), 102.

96 Esquirol, "Monomania," *Mental Maladies: A Treatise on Insanity* (Philadelphia: Lea and Blanchard, 1845), 320–76.

97 See Leonard Keene Hirshberg, "Why Insanity Specialists Often Become Insane," *Washington Post*, December 24, 1916, MT5.

98 Lever, "Post-Mortem Recollections of a Medical Lecturer," 627.

99 Samuel Warren, *Passages from the Diary of a Late Physician* (Edinburgh: W. Blackwood and Sons, 1864), 297.

100 Moriz Rosenthal, Jean Martin Charcot, and Leopold Putzel, *A Clinical Treatise on the Diseases of the Nervous System*, trans. Leopold Putzel (New York: William Wood, 1879), 326.
101 Edgar Allan Poe, "The Psyche Zenobia (How to Write a Blackwood Article)," in *Tales of the Grotesque and Arabesque* (Philadelphia: Lea & Blanchard, 1840), 213–28.
102 Edgar Allan Poe, "The Scythe of Time (A Predicament)," in *Tales of the Grotesque and Arabesque* (Philadelphia: Lea & Blanchard, 1840), 229–42.
103 Poe, "A Predicament."
104 Edgar Allen Poe, "The Premature Burial," *Dollar Newspaper*, July 31, 1844.
105 Francis Wharton, Moreton Stillé, Frank Hunter Bowlby, James Hendrie Lloyd, Robert Amory, Robert Leonard Emerson, and Truman Abbe, *Wharton and Stillé's Medical Jurisprudence*, vol. 1 (Rochester, NY: Lawyer's Co-operative, 1905).
106 "The Proposed Premature Burial Act," *American Lawyer*, vol. 6, October 1898, 10.
107 "Concerning Premature Burial," *Harper's Bazaar*, vol. 33, August 18, 1900, 1027.
108 "You Cannot Be Buried Alive," *New York Times*, July 24, 1898, SM10.
109 "Will Be Buried Alive," *Chicago Tribune*, February 17, 1889, 25.
110 Franz Mesmer, "On the Discovery of Animal Magnetism," in Franz Mesmer, *Mesmerism: A Translation of the Original Scientific and Medical Writings of F. A. Mesmer*, trans. George J. Bloch (Los Altos, CA: William Kaufmann, 1980), 51.
111 Nicolas Bergasse, *Le magnetisme animal, ou sur la théorie du monde et des êtres organisés* (Paris: La Haye, 1784), 103.
112 Jean Sylvain Bailley and Benjamin Franklin, *De l'examen du magnétisme animal* (Geneva: Slatkine, [1784] 1980).
113 "Dissertation by F. A. Mesmer, Doctor of Medicine, on His Discoveries," in Franz Mesmer, *Mesmerism*, 121.
114 Francis Sitwell, *Mesmerism Considered; in Connexion with Personal Responsibility* (Glasgow: William MacKenzie, 1852), 11.
115 Timothy Shay Arthur, *Agnes; or, The Possessed: A Revelation of Mesmerism* (Philadelphia: T. B. Peterson, 1848), 2.
116 Caen Duvard, "Case of Catalepsy with Transposition of the Senses," *Medical Examiner* 1, no. 13 (August 27, 1842): 559.
117 Wendy Moore, *The Mesmerist: The Society Doctor Who Held Victorian London Spellbound* (London: Orion, 2016).
118 Anonymous, *A Full Discovery of the Strange Practices of Dr. Elliotson on the Bodies of His Female Patients!* (London: E. Hancock, 1842); Thomas Wakley (pseud.), *Undeniable Facts Concerning the Strange Practices of Dr. Elliotson, . . . with His Female Patients; and His Medical Experiments upon the Bodies of . . . E. and J. Okey, etc.* (London: 1842).
119 Pierre Toutain-Dorbec, *The Power of Mesmerism* [1892] (New York: Grove Press, 1969).

120 Robert Darnton, *Mesmerism and the End of the Enlightenment in France* (Cambridge, MA: Harvard University Press, 1968), 83.
121 Ann Braude, *Radical Spirits: Spiritualism and Women's Rights in Nineteenth-Century America* (Bloomington: Indiana University Press, 2001); Alex Owen, *The Darkened Room: Women, Power, and Spiritualism in Late Victorian England* (Chicago: University of Chicago Press, 2004).
122 Sheriden Le Fanu, "Green Tea," in *In a Glass Darkly* (London: Richard Bentley and Son, 1886), 16.
123 Le Fanu, "Green Tea," 41.
124 Le Fanu, "Green Tea," 42.
125 For Lovecraft's own account of "cosmic horror," see Howard Phillips Lovecraft, *Supernatural Horror in Literature* (New York: Dover, [1927] 1973). For a larger overview, see Brian Stableford, "The Cosmic Horror," in *Icons of Horror and the Supernatural: An Encyclopedia of Our Worst Nightmares*, vol. 2, ed. S. T. Joshi (Westport, CT: Greenwood, 2006), 65–96.
126 Le Fanu, "Green Tea," 50.
127 Le Fanu, "Green Tea," 53.
128 Le Fanu's choice of green tea as the putative catalyst for Jennings's downfall was not entirely random. Joshua Burgess's tract on madness in relation to "vegetative vital force" warned against the use of green tea and other "diluent and enervating fluids," while Le Fanu himself is said to have been inspired by the then recent case of nuns at a Canadian convent said to have been driven mad by excessive consumption of green tea: see Joshua Burgess, *The Medical and Legal Relations of Madness* (London: Churchill, 1858), 61; see also Edward Percival, *Account of a Petechial Febricula; Some Brief Notices of the Deleterious and Medicinal Effects of Green Tea; a Case of Dropsy* (Dublin: Hodges and M'Arthur, 1817).
129 Edward Page Mitchell, "The Professor's Experiment" (1880), in *The Crystal Man: Landmark Science-Fiction* (New York: Doubleday, 1973), 142.
130 For a history of the SPR, see Janet Oppenheim, *The Other World: Spiritualism and Psychical Research in England, 1850–1914* (Cambridge: Cambridge University Press, 1988).
131 William Fletcher Barrett, "On Some Phenomena Associated with Abnormal Conditions of Mind," *Proceedings of the Society for Psychical Research* 1 (1882): 244.
132 Frank Podmore, *Apparitions and Thought Transference* (London: Charles Scribner's Sons, 1898).
133 Podmore was responding here to the psychic phenomenon of seeing or dreaming about an absent individual, only to learn shortly thereafter that the person had passed away at almost the exact moment of the vision or dream. This thesis was also advocated by Bernard Hollander in the early twentieth century: see "How to See Ghosts: Scientist Says Specters Are Living Thoughts Projected into Space by the Personality at the Death Moment," *Chicago Daily Tribune*, June 2, 1907, F7. Ambrose Bierce used this premise in his short ghost story

"A Wireless Message" (1905) and in "You *May* Telephone from Here" (1909), both in Ambrose Bierce, *The Complete Short Stories of Ambrose Bierce* (Lincoln: University of Nebraska Press, 1984).

134 For a history of spirit photography's emergence after the Civil War, see Louis Kaplan, *The Strange Case of William Mumler, Spirit Photographer* (Minneapolis: University of Minnesota Press, 2008).

135 Tom Gunning, "Phantom Images and Modern Manifestations: Spirit Photography, Magic Theater, Trick Films, and Photography's Uncanny," in *Fugitive Images: From Photography to Video*, ed. Patrice Petro (Bloomington: Indiana University Press, 1995), 58. In Paris, Hippolyte Ferdinand Baraduc claimed to have "photographed" thought and emotion on special plates, including a "nebulous globe" that exited his wife shortly after her death: Hippolyte Ferdinand Baraduc, *Iconographie de la force vitale cosmique od: Extrait de l'âme humaine, ses mouvements, ses lumières* (Paris: Paul Ollendorff, 1897).

136 The mechanism here is much like astral projection, the occultist model for magically thinking that a spiritual essence might temporarily exit the body. Such experiences frequently invoke a type of umbilicus linking the drifting spirit body back to its unconscious material host. One astral projector recalls seeing "a small cord, like a spider's web, running from my shoulders back to my body and attaching to it at the base of the front of the neck. I was satisfied with the conclusion that by means of that cord I was using the eyes of my body, and, turning, walked down the street." The full testimony is in Frederic Myers, *Human Personality and Its Survival of Bodily Death*, vol. 2. (New York: Longmans, Green, 1904), 317–19.

137 William Jackson Crawford, *Reality of Psychic Phenomena*. (New York: E. P. Dutton, 1918), 242–43.

138 Douglas MacDougall, "Hypothesis Concerning Soul Substance Together with Experimental Evidence of the Existence of Such Substance," *Journal of the American Society for Psychical Research* 1, no. 5 (May 1907): 237–44.

139 See Josiah Stickney Lombard, *Experimental Researches on the Regional Temperature of the Head: Under Conditions of Rest, Intellectual Activity, and Emotion* (London: H. K. Lewis, 1879). A study from the same era equated increased mental activity with the composition of the urine, and in particular the presence of alkaline phosphates: see H. Byasson, *Essai sur la relation qui existe a l'etat physiologique entre l'activites cerebrale et la composition des urines* (Paris: Germer Baillière, 1868).

140 Angelo Musso, *Application de la balance à l'étude de la circulation du sang chez l'homme* (Turin: Hermann Loescher, 1884). See also Stefano Sandrone, Marco Bacigaluppi, Marco R. Galloni, Stefano F. Cappa, Andrea Moro, Marco Catani, Massimo Filippi, Martin M. Monti, Daniela Perani, and Gianvito Martino, "Weighing Brain Activity with the Balance: Angelo Mosso's Original Manuscripts Come to Light," *Brain* 37, no. 2 (2013): 621–33.

141 Elliot S. Valenstein, *The War of the Soups and the Sparks: The Discovery of Neurotransmitters and the Dispute over How Nerves Communicate* (New York: Columbia University Press, 2005).

142 See Richard Rapport, *Nerve Endings: The Discovery of the Synapse* (New York: W. W. Norton, 2005). As early as 1874, meanwhile, Edward Tylor Richardson had proposed a "theory of nervous ether" to explain the capacity of nervous tissue to respond to the stimuli of pressure, hypothesizing that the transmission of nervous impulses was not a conductive function of "electrical fluid" but, rather, an inductive function of this internal ether thought to suffuse the spaces between all nerve molecules: Edward Tylor Richardson, "Theory of the Nervous Ether," *Recreations in Popular Science* (Boston: Estes and Lauriat, 1874): 362–74.

143 Oliver Lodge, *Ether and Reality* (London: Hodder and Stoughton, 1925), 173. For a more complete account of the ether in cultural history, see Joe Milutis, *Ether: The Nothing That Connects Everything* (Minneapolis: University of Minnesota Press, 2006).

144 Daniel Paul Schreber, *Memoirs of My Nervous Illness* (New York: NYRB Classics, 2000), 19.

145 Schreber, *Memoirs of My Nervous Illness*, 20.

146 Schreber, *Memoirs of My Nervous Illness*, 21.

147 Schreber, *Memoirs of My Nervous Illness*, 24.

148 Eric Santner explores the Lacanian implications of Schreber's promotion as a psychotic trigger: Eric Santner, *My Own Private Germany: Daniel Paul Schreber's Secret History of Modernity* (Princeton, NJ: Princeton University Press, 1997).

149 Schreber, *Memoirs of My Nervous Illness*, 33.

150 Schreber, *Memoirs of My Nervous Illness*, 66.

151 Schreber, *Memoirs of My Nervous Illness*, 40.

152 Anticipating resistance from his readers, Schreber observes, "Religiously minded people who are filled with the concept of God's omnipotence, omniscience and loving kindness must find it incomprehensible that God should here be depicted as so lowly a Being that He can be surpassed both morally and mentally by one single human being. However, I must emphasize that my superiority in both respects is to be understood *in the most relative sense*": Schreber, *Memoirs of My Nervous Illness*, 173. In other words, Schreber understands the crisis facing the order of the universe, even as God does not, but only because of his singular and extraordinary entanglement with God's nerve rays.

153 Schreber, *Memoirs of My Nervous Illness*, 116.

154 Schreber, *Memoirs of My Nervous Illness*, 147–48.

155 Schreber, *Memoirs of My Nervous Illness*, 118.

156 Schreber, *Memoirs of My Nervous Illness*, 147.

157 Schreber, *Memoirs of My Nervous Illness*, 146.

158 Schreber, *Memoirs of My Nervous Illness*, 296–99.
159 Schreber, *Memoirs of My Nervous Illness*, 59.
160 Schreber, *Memoirs of My Nervous Illness*, 46.
161 Schreber, *Memoirs of My Nervous Illness*, 245.
162 Schreber, *Memoirs of My Nervous Illness*, 164.
163 Schreber, *Memoirs of My Nervous Illness*, 164.
164 Schreber, *Memoirs of My Nervous Illness*, 121.
165 Schreber, *Memoirs of My Nervous Illness*, 122.
166 Schreber, *Memoirs of My Nervous Illness*, 178.
167 Schreber, *Memoirs of My Nervous Illness*, 123.
168 Schreber, *Memoirs of My Nervous Illness*, 147.
169 Ole Frahm discusses Schreber's rather uncanny anticipation of radio in "Radio und Schizophrenie: Anmerkungen zu Daniel Paul Schrebers Radiotheorie avant la letter," *Kultur und Gespenster* 14 (Autumn 2013): 198–229.
170 *Memoirs of My Nervous Illness* was originally published as *Denkwürdigkeiten eines Nervenkranken* (Leipzig: Oswald Mutze, 1903).
171 Sigmund Freud, "Psychoanalytic Notes upon an Autobiographical Account of a Case of Paranoia" (1911), in *The Standard Edition of the Complete Psychological Works of Sigmund Freud*, 24 vols., ed. James Strachey, (London: Hogarth, 1958), 12:9–82.
172 Schreber's case file has passed from Freud to Jacques Lacan, Gilles Deleuze, Félix Guattari, Michel de Certeau, Michel Foucault, Elias Canetti, and Friedrich Kittler, to name only a few luminaries of twentieth-century thought. Schreber has also been central to many histories of psychiatry and modernity. Notable contributions include Zvi Lothane, *In Defense of Schreber: Soul Murder and Psychiatry* (Hillsdale, NJ: Analytic, 1992); Santner, *My Own Private Germany*; Morton Schatzman, *Soul Murder: Persecution in the Family* (New York: Random House, 1973).
173 This thesis becomes a logical proof: "I (a man) love him"; "I do not love him; I hate him"; "I do not love him—I hate him because HE PERSECUTES ME": see Freud, "Psychoanalytic Notes upon an Autobiographical Account of a Case of Paranoia," 12:63.
174 Two of the best-known titles in this genre are by the psychoanalyst-turned-hypnotherapist François Roustang. In *Un destin si funeste* (1976), Roustang considers the relationship between Freud and his disciples, emphasizing how the fundamentally "asocial" aspects of transference (and thus psychoanalysis) led to the many notorious conflicts between Freud the mentor and his various students. *Un destin si funeste* appeared in English translation as François Roustang, *Dire Mastery*, trans. Ned Lukacher (Baltimore: Johns Hopkins University Press, 1982). This critique continued in François Roustang, *Psychoanalysis Never Lets Go*, trans. Ned Luckacher (Baltimore: Johns Hopkins University Press, [1980] 1983). Here Roustang examines the relationship among transference,

hypnosis, and telepathy in Freud's work, centering on Freud's anxiety over the role of "suggestion" in all three phenomena.

175 John Farrell aligns Freud with a paranoid streak found in many of modernity's leading intellectuals. Farrell argues that "Freud's personal paranoia combined with the resources of suspicion dominant in modernity to produce the superbly persuasive intellectual and rhetorical structure that is psychoanalysis": John Farrell, *Freud's Paranoid Quest: Psychoanalysis and Modern Suspicion* (New York: New York University Press, 1996), 4. Psychoanalysis, in other words, is an inherently paranoid discourse. In Farrell's reading, the paranoid Judge Schreber was thus a "supreme rhetorical ally" for Freud. "His condition displays the cunning involvement of reason in madness: the judge's juridical aplomb, his theological fertility, his casuistical brilliance, and his powers of psychological observation, all of these are humorous triumphs for the Freudian method and reflective of its own qualities": Farrell, *Freud's Paranoid Quest*, 194.

176 Freud, "Psychoanalytic Notes upon an Autobiographical Account of a Case of Paranoia," 79.

177 Friedrich A. Kittler, *Discourse Networks 1800/1900*, trans. Michael Metteer (Stanford, CA: Stanford University Press, 1992), 294.

178 Oliver Lodge, *Life and Matter* (London: Williams and Norgate, 1906), 97.

179 Kittler, *Discourse Networks 1800/1900*, 299.

180 Freud announces the aim of the project by writing, "The intention of this project is to furnish us with a psychology which shall be a natural science: its aim, that is, is to represent psychical processes as quantitatively determined states of specifiable material particles and so to make them plain and void of contradictions. The project involves two principal ideas: 1. That what distinguishes activity from rest is to be regarded as a quantity (Q) subject to the general laws of motion. 2. That it is to be assumed that the material particles in question are the neurones": Sigmund Freud, "Project for a Scientific Psychology" (1895), in *The Standard Edition of the Complete Psychological Works of Sigmund Freud*, 1:283.

181 Sigmund Freud, "Letter to Wilhelm Fliess (May 25, 1895)," in *The Complete Letters of Sigmund Freud to Wilhelm Fliess, 1887–1904*, ed. Jeffrey M. Masson (Cambridge, MA: Harvard University Press, 1985), 1:129.

182 Kittler, *Discourse Networks 1800/1900*, 293.

183 Freud's most extended discussion of "magical thinking" can be found in "Totem and Taboo" (1913), in *The Standard Edition of the Complete Psychological Works of Sigmund Freud*, 13:1–162.

184 Pamela Thurschwell, *Literature, Technology and Magical Thinking, 1880–1920* (Cambridge: Cambridge University Press, 2001).

185 For a more detailed discussion of Ferenczi and telepathy, see Thurschwell, *Literature, Technology and Magical Thinking*, 115–50.

186 Ernest Jones, "Letter to Sigmund Freud (March 17, 1911)," in Freud and Jones, *The Complete Correspondence of Sigmund Freud and Ernest Jones*, 97.

187 These claims are central to Paul Roazen's *Brother Animal*, a history of the "inner circle" focusing on the escalating tension between Freud and Tausk. Based in large part on the journal of their mutual confidant, Lou Andres-Salome, Roazen portrays Freud as unnerved by Tausk, whom he believed "could take an idea of Freud's and develop it before Freud himself had quite finished with it": Paul Roazen, *Brother Animal: The Story of Freud and Tausk* (New York: Alfred A. Knopf, 1969), 78. Freud lamented that Tausk's uncanny ability to anticipate his thought forced him to engage in "premature discussion" of developing concepts. Tausk committed suicide on July 3, 1919, a tragedy that Roazen implies stemmed in no small part from Freud's continuing hostility toward him. Afterward, Freud confided to Helene Deutsch that he would "not miss" Tausk, as Tausk had always left him with an "uncanny impression": Roazen, *Brother Animal*, 170. See also Sigmund Freud, "Victor Tausk" (1919), in *The Standard Edition of the Complete Psychological Works of Sigmund Freud*, 17:273–76.

This portrait of Freud as a paranoid sadist did not sit well with other Freudians. In a testament to the rising stakes of biographical melodrama in psychoanalysis, Kurt R. Eissler, analyst and director of the Freud Archives in New York City, wrote not one but two books refuting Roazen's claims: see Kurt Eissler, *Talent and Genius: The Fictitious Case of Tausk contra Freud* (New York: Quadrangle, 1971); Kurt Eissler, *Victor Tausk's Suicide* (New York: International Universities Press, 1983). Roustang examines the struggle between Eissler and Roazen (over Tausk and Freud) in *Dire Mastery*, 76–106.

188 Sigmund Freud, "Psychoanalysis and Telepathy" (1921), in *The Standard Edition of the Complete Psychological Works of Sigmund Freud*, 19:177.

189 Sigmund Freud, "Dreams and Telepathy" (1922), in *The Standard Edition of the Complete Psychological Works of Sigmund Freud*, 18:195–220.

190 Sigmund Freud, "The Occult Significance of Dreams" (1925), in *The Standard Edition of the Complete Psychological Works of Sigmund Freud*, 19:135–40.

191 Sigmund Freud, "Letter to Ernest Jones (March 7, 1926), in Sigmund Freud and Ernest Jones, *The Complete Correspondence of Sigmund Freud and Ernest Jones, 1908–1939*, ed. R. Andrew Paskauskas (Cambridge, MA: Harvard University Press, 1993), 597.

192 Freud discusses "omnipotence of thought" and "magical thinking" at length in "Totem and Taboo."

193 Freud, "The Occult Significance of Dreams," 135–41. He repeats this claim in "Dreams and Occultism" (1933), In *The Standard Edition of the Complete Psychological Works of Sigmund Freud*, 22:31–56.

194 Freud, "The Occult Significance of Dreams."

195 Helene Deutsch, "Occult Processes Occurring during Psychoanalysis," *Imago* 12 (1926): 418–33. Other work on this topic includes H. J. Ehrenweld, "Telepathy in the Psychoanalytic Situation," *British Journal of Medical Psychology* 20 (1944): 51–62; Nandor Fodor, "Telepathy in Analysis," *Psychiatric Quarterly* 21 (1947):

171–89; Fanny Hann-Kende, "On the Role of Transference and Counter-Transference in Psychoanalysis," *Internationale Zeitschrift für Psychoanalyse* 22 (1936): 478–86; Geraldine Pederson-Krag, "Telepathy and Repression," *Psychoanalytic Quarterly* 16 (1947): 61–68; M. L. Peerbolte, "Psychoanalysis and Parapsychology," *Internationale Zeitschrift für Psychoanalyse* 26, no.1 (1941): 93–94; L. J. Saul, "Telepathic Sensitiveness as a Neurotic Symptom," *Psychoanalytic Quarterly* 7 (1938): 329–35.

196 John Forrester, *The Seductions of Psychoanalysis: Freud, Lacan, and Derrida* (Cambridge: Cambridge University Press, 1992), 251.

197 George Devereux, "A Summary of Istvan Hollos' Theories," in *Psychoanalysis and the Occult*, ed. George Devereux (New York: International Universities Press, 1953), 200.

198 Devereux, "A Summary of Istvan Hollos' Theories," 201.

199 Sigmund Freud, "On Narcissism: An Introduction" (1914), in *The Standard Edition of the Complete Psychological Works of Sigmund Freud*, 14:81–105.

200 Géza Róheim, *Magic and Schizophrenia* (New York: International Universities Press, 1955), 82–83.

201 Róheim, *Magic and Schizophrenia*, 95.

202 This patient's confabulation of radium, rays, and vision aligns him with the occultists Adorno so excoriated for their continuing investment in technomysticism. "Occultists rightly feel drawn towards childishly monstrous scientific fantasies," Adorno writes. "The confusion they sow between their emanations and the isotopes of uranium is ultimate clarity. The mystical rays are modest anticipations of technical ones": Theodor W. Adorno, *Minima Moralia* (London: Verso, [1951] 2005), 238–41. Adorno also endorsed a theory of regression, opening his essay with the words, "The tendency to occultism is a symptom of regression in consciousness."

203 Róheim, *Magic and Schizophrenia*, 95.

204 William Merriam Rouse, "The Dead Man's Thoughts," *Munsey's Magazine*, June 1921, 642–43.

205 Rouse, "The Dead Man's Thoughts," 649.

206 It is worth noting just how skeptical, even playful, Freud himself was in conjuring this realm at the occult border of known psychoanalytic theory. "What follows is speculation, often far-fetched speculation, which the reader will consider or dismiss according to his individual predilection," he writes. "It is further an attempt to follow out an idea consistently, out of curiosity to see where it will lead": Sigmund Freud, "Beyond the Pleasure Principle" (1920), in *The Standard Edition of the Complete Psychological Works of Sigmund Freud*, 18:7–64.

207 Freud, "Beyond the Pleasure Principle," 18:20.

208 Freud, "Beyond the Pleasure Principle," 18:20.

209 Freud, "Beyond the Pleasure Principle," 18:21.

210 Freud, "Beyond the Pleasure Principle," 18:21.
211 Marshall McLuhan, *Understanding Media: The Extensions of Man* (Boston: MIT Press, 1994), 43.
212 Schreber, *Memoirs of My Nervous Illness*, 277.
213 Sigmund Freud, "Recommendations to Physicians Practising Psycho-analysis" (1912), in *The Standard Edition of the Complete Psychological Works of Sigmund Freud*, 12:111–20.
214 Freud, "Recommendations to Physicians Practising Psycho-analysis," 12:115–16.
215 Michael Eigen, *The Psychotic Core* (Landham, MD: Jason Aronson, 1993), 330.

Chapter 4. The System

1 Renee Sechehaye and Marguerite Sechehaye, *Autobiography of a Schizophrenic Girl: Reality Lost and Gained, with Analytic Interpretation* (New York: Grune and Stratton, 1951), 59.
2 Sechehaye and Sechehaye, *Autobiography of a Schizophrenic Girl*, 59.
3 Sechehaye and Sechehaye, *Autobiography of a Schizophrenic Girl*, 6.
4 Sechehaye and Sechehaye, *Autobiography of a Schizophrenic Girl*, 33.
5 Sechehaye and Sechehaye, *Autobiography of a Schizophrenic Girl*, 35.
6 Sechehaye and Sechehaye, *Autobiography of a Schizophrenic Girl*, 35.
7 Michel Foucault, *The History of Sexuality* (New York: Pantheon, 1978), 139.
8 Foucault, *The History of Sexuality*, 139.
9 Sechehaye and Sechehaye, *Autobiography of a Schizophrenic Girl*, 35.
10 Thomas Percival's *Medical Ethics, or a Code of Institutes and Precepts, Adapted to the Professional Conduct of Physicians and Surgeons* (Manchester: S. Russell, 1803).
11 Michel Foucault, *Psychiatric Power: Lectures at the Collège de France, 1973–1974*, vol. 1 (New York: Macmillan, 2008), 20. Foucault's account is based on Pinel's discussion of the case.
12 Foucault, *Psychiatric Power*, 20.
13 Foucault, *Psychiatric Power*, 147.
14 Charles Caldwell, *Facts in Mesmerism, and Thoughts on Its Causes and Uses* (Louisville, KY: Prentice and Weissinger, 1842), 17.
15 Esquirol quoted in James Copeland, *A Dictionary of Practical Medicine* (London: Longman, Green, Brown, Longmans, and Roberts, 1858), 445.
16 "Jonathan Kentucky's Journal, no. VI," *New Monthly Magazine and Literary Journal*, vol. 2, no. 11, 1821, 560.
17 James Cowles Prichard, *A Treatise on Insanity and Other Disorders Affecting the Mind* (London: Sherwood, Gilbert, and Piper, 1835), 32.
18 "Electricity Was Her Nemesis," *Atlanta Constitution*, November 11, 1897, 7. Psychiatric studies in the 1950s, meanwhile, expressed some surprise that many

patients remained highly suspicious of, and even paranoid about, electroconvulsive therapy (ECT), even after the physician had patiently explained that jolting the nervous system with massive levels of electricity would be in the patient's best interest: Alfred Gallinek, "Fear and Anxiety in the Course of Electroshock Therapy," *American Journal of Psychiatry* 113, no. 5 (November, 1956): 428–34. A study from 1986 reported that many ECT candidates had "been put off by the film *One Flew over the Cuckoo's Nest*": C. P. L. Freeman and K. E. Cheshire, "Attitude Studies on Electroconvulsive Therapy," *Journal of ECT* 2, no. 1 (1986): 31–42.

19 William Belcher, *Address to Humanity: Containing, A Letter to Dr. Thomas Monro; a Receipt to Make a Lunatic, and Seize His Estate; and a Sketch of a True Smiling Hyena* (London: Allen and West, 1796), 9.

20 Belcher, *Address to Humanity*, 5.

21 "Insanity," *Atkinson's Casket* 9, no. 4 (April 1834): 154.

22 William Griggs, *Lunacy versus Liberty: A Letter on the Defective State of the Law, as Regards Insane Persons, and Private Asylums* (London: W. Griggs, 1832), 7.

23 "The Commissioners of Lunacy," *The Observer*, August 27, 1849, 3.

24 "The Commissioners of Lunacy," 3.

25 "The Commissioners of Lunacy," 3.

26 The case of James Tilly Matthews has attracted the attention of several historians and at least one novelist: see Greg Hollingshead, *Bedlam: A Novel of Love and Madness* (New York: Thomas Dunne, 2006). The summation of Matthews's activities before his institutionalization that follows comes from Mike Jay, *The Air Loom Gang: The Strange and True Story of James Tilly Matthews and His Visionary Madness* (New York: Four Walls Eight Windows, 2004).

27 Jay, *The Air Loom Gang*, 62.

28 John Haslam, *Illustrations of Madness: Exhibiting a Singular Case of Insanity and a No Less Remarkable Difference in Medical Opinion: Developing the Nature of Assailment, and the Manner of Working Events; with a Description of the Tortures Experienced by Bomb-Bursting, Lobster-Cracking, and Lengthening the Brain* (London: G. Hayden, 1810).

29 Haslam, *Illustrations of Madness*, 19.

30 Haslam, *Illustrations of Madness*, 31, 33, 43.

31 Haslam, *Illustrations of Madness*, 31.

32 Haslam, *Illustrations of Madness*, 39.

33 Haslam, *Illustrations of Madness*, 34.

34 Haslam, *Illustrations of Madness*, lxvii.

35 Nellie Bly, *Ten Days in a Mad-House* (New York: Ian L. Munro, 1887).

36 Edgar Allan Poe, "The System of Doctor Tarr and Professor Fether," *Graham's Magazine* 27, no. 5 (November, 1845): 193.

37 One frequently reported and no doubt apocryphal incident speaks to the Victorian public's delight in seeing psychiatry's growing and dubious disciplinary power mocked and countermanded. A lunatic is placed under escort for a trip to the asylum, told only that he is to take a brief excursion for pleasure in the

countryside. After they arrive in the city of the asylum late one evening, the lunatic's escort decides they should spend the night at an inn and proceed with the actual institutionalization in the morning. Waking early while his escort is still asleep, the lunatic discovers the magistrate's orders for his confinement in the escort's pocket. Showing "that cunning which madmen not unfrequently display," the lunatic proceeds ahead to the asylum and informs its director he will be bringing a new charge later that day. "He's a very queer fellow, and has got very odd ways," says the lunatic. "For instance, I should not wonder if he was to say I was the madman and that he was bringing me; but you must not believe him, and not believe a word he says." Obtaining the director's consent, the lunatic returns to the inn, where his escort is still asleep. Later that day, the scheme comes to its inevitable conclusion: the escort, against all protestation, has his head shaved and is put in a straitjacket while the lunatic is free (at least temporarily) to go on his way. The first reference to this story is "A Lunatic's Cunning," in *The Flowers of Anecdote, Wit, Humor, Gaiety, and Genius* (London: Charles Tilt, 1829), 147. Reprinted many times, this same account appeared, more or less verbatim, as an example of legal precedent in Francis Wharton and Moreton Stillé, *Medical Jurisprudence* (Philadelphia: Kay and Brother, 1855), 94.

38 George Cheyne, *The English Malady* (London: G. Strahan, 1733), 4–5.
39 Cheyne, *The English Malady*, i.
40 Cheyne, *The English Malady*, 54.
41 Describing the impact of hot, dry air on the body, for example, Cheyne argued that such conditions render the nerves "too crisp, over elastick, and brittle, and so forces on the Circulation, and sends about the Juices with too great Force, Rapidity, and Violence, instead of that calm and uniform manner, in 'which the Functions, and Secretions of the animal Economy, are naturally perform'd, and that due Balance, which ought, naturally to be between the Solids and Fluids": Cheyne, *The English Malady*, 10.
42 Thomas Trotter, *A View of the Nervous Temperament: Being a Practical Inquiry into the Increasing Prevalence, Prevention, and Treatment of those Diseases Commonly Called Nervous, Bilious, Stomach and Liver Complaints, Indigestion, Low Spirits, Gout, &c.* (London: Longman, Hurst, Rees, and Orme, 1807).
43 Trotter, *A View of the Nervous Temperament*, 145.
44 Trotter, *A View of the Nervous Temperament*, 44. In nominating city life as the great cause of nervous disorder, Trotter attempts to match pathology with type, outlining the unique nervous complaints attending the characteristic occupants of the city: "1. Literary men. 2. Men of business. 3. The idle and dissipated. 4. The artificer and manufacturer. 5. Those employed in drudgery. 6. Persons returned from the colonies." The seventh category is reserved for "the female sex; consisting of the higher, middling, and lower orders of women": Trotter, *A View of the Nervous Temperament*, 37.
45 Michel Foucault, *History of Madness* (London: Routledge, 2013), 295.
46 Foucault, *History of Madness*, 295.

47 Trotter, *A View of the Nervous Temperament*, 221.
48 Trotter, *A View of the Nervous Temperament*, xi. Offering a more optimistic thesis was Robert Verity, *Changes Produced in the Nervous System by Civilization* (London: Highley, 1837). In an airtight tautology, Verity proposed that English civilization excelled because of England's superior nervous constitution, while England's superior nervous constitution was a product of the superiority of English civilization. Rather than produce decadence and enervation, England's ascendency as the premiere global power suggested a feedback loop of nerve and civilization in which each amplified the other toward eventual perfection (or, at the very least, continued dominance).
49 Iwan Rhys Morus, "The Nervous System of Britain: Space, Time and the Electric Telegraph in the Victorian Age," *British Journal of the History of Science* 33, no. 4 (2000): 470.
50 George Wilson, *The Progress of the Telegraph: Lecture* (Cambridge: Macmillan, 1859), 24.
51 "The Human Brain; An Instructive Lecture by Dr. Van Slyck," *Los Angeles Times*, February 8, 1890, 7.
52 As James Carey writes, the telegraph became not simply an instrument for communication, but also a concept for thinking about communications: see James W. Carey, "Technology and Ideology: The Case of the Telegraph," *Prospects* 8 (1983): 303–25.
53 Benedict Anderson, *Imagined Communities: Reflections on the Origin and Spread of Nationalism* (London: Verso, 2006).
54 As Anderson writes, "The idea of a sociological organism moving calendrically through homogenous, empty time is a precise analogue of the idea of the nation, which is also conceived as a solid community moving steadily down (or up) history": Anderson, *Imagined Communities*, 26.
55 Anderson, *Imagined Communities*, 7.
56 Anderson, *Imagined Communities*, 32–36. Even before the telegraph arrived to accelerate the gathering and distribution of the news, the press sought new technologies that could compress the space and time of their reporting and thus bring the "news" and its public closer to an asymtopic simultaneity. In 1846, accordingly, five newspapers in New York City joined forces to create the Associated Press, financing a "Pony Express" route that could deliver updates on the Mexican War in advance of the US Post Office.
57 "The Nerves of the Continent," *The Friend*, vol. 19, no. 50, September 5, 1846, 394.
58 "The Magnetic Telegraph," *Harbinger*, vol. 1, no. 7, July 26, 1845, 104.
59 Michael Angelo Garvey, *The Silent Revolution, or, The Future Effects of Steam and Electricity upon the Condition of Mankind* (Dublin: William and Frederick G. Cash, 1852), 103.
60 "Modern Telegraphy," *Scientific American* 2, no. 23 (June 2, 1860): 356.
61 William Horatio Barnes, *The Body Politic*, 158.
62 Barnes, *The Body Politic*, 102.

63 Barnes, *The Body Politic*, 171.
64 Herbert Spencer, "The Social Organism," *Westminster Review* 73 (January, 1860): 54.
65 Spencer, "The Social Organism," 56
66 Spencer, "The Social Organism," 66.
67 Spencer, "The Social Organism," 67.
68 Spencer, "The Social Organism," 68.
69 Spencer, "The Social Organism," 68.
70 "Diseases of Overworked Men," *Scientific American* 10, no. 13 (March 26, 1864): 208.
71 George Miller Beard, *American Nervousness: Its Causes and Consequences; a Supplement to Nervous Exhaustion (Neurasthenia)* (New York: G. P. Putnam's Sons, 1881), vi. As Tom Lutz has argued, the ongoing association of neurasthenia with civilized refinement and intellectual accomplishment made the condition "a mark of distinction, of class, of status, of refinement": Tom Lutz, *1903: American Nervousness and the Economy of Cultural Change* (Palo Alto, CA: Stanford University Press, 1989), 6.
72 Beard, *American Nervousness*, 146.
73 Beard, *American Nervousness*, 11.
74 Beard, *American Nervousness*, 99.
75 Timothy J. McGillicuddy, *Functional Disorders of the Nervous System in Women* (New York: William Wood, 1896).
76 Beard, *American Nervousness*, 96.
77 Beard, *American Nervousness*, 105.
78 T. Jackson Lears, *No Place of Grace: Anti-Modernism and the Transformation of American Culture, 1880–1920* (Chicago: University of Chicago Press, 1992), 52–53.
79 Gustav Liebig, *Practical Electricity in Medicine and Surgery* (Philadelphia: F. A. Davis, 1890), 26.
80 Carolyn Thomas de la Peña, *The Body Electric: How Strange Machines Built the Modern American* (New York: New York University Press, 2003), xx. 9.
81 Given the state of accredited medical practice for impotence in late nineteenth-century urology, the appeal of these devices can be better understood. Hoping to introduce more precise electrotherapeutics in cases of prostatitis and impotence, one physician derided the contemporary surgical approach that "looked for stricture in every case of impotence, and if one could not be induced to appear in the deeper parts of the urethra by the irritation of abnormally large sounds or bulbous probes, ... remorselessly divided the inoffending meatus itself, whose only fault could have been to act as a barrier to useless and possibly harmful stretching of the important structures deeper down": Betton G. Massey, "Electricity in the Treatment of Chronic Prostatitis and other Conditions Underlying Impotence in Men," *Proceedings* 15 (1894): 29–30. Small wonder that so many men chose instead to send in the mail for a discreet belt that would gently tingle their loins.

82 "Telephone Insanity: German Alienist Says 'Central' Drives Men to Madness," *New York Times*, May 5, 1913, 3.
83 "Afflicted with Hello-Mania," *Chicago Daily Tribune*, August 23, 1890, 3.
84 "Telephonic Insanity," *New York Times*, August 19, 1890, 5.
85 "Love's Gift of Insanity," *Chicago Tribune*, July 9, 1896, 13.
86 "Driven Crazy by Love," *New York Times*, January 21, 1889.
87 *Milwaukee Journal*, February 3, 1892, 8.
88 Mark Essig, *Edison and the Electric Chair: A Story of Light and Death* (New York: Bloomsbury, 2005).
89 "Insanity Caused by Electricity: James Grant a Raving Maniac from Using a Telephone during a Storm," *Chicago Daily Tribune*, May 6, 1892, 1. Other linemen faced more direct threats from insanity, as in the case of a telephone worker sent to repair the line at an "Insane Hospital" in Indianapolis who found himself under attack by "a maniac" who believed the worker had hidden stolen money in the walls: see "Linemen's Adventure with a Maniac," *Los Angeles Times*, October 15, 1902.
90 Philip Coombs Knapp, *Accidents from the Electrical Current: A Contribution to the Study of the Action of Currents of High Potential upon the Human Organism* (Boston: Damrell and Upham, 1890), 2.
91 Knapp, *Accidents from the Electrical Current*, 25.
92 Knapp, *Accidents from the Electrical Current*, 35.
93 Edwin Lancelot Hopewell-Ash, *The Problem of Nervous Breakdown* (New York: Macmillan, 1920), 64.
94 "Telephonic Insanity," *Rocky Mountain News*, September 1, 1890.
95 "Telephonic Insanity" (*Rocky Mountain News*), col. A. See also "Telephone Girls Insane," *New York Sun*, October 7, 1890, 6.
96 Andreas Killen, *Berlin Electropolis: Shock, Nerves, and German Modernity* (Berkeley: University of California Press, 2005), 162.
97 Josephine Clara Goldmark and Louis Dembitz Brandeis, *Fatigue and Efficiency: A Study in Industry* (New York: Charities Publication Committee, 1912), 348.
98 Killen, *Berlin Electropolis*, 25.
99 Victor Tausk, "On the Origin of the 'Influencing Machine' in Schizophrenia" (1919), in *The Psycho-Analytic Reader*, ed. Robert Fliess (New York: International Press, 1948), 61.
100 Frederick Peterson, "Extracts from the Autobiography of a Paranoiac," Reprint from *The American Journal of Psychology*, (January, 1889): 23.
101 Peterson, "Extracts from the Autobiography of a Paranoiac," 23–24. Schreber discussed a similarly intermedial component to his delusional system, what he termed "the writing-down system." This system developed shortly after the advent of the "tying-to-celestial-bodies": "Books or other notes are kept in which for years have been *written-down* all my thoughts, all my phrases, all my necessaries, all the articles in my possession or around me, all persons with whom I come into contact." Crucially, the "writers" in this "writing-down sys-

tem" are little more than automatons. "I presume the writing down is done by creatures given human shape on distant celestial bodies . . . , but lacking all intelligence; their hands are led automatically, as it were, by passing rays for the purpose of making them write-down, so that later rays can again look at what has been written": Daniel Paul Schreber, *Memoirs of My Nervous Illness* (New York: NYRB Classics, 2000), 123. The image of human automatons writing down Schreber's every word and action also suggests an immense cosmic bureaucracy involved in producing a textual body of absolute visibility that Foucault locates at the center of disciplinary power.

102 Anderson, *Imagined Communities*, 35.
103 Peterson, "Extracts from the Autobiography of a Paranoiac," 23–24.
104 Susan Douglas, *Inventing American Broadcasting, 1899–1922* (Baltimore: Johns Hopkins University Press, 1989).
105 "Chicago Crank Has Woes: Chas Keating Arrested while Seeking Thomas A. Edison," *Chicago Tribune*, August 30, 1901, 9. Edison's legend was so great that these "cranks" even included his wife in their delusions: see "Annoyed Inventor Edison's Wife," *Washington Post*, July 1, 1894, 1. In 1929, a psychologist seeking to differentiate various modes of paranoia proposed the category of "inventive paranoia," a condition in which "the individual believes himself to be a great inventor and besieges offices with his many inventions." Such cases, however, rarely resulted in institutionalization in that these delusions were "not likely to bring [the individuals] into sharp conflict with society": see Vivian E. Fisher, *An Introduction to Abnormal Psychology* (New York: Macmillan, 1929), 304. Fisher notes that one individual submitted a patent for making gold out of corn husks.
106 Garrett P. Serviss, "Edison's Conquest of Mars," *New York Evening Journal*, January–February 1898. Edison also appeared in newspaper stories, reported as "fact," that seem dubious at best. "A Queer Yarn about Edison," for example, details Edison's role in improvising an electrical device to save a cataleptic teenage girl. Edison, who is not recognized by the girl's rube parents, awakens her with an electrical coil, causing the girl to grab Edison by the neck. The parents suspect the device is a trick to "win the affections" of their daughter. After escorting Edison from this misunderstanding, a friend returns to the parents and explains that the man who saved their daughter is "deaf" and a "lunatic" and therefore has no interest in marrying the young girl: "A Queer Yarn about Edison," *Chicago Tribune*, November 11, 1887, 10.
107 John Clute and Peter Nicholls, *The Encyclopedia of Science Fiction* (New York: St. Martin's, 1995).
108 "Electric Bob's Big Black Ostrich," *New York Five Cent Library*, no. 55, August 26, 1893, 1–15.
109 Edward N. Flint, "A Case of Paranoia," *Journal of Nervous and Mental Disease* 20 (1893): 573.
110 Edward N. Flint, "A Case of Paranoia," 578.

111 William Walker Atkinson, *Thought-Force in Business and Everyday Life* (New York: Sydney Flower, 1900), 49.
112 Proponents of the New Thought found much of their inspiration in the teachings of Phineas Parkhurst Quimby, a physician from New England who theorized all disease to be a function of mind and belief. Quimby subscribed to the idea that thought alone could make a person ill, a doctrine that also became the foundation of Mary Baker Eddy's Christian Science movement: Phineas P. Quimby, "Is Disease a Belief?" (1859), in *The Quimby Manuscripts*, ed. Horatio W. Dresser (New York: Thomas Y. Crowell, 1921), 186.
113 William Walker Atkinson, *Mind Power: The Secret of Mental Magic* (Chicago: Advanced Thought, 1912), 7.
114 Atkinson, *Mind Power*, 10. Atkinson eventually found a valuable collaborator in Baba Bharata, a yogi who journeyed from India to Chicago for the Columbian Exposition of 1893. Together, Atkinson and Bharata co-wrote a number of books integrating principles of Hindu mysticism, Quimby's teachings, and benchmarks of Christian spirituality. Appearing under the pseudonym Yogi Ramacharaka, these books were among the first to bring Yoga philosophy to North American readers and remain to this day among the biggest-selling titles in metaphysical publishing. Their most successful book is *Advanced Course in Yogi Philosophy and Oriental Occultism* (1904).
115 Dale Carnegie, *How to Win Friends and Influence People* (New York: Simon and Schuster, 1937); Norman Vincent Peale, *The Power of Positive Thinking* (New York: Prentice Hall, 1952).
116 William Walker Atkinson, *Nuggets of the New Thought* (Chicago: Psychic Research, 1902), 89.
117 Atkinson, *Nuggets of the New Thought*, 89.
118 William Walker Atkinson, *Practical Mental Influence and Mental Fascination* (Chicago: Advanced Thought, 1908), 26.
119 Atkinson, *Mind Power*, 36.
120 Atkinson, *Mind Power*, 38–39.
121 Atkinson, *Mind Power*, 29.
122 Atkinson, *Mind Power*, 30.
123 Atkinson, *Mind Power*, 99–100.
124 Atkinson, *Mind Power*, 266.
125 Atkinson, *Practical Mental Influence*, 68.
126 Atkinson, *Nuggets of the New Thought*, 54.
127 Dion Fortune, *Psychic Self-Defense* (London: Rider, 1930). In addition to her non-fiction writing, Fortune wrote a trio of novels based on occult themes: *The Demon Lover* (1927), *The Winged Bull* (1935), and *The Goat-Footed God* (1936).
128 Fortune, *Psychic Self-Defense*, 8.
129 This concern over novices' blundering into an occult crisis remains a central concern of those who teach psychic self-defense. "Occult activity also, if undertaken without due knowledge and care, can open dangerous doorways to

powerful forces, which may affect other people besides the operator": Melita Denning and Osborne Phillips, *Psychic Self-Defense and Well-Being* (St. Paul, MN: Llewellyn, 1980), 11.

130 Fortune, *Psychic Self-Defense*, 55.
131 Fortune, *Psychic Self-Defense*, 61.
132 Fortune, *Psychic Self-Defense*, 43.
133 Those involved in therapy and childcare are thought to be especially vulnerable to psychic attack. "Are you a therapist or a healer? Do you use guided imagery or self-hypnosis tapes? Do you find people naturally gravitate to you with their troubles?" If so, warns Judy Hall, you need psychic protection: Judy Hall, *The Art of Psychic Protection* (Chicago: Findhorn, 1996). Denning and Phillips advise that the "housewife" should also learn strategies of psychic self-defense, as she is "the center of her family's demands" and, "as the chief buyer of the family, is subject to the advertising and sales pressures of the total consumption-oriented economy": Denning and Phillips, *Psychic Self-Defense and Well-Being*, 3.
134 Morton Prince, *The Unconscious: The Fundamentals of Human Personality, Normal and Abnormal* (New York: Macmillan, 1914), 178.
135 Wilhelm Stekel, *Twelve Essays on Sex and Psychoanalysis*, trans. S. A. Tannenbaum (New York: Critic and Guide, 1922), 78.
136 James Oppenheim, *Your Hidden Powers* (New York: Alfred A. Knopf, 1923), 1.
137 Oppenheim, *Your Hidden Powers*, 4.
138 Oppenheim, *Your Hidden Powers*, 5.
139 See "Human Radio Emanations," *New York Times*, September 28, 1927, 27. For a full account of Cazzamali's findings, see also "Says Human Brain Emits Radio Waves," *New York Times*, August 21, 1925, 1; "Radio's Aid Is Invoked to Explore Telepathy," *New York Times*, August 30, 1925, XX3. These conclusions were later endorsed by the German neurologist N. W. Krainsky: see N. W. Krainsky, "Nerven-Psychische Emission und Radio-Prozesse im Lebenden Organismus," *Monatsberichte* 1 (1936): 13–54. News that doctors in Edinburgh had created the "encephalophone" led one reporter to recall the story of a British physician who converted brainwaves into "audible buzzes and clicks" for his audience. On one occasion, we are told, the doctor's device picked up a transmission of "God Save the King," causing the audience to rise "in respect." The reporter then goes on to argue waggishly that the new encephalophone, a device capable of converting brainwaves into audible tones, will be of immense interest to "modernist" composers. "We can imagine Shostakovich, Prokofieff or Stravinsky developing the trills, warbles and the cacophonies into some weird tone-poem which will interpret realistically what is passing in the mind of a schizophrenic or an epileptic in seizure": "Singing Brains," *New York Times*, March 9, 1943, 22.
140 "Radio's Aid Is Invoked to Explore Telepathy," XX3. Not long after Cazzamali's experiments, Sir Oliver Lodge conducted a reverse experiment in wireless telepathy, broadcasting his "impressions" on the airwaves and inviting listeners

to send in any messages they might receive: see V. J. Woolley, "The Broadcast Experiment in Mass Telepathy," *Proceedings of the Society for Psychical Research* 5, no. 38 (1928): 1–9. Radio experiments in telepathic transmission were attempted again in 1938: see L. D. Goodfellow, "A Psychological Interpretation of the Results of the Zenith Radio Experiments in Telepathy," *Journal of Experimental Psychology* 23 (1938): 601–32. Predictably, such experiments were attempted once again with television in 1957: see D. Michie and D. J. West, "A Mass ESP Test Using Television," *Journal of the Society for Psychical Research* 39 (1957): 113–33.

141 Edmund Shaftesbury, *Thought Transference; or, The Radio-Activity of the Human Mind; Based on the Newly Discovered Laws of Radio-Communication between Brain and Brain* (Meriden, CT: Ralston Society, 1927), 3.

142 The definitive history of this transition remains Douglas, *Inventing American Broadcasting*.

143 Benjamin Kidd, *The Science of Power* (New York: G. P. Putnam's Sons, 1918), 130.

144 Adam Lipsky, *Man the Puppet: The Art of Controlling Minds* (New York: Frank-Maurice, 1925), 255–56.

145 Lipsky, *Man the Puppet*, 23.

146 Lipsky, *Man the Puppet*, 98.

147 The "occult" dimensions of taste have figured in recent science fiction: see esp. William Gibson, *Pattern Recognition* (New York: G. P. Putnam's Sons, 2003).

148 Edward L. Bernays, *Propaganda* (New York: H. R. Liveright, 1928), 9.

149 James A. Brussel, "Autocatharsis as a Therapeutic Measure," *Psychiatric Quarterly* 10, no. 4 (1936): 552–74.

150 Brussel, "Autocatharsis as a Therapeutic Measure," 567.

151 Brussel, "Autocatharsis as a Therapeutic Measure," 568.

152 Brussel, "Autocatharsis as a Therapeutic Measure," 571–72.

153 Barbara O'Brien, *Operators and Things* (New York: Ace, 1958).

154 O'Brien, *Operators and Things*, 43.

155 O'Brien, *Operators and Things*, 42.

156 O'Brien, *Operators and Things*, 48.

157 O'Brien, *Operators and Things*, 93–95.

158 O'Brien, *Operators and Things*, 26. While psychotic, O'Brien learns that her "contract" was originally owned by her employer before it passed to Hadley. Later, her employer complains to her new operators that O'Brien, a "top-grade horse," is being ruined by the experiment. Companies rely on "horses" and "broncos" to perform certain functions. While horses "stew and worry," broncos "kick up their heels" and "plunge right in": O'Brien, *Operators and Things*, 54–55.

159 O'Brien, *Operators and Things*, 28.

160 O'Brien, *Operators and Things*, 52.

161 Sechehaye and Sechehaye, *Autobiography of a Schizophrenic Girl*, 33.

162 Paula Elkisch, "Significant Relationship between the Human Figure and the Machine in the Drawings of Boys," *American Journal of Orthopsychiatry* 22, no. 2 (1952): 379.

163 Elkisch made these selections according to Jacob Moreno's system of "sociometery": see Jacob Levy Moreno, "Foundations of Sociometry: An Introduction," *Sociometry* 4, no. 1 (February, 1941): 15–35.
164 Elkisch, "Significant Relationship between the Human Figure and the Machine in the Drawings of Boys," 379. Elkisch briefly mentions a third boy from another study who was "severely disturbed" and expressed his "exaggerated motility in his drawing of fantastic machines. His own self, on the other hand, had faded away; it was 'eaten up' by what he called 'the man in the machine.'"
165 Elkisch, "Significant Relationship between the Human Figure and the Machine in the Drawings of Boys," 379.
166 Bruno Bettelheim, "Joey," in Bruno Bettelheim, *The Empty Fortress* (New York: Simon and Schuster, 1967), 233–342.
167 Bettelheim's tenure at the Orthogenic School eventually became a point of great controversy. After Bettelheim's suicide in 1990, several of the school's former students came forward with allegations of physical and sexual abuse. An article in *Newsweek* further alleged that Chicago's psychiatric community knew about Bettelheim's proclivity for severe methods (nicknaming him "Beno Brutalheim") but did nothing to intervene: see Nina Darnton, "'Beno Brutalheim'?" *Newsweek*, September 10, 1990. Other staff members defended Bettelheim but conceded he was a supporter of corporal punishment.
168 Bruno Bettelheim, "Joey: A Mechanical Boy," *Scientific American* 3 (1959): 116–27; "Motors Replace Love: Boy Mentally Turns Himself into a Machine," *Los Angeles Times*, February 27, 1959, 10.
169 Bettelheim, *The Empty Fortress*, 235.
170 Bettelheim, *The Empty Fortress*, 236.
171 Bettelheim, *The Empty Fortress*, 253–54.
172 This account of autism is generally attributed to Leo Kanner, "Autistic Disturbances of Affective Contact," *Nervous Child* 2 (1943): 217–50.
173 Bettelheim, *The Empty Fortress*, 244.
174 Bettelheim, *The Empty Fortress*, 235.
175 Acknowledging the ultimate "heat-death" of the universe, Wiener writes, "In a very real sense we are shipwrecked passengers on a doomed planet. Yet even in a shipwreck, human decencies and human values do not necessarily vanish, and we must make the most of them. We shall go down, but let it be in a manner to which we may look forward as worthy of our dignity": Norbert Wiener, *The Human Use of Human Beings* (New York, Avon, 1954).
176 Weiner, *The Human Use of Human Beings*, 95.
177 Weiner, *The Human Use of Human Beings*, 16.
178 Bernard Dionysius Geoghegan, "From Information Theory to French Theory: Jakobson, Lévi-Strauss, and the Cybernetic Apparatus," *Critical Inquiry* 38, no. 1 (2011): 98.
179 Norbert Wiener, *Cybernetics: Control and Communication in the Animal and Machine* (New York: John Wiley and Sons, 1948), 173–74.

180 See N. Katherine Hayles, *How We Became Posthuman: Virtual Bodies in Cybernetics, Literature, and Informatics* (Chicago: University of Chicago Press, 1999), 70–72.

181 Bruno Bettelheim, *The Informed Heart: Autonomy in a Mass Age* (Glencoe, IL: Free Press, 1960), vii.

182 Bettelheim, *The Informed Heart*, 45. Ted Kaczynski would make a similar argument in his Unibomber "manifesto" of 1995: see Theodore Kaczynski, *Technological Slavery: The Collected Writings of Theodore J. Kaczynski, a.k.a. "The Unabomber"* (Los Angeles: Feral House, 2010).

183 Bettelheim, *The Informed Heart*, 55–56.

184 Wiener, *The Human Uses of Human Beings*, 51.

185 Wiener, *The Human Uses of Human Beings*, 52.

186 Bettelheim, *The Informed Heart*, 267.

187 Bettelheim, *The Empty Fortress*, 234.

188 After languishing for many years in obscurity, Joey the mechanical boy has begun to gain interest among a growing number of scholars and artists. While older scholarship on Joey, confined primarily to studies of autism and psychoanalysis, followed Bettelheim's assumption that he should be delivered from his mechanical state, more recent discussions, informed by various convergences of the neurodiversity movement, technology studies, and post-structuralist theory are critical of Bettelheim's naïve humanism and more celebratory of Joey's technical adaptations. Much as Schreber served as the preeminent psychotic ambassador of modernity and Freudian theory, Joey stands a good chance of taking on a similar role in the literature of cybernetics, transhumanism, and object-oriented ontology. In a provocative bid to redeem Joey's pathology, Steven Thompson identifies an "orthodox" and "unorthodox" account of this famous case. In the orthodox reading, Bettelheim as old-fashioned humanist works to save Joey from the antiseptic emotional life of mechanized existence in a mechanized society. Thompson's "unorthodox" account approaches Joey as "a design analysis, revealing how Joey realised his own therapy, through a process that enables his selfhood as an emergent condition that accepted continuum rather than the resolution of heterogeneous entities." Joey, in other words, is not saved from mechanized life by Bettelheim but instead uses machine logic to discover and construct his selfhood: see Stephen Thompson, "Joey the Mechanical Boy," in *Transtechnology Research Reader*, ed. Martha Blassnigg, Hannah Drayson, Michael Punt, John Vines, and Brigitta Zics (Plymouth, UK: University of Plymouth, 2010), 85–97. For more recent work invoking Joey, see Sarah Reddington and Deborah Price, "Cyborg and Autism: Exploring New Social Articulations via Posthuman Connections," *International Journal of Qualitative Studies in Education* 29, no. 7 (2016): 882–92; Amit Pinchevski and John Durham Peters, "Autism and New Media: Disability between Technology and Society," *New Media and Society* 18, no 11 (2016): 2507–23. Two drawings by Joey were included in the gallery exhibition "The Universal Addressability

of Dumb Things," curated by Mark Leckey for Nottingham Contemporary, April 27–June 30, 2013. In 2011, the artists Ian Haig and Kotoe Ishii collaborated on an installation piece, "The Joey Machine," a sculptural interpretation of the mechanized bed Joey used to "live him."

189 Bettelheim, *The Empty Fortress*, 271.
190 As is standard in psychoanalytic case studies, "Joey" is a pseudonym. Given the importance of this kangaroo fantasy in "Joey's" recovery, one can assume Bettelheim picked this particular name to evoke a baby kangaroo, also known as a "joey."
191 Bettelheim, *The Empty Fortress*, 290.
192 Bettelheim, *The Empty Fortress*, 285.
193 Bettelheim, *The Empty Fortress*, 276.
194 Bettelheim, *The Empty Fortress*, 304.
195 Bettelheim appears to base this interpretation on details of the drawing near the "hen electric's" back wheel. It is unclear (to me, anyway) whether this part of the drawing depicts a fetus or some type of gear or fan-belt system.
196 Ray Kurzweil, *The Age of Spiritual Machines: When Computers Exceed Human Intelligence* (New York: Penguin, 2000).
197 Wiener, *The Human Use of Human Beings*, 57. Wiener also endorsed the possibility of human teleportation, a prediction that Jacques Lacan found particularly amusing. See his discussion of Wiener in Jacques Lacan, *The Psychoses, The Seminar of Jacques Lacan, Book III, 1955–1956*, ed. Jacques-Alain Miller, trans. Russell Grigg (New York: W. W. Norton, 1993), 37.
198 In 2013, Kurzweil predicted that whole brain emulation would be possible by 2045, a project that was endorsed by the Russian investor Dmitry Itskov when he created the 2045 Initiative, a "project aims to create technologies enabling the transfer of a [sic] individual's personality to a more advanced non-biological carrier, and extending life, including to the point of immortality": see "2045 Strategic Social Initiative," January 1, 2016, http://2045.com/read-us. Proponents foresee four stages in this path toward cybernetic eternity. Avatar A (2015–20) would involve a brain able to remotely control a robot body via a brain-computer interface, or BCI. Avatar B (2020–25) would realize the uncanny nightmare of innumerable pulp writers: transplantation of a human brain into a new vessel. Avatar C (2030–35) would see "human personality" transferred into an artificial brain, the prelude to Avatar D (2040–45), in which a "hologram-like avatar" becomes the ultimate repository of human consciousness. Kurzweil's new project argues that the dead might be resurrected by entering all of their personal data into computers to generate life-like avatars. Adding an oedipal cant to these prognostications, Kurzweil is hopeful that he might bring back his own father through such technology: see Ray Kurzweil, *The Singularity Is Near: When Humans Transcend Biology* (New York: Penguin, 2005).
199 Joshua L. Morgan and Jeff W. Lichtman, "Why Not Connectomics?" *Nature Methods* 10, no. 6 (2013): 494–500.

200 Kenneth J. Hayworth, "Electron Imaging Technology for Whole Brain Neural Circuit Mapping," *International Journal of Machine Consciousness* 4, no. 1 (2012): 89. Hayworth is correct in this assumption: much of neuroscience does indeed believe that human beings are "intelligent robots," a symptom, it should be noted, that is also commonly encountered among those diagnosed with schizophrenia, an illness frequently distinguished by a tendency to literalize metaphors.

201 Sigmund Freud, "The Future of an Illusion" (1927), in *The Standard Edition of the Complete Psychological Works of Sigmund Freud*, 21:3–57.

202 Hayles, *How We Became Posthuman*.

203 Admittedly, this dream of positivist immortality is slightly less secure. Religion promises the boredom of an ego living forever in the spiritual afterlife. Posthuman futurism, meanwhile, imagines an ego that can survive for as long as the laws of physics are in operation, essentially kicking the can of ego crisis down the road a few decades, centuries, or millennia. (That is, after the Big Collapse bookends the Big Bang, you are on your own.)

Chapter 5. Targeted Individuals

1 Francis E. Dec, "Gangster Computer God Worldwide Secret Containment Policy," http://www.bentoandstarchky.com/dec/containmentpolicy.html.
2 Francis E. Dec, "The Empirical Scientific Agnostic Religion of Astrocism," http://www.bentoandstarchky.com/dec/astrocism.htm.
3 Diane Kossy, *Kooks: A Guide to the Outer Limits of Human Belief* (Los Angeles: Feral House, 1994), 179.
4 See the Official Francis E. Dec Fan Club website, http://www.bentoandstarchky.com.
5 Francis E. Dec, "Master-Race Frankenstein Controls" (ca. 1984–85), http://www.bentoandstarchky.com/dec/mrfrc.htm.
6 Dec, "Master-Race Frankenstein Controls."
7 Francis E. Dec, "Rant No. 4," http://www.bentoandstarchky.com/dec/rants.htm.
8 Frances E. Dec, "Letter Addressed to First and Second Appellate Division, Superior Court, New York City; Court of Appeals, Albany, New York; and US Supreme Court, Washington, DC (October 21, 1976)," http://www.bentoandstarchky.com/dec/scappeal.htm. Dec's "fans" refer to it as the "To All Judges" letter.
9 Erich Von Däniken, *Chariots of the Gods* (New York: G. P. Putnam's Sons, 1968). Von Däniken followed up his bestseller with *Gods from Outer Space* (New York: G. P. Putnam's Sons, 1972). Von Däniken was not the first to suggest that the Earth had been visited by aliens. Four years before *Chariots of the Gods?* was released, W. R. Drake's *Gods or Spacemen?* (Amherst WI: Amherst, 1964) offered a similar thesis. Von Däniken's book was central to a larger resurgence in popular Forteanism in the early 1970s, a publishing

phenomenon that also included several books on the Bermuda Triangle, Satanism, Bigfoot, and UFOS. Such speculation has become so entrenched over the past forty years that is has generated its own abbreviation: AAT (alien astronaut theory).

10 Francis E. Dec, "Astrocism: The True Religion of the Slovene People," http://www.bentoandstarchky.com/dec/astrocism.htm.

11 Eschatology is a particular virulent incubator of delusional reference, a product of the Bible's historical distance and allegorical style. William Miller, leader of the Millerites, predicted in 1822 that the world would come to an end in 1843, a conclusion based on his detailed analysis of the Book of Daniel. More recently, Reverend Austin Miles invoked Deuteronomy 28:43 as proof that the Bible predicted the terrorist attacks of 9/11: "The stranger (unknown people) that is within thee shall get up above thee very high (hijacked airplanes); and thou (you) shalt come down very low . . . (everything leveled by the bombings)": Austin Miles, "Did Bible Predict 9–11 Attacks? Rev. Austin Miles Says Yes," blog post, *Christian Coalition*, http://www.cc.org/blog/did_bible_predict_911_attacks_rev_austin_miles_says_yes, accessed January 1, 2016. Also popular in this community is competitive speculation about the identity of the Antichrist. The pope, whoever he may be, is frequently a leading contender. As of this writing, however, former President Barack Obama leads the field as the main suspect: see Paul Harris, "One in Four Americans Think Obama May be the Antichrist, Survey Says," *The Guardian*, April 2, 2013. One of the more unusual theories posits that Microsoft's founder, Bill Gates, is the antichrist, a conclusion based on mathematical conversions. As one writer notes, "BILL GATES III" converted into ASCII creates a series of numbers that equal 666, as do "WINDOWS 95" and "MS-DOS 6.11": David Tormsen, "10 Individuals Surprisingly Identified as the Antichrist," January 6, 2016, https://listverse.com/2016/01/06/10-individuals-surprisingly-identified-as-the-antichrist, accessed January 1, 2017.

12 Jack T. Chick, *My Name? . . . In the Vatican?*, Chick Tract (Rancho Cucamonga, CA: Chick Publications, 1980).

13 Dec, "Astrocism." Here Dec echoes Jack Chick's contention that "Catholicism controls its members from the cradle to the grave": Jack T. Chick, *Are Roman Catholics Christians?* (Rancho Cucamonga, CA: Chick Publications, 1985).

14 Dec, "Gangster Computer God Worldwide Containment Policy."

15 Dec, "Gangster Computer God Worldwide Containment Policy."

16 For a biography of Freeman, see Jack El-Hai, *The Lobotomist: A Maverick Medical Genius and His Tragic Quest to Rid the World of Mental Illness* (New York: John Wiley and Sons, 2005).

17 David R. McLean, "Nuts and Screwballs," *Studies in Intelligence* 9 (1965): 79–89.

18 The idea that atomic power might animate an otherwise dormant nervous system saw its apotheosis in *Fiend without a Face* (1958). Also a staple of late-night

television, this film features hovering brains attached to prehensile spinal columns, brought to life by the confluence of a "mentalist's" thought projections and radiation from a nearby nuclear reactor.

19 The first appearance of the term "science fiction" is in William Wilson, *A Little Earnest Book upon a Great Old Subject* (London: Darton, 1851), 139–40. In a discussion of R. H. Horne's story "The Poor Artists: or, Seven Eye-Sights and One Object," Wilson describes science fiction as a welcome new form "in which the revealed truths of Science may be given, interwoven with a pleasing story which may itself be poetical and *true*—thus circulating a knowledge of the Poetry of Science, clothed in a garb of the Poetry of life." As early as 1890, Patrick Stokes considered the philosophical implications of what he called the "so-called science fiction scenarios ... mind-swaps, implanted memories, brain transplants, human fission and fusion, teleportation": Patrick Stokes, "Anti-Climacus and Neo-Lockeanism," *Locus* 1 (1890): 330.

20 Paul Alkon traces the origins of the genre to utopian fiction of the eighteenth century, citing Samuel Madden's *Memoirs of the Twentieth-Century*, written in 1733, as "the first utopia set ahead in time rather on some imaginary island." Particularly influential in establishing speculative fictions of the future, Alkon argues, was Louis-Sebastien Mercier's *L'an 2440* (The year 2440), published in 1771: see Paul K. Alkon, *Science Fiction before 1900: Imagination Discovers Technology* (New York: Routledge, 2013), 21.

21 "Description of the Journey to Mars, and Wonder Information Furnished by Madam Ehrenborg," in *A Book Written by the Spirits of the So-Called Dead, with Their Own Materialized Hands, by the Process of Independent Slate-Writing, through Mrs. Lizzie S. Green and Others, as Mediums*, comp. C. G. Helleberg (Cincinnati: C. G. Helleberg, 1883), 54.

22 Theodore Flournoy, *From India to the Planet Mars: A Case of Multiple Personality with Imaginary Languages*, ed. Sonu Shamdasani, trans. Daniel B. Vermilye (Princeton, NJ: Princeton University Press, [1899] 1994).

23 Tzvetan Todorov, *The Fantastic: A Structural Approach to a Literary Genre* (Ithaca, NY: Cornell University Press, 1975).

24 David Durant, "Ann Radcliffe and the Conservative Gothic," *Studies in English Literature 1500–1900* 22, no. 3 (1982): 519–30.

25 Hugh B. Cave, "The Murder Machine," *Astounding Stories of Super-Science* (September 1930): 377.

26 Stanton A. Coblentz, "The Radio Mind-Ray," *Astounding Stories* (June 1934): 90–97.

27 S. P. Meek, "The Ray of Madness," *Astounding Stories of Super-Science* (April 1930): 112–26.

28 Rudolf Ekstein, "Evaluation of an Adolescent Girl," in Rudolf Ekstein and Elaine Caruth, *Children of Time and Space, of Action and Impulse* (New York: Appleton-Century-Crofts, 1966), 35.

29 Ekstein, "Work with Severely Disturbed Girl," in Ekstein and Caruth, *Children of Time and Space*, 85. A study published in 1999 advises that it is "helpful to clinicians, working with children and adolescents, to understand the spectrum of alien or extraterrestrial culture." The authors argue, "A fixed belief in the paranormal may be seen in chronic psychiatric disorders, with these beliefs providing a psychotic rationalization for a delusional world." They cite the case of a fourteen-year old boy "fascinated with *Star Trek* from a young age" who became convinced that he had been transported to a spaceship where "he met his *Star Trek* friends amongst the other aliens. . . . He decided that a female physician on the ship had operated on his brain, providing him with special schizophrenic intelligence": Sandra Fishman and Raymond Fishman, "Cultural Influences on Symptom Presentation in Childhood," *Journal of the American Academy of Child and Adolescent Psychiatry* 38, no. 6 (1999): 782–83.

30 See "Schizophrenic SF?" *Time*, September 6, 1954; Robert Plank, "The Reproduction of Psychosis in Science Fiction," *International Record of Medicine and General Practice Clinics* 167, no. 7 (1954): 407. Other publications by Plank on science fiction and psychiatry include Robert Plank, *The Emotional Significance of Imaginary Beings: A Study of the Interaction between Psychopathology, Literature, and Reality in the Modern World* (Waukesha, WI: Thomas, 1968); Robert Plank, "The Expedition to the Planet of Paranoia," *Extrapolation* 22, no. 2 (1981): 171–85; Robert Plank, "Names and Roles of Characters in Science Fiction," *Names* 9, no. 3 (1961): 151–59. Plank was not alone in turning psychoanalytic interest toward science-fiction: see also Ednita Bernabeu, "Science Fiction: A New Mythos," *Psychoanalytic Quarterly* 26, no. 4 (1957): 527.

31 Plank, "The Reproduction of Psychosis in Science Fiction," 407.
32 Fredric Wertham, *Seduction of the Innocent* (New York: Rinehart, 1954).
33 "Schizophrenic SF?"
34 "Schizophrenic SF?"
35 Franklin D. Jones, "The Schizophrenic Theme in Science Fiction," presentation at Senior Residents' Symposium, Department of Psychiatry and Neurology, Walter Reed Army Medical Center, Washington, DC, June 11, 1965.
36 Colin Greenland, *Entropy Exhibition: Michael Moorcock and the British 'New Wave' in Science Fiction* (London: Routledge, 2013), 56.
37 For a collection of Powers's work, see Jane Frank, *The Art of Richard Powers* (London: Paper Tiger, 2001).
38 Scott Bukatman, *Terminal Identity: The Virtual Subject in Postmodern Science Fiction* (Durham, NC: Duke University Press, 1993); Fredric Jameson, *Archaeologies of the Future: The Desire Called Utopia and Other Science Fictions* (London: Verso, 2005).
39 Philip K. Dick, *The Exegesis of Philip K. Dick*, ed. Pamela Jackson and Jonathan Lethem (Boston: Houghton Mifflin Harcourt, 2011), 367.

40   A similar conceit informs Kurt Vonnegut's *Slaughterhouse-Five* (New York: Delacorte, 1969), in which the novel's protagonist, Billy Pilgrim, becomes "unstuck in time."
41   Dick, *The Exegesis of Philip K. Dick*, 210.
42   Although these two months in 1974 proved the most crucial in Dick's revelations, he later traces his psychotic journey back to a day in 1970 when he kept playing a Paul McCartney record over and over: Dick, *The Exegesis of Philip K. Dick*, 194.
43   Writes Dick, "I've watched my cat, now, as he sits out on the sundeck at night; he is beyond doubt considering the sidereal world above him and not moving objects below—when he comes in the house an hour or two later he seems modified, as if he has been taught a lesson during that period and knows it": Dick, *The Exegesis of Philip K. Dick*, 9
44   Dick, *The Exegesis of Philip K. Dick*, 235.
45   Dick, *The Exegesis of Philip K. Dick*, xix. Jackson and Lethem appear most convinced by the possibility that Dick suffered from temporal lobe epilepsy, a condition that can stimulate prolonged episodes of manic behavior.
46   Dick, *The Exegesis of Philip K. Dick*, 206–7.
47   Dick, *The Exegesis of Philip K. Dick*, 207.
48   Dick, *The Exegesis of Philip K. Dick*, 11–12.
49   Dick, *The Exegesis of Philip K. Dick*, 3.
50   Dick, *The Exegesis of Philip K. Dick*, 461.
51   No doubt influenced by contemporary speculation over ESP research in the Soviet Union, Dick also thought that his experiences might have been part of a "psi" experiment. "However," he writes, "it is equally probable that in March 1974 an actual concerted telepathic transmission effort was made in Leningrad vis-à-vis me and my ideas, perhaps, to test out and see if I was telepathically sensitive": Dick, *The Exegesis of Philip K. Dick*, 138.
52   Dick, *The Exegesis of Philip K. Dick*, 89.
53   Dick, *The Exegesis of Philip K. Dick*, 97.
54   Robert Plank, "Communication in Science Fiction," ETC :*A Review of General Semantics* 11, no. 1 (Autumn 1953): 16–20.
55   Plank, "Communication in Science Fiction," 18.
56   This speculation was not merely hypothetical, as a number of inventors in the 1920s and '30s claimed to be working on various ray weapons, including Harry Grindell Matthews in 1923 and Nikolas Tesla in the early 1930s. For most of 1924, Matthews encouraged press speculation that England, France, and the United States were in a bidding war for his "death-ray" technology. Matthews showcased this device in a short documentary film that featured the inventor using his prototype to illuminate a light bulb, ignite gunpowder, and execute a rat, all at a distance through the open air: "'Death Ray' Shown Vividly in Movie," *New York Times*, November 3, 1924, 21. For a more thorough discussion of Matthews's ray, see "'Diabolic Ray' Makes Scientists Wonder," *New York Times*, June 1, 1924, 3.

57 Cast in technical histories as the brilliant but unlucky foil to the more famous Thomas Edison, Nikolas Tesla has been associated over the past century with all manner of secret and suppressed technologies. Some maintain that Tesla, not an asteroid, was responsible for the immense explosion in 1908 known as the Tunguska event. William Lyne has been particularly prolific in associating Tesla with secret affordances. Lyne believes the government took control of Tesla's space propulsion system and then worked "to blur the facts and disjoint reality, thus protecting the archaic technology and resources of coercive-monopolist, corporate-state interests from the competition of a truly free market": William Lyne, *Occult Ether Physics: Tesla's Hidden Space Propulsion System and the Conspiracy to Conceal It* (Lamy, NM: Creatopia, 1997); William Lyne, *Space Aliens from the Pentagon* (Lamy, NM: Creatopia, 1993).

58 For the text of Reagan's speech, see Ronald Reagan, "Address to the Nation on Defense and National Security," March 23, 1983, Ronald Reagan Presidential Library and Museum, https://www.reaganlibrary.gov/sites/default/files/archives/speeches/1983/32383d.htm.

59 Alex Constantine, *Psychic Dictatorship in the USA* (Los Angeles: Feral House, 1995), 43.

60 Constantine, *Psychic Dictatorship in the USA*, 39.

61 See "Who Killed All Those British Star Wars Scientists?" http://rense.com/general78/sci.htm, January 1, 2016.

62 Gary Allen and Larry Abraham, *None Dare Call It Conspiracy* (Cutchogue, NY: Buccaneer, 1971). The Gemstone File began circulating in 1975 as a photocopied flier. Attributed to Bruce Porter Roberts, the document proposes a vast conspiracy of global power involving Howard Hughes, Aristotle Onassis, Joseph P. Kennedy, and other prominent figures of the era. Roberts began gathering his data after Hughes allegedly stole his idea for manufacturing synthetic rubies (thus, Gemstone). For a more detailed account, see Stephanie Caruana, *The Gemstone File: A Memoir* (Bloomington, IN: Trafford, 2006).

63 Cathy O'Brien and Marquart Ewing Phillips, *Trance Formation of America* (Reality Marketing, 1995), 160.

64 O'Brien and Phillips, *Trance Formation of America*, 160.

65 Mark Fenster, *Conspiracy Theories: Secrecy and Power in American Culture* (Minneapolis: University of Minnesota Press, 1999), 63.

66 Richard Hofstadter, "The Paranoid Style in American Politics," *Harper's Magazine*, vol. 229, no. 1374 (1964), 77–86.

67 Len Manovich dates "Web 2.0" to around 2005: Lev Manovich, "The Practice of Everyday (Media) Life: From Mass Consumption to Mass Cultural Production?" *Critical Inquiry* 35, no. 2 (2009): 319–31.

68 In one of the campaign's many astounding moments, Trump produced a picture of the father of his rival Ted Cruz, in Cuba, standing next to Lee Harvey Oswald, implying that the senior Cruz was perhaps complicit in the assassination of Kennedy.

69 Cecilia Kang, "Fake News Onslaught Targets Pizzeria as Nest of Child-Trafficking," *New York Times*, November 21, 2016.
70 For a history of this movement, see Sylvia Noble Tesh, *Uncertain Hazards: Environmental Activists and Scientific Proof* (Ithaca, NY: Cornell University Press, 2000).
71 Sharon Weinberger, "Mind Games," *Washington Post Magazine*, January 14, 2007.
72 Naylor also told the interviewer,

> I realized at one point that I was being followed, and then I began to see the surveillance that was going past the road on my house. And so, these cars began to surveil me. People began to follow me around, and it did, it was very disrupting to think that your privacy was being violated, and for no reason that I could come up with. Since I'm not, basically, a political writer, I'm a fiction writer, for the most part. And so, I just didn't, I didn't understand it. I knew about CoIntelpro, which is because I'm African-American, and in those years, the FBI did many shameful things to disrupt black nationalist organizations. (Gloria Naylor, interview with Ed Gordon, National Public Radio, January 23, 2006, transcript, https://www.npr.org/templates/story/story.php?storyId=5168026)

73 See Nancy Jo Sales, "The Quaid Conspiracy," *Vanity Fair*, December 1, 2010. The status of the "Quaid Conspiracy" is difficult to evaluate, given the recent rise of celebrity marketing based on erratic behavior. After winning the Oscar for his performance in *Walk the Line* (2005), for example, Joaquin Phoenix announced he was retiring from acting to become a professional rapper. For the next year, Phoenix lived a persona calculated to make the public suspect he might be having a mental breakdown—in the end, this all turned out to be a "performance" piece for the documentary *I'm Still Here* (2010). In 2013–14, meanwhile, the actor Shia LaBeouf attracted headlines through his seemingly unstable behavior: disrupting a Broadway performance of *Cabaret*; attending a movie premiere wearing a paper bag over his head (with the phrase "I'm not famous anymore" written on it); and renting an art gallery in Los Angeles, where he sat at a desk and cried as the public entered, one at a time, to sit across from him. The fact that the Quaids have yet to translate their "crazy" coverage into any form of economic or symbolic capital suggests a certain authenticity, as does their apparent commitment to living in their car for long periods of time.
74 Titles include Michael Fleming, *Stalked by the FBI: COINTELPRO Targeted Individuals* (self-pub., Amazon Digital, 2014); Steven Lloyd, *My Rocky New Age Road to the Kryst: A True Account of My Becoming a Targeted Individual* (self-pub., CreateSpace, 2014); Renee Pittman, *Diary of an Angry Targeted Individual* (self-pub., Amazon Digital, 2014); Sharon Rose Poet, *Ramblings of a Targeted Individual* (self-pub., Amazon Digital, 2014); Steven Starks, *Threat Assessment of Directed Energy Weapon (DEW) on Targeted Individuals and Those Experiencing Electronic Harassment* (self-pub., Amazon Digital, 2014).

75 In 1996, the organizational psychologist Heinz Leymann discussed the phenomena of "workplace mobbing," a practice in which an unpopular employee becomes the target of sustained abuse by fellow workers, ostensibly to make the target employee leave: Heinz Leymann, "The Content and Development of Mobbing at Work," *European Journal of Work and Organizational Psychology* 5, no. 2 (1996): 165–84. See also Noa Davenport, Ruth Distler Schwartz, and Gail Pursell Elliott, *Mobbing: Emotional Abuse in the American Workplace* (Ames, IA: Civil Society, 1999). In cause stalking, meanwhile, a political group will target an opponent with a round-the-clock program of harassment to signal an imminent threat. Opponents to abortion have been accused of carrying their protests beyond picketing a clinic to "cause stalking" physicians (slashing their tires, killing their pets, threatening the safety of spouses or children). For a discussion of cause stalking, see Charisse Tia Maria Coston, *Victimizing Vulnerable Groups: Images of Uniquely High-Risk Crime Targets* (Westport, CT: Praeger, 2004), 282.

76 Elizabeth Sullivan, *My Life Changed Forever: The Years I Have Lost as a Target of Organized Stalking* (Conshohocken, PA: Infinity, 2012), 5.

77 John Hall, *A New Breed: Satellite Terrorism in America* (New York: Strategic, 2009).

78 This quotation, widely circulated in the TI community, is attributed to Cathy Meadows, a clinical psychologist said to specialize in cases involving "Victims of Whistle-Blower Retaliation and of Retaliatory Harassment and Surveillance." See Meadows at https://www.stopgangstalkingcrimes.com.

79 Regina Cullen recounts this pattern in "The Travelling Torture Chamber," in *Paranoid Women Collect Their Thoughts*, ed. Joan D'Arc (Providence, RI: Paranoia, 1996). Writes Cullen, "I managed to move from the bedsit but only had one free night before it began there, and in the ensuing years I was followed many places. Sometimes, in outrage at being forced out of my home, I would return in the middle of the night to find complete peace and quiet, but ten or twenty minutes later the frequency assault would begin again": Cullen, "The Travelling Torture Chamber," 2.

80 Allan H. Frey, "Human Auditory System Response to Modulated Electromagnetic Energy," *Journal of Applied Physiology* 17, no. 4 (1962): 689–92.

81 Frey, "Human Auditory System Response to Modulated Electromagnetic Energy."

82 Frey, "Human Auditory System Response to Modulated Electromagnetic Energy."

83 Cullen, "The Traveling Torture Chamber," 2.

84 Recently, popular history has demonstrated a growing fascination for Hitler's alleged interest in the occult and new super-technologies. Historians have also long emphasized the growing sophistication of the V-2 rocket program and the Nazis' efforts in creating atomic weaponry as chilling evidence that the Allied Forces won the war just in time. Marrying this occultism to the advanced accomplishments of Nazi science creates a terrifying "What if?" narrative in popular history. The idea of Germany winning World War II has also become

its own subgenre of science fiction. Philip Dick took up this premise in *The Man in the High Castle* (New York: G. P. Putnam's Sons, 1962), and in the 1980s Gregory Benford and Martin Greenberg edited the anthology *Hitler Victorious: 11 Stories of the German Victory in World War II* (New York: Berkley, 1986).

85 Numerous books allege links between Hitler and occult practices, locating the roots of the National Socialist Party in an odd combination of Nietzsche and mysticism. Titles include Michael FitzGerald, *The Nazi Occult War: Hitler's Compact with the Forces of Evil* (London: Arcturus, 2013); Nicholas Goodrick-Clarke, *The Occult Roots of Nazism: Secret Aryan Cults and Their Influence on Nazi Ideology* (London: I. B. Tauris, 1985); Peter Levenda, *Alliance: A History of Nazi Involvement with the Occult* (London: A&C Black, 2002); Paul Roland, *Nazis and the Occult: The Dark Forces Unleashed by the Third Reich* (London: Arcturus, 2012); Dusty Sklar, *The Nazis and the Occult* (New York: Dorset, 1990); Bill Yenne, *Hitler's Master of the Dark Arts: Himmler's Black Knights and the Occult Origins of the SS* (Minneapolis: Zenith, 2010). For a debunking of these myths, see Ken Anderson, *Hitler and the Occult* (New York: Prometheus, 1995).

86 "Brain Research by Soviet Cited," *New York Times*, April 13, 1958, 57.

87 See Bernice Glatzer Rosenthal, *The Occult in Russian and Soviet Culture* (Ithaca, NY: Cornell University Press, 1993), 194.

88 See Leonid Vasiliev, "Is Transmission of Muscular Power at a Distance Possible?" in *Mysterious Phenomena of the Human Psyche* (New Hyde Park, NY: University Books, 1965), 169–85. Morrow concedes that the publication of Vasiliev's work in English, after languishing in exile for so many years, might well have been a bid to stoke fears in the West of superior Soviet achievements in parapsychological research.

89 Sheila Ostrander and Lynn Schroeder, *Psychic Discoveries behind the Iron Curtain* (New York: Bantam, 1971).

90 "Moscow Microwaves," *Time*, February 23, 1976.

91 "The Microwave Furor," *Time*, March 22, 1976. Oddly, these accusations of microwave bombardment arose again in 2017, this time at the US Embassy in Cuba: see Gardiner Harris, "16 Americans Sickened after Attack on Embassy in Havana," *New York Times*, August 24, 2017.

92 Bradley Wells, "The Russian Woodpecker: A Continuing Nuisance," *Ham Radio Magazine*, vol. 17, 1984, 37–45.

93 Perhaps the most famous advocate of this theory was Ira Einhorn. In "A Disturbing Communiqué," published in *CoEvolution Quarterly* in 1977, Einhorn noted a resurgent interest in the theories of Nikola Tesla—particularly his ideas about the long-distance broadcasting of electricity in the air. Following the revelation of the US Embassy's microwave bombardment, the Russian Woodpecker suggested the Soviets were implementing a technology to broadcast mind-controlling "alpha waves" to the masses. Einhorn also claimed to have knowledge that the United States had constructed a similar array in New Zealand and promised to share more details about the project in a forthcom-

ing book. Shortly after publishing the article, however, Einhorn was arrested for the murder of his girlfriend Holly Maddux. Dubbed the "Unicorn Killer," Einhorn fled the United States in 1981 and disappeared. Convicted *in absentia* in 1993, Einhorn remained missing until 1997, when police located him living under an alias in Champagne-Mouton, France. After returning to the United States, he appeared in court in 2001, maintaining his innocence and attributing the murder of Maddux to his previous research in "psychotronic" CIA technologies. The CIA, he maintained, had framed him to discredit his reporting: see Ira Einhorn, "A Disturbing Communiqué," *CoEvolution Quarterly* 16 (Winter 1977), 76–78. Einhorn published a more extended account of his story in *Prelude to Intimacy* (self-pub., Lulu.com, 2005).

94 John B. Alexander, "The New Mental Battlefield: Beam Me Up, Spock," *Military Review* 60, no. 12 (1980): 47–54.

95 Donald Bain, *The Control of Candy Jones* (Chicago: Playboy, 1976).

96 As Rebecca Lemov notes in her account of Cameron, it is not entirely clear whether he knew his funding source was the CIA. Lemov argues Cameron should be seen as "a reflected portrait of the future as groups of forward-looking men and women in the behavioral sciences' postwar world imagined it": Rebecca Lemov, "Brainwashing's Avatar: The Curious Career of Dr. Ewen Cameron," *Grey Room* 45 (Fall 2011): 86.

97 D. Ewen Cameron and S. K. Pande, "Treatment of the Chronic Paranoid Schizophrenic Patient," *Canadian Medical Association Journal* 78, no. 2 (1958): 92.

98 D. Ewen Cameron, John G. Lohrenz, and K. A. Handcock, "The Depatterning Treatment of Schizophrenia," *Comprehensive Psychiatry* 3, no. 2 (1962): 65–76.

99 Cameron et al., "The Depatterning Treatment of Schizophrenia."

100 Klein proposes a trajectory from Cameron's "shock" therapy, as codified by KUBARK, and the later abuses of Abu Ghraib during the Iraq War: see Naomi Klein, *The Shock Doctrine: The Rise of Disaster Capitalism* (New York: Macmillan, 2007), xx.

101 Jose M. R. Delgado, Vernon Mark, William Sweet, Frank Ervin, Gerhard Weiss, George Bach-Y-Rita, and Rioji Hagiwara, "Intracerebral Radio Stimulation and Recording in Completely Free Patients," *Journal of Nervous and Mental Disease* 147, no. 4 (October 1968): 329–40.

102 Delgado et al., "Intracerebral Radio Stimulation and Recording in Completely Free Patients," 336.

103 Delgado et al., "Intracerebral Radio Stimulation and Recording in Completely Free Patients," 335.

104 Delgado et al., "Intracerebral Radio Stimulation and Recording in Completely Free Patients," 337.

105 José M. R. Delgado, *Physical Control of the Mind: Toward a Psychocivilized Society* (New York: Harper and Row, 1969).

106 Delgado, *Physical Control of the Mind*, 249.

107 Delgado, *Physical Control of the Mind*, 262.

108 Delgado, *Physical Control of the Mind*, 258. For Delgado's work on electronically agitating monkeys, see José M. R. Delgado, "Aggressive Behavior Evoked by Radio Stimulation in Monkey Colonies," *American Zoologist* 6, no. 4 (1966): 669–81.

109 Vernon H. Mark and Frank R. Ervin, *Violence and the Brain* (New York: Harper and Row, 1970).

110 Jonathan Metzl, *The Protest Psychosis* (Boston: Beacon, 2009), 100. See also Walter Bromberg and Franck Simon, "The 'Protest' Psychosis: A Special Type of Reactive Psychosis," *Archives of General Psychiatry* 19, no. 2 (1968): 155. For more on the relationship between race and psychiatric diagnosis, see Dinesh Bhugra and Oyedeji Ayonrinde, "Racism, Racial Life Events, and Mental Ill Health," in *Clinical Topics in Cultural Psychiatry*, ed. Rahul Bhattacharya, Sean Cross, and Dinesh Bhugra (London: RCPsych, 2010), 39–51.

111 Vernon H. Mark, William H. Sweet, and F. R. Ervin, "Role of Brain Disease in Riots and Urban Violence," *Journal of the American Medical Association* 201, no. 11 (1967): 895.

112 B. J. Mason, "Brain Surgery to Control Behavior," *Ebony*, February 1973, 66. *Ebony*'s coverage contrasted sharply with an early piece in *Life Magazine* that celebrated the possibilities of addressing violence through psychosurgery: see "The Psychobiology of Violence," *Life Magazine*, June 21, 1968.

113 Conspiracy theorists and TIs are particularly troubled by Agenda 21, a plan offered in 1993 by the United Nations and designed to encourage more global cooperation on issues of environmental sustainability: see Jose Antonio Ocampo, *Agenda 21: Earth Summit: The United Nations Programme of Action from Rio* (New York: United Nations, 1993). See also Illena Johnson Paugh, *Agenda 21: Environmental Piracy* (self-published, 2012).

114 Officially under the jurisdiction of Edwards Air Force Base, Area 51 is a top-secret military facility operating within the borders of the Nevada Test and Training Range. Believed to be a testing ground for experimental flight technology, Area 51 for many years also has been a site of immense interest to ufologists. If the US government had actually discovered some type of extraterrestrial technology, goes the reasoning, Area 51 would be the logical facility for testing and perhaps replicating these alien devices. For a recent history of the site's activities, see Annie Jacobson, *Area 51: An Uncensored History of America's Top Secret Military Base* (New York: Hachette, 2011). For a document more typical of the UFO community, see Grant Cameron and T. Scott Crain, Jr., *UFOs, Area 51, and Government Informants: A Report on Government Involvement in UFO Crash Retrievals* (self-published, CreateSpace, 2013).

115 Kurt Nimmo, "Hurricane Sandy: Divine Wind for Obama," October 26, 2012, http://www.infowars.com/hurricane-sandy-divine-wind-for-obama, accessed January 1, 2016.

116 Elana Freeland, *Chemtrails, HAARP, and the Full Spectrum Dominance of Planet Earth* (Los Angeles: Feral House, 2014).

117 "Method and Apparatus for Altering a Region in the Earth's Atmosphere, Ionosphere, and/or Magnetosphere," US Patent no. 4,686,605, August 11, 1987.
118 "Method and Apparatus for Altering a Region in the Earth's Atmosphere, Ionosphere, and/or Magnetosphere."
119 "Method and Apparatus for Altering a Region in the Earth's Atmosphere, Ionosphere, and/or Magnetosphere."
120 Freeland, *Chemtrails, HAARP, and the Full Spectrum Dominance of Planet Earth*, 87.
121 Freeland, *Chemtrails, HAARP, and the Full Spectrum Dominance of Planet Earth*, 87.
122 Morgellons disease remains a controversial and mysterious diagnosis. Morgellons presents as an intense itching or burning sensation accompanied by small fibers protruding from the affected area. The co-presence of acute anxiety and behavior associated with paranoia has led many to designate Morgellons a neuropsychiatric disorder, while others (especially sufferers) maintain that it is some form of contamination by a parasite or toxin: see Caroline S. Koblenzer, "The Challenge of Morgellons Disease," *Journal of the American Academy of Dermatology* 55.5 (2006): 920–22; Virginia R. Savely, Mary M. Leitao, and Raphael B. Stricker, "The Mystery of Morgellons Disease," *American Journal of Clinical Dermatology* 7, no. 1 (2006): 1–5.
123 Jerry E. Smith, *HAARP: The Ultimate Weapon of the Conspiracy* (Kempton, IL: Adventures Unlimited, 1998). Like many conspiracy writers, Smith believes that the philosophy guiding these plots stems from European traditions of radical materialism wherein there is "no soul" and man is just a "hunk of meat." Smith ascribes much of this philosophy to the "Austrian doctor and drug addict" Sigmund Freud and the experimental psychology of Wilhelm Max Wundt.
124 Sharon Rose Poet, *Technological Holocaust: Targeted in America* (Mt. Vernon, NH: Poetic Publications, 2013), 48.
125 James Lico, "The Mass Shootings Keep Happening Because Targeted Individuals Are Being Tortured," blog post, TI=HT, http://jameslico.com.
126 Michael Hardt and Antonio Negri, *Empire* (Cambridge, MA: Harvard University Press, 2001).
127 Louis Althusser, "Ideology and Ideological State Apparatuses," in *Lenin and Philosophy and Other Essays*, trans. Ben Brewster (London: New Left Books, 1971), 85–126.
128 The proximity of the Aurora shooting to Columbine High School has made Colorado a prominent target of suspicion in the conspiracy community. The odd focus of much of this suspicion is the recently constructed Denver International Airport. Speculation centers on the airport serving as a secret research lab for the government or a subterranean headquarters for the Freemasons or some other occultist society. This theory is based on (1) immense and allegedly unexplained cost overruns in building the airport; (2) runways arranged to form a type of "swastika"; (3) a Masonic symbol engraved in the airport's dedication marker; (4) claims that several five-story facilities were constructed beneath the airport; (5) odd murals in Terminal 5 ("In Peace and

Harmony with Nature" and "Children of the World Dream of Peace," both by Leo Tanguma) that allegedly depict the rise of the New World Order; and (6) "Blucifer," an immense sculpture of a blue horse (with glowing red eyes) that greets visitors as they enter the airport grounds. During the fabrication of the sculpture, largely interpreted as representing "Death—The Fourth Horseman of the Apocalypse," the piece fell on and killed its sculptor, Luis Jiménez: see J. Stolwijk, "Denver's Airport of Doom: The Story behind the World's Possibly Most Controversial Airport," *Leonardo Times*, vol. 18, no. 2, 2014.

129 In conspiracy circles, a "false-flag" operation is an event staged to discredit a particular political faction. Hitler's burning of the Reichstag is the classic example. According to this logic, Obama's agents staged the mass shooting to stir enmity against gun owners and their main political lobby, the National Rifle Association.

130 The close inspection of official photographs has long been a central pursuit in conspiracy theory. For many years, Kennedy conspiracy theorists maintained that the famous photograph of Lee Harvey Oswald (holding a rifle while standing in his back yard) had been altered in some way. The main point of contention involved the direction of the shadows issuing from Oswald's head and body. After examining the photo using 3D modeling technology, Hany Farid of Dartmouth has claimed it is legitimate: Hany Farid, "The Lee Harvey Oswald Backyard Photos: Real or Fake?" *Perception* 38, no. 11 (2009): 1731–34. Farid has also used computer modeling to study frames of the Zapruder film, the key primary document of Kennedy's assassination: Hany Farid, "A 3D Lighting and Shadow Analysis of the JFK Zapruder film (Frame 317)," Technical Report no. TR2010–677, 2010, Dartmouth College, Hanover, NH.

131 Alan Prendergast, "James Holmes: Inmate's Strange Tale of 'Confession' and Suicide Efforts," *Westword*, November 20, 2012, http://www.westword.com/news/james-holmes-inmates-strange-tale-of-confession-and-suicide-efforts-5861525, accessed January 1, 2016.

132 "DARPA Neuroscience Research and the Batman Massacre: James Holmes Father Linked to DARPA!" Before It's News, July 25, 2012, http://beforeitsnews.com/power-elite/2012/07/darpa-neuroscience-research-and-the-batman-massacre-james-holmes-father-linked-to-darpa-2434319.html, accessed January 1, 2016. Grace Powers provides her own account in a news release titled, "Batman Massacre: Why and Who and How," July 28, 2012, http://www.helpfreetheearth.com/news617_batmanwhohow.html.

133 Nick Allen, "Batman Colorado Shooting: James Holmes Fixated by Altered States of Mind," *The Telegraph*, July 23, 2012.

134 "Temporal Illusions Are a Form of Time Travel (i.e. James Holmes)," http://www.godlikeproductions.com/forum, accessed January 1, 2016. In a presentation posted on YouTube in 2006, Holmes shares his interest in "temporal illusions" and "subjective reality," citing the influence of his "mentor" John Jacobson at the

Computational Neurology Lab, University of California, San Diego. Conspiracy theorists frequently refer to an article co-written by two other scientists at the lab as contributing to the plausibility of time travel: see David M. Eagleman and Terrence J. Sejnowski, "Untangling Spatial from Temporal Illusions," *Trends in Neurosciences* 25, no. 6 (2002): 293.

135 "'Dark Knight Rises' Scene Eerily Shows 'Sandy Hook' Written on Map," Infowars.com, December 17, 2012, https://www.infowars.com/dark-knight-rises-shows-sandy-hook-written-on-map, accessed January 1, 2016.

136 "'Dark Knight Rises' Scene Eerily Shows 'Sandy Hook' Written on Map."

137 *The Notebook of James Holmes*, https://www.scribd.com/doc/266822752/The-Notebook-of-James-Holmes.

138 Sari Horowitz, Steve Vogel, and Michael Laris, "Officials: Navy Yard Shooter Carved Odd Messages into his Gun before Carnage," *Washington Post*, September 18, 2013.

139 Renee Pittman provides a timeline of these contacts in *The Targeting of Myron May: Florida State University Shooting* (self-pub., CreateSpace, 2015).

140 Pittman, *The Targeting of Myron May*.

141 "The Laws of the Cosmos: Wisely Follow or Blindly Suffer—The Definitive Law Guide to Spiritual Success"; "The Cosmo Way: A W(H)olistic Guide for the Total Transformation of Melanated People, Volume 1: The Detox"; and "The Cosmo Way: A W(H)olistic Guide for the Total Transformation of Melanated People, Volume 2: The Ascension": see Michael Schaub, "The Bizarre Books by Baton Rouge Police Shooter Gavin Eugene Long, a.k.a. Cosmo Setepenra," *Los Angeles Times*, July 16, 2016.

142 Vaughan Bell, "Online Information, Extreme Communities and Internet Therapy: Is the Internet Good for Our Mental Health?" *Journal of Mental Health* 16, no. 4 (2007): 445–57. Bell cites "pro-anorexia" websites as a prominent example.

143 Vaughan Bell, C. Maiden, A. Munoz-Solomando, and V. Reddy V, "'Mind Control' Experiences on the Internet: Implications for the Psychiatric Diagnosis of Delusions," *Psychopathology* 39, no. 2 (2006): 87–91.

144 Presidential Commission for the Study of Bioethical Issues, meeting 5, session 6, May 18, 2011, New York City. In his opening remarks, the moderator notes that a call for public comment on bioethics listed in the *Federal Register* received three hundred applications to address the committee. At a subsequent meeting of the Commission in Philadelphia, Dr. Walter J. Koroshetz of the National Institutes of Health offered comments that many TIs would find troubling:

> One technology which is a little bit off the grid, not that well-known, but I have been struck by the fact that it could be transformed on the short-term. And that's what's called MR-focused ultrasound. So it's a technology that's now being used so it's noninvasive stimulation of brain with ultrasound waves that can be targeted to a one millimeter spot. So Frank, what it is you may remember from—was one of the pioneers. So they're currently

using it to make lesions, but the really interesting part is that energies below lesions you can potentially either stimulate or shut off the brain with that and potentially without doing harm to the nervous system. If that plays out, that opens up the ability to interrogate all deep structures in the brain, turning them on and off. Seeing you know, in mental health conditions does it—you know, finding areas like Helen found just all over the brain. That would be the one thing that I think is a long shot, but I see as potentially really unbelievably short-term transformative. (Presidential Commission for the Study of Bioethical Issues, meeting 14, session 8, August 20, 2013, Philadelphia)

145 "How to Accept Social Isolation for Targeted Individuals," http://www.wikihow.com/Accept-Social-Isolation-for-Targeted-Individuals.
146 Like those deemed psychotic in previous centuries, targeted individuals recognize that contact with a psychiatrist is likely to compromise their liberty. "If you can avoid, do not go to psychiatrist. If you can avoid, do not take anti-depression pills. Do not take Paxil. Be aware of a sudden change in your mood. Emotions like sadness, shyness, anxieties are not an automatic sign of mental disorder or chronic depression. These are normal human emotions": "Survival Guide," Targeted Individuals 101, n.d., https://sites.google.com/site/targetedindividuals101/survival-guide, accessed January 1, 2016.
147 "Help for Targeted Individuals," http://www.targetedinamerica.com/helpforti.html, accessed January 1, 2016.
148 "General Overview," TI Protects: Justice for Human Experimentation Victims, n.d., http://tiprotects.com, accessed January 1, 2016.
149 Such products can be found at online stores such as LessEMF.com, http://www.lessemf.com/personal.html.
150 See http://quwave.com.
151 If the baseball cap proves ineffective, the company also manufactures a lined nylon "skull cap with ear flaps" under the trade name Brain Coat.

Epilogue

1 Matt Bean, "*Matrix* Makes Its Way into Court as Defense Strategy," May 21, 2003, CNN.com, accessed January 1, 2016.
2 Janice Morse, "Insanity Plea Made in Killing," *Cincinnati Enquirer*, August 15, 2002.
3 Mark Schone, "The Matrix Defense," *Boston Globe*, November 9, 2003.
4 Jean Baudrillard, "The Matrix Revisited" in *The Conspiracy of Art* (New York: Semiotext(e), 2005), 201–4.
5 When Charles Manson masterminded the notorious Helter Skelter murders in 1969, he arranged to have the wallet of a white victim left in the bathroom of a gas station in an African American neighborhood. The goal was to allow

the media to link a murder in Beverly Hills with militant blacks in Compton, thereby igniting the race war that Manson believed was inevitable.
6 David Lamb and Stephen Braun, "Snipers' Motives Start to Emerge," *Los Angeles Times*, December 14, 2003.
7 David Lamb and Stephen Braun, "Snipers' Motives Start to Emerge." Manson believed the Helter Skelter murders would incite a race riot, leading to a period of black rule. This was to be followed by Manson and his followers' emerging from their Death Valley encampment to assert their rightful place as the new white leaders.
8 Max Fischer, "Stephen K. Bannon's CPAC Comments, Annotated and Explained," *New York Times*, February 24, 2017.
9 In George Orwell's *1984*, the authoritarian state broadcasts a daily "two minutes hate" against its enemies. See George Orwell, *Nineteen Eighty-Four* (London: Secker & Warburg, 1949), 3.
10 Kyle Mantyla, "Mark Taylor: Freemasons and the Illuminati Are Using a Special Frequency to Change DNA and Make People Hate Trump," *Right Wing Watch*, August 31, 2017.
11 Joel Gold and Ian Gold, "The 'Truman Show' Delusion: Psychosis in the Global Village," *Cognitive Neuropsychiatry* 17, no. 6 (2012): 455–72.
12 "Reality TV Can Drive You Nuts," *New York Post*, July 24, 2008. See also Sarah Kershaw, "Look Closely, Doctor, Do You See the Camera?," *New York Times*, August 28, 2008. For a more detailed discussion of the "Truman Show delusion," see Mark Deuze, "Media Life," *Media, Culture and Society* 33, no. 1 (2011): 137–48.
13 Andrew Marantz, "Unreality Star," *New Yorker* (September 6, 2013), 32–37.
14 Joel Gold and Ian Gold, *Suspicious Minds: How Culture Shapes Madness* (New York: Simon and Schuster, 2015).
15 Gold and Gold, *Suspicious Minds*, 209.
16 Gold and Gold, *Suspicious Minds*, 220.
17 Gold and Gold, *Suspicious Minds*, 220.
18 Joshua Gamson, "The Unwatched Life Is Not Worth Living: The Elevation of the Ordinary in Celebrity Culture," *PMLA* 126, no. 4 (2011), 1061–69.
19 Michael A. Fuoco, Jerome L. Sherman, and Sadie Gurman, "McCain Volunteer Admits to Hoax," *Pittsburgh Post-Gazette*, October 25, 2008.
20 Julie Westhoff, "Herald Receives Letter from Pipe Bomb Suspect; Suspect Apprehended," *Badger Herald* (University of Wisconsin, Stout), May 7, 2002.
21 Helder's manifesto is posted online at http://www.thesmokinggun.com/file/luke-helder-manifesto.
22 Jean Baudrillard, *The Perfect Crime*, trans. Chris Turner (London: Verso, 1995), 8.
23 Chris Turner, the translator of *The Perfect Crime*, explains his choice of "alter-ation" as a neologism meant to capture Baudrillard's drawing on both French and English meanings of the verb *altérer*. Turner defines "alter-ation" as "involving a *negative* alteration, a change *for the worse*": Jean Baudrillard, *The Perfect Crime*, 153.

24 Baudrillard, *The Perfect Crime*, 8.
25 Baudrillard, *The Perfect Crime*, 25.
26 Jean Baudrillard, *The Intelligence of Evil; or, The Lucidity Pact*, trans. Chris Turner (London: Bloomsbury, 2005), 14.
27 Fredric Jameson, *Postmodernism, or, The Cultural Logic of Late Capitalism* (Durham, NC: Duke University Press, 1991).
28 While not futurists per se, Judith Butler, Ernesto Laclau, and Slavoj Žižek examine the fate of difference and the quest for the universal in their collaborative work, *Contingency, Hegemony, Universality: Contemporary Dialogues on the Left* (London: Verso, 2000).
29 The idea of storing brain data within a digital brain avatar is reminiscent of the mechanism behind "mad cow" disease, a disorder apparently created by feeding beef meal to cows.
30 Donna Haraway, "A Cyborg Manifesto: Science, Technology, and Socialist-Feminism in the Late Twentieth Century," in *Simians, Cyborgs and Women: The Reinvention of Nature* (New York; Routledge, 1991), 149–81.
31 Gilles Deleuze and Félix Guattari, *Anti-Oedipus*, trans. Robert Hurley, Mark Seem, and Helen R. Lane (Minneapolis: University of Minnesota Press, [1972] 1983); Gilles Deleuze and Félix Guattari, *A Thousand Plateaus*, trans. Brian Massumi (Minneapolis: University of Minnesota Press, [1980] 1987).
32 Deleuze and Guattari, *Anti-Oedipus*, 5.
33 Deleuze and Guattari, *Anti-Oedipus*, 59.
34 Deleuze and Guattari, *Anti-Oedipus*, 59.
35 A trace of egoistic agency remains even in the wildly careening paths of Deleuze and Guattari's desiring machine ("it" wants a glass of milk, apparently, as opposed to a tumbler of whisky, a stick in the eye, or a Mercedes E-Class convertible with leather seats and full navigation package).
36 See Gilles Deleuze, "Postscript on Control Societies," in Gilles Deleuze, *Negotiations, 1972–1990*, trans. Martin Joughin (New York: Columbia University Press, 1995), 177–82.
37 Deleuze, "Postscript on Control Societies."
38 This recalibration can already be seen in the realm of arts and leisure, sinkholes of meaningful experience that are now being drained through data rationalism. Why spend precious time perusing the shelves of a dusty bookstore or library when an algorithm has already predicted what "I," at his exact historical juncture of my selfhood, would most enjoy (or worse, "benefit from") reading? God forbid anyone encounter anything *by accident*. In the Amazonian age that precedes the advent of teleportation, there will come a time when all public space is haunted, and the only lingering encounters between embodied subjects will involve unfortunate collisions between UPS trucks and cyclists delivering takeout food.
39 In "San Junipero" (2016), a popular episode of the science-fiction series *Black Mirror*, elderly lesbians who fall in love as young women in a computer simulation

of a 1980s beach resort are free to spend eternity exploring a relationship denied them in meat life (and listening to Depeche Mode . . . forever). How, exactly, the couple will avoid the crippling psychodynamics inculcated by their previous existence remains unexplained. Like a video game, life as an immortal avatar apparently allows one to hit the "play" button again, Mr. and Ms. Pac-Man unencumbered by the trauma of having just been ripped apart by angry ghosts.

40 This stasis is temporary given that the universe, as Norbert Wiener reminds us, is destined to entropy and collapse.

Abramson, H. A., M. E. Jarvik, and M. W. Hirsch. "Lysergic Acid Diethylamide (LSD-25): X. Effect on Reaction Time to Auditory and Visual Stimuli." *Journal of Psychology* 40, no. 1 (1955): 39–52.
Achté, Karl Aimo. *Der Verlauf der Schizophrenien und der Schizophreniformen Psychosen: Eine vergleichende Untersuchung der Veränderungen in den Krankseitsbildern, der Prognosen und des Verhältnisses zwischen dem Kranken und dem Arzt in den Jahren 1933–1935 und 1953–1955.* Copenhagen: Ejnar Munksgaard, 1961.
Acland, Charles R. *Swift Viewing: The Popular Life of Subliminal Influence.* Durham, NC: Duke University Press, 2012.
Adams, George. *An Essay on Electricity, Explaining the Principles of that Useful Science; and Describing the Instruments, Contrived either to Illustrate the Theory or Render the Practice Entertaining.* London: J. Dillon, 1799.
A Dissertation upon the Nervous System and Its Influence upon the Soul. London: 1780.
Adorno, Theodor W. *Minima Moralia.* London: Verso, [1951] 2005.
Agresti, Enzo. "Studio delle varianti cliniche dei temi e dei contenuti deliranti in epoche diverse. Confronto dei vari tipi di delirio a distanza di circa un secolo." *Rivista di Patolologia Nervosa e Mentale* 80 (1959): 845–65.
Aldini, Giovanni. *An Account of the Galvanic Experiments Performed by John Aldini on the Body of a Malefactor Executed at Newgate.* London: Cuthell and Martin, 1803.
Aldini, Giovanni. *General Views on the Application of Galvanism to Medical Purposes; Principally in Cases of Suspended Animation,* London: J. Callow, 1819.

Alexander, John B. "The New Mental Battlefield: Beam Me Up, Spock." *Military Review* 60, no. 12 (1980): 47–54.

Alivisatos, A. Paul, Miyoung Chun, George M. Church, Ralph J. Greenspan, Michael L. Roukes, and Rafael Yuste. "The Brain Activity Map Project and the Challenge of Functional Connectomics." *Neuron* 74, no. 6 (2012): 970–74.

Alkon, Paul K. *Science Fiction before 1900: Imagination Discovers Technology.* New York: Routledge, 2013.

Allen, Gary, and Larry Abraham. *None Dare Call It Conspiracy.* Cutchogue, NY: Buccaneer, 1971.

Althusser, Louis, "Ideology and Ideological State Apparatuses." In *Lenin and Philosophy and Other Essays*, trans. Ben Brewster, 85–126. London: New Left Books, 1971.

"A Lunatic's Cunning." In *The Flowers of Anecdote, Wit, Humor, Gaiety, and Genius*, 147–49. London: Charles Tilt, 1829.

American Psychiatric Association, ed. *The Diagnostic and Statistical Manual of Mental Disorders*, 4th ed. (DSM-IV). Washington, DC: American Psychiatric Association, 1994.

American Psychiatric Association, ed. *The Diagnostic and Statistical Manual of Mental Disorders*, 5th ed. (DSM-V) Washington, DC: American Psychiatric Association, 2013.

American Psychiatric Association, ed. *Schizophrenia Spectrum and Other Psychotic Disorders: DSM-V Selections.* Washington, DC: American Psychiatric Association, 2016.

Anderson, Benedict. *Imagined Communities: Reflections on the Origin and Spread of Nationalism.* London: Verso, 2006.

Anderson, Ken. *Hitler and the Occult.* New York: Prometheus, 1995.

Andrejevic, Mark. *Infoglut: How Too Much Information Is Changing the Way We Think and Know.* New York: Routledge, 2013.

Andrejevic, Mark. "Surveillance in the Digital Enclosure." *Communication Review*, 10 (2007): 295–317.

Andrews, George C. *Extra-Terrestrials among Us.* Woodbury, MN: Llewellyn, 1986.

Anonymous. *A Full Discovery of the Strange Practices of Dr. Elliotson on the Bodies of His Female Patients!* London: E. Hancock, 1842.

Anonymous. *Man, More than a Machine.* London: W. Owen, 1752.

Arthur, Timothy Shay. *Agnes; or, The Possessed: A Revelation of Mesmerism.* Philadelphia: T. B. Peterson, 1848.

Atkinson, William Walker. *Mind Power: The Secret of Mental Magic.* Chicago: Advanced Thought, 1912.

Atkinson, William Walker. *Nuggets of the New Thought.* Chicago: Psychic Research Company, 1902.

Atkinson, William Walker. *Practical Mental Influence and Mental Fascination.* Chicago: Advanced Thought, 1908.

Atkinson, William Walker. *Thought-Force in Business and Everyday Life.* New York: Sydney Flower, 1900.
Atwood, George E., Donna M. Orange, and Robert D. Stolorow. "Shattered Worlds/Psychotic States: A Post-Cartesian View of the Experience of Personal Annihilation." *Psychoanalytic Psychology* 19, no. 2 (2002): 281–306.
"Automaton Extraordinary." *Scientific American* 48, no. 3 (March 25, 1848): 272.
Aviv, Rachel. "Which Way Madness Lies: Can Psychosis Be Prevented?" *Harper's Magazine*, December 2010, 35–46.
Bach, Sheldon. "Narcissism, Continuity, and the Uncanny." In *Narcissistic States and the Therapeutic Process*, 111–28. New York: Rowman and Littlefield, 1985.
Bailey, James Blake. *The Diary of a Resurrectionist, 1811–1812: To Which Are Added an Account of the Resurrection Men in London and a Short History of the Passing of the Anatomy Act.* London: Swan Sonnenschein, 1896.
Bailley, Jean Sylvain, and Benjamin Franklin. *De l'examen du magnétisme animal.* Geneva: Slatkine, [1784] 1980.
Bain, Donald. *The Control of Candy Jones.* Chicago: Playboy, 1976.
Baraduc, Hippolyte Ferdinand. *Iconographie de la force vitale cosmique od: Extrait de l'âme humaine, ses mouvements, ses lumières.* Paris: Paul Ollendorff, 1897.
Barkun, Michael. "Religion, Militias and Oklahoma City: The Mind of Conspiratorialists." *Terrorism and Political Violence* 8, no. 1 (1996): 50–64.
Barnes, William Horatio. *The Body Politic.* Cincinnati: Moore, Wilstach and Baldwin, 1866.
Barrett, William Fletcher. "On Some Phenomena Associated with Abnormal Conditions of Mind." *Proceedings of the Society for Psychical Research* 1 (1882): 238–44.
Barth, Alfred, and Bernd Küfferle. "Development of a Proverb Test for Assessment of Concrete Thinking Problems in Schizophrenic Patients." *Der Nervenarzt* 72, no. 11 (2001): 853–58.
Baudrillard, Jean. *The Ecstasy of Communication*, trans. Bernard Schultz and Caroline Schultz. New York: Semiotext(e), 1988.
Baudrillard, Jean. *The Intelligence of Evil; or, The Lucidity Pact*, trans. Chris Turner. London: Bloomsbury, 2005.
Baudrillard, Jean. "The Matrix Revisited." In *The Conspiracy of Art*, 201–4. New York: Semiotext(e), 2005.
Baudrillard, Jean. *The Perfect Crime*, trans. Chris Turner. London: Verso, 1995.
Baudrillard, Jean. *Screened Out*, trans. Chris Turner. London: Verso, 2002.
Baudrillard, Jean. *Simulations.* New York: Semiotext(e), [1981] 1994.
Baudrillard, Jean. *The System of Objects.* London: Verso, 1996.
Baum, Frank L., *The Master Key: An Electrical Fairy Tale Founded upon the Mysteries of Electricity and the Optimism of Its Devotees. It Was Written for Boys, but Others May Read It.* New York: Bowen-Merrill, 1901.
Bazin, André. "The Myth of Total Cinema." In *What Is Cinema?* vol. 1, trans. Hugh Gray, 17–22. Berkeley: University of California Press, 1967.

Beard, George Miller. *American Nervousness: Its Causes and Consequences; a Supplement to Nervous Exhaustion (Neurasthenia)*. New York: G. P. Putnam's Sons, 1881.

Beaudreau, Sherry Ann, and Stanley Finger. "Medical Electricity and Madness in the 18th Century: The Legacies of Benjamin Franklin and Jan Ingenhousz." *Perspectives in Biology and Medicine* 49, no. 3 (Summer 2006): 330–45.

Belcher, William. *Address to Humanity: Containing, a Letter to Dr. Thomas Monro; a Receipt to Make a Lunatic, and Seize His Estate; and a Sketch of a True Smiling Hyena*. London: Allen and West, 1796.

Bell, Michael F. *The Invisible Crime: Illegal Microchip Implants and Their Use against Humanity*. Chandler, AZ: Brighton, 2011. Kindle.

Bell, Vaughn. "Online Information, Extreme Communities and Internet Therapy: Is the Internet Good for Our Mental Health?" *Journal of Mental Health* 16, no. 4 (2007): 445–57.

Bell, Vaughn, Ethan Grech, Cara Maiden, Peter W. Halligan, and Hadyn D. Ellis. "'Internet Delusions': A Case Series and Theoretical Integration." *Psychopathology* 38, no. 3 (2005): 144–50.

Bell, Vaughn, Cara Maiden, Antonio Muñoz-Solomando, and Venu Reddy. "'Mind Control' Experiences on the Internet: Implications for the Psychiatric Diagnosis of Delusions." *Psychopathology* 39, no. 2 (2006): 87–91.

Belli, Stefano. "A Psychobiographical Analysis of Brian Douglas Wilson: Creativity, Drugs, and Models of Schizophrenic and Affective Disorders." *Personality and Individual Differences* 46, no. 8 (2009): 809–19.

Benford, Gregory, and Martin Greenberg, eds. *Hitler Victorious: 11 Stories of the German Victory in World War II*. New York: Berkley, 1986.

Bentall, Richard P. *Madness Explained: Psychosis and Human Nature*. London: Penguin, 2004.

Benz, Ernst. *The Theology of Electricity: On the Encounter and Explanation of Theology and Science in the Seventeenth and Eighteenth Centuries*. Eugene, OR: Pickwick, 1999.

Bergasse, Nicolas. *Le magnetisme animal, ou sur la théorie du monde et des êtres organisés*. Paris: La Haye, 1784.

Berke, Joseph, and Mary Barnes. *Mary Barnes: Two Accounts of a Journey through Madness*. London: MacGibbon and Kee, 1971.

Bernabeu, Ednita. "Science Fiction: A New Mythos." *Psychoanalytic Quarterly* 26, no. 4 (1957): 527–35.

Bernays, Edward L. *Crystallizing Public Opinion*. New York: Boni and Liveright, 1927,

Bernays, Edward L. *Propaganda*, New York: H. R. Liveright, 1928.

Bettelheim, Bruno. *The Empty Fortress*. New York: Simon and Schuster, 1967.

Bettelheim, Bruno. *The Informed Heart: Autonomy in a Mass Age*. Glencoe, IL: Free Press, 1960.

Bettelheim, Bruno. "Joey: A Mechanical Boy." *Scientific American* 3 (1959): 116–27.
Bhatia, Manjeet Singh. "Cell Phone Dependency—A New Diagnostic Entity." *Delhi Psychiatry Journal* 11, no. 2 (2008): 123–24.
Bhugra, Dinesh, and Oyedeji Ayonrinde. "Racism, Racial Life Events, and Mental Ill Health." In *Clinical Topics in Cultural Psychiatry*, ed. Rahul Bhattacharya, Sean Cross, and Dinesh Bhugra, 39–51. London: RCPsych, 2010.
Bhugra, Dinesh, and Kamaldeep Bhui. "Cross-Cultural Psychiatric Assessment." *Advances in Psychiatric Treatment* 3, no. 2 (1997): 103–10.
Bhugra, Dinesh, and Kamaldeep Bhui. "Cross-Cultural Psychiatric Assessment." In *Clinical Topics in Cultural Psychiatry*, ed. Rahul Bhattachary, Sean Cross, and Dinesh Bhugra, 247–60. London: RCPsych, 2010.
Bierce, Ambrose. *The Complete Short Stories of Ambrose Bierce*. Lincoln: University of Nebraska Press, 1984.
Bleuler, Eugen. *Dementia Praecox or the Group of Schizophrenias* (1911). New York: New York International Universities Press, 1952.
Bly, Nellie. *Ten Days in a Mad-House*. New York: Ian L. Munro, 1887.
Bocij, Paul. *Cyberstalking: Harassment in the Internet Age and How to Protect Your Family*. Westport, CT: Greenwood, 2004.
Bohlken, Jens, and Stefan Priebe. "Political Change and Course of Affective Psychoses: Berlin 1989–90." *Psychiatry Research* 37, no. 1 (1991): 1–4.
Bondeson, Jan. *Buried Alive: The Terrifying History of Our Most Primal Fear*. New York: W. W. Norton, 2001.
Boorstin, Daniel. *The Image: A Guide to Pseudo-Events in America*. New York: Atheneum, 1962.
Bouchal, M. "Changes in the Thematic Content of the Symptoms of Schizophrenia and Paraphrenia under the Influence of Social and Historic Development." *Ceskoslovenská psychiatrie* 54, no. 3 (1958): 149–53.
Bourdieu, Pierre. *Distinction: A Social Critique of the Judgement of Taste*. Cambridge, MA: Harvard University Press, 1984.
Bourque, F., E. Van der Ven, and A. Malla. "A Meta-analysis of the Risk for Psychotic Disorders among First- and Second-Generation Immigrants." *Psychological Medicine* 41, no. 5 (2011): 897–910.
Bowers, Malcolm B., Jr., and Daniel X. Freedman. "'Psychedelic' Experiences in Acute Psychoses." *Archives of General Psychiatry* 15, no. 3 (1966): 240–48.
Bradford, Peter, and Richard Wurman. *Information Architects*. New York: Graphis 1996.
Braude, Ann. *Radical Spirits: Spiritualism and Women's Rights in Nineteenth-Century America*. Bloomington: Indiana University Press, 2001.
Brecht, Bertolt. "A Short Organum for the Theatre." In *Brecht on Theatre: The Development of an Aesthetic*, ed. and trans. John Willett. London: Methuen, 1964. 179–205.

Brennan, Teresa. *History after Lacan*. London: Routledge, 2002.
Brian, Denis. *Sing Sing: The Inside Story of a Notorious Prison*. Amherst, NY: Prometheus, 2005.
Bromberg, Walter, and Franck Simon. "The 'Protest' Psychosis: A Special Type of Reactive Psychosis." *Archives of General Psychiatry* 19, no. 2 (1968): 155–60.
Brown, Isaac Baker. *On the Curability of Certain Forms of Insanity, Epilepsy, Catalepsy, and Hysteria in Females*. London: Robert Hardwicke, 1866.
Brussel, James A. "Autocatharsis as a Therapeutic Measure." *Psychiatric Quarterly* 10, no. 4 (1936): 552–74.
Bukatman, Scott. *Terminal Identity: The Virtual Subject in Postmodern Science Fiction*. Durham, NC: Duke University Press, 1993.
Burgess, Joshua. *The Medical and Legal Relations of Madness; Showing a Cellular Theory of Mind, and of Nerve Force, and also of Vegetative Vital Force*. London: John Churchill, 1858.
Burnham, Donald L. "Some Problems in Communication with Schizophrenic Patients." *Journal of the American Psychoanalytic Association* 3, no. 1 (1955): 67–81.
Bush, George. *Anastasis: or, The Doctrine of the Resurrection of the Body, Rationally and Scripturally Considered*. New York: Wiley and Putnam, 1845.
Butler, Judith, Ernesto Laclau, and Slavoj Žižek. *Contingency, Hegemony, Universality: Contemporary Dialogues on the Left*. London: Verso, 2000.
Byasson, H. *Essai sur la relation qui existe a l'etat physiologique entre l'activites cerebrale et la composition des urines*. Paris: G. Baillière, 1868.
Caldwell, Charles. *Facts in Mesmerism, and Thoughts on Its Causes and Uses*. Louisville, KY: Prentice and Weissinger, 1842.
Cameron, D. Ewen, John G. Lohrenz, and K. A. Handcock. "The Depatterning Treatment of Schizophrenia." *Comprehensive Psychiatry* 3, no. 2 (1962): 65–76.
Cameron, D. Ewen, and S. K. Pande. "Treatment of the Chronic Paranoid Schizophrenic Patient." *Canadian Medical Association Journal* 78, no. 2 (1958): 92.
Cameron, Grant, and T. Scott Crain, Jr., *UFOs, Area 51, and Government Informants: A Report on Government Involvement in UFO Crash Retrievals*. Self-published, CreateSpace, 2013.
Campbell, Hugh. *A Treatise on Nervous Exhaustion and the Diseases Induced by It*. London: Henry Renshaw, 1875.
Canguilhem, Georges. "Machine and Organism." In *Incorporations*, 44–70. New York: Zone, 1992.
Cannon, Brooke, and Lorraine Masinos Kramer. "Delusion Content across the 20th Century in an American Psychiatric Hospital." *International Journal of Social Psychiatry* 58, no. 3 (2012): 323–27.
Carey, James W. "Technology and Ideology: The Case of the Telegraph." *Prospects* 8 (1983): 303–25.
Carey, James W., and John J. Quirk. "The Mythos of the Electronic Revolution." *American Scholar* 39, no. 3 (1970): 395–424.

Carnegie, Dale. *How to Win Friends and Influence People*. New York: Simon and Schuster, 1937.

Caruana, Stephanie. *The Gemstone File: A Memoir*. Bloomington, IN: Trafford, 2006.

Catania, Kenneth C. "Leaping Eels Electrify Threats, Supporting Humboldt's Account of a Battle with Horses." *Proceedings of the National Academy of Sciences* 113, no. 25 (2016): 6979–84.

Caughey, John. *Imaginary Social Worlds: A Cultural Approach*. Lincoln: University of Nebraska Press, 1984.

Cavallo, Tiberius. *An Essay on the Theory and Practice of Medical Electricity*. London: Elmsly, Dilly, Bowen, 1781.

Cavell, Stanley. "The Fact of Television." *Daedalus* 111, no. 4 (Fall 1982): 75–96.

Cermolacce, M., L. Sass, and J. Parnas. "What Is Bizarre in Bizarre Delusions? A Critical Review." *Schizophrenia Bulletin* 36, no. 4 (2010): 667–79.

Chadwick, Peter K. "Peer-Professional First-Person Account: Schizophrenia from the Inside—Phenomenology and the Integration of Causes and Meanings." *Schizophrenia Bulletin* 33, no. 1 (2007): 166–73.

Chamberlin, O. K. *Electricity, Wonderful and Mysterious Agent*. New York: John F. Trow, 1862.

Cheyne, George. *The English Malady*. London: G. Strahan, 1733.

Chick, Jack T. *Are Roman Catholics Christians?* Chick Tract. Rancho Cucamonga, CA: Chick Publications, 1985.

Chick, Jack T. *My Name? . . . In the Vatican?* Chick Tract. Rancho Cucamonga, CA: Chick Publications, 1980.

Christakis, D. A., J. S. B. Ramirez, and J. M. Ramirez. "Overstimulation of Newborn Mice Leads to Behavioral Differences and Deficits in Cognitive Performance." *Scientific Reports* 2 (2012): 546.

Cline, Ernest. *Ready Player One*. New York: Random House, 2011.

Clute, John, and Peter Nicholls. *The Encyclopedia of Science Fiction*. New York: St. Martin's, 1995.

Cobb, Matthew. "Exorcizing the Animal Spirits: Jan Swammerdam on Nerve Function." *Nature Reviews Neuroscience* 3, no. 5 (2002): 395–400.

Cochrane, Peter. *Tips for Time Travelers*. New York: McGraw-Hill, 1999.

Conrad, Klaus. *Die beginnende Schizophrenie. Versuch einer Gestaltanalyse des Wahns*. Stuttgart: Georg Thieme, 1958.

Constantine, Alex. *Psychic Dictatorship in the USA*. Los Angeles: Feral House, 1995.

Cooper, John E. *Psychiatric Diagnosis in New York and London: A Comparative Study of Mental Hospital Admissions*. Maudslay Monograph no. 20. London: Oxford University Press, 1972.

Copeland, James. *A Dictionary of Practical Medicine*. London: Longman, Green, Brown, Longmans, and Roberts, 1858.

Coston, Charisse Tia Maria, ed. *Victimizing Vulnerable Groups: Images of Uniquely High-Risk Crime Targets*. Westport, CT: Praeger, 2004.

Cowen, Joseph Robert. "A Note on the Meaning of Television to a Psychotic Woman." *Bulletin of the Menninger Clinic* 23 (1959): 202–3.

Crawford, William Jackson. *Reality of Psychic Phenomena*. New York: E. P. Dutton, 1918.

Cullen, Regina. "The Travelling Torture Chamber." In *Paranoid Women Collect Their Thoughts*, ed. Joan D'Arc, 1–6. Providence, RI: Paranoia, 1996.

Darnton, Robert. *Mesmerism and the End of the Enlightenment in France*. Cambridge, MA: Harvard University Press, 1968.

Davenport, Noa, Ruth Distler Schwartz, and Gail Pursell Elliott. *Mobbing: Emotional Abuse in the American Workplace*. Ames, IA: Civil Society, 1999.

Davy, Sir Humphry. *A Discourse, Introductory to a Course of Lectures on Chemistry*. London: Johnson, Cadell, Davies, 1802.

De Hert, Marc, Geerdt Magiels, and Erik Thys. *The Secret of the Brain Chip: A Self-Help Guide for People Experiencing Psychosis*. Brussels: EPO Press, 2003.

De La Peña, Carolyn Thomas. *The Body Electric: How Strange Machines Built the Modern American*. New York: New York University Press, 2003.

Delbourgo, James. *A Most Amazing Scene of Wonders: Electricity and Enlightenment in Early America*. Cambridge, MA: Harvard University Press, 2006.

Deleuze, Gilles. "Postscript on Control Societies." In Gilles Deleuze, *Negotiations, 1972–1990*, trans. Martin Joughin, 177–82. New York: Columbia Press, 1995.

Deleuze, Gilles, and Félix Guattari. *Anti-Oedipus*, trans. Robert Hurley, Mark Seem, and Helen R. Lane. Minneapolis: University of Minnesota Press, [1972] 1983.

Deleuze, Gilles, and Félix Guattari. *A Thousand Plateaus*, trans Brian Massumi. Minneapolis: University of Minnesota Press, [1980] 1987.

Delgado, Jose M. R. "Aggressive Behavior Evoked by Radio Stimulation in Monkey Colonies." *American Zoologist* 6, no. 4 (1966): 669–81.

Delgado, Jose M. R. *Physical Control of the Mind: Toward a Psychocivilized Society*. New York: Harper and Row, 1969.

Delgado, Jose M. R., Vernon Mark, William Sweet, Frank Ervin, Gerhard Weiss, George Bach-Y-Rita, and Rioji Hagiwara. "Intracerebral Radio Stimulation and Recording in Completely Free Patients." *Journal of Nervous and Mental Disease* 147, no. 4 (October 1968): 329–40.

Denning, Melita, and Osborne Phillips. *Psychic Self-Defense and Well-Being*. St. Paul, MN: Llewellyn, 1980.

De Pauw, Karel W., and T. Krystyna Szulecka. "Dangerous Delusions: Violence and the Misidentification Syndromes." *British Journal of Psychiatry* 152, no. 1 (1988): 91–96.

Derrida, Jacques, and Bernard Stiegler. *Echographies of Television*. Cambridge: Polity, 2002.

Desbeaux, Émile. *Physique populaire*. Paris: Librairie Marpon et Flammarion, 1891.

"Description of the Journey to Mars, and Wonder Information Furnished by Madam Ehrenborg." In *A Book Written by the Spirits of the So-Called Dead*, with Their Own Materialized Hands, by the Process of Independent Slate-Writing, through Mrs. Lizzie S. Green and Others, as Mediums,* comp. C. G. Helleberg, 54–107. Cincinnati, OH: C. G. Helleberg, 1883.

Desmaze, Charles. *Histoire de la médecine légale en France: D'après les lois, registres et arrêts criminels.* Paris: Charpentier, 1880.

Deuze, Mark. "Media Life." *Media, Culture and Society* 33, no. 1 (2011): 137–48.

Deutsch, Helene. "Occult Processes Occurring during Psychoanalysis." *Imago* 12 (1926): 418–33.

Devereux, George. "A Summary of Istvan Hollos' Theories." In *Psychoanalysis and the Occult*, ed. George Devereux, 199–203. New York: International Universities Press, 1953.

Dick, Philip K. *The Exegesis of Philip K. Dick*, ed. Pamela Jackson and Jonathan Lethem. Boston: Houghton Mifflin Harcourt, 2011.

Dick, Philip K. *The Man in the High Castle.* New York: G. P. Putnam's Sons, 1962.

"Diseases of Overworked Men." *Scientific American* 10, no. 13 (March 26, 1864): 208.

Doane, Mary Ann. "Information, Crisis, Catastrophe." In *Logics of Television: Essays in Cultural Criticism*, 222–39. Bloomington: Indiana University Press, 1990.

Douglas, Robert. *Adventures of a Medical Student.* New York: Burgess, Stringer, 1848.

Douglas, Susan. *Inventing American Broadcasting, 1899–1922.* Baltimore: Johns Hopkins University Press, 1989.

Drake, W. R. *Gods or Spacemen?* Amherst, WI: Amherst, 1964.

Dubuffet, Jean, ed., *L'Art Brut*, vol. 3. Lausanne: Collection de l'Art Brut, 1965.

Dubuffet, Jean. *L'art brut préféré aux arts culturels.* Paris: Galerie René Drouin, 1949.

Duncan, David Ewing. "Implanting Hope." *Technology Review* 108, no. 3 (2005): 48–54.

Durant, David. "Ann Radcliffe and the Conservative Gothic." *Studies in English Literature 1500–1900* 22, no. 3 (1982): 519–30.

Duvard, Caen. "Case of Catalepsy with Transposition of the Senses." *Medical Examiner* 1, no. 13 (August 27, 1842): 558–60.

Eagleman, David M., and Terrence J. Sejnowski. "Untangling Spatial from Temporal Illusions." *Trends in Neurosciences* 25, no. 6 (2002): 293.

Eggers, David. *The Circle.* New York: Vintage, 2013.

Eigen, Michael. *The Psychotic Core.* Landham, MD: Jason Aronson, 1993.

Einhorn, Ira. "A Disturbing Communiqué," *CoEvolution Quarterly* 16 (Winter 1977), 76–78.

Eissler, Kurt. *Talent and Genius: The Fictitious Case of Tausk contra Freud.* New York: Quadrangle, 1971.

Eissler, Kurt. *Victor Tausk's Suicide.* Madison, CT: International Universities Press, 1983.

Ekstein, Rudolf, and Elaine Caruth. *Children of Time and Space, of Action and Impulse.* New York: Appleton-Century-Crofts, 1966.

El-Hai, Jack. *The Lobotomist: A Maverick Medical Genius and His Tragic Quest to Rid the World of Mental Illness.* New York: John Wiley and Sons, 2005.

Elkisch, Paula. "Significant Relationship between the Human Figure and the Machine in the Drawings of Boys." *American Journal of Orthopsychiatry* 22, no. 2 (1952): 379.

Ellis, John. *Seeing Things: Television in the Age of Uncertainty*. London: I. B. Tauris, 2000.

Epstein, Seymour, and Margaret Coleman. "Drive Theories of Schizophrenia." *Psychosomatic Medicine* 32, no. 2 (1970): 113–40.

Ehrenweld, H. J. "Telepathy in the Psychoanalytic Situation." *British Journal of Medical Psychology* 20 (1944): 51–62.

Essig, Mark. *Edison and the Electric Chair: A Story of Light and Death*. New York: Bloomsbury, 2005.

Esquirol, Jean-Étienne Dominique. *Mental Maladies: A Treatise on Insanity*. Philadelpha: Lea and Blanchard, 1845.

"Experiments upon the Body of Morris, Executed Jan. 15, 1841." *Medical Examiner* 4, no. 4 (January 23, 1841): 58–61.

Farid, Hany. "A 3D Lighting and Shadow Analysis of the JFK Zapruder Film (Frame 317)." Technical Report no. TR2010–677, 2010. Dartmouth College, Hanover, NH.

Farid, Hany. "The Lee Harvey Oswald Backyard Photos: Real or Fake?" *Perception* 38, no. 11 (2009): 1731–34.

Faris, Robert E. Lee, and Henry Warren Dunham. *Mental Disorders in Urban Areas: An Ecological Study of Schizophrenia and Other Psychoses* (1939). Chicago: University of Chicago Press, 1965.

Farrell, John. *Freud's Paranoid Quest: Psychoanalysis and Modern Suspicion*. New York: New York University Press, 1996.

Fenster, Mark. *Conspiracy Theories: Secrecy and Power in American Culture*. Minneapolis: University of Minnesota Press, 1999.

Feuer, Jane. "The Concept of Live Television: Ontology as Ideology." In *Regarding Television: Critical Approaches*, E. Ann Kaplan, ed., 12–23. Los Angeles: American Film Institute, 1983.

Fetridge, William Pembroke. "Germany." In *Harper's Hand-book for Travellers in Europe and the East*, 340–41. New York: Harper and Brothers, 1871.

Field, Matthew D. "Is Belief in Spiritualism Ever Evidence of Insanity Per Se?" *Medico-Legal Journal* 6 (1888): 489–95.

Finger, Stanley. "Benjamin Franklin, Electricity, and the Palsies: Historical Neurology." *Neurology* 66, no. 11 (May 23, 2006): 1559–63.

Finger, Stanley, and Mark B. Law. "Karl August Weinhold and His 'Science' in the Era of Mary Shelley's *Frankenstein*: Experiments on Electricity and the Restoration of Life." *Journal of the History of Medicine and Allied Sciences* 53 (1998): 161–80.

Finster, Howard, and Tom Patterson. *Howard Finster, Stranger from Another World: Man of Visions Now on This Earth*. New York: Abbeville Press, 1989.

First, Michael B., Allen France, and Harold Alan Pincus. DSM-IV-TR Guidebook. American Psychiatric Publishing, Inc., 2004.
Fisher, Vivian E. *An Introduction to Abnormal Psychology*. New York: Macmillan, 1929.
Fishman, Sandra, and Raymond Fishman. "Cultural Influences on Symptom Presentation in Childhood." *Journal of the American Academy of Child and Adolescent Psychiatry* 38, no. 6 (1999): 782–83.
FitzGerald, Michael. *The Nazi Occult War: Hitler's Compact with the Forces of Evil*. London: Arcturus, 2013.
Fleming, Michael. *Stalked by the FBI: COINTELPRO Targeted Individuals*. Self-published, Amazon Digital, 2014.
Flint, Edward N. "A Case of Paranoia." *Journal of Nervous and Mental Disease* 20 (1893): 567–78.
Flournoy, Theodore. *From India to the Planet Mars: A Case of Multiple Personality with Imaginary Languages*, ed. Sonu Shamdasani, trans. Daniel B. Vermilye. Princeton, NJ: Princeton University Press, [1899] 1994.
Fodor, Nandor. "Telepathy in Analysis." *Psychiatric Quarterly* 21 (1947): 171–89.
Forrester, John. *The Seductions of Psychoanalysis: Freud, Lacan, and Derrida*. Cambridge: Cambridge University Press, 1992.
Fortune, Dion. *Psychic Self-Defense*. London: Rider, 1930.
Foster, Jr., John S.; Gjelde, Earl; Graham, William R.; Hermann, Robert J.; Kluepfel, Henry M.; Lawson, Richard L.; Soper, Gordon K.; Wood, Lowell L.; Woodard, Joan B. *Report of the Commission to Assess the Threat to the United States from Electromagnetic Pulse (EMP) Attack: Critical National Infrastructures*. April 2008. http://www.empcommission.org/docs/A2473-EMP_Commission-7MB.pdf.
Foucault, Michel. *Discipline and Punish*, trans. Alan Sheridan. New York: Vintage, 1979.
Foucault, Michel. *History of Madness*. London: Routledge, 2013.
Foucault, Michel. *The History of Sexuality*. New York: Pantheon, 1978.
Foucault, Michel. *Psychiatric Power: Lectures at the Collège de France, 1973–1974*, vol. 1. New York: Macmillan, 2008.
Frahm, Ole. "Radio und Schizophrenie: Anmerkungen zu Daniel Paul Schrebers Radiotheorie avant la letter." *Kultur und Gespenster* 14 (Autumn 2013): 198–229.
Frank, Jane. *The Art of Richard Powers*. London: Paper Tiger, 2001.
Franz, Victoria A., Carol R. Glass, Diane B. Arnkoff, and Mary Ann Dutton. "The Impact of the September 11th Terrorist Attacks on Psychiatric Patients: A Review." *Clinical Psychology Review* 29, no. 4 (2009): 339–47.
Fraser, George A., ed. *The Dilemma of Ritual Abuse: Cautions and Guides for Therapists*. Washington, DC: American Psychiatric Press, 1997.
Freeland, Elana. *Chemtrails, HAARP, and the Full Spectrum Dominance of Planet Earth*. Los Angeles: Feral House, 2014.
Freeman, C. P. L., and K. E. Cheshire. "Attitude Studies on Electroconvulsive Therapy." *Journal of ECT* 2, no. 1 (1986): 31–42.

Freeman, Daniel, and Jason Freeman. *Paranoia: The 21st-Century Fear*. London: Oxford University Press, 2008.

Freud, Sigmund. "Beyond the Pleasure Principle" (1920). In *The Standard Edition of the Complete Psychological Works of Sigmund Freud*, 24 vols., ed. James Strachey, 18:7–64. London: Hogarth, 1955.

Freud, Sigmund. "Civilization and Its Discontents" (1930). In *The Standard Edition of the Complete Psychological Works of Sigmund Freud*, 24 vols., ed. James Strachey, 21:59–148. London: Hogarth, 1955.

Freud, Sigmund. "Dreams and Occultism" (1932). In *The Standard Edition of the Complete Psychological Works of Sigmund Freud*, 24 vols., ed. James Strachey, 22:31–56. London: Hogarth, 1955.

Freud, Sigmund. "Dreams and Telepathy" (1922). In *The Standard Edition of the Complete Psychological Works of Sigmund Freud*, 24 vols., ed. James Strachey, 18:195–220. London: Hogarth, 1955.

Freud, Sigmund. "The Future of an Illusion" (1927). In *The Standard Edition of the Complete Psychological Works of Sigmund Freud*, 24 vols., ed. James Strachey, 21:5–58. London: Hogarth, 1955.

Freud, Sigmund. "Letter to Ernest Jones (March 7, 1926)." In Sigmund Freud and Ernest Jones, *The Complete Correspondence of Sigmund Freud and Ernest Jones, 1908–1939*, ed. R. Andrew Paskauska, 596–97. Cambridge, MA: Harvard University Press, 1993.

Freud, Sigmund. "Letter to Wilhelm Fliess (May 25, 1895)." In *The Complete Letters of Sigmund Freud to Wilhelm Fliess, 1887–1904*, ed. Jeffrey M. Masson. Cambridge, MA: Harvard University Press, 1985.

Freud, Sigmund. "Neurosis and Psychosis" (1924). In *The Standard Edition of the Complete Psychological Works of Sigmund Freud*, 24 vols., ed. James Strachey, 19:149–53. London: Hogarth, 1955.

Freud, Sigmund. "The Occult Significance of Dreams" (1925). In *The Standard Edition of the Complete Psychological Works of Sigmund Freud*, 24 vols., ed. James Strachey, 19:135–40. London: Hogarth, 1955.

Freud, Sigmund. "On Narcissism: An Introduction" (1914). In *The Standard Edition of the Complete Psychological Works of Sigmund Freud*, 24 vols., ed. James Strachey, 14:67–102. London: Hogarth, 1955.

Freud, Sigmund. "Project for a Scientific Psychology" (1895). In *The Standard Edition of the Complete Psychological Works of Sigmund Freud*, 24 vols., ed. James Strachey, 1:283–392. London: Hogarth, 1955.

Freud, Sigmund. "Psychoanalysis and Telepathy" (1921). In *The Standard Edition of the Complete Psychological Works of Sigmund Freud*, 24 vols., ed. James Strachey, 18:173–94. London: Hogarth, 1955.

Freud, Sigmund. "Psychoanalytic Notes upon an Autobiographical Account of a Case of Paranoia" (1911). In *The Standard Edition of the Complete Psychological Works of Sigmund Freud*, 24 vols., ed. James Strachey, 12:9–82. London: Hogarth, 1955.

Freud, Sigmund. "Recommendations to Physicians Practising Psycho-Analysis" (1912). In *The Standard Edition of the Complete Psychological Works of Sigmund Freud*, 24 vols., ed. James Strachey, 12:111–20. London: Hogarth, 1955.

Freud, Sigmund. "Totem and Taboo" (1913). In *The Standard Edition of the Complete Psychological Works of Sigmund Freud*, 24 vols., ed. James Strachey, 13:1–162. London: Hogarth, 1955.

Freud, Sigmund. "The 'Uncanny'" (1919). In *The Standard Edition of the Complete Psychological Works of Sigmund Freud*, 24 vols., ed. James Strachey, 17:218–56. London: Hogarth, 1955.

Freud, Sigmund. "Victor Tausk" (1919) In *The Standard Edition of the Complete Psychological Works of Sigmund Freud*, 24 vols., ed. James Strachey, 17:273–76. London: Hogarth, 1955.

Frey, Allan H. "Human Auditory System Response to Modulated Electromagnetic Energy." *Journal of Applied Physiology* 17, no. 4 (1962): 689–92.

Froese, Arno. *The Coming Digital God*. West Columbia, SC: Midnight Call Ministries, 2001.

Fry, Peter Vincent. *Apocalypse Unknown: The Struggle to Protect America from an Electromagnetic Pulse Catastrophe*. CreateSpace Independent Publishing Platform, 2013.

Fry, Peter Vincent. *Blackout Wars: State Initiatives to Achieve Preparedness against an Electromagnetic Pulse (EMP) Catastrophe*. CreateSpace Independent Publishing Platform, 2015.

Fry, Peter Vincent. *Electric Armageddon: Civil-Military Preparedness for an Electromagnetic Pulse Catastrophe*. CreateSpace Independent Publishing Platform, 2013.

Gallinek, Alfred. "Fear and Anxiety in the Course of Electroshock Therapy." *American Journal of Psychiatry* 113, no. 5 (November, 1956): 428–34.

Gallois, M. L. "Experiments on the Principle of Life: Especially on That of the Motions of the Heart, and on the Seat of this Principle." *New England Journal of Medicine, Surgery and Collateral Branches of Science* 3, no. 1 (1814): 11–20.

Galvani, Luigi. *Effects of Electricity on Muscular Motion*. Norwalk, CT: Burndy Library, [1791] 1953.

Gamson, Joshua. "The Unwatched Life Is Not Worth Living: The Elevation of the Ordinary in Celebrity Culture." PMLA 126, no. 4 (2011): 1061–69.

Garvey, Michael Angelo. *The Silent Revolution, or, The Future Effects of Steam and Electricity upon the Condition of Mankind*. London: William and Frederick G. Cash, 1852.

Gavin, B. E., B. D. Kelly, A. Lane, and E. O'Callaghan. "The Mental Health of Migrants." *Irish Medical Journal* 109, no. 1 (2016): 229–30.

Gaygen, Daniel. "Effects of Ambient Music Exposure on Simulated Buy Decisions." *International Journal of Business and Social Science* 4, no. 4 (2013): 184–94.

Geoghegan, Bernard Dionysius. "From Information Theory to French Theory: Jakobson, Lévi-Strauss, and the Cybernetic Apparatus." *Critical Inquiry* 38, no. 1 (2011): 96–126.

Gibson, William. *Pattern Recognition*. New York: G. P. Putnam's Sons, 2003.

Glass, George S. "Psychedelic Drugs, Stress, and the Ego: The Differential Diagnosis of Psychosis Associated with Psychotomimetic Drug Use." *Journal of Nervous and Mental Disease* 156, no. 4 (1973): 232–41.

Gold, Joel, and Ian Gold. *Suspicious Minds: How Culture Shapes Madness*. New York: Simon and Schuster, 2015.

Gold, Joel, and Ian Gold. "The 'Truman Show' Delusion: Psychosis in the Global Village." *Cognitive Neuropsychiatry* 17, no. 6 (2012): 455–72.

Goldmark, Josephine Clara, and Louis Dembitz Brandeis. *Fatigue and Efficiency: A Study in Industry*. New York: Charities Publication Committee, 1912.

Goodfellow, L. D. "A Psychological Interpretation of the Results of the Zenith Radio Experiments in Telepathy." *Journal of Experimental Psychology* 23 (1938): 601–32.

Goodrick-Clarke, Nicholas. *The Occult Roots of Nazism: Secret Aryan Cults and Their Influence on Nazi Ideology*. London: I. B. Tauris, 1985.

Grant, Brian W. *Schizophrenia, a Source of Social Insight*. Philadelphia: Westminster Press, 1975.

Grau, Carles, Romuald Ginhoux, Alejandro Riera, Thanh Lam Nguyen, Hubert Chauvat, Michel Berg, Julià L. Amengual, Alvaro Pascual-Leone, and Giulio Ruffini. "Conscious Brain-to-Brain Communication in Humans Using Noninvasive Technologies." *PLoS One* 9, no. 8 (2014): e105225.

Greenfeld, Liah. *Mind, Modernity, Madness*. Cambridge, MA: Harvard University Press, 2013.

Greenland, Colin. *Entropy Exhibition: Michael Moorcock and the British "New Wave" in Science Fiction*. London: Routledge, 2013.

Greenway, John. "Galvanism as Therapeutic Agent: Perkins's 'Metallic Tractors' and the Placebo Effect." *ANQ* 14, no. 4 (2001): 24–37.

Griggs, William. *Lunacy versus Liberty: A Letter on the Defective State of the Law, as Regards Insane Persons, and Private Asylums*. London: W. Griggs, 1832.

Gunning, Tom. "Phantom Images and Modern Manifestations: Spirit Photography, Magic Theater, Trick Films, and Photography's Uncanny." In *Fugitive Images: From Photography to Video*, ed. Patrice Petro, 42–71. Bloomington: Indiana University Press, 1995.

Gurland, Barry J., Joseph L. Fleiss, John E. Cooper, Robert E. Kendell, and Robert Simon. "Cross-National Study of Diagnosis of the Mental Disorders: Some Comparisons of Diagnostic Criteria from the First Investigation." *American Journal of Psychiatry* 125, no. 10S (1969): 30–39.

Hall, John. *A New Breed: Satellite Terrorism in America*. New York: Strategic, 2009.

Hall, Judy. *The Art of Psychic Protection*. Forres, UK: Findhorn, 1996.

Hann-Kende, Fanny. "On the Role of Transference and Counter-Transference in Psychoanalysis." *Internationale Zeitschrift für Psychoanalyse* 22 (1936): 478–86.

Haraway, Donna J. "A Cyborg Manifesto: Science, Technology, and Socialist-Feminism in the Late 20th Century." *International Handbook of Virtual Learn-*

ing Environments, ed. Joel Weiss, Jason Nolan, Jeremy Hunsinger, and Peter Trifonas (Dordrecht: Springer, 2006): 117–58.

Haraway, Donna J. *Primate Visions: Gender, Race, and Nature in the World of Modern Science*. New York: Routledge, 1989.

Harber, Francis. *Schizophrenia, Obsession, Exorcism, Reincarnation, and Mediums*. New York: Vantage, 1976.

Hardt, Michael, and Antonio Negri. *Empire*. Cambridge, MA: Harvard University Press, 2001.

Hart, Cheney. "An Account of a Cure of a Paralytic Arm, by Electricity: In a Letter from Cheney Hart, MD, to Mr. William Watson, FRS." *Philosophical Transactions* 49 (1755): 558–63.

Hartmann, Franz. *Buried Alive: An Examination into the Occult Causes of Apparent Death, Trance, and Catalepsy*. Boston: Occult, 1895.

Haslam, John. *Illustrations of Madness: Exhibiting a Singular Case of Insanity and a No Less Remarkable Difference in Medical Opinion: Developing the Nature of Assailment, and the Manner of Working Events; with a Description of the Tortures Experienced by Bomb-Bursting, Lobster-Cracking, and Lengthening the Brain*. London: G. Hayden, 1810.

Haslam, John. *Observations on Madness and Melancholy: Including Practical Remarks on Those Diseases; Together with Cases: and an Account of the Morbid Appearances on Dissection*. London: J. Callow, 1809.

Hay, Celestine. "Command-Automatism and Echopraxia to Television." *American Journal of Psychiatry* 112, no. 1 (1955): 65.

Hayles, N. Katherine. *How We Became Posthuman: Virtual Bodies in Cybernetics, Literature, and Informatics*. Chicago: University of Chicago Press, 1999.

Hayworth, Kenneth J. "Electron Imaging Technology for Whole Brain Neural Circuit Mapping." *International Journal of Machine Consciousness* 4, no. 1 (2012): 87–108.

Heidegger, Martin. *The Question of Technology and Other Essays*, trans. William Lovitt. New York: Harper and Row, 1977.

Hill, Joel Milam. "Hallucinations in Psychoses." *Journal of Nervous and Mental Disease* 83, no. 4 (1936): 405–21.

Hinduja, Sameer, and Justin W. Patchin. "Bullying, Cyberbullying, and Suicide." *Archives of Suicide Research* 14, no. 3 (2010): 206–21.

Hirjak, Dusan, and Thomas Fuchs. "Delusions of Technical Alien Control: A Phenomenological Description of Three Cases." *Psychopathology* 43, no. 2 (2010): 96–103.

Hoerl, Christoph. "On Thought Insertion." *Philosophy, Psychiatry, and Psychology* 8, nos. 2–3 (June–September 2001): 189–200.

Hollingshead, Greg. *Bedlam: A Novel of Love and Madness*. New York: Thomas Dunne, 2006.

Holloway, Donell, and Lelia Green. "The Internet of Toys." *Communication Research and Practice* 2, no. 4 (2016): 1–14.

Hopewell-Ash, Edwin Lancelot. *The Problem of Nervous Breakdown.* New York: Macmillan, 1920.

Hopper, Kim, and Joseph Wanderling. "Revisiting the Developed versus Developing Country Distinction in Course and Outcome in Schizophrenia: Results from ISoS, the WHO Collaborative Follow-Up Project." *Schizophrenia Bulletin* 26, no. 4 (2000): 835–46.

Horkheimer, Max. "The Concept of Man" (1957). In *Critique of Instrumental Reason*, trans. Matthew J. O'Connell, 1–33. London: Verso, 2012.

Horkheimer, Max, and Theodor Adorno. "The Culture Industry: Enlightenment as Mass Deception." In *Dialectic of Enlightenment*, trans. John Cumming, 120–67. London: Verso, 1972.

Horner, William E. "Observations and Experiments on Certain Parts of the Nervous System." *Philadelphia Journal of the Medical and Physical Sciences* (July 1, 1820): 285–99.

Hosokawa, Shuhei. "The Walkman Effect." *Popular Music* 4 (1984): 165–80.

Huntley, Noel. *ETs and Aliens: Who Are They? and Why Are They Here?* Bloomington, IN: Xlibris, 2002.

Jacobson, Annie. *Area 51: An Uncensored History of America's Top Secret Military Base.* New York: Hachette, 2011.

Jameson, Fredric. *Archaeologies of the Future: The Desire Called Utopia and Other Science Fictions.* London: Verso, 2005.

Jameson, Fredric. *Postmodernism, or, The Cultural Logic of Late Capitalism.* Durham, NC: Duke University Press, 1991.

Jaspers, Karl. *General Psychopathology* (1913), trans. J. Hoenig and Marian W. Hamilton. Chicago: University of Chicago Press, 1963.

Jaspers, Karl. *General Psychopathology*, 7th ed., trans. J. Hoenig and Marian W. Hamilton. Baltimore: Johns Hopkins University Press, 1997.

Jay, Mike. *The Air Loom Gang: The Strange and True Story of James Tilly Matthews and His Visionary Madness.* New York: Four Walls Eight Windows, 2004.

Jeffrey, Grant R. *Surveillance Society: The Rise of the Antichrist.* Oklahoma City, OK: Frontier Research, 2000.

Johnson, Matt. "Fear and Power: From Naivete to a Believer in Cult Abuse." *Journal of Psychohistory* 21, no. 4 (1994): 435–41.

Jones, Ernest. "Letter to Sigmund Freud (March 17, 1911)." In Sigmund Freud and Ernest Jones, *The Complete Correspondence of Sigmund Freud and Ernest Jones, 1908–1939*, ed. R. Andrew Paskauskas. Cambridge, MA: Harvard University Press, 1995.

Jones, Franklin D. "The Schizophrenic Theme in Science Fiction." Presentation at Senior Residents' Symposium, Department of Psychiatry and Neurology, Walter Reed Army Medical Center, Washington DC, June 11, 1965.

Kaczynski, Theodore. *Technological Slavery: The Collected Writings of Theodore J. Kaczynski, a.k.a. "The Unabomber."* Los Angeles: Feral House, 2010.

Kahan, Dan M., Ellen Peters, Erica Dawson, and Paul Slovic. "Motivated Numeracy and Enlightened Self-Government." *Behavioural Public Policy* 1, no. 1 (May 2017): 54–86.
Kanner, Leo. "Autistic Disturbances of Affective Contact." *Nervous Child* 2 (1943): 217–50.
Kantor, Elizabeth D., C. D. Rehm, J. S. Haas, A. T. Chan, and E. L. Giovannucci. "Trends in Prescription Drug Use among Adults in the United States from 1999–2012." *Journal of the American Medical Association* 314, no. 17 (2015): 1818–30.
Kaplan, Louis. *The Strange Case of William Mumler, Spirit Photographer*. Minneapolis: University of Minnesota Press, 2008.
Kapur, Shitij. "Psychosis as a State of Aberrant Salience: A Framework Linking Biology, Phenomenology, and Pharmacology in Schizophrenia." *American Journal of Psychiatry* 160, no. 1 (2003): 13–23.
Kazantzis, Nikolaos, Frank P. Deane, Devin R. Ronan, and Luciano L'Abate, eds. *Using Homework Assignments in Cognitive Behavior Therapy*. New York: Routledge, 2005.
Keith, Jim. *Mass Control: Engineering Human Consciousness*. Atlanta, GA: IllumiNet, 1999.
Kibzey, A. T. "Folie à Deux: A Case of Familial Psychosis." *Psychiatric Quarterly* 22, nos. 1–4 (1948): 718–28.
Kidd, Benjamin. *The Science of Power*. New York: G. P. Putnam's Sons, 1918.
Killen, Andreas. *Berlin Electropolis: Shock, Nerves, and German Modernity*. Berkeley: University of California Press, 2005.
King, Anna Lucia Spear, Alexandre Martins Valença, Adriana Cardoso Silva, Federica Sancassiani, Sergio Machado, and Antonio Egidio Nardi. "'Nomophobia': Impact of Cell Phone Use Interfering with Symptoms and Emotions of Individuals with Panic Disorder Compared with a Control Group." *Clinical Practice and Epidemiology in Mental Health* 10 (2014): 28–35.
King, L. Percy. "Criminal Complaints: A True Account by L. Percy King." In *The Inner World of Mental Illness*, ed. Bert Kaplan. New York: Harper and Row, 1964.
Kite, Charles. *Essay on the Recovery of the Apparently Dead*. London: C. Dilly, 1751.
Kittler, Friedrich A. *Discourse Networks 1800/1900*, trans. Michael Metteer. Stanford, CA: Stanford University Press, 1992.
Klein, Naomi. *The Shock Doctrine: The Rise of Disaster Capitalism*. New York: Macmillan, 2007.
Kleinberg-Levin, David Michael, ed. *Pathologies of the Modern Self: Postmodern Studies on Narcissism, Schizophrenia, and Depression*. New York: New York University Press, 1987.
Knapp, Philip Coombs. *Accidents from the Electrical Current: A Contribution to the Study of the Action of Currents of High Potential upon the Human Organism*. Boston: Damrell and Upham, 1890.

Ko, Minjin, Kyoungwoo Bae, Gyuhwan Oh, and Taiyoung Ryu. "A Study on New Gameplay Based on Brain-Computer Interface." Proceedings of the 2009 DIGRA International Conference: Breaking New Ground: Innovation in Games, Play, Practice, and Theory, http://www.digra.org/digital-library/publications/a-study-on-new-gameplay-based-on-brain-computer-interface.

Koblenzer, Caroline S. "The Challenge of Morgellons Disease." *Journal of the American Academy of Dermatology* 55, no. 5 (2006): 920–22.

Korngold, Murray. "LSD and the Creative Experience." *Psychoanalytic Review* 50, no. 4 (1963): 682–85.

Kossy, Diane. *Kooks: A Guide to the Outer Limits of Human Belief*. Los Angeles: Feral House, 1994.

Kovel, Joel. "Schizophrenic Being and Technocratic Society." In *Pathologies of the Modern Self: Postmodern Studies on Narcissism, Schizophrenia, and Depression*, ed. David Michael Kleinberg-Levin, 330–48. New York: New York University Press, 1987.

Kraepelin, Emil. *Lectures on Clinical Psychiatry*. New York: William Wood and Company, 1917.

Krainsky, N. W. "Nerven-Psychische Emission und Radio-Prozesse im Lebenden Organismus." *Monatsberichte* 1 (1936): 13–54.

Kramer, Morton. "Cross-National Study of Diagnosis of the Mental Disorders: Origin of the Problem." *American Journal of Psychiatry* 125, no. 10S (1969): 1–11.

Kranz, Heinrich. "Das Thema des Wahns im Wandel der Zeit." *Fortschritte der Neurologie und Psychiatrie und Grenzbeibiete* 23, nos. 1–2 (1955): 58–72.

Kraus, Alfred. "Phenomenology of the Technical Delusion in Schizophrenics." *Journal of Phenomenological Psychology* 25, no. 1 (1994): 51–69.

Krishna, Nithin, Bernard A. Fischer, Moshe Miller, Kelly Register-Brown, Kathleen Patchan, and Ann Hackman. "The Role of Social Media Networks in Psychotic Disorders: A Case Report." *General Hospital Psychiatry* 35, no. 5 (2013): 576.

Kristeva, Julia. *Powers of Horror*, ed. Leon S. Roudiez. New York: Columbia University Press, 1982.

Kulhara, Parmanand. "Outcome of Schizophrenia: Some Transcultural Observations with Particular Reference to Developing Countries." *European Archives of Psychiatry and Clinical Neuroscience* 244, no. 5 (1994): 227–35.

Kuo, Joseph, and Hai-Gwo Hwu. "Internet-Related Delusional Disorder." *Taiwanese Journal of Psychiatry* 21, no. 1 (2007): 66–71.

Kurzweil, Ray. *The Age of Spiritual Machines: When Computers Exceed Human Intelligence*. New York: Penguin, 2000.

Kurzweil, Ray. *The Singularity Is Near: When Humans Transcend Biology*. New York: Penguin, 2005.

La Beaume, Michael. *Remarks on the History and Philosophy but Particularly the Medical Efficacy of Electricity*. London: F. Warr, 1820.

Lacan, Jacques. *The Four Fundamental Concepts of Psychoanalysis: The Seminar of Jacques Lacan, Book XI*, trans. Alan Sheridan. London: Hogarth and Institute of Psycho-Analysis, 1977.

Lacan, Jacques. *The Psychoses, The Seminar of Jacques Lacan, Book III, 1955–1956,* ed. Jacques-Alain Miller, trans. Russell Grigg. New York: W. W. Norton, 1993.

Lacan, Jacques. *Speech and Language in Psychoanalysis,* trans. Anthony Wilden. Baltimore: Johns Hopkins University Press, 1981.

Laing, R. D. *The Politics of Experience.* New York: Ballantine, 1968.

Laing, R. D. *The Politics of the Family, and Other Essays.* London: Routledge, 1971.

Lane, Christopher. *Shyness: How Normal Behavior Became a Sickness.* New Haven, CT: Yale University Press, 2008.

Lasswell, Harold D. "The Theory of Political Propaganda." *American Political Science Review* 21, no. 3 (1927): 627–31.

Leader, Darian. *What Is Madness?* London: Penguin, 2011.

Lears, T. Jackson. *No Place of Grace: Anti-Modernism and the Transformation of American Culture, 1880–1920.* Chicago: University of Chicago Press, 1992.

Le Bon, Gustave. *The Crowd: A Study of the Popular Mind.* London: T. Fisher Unwin, 1893.

LeDoux, Joseph. *Synaptic Self.* New York: Penguin, 2002.

Le Fanu, Sheridan. "Green Tea." In *In a Glass Darkly,* 1–54. London: Richard Bentley and Son, 1886.

Legge, F. "The Nature of Hallucinations." In *The Living Age,* vol. 235 (Boston: Living Age, 1902): 249–51.

Lemov, Rebecca. "Brainwashing's Avatar: The Curious Career of Dr. Ewen Cameron." *Grey Room* 45 (Fall 2011): 60–87.

Lenz, Hermann. *Vergleichende Psychiatrie.* Vienna: Wilhelm Maudrich, 1964.

Leudar, Ivan, Philip Thomas, D. McNally, and A. Glinski. "What Voices Can Do with Words: Pragmatics of Verbal Hallucinations." *Psychological Medicine* 27, no. 4 (1997): 885–98.

Levenda, Peter. *Alliance: A History of Nazi Involvement with the Occult.* London: A&C Black, 2002.

Leventhall, Geoff, Peter Pelmear, and Stephen Benton. *A Review of Published Research on Low Frequency Noise and Its Effects.* London: Nobel House, 2003.

Leymann, Heinz. "The Content and Development of Mobbing at Work." *European Journal of Work and Organizational Psychology* 5, no. 2 (1996): 165–84.

Liao, Paul, Alexis Smith, and Connie Wang. "Convenience and Safety versus Privacy: The Ethics of Radio Frequency Identification." In *Confronting Information Ethics in the New Millennium,* ed. Laurie Burkhart, Jake Friedberg, Trevor Martin, Kavitha Sharma, and Morgan Ship, 115–23. Boulder, CO: Leeds School of Business, 2007.

Liebig, Gustav. *Practical Electricity in Medicine and Surgery.* Philadelphia: F. A. Davis, 1890.

Lipsky, Adam. *Man the Puppet: The Art of Controlling Minds.* New York: Frank-Maurice, 1925.

Littell, S. "On the Influence of Electrical Fluctuations as a Cause of Disease." *Littell's Living Age* (October 10, 1857): 699.

Lloyd, Steven. *My Rocky New Age Road to the Kryst: A True Account of My Becoming a Targeted Individual*. Self-published, CreateSpace, 2014.

Locke, John, *An Essay Concerning Human Understanding*, (1690). London: T. Tegg and Son, 1836.

Lodge, Oliver. *Ether and Reality*. London: Hodder and Stoughton, 1925.

Lodge, Oliver. *Life and Matter*. London: Williams ad Norgate, 1906.

Lombard, Josiah Stickney. *Experimental Researches on the Regional Temperature of the Head: Under Conditions of Rest, Intellectual Activity, and Emotion*. London: H. K. Lewis, 1879.

Lothane, Zvi. *In Defense of Schreber: Soul Murder and Psychiatry*. Hillsdale, NJ: Analytic, 1992.

Lowndes, Francis. *Observations on Medical Electricity: Containing a Synopsis of All the Diseases in which Electricity Has Been Recommended or Applied with Success*. London: Stuart, 1787.

Lovecraft, Howard Phillips. *Supernatural Horror in Literature*. New York: Dover, [1945] 1973.

Lutz, Tom. *1903: American Nervousness and the Economy of Cultural Change*. Palo Alto, CA: Stanford University Press, 1989.

Lyne, William. *Occult Ether Physics: Tesla's Hidden Space Propulsion System and the Conspiracy to Conceal It*. Lamy, NM: Creatopia, 1997.

Lyne, William. *Space Aliens from the Pentagon*. Lamy, NM: Creatopia, 1993.

Lyotard, Jean-François. *The Postmodern Condition: A Report on Knowledge*. Minneapolis: University of Minnesota Press, 1984.

MacDougall, Douglas. "Hypothesis Concerning Soul Substance Together with Experimental Evidence of the Existence of Such Substance." *Journal of the American Society for Psychical Research* 1, no. 5 (May 1907): 237–44.

MacGregor, John M. *Henry Darger: In the Realms of the Unreal*. New York: Delano Greenidge, 2002.

Machado, Arlindo. "A Microchip Inside the Body." *Performance Research* 4, no. 2 (1999): 8–12.

Mackay, Charles. *Extraordinary Popular Delusions and the Madness of Crowds*. London: Richard Bentley, 1841.

Maclagan, David. "Has 'Psychotic Art' Become Extinct?" In *Arts, Psychotherapy and Psychosis*, ed. Katherine Killick and Joy Schaverien. New York: Routledge, 2003.

Maeterlinck, Maurice. *The Unknown Guest and Other Essays*. London: Methuen, 1914.

Maher, Brendan A. *Anomalous Experience and Delusional Thinking: The Logic of Explanations*. Somerset, NJ; John Wiley and Sons, 1988.

Mander, Jerry. *Four Arguments for Eliminating Television*. New York: William Morrow, 1978.

Manovich, Lev. "The Practice of Everyday (Media) Life: From Mass Consumption to Mass Cultural Production." *Critical Inquiry* 35, no. 2 (2009): 319–31.

Marcolin, M. A. "The Prognosis of Schizophrenia across Cultures." *Ethnicity and Disease* 1, no. 1 (1991): 99–104.

Mark, Vernon H., and Frank R. Ervin. *Violence and the Brain*. New York: Harper and Row, 1970.

Mark, Vernon H., William H. Sweet, and F. R. Ervin. "Role of Brain Disease in Riots and Urban Violence." *Journal of the American Medical Association* 201, no. 11 (1967): 895.

Marrs, Jim. *The Trillion-Dollar Conspiracy: How the New World Order, Man-Made Diseases, and Zombie Banks Are Destroying America*. New York: William Morrow Paperbacks, 2011.

Marshall, John S. "Communications." *Medical and Surgical Reporter* 54, no. 1327 (March 1886): 388.

Marx, Karl. *The Eighteenth Brumaire of Louis Bonaparte*. New York: International Publishers, 1963.

Marx, Leo. *The Machine in the Garden: Technology and the Pastoral Ideal in America*. Oxford: Oxford University Press, 1964.

Massey, Betton G. "Electricity in the Treatment of Chronic Prostatitis and other Conditions Underlying Impotence in Men." *Proceedings* 15 (1894): 29–33.

Maudsley, Henry. "Is Insanity on the Increase?" *British Medical Journal* 1, no. 576 (1872): 36–39.

McCarthy-Jones, Simon. "The Concept of Schizophrenia is Coming to End—Here's Why," *The Conversation*, August 24, 2017, https://theconversation.com/the-concept-of-schizophrenia-is-coming-to-an-end-heres-why-82775.

McGee, Ellen M. "Bioelectronics and Implanted Devices." In *Medical Enhancement and Posthumanity*, vol. 2., ed. Bert Gordijn and Ruth Chadwick, 207–24. Berlin: Springer Science and Business Media, 2008.

McGillicuddy, Timothy J. *Functional Disorders of the Nervous System in Women*. New York: William Wood and Company, 1896.

McIntyre, Alistair. *A Journey into Madness*. London: Chipmunka, 2007.

McLean, David R. "Nuts and Screwballs." *Studies in Intelligence* 9 (1965): 79–89.

McLuhan, Marshall. *Understanding Media: The Extensions of Man*. New York: McGraw-Hill, 1964.

Mercier, Charles Arthur. *A Text-Book of Insanity*. New York: Macmillan, 1902.

Mesmer, Franz. *Mesmerism: A Translation of the Original Scientific and Medical Writings of F. A. Mesmer*, trans. George J. Bloch. Los Altos, CA: William Kaufmann, 1980.

Mettrie, Julien Offray de La. *Man a Machine*. Cambridge: Cambridge University Press, [1748] 1996.

Metzl, Jonathan. *The Protest Psychosis*. Boston: Beacon, 2009.

Michael, Katina, and M. G. Michael. "Homo Electricus and the Continued Speciation of Humans." In *The Encyclopedia of Information Ethics and Security*, ed. Marian Quigley, 312–18. Hershey, PA: Information Science Reference, 2007.

Michie, D., and D. J. West. "A Mass ESP Test Using Television." *Journal of the Society for Psychical Research* 39 (1957): 113–33.

Milanovich, Norma J., Betty Rice, and Cynthia Ploski. *We, the Arcturians*. Albuquerque, NM: Athena, 1990.

Milutis, Joe. *Ether: The Nothing That Connects Everything*. Minneapolis: University of Minnesota Press, 2006.

Miller, David K. *Spiritual Technology for the Fifth-Dimensional Earth*. Flagstaff, AZ: Light Technology, 2008.

Miller, Jacques-Alain. "The Invention of Delusion," trans. Gary Marshall. *International Lacanian Review* 5 (2009): 1–29.

Miller, William Snow. "Elisha Perkins and His Metallic Tractors." *Yale Journal of Biology and Medicine* 8, no. 1 (1935): 41–57.

"Modern Telegraphy." *Scientific American* 2, no. 23 (June 2, 1860): 356–57.

Monden, Marcel A. H. "Development of Psychopathology in International Tourists." In *Psychological Aspects of Geographical Moves: Homesickness and Acculturation Stress*, ed. Miranda A. L. van Tilburg and Ad J. J. M. Vingerhoets, 213–226. Amsterdam: Amsterdam University Press, 1997.

Moore, Wendy. *The Mesmerist: The Society Doctor Who Held Victorian London Spellbound*. London: Orion, 2016.

Moreno, Jacob Levy. "Foundations of Sociometry: An Introduction." *Sociometry* 4, no. 1 (February, 1941): 15–35.

Morgan, Joshua L., and Jeff W. Lichtman. "Why Not Connectomics?" *Nature Methods* 10, no. 6 (2013): 494–500.

Morison, Alexander. *Cases of Mental Disease, with Practical Observations on Medical Treatment*. London: Longman and S. Highley, 1828.

Morrison Anthony P. "A Cognitive Analysis of the Maintenance of Auditory Hallucinations: Are Voices to Schizophrenia What Bodily Sensations Are to Panic?" *Behavioral and Cognitive Psychotherapy* 26, no. 4 (1998): 289–302.

Morus, Iwan Rhys. "'The Nervous System of Britain': Space, Time and the Electric Telegraph in the Victorian Age." *British Journal for the History of Science* 33, no. 4 (2000): 455–75.

Munger, Sean. "Bill Clinton Bugged My Brain: Delusional Claims in Federal Courts." *Tulane Law Review* 72 (1997): 1809–52.

Musso, Angelo. *Application de la balance à l'étude de la circulation du sang chez l'homme*. Turin: Hermann Loescher, 1884.

Myers, Frederic. *Human Personality and Its Survival of Bodily Death*, vol. 2. New York: Longmans and Green, 1904.

"Nervous Strain." *Journal of the American Medical Association* 45 (1905): 404.

Newland, Constance. *My Self and I*. New York: Coward-McCann, 1962.

Nietzsche, Friedrich. *The Will to Power*, trans. Walter Kaufmann and R. J. Hollingdale. New York: Vintage, 1968.

Noffsinger, Stephen G., and Fabian M. Saleh. "Ideas of Reference about Newscasters." *Psychiatric Services* 51, no. 5 (2000): 679.

Nordau, Max S. *Degeneration*. New York: D. Appleton, 1895.
Nordau, Max. *Degeneration*. Lincoln: University of Nebraska Press, [1892] 1993.
Nye, David E. *Electrifying America: Social Meanings of a New Technology, 1880–1940*. Cambridge, MA: MIT Press, 1992.
O'Brien, Barbara. *Operators and Things*. New York: Ace, 1958.
O'Brien, Cathy, and Marquart Ewing Phillips. *Trance Formation of America*. Reality Marketing, 1995.
Ocampo, Jose Antonio. *Agenda 21: Earth Summit: The United Nations Programme of Action from Rio*. New York: United Nations, 1993.
Oh, Seung Wook, Julie A. Harris, Lydia Ng, and Brent Winslow et al. "A Mesoscale Connectome of the Mouse Brain." *Nature* 508 (April 10, 2014): 207–14.
Olcott, Henry Steel. *The Vampire*. Wheaton, IL: Theosophical, 1920.
Oppenheim, James. *Your Hidden Powers*. New York: Alfred A. Knopf, 1923.
Oppenheim, Janet. *The Other World: Spiritualism and Psychical Research in England, 1850–1914*. Cambridge: Cambridge University Press, 1988.
Orwell, George. *Nineteen Eighty-Four*. London: Secker & Warburg, 1949.
Ostrander, Sheila, and Lynn Schroeder. *Psychic Discoveries behind the Iron Curtain*. New York: Bantam, 1971.
Owen, Alex. *The Darkened Room: Women, Power, and Spiritualism in Late Victorian England*. Chicago: University of Chicago Press, 2004.
Owen, Alex. *The Place of Enchantment: British Occultism and the Culture of the Modern*. Chicago: University of Chicago Press, 2007.
Pacherie, Elisabeth, Melissa Green, and Tim Bayne. "Phenomenology and Delusions: Who Put the 'Alien' in Alien Control?" *Consciousness and Cognition* 15, no. 3 (2006): 566–77.
Packard, Vance. *The Hidden Persuaders*. New York: David McKay, 1957.
Panagiota, Petkou. "Getting Dirty with the Body: Abjection in Mary Shelley's *Frankenstein*." *Gramma* 11 (2003): 31–38.
Pandya, Anand, and Peter J. Weiden. "Trauma and Disaster in Psychiatrically Vulnerable Populations." *Journal of Psychiatric Practice* 7, no. 6 (2001): 426–31.
Paugh, Illena Johnson. *Agenda 21: Environmental Piracy*. Self-published, 2012.
Pazder, Lawrence. *Michelle Remembers*. New York: Pocket Books, 1980.
Peale, Norman Vincent. *The Power of Positive Thinking*. New York: Prentice Hall, 1952.
Pederson-Krag, Geraldine. "Telepathy and Repression." *Psychoanalytic Quarterly* 16 (1947): 61–68.
Peerbolte, M. L. "Psychoanalysis and Parapsychology." *Psychiatrische en Neurologische Biaden* 42 (1938): 632.
Percival, Edward. *Account of a Petechial Febricula; Some Brief Notices of the Deleterious and Medicinal Effects of Green Tea; a Case of Dropsy*. Dublin: Hodges and M'Arthur, 1817.
Percival, Thomas. *Essays Medical and Experimental*, vol. 2. London: J. Johnson, 1773.
Percival, Thomas. *Medical Ethics, or a Code of Institutes and Precepts, Adapted to the Professional Conduct of Physicians and Surgeons*. Manchester: S. Russell, 1803.

Perkins, Benjamin Douglas. *The Influence of Metallic Tractors on the Human Body.* London: J. Johnson, 1798.

Perkins, Rodney, and Forrest Jackson. *Cosmic Suicide: The Tragedy and Transcendence of Heaven's Gate.* Dallas, TX: Pentaradial Press, 1997.

Peters, John Durham. "Broadcasting and Schizophrenia." *Media, Culture and Society* 32, no. 1 (2010): 123–40.

Peterson, Frederick. "Extracts from the Autobiography of a Paranoiac," Reprint from *The American Journal of Psychology* (January, 1889).

"Physiological Experiments." *The Medico-Chirurgical Review* 1, no.2 (London: G. Hayden, 1824), 440–46.

Pinchevski, Amit, and John Durham Peters. "Autism and New Media: Disability between Technology and Society." *New Media and Society* 18, no. 11 (2016): 2507–23.

Pittman, Renee. *Diary of an Angry Targeted Individual.* Self-published, Amazon Digital, 2014.

Pittman, Renee. *The Targeting of Myron May: Florida State University Shooting.* Self-published, CreateSpace, 2015.

Plank, Robert. "Communication in Science Fiction," *ETC : A Review of General Semantics* 11, no. 1 (Autumn 1953): 16–20.

Plank, Robert. *The Emotional Significance of Imaginary Beings: A Study of the Interaction between Psychopathology, Literature, and Reality in the Modern World.* Waukesha, WI: Thomas, 1968.

Plank, Robert. "The Expedition to the Planet of Paranoia." *Extrapolation* 22, no. 2 (1981): 171–85.

Plank, Robert. "Names and Roles of Characters in Science Fiction." *Names* 9, no. 3 (1961): 151–59.

Plank, Robert. "The Reproduction of Psychosis in Science Fiction." *International Record of Medicine and General Practice Clinics* 167, no. 7 (1954): 407.

Plass-Oude, Danny, Boris Reuderink, Bram van de Laar, Hayrettin Gürkök, Christian Mühl, Mannes Pohl, Anton Nijholt, and Dirk Heylen. "Brain-Computer Interfacing and Games." *Brain-Computer Interfaces* (2010): 149–78.

Podmore, Frank. *Apparitions and Thought Transference.* London: Charles Scribner's Sons, 1898.

Poe, Edgar Allan. "The Man of the Crowd," *Burton's Gentleman's Magazine*, December 1840, 267–70.

Poe, Edgar Allan. *Tales of the Grotesque and Arabesque.* Philadelphia: Lea & Blanchard, 1840.

Poet, Sharon Rose. *Ramblings of a Targeted Individual.* Self-published, Amazon Digital, 2014.

Poet, Sharon Rose. *Technological Holocaust: Targeted in America.* Mt. Vernon, NH: Poetic Publications, 2013.

"Power of Galvanism." *The Lancet* 2 (1842–43): 815.

Prichard, James Cowles. *A Treatise on Insanity and Other Disorders Affecting the Mind*. London: Sherwood, Gilbert, and Piper, 1835.

Priestley, Joseph. *A Free Discussion of the Doctrines of Materialism, and Philosophical Necessity, in a Correspondence between Dr. Price, and Dr. Priestley. To which Are Added, by Dr. Priestley, an Introduction, Explaining the Nature of the Controversy, and Letters to Several Writers, etc*. London: J. Johnson and T. Cadell, 1778.

Priestley, Joseph. *The History and Present State of Electricity*. London: J. Dodsley, J. Johnson, B. Davenport, and T. Cadell, 1767.

Prince, Morton. *The Unconscious: The Fundamentals of Human Personality, Normal and Abnormal*. New York: Macmillan, 1914.

Quimby, Phineas P. "Is Disease a Belief?" (1859). In *The Quimby Manuscripts*, ed. Horatio W. Dresser, 186. New York: Thomas Y. Crowell, 1921.

Rabinbach, Anson. *The Human Motor: Energy, Fatigue, and the Origins of Modernity*. Berkeley: University of California Press, 1992.

Rahimi, Ali, Ben Recht, Jason Taylor, and Noah Vawter. "On the Effectiveness of Aluminium Foil Helmets: An Empirical Study." Massachusetts Institute of Technology, Cambridge, MA, February 17, 2005.

Rapport, Richard. *Nerve Endings: The Discovery of the Synapse*. New York: W. W. Norton, 2005.

Raza, Nadeem, Viv Bradshaw, and Matthew Hague. *Applications of RFID Technology*. London: Institute of Electrical Engineers, 1999.

Reddington, Sarah, and Deborah Price. "Cyborg and Autism: Exploring New Social Articulations via Posthuman Connections." *International Journal of Qualitative Studies in Education* 29, no. 7 (2016): 882–92.

Reitman, Francis. *Psychotic Art*. Madison, CT: International Universities Press, 1951.

Richardson, Edward Tylor. "Theory of the Nervous Ether," in *Recreations in Popular Science*, 362–74. Boston: Estes and Lauriat, 1874.

Roazen, Paul. *Brother Animal: The Story of Freud and Tausk*. New York: Alfred A. Knopf, 1969.

Róheim, Géza. *Magic and Schizophrenia*. Madison, CT: International Universities Press, 1955.

Rokeach, Milton. *The Three Christs of Ypsilanti*. New York: NYRB Classics, 2011.

Roland, Paul. *Nazis and the Occult: The Dark Forces Unleashed by the Third Reich*. London: Arcturus, 2012.

Rose, David. *Enchanted Objects: Design, Human Desire, and the Internet of Things*. New York: Simon and Schuster, 2014.

Rosen, Christine. "The Age of Egocasting." *New Atlantis* 7 (Fall 2004–Winter 20005): 51–72.

Rosenhan, David L. "On Being Sane in Insane Places." *Science* 179, no. 4070 (1973): 250–58.

Rosenthal, Bernice Glatzer. *The Occult in Russian and Soviet Culture*. Ithaca, NY: Cornell University Press, 1993.

Rosenthal, Moriz, Jean Martin Charcot, and Leopold Putzel. *A Clinical Treatise on the Diseases of the Nervous System*, trans. Leopold Putzel. New York: William Wood, 1879.

Ross, Colin A. *Satanic Ritual Abuse: Principles of Treatment*. Toronto: University of Toronto Press, 1995.

Roustang, François. *Dire Mastery*, trans. Ned Lukacher. Baltimore: Johns Hopkins University Press, 1982.

Roustang, François. *Psychoanalysis Never Lets Go*, trans. Ned Luckacher. Baltimore: Johns Hopkins University Press, [1980] 1983.

Rovers, A. F., L. M. G. Fejis, G. J. M. van Boxtel, and P. J. M. Cluitmans. "Flanker Shooting Game: Model-Based Design of Biofeedback Games." *Proceedings of the International Conference on Designing Pleasurable Products and Interfaces* (2009): 483–94.

Ryder, Garrett B. "Delusional Dish Syndromes." *Irish Journal of Psychological Medicine* 9, no. 2 (November 1992): 134.

Sadock, Benjamin J., and Virginia A. Sadock. *Kaplan and Sadock's Synopsis of Psychiatry: Behavioral Sciences/Clinical Psychiatry*. Philadelphia: Lippincott, Williams, and Wilkins, 2011.

Sachs, Hanns. "The Delay of the Machine Age." *Psychoanalytic Quarterly* 2, nos. 3–4 (1933): 404–24.

Saitō, Tamaki. *Social Withdrawal: Adolescence without End*, trans. Jeffrey Angles. Minneapolis: University of Minnesota Press, 2012.

Sanders, Ed. *The Family: The Story of Charles Manson's Dune Buggy Attack Battalion*. New York: E. P. Dutton, 1971.

Sandrone, Stefano, Marco Bacigaluppi, Marco R. Galloni, Stefano F. Cappa, Andrea Moro, Marco Catani, Massimo Filippi, Martin M. Monti, Daniela Perani, and Gianvito Martino. "Weighing Brain Activity with the Balance: Angelo Mosso's Original Manuscripts Come to Light." *Brain* 137, no. 2 (2013): 621–33.

Santner, Eric. *My Own Private Germany: Daniel Paul Schreber's Secret History of Modernity*. Princeton, NJ: Princeton University Press, 1998.

Sarasin, Philipp. "The Body as Medium: Nineteenth-Century European Hygiene Discourse." *Grey Room* 29 (2007): 48–65.

Sartre, Jean-Paul. *Nausea*. New York: New Directions, 1964.

Sass, Louis A. "Introspection, Schizophrenia, and the Fragmentation of Self." *Representations* 19 (1987): 1–34.

Sass, Louis A. "The Land of Unreality: On the Phenomenology of the Schizophrenic Break." *New Ideas in Psychology* 6, no. 2 (1988): 223–42.

Sass, Louis A. *Madness and Modernism: Insanity in the Light of Modern Art, Literature, and Thought*. New York: Basic, 1992.

Saul L. J. "Telepathic Sensitiveness as a Neurotic Symptom." *Psychoanalytic Quarterly* 7 (1938): 329–35.

Savage, Charles. "Variations in Ego Feeling Induced by D-Lysergic Acid Diethylamide (LSD-25)," *Psychoanalytic Review* 42, no. 1 (January 1955): 10–11.

Savage, Charles, and Louis Cholden. "Schizophrenia and the Model Psychoses." *Journal of Clinical and Experimental Psychopathology* 17, no. 4 (1956): 405–13.
Savely, Virginia R., Mary M. Leitao, and Raphael B. Stricker. "The Mystery of Morgellons Disease." *American Journal of Clinical Dermatology* 7, no. 1 (2006): 1–5.
Schatzman, Morton. *Soul Murder: Persecution in the Family*. New York: Random House, 1973.
Scher, L. "Sociopolitical Events and Technical Innovations May Affect the Content of Delusions and the Course of Psychotic Disorders." *Medical Hypotheses* 55, no. 6 (2000): 507–9.
Schneider, Kurt. *Clinical Psychopathology*. New York: Grune and Stratton, 1959.
Schreber, Daniel Paul. *Denkwürdigkeiten eines Nervenkranken*. Leipzig: Oswald Mutze, 1903.
Schreber, Daniel Paul. *Memoirs of My Nervous Illness*. New York: NYRB Classics, 2000.
Sconce, Jeffrey. *Haunted Media: Electronic Presence from Telegraphy to Television*. Durham, NC: Duke University Press, 2000.
Sechehaye, Renee, and Marguerite Sechehaye. *Autobiography of a Schizophrenic Girl: Reality Lost and Gained, with Analytic Interpretation*. New York: Grune and Stratton, 1951.
Serazio, Michael. "Selling (Digital) Millennials: The Social Construction and Technological Bias of a Consumer Generation." *Television and New Media* 16, no. 7 (2015): 599–615.
Shaftesbury, Edmund. *Thought Transference; or, The Radio-Activity of the Human Mind; Based on the Newly Discovered Laws of Radio Communication between Brain and Brain*. Meriden, CT: Ralston Society, 1927.
Shapiro, Stanley. "A Study of Psychiatric Syndromes Manifested at an International Airport." *Comprehensive Psychiatry* 17, no. 3 (1976): 453–56.
Shelley, Mary. *Frankenstein; or, The Modern Prometheus*. London: Lackington, Hughes, Harding, Mayor and Jones, 1818.
Shelley, Mary. *Frankenstein: Or the Modern Prometheus*. London: Colburn and Bentley, 1831.
Shelton, Don. *The Real Mr. Frankenstein: Sir Anthony Carlisle, Medical Murders, and the Social Genesis of Frankenstein*. Auckland: Portmin, 2012.
Siegel, Ronald K. "Dr. Tolman's Flying Influence Machine." In *Whispers: The Voices of Paranoia*, 53–89. New York: Simon and Schuster, 1996.
Siirala, Martii, Silvano Arieti, and Harold Kelman. "Schizophrenia: A Human Situation." *American Journal of Psychoanalysis* 23, no. 1 (1963): 39–57.
Simmel, Georg. "The Metropolis and Mental Life" (1903). In *The Sociology of Georg Simmel*, trans. Kurt Wolff, 409–35. New York: Free Press, 1950.
Sitwell, Francis. *Mesmerism Considered; in Connexion with Personal Responsibility*. Glasgow: William MacKenzie, 1852.
Sklar, Dusty. *The Nazis and the Occult*. New York: Dorset, 1990.
Skodlar, B., M. Z. Dernovsek, and M. Kocmur. "Psychopathology of Schizophrenia in Ljubljana (Slovenia) from 1881 to 2000: Changes in the Content

of Delusions in Schizophrenia Patients Related to Various Sociopolitical, Technical and Scientific Changes." *International Journal of Social Psychiatry* 54 (2008): 101–11.

Smith, William. *A Dissertation upon the Nerves*. London: W. Owen, 1768.

Smith, Jerry E. HAARP: *The Ultimate Weapon of the Conspiracy*. Kempton, IL: Adventures Unlimited, 1998.

Smyth, M. G. "A Glossary of Television-Related Symptoms in Psychosis." *Psychiatric Bulletin* 21 (1997): 545–46.

Spencer, Herbert. "The Social Organism," *Westminster Review* 73 (January, 1860): 51–68.

Spitzka, Edward Charles. *Insanity: Its Classification, Diagnosis and Treatment*. New York: E. B. Treat, 1887.

Spry, Edward. "Account of a Locked Jaw, and Paralysis, Cured by Electricity: By Dr. Edward Spry, of Totness, in a Letter to Charles Morton, MD Sec. RS." *Philosophical Transactions* (1767): 88–91.

Stableford, Brian. "The Cosmic Horror." In *Icons of Horror and the Supernatural: An Encyclopedia of Our Worst Nightmares*, vol. 2, ed. S. T. Joshi, 65–96. Westport, CT: Greenwood, 2006.

Starks, Steven. *Threat Assessment of Directed Energy Weapon (DEW) on Targeted Individuals and Those Experiencing Electronic Harassment*. Amazon Digital Services, 2014.

Steele, Ken, and Claire Berman. *The Day the Voices Stopped: A Memoir of Madness and Hope*. New York: Basic, 2001.

Stekel, Wilhelm. *Twelve Essays on Sex and Psychoanalysis*, trans. S. A. Tannenbaum. New York: Critic and Guide, 1922.

Stokes, Patrick. "Anti-Climacus and Neo-Lockeanism." *Locus* 1 (1890): 330.

Stompe, Thomas, Gerhard Ortwein-Swoboda, Kristina Ritter, and Hans Schanda. "Old Wine in New Bottles? Stability and Plasticity of the Contents of Schizophrenic Delusions." *Psychopathology* 36, no. 1 (2003): 6–12.

Stout, Ronnie G., and Rokeya S. Farooque. "Negative Symptoms, Anger, and Social Support: Response of an Inpatient Sample to News Coverage of the September 11 Terrorist Attacks." *Psychiatric Quarterly* 74, no. 3 (2003): 237–50.

Strindberg, August. *Inferno and From an Occult Diary*. New York: Penguin, 1979.

Sullivan, Elizabeth. *My Life Changed Forever: The Years I Have Lost as a Target of Organized Stalking*. Conshohocken, PA: Infinity, 2012.

Szasz, Thomas S. "Involuntary Hospital Commitment." In *Ideology and Insanity: Essays on the Psychiatric Dehumanization of Man*, 113–39. Syracuse, NY: Syracuse University Press, 1991.

Szasz, Thomas S. *Schizophrenia: The Sacred Symbol of Psychiatry*. Syracuse, NY: Syracuse University Press, 1988.

Szasz, Thomas S. *The Second Sin*. London: Routledge and Kegan Paul, 1974.

Szasz, Thomas S. *The Therapeutic State: Psychiatry in the Mirror of Current Events*. New York: Prometheus, 1984.

Tausk, Victor. "On the Origin of the 'Influencing Machine' in Schizophrenia." In *The Psycho-Analytic Reader*, ed. Robert Fliess, 31–64. New York: International Press, 1948.

Taylor, Mark, and Kym Jenkins. "The Psychological Impact of September 11 Terrorism on Australian Inpatients." *Australasian Psychiatry* 12, no. 3 (2004): 253–55.

Tebb, William, and Edward Perry Vollum. *Premature Burial and How It May Be Prevented, with Special Reference to Trance Catalepsy, and Other Forms of Suspended Animation*. London: Swan Sonnenschein, 1905.

Tesh, Sylvia Noble. *Uncertain Hazards: Environmental Activists and Scientific Proof*. Ithaca, NY: Cornell University Press, 2000.

Thacker, Eugene. *Biomedia*. Minneapolis: University of Minnesota Press, 2004.

Thompson, Stephen. "Joey the Mechanical Boy." In *Transtechnology Research Reader*, ed. Martha Blassnigg, Hannah Drayson, Michael Punt, John Vines, and Brigitta Zics, 85–97. Plymouth, UK: University of Plymouth, 2010.

Thurschwell, Pamela. *Literature, Technology and Magical Thinking, 1880–1920*. Cambridge: Cambridge University Press, 2001.

Tiffany, Joel. *Lectures on Spiritualism: Being a Series of Lectures on the Phenomena and Philosophy of Development, Individualism, Spirit, Immortality, Mesmerism, Clairvoyance, Spiritual Manifestations, Christianity, and Progress, Delivered at Prospect Street Church, in the City of Cleveland, during the Winter and Spring of 1851*. Cleveland, OH: J. Tiffany, 1851.

Todorov, Tzvetan. *The Fantastic: A Structural Approach to a Literary Genre*. Ithaca, NY: Cornell University Press, 1975.

Toffler, Alvin. *Future Shock*. New York: Random House, 1970.

Torrey, E. Fuller, Peter Lurie, Sidney M. Wolfe, and Mary Zdanowicz. "Threats to Radio and Television Personnel in the United States by Individuals with Severe Mental Illnesses." HRG Publication no. 1501. Public Citizen's Health Research Group, Washington, DC, and Treatment Advocacy Center, Arlington, VA, December 15, 1999.

Torrey, E. Fuller, and Robert H. Yolken. "Could Schizophrenia Be a Viral Zoonosis Transmitted from House Cats?" *Schizophrenia Bulletin* 21, no. 2 (1995): 167–71.

Toutain-Dorbec, Pierre. *The Power of Mesmerism* (1892). New York: Grove Press, 1969.

Triebwasser, Joseph, Eran Chemerinski, Panos Roussos, and Larry J. Siever. "Paranoid Personality Disorder." *Journal of Personality Disorders* 27, no. 6 (2013): 795–805.

Trotter, Thomas. *A View of the Nervous Temperament: Being a Practical Inquiry into the Increasing Prevalence, Prevention, and Treatment of those Diseases Commonly Called Nervous, Bilious, Stomach and Liver Complaints, Indigestion, Low Spirits, Gout, [et]c*. London: Longman, Hurst, Rees, and Orme, 1807.

Tucker, Tom. *Bolt of Fate: Benjamin Franklin and His Fabulous Kite*. New York: Public Affairs, 2003.

Uemoto, M., N. Moriyama, H. Hamada, M. Onishi, K. Fujiya, A. Koizumi, and S. Watanabe. "Maladies mentales chez les Japonais à Paris." *Annales Médico-Psychologiques* 140, no. 7 (1982): 717–27.

Valenstein, Elliot S. *The War of the Soups and the Sparks: The Discovery of Neurotransmitters and the Dispute over How Nerves Communicate.* New York: Columbia University Press, 2005.

Vardy, Michael M., and Stanley R. Kay. "LSD Psychosis or LSD-Induced Schizophrenia? A Multimethod Inquiry." *Archives of General Psychiatry* 40, no. 8 (1983): 877–83.

Vasiliev, Leonoid. "Is Transmission of Muscular Power at a Distance Possible?" In *Mysterious Phenomena of the Human Psyche*, 169–85. New Hyde Park, NY: University Books, 1965.

Verity, Robert. *Changes Produced in the Nervous System by Civilization.* London: Highley, 1837.

Verne, Jules. *20,000 Leagues under the Sea* (1870), trans. Anthony Bonner. New York: Bantam, 1962.

Virtue, Doreen. *How to Hear Your Angels.* Carlsbad, CA: Hay House, 2007.

Von Däniken, Erich. *Chariots of the Gods? Unsolved Mysteries of the Past.* New York: G. P. Putnam's Sons, 1968.

Von Däniken, Erich. *Gods from Outer Space.* New York: G. P. Putnam's Sons, 1972.

Vonnegut, Kurt. *Slaughterhouse-Five.* New York: Delacorte, 1969.

Vossler, Andreas. "Internet Infidelity 10 Years On: A Critical Review of the Literature." *Family Journal* 24, no. 4 (2016): 359–66.

Wakley, Thomas (pseud.). *Undeniable Facts Concerning the Strange Practices of Dr. Elliotson, . . . with His Female Patients; and His Medical Experiments upon the Bodies of . . . E. and J. Okey, etc.* London, 1842.

Warneke, Brett, Matt Last, Brian Liebowitz, and Kristofer S. J. Pister. "Smart Dust: Communicating with a Cubic-Millimeter Computer." *Computer* 34, no. 1 (2001): 44–51.

Warren, Carol. *Madwives: Schizophrenic Women in the 1950s.* New Brunswick, NJ: Rutgers University Press, 1987.

Warren, Samuel. *Passages from the Diary of a Late Physician.* Edinburgh: W. Blackwood and Sons, 1864.

Watson, William. "Observations upon the Effects of Electricity Applied to a Tetanus, or Muscular Rigidity, of Four Months Continuance." *Philosophical Transactions* 53 (1763): 10–26.

Watts, Geoff. "Thomas Stephen Szasz." *The Lancet* 380, no. 9851 (2012): 1380.

Weiner, Susan K. "First Person Account: Living with the Delusions and Effects of Schizophrenia." *Schizophrenia Bulletin* 29, no. 4 (2003): 877–79.

Weinhold, Karl August. *Versuche über das Leben und seine Grundkräfte auf dem Wege der Experimental-Physiologie.* Madgeburg, Germany: Creutz, 1817.

Weinschenk, Susan. "Why We're All Addicted to Texts, Twitter, and Google." *Psychology Today* (blog), posted September 11, 2012. https://www.psychologytoday.com/blog/brain-wise/201209/why-were-all-addicted-texts-twitter-and-google.

Weiser, Mark, Rich Gold, and John Seely Brown. "The Origins of Ubiquitous Computing Research at PARC in the late 1980s." *IBM Systems Journal* 38, no. 4 (1999): 693–96.
Wertham, Fredric. *Seduction of the Innocent*. New York: Rinehart, 1954.
Wharton, Francis and Moreton Stillé. *Medical Jurisprudence*. Philadelphia: Kay and Brother, 1855.
White, Alexander. "Corporeal Contraband: A History of the Resurrectionist Movement in Britain and Canada." *University of Toronto Medical Journal* 86, no. 3 (2009): 113–16.
Whytt, Robert. *Observations on the Nature, Causes, and Cure of Those Disorders Which Have Been Commonly Called Nervous, Hypochondriac, or Hysteric: to Which Are Prefixed Some Remarks on the Sympathy of the Nerves*. Edinburgh: Becket, Du Hondt, and Balfour, 1765.
Wiener, Norbert. *Cybernetics: Control and Communication in the Animal and the Machine*. New York: John Wiley and Sons, 1948.
Wiener, Norbert. *The Human Use of Human Beings*. New York: Avon, 1954.
Wiertz, Antoine. "Thoughts and Visions of a Severed Head" (1870). In Walter Benjamin, *The Work of Art in the Age of Its Technological Reproducibility, and Other Writings on Media*. Cambridge, MA: Harvard University Press, 2008.
Wilkinson, John. *The Case of Mister Winder, Who Was Cured of a Paralysis by Flash of Lightning*. Göttingen, Germany: Podwig and Barmeier, 1765.
Williams, B. Brown. *Mental Alchemy: A Treatise on the Mind, Nervous System, Psychology, Magnetism, Mesmerism, and Diseases*. New York: Fowlers and Wells, 1852.
Williams, Raymond. *Marxism and Literature*. Oxford, UK: Oxford University Press, 1977.
Wilson, George. *The Progress of the Telegraph: Lecture*. Cambridge: Macmillan, 1859.
Wilson, William. *A Little Earnest Book upon a Great Old Subject*, London: Darton, 1851,
Windholz, George. "Pavlov's Concept of Schizophrenia as Related to the Theory of Higher Nervous Activity." *History of Psychiatry* 4, no. 16 (1993): 511–26.
Winslow, Jacques-Bénigne, and Jacques-Jean Bruhier. *The Uncertainty of the Signs of Death, and the Danger of Precipitate Interments and Dissections, Demonstrated*. Dublin: George Faulkner, 1746.
Woods, Angela. *The Sublime Object of Psychiatry: Schizophrenia in Clinical and Cultural Theory*. Oxford: Oxford University Press, 2011.
Woolley, V. J. "The Broadcast Experiment in Mass Telepathy." *Proceedings of the Society for Psychical Research* 5, no. 381928: 1–9.
Wright, Lawrence. *Going Clear: Scientology, Hollywood, and the Prison of Belief*. New York: Vintage, 2013.

Xavier, Rose Mary, and Allison Vorderstrasse. "Neurobiological Basis of Insight in Schizophrenia: A Systematic Review." *Nursing Research* 65, no. 3 (2016): 224–37.

Yenne, Bill. *Hitler's Master of the Dark Arts: Himmler's Black Knights and the Occult Origins of the SS*. Minneapolis: Zenith, 2010.

INDEX

1996 (2004), 259–60
2001: A Space Odyssey (1968), 255
9/11, 45, 49, 63–64, 73, 275, 293

"aberrant salience," 46, 52
Abbott, Greg, 74
Acland, Charles, 336n93
Active Denial System (ADS), 90. *See also* Directed Energy Weapons
Adler, Alfred, 167, 217
adolescents, 68, 71, 72, 87–88, 108–9, 175–76, 246–47, 319n141, 321n155, 371n29
Adorno, Theodor, 3, 9, 354n202
advertising, 1, 2 (*figure 1.1*), 44, 45, 106–8, 210–11, 281–82, 283; 291–92, 321n155, 336n93, 363n133
African Americans, 278, 287, 292; and conspiracy theory, 102, 258; and diagnostic bias, 10, 11, 268; and targeted individuals, 278, 374n72
Agenda 21, 378n113
Agnes, The Possessed (1848), 147
Ailes, Roger, 63
"Air Loom," 184–85 (*figure 4.2*). *See also* Matthews, James Tilley
Al-Qaeda, 69

Aldini, Giovanni, 127, 128 (*figure 3.1*), 129
Alexis, Aaron, 276, 278
algorithms, 61, 67–68, 69, 104, 107–10, 291, 384n38
alienation, 10, 11, 12, 44, 46, 53, 70, 71, 176, 246, 295
Allman, Paul Limbert, 306–7n4
Althusser, Louis, 273
Amazing Stories, 246
Amazon.com, 108, 320n148, 384n38
American Nervousness (1881) 16, 195–97, 359n71
anatomo-politics, 177–78, 222, 231. *See also* Foucault, Michel
Anatomy Act of 1832, 127, 344n56
Anderson, Benedict, 191, 204, 358n56
Andrejevic, Mark, 17, 68
Andres-Salome, Lou, 352–53n187
Andrews, Erin, 320n149
androids, 29, 249
animal magnetism, 145, 182, 206. *See also* magnetism; mesmerism
Ansley, Tonda, 285
Anthropocene, 296
Antichrist, 243, 334n76, 369n11
Anti-Oedipus, The (1972), 297–98
"anti-psychiatry," 8–9, 303–4n27

apophany, 46, 49, 50, 83 (figure 2.1), 216, 313n80
Apple Corporation, 4, 320n148
Aquino, Michael, 113, 337–38n104
Arcturians, 95, 9, 327n37, 327n38, 328n40.
    See also extraterrestrials
Area 51, 268, 378n114
Artaud, Antonin, 9
Arthur, Timothy Shay, 147
artificial intelligence (AI), 234, 253
astral projection, 173, 293, 346n90, 349n136
asylums, 15, 179–87, 206, 356n37
Atkinson, William Walker, 207–11, 214,
    362n114. See also New Thought
autism, 14, 73, 103, 104, 223–24, 228, 229,
    366n188
automaton, 129, 133–34, 176, 222, 228, 234–35,
    244, 249, 311n45, 323n2, 360–61n101, 367n198,
    368n200

Baba Bharta, 362n114
Ballard, J. G., 249
Bannon, Steve, 288
Banta, Emil, Dr., 141
Barnes, Mary, 312n57
Barnes, William Horatio, 192–93
Barrett, William, 153–54, 168
Barthelme, Donald, 306–7n4
Bataille, Georges, 315n92
Baudrillard, Jean, 9, 73, 75, 276, 286–87, 293,
    335–36n89, 383n23; and "the ecstasy of com-
    munication," 60–62, 75, 252; and integral
    reality, 295, 298–300; and radical illusion,
    286–87, 290, 293–96; and simulation, 73,
    286, 293, 295; and "superconductivity," 63,
    64, 287, 293; and "virtual credibility," 73–74
Baum, Frank, 5, 40
Bayne, Tim, 316n110
Beard, George, 16, 195–97
Beatles, The (band), 29, 108, 291, 309n23,
    309n24
Beatles, The ("White Album"), 29, 309n23
Beckett, Samuel, 9
Beckham, Alistair, 256
Belcher, William, 181–82
Bell, Alexander Graham, 6, 43
Bell, Michael, 329n49, 329n50
Benjamin, Walter, 136
Bentall, Richard, 14
Bernays, Edward, 2, 215–16
Bettelheim, Bruno, 223–31, 232–33 (figures 4.7,
    4.8, 4.9), 365n167; 366n188; and autism, 229;

and cybernetics, 225–27, 235; and homeo-
    stasis, 225
"Beyond the Pleasure Principle" (1920), 171–72,
    354n206. See also Freud, Sigmund
Biden, Joe, 102
Bierce, Ambrose, 348–49n133
"Big Data," 71, 73, 107, 108, 235–36, 294–298,
    321n155, 384n38
biopolitics, 177–78, 182, 183, 187, 203, 222, 231,
    298, 299. See also Foucault, Michel
Birch, John, 124
"bizarre" delusions, 86–87, 90, 92. See also
    delusions
Black Lives Matter, 278
Bleuler, Eugen, 7, 8, 10, 33, 245
Bly, Nellie, 186 (figure 4.3), 187
body politic, 5, 177–78, 187, 190–94, 202, 216.
    See also public sphere
Bondeson, Jan, 138
Book of Genesis, 95, 124–25
Book of Revelations, 103, 243–44, 334n76
Boorstin, Daniel, 3
Bourdieu, Pierre, 108
Braid, James, 146. See also hypnosis
brain, 43, 47, 49, 71, 79, 86, 90–91, 92, 106, 139,
    140, 141, 151–52, 154, 162, 164, 170, 184–86,
    210, 237–39, 250, 260, 263, 267, 305n46,
    325n18, 331–32n63, 381n144; and cybernetics,
    56, 60, 234, 251; and electricity, 124, 203; and
    electronic stimulation, 265–66; and energetic
    control, 25, 32, 87, 99–100, 205, 245, 256, 271,
    282; and mind, 120, 126, 192; and neurasthe-
    nia, 195–96; and neurology, 8, 32, 35, 103, 156,
    157; and posthumanism, 80, 234–35, 296,
    299, 367n198; and psychoanalysis, 168; and
    schizophrenia, 11, 14; and telegraphy, 190–92;
    and telepathy, 42, 203, 213–14, 220, 363n139,
    369–70n18; and willpower, 121, 126. See also
    brain chips
brain chips, 23, 65, 66, 83 (figure 2.1), 84–85,
    90–91, 97–98, 100, 102–7, 109, 112–14, 116,
    331n62, 335n88, 339n107. See also microchips
Brain Gate, 90–91
brainwashing, 263, 266
Brennan, Teresa, 77–78
Breton, Andre, 315n92
Breuer, Joseph, 164
Brill, A. A., 10
British Broadcasting Corporation (BBC), 53, 54,
    214, 318n133
British Telecom, 113, 114

Britton, Doc, 238
broadcasting, 24–25, 29–30, 53, 57, 60, 65, 203, 204, 212–15, 251, 258, 264, 271, 288, 376n93
Bromberg, Walter, 10–11, 268
Burgess Joshua, 348n128
Burke, Bill, 98
Burroughs, William S., 249
Bush, George, 135, 158
Bush, George H. W., 256–57
Bush, George W., 45, 49
Butler, Judith, 384n28

Cajal, Santiago Ramón y, 156, 168
Cameron, Donald Ewen, 265, 271, 377n96
Campbell, Hugh, 125
Canetti, Elias, 351n172
Canguilhem, Georges, 119
Capgras Delusion, 311n45. *See also* delusions
capitalism, 10, 12, 41, 69, 75, 76, 109–10, 272, 292, 296, 297, 335–36n89
Capshaw, Kate, 112
Carmichael, Leonard, 263
Carnegie, Dale, 208
Carradine, David, 260
Casagrande, Vicki, 101, 331n63
catalepsy, 136–44, 139 (*figure 3.3*), 147, 148, 150, 346n90, 361n106
cathexis, 163–65, 166 (*figure 3.7*), 168–69, 172, 225, 228, 352n180
Catholicism, 243–44, 369n11. *See also* Christianity
Caughey, John, 29, 309n23
Cavallo, Tiberius, 124
Cave, Hugh B., 246
Cavell, Stanley, 301–2n3
Cayce, Edgar, 327n37
Cazzamali, Fernando, 213–14, 363n139
celebrity stalking, 28–29, 66, 260
Central Intelligence Agency (CIA), 30, 31, 32, 94, 98, 106, 237, 242, 244, 256, 264–65, 271, 376–77n93, 377n96
Chadwick, Peter, 53
Chapman, Mark David, 29
chemtrails, 268–69, 271
Chevalier, W., 131, 132 (*figure 3.2*)
Cheyne, George, 187–88, 189, 195, 357n41
Chick, Jack, 243–44
Chittendale, Sterne, 117–18
Christianity, 40, 95, 103, 121, 129, 135, 146, 151, 243, 244, 249–50, 327n37, 362n112, n114, 369n11

Christie, Chris, 269
cities, 4–5, 11, 12, 57, 66, 78–79, 187–91, 197, 202, 209, 221, 235, 268, 357n44
Citizen's Commission of Human Rights, 303–4n27. *See also* Scientology; Szasz, Thomas
Civilization and Its Discontents (1930), 59, 76
Clarke, Arthur C., 253
Cline, Ernest, 115
Clinton, Hillary, 26 (*figure 1.1*), 258
Clinton, William Jefferson, 257–58
Clute, John, 205
Clydsdale, Matthew, 128–29
Cobbe, Frances, 343n55
Cochrane, Peter, 113–14, 339n197
"Cold War," 6, 16, 208, 244, 262–64. *See also* Soviet Union
Cole, Mark, 103
Columbia Broadcasting System (CBS), 21, 74, 214
communism, 106, 218, 238, 244, 257, 263
computer generated imagery (CGI), 114, 285
computers, 3, 18, 23, 30, 68, 69, 79, 81, 90, 95, 98, 105, 107, 108, 110, 113–15, 227, 234–35, 236, 238–41, 243, 244, 256, 330n50, 333n71, 336n91, 338n105, 367n198
"concrete thinking," 36, 51, 311n46, 315n96
conduction: and electricity, 160, 190; and nerves, 120, 124–26, 140–41, 145, 154–56, 178, 224, 297, 350n142; and Schreber, 158, 162–64; and telepathy, 169, 172–74, 212. *See also* galvanism
Conrad, Klaus, 45, 46
conspiracy theory, 64, 74, 238, 248, 256–58, 259, 262, 264, 279, 283, 325n16, 373n62, 378n113, 379n123, 379n128, 380n129, 380n130, 380n134; and HAARP, 269–72; and James Holmes, 273–76
Constantine, Alex, 255–56
Cooke, Josh, 285–86
Cooper, David, 8, 303–4n27, 312n57
Corbett, Sherry Lee, 285
Crawford, William, 154–55
Creature with the Atom Brain (1956), 245
Crist, Judith, 28
Crumb, Robert, 238
cults, 29, 309n23
cybernetics, 56–57, 61, 63–65, 69, 70, 78, 80, 109, 134, 178, 251, 256, 283, 291, 293, 295, 300; and "Joey," 225–31, 232 (*figure 4.7*), 233 (*figures 4.8, 4.9*), 366n188; and posthumanism, 234–36, 367n198. *See also* Wiener, Norbert
cyborgs, 7, 18, 61, 234, 297, 311n45, 339n107

Dali, Salvador, 315n92
Dalton, Jason, 70
Darger, Henry, 40
Dark Knight Rises, The (2012), 273, 275, 276
Darlington, Thomas, 43, 44, 49
Darnton, Robert, 148–50
Davy, Humphry, 129–30
de Certeau, Michel, 351n172
de Clérambault Gaëtan, 13, 316n104
de la Mettrie, Julien Offray, 121, 122, 126, 131
de la Pena, Carolyn Thomas, 197
de Vaucanson, Jacques, 129
deanimation. *See* catalepsy
death ray. *See* ray gun
DeBuffet, Jean, 38, 312n59. *See also* l'art brut
Dec, Francis E., 237–45, 240 (*figure 5.1*), 257
decapitation, 121, 126–28, 135–36, 143, 221, 341
Defense Advanced Research Projects Agency (DARPA) 6, 90–91, 92, 98, 103, 116, 264, 274–76, 325n16
Delbourgo, James, 129
Deleuze, Gilles, 9, 297–98, 303n27, 351n172, 384n35
Delgado, Jose Manuel Rodriguez, 265–67, 267 (*figure 5.4*), 271
delusional formation. *See* delusions: and formation
delusions, 105, 113, 78, 84–85, 164, 177, 181, 187, 228, 237, 242; and conspiracy theory, 257–58, 275–76; and content, 31–32, 35–42, 51; definition of, 34, 86–87, 92–93, 289–90; and depth of conviction, 92–93, 98, 326n29; and diagnosis, 19, 31–35, 85, 104, 116, 183, 279; as discourse, 33–34, 38–42, 50–54, 85, 98, 183; and electricity, 116–19, 182, 203, 207; and electromagnetism, 24, 118, 119, 182, 203–7; and electronics, 4, 18–19, 23–30, 57–59, 82–85, 97, 175–76, 187, 199–100, 204, 216–19, 237–41, 285–86, 290–93, 299–300; of erotomania, 28, 30, 62; and extraterrestrials, 95–97; and falsity, 92–93, 98; as "faulty reason," 47–50, 54; and form, 31–32, 35–42; and formation, 42, 44–54, 279; of grandiosity, 30, 35, 183, 219, 290; and incorrigibility, 92, 313–14n83; of influence, 23–27, 58, 62, 82–85, 184, 203, 237–41, 252; and "lack of insight," 92, 326n29; and magnetism, 203–4, 206; and the masses, 2–3, 206, 216–19, 220–21; and meaning, 13–14, 57–59, 85; and modernity, 18, 78, 200, 206, 216–19, 220–21, 239, 283, and psychiatry, 30–34, 86–87, 92–93; of reference, 23, 27–30,

53–54, 58, 62–63, 65, 73–75, 288–90; and religion, 93–95, 243, 244; as revelation, 50–54; and science fiction, 246–48, 285–86; as a spectrum, 104–5, 116; and Tausk, 25, 27, 35–37, 167; and technology, 3–4, 18, 24–25, 36, 57–59, 178, 184–85, 200, 203–7, 219, 239
demonic possession, 97, 144, 146, 151–52, 181, 329n47
depatterning, 265
depersonalization, 45–46, 175
depression, 7, 9, 10, 12, 15, 34, 82, 382n146
derealization, 45–46
Derrida, Jacques, 3, 9
Descartes, René, 80, 119–21, 129, 133, 135, 235
Deutsch, Helene, 168, 352–53n187
Devil Girl from Mars, The (1954), 246–47, 247 (*figure 5.2*)
Diagnostic and Statistical Manual of Mental Disorders (DSM); 94, 183, 310n37; DSM-IV (1994), 86–87; DSM-V (2013), 14, 33–34, 92–93, 104, 303n24
Dick, Philip K., 80, 108, 249–53; 372n42, 43, 51
Directed Energy Weapons (DEW), 18, 57, 101–2, 254–55, 261, 264, 272, 279, 282, 333n71, 372n56
disequilibrium. *See* homeostasis
Disneyland, 261, 322n171
Distribution d'effluves avec machine centrale et tableau métrique, 38–40, 41
Doane, Mary Ann, 63
Donald Duck, 41–42, 54
Douglas, Robert, 133
Downs, Hugh, 28
Doyle, Sir Arthur Conan, 42
Dreamscape, 98
Du Maurier, George, 148

Ebony, 268, 278n112
ectoplasm, 154–55, 155 (*figure 3.5*)
Eddy, Mary Baker, 362n112
Edison, Thomas, 5, 6, 24, 43, 204–5, 207, 290, 331n62, 361n105 andn106, 373n57
Eggers, Dave, 67
ego, 17–18, 36, 58, 65, 166, 215–16, 223, 250, 280; and anatomy, 120, 130, 132, 136, 137–39, 146, 150, 162; and cybernetics, 231–36, 293; and data, 68, 292; and Lacan, 13–14, 50–54, 80, 295; and modernity, 76–81; and paranoia, 36, 239, 290; and posthumanism, 60, 78–81, 234–36, 296–300, 368n203; and schizophrenia, 45, 56, 174; and telepathy, 168, 173

egocasting, 65, 291
Eigen, Michael, 173–74
Einhorn, Ira, 376–77n93
Einstein, Albert, 156, 218, 219
Eissler, Kurt R., 353n187
Ekstein, Rudolf, 246, 247
electricity, 4–7, 122, 126, 133, 145, 158, 168, 173, 177, 205, 214, 229, 246, 254, 291, 344–45n64, 360n89, 376n93; and the body, 78, 118, 119, 122–24, 125–29, 133–35, 139–44, 146, 151, 172, 195–97, 200–1, 212, 223–25, 230–34, 266–68, 308n10, 344n60; delusions involving, 24, 27, 35, 41, 43, 48, 95, 99–100, 117–19, 175–76, 178, 181, 182–83, 200, 203, 205, 207, 222, 239, 244, 251–52, 340n11; and homeostasis, 140, 151, 195–97, 225; and medicine, 122–24, 126, 133, 196–97, 266–68, 355–56n19, 359n81, 361n106; and spirit, 124–25, 135; and telegraphy, 190–93. *See also* electronics; galvanism; delusions
electroconvulsive therapy (ECT), 124, 221, 265, 355–56n18
electrocution, 25, 123, 173, 200–1
electromagnetic frequency pollution, 317n129, 376n91
electromagnetic pulse (EMP), 6, 302–3n18
electropsychometer (E-meter), 96, 328n41
electroshock. *See* electroconvulsive therapy (ECT)
electronic brain stimulation (ESB), 266–67. *See also* electroconvulsive therapy
electronics, 1, 4–7, 18–19, 23–25, 34, 37, 41, 47, 57–70, 85, 87–89, 98, 100, 101–3, 105, 160, 172, 174, 178, 187, 190, 194, 199–201, 215, 229–30, 235–36, 237–39, 259–66, 279–83, 288, 290, 293, 294, 297, 299, 328–29n44, 333n71, 334n76. *See also* electricity; telegraphy; telephony; television; virtual reality
Elkisch, Paula, 223, 365n164
Elliotson, John, Dr., 148–49. *See also* mesmerism
Ellis, John, 70
Ellul, Jacques, 17
Enlightenment, the, 5, 47, 73, 119–22, 129–30, 176, 235, 294
equilibrium. *See* homeostasis
"erotomania," 28, 30, 62
Ervin, Frank, 267–68
eschatology, 243–44, 369n11
Esquirol, Jean-Étienne Dominique, 24, 140, 181, 308n10

ether, 25, 42, 61, 156–57, 164, 170, 214, 308n13, 350n142
European Union, 326n25, 334n74
Eviltron, 88–89, 89 (*figure 2.2*)
Exegesis of Philip K. Dick, The (2011), 250–52
explanationism, 47–49, 316n110. *See also* delusions
extrasensory perception (ESP), 372n51. *See also* telepathy
extraterrestrials, 94–97, 220, 243, 245, 246–47, 255, 327n37, 327n38, 327n39, 328n40, 328n42, 326n43, 328n44, 338n105, 371n29; 378n114; *See also* Arcturians; Scientology

Facebook, 64, 71, 72, 278, 280, 291
"fake news," 16, 282, 288
"false-flag" operation, 74, 274, 380n129
Fanning, William J., 254
"fantastic," the, 152, 245–46, 248–49
Faraday, Michael, 5
Federal Bureau of Investigation (FBI), 90, 98, 106, 274, 276, 318n35
Federal Communications Commission (FCC) 62, 63, 318n136
Fenster, Mark, 257
Ferenczi, Sandor, 166, 168
Fessenden, Reginald, 43
Feuer, Jane, 61
Finster, Howard, 40, 312n61
Flechsig, Paul, Dr., 157, 159, 162, 164, 165 (*figure 3.6*)
Fleming, Ian, 242
"flight of ideas," 51, 139, 315n96
Flournoy, Theodore, 245
Folie et déraison: Histoire de la folie à l'âge classique (1961), 8, 303n20. *See also* Foucault, Michel
Force Trainer, 91, 325n19
Forrester, John, 168
Fortune, Dion, 211–12, 214, 362n128
Foster, George, 127
Foster, Jodie, 29
Foster, Vince, 258
Foucault, Michel, 5, 290, 297, 298; on biopolitics, 177–78; on "madness," 7–9, 93, 180, 189, 303n20, 351n72, 360–61n101
Fox News, 63, 102, 258
Frahm, Ole, 351n169
Frankenstein (1818; 1831), 129–35, 132 (*figure 3.2*), 137, 138–39, 140, 145, 150, 193, 200, 235, 238–41, 240 (*figure 5.1*), 243–45, 344–45n64

INDEX 423

Franklin, Benjamin, 5, 122, 123, 124, 145, 341n26, 342n39
Freeland, Elana, 269–71
Freeman, Daniel, 16, 104–5
Freeman, Jason, 16, 104–5
Freeman, Walter, 244
Freemasons, 97, 207, 209, 262, 288, 379–80n128
French Revolution, 135, 148–49, 181
Freud, Sigmund, 24, 25, 35, 42, 50, 54, 64, 76, 171–72, 209, 216, 217–19, 221, 222, 226, 235, 292, 297, 323n2, 336–37n100, 351n174, 352n175, 352–53n187, 354n206, 366n188, 379n123; and cathexis, 164–65, 228, 166 (*figure 3.7*), 352n180; on delusions, 52, 62, 164, 169, 280; on magical thinking, 165, 169–70; on paranoia, 36, 163–64, 351n173; and the "principle of constancy," 16, 164, 225; on Prosthetic Gods, 59, 76, 80; on Schreber, 163–65, 173; and telepathy, 166–69; on the uncanny, 55; and the unconscious, 172, 212–13, 328n41
Frey, Allan, 262, 271
Froese, Arno, 334n76
From India to the Planet Mars (1900), 245
Fry, Peter, 302–3n18

Gaines, William, 1
Gallois, M. L., 126–27
Galvani, Luigi, 125–28, 188. *See also* galvanism
Galvanic Belt, 196–97, 198 (*figure 4.4*)
galvanism, 125–28, 129, 131, 133–43, 145, 146, 150, 157, 173, 190, 193, 197–98, 200, 244, 344n64
Gamson, Joshua, 292
"gang-stalking," 260–61, 375n75
Garvey, Michael, 192
Gates, Bill, 369n11
Geoghegan, Bernard, 226
ghosts. *See* spirits
Gie, Robert, 38–40, 39 (*figure 1.2*)
Ginter, John, 100
Girard, Harlan, 259, 262
God, 80–81, 90, 94–95, 97, 102, 113, 119, 125, 129–33, 135, 141, 177, 235, 243, 250, 255, 287, 312n61, 327–28n35; and Daniel Schreber, 157–63, 350n152; and Francis Dec, 237–41, 243, 244
Goffman, Erving, 292
Goebbels, Joseph, 216
Gohmert, Louis, 74
Gold, Ian, 288–90
Gold, Joel, 288–90
Golgi, Camillo, 156

Grant, Brian W., 55
Grant, Jeffrey, 334n76
Green, Melissa, 316n110
"Green Tea" (1869), 150–52, 348n128
Greenfeld, Liah, 9
Greenland, Colin, 248
Guattari, Félix, 8, 9, 297, 303–4n27, 351n172, 384n35
Guest, Jim, 101
Gunning, Tom, 154
Gurney, Edmund, 153

Haig, Ian, 366–67n188
Hall, John, 260
hallucinations, 11, 14, 33, 34, 39, 87, 118, 152, 154, 249–50, 268, 318n133; auditory, 23, 24, 27–28, 32, 43–44, 46, 62, 82, 89, 256, 308n8, 319n142
Haraway, Donna, 78, 297
Harber, Francis, 97, 329n47
Hardt, Michael, 273
Harrison, George, 29
Haslam, Joseph, 15, 24, 184–86, 185 (*figure 4.2*)
Hayles, Katherine, 226, 235
Heaven's Gate, 29
Hegel, Georg Wilhelm Friedrich, 50
Heidegger, Martin, 17, 50, 54, 77
Helder, Lucas, 292–93
"Hello Barbie," 110–12, 111 (*figure 2.4*)
Helms, Richard, 264
Herbert, John, Mrs., 137
Heston, Charlton, 90
Hewitt, Jennifer Love, 113, 116, 338n105, 339n114
High Frequency Active Auroral Research Project (HAARP), 268–72, 282
hikikomori, 72, 77 (*figure 1.3*)
Hill, Barney, 329n45
Hill, Betty, 329n45
Hinckley, John, 29
Hitler, Adolf, 218, 263, 375–76n84, 376n85, 380n129
Hofstadter, Richard, 257
Hollos, Istvan, 168–69
Hollywood, 114–15, 202, 253, 258, 260, 272, 276, 287, 337–38n104
Holmes, James, 273–76, 277 (*figure 5.6*), 380–81n134
Holmes, Robert, 274
Holosonics, 89
homeostasis, 120–21, 126, 140, 152, 159, 164, 187–88, 192, 193, 195, 225, 229–30, 295, 297, 300
Horkheimer, Max, 3, 69

Hosokawa, Shuhei, 319n141
Hubbard, L. Ron, 96, 328n40, 328n43, 328n44
Huckabee, Mike, 63
Hughes, Howard, 373n62
HUMANCENTiPad, 111 (figure 2.3), 336n97
Huysmans, Joris-Karl, 336–37n100
hypnosis, 42, 136, 137, 144, 145–46, 150, 154, 167, 173, 213, 264, 271, 274, 351n174. *See also* mesmerism
hysteria, 14, 42, 75, 147, 164, 166, 169, 196, 201, 202

Illuminati, 85, 262, 288
induction, 43, 49, 150, 153–56, 157, 160, 162–63, 168–70, 172–74, 178, 203–4, 208, 210, 350n142
Industrial Revolution, 4–5, 24, 85, 177, 191
"influencing machine," 18, 25, 27, 35–37, 42, 52, 119, 167, 174, 176–78, 183–84, 203, 254–55, 257, 276, 290–91, 301n3. *See also* Tausk, Victor
information, 75, 76, 102, 164, 190, 252, 254–55, 262, 276, 279, 287, 290–96, 298–99; Age of, 6, 56, 67, 85, 290–91; and cybernetics, 56, 60, 65, 79, 80, 91, 225, 231, 234–36; and data harvesting, 67–68, 69, 91–92, 98, 108–12; ego as, 7, 78, 114, 234–36; and "overload," 16–17, 58, 61, 63, 72–75, 81, 239
Ingenhousz, Jan, 123–24
insanity, 3, 7, 15–16, 24, 42–44, 137, 139–41, 179, 182–87, 199, 202, 360n89. *See also* paranoia; psychosis; schizophrenia
Institute for Creative Technologies (ICT), 114–15, 116
Institute of Electrical and Electronics Engineers (IEEE), 331n62
Internet, 4, 18, 30, 60, 63, 66, 72–73, 77 (figure 1.3), 79, 91, 113, 276, 279, 280–81, 320n147, 321n152, 323n189, 338n105
"Internet of things," 18, 80, 106, 234, 299
International Classification of Diseases (ICD), 33, 310n37
"Intracerebral Radio Stimulation and Recording in Completely Free Patients" (1968), 266–67
iPhone, 65, 319n142, 320n147, 320n148
Ishii, Kotoe, 366–67n188
Itskov, Dmitry, 367n198

Jackson, Pamela, 250
Jack the Ripper, 5, 302n11
Jacobs, Brandon, 331n62
Jacobson, John, 380–81n134
Jade Helm, 15, 74
Jameson, Fredric, 9, 75, 296
Jaspers, Karl, 31–32, 44, 48, 289, 316n103
Jay, Mike, 185
Jenkinson, Robert Banks, 183
Jesus Christ, 94, 313–14n83, 327n37. *See also* Christianity
"Joey, the Mechanical Boy," 222–35, 366n188
Johnson, Micah Xavier, 278
Jones, Alex, 269, 275
Jones, Candy, 264–65
Jones, Ernest, 166–67
Jones, Franklin D., 248
Jones, George C., 99, 330n56
Josef H., 118–19
Joyce, James, 163
Judaism, 112, 167, 244
Jung, Carl, 163, 166, 167, 217, 218
Jurassic Park (1993), 114

Kac, Eduardo, 320n147
Kaczynski, Ted, 366n182
Kannenberg, Ida, 327–28n39
Kapur, Shitji, 46
Katzman, Sam, 245
Kennedy, John F., 256, 264, 373n68, 380n130
Kennedy, Joseph P., 373n62
Kidd, Benjamin, 215
King George III, 179–80
King Louis XIV, 145
Kittler, Friedrich, 9, 59–60, 164, 165, 351n172
Klein, Naomi, 265, 377n100
Kleinberg-Levin, David Michael, 9
Koestler, Arthur, 252
Koresh, David, 90
Koroshetz, Walter, 381–82n144
Kossy, Diane, 238
Kovel, Joel, 9–10
Kraepelin, Emil, 7, 25, 48, 316n116
Kramer, Heinrich, 336–37n100
Kraus, Alfred, 30
Kristeva, Julia, 130, 132
Kubie, Lawrence, 226
Kubrick, Stanley, 255
Kucinich, Denis, 101–2
Kurzweil, Ray, 114, 231, 234, 367n198

La Bas (1891), 337n100
La Beaume, Michael, 140

LaBeouf, Shia, 374n73
Lacan, Jacques, 13–14, 50–52, 54–55, 75, 77, 79, 80, 293, 295, 297, 298 305n46, 315n91, 315n92, 316n104, 323n2, 351n172, 367n197
Laclau, Ernesto, 384n28
Lafontaine, Charles, 146
Laing, R. D., 8, 9, 12, 312n57
Lanza, Adam, 273–76
Laswell, Howard, 1
LaVey, Anton, 113
Le Bon, Gustave, 3, 215
Le Fanu, Sheriden, 150–52, 348n128
Leader, Darien, 44, 46, 51, 52, 315n94
Lears, T. Jackson, 197
Leduc, Don, 332n64
Leavis, F. R., 1
Ledger, Heath, 260, 275
LeDoux, Joseph, 103, 305n46, 335n81
Lemov, Rebecca, 377n96
Lennon, John, 29
Lethem, Jonathan, 250, 372n45
Letterman, David, 29
Lever, Charles, 139–41, 142
Lévi-Strauss, Claude, 9
Leymann, Heinz, 375n75
Lichtman, Jeff, 234
Lindsay, Hal, 243
Lippard, George, 189
Lipsky, Adam, 215
lobotomy. *See* psychosurgery
Locke, John, 47, 54
Lodge, Sir Oliver, 156–57, 164, 363–64n140
Lombard, J. S., 156
Long, Gavin Eugene, 278
Lothane, Zvi, 165 (*figure 3.6*), 351n172
Lovecraft, H. P., 151, 243, 246
Lowndes, Francis, 123
Luckhurst, Roger, 153
Lutz, Tom, 359n71
Lyne, William, 373n57
Lyotard, Jean-François, 75
lysergic acid diethylamide (LSD), 29, 55–56, 271, 309n24, 316–17n116

McCain, John, 292
McCarthy-Jones, Simon, 14
McCartney, Paul, 309n24, 372n42
McCulloch, Warren, 226
MacDougall, Duncan, 155–56
McGee, Ellen M., 79–80
McGillicuddy, Timothy, 196

McLean, David R., 244
McLuhan, Marshall, 58, 59, 171–72
McVeigh, Timothy, 31
Mackay, Charles, 3, 215
Maclagan, David, 38–39, 40
MAD Magazine, 1, 2 (*figure 1.1*), 243
Madam Ehrenborg, 245
Madden, Samuel, 370n20
Maddux, Holly, 376–77n93
Maeterlinck, Maurice, 42, 312n64
"magical thinking," 165–66, 169, 253, 325n19
magnetism, 4, 24, 27, 118, 126, 135, 145–46, 159, 173, 182, 183, 184, 203, 205–7, 212, 245. *See also* animal magnetism; electricity; electromagnetism; mesmerism
Maher, Brendan A., 324n6
malingering, 34, 187, 310–11n41
Malvo, Lee Boyd, 286–88, 289 (*figure E.1*)
Mander, Jerry, 2, 301–2n3
mania, 117–18, 139, 140, 200, 360n89
Manson, Charles, 29, 287, 309n23, 382–83n5, 383n7
Marconi, Guglielmo, 6, 24, 43, 170, 204, 207, 208
Mark, Vernon, 267
marketing. *See* advertising
Mars, 205, 245, 246–47, 249, 254 (*figure 5.3*)
Mars Attacks cards (1962), 254 (*figure 5.3*)
Marsh, Richard, 148
"Martha Mitchell Effect," 324n6
Marx, Karl, 10, 58, 218
Marxism, 70, 109, 273, 292
materialism, 121, 122, 129, 130, 134, 150, 152–53, 235, 271, 279, 379n123
Mattel, 91, 110
Matthews, Harry Grindell, 372n56
Matthews, James Tilley, 183–85, 185 (*figure 4.2*), 186, 356n26
Matrix, The (1999), 285–87, 289, 290, 298, 300, 335n87
"*Matrix* Defense," 286
Maudsley, Henry, 15
May, Myron, 278
Meadows, Cathy, 375n78
mediumship, 137, 150, 153, 167, 196. *See also* spiritualism
MEDUSA (Mob Excess Deterrent Using Silent Audio), 90
Memoirs of My Nervous Illness (1903), 157–65
Mendoza, Jesus, 101, 332n64
Mercier, Charles Arthur, 24, 308n12

Mesmer, Franz, 145–46, 150
mesmerism, 145–50, 149 (*figure 3.4*), 185.
    See also hypnosis
"Method and Apparatus for Altering a Region in the Earth's Atmosphere, and/or Magnetosphere" (1987), 269, 270 (*figure 5.5*)
Metzl, Jonathan, 10, 267–68
microchip, 31, 85, 92, 99, 102, 106, 320n147, 326n25, 329n49, 330n50, 330n53, 331n62, 334n74, 335n81. *See also* brain chip
microwaves, 18, 23, 90, 101, 259, 260, 262, 263, 271, 282, 333n71, 376n91, 376n93
microwave oven, 57, 261
"microwave auditory effect" (MAE), 262
Mieseges, Vadim, 285
"Mike, the Headless Chicken," 341n22
Milanovich, Norma, 95, 327n38
Miller, Jacques-Alain, 315–16n101, 316n104
Millerites, 369n11
Mind Molester, 88
"mind control," 97, 100–2, 106, 113, 255, 256–57, 261, 263, 264, 266, 271, 274, 279, 282, 327–28n39, 376n93
MindFlex, 91, 325n19
Mink, Eric, 22
Mitchell, Edward Page, 152–53
Mitchell, John, 324n6
Mitchell, Martha, 324n6
MK-ULTRA, 264–65, 271, 290
modernism, 9, 163, 248, 297, 315n92, 363n139
modernity, 3, 4–7, 9–12, 16–18, 40–41, 53, 75–76, 92, 105, 129, 133, 160, 163, 171, 174, 191, 196–97, 202, 223, 227, 235, 252, 283, 298, 351n172, 352n175, 366n188
Monet, Claude, 37
monomania, 140–41, 199
Montgomery, Campbell, 22
Moorcock, Michael, 248
Moore, Gordon E., 105
"Moore's Law," 105, 114, 335n86
Morgan, J. L., 234
Morgan, J. P., 218, 219
Morgellons Disease, 379n122
Morrow, Felix, 263
Morse, Samuel, 197
Morus, Iwan Rhys, 190
Mosquito, The, 87–88
Mosso, Angelo, 156
Muhammad, John Lee, 286–87
Murdoch, Rupert, 63, 258
Myers, Fredric W. H., 153, 166

Nagle, Matthew, 90
nanotechnology, 85, 102, 326n28
Napolis, Diane, 112–16, 336–37n100, 337n104, 338n105
"Natalija A.," 27, 36–37, 38, 48
National Bioethics Advisory Board, 101
National Broadcasting Company (NBC), 22, 28, 214
National Institute of Health (NIH), 23, 274–75, 381–82n144
National Rifle Association, 380n129
National Security Agency (NSA), 106, 112–13, 116
Nausée, La (1938), 45–46
Naylor, Gloria, 259–60, 374n72
Nazism, 97, 216–17, 218, 219, 245, 263, 271, 375n84, 376n85
Negri, Antonio, 273
neoliberalism, 12, 15, 283, 284, 291
nervous system, 1, 135, 148, 164, 234, 246, 263, 202, 222, 235, 350n142, 357n41; and anatomy, 120; and catalepsy, 139–40, 141, 142; and galvanism, 122, 125–29, 133, 134, 173, 224; and homeostasis, 78, 121, 152, 165, 189, 195–97, 357n41; and mechanical control, 49, 110, 134, 369–70n18, 381–82n144; and media, 49, 59–60, 63, 113, 172, 178, 200, 283, 291; and mediumship, 154–55; and Schreber, 157–62; and telegraphy, 190–93, 194–95; and telepathy, 169
neurasthenia, 195–97, 208, 359n71
neurobiology. *See* neurology
neurodiversity movement, 14
neurology, 8, 32, 35, 42, 44, 104, 135, 140, 142, 157, 168, 208, 213, 226, 246, 250, 263, 276, 314n84
New Age, 94, 208
New Thought, 207–11, 213, 362n112
New World Order, 106, 257, 272, 273, 379–80n128
New Worlds, 248
Newland, Constance, 316–17n116
newscasters, 21–23, 28, 54, 62–63
newspapers, 16, 53, 63, 75, 79, 191, 197, 200, 201, 203, 204, 219, 358n56
Nicholls, Peter, 205
Niemoller, Martin, 99
Nietzsche, Friedrich, 3, 5, 16, 54, 210
Nimmo, Kurt, 269
Nineteen Eighty-Four (1949), 253, 320n148
Nixon, Richard, 324n6

INDEX   427

nomophobia, 65
Nordau, Max, 16, 41, 118
Noriega, Manuel, 90
Norris, Chuck, 74

Obama, Barack, 74, 102–3, 258, 269, 272–74, 292, 321n152, 333–34n73, 369n11, 380n129
"Obama Brain Initiative," 103
O'Brien, Barbara, 219–22, 364n158
O'Brien, Cathy, 256–57
occultism, 150–51, 163, 165, 167–68, 173, 183, 185, 196, 207, 208, 211–13, 215, 219, 235, 250, 263, 275, 309n23, 336–37n100, 349n136, 354n202, 362n127, 362n129, 364n147, 375–76n84, 376n85, 379n128
Odd Fellows, 206, 207, 209
Oetinger, Friedrich, 124–25, 158
Okey, Elizabeth, 148
Okey, Jane, 148
"On the Origins of the Influencing Machine in Schizophrenia," 25–27, 35–37
Operation Paperclip, 263
Operators and Things (1958), 219–22
Oppenheim, James, 213
Orwell, George, 253, 288, 320n148
Oswald, Lee Harvey, 256, 264, 274, 373n68, 380n130
Owen, Alex, 312–13n65

paranoia, 13, 15, 48, 57, 75, 84, 88, 97, 106, 113, 217–18, 243, 249, 361n105; in business, 209, 222; and conspiracy theory, 73, 257–58, 272; and diagnosis, 50–51, 94, 104–5; and electronic media, 24–25, 30, 36, 48, 57, 62–64, 102–4, 107, 118, 164, 202, 203–7, 259–62; and Francis E. Dec, 237–42; and Freud, 36–37, 163–64, 167, 169, 171, 352n175, 352–53n187; and modernity, 16, 178, 352n175; and physicians, 181–87, 203–4; political, 73, 102–4, 106, 257–58, 272, 335n84; and schizophrenia, 8, 11, 22, 23, 29, 50, 76, 184, 253; and surveillance, 91, 253, 289–90; and targeted individuals, 259–62, 281. *See also* psychosis; schizophrenia; delusions
Pavlov, Ivan, 75–76, 263, 271
Pazder, Lawrence, 337n100
Peale, Norman Vincent, 208
Pearson, Ian, 114, 339n112
Percival, Thomas, 123, 179
Perfect Crime, The (1996), 294–95, 383n23
Perkins, Benjamin Douglas, 126

Peters, John Durham, 53
Peterson, Albert, 102
Peterson, Frederick, 203
Petkou, Panagiota, 131
pharmacology, 12, 14–15, 87, 250
Physical Control of the Mind (1969), 266–67. *See also* Delgado, Jose Manuel Rodriquez
physicians, 15, 141; as diagnostician, 33, 84, 93, 97; in fiction, 133, 139, 142, 147, 150–53, 371n29; as persecutors, 56, 179–87, 203–4
Pittman, Renee, 278
Plank, Robert, 247–48, 252–53, 371n30
Podmore, Frank, 154, 348n133
Poe, Edgar Allan, 5, 143, 144, 187
positivism, 34, 231, 235, 294–96, 298, 368n203
posthumanism, 59, 78–81, 231, 234–36, 296–300, 368n203
"Post-mortem Recollections of a Medical Lecturer" (1836), 139–41
postmodernity, 75, 249, 296
Poulsen, Valdemar, 43, 314n87
power, 9, 18–19, 53, 56–57, 62, 64, 74–75, 104, 119, 177, 187, 203, 276, 360–61n101; biopolitical, 177–78, 179, 183, 203; electro-political, 4, 190, 192, 219, 231, 242, 246, 255, 259–61, 271–72, 281, 283, 290–93, 298, 299; 355n88; energetic, 4, 6, 58–59, 118–19, 122, 173, 200, 205, 224, 262; political, 5, 34, 57, 58, 60, 62, 69, 78, 85, 97–99, 107, 177–78, 193–94, 207, 211, 215, 218, 220, 221–22, 239–41, 253, 256, 257, 272–73, 288, 298, 299; mesmeristic, 145–50, 173, 185, 206, 207; mind, 174, 207–10, 211, 214, 215, 219, 220, 264; nervous, 120–21, 123–27, 134, 137, 145, 150, 154, 159–61, 173, 196–97, 251; psychiatric, 7–9, 97, 179–87, 265–68, 303n20; 323n2, 356–57n37. *See also* willpower
Powers, Richard, 248
premature burial, 138–41, 139 (*figure 3.3*), 143–44, 346n93
Presidential Commission for the Study of Bioethical Issues, 279, 381–82n144
Priestley, Joseph, 122–23
primary delusion, 31–32, 40, 52, 289. *See also* delusions
Prince, Morton, 213
privacy, 66–68, 72, 79–80, 91, 99, 101, 109, 110–12, 214, 260, 290, 374n72
prodrome, 44–46, 52, 53, 71–72, 82, 87–88, 114, 118, 175, 281, 283
Project Artichoke, 264

"Prosthetic God" 59–60, 76–78, 80, 81, 300. See also Freud, Sigmund; prosthetic irritation
prosthetic irritation, 59–75; and addiction, 65–66; and algorithmic management, 67–69; and convergence, 60–61; and cybernetic penetration, 64–65; and entertainment, 70–71; and information, 72–75; and labor, 69–70; and "liveness," 61–62, 64; and "news" 62–64; and privacy, 66–68; and relationships, 71–72; and superconductivity, 63–64; and surveillance, 66–67
"protest psychosis," 10–11, 268
Protestantism, 243–44. See also Christianity
Prunier, Théotime, 136
psychiatry, 10, 15, 19, 23, 104, 141, 221, 226, 227, 250, 281, 308n12, 315n94, 328n41, 355–56n18, 382n146; and diagnostic criteria, 4, 30–34, 35, 38, 47–48, 50–51, 65, 85, 86–87, 104–5, 238, 279, 304n36, 307–8n6, 310n37, 310–11n41, 314n84, 324n6, 326n29, 378n110; and neurobiology, 8–9; and power, 4, 7–9, 97, 179–87, 265–68, 303n20; 323n2, 356–57n37; and schizophrenia, 7–13, 14, 18, 75–76, 104, 245, 315n96. See also anti-psychiatry; psychoanalysis
psychic attack, 211–12, 282, 283 (figure 5.7), 363n133
Psychic Discoveries Behind the Iron Curtain (1971), 263
psychic driving, 265
psychic vampirism. See psychic attack
psychoanalysis, 10, 36–38, 76–77, 163–69, 172, 175–76, 208, 212, 213, 218, 221, 223, 226, 228, 231, 247, 266, 323n2, 328n41, 351n174, 352n175, 352–53n187, 354n206, 366n188. See also Freud, Sigmund; Lacan, Jacques
"Psychoanalytic Notes upon an Autobiographical Account of a Case of Paranoia" (1911), 163–164. See also Freud, Sigmund
psychosis, 1, 4, 8, 10, 15, 18, 36, 48, 53, 59, 80, 84, 94, 107, 118, 173–74, 216, 221, 245, 259, 300; and art, 38–42, 312n56, 312n57, 312n59, 312n61; and delusions, 31–34, 85; and diagnostic criteria, 31–34, 85; and environment, 14–15; and immigrants, 11, 216, 304–5n39; and magical thinking, 169; and meaning, 50–52; and neurobiology, 13–14, 32, 35, 87; politics of evaluation, 7, 18–19, 34; prodromal phase, 44–46, 72, 82; and psychoanalysis, 13–14; and race, 10, 268, 304n36; and science fiction, 246–49, 256; "triggers," 51–52, 315n99. See also paranoia; schizophrenia

psychosurgery, 226, 244–45, 265–67, 268, 330n50, 378n112
Psychotic Art, 40
psychotronics, 262–64, 273, 282, 283 (figure 5.7), 376–77n93
public mind, 1–3, 191–93, 211, 215
"public sphere," 3, 63–64, 191, 203–4, 219, 279, 291, 358n56

Quaid, Evi, 260, 374n73
Quaid, Randy, 260, 374n73
Quimby, Phineas Parkhurst, 362n112, 362n114
QuWave, 282, 283 (figure 5.7)

Rabinbach, Anson, 125–26
radiation, 102, 204, 282, 369–70n18
radio, 6, 18, 23–25, 28–30, 53, 54, 58, 59, 60, 61, 64, 65, 66, 74–75, 79, 84, 102, 105, 204, 213–19, 224, 230, 238–41, 244–46, 252, 262–64, 266, 269, 282, 308n13, 351n169, 363–64n140. See also wireless
radio frequency identification (RFID), 91, 92, 98–99, 107, 330n53, 334n74
"Radio Mind-Ray, The" (1934), 246
radiology, 329n49, 331n62
Rather, Dan, 21–22, 60, 62, 306–7n4
Ray, Margaret, 29
ray gun, 169, 254–55, 254 (figure 5.3), 372n56
Raza, Ghyslain, 67, 321n152
Ready Player One (2018), 115–16
Reagan, Ronald, 29, 255–57, 269
reflectionism, 35–42, 47
Reitman, Francis, 39–40
remote viewing (RV), 263–64, 282
resurrectionists, 127, 344n56, 345n75
Reynolds, George W. M., 189
Richardson, Edward Tylor, 350n142
ringxiety, 65
Roazen, Paul, 352–53n187
Robbins v. Lower Merion School District, 67
Roberts, Bruce Porter, 373n62
Roberts, John, 102, 333n72
robot. See automaton
Roheim, Geza, 169–70
Rokeach, Milton, 313–14n83
"Role of Brain Disease in Riots and Urban Violence, The" (1967), 268
Romains, Jules, 218
Romney, Mitt, 67, 269, 273, 321n152
Roquentin, Antoine, 45–46
Rosen, Christine, 65

INDEX 429

"Rosenhan Experiment," 310–11n41
Rosenhan, David, 310–11n41
Rouse, William, 170
Roustang, Francois, 351n174, 352–53n187
Russell, Bertrand, 218
Russian Woodpecker, 264, 376–77n93

Sachs, Hanns, 340–41n15
Saito, Tamaki, 72
Sanders, Bernie, 272
Sandy Hook Elementary School, 73–74, 273, 275
Santner, Eric, 315n99, 351n172
Sappell, Joel, 328n43
Sarasin, Philipp, 120
Sartre, Jean-Paul, 45–46
Sass, Louis S., 9, 45
Satanic Ritual Abuse, 113, 336–37n100
Satanism, 112–13, 116, 273, 275, 336–37n100, 338n105, 339n109, 368–69n9
satellites, 23, 41, 82–84, 83 (*figure 2.1*), 87, 252, 255, 261
Saussure, Ferdinand, 50
schizophrenia, 22–23, 25, 29, 36–40, 50–51, 54, 57, 80, 94–95, 113, 169, 175, 221, 245, 256, 261, 265, 303n27, 331n46, 312n57, 319n141; diagnostic criteria of, 7, 8, 10, 13–14, 32–34, 86–87, 97, 104, 267–68, 307n6, 315n96; etiology of, 8–9, 11–12, 31, 75; history of, 7–8, 10–11, 16, 55–56, 245; as insight, 55–57; and media, 2, 18, 21–23, 53–54, 56–57, 61–63, 75, 114, 216–19, 301n3, 371n29; and modernity, 9–10, 16, 18, 53, 75, 297; prodrome of, 44–46; and science fiction, 247–50. *See also* psychosis
Schneider, Kurt, 32–33
Schreber, Daniel Paul, 157–62, 163–66, 167, 171–73; 315n99, 350n152, 351n172, 352n175, 360–61n101, 366n188
Schwarzenegger, Arnold, 253
science fiction, 9, 96, 129, 220, 228, 234, 245–55, 256, 259, 271, 283, 285, 293–94, 364n147, 370n19, 370n20, 371n29, 375–76n84, 384–85n39
scientific marvelous, 169, 245–46, 256, 283
Scientology, 8, 96, 303–4n27, 328n40–44
Scorsese, Martin, 29
Sechehaye, Marguerite, 175
Sechehaye, Renee, 175–76, 178, 222
secondary delusion, 31–32, 52, 289. *See also* delusions
Secret of the Brain-Chip, The, 82–85, 83 (*figure 2.1*), 87, 114

selfies, 291
Seltzer, Ed, 102, 334n75
Serazio, Michael, 108
Serviss, Garrett P., 205
sexting, 67
Shaftsbury, Edmund, 214
Shakur, Tupac, 287
Shelley, Mary, 129–34, 138, 344n64
Sidgwick, Henry, 153
Siegel, Ronald, 87
Siirala, Martti, 55
Si-Ming, Huang, 100–1
Simmel, Georg, 5, 41
Simon, Franck, 10–11, 268
Singularity, 234, 299, 300
Skype, 66
Slater, Ben, 320n147
"smart dust," 91–92
Smirnov, Igor, 90
Smith, Helene, 245
Smith, Jerry, 271
Smith, Michelle, 336–37n100
Smith, William, 121–22
Snake Pit, The (1948), 10
"social anxiety disorder," 12
social body. *See* body politic
social media, 61, 64, 66, 68, 71–72; 107–8, 278, 280–81, 288, 291, 323n189
"Social Organism, The" (1860), 193–95
Society for Psychical Research (SPR), 153–54, 156, 166–67
Sollers, Phillip, 319n141
sonic nausea, 88
Soul Catcher Chip, 113–14, 116
Soviet Union, 255, 263, 372n51, 376n88
"spectrum disorders," 14, 104–5, 116
Spencer, Herbert, 193–95
Spielberg, Steven, 112–16
spirit photography, 154, 349n135
spirits, 96, 97, 125, 134, 135, 151–52, 154, 154, 158, 173, 181, 217–18, 219, 308n13, 309n24, 329n47, 339n107, 349n136
spiritualism, 94, 150, 152–57, 155 (*figure 3.5*), 158, 196, 208, 213, 245, 326–27n35
spirituality, 31, 94, 97, 114, 121, 125, 126, 131, 145, 153–57, 158, 211, 249, 297, 312–13n65, 326n35, 338n105, 362n114, 368n203
Sprenger, James, 336–37n100
Stalin, Joseph, 263
Stapleton, Howard, 87
Star Trek, 108, 255, 371n29

Star Trek: The Next Generation, 29
Star Wars, 67, 91, 108, 255, 321n152
Stargate Project, 264
Steele, Kenneth, 27–28
Stekel, Wilhelm, 213
Sterling, Alton, 278
Stevenson, Robert Louis, 127
Stiegler, Bernard, 17
"stimoceiver," 266–67, 271
Stipe, Michael, 21
Stoker, Bram, 148
Strategic Defense Initiative (SDI), 255–56, 269
stress, 15, 16, 17, 68, 76, 78–79, 171, 197, 202
Strindberg, August, 117–18, 340n11
subliminal messaging, 89, 90, 107, 336n93
Sue, Eugene, 189
Sullivan, Elizabeth, 260, 261
surveillance, 31, 67, 94, 109, 113, 214, 253, 259, 289–90, 374n72
Suspicious Minds: How Culture Shapes Madness (2014), 289–90
Sweet, William H., 268
Szasz, Thomas, 7–10, 94–95, 303n22, 303–4n27

Tager, William, 21–23, 62
Targeted Individuals (TIs), 259–72, 276, 278–84, 381–82n144, 382n146
Tausk, Victor, 25–27, 31, 35–38, 42, 48, 118–19, 167, 203, 290, 301n3, 352–53n187
Taxi Driver (1976), 29
Tebb, William, 139 (*figure 3.3*), 144
technical delusion, 3–4, 18–19, 30, 31, 35, 37, 48, 50, 56, 57, 59, 78, 85, 87, 98, 105, 169, 178, 187, 204, 283, 290, 293, 297, 299
teenagers. *See* adolescence
telebiostimulation, 101, 331–32n63
telegraphy, 24, 61, 150, 158, 160, 170, 183, 190–98, 202, 204, 212, 358n56
telekinesis, 91, 95, 173, 246, 263, 325n19
telepathy, 23, 42–44, 46–47, 49, 91, 95, 108, 145–46, 153–54, 165, 167–69, 173, 203, 204, 207–8, 212–14, 217, 219–21, 246, 253–54, 256, 262–63, 308n13, 314n87, 351n174, 363–64n140, 372n51
"Telepathic Vision and Sound," 42–44, 46–52
telephone linemen, 200, 201 (*figure 4.5*), 360n89
telephone operators, 172–73, 199, 201–2, 314n87
telephony, 24, 35, 44, 49, 59, 69, 164, 172, 198–2, 225, 314n87, 317n129
teleportation, 87, 96, 338n105, 367n197, 370n19, 384n38

television, 1, 2 (*figure 1.1*), 6, 18, 22, 23, 25, 28, 53–54, 56–59, 61–66, 70, 84, 229, 239, 241, 256, 263, 288, 300, 301n3, 307n6, 308n16, 318n131, 318n137, 363–64n140
Tesla, Nikola, 6, 43, 254, 372n56, 373n57, 376–77n93
Thacker, Eugene, 326n28
Theosophy, 263
"Thunderstruck, The" (1836), 141–42
Thompson, Steven, 366n188
Thompson, Victor, 42–44, 46–52, 314n87, 314n89
"thought broadcasting" 23, 62, 80, 184, 203, 206, 214, 219
"thought echo," 13, 62
"thought insertion," 23, 184, 308n8
thought transference, 153, 154, 165, 167–69. *See also* telepathy
Three Christs of Ypsilanti, The, 313–14n83
Thurschwell, Pamela, 166
TIs. *See* Targeted Individuals
Tiffany, Joel, 134
Today Show, The, 22, 28
Todorov, Tzvetan, 245–46
Tomlin, Lily, 85
transference, 168, 173, 323n2, 351n174
Three Stigmata of Palmer Aldritch, The (1965), 249
time travel, 96, 249, 254, 275, 276, 338n105, 380–81n134
tin-foil hat, 25, 26 (*figure 1.1*), 60, 282–84, 308–9n17, 382n151
Tinder, 71
TiVo, 109
Todd, Ashley, 292
Toffler, Alvin, 16–17, 108
trema. *See* prodrome
Trilateral Commission, 106, 272
Trotter, Thomas, 188–89, 190, 195, 357n44
Truman Show Delusion, The (TSD), 288–90
Trump, Donald J., 17, 26 (*figure 1.1*), 74, 258, 272, 288, 335n84, 373n68
"Truthers," 73
Tunguska Event, 373n57
Turner, Chris, 383n23
Twenty-Thousand Leagues under the Sea (1870), 5
Twitter, 64, 280, 288, 291. *See also* social media

U2, 66, 320n148
Uber, 70

Ubik (1969), 251, 252
"Ubik." *See* "Zebra" and VALIS
"ubiquitous computing," 68, 106, 336n91
unbizarre delusions, 86–87, 90, 92. *See also* delusions
unconscious, 36, 42, 166, 168–69, 172–73, 222–23, 215, 221, 235, 296, 328n41, 340–41n15. *See also* Freud, Sigmund
unidentified flying object (UFO), 95, 254, 327–28n39, 329n45, 368–69n9, 378n114
United Nations (UN), 98, 269, 272, 378n113
United States Patent Office, 100, 269, 270 (*figure 5.5*), 336n93
Universal Price Code (UPC), 102–3, 334n76
University of Southern California, 114–15
Urantia Book, The, 95–96
Ure, Andrew, 128

Vallee, Rudy, 28
Valli, Frankie, 27–28
vampires, 109, 346n90
Van Gogh, Vincent, 37, 39
Vasiliev, L. L., 263, 376n88
"Vast Active Living Intelligence System" (VALIS), 252. *See also* VALIS
VeriChip, 98–99, 330n53. *See also* microchips; radio frequency identification
Verity, Robert, 358n48
Verne, Jules, 5, 245
Vicars, Edmund, 182–83
video cassette recorder (VCR), 70
video games, 90, 115, 274, 276, 286, 287, 325n18, 384–85n39
Violence and the Brain (1969), 267–68
virtual reality, 35, 60, 80, 105, 112–13, 115, 249, 285–86, 293–94
Virtue, Doreen, 93–94
vivisection, 343n55
Voice to Skull (V2K), 262, 271, 272, 279, 282
Vollum, Edward Perry, 139 (*figure 3.3*), 144
Volta, Alessandro, 5, 125
Von Daniken, Erich, 243, 368–69n9
Von Haller, Albrecht, 120, 126
Von Hemholtz, Hermann, 125–26
Von Kempelen, Wolfgang, 129
Vonnegut, Kurt, 372n40

Wachowski, Andrew, 286
Wachowski, Laurence, 286
Wagner, Jane, 85
Wain, Louis, 312n56

Walbert, James, 101, 333n66
Walkman (Sony), 64, 65, 319n141, 319n142
Walters, Barbara, 28
War of the Worlds (1898), 205, 254
Ward, Mary Jane, 10
Warner Brothers, 115
Warren, Carol, 10
Warren, Samuel, 141
Washington, George, 126
Watson, William, 122
webcams, 3, 66–67
Weber, Max, 41
Weiner, Anthony, 67, 321n152
Weiner, Susan, 74–75
Weinhold, Karl August, 127, 343n54
Welkos, Robert W., 328n43
Weiser, Mark, 106
Wells, H. G., 114, 205, 245, 254
Wertham, Frederic, 247
West, Benjamin, 341n26
Wharton, Francis, 144
"What's the Frequency, Kenneth?" (song), 21
What's the Frequency, Kenneth? (play), 22, 306–7n4
White, Norman, 28
whole brain emulation (WBE), 234–36, 296–97, 299, 367n198
Whytt, Robert, 120
Wiener, Norbert, 56, 225–28, 231, 234–35, 291, 365n175, 367n197, 385n40. *See also* cybernetics
Wiertz, Antoine, 135–36
Wikipedia, 73
Wilden, Anthony, 50, 315n91
willpower, 119, 137, 141, 146–48, 162, 173, 178, 197, 209–10, 283
Williams, Raymond, 37–38
Wilson, George, 190
Wilson, William, 370n19
Winfrey, Oprah, 259, 336–37n100
Winky Dink, 251
Winslow, Jacques-Benigne, 138
Winter, Chris, 114
wireless, 5–6, 24, 25, 42–44, 46, 57, 58, 79, 92, 103, 113, 204, 207–8, 213–14, 219, 246, 254, 314n87, 363–64n140
Woods, Angela, 9–10
"word salad," 51, 315n96
World Health Organization (WHO), 12
World War I, 252, 254
World War II, 239, 262, 263, 375–76n84, 376n85

Wundt, Wilhelm Max, 379n123
Wyndham, John, 253

X-ray, 18, 27, 31, 59, 97, 207, 254, 331n62
Xenu, 96, 97, 328n42, 328n43

YouTube, 67

"Zebra," 250, 251, 252, 254. *See also* Dick, Philip K.
Zenith Radio Corporation, 25, 250–51, 308n16
Žižek, Slavoj, 9, 384n28
Zodiac Killer, 293
zombies, 245, 346n90

www.ingramcontent.com/pod-product-compliance
Lightning Source LLC
Chambersburg PA
CBHW061341300426
44116CB00011B/1939